When should I travel to get the best airfare?
Where do I go for answers to my travel questions?
What's the best and easiest way to plan and book my trip?

www.frommers.travelocity.com

Frommer's, the travel guide leader, has teamed up with **Travelocity.com**, the leader in online travel, to bring you an in-depth, easy-to-use resource designed to help you plan and book your trip online.

At **www.frommers.travelocity.com**, you'll find free online updates about your destination from the experts at Frommer's plus the outstanding travel planning and purchasing features of Travelocity.com. Travelocity.com provides reservations capabilities for 95 percent of all airline seats sold, more than 47,000 hotels, and over 50 car rental companies. In addition, Travelocity.com offers more than 2,000 exciting vacation and cruise packages. Travelocity.com puts you in complete control of your travel planning with these and other great features:

Expert travel guidance from Frommer's - over 150 writers reporting from around the world!

Best Fare Finder - an interactive calendar tells you when to travel to get the best airfare

Fare Watcher - we'll track airfare changes to your favorite destinations

Dream Maps - a mapping feature that suggests travel opportunities based on your budget

Shop Safe Guarantee - 24 hours a day / 7 days a week live customer service, and more!

Whether traveling on a tight budget, looking for a quick weekend getaway, or planning the trip of a lifetime, Frommer's guides and Travelocity.com will make your travel dreams a reality. You've bought the book, now book the trip!

Also available from Hungry Minds:

the Unofficial Guide® to South Florida

Including Miami & The Keys

1st Edition

Marcia Levin
and
Joe Surkiewicz
with Molly Arost Staub

Hungry Minds™

Best-Selling Books • Digital Downloads • e-Books • Answer Networks • e-Newsletters
Branded Web Sites • e-Learning

New York, NY ✦ Cleveland, OH ✦ Indianapolis, IN

For my husband Morton, who has made the highways of my life much more easy to transit and whose constant support has always encouraged new adventures—M.L.

To Ann Lembo, Esquire—best friend . . . and counselor—J.S.

Please note that prices fluctuate in the course of time, and travel information changes under the impact of many factors that influence the travel industry. We therefore suggest that you write or call ahead for confirmation when making your travel plans. Every effort has been made to ensure the accuracy of information throughout this book, and the contents of this publication are believed correct at the time of printing. Nevertheless, the publishers cannot accept responsibility for errors or omissions or for changes in details given in this guide or for the consequences of any reliance on the information provided by the same. Assessments of attractions and so forth are based upon the author's own experience and therefore, descriptions given in this guide necessarily contain an element of subjective opinion, which may not reflect the publisher's opinion or dictate a reader's own experience on another occasion. Readers are invited to write to the publisher with ideas, comments, and suggestions for future editions.

Your safety is important to us, so we encourage you to stay alert and be aware of your surroundings. Keep a close eye on cameras, purses, and wallets, all favorite targets of thieves and pickpockets.

Published by Hungry Minds, Inc.
909 Third Avenue
New York, New York 10022

Produced by Menasha Ridge Press

Unofficial Guide is a registered trademark of Hungry Minds, Inc. All other trademarks are property of their respective owners.

ISBN 0-7645-6247-9

ISSN 1534-9152

Manufactured in the United States of America

10 9 8 7 6 5 4 3 2 1

First edition

Contents

List of Maps

Acknowledgments

People from Miami are crazy about their town: they use words like young, vibrant, spicy, and seductive to describe its fun-in-the-sun climate, vibrant multiethnic culture, and lush, tropical beauty. Because Miami is not a prim and proper place, it wasn't always easy to get a handle on this unconventional city. Luckily, we got some help along the way.

Thanks to Michelle Abram of the Miami Convention and Visitors Bureau, who was unstinting in her efforts—almost always requested at the last minute—to get us all kinds of arcane information (for example, the latest crime statistics) and a fix on a convenient, yet cheap, hotel.

Captain Jeff Cardenas, owner of The Salt Water Angler in Key West, took the time to explain to a novice the ins and outs of deep-sea fishing. Captain Ed Sides shared 20 years of scuba diving expertise for our section on underwater exploration.

To fulfill their task, the hotel inspection team of Grace Walton and Shannon Dobbs endured sore feet, a cramped South Beach hotel room, and perennial parking hassles in Miami Beach. (But the weather was great.)

Finally, many thanks to Molly Merkle, Holly Cross, Chris Mohney, Annie Long, Steve Jones, and Ann Cassar, the pros who managed to transform all this effort into a book.

—*Joe Surkiewicz*

About Our Authors

Marcia Levin wrote our Broward County, Southwest Florida, and Planning chapters and has called South Florida home for most of her life. A veteran travel writer, she has authored several guidebooks and written about Florida, the Caribbean, and cruising for newspapers, magazines, and the Internet. Marcia is chairman of the Atlantic-Caribbean Chapter of Society of American Travel Writers, as well as a board member of the society. She and her husband live in Hollywood, Florida.

Joe Surkiewicz is the lead writer of four *Unofficial Guides* and the author of two mountain bike guidebooks for Menasha Ridge Press. Joe penned our Miami-Dade County, The Florida Keys, and Everglades National Park chapters. When not riding his bike or savoring the films of MGM movie diva Norma Shearer, Joe is an award-winning legal reporter at *The Daily Record* in Baltimore. He lives in Baltimore with attorney/soul mate/best-riding-buddy Ann Lembo and their two ornery (but insufferably cute) cats.

Molly Arost Staub contributed our chapter on Palm Beach County, which she also calls home. For more than 20 years, she has been writing for many major publications, as well as Internet sites, and has covered all phases of travel from honeymoon destinations to traveling with grandchildren. She has also written extensively about dining in Broward and Palm Beach Counties.

Karen Feldman wrote the nightlife and dining sections for our Southwest Florida chapter. Her specialties include food, dining, and travel. Her articles have been published in newspapers and magazines across the country. She's authored two books on fund-raising events for non-profit groups. Karen lives in Fort Myers, Florida.

Tara Solomon contributed the shopping and nightlife sections for the Miami-Dade chapter and the nightlife section for The Keys. She is a writer and owner of a multi-disciplinary marketing and creative arts firm, TARA, Ink., based in Miami Beach. Her weekly advice column for *The Miami Herald,* "The Advice Diva," is syndicated through Knight-Ridder. Still affectionately referred to as "The Queen of the Night," Tara penned a nightlife column for *The Herald* from 1993 to 1998. Her work has been published in numerous national and local publications.

Terry Zarikian has served as culinary editor of *Selecta Magazine* for the last 14 years. He owned the critically acclaimed L'Allouete restaurants from 1983 to 1985. He is also the founder of Shapiro & Zarikian, Inc, a public relations, special events, and promotions company. Terry wrote our dining sections for Miami-Dade and The Keys.

Introduction

About This Guide

The Unofficial Guide to South Florida is just exactly that. It is a collection of information about some of the hottest Florida tourist destinations of the new millennium, with emphasis on Palm Beach and Broward Counties, Southwest Florida along the Gulf of Mexico, and of course the always popular Greater Miami and Florida Keys.

These areas are among the fastest growing in the United States. All have outstanding beaches, wonderful hotels and restaurants, some of the most exciting shopping opportunities around, every professional spectator sport imaginable, and excellent tourist attractions. This book will tell you if it's not worth the wait for the mediocre food served in a well-known restaurant, we'll complain loudly about overpriced and inconveniently located hotel rooms, and we'll keep you away from the crowds and congestion for a break now and then. We'll point out good values and tell you what we consider a waste of time and money, hopefully making your visit more fun, efficient, and economical.

And in the process we'll explain why "South Florida" is no longer just Miami, Miami Beach, and the Florida Keys. Southwest Florida, for example, places high priorities on nature and ecology, and this concern is evident at many tourist attractions. Consider more than one million acres of nature sanctuaries, many with paths or boardwalks over unspoiled wetlands, where tourists can explore virginal Florida and see outstanding examples of wildlife thriving in natural settings.

Palm Beach County has traditionally been a winter home for the Kennedys, Trumps, and dozens of other heavy hitters whose names haven't yet made the tabloids. But Palm Beach at the beginning of the 21st century is also a thriving community, where young families and active retirees coexist, and development after development sidles westward from the ocean toward the Everglades. Growth is a fact of life.

A similar situation exists in Broward County, with myriad new communities, the world's second-largest cruise port, a state-of-the-art airport, and the largest outlet shopping mall (more than 200 stores) in the world. Broward County's beaches of Hollywood, Dania Beach, Fort Lauderdale, Pompano Beach, and Deerfield Beach have been designated the first of Florida's "Blue Wave Beaches." This designation reflects their favorable water quality, beach and intertidal conditions, safety, service, habitat conservation, public information and education, and erosion management.

Then, with a strong Spanish accent, there's Miami—with its strong doses of Latin culture and remarkable natural beauty. Miami is much more than pictured on film or TV. It is not a hotbed of crime and not merely a sleepy winter retreat from the ice and cold of the Northeast. Today, the Miami area attracts people year-round from all around the globe and offers that proverbial something for everyone . . . all in gorgeous living color.

Finally, the Florida Keys conjure up black-and-white images of Humphrey Bogart in *Key Largo* weathering a hurricane in an old clapboard house, bedeviled by a nasty Edward G. Robinson. Or you might picture a robust Ernest Hemingway imbibing at Sloppy Joe's and penning yet another masterpiece in his study. Others flash on ex-hippies and artists reliving the late 1960s in laid-back Key West.

Many of these romantic images stem from a flow of fiction, film, and hyperbole. Today's reality is that the Keys are a tropical mecca for tourists, divers, and sport fishers, drawing more than a million visitors each year. An early and earthy rum-soaked sleaziness was largely pushed aside by restoration, revitalization, and the good intentions of the tourist industry.

HOW *UNOFFICIAL GUIDES* ARE DIFFERENT

Readers care about the author's opinion. The author, after all, is supposed to know what he or she is talking about. This, coupled with the fact that the traveler wants quick answers (as opposed to endless alternatives), dictates that authors should be explicit, prescriptive, and above all, direct. *The Unofficial Guide* tries to do just that. It spells out alternatives and recommends specific courses of action. It simplifies complicated destinations and attractions and allows the traveler to feel in control in the most unfamiliar environments. The objective of *The Unofficial Guide* is not to have the most information or all of the information; it aims to have the most accessible, useful information, unbiased by affiliation with any organization or industry.

Our authors and research team are completely independent from the attractions, restaurants, and hotels we describe. *The Unofficial Guide to South Florida* is designed for individuals and families traveling for the fun of it, as well as for business travelers and convention-goers, especially those visiting South Florida for the first time. The guide is directed at value-conscious, consumer-oriented adults who seek a cost-effective (though not spartan) travel style.

SPECIAL FEATURES

The *Unofficial Guide* incorporates the following special features:

- A retracing of South Florida's fascinating history.

- "Best of" listings giving our well-qualified opinions on everything ranging from beaches to golf, or from museums to the best views in South Florida.

- Listings keyed to your interests, so you can pick and choose.

- Advice to sight-seers on how to avoid crowds, advice to business travelers on how to avoid traffic and excessive cost.

- Maps to make it easy to find the places you want to go and avoid places you don't.

- Expert advice on avoiding crime.

- Hotel tables that help narrow your choices fast, according to your needs.

- Shorter listings that include only those restaurants, clubs, and attractions we think are worth considering.

- A detailed index and table of contents to help you find things quickly.

COMMENTS AND SUGGESTIONS FROM READERS

We expect to learn from our mistakes, as well as from the input of our readers, and to improve with each book and edition. Many of those who use the *Unofficial Guides* write to us making comments or sharing their own discoveries and lessons learned in South Florida. We appreciate all such input, both positive and critical, and encourage our readers to continue writing.

How to Write the Authors:

Marcia Levin and Joe Surkiewicz
The Unofficial Guide to South Florida, Including Miami & The Keys, 1st Edition
P.O. Box 43673
Birmingham, AL 35243

When you write, be sure to put your return address on your letter as well as on the envelope—sometimes envelopes and letters get separated. And remember, our work takes us out of the office for long periods of time, so forgive us if our response is delayed.

Reader Survey

At the back of this guide you will find a short questionnaire that you can use to express opinions concerning your South Florida visit. Clip the questionnaire along the dotted line and mail it to the above address.

HOW INFORMATION IS ORGANIZED

To give you fast access to information about the best of South Florida, we've organized material in several formats.

Hotels   With so many South Florida hotels available and seeking your business, choosing the right one for you can be an imposing proposition. We simplify the process through maps, ratings, and rankings that allow you to quickly focus your decision-making process. We do not go on page after page describing lobbies and rooms which may sound much the same in the final analysis. Instead, we concentrate on the variables that differentiate one hotel from another: location, size, room quality, services, amenities, and cost.

Attractions   Since visiting area attractions is high on the priority list for most tourists, we've provided detailed profiles of the best attractions in each South Florida destination. We rate each attraction by age group to help you decide which attractions are right for you. And we provide recommendations on other things to do nearby so you can plan a full day of sight-seeing.

Restaurants   We provide a lot of detail when it comes to restaurants. Because you will probably eat a dozen or more restaurant meals during your stay, and because not even you can predict what you might be in the mood for on Saturday night, we provide detailed profiles of the best restaurants in South Florida.

Entertainment and Nightlife   Visitors frequently try several different clubs or nightspots during their stay. Because clubs and nightspots, like restaurants, are usually selected spontaneously after arriving in South Florida, we believe detailed descriptions are warranted. The best nightspots and lounges in South Florida are profiled under nightlife in all chapters.

Part One

Planning Your Visit to South Florida

A Brief History of South Florida

South Florida's background is a mélange of Southern history and the great American tradition of immigration. It is a mix of Spanish colonists and Cuban fishermen, of Native Americans and adventuresome cowboys, of corporate honchos who discovered Florida as a luxe vacation destination, and of men and women of the U.S. armed forces stationed in the region during World War II.

Over the generations, South Florida has become a center for active retirees. Hundreds of thousands of men and women who worked hard all their lives settled in the sun to avoid winters of snow, slush, and sleet. This current crop of retirees won't be found rocking on the front porch of a beach hotel. Instead, these active seniors are playing tennis and golf, enjoying boating and water sports, taking classes at any of the many universities in the area, and enjoying cultural offerings. And many are still working. Retirees coexist harmoniously with young families, singles, and couples.

A Discovery Even Better than the Fountain of Youth

Though he never found the Fountain of Youth, Ponce de Leon did claim what is now southwest Florida for Spain in 1521 (on his second voyage to Florida). Though Ponce de Leon was wounded by Native Americans shortly after arriving on the coast of southwest Florida, and his expedition withdrew and sailed for Cuba (where he died shortly after landing), Spanish involvement continued in Florida for the next 300 years. In 1783 the Spanish, via the Treaty of Paris, protected the coast and shipping in the area. They simultaneously converted the Calusa Indians, a tribe of fierce warriors whose roots can be found along the coastal and barrier islands as far back as 5000 B.C., but war and disease eventually wiped out the tribe.

The United States bought the territory of Florida from Spain in 1821. Later Seminoles from Georgia and Alabama moved south to escape slavery and served as interpreters and advisors to the Indians through the Third Seminole War, which ended in 1856.

Early Floridians

Early settlers in South Florida were Native Americans and people who moved south from Georgia and Alabama in search of the "better life." The area's history is also a primer illustrating the positive contributions of immigrants and their assimilation into the fabric of community life. This mix-and-match population created a rich and varied culture in the region addressed in this book: Southern Florida between the Atlantic Ocean and the Gulf of Mexico, from Palm Beach County, across to Lee County, and south through Broward County, Miami-Dade, and down through the Florida Keys.

Traditionally, residents of the Northeast corridor of the United States have left snow and slush behind and opted for the sunshine of Florida's Atlantic Coast. Midwesterners, on the other hand—folks from Ohio, Indiana, Illinois, and Michigan—make their Florida homes in communities along the Gulf of Mexico.

South Florida doesn't reflect a great deal of history prior to the arrival of the railroad into South Florida in the 1890s, but it has been in the headlines ever since.

Tracking Florida

For the rich and famous of the day, Palm Beach at the end of the 19th century was a wonderful site for a winter vacation home. It was made up of private estates, clubs, and broad beaches. Legend has it that Palm Beach got its name from the remnants of a Spanish ship carrying a load of coconuts from Trinidad that washed ashore north of Hypoluxo.

When Henry Flagler, a founding partner in Standard Oil, first brought his rail line to Palm Beach in 1893, he chose not to continue south into Miami—a distance of some 65 miles. After a killer freeze struck Florida during the winter of 1894–1895, destroying the year's citrus crops, Flagler decided to take his train farther south. The frost hadn't touched Miami-area crops, and in spite of himself, Flagler completed the line to Miami on April 15, 1896.

The story that grew up around the railroad's arrival focuses on Julia Tuttle, a dedicated woman who wanted to create a city at the mouth of the Miami River. Born in Cleveland, she settled on the north bank of the Miami River in 1891. She searched for a railroad mogul who would bring a line south. When the frost of 1894–1895 depleted crops in Palm Beach, Tuttle sent a simple but eloquent message to Flagler—a single orange blossom.

Whether the story is true or not, the train headed south and all 300 Miami residents turned out to greet the locomotive. Before the turn of the century, Miami had a newspaper. Soon churches and schools were established, and the city was calling itself "America's sun porch." Flagler brought his railroad to the southern tip of Florida, to Key West, in 1912.

Once the railroad arrived, a land boom quickly developed and real estate was hot as the Florida sun. Low-priced South Florida land sites were offered for sale across the nation. The fact that many of these lots were under water, much was swampland, and some didn't even exist, laid the groundwork for South Florida's reputation as an area of fast-talking salesmen where "anything goes." (A reputation, some would say, that still has more than a grain of truth.) But nature works in strange ways: in 1926 a hurricane devastated the area. Those garrulous salesmen took their pitches elsewhere, and South Florida suffered fairly hard financial times until World War II.

World War II and the Aftermath

During World War II, military personnel enjoyed Florida's broad white sand beaches while on rest and relaxation breaks from training in Miami. Many made a mental note of the beauty of the region and at the end of World War II returned to establish homes and families, taking advantage of Veteran's Administration low-interest rate mortgages and low down payments. The construction industry—and the entire area—entered into another boom phase.

In the 1950s the region was largely a winter home for wealthy families from the Northeast and Midwest. At the same time, some Broward County neighborhoods became bedroom communities for Miami's workers. Summertime found many hotels shuttered and restaurants closed in Miami-Dade (then called Dade County), Broward, and Palm Beach Counties. Traffic slowed considerably, and the area was made up of many sleepy Southern towns.

Large luxury hotels began appearing along the Atlantic Ocean, and in Miami-Dade and Broward Counties beachfronts were sacrificed to developers, as the boom continued into the 1960s.

Cuban Immigration

In 1960 Fidel Castro came to power in Cuba (only 90 miles south of Key West), triggering the first wave of Cuban immigration. (Cuban immigration to South Florida continues to this day, and special laws allow illegal immigration.) The Cuban Missile Crisis of October 1962 again put the region in the news when Castro's guns and Russia's missiles were aimed at South Florida. Four decades later, Miami has become what many consider the most Latin city in the United States, where strong, hot café Cubano is the wakeup drink of choice for more than half the population.

The 1970s

In the 1970s, Fort Lauderdale gained its greatest fame (and some notoriety), when it became the spring break capital of the United States. Some 350,000 college kids from all over the country—thanks to film stars George Hamilton and Connie Francis in the movie *Where The Boys Are*—thought Fort Lauderdale was the heart of the action, and beer-guzzling and wet T-shirt contests were de rigueur.

While the kids were in Fort Lauderdale, Miami was becoming a major player in international banking and business. As the gateway to Latin America, huge office buildings began dotting the Miami skyline.

Notoriety and Another Boom

South Florida had its share of notoriety in the 1980s. An enormous Cuban immigration, the resultant tent cities where newly arrived Cubans lived for months, and horrendous crime stats straight out of *Miami Vice* underscored the decade.

All the while, growth continued, and Florida became an international tourist destination for the first time. Miami's South Beach was redeveloped, and the Art Deco District attracted photographers from around the globe. The fashion press shot beautiful men and women against a backdrop of pastel hotels, white sand, and a turquoise blue sea. The publicity worked—huge numbers of tourists began arriving daily from Germany, Scandinavia, Great Britain, and all across Europe.

Disaster Strikes Again

Devastating Hurricane Andrew hit South Florida in 1992, causing nearly $20 billion in damages. Many Miami-area families, whose homes were wiped out by the strong hurricane, relocated to Broward and Palm Beach Counties and Florida's southwest coast.

But as the century ended and the area made tremendous efforts to rebuild itself, South Florida again has become a world-class tourist destination—extending across the state to Southwest Florida and down through the Florida Keys.

South Florida Today

The year 2000 saw the saga of Elian Gonzalez on nightly newscasts. Stories of Florida consumer scams and political graft also made headlines, and the year ended with the drama of the hanging chads in the presidential election of 2000.

On the positive side, the region has cleaned up its act. South Florida—from coast to coast—has seen lower crime figures and an improved quality of life. Despite bad press, leisure and business travel have increased; convention centers are doing big business; and hotels and motels are full.

Nothing, it seems, can beat incredible weather, fresh ocean breezes, and state-of-the-art hotels and restaurants. Shopping venues in South Florida can compete with those anywhere else in the world, and the tourist attractions offer that proverbial something for everyone. South Florida is a 21st-century destination.

Palm Beach County   Since Flagler's time and to the present, Palm Beach has been synonymous with a standard of life to which few people in the country could aspire. In many ways, some areas of Palm Beach County remain a special bastion for the wealthy. In tony Boca Raton, for example, many elegant homes and high-priced condos with $1-million-plus price tags sprawl westward from the ocean. In Spanish, Boca Raton means "mouth of the rat," supposedly a term sailors used to describe a hidden rock that destroys ship's cables.

Broward County   What was once a tiny beach strip of development one and a half miles long is today considered Greater Fort Lauderdale. This name encompasses 30 municipalities and 1,200 square miles extending from the Atlantic Ocean to the depths of the Everglades, from the Palm Beach county line to the Miami-Dade county line, and everything in between.

Big bucks have recently been spent in Greater Fort Lauderdale, including $502.5 million in new attractions and a $334-million expansion and renovation of the Fort Lauderdale/Hollywood International Airport. In 2000, 7.5 million visitors experienced Greater Fort Lauderdale. Nicki E. Grossman, president of the Greater Fort Lauderdale Convention & Visitors Bureau, says "no other destination in the country can claim a greater commitment to tourism and growth than this community."

Miami-Dade County   In the new millennium, Miami is a key business center for Latin America and a multinational capital where German, Dutch, Spanish, French, Creole, Portuguese, Yiddish, and Italian might be spoken on any corner. A rich tapestry of cultures is the result. Northeastern and Midwestern accents are commonplace, and soft Southern drawls are widespread. Miami is a true melting pot.

Miami has also become the "cruise capital of the world," with dozens of cruise ships calling the beautiful port home and making its huge airport the number-one gateway for both cargo and passengers traveling to the Caribbean and Latin America.

Southwest Florida   On Florida's southwest coast, Lee and Collier Counties and the cities of Fort Myers, Fort Myers Beach, and Naples are popular tourist destinations. The Lee Island Coast, named for Confederate General Robert E. Lee (even though he never visited the area), was settled in 1887. The current population of Fort Myers alone is 500,000, approximately 150,000 more people than in 1990. One of the state's primary growth areas, close to two million tourists visited southwest Florida in 1999.

The story of South Florida's growth—both in tourism and numbers of residents—has one common chord: People looking for a comfortable life. South Florida continues to offer that and more.

When to Go

They don't call Florida the Sunshine State without good reason: During the winter months, South Florida is a mecca for sun-seeking vacationers escaping icy blasts and snowdrifts in less temperate climes. From November through April, South Florida's sub-tropical climate offers—but doesn't guarantee—blue skies, warm sunshine, and low humidity. It's been called paradise by the more poetic, and when the weather is perfect, paradise it is. What else would you call temperatures in the 70s, low humidity, and bright blue skies? And it's perfection more times than not.

Consequently, it's no surprise that the winter months are South Florida's peak tourist season. The "winter season" generally starts just before Christmas and ends just after Easter. Christmas week, the busiest week of the year, pushes tourist facilities, restaurants, and hotels to their limit throughout South Florida. Lines get long at major tourist destinations, small attractions get inundated, and finding a hotel room that's both convenient and affordable is difficult. Other busy times are major football weekends, or during large conventions that tax area hotels and facilities to the max.

Our advice: If at all possible, avoid touring the area during Christmas week and major holidays such as Easter and Thanksgiving. The period after Thanksgiving through the week before the winter holidays offers manageable crowds at attractions, beaches, and restaurants—and finding a reasonably priced hotel room is easier.

While the crowds recede to some extent after New Year's Day, things really pick up in mid-January as affluent Northerners and Midwesterners

South Florida's Average Monthly Temperatures					
	High	**Low**		**High**	**Low**
January	74	63	July	88	76
February	76	63	August	88	77
March	77	65	September	86	76
April	79	68	October	83	72
May	83	72	November	79	67
June	85	76	December	76	67

who own property in South Florida settle into their winter digs. The winter season remains in full swing through Easter, and Easter week is almost as crowded as the winter holidays. These months are the best time to visit the Everglades (it's the dry season, so mosquitoes are usually scarce and animal life congregates around the remaining water). The time between Easter and the beginning of summer is slower—highways are less traveled, and restaurants and hotels are less busy.

THE SUMMER SEASON

The action picks up toward the middle of June with the arrival of families on vacation toting school-aged children along. The "summer season" continues through mid-August when the kids head back to school. While the region doesn't get as crowded during the summer as it does in the winter months, summer is South Florida's other major tourist season. Additionally, the Miami area has traditionally been a major summer destination for South Americans who head north to shop and escape their winter. The July 4th and Labor Day weekends see great crowds heading south once again. Hotel prices are lower than winter rates, and with moderately priced airfares, a holiday weekend in South Florida is definitely do-able.

If you plan to visit this subtropical region during the summer, keep two things in mind: This is the rainy season, characterized by ferocious, though usually brief, afternoon thunderstorms, high temperatures, and often equally high humidity. Comfort, as well as crowd avoidance, dictates that touring, tennis, golf, and sight-seeing should be done early in the day. Here's another caveat to summer visits to South Florida. Natives (usually defined as residents who have lived here at least five years) think of South Florida summers the way folks in Maine think of their winters: You really haven't arrived until you've survived at least one. Keep that in mind if you've never ventured farther south than Orlando between June and September, and you're contemplating a summer trip to South Florida. The intensity of the sun, high temperatures, and humidity can be oppressive. Keep in mind that high temperatures don't tell the whole story: Most natives pay more attention to a weather forecast's humidity levels than the day's high temperature (80 percent is comfortable; the high 90s are not).

But don't let tales of heat and humidity keep you away. We definitely recommend South Florida's off-season. Remember that everything is air-conditioned, and unless you plan to run a marathon or trek through the Everglades, those few minutes outdoors won't hurt anyone. Locals, in fact, keep a cotton sweater handy, as some public places are over-air-conditioned.

THE SHOULDER SEASONS

The two "shoulder" periods between the major tourist seasons—mid-April through early June and September through mid-December—offer visitors the best chance of avoiding large crowds, packed attractions, and expensive lodging. The weather is usually pleasant and dry (though rainier than the winter months).

Note, however, that South Florida's hurricane season lasts from June to November. Statistically, there's not much chance that one of the huge tropical storms will hit during your visit—and if it does, there will be plenty of warning. Evacuation routes are well marked, and newspaper editors and television anchors are only too eager to share their information with the immediate world.

AVOIDING CROWDS

In general, popular tourist sights are busier on weekends than weekdays, and Saturdays are busier than Sundays. The winter season is by far the busiest time of year at most attractions, with some exceptions: The relatively low number of school-aged children in town during the winter (except for holidays) means that kid-friendly places such as the Seaquarium in Miami, Butterfly World in Broward, and Lion Country Safari in Palm Beach may not be as crowded, compared to summer.

Driving in South Florida's rush-hour traffic, especially on the Florida Turnpike (also called Ronald Reagan Turnpike), I-95, US 1, I-75, or US 41 (also called Tamiami Trail) on the Gulf Coast should be avoided if possible. If not possible, do what you do in your home town in traffic. Relax, listen to the radio, and know it's going to thin out eventually. If you're driving into South Florida on a weekday, avoid hitting town between 7:30 a.m. and 9 a.m., and 4 p.m. to 6 p.m. Expect equally heavy traffic on the two east-west expressways that connect with I-95 near downtown: the Dolphin Expressway (Route 836) and the Airport Expressway (Route 112). US 1 below downtown is the only route to Coconut Grove, Coral Gables, and points south; rush-hour gridlock is the norm. The Turnpike makes a terrific alternate route to the Florida Keys, bypassing Miami and mucho traffic.

The same caveats apply to Broward and Palm Beach Counties as well as to Southwest Florida. Time your arrival or departure to midday hours (although in season, highways and expressways seem gridlocked all day long), and avoid rush hours if you possibly can. Remember that a lot of the automobiles on the road are those of visitors—just read the license plates to realize that everyone's pretty much in the same boat. Most of these drivers are as unfamiliar with the roadways as you are, and if patience was ever a virtue, this is the time to be virtuous.

Gathering Information

Florida information is available in a variety of sources from Visit Florida Headquarters: (888) 7FLA-USA; www.flausa.com; Visit Florida Headquarters, P.O. 1100, Tallahassee, FL 32302-1100. Vacation guides are available for domestic and international visitors, including versions for the United States, the United Kingdom, Germany, France, and Spain.

Palm Beach County Palm Beach County Convention & Visitors Bureau, 1555 Palm Beach Lakes Boulevard, Suite 204, West Palm Beach, FL 33401; phone (561) 471- 3995; fax (561) 471-3990; www.palmbeachfl.com.

Broward County Greater Fort Lauderdale Convention & Visitors Bureau, 1850 Eller Drive, Suite 303, Fort Lauderdale, FL 33315; phone (800) 22-SUNNY (in the U.S. and Canada) or (954) 765-4466; fax (954) 765-4467; www.sunny.org.

Miami-Dade County Visitor Service Center at the Greater Miami Convention and Visitors Bureau, 701 Brickell Avenue, Suite 2700, Miami, Florida 33131; phone (800) 933-8448 or (305) 539-3034); www.tropi coolmiami.com.

The Florida Keys Florida Keys and Key West, phone (800) FLA-KEYS (352-5397); www.fla-keys.com

Southwest Florida Lee Island Coast Visitor & Convention Bureau, 2180 W. First Street, Suite 100, Fort Myers, FL 33901; phone (800) 237-6444; www.leeislandcoast.com.

Tourism Alliance of Collier County, 5395 Park Central Court, Naples, FL 34109; phone: (800) 688-3600 or (941)597-8001; www.visit-naples.com.

Official Florida Welcome Centers for Motorists

I-95 7 miles north of Yulee on I-95 South; phone (904) 225-9182; fax (904) 225-0064.

I-75 4 miles north of Jennings on I-75 South; phone (904) 938-2981; fax (940)-938-1292.

I-10 16 miles west of Pensacola on I-10 East; phone (850) 944-0442; fax (850) 944-3675.

The Capitol Plaza Level, The Capitol, Tallahassee, 32301; phone (850) 488-6167; fax (850) 414-2560.

U.S. 231 3 miles north of Campbellton; phone/fax (850) 263-3510.

Websites from the Society for the Advancement of Travel for the Handicapped	
www.access-able.com	Access-Able Travel Source
www.disabilitytravel.com	Accessible Journeys
www.accessiblevans.com	Accessible Vans of America
www.blvd.com/wg	Wheelchair Getaways

South Florida Destinations

Okay. You've made one decision, now it's time for another. You've decided to go to Florida, now the decision is where exactly you should go in the Sunshine State. The choices are many and varied. Should you head to the wonderful vacation areas on the state's Gulf of Mexico coast? Maybe you'd rather stay along the Atlantic Ocean? The beaches of Florida's southwest coast, where ecotourism is practiced as well as preached, or the Sunshine State's "Gold Coast," with its high-rise hotels and condos lining the seashore? It really all depends on what you're looking for. If you're interested in glitz and glamour (and don't knock it if you haven't tried it), then Palm Beach, Broward County, or Miami-Dade might be your cup of tea. Are you and your family more interested in the outdoors, nature, and possibly getting up close and personal with panthers, bison, birds, and alligators? Try the southwest coast or the Florida Keys. We've put together information on all these areas. You make the call.

PALM BEACH COUNTY

Though Palm Beach is similar in some ways to other South Florida tourist destinations, in many ways, it is worlds apart. Consider the Palm Beach Polo & Country Club, where Princes Charles has played the game; Worth Avenue, a pricey, upscale street of some 200 shops with designer names and big bucks price tags; and charming, intimate restaurants that appeal to transplanted Northeasterners eager to replicate the East Side of New York, except with palm trees and an average year-round temperature of 78 degrees. And Palm Beach has close to 150 golf courses—more than any county in the nation.

Palm Beach winter residents are often the grandchildren of Palm Beach winter residents. It's not necessarily a genetic thing, but those who love the good life love Palm Beach. Think Trump, Kennedy, Pulitzer (okay, think scandal), but also think about a lifestyle that has been written about and talked about for the better part of the last 50 years. Then think of megabucks property owners who have always enjoyed the Atlantic Ocean at their back door and exclusive private clubs as their playgrounds.

That's probably too broad a brush with which to paint all winter residents. Heading west from the ocean, there are literally dozens of condominium and town home complexes that are more affordable and provide a (somewhat) toned-down lifestyle. Two elegant old hotels, each redone at a tremendous cost, are The Breakers and the Boca Raton Hotel and Resort. Each is a timeless establishment where generations have gone for sun and fun.

Today's Palm Beach County visitor—and there were more than a million last year—could be anyone from a high-pressure business exec to a retiree on a fixed income to a typical family tourist. The region's appeal, in this new century, is more egalitarian.

BROWARD COUNTY

Broward is Palm Beach's neighbor to the south. Just under 500 daily airline arrivals and departures are scheduled at the Fort Lauderdale/Hollywood International Airport, recently redone at a cost of about $700 million and still one of the state's most user-friendly airports. It is considered the fourth-fastest-growing airport in the United States and the world. The average stay of Greater Fort Lauderdale visitors is just under five days. Port Everglades, the cruise port just minutes from the airport, is the number two cruise port in the world (Miami is number one). While winter holiday vacations find the area busier than ever, summer family vacations in Greater Fort Lauderdale are increasingly popular. Families from Europe and South America also enjoy the area.

Many tourists come via package tie-ins to Disney vacations, while two-income couples choose the area for frequent getaways, jetting south three or four times a year. Sophisticated, upscale visitors will target the upcoming St. Regis, a five-star hotel to be built on Fort Lauderdale Beach; and the Seminole Hard Rock Hotel and Casino, a 750-room property under construction on the Seminole Indian Reservation in Hollywood.

One of Greater Fort Lauderdale's major tourist attractions is the Sawgrass Mills Shopping Center, visited by 24 million in 1999—a figure only 2 million less than those at the Magic Kingdom at Walt Disney World. Sawgrass Mills is the world's largest discount and entertainment mall, with more than 2,780 brand-name and designer outlets, discount stores, specialty shops, and restaurants. Stores include Saks Fifth Avenue, Levi Strauss, Benetton, Ann Taylor, and DKNY.

The Fort Lauderdale area is another haven for golfers, with more than 50 of the most affordable courses in the United States. They include municipal, public, semi-private and private, and various night-driving ranges.

MIAMI-DADE COUNTY

In Miami-Dade, the two words "Miami Beach" say it all. And in Miami Beach, South Beach, called SoBe by locals and repeat visitors, is the epicenter of the world of glamour, fashion, and photography. Some folks call it the "American Riviera."

SoBe hotels and restaurants are frequented by beautiful people, all with midriffs bare, earrings dangling, and trousers tight as humanly possible— men and women alike. These are people whose images you might find in fashion magazines, on television's tabloid shows, and in the newspaper tabloids themselves. Dennis Rodman, Gloria Estefan (she and her husband Emilio own Lario's Restaurant in SoBe), Madonna, and Rosie O'Donnell are just some of the celebs who hang out in the area. Actor Robert De Niro has an apartment nearby, and the late Gianni Versace was killed on the front steps of his palatial estate on Ocean Drive. Cher bought, then sold, a pricey piece of property here, and other stars of film and TV are spotted regularly in the area. Fifty years ago, European-born grandmas and grandpas sat on the porches of these now redone and very glamorous hotels and rocked away their days. Now, beautiful boys and girls sleep during the day and rock away the nights at restored old hotels where glitz and glamour are the operative words.

Don't miss touring the Art Deco hotels or strolling down Ocean Drive and people-watching. And if you want to be a part of the scene and stay at SoBe or dine at any of a dozen or so great eateries, feel free. Just be prepared that it's definitely a serious safari into la vida loca.

SoBe is really only a two-mile strip on the south end of Miami Beach. Miami-Dade is much more: Central Miami Beach, North Miami Beach, Little Havana, Little Haiti, Coral Gables, Coconut Grove, and the new city of Aventura are all integral parts of Miami. Each area has its own flavor and much to offer tourists.

In mid-Miami Beach, two temples to excess were built in the 1950s, and the Fontainebleau and Eden Roc still do a great job as mega-hotels. Both are oceanfront, and both have been redone and updated. Not quite the hotspots they once were—Frank Sinatra, Harry Belafonte, Milton Berle, and Nat King Cole once starred in their showrooms—both are still good choices.

Michael Aller, tourism and convention director and chief of protocol for the City of Miami Beach, notes a change in the diversity of the community, which has gone from 90 percent Jewish to 50 percent Hispanic. He says change began in the late 1970s when the Jewish community began its trek northward into Broward and Palm Beach Counties. "The elderly, on fixed incomes and without additional help, were stuck here in the midst of what became 'crack city.'" As South Beach began to draw investors and create its upscale hard edge, Miami Beach changed. The average age dropped from

69 to 41, and a more diverse community resulted. The communities of Surfside, Bal Harbour, and Sunny Isles are respectively dominated by Jewish and Canadian tourists and retirees, as well as middle-of-the road tourists who want to be close to the beach. Latin visitors enjoy the Surfside region but also opt for Coral Gables and Coconut Grove. Families tend to stay close to the beach, but many attractions are far inland. A rental car is almost a necessity for this sprawling region.

THE FLORIDA KEYS

The Florida Keys are the string of islands between the Atlantic Ocean and the Gulf of Mexico. This is a favorite destination for outdoorsy types— those who enjoy fishing and a world-class array of marine life. Great snorkeling and diving can also be found here, around the only coral reef in the continental United States.

Day-trippers generally only make it to the Upper Keys, but the Middle Keys (e.g. Marathon) and Key West are great options for a longer stay. Many families vacation off-season in the Keys, where during high season (from late November until Easter) it is just as crowded as mainland Florida.

SOUTHWEST FLORIDA

In Lee County, tourist hotspots include Sanibel and Captiva Islands, Fort Myers Beach, Fort Myers, Cape Coral, Bonita Springs and beaches, Pine Island, Boca Grande, Lehigh Acres, and North Fort Myers; these make up the Lee Island Coast. Farther south along the Gulf of Mexico, a long-standing popular tourist draw is Greater Naples, while Marco Island and the Everglades also attract visitors. These beaches are powdery white, and many are part of wonderful sprawling parks offering recreational settings. In Naples alone, accommodations range from small bed-and-breakfasts to the Ritz-Carlton, where a three-story spa was recently opened. Another local favorite is the traditional, family-owned Naples Beach Hotel, which recently added a 75,000-square-foot meeting facility, a golf pro shop, locker rooms, a restaurant and bar, ballrooms, and a spa.

In 1900 the population of Fort Myers was less than 1,000. It was still a tiny town when inventor Thomas Alva Edison, auto tycoon Henry Ford, and tire mogul Harvey Firestone made Fort Myers their winter home before the dawn of the 20th century. Today the county is home to 370,000 full-time residents, while the population practically doubles during winter months.

The Fort Myers and Lee County area has a history rich in tales of Native Americans, Spanish Colonials, and pirates. Superimposed on this exciting background is the growth of a small southern town into an imposing city, where new construction is perpetual and tourists are attracted by many historic homes and sites as well as state-of-the-art accommodations.

These Gulf beaches have become so famous with shell collectors that the shelling posture has been called the Sanibel Stoop and the Captiva Crouch! And while water sports are always a big draw, the area's tennis and golf facilities consistently rank among the best in the country. Babcock Wilderness Experience in Boca Grande and Everglades National Park (home to 1.5 million acres of the largest wetland ecosystem in the country) are havens for those inclined to explore natural environments and view endangered species.

Naples is a "preppy" winter destination, with shop after shop filled with plaid golf pants and hundreds of tiny alligators on knit shirts in colors Crayola never dreamed of. The entire west coast is a prime vacation area for Midwesterners, as well as Canadians who eschew the glitzier Atlantic vacation destinations for the charm and beauty of the Gulf Coast on the southwest part of the state. Simply put, tourists who want a laid-back vacation might well opt for the Fort Myers or Naples areas.

The Beaches

Any visit to Florida must include that popular "day at the beach." Expect clean white sand, broad beaches, plenty of room for blankets or rental lounges, and sun and sea to make even the most dedicated landlubber get his feet wet. Whether the Atlantic Ocean or the Gulf of Mexico, millions of tourists annually look forward to beaching it. At one time, a visit to South Florida had no other purpose. Today, with many more attractions designed to eat up a vacation, beaches remain a major objective of a Florida visit. Sun worshippers in beachfront hotels merely have to throw on a cover-up, walk out the door, and voila! You're on the beach.

According to Stephen "Dr. Beach" Leatherman, eight of the top beaches in the country can be found on Florida's 1,800 miles of coastline. Leatherman, professor and director of the International Hurricane Center at Florida International University, is an authority on beach quality and coastal erosion studies. All Florida water sports—sailing, swimming, windsurfing, water skiing, boating, deep-sea fishing, parasailing, and scuba diving—are among the best in the world. These are postcard-pretty beaches where families play together and where romantic couples romp in the surf. Generally speaking, beaches are open from dawn to dusk, with lifeguards on duty during daylight hours.

PALM BEACH COUNTY

Palm Beach boasts 47 miles of clean, white sand. Outstanding beaches include **Carlin Park, Coral Cave Park,** and **Jupiter Beach Park** in Jupiter; **John D. MacArthur Beach State Park** on Singer Island; **Lake Worth**

Beach and **Phipps Ocean Park** at Lake Worth; **Lantana Park & Beach** at Lantana; and **Spanish River Park** at Boca Raton.

BROWARD COUNTY

The Washington-based Clean Beaches Council, the first national environmental beach certification organization in the United States, recently named Greater Fort Lauderdale beaches as Blue Wave Beaches, defined as safe, clean, and user-friendly. **Hollywood, Dania Beach, Fort Lauderdale Beach, Pompano Beach,** and **Deerfield Beach** are the state's only beaches to qualify. These beaches receive Blue Wave flags, public information kiosks, and beach entrance boundary markers. Greater Fort Lauderdale has also been named one of the top diving destinations in the country.

Hollywood Beach is popular because of its Broadwalk (cq) running parallel to the ocean as well as dozens of little restaurants, many French in origin and geared to the French-Canadian tourists who winter in the area. It's a good family beach with many lifeguard stations. Fort Lauderdale Beach is crowded, and the images of *Where the Boys Are* still linger. This is another popular family favorite with lifeguard stations at the ready. Deerfield Beach is a much less crowded beach, but restaurants and cafes aren't as numerous as along Hollywood or Fort Lauderdale Beach.

MIAMI-DADE COUNTY

One of "Dr. Beach" Leatherman's top beaches is **South Beach** on Miami Beach. Look for beautiful people of all ages and sexual persuasions—and definitely all nationalities. South Beach has become one of the most desired photographic locations in the nation, and fashion shoots for publications from all around the globe have been set along Ocean Drive. You'll also see topless bathers, so save the family beach experience for northern beaches along the ocean. European visitors and the beautiful people from all over the world have found their favorite beach.

Crandon Park Beach on the Rickenbacker Causeway to Key Biscayne is a popular destination for families and picnickers. **Haulover Park** at the north end of Miami Beach is another popular spot. Farther south, **Matheson Hammock Park** offers a small beach on Biscayne Bay with a terrific view of the Miami skyline.

Wherever you have beaches you have parking problems. Weekends are especially crowded, and we suggest using metered parking, pay lots, or garages. Don't try to park on the street—it could turn into a very costly day at the beach indeed, due to militant enforcement of parking regulations. The early arrival gets the parking space. Of course, if your hotel is on the Gulf or the Ocean, walking to the beach is a nice option.

SOUTHWEST FLORIDA

Some of the best beaches in Southwest Florida are in Lee and Collier Counties. These are white sugar sand beaches, world famous for shelling. Possibilities include **Fort Myers Beach,** the beach at the **Sanibel Lighthouse** (located on Sanibel Island's southern tip by the picturesque, century-old lighthouse), and **Turner Beach** (situated between Sanibel and Captiva Islands.) **Captiva Island** has been ranked as one of the country's most romantic beaches for two consecutive years by "Dr. Beach" Leatherman, and the late Anne Morrow Lindbergh used the Captiva beaches for her novel *A Gift from the Sea.* These beaches are the best seats in town for watching dolphins frolicking in the Gulf or for enjoying a spectacular sunset.

Naples and the tiny four-mile stretch of **Marco Island** are other area beaches popular with tourists and locals alike. In Naples, **Clam Pass** and **Delnor-Wiggins** have regularly made "Dr Beach's" top 20 national best beaches survey.

Considerations for Outdoor Recreation

HANDLING FLORIDA WEATHER

Some of us on *The Unofficial Guide* research team have resided in South Florida for many years—and enjoyed it. We've lived with heat, humidity, no perceptible change of season, and even the occasional hurricane. We've survived. We've survived rather well, we like our tropical lifestyle, and very few of us return to our northern roots voluntarily. We never have to worry about shoveling the driveway, sky-high heating bills, buying cold-weather clothes, or chopping wood for the fireplace. It's a trade-off, and Floridians think they get the best of the bargain. We do, though, have summer storms—complete with world-class lightning shows—that can be a daily occurrence and usually strike in late afternoon. (A good reason to get in your fitness regime early in the morning.) And the much-heralded heat and humidity are always mitigated by a breeze off the ocean. It's never as bad as a major northern city in a summer heat wave.

While the breezes are augmented by the ubiquitous air conditioning, we agree that living or vacationing in the South Florida climate takes some getting used to. Just as vacationers do, we locals must deal with keeping the sun's rays off our bodies and avoiding heat exhaustion. That's hard to do if you live any kind of an active lifestyle. Whether you walk, run, jog, play tennis or golf, swim or do water exercises, you will be in the sun and heat for some time. Even if you do little more than walk to your car in a parking lot, you are exposed to the sun. Working out outdoors increases the challenge. Caution is important if you plan to spend time outdoors.

Use Plenty of Sunscreen It's probably a good idea to talk to a dermatologist before heading south and get his recommendations for sunscreen. Remember to cover those "danger zones": the back of the neck, shoulders, face, and behind the ears. If thinning hair is a problem, cover the scalp or wear a hat. Reapply sunscreen when sweat or water wash the original application away. Work out early in the day or late in the afternoon, especially in late spring, summer, and fall. Think about how marvelous it could be to exercise outdoors in fall and winter when snowstorms are threatening most of the country. The thought might even cool you off. Increase your exposure by about 10 minutes a day. After a week, most of us—covered in sunscreen of course—can spend up to an hour at a time in the sun. Remember that South Florida shares the same latitude as the Sahara Desert.

Drink Plenty of Water Carry a bottle of water around with you and keep hydrated. Avoid sweet drinks—colas and fruit drinks don't hydrate as well as water, and alcohol or even tea can act as dehydrators.

Stick to Light-Colored Clothes Wear pastels and whites. When that tropical sun bakes down during summer months you'll be much more comfortable than in darker hues. And baby powder isn't just for babies anymore. A thin coat in socks works wonders and cuts down on odors as a bonus.

TENNIS AND GOLF

Most South Florida tennis and golf players know that heat and humidity result in a real workout on the course or court. Most tennis players opt for early-morning or evening games. (Another reason why many South Florida courts are lighted and why golf courses often offer reduced fees for afternoon play.) Weekends, when local residents hit the links, are always busy (regardless of season), and getting a morning tee time or court is difficult.

Plan on teeing off either before 9 a.m. or after 4 p.m. to play nine holes. Avoid the links in the middle of the day, and be wary of sudden tropical rainstorms. Florida is the lightning capital of the world, and the golf course is not a fun place to be when storms roll in. We suggest asking your hotel to book tee times or tennis courts in advance of your arrival whenever possible.

SWIMMING HAZARDS: IT'S A WILD OCEAN OUT THERE

Folks on a visit to the shores of South Florida beaches need to keep a few things in mind to enjoy a safe and pleasant trip. To get the low-down on beach hazards and common-sense safety guidelines, we called Larry Pizzi, operations supervisor of the Miami Beach lifeguards.

On the Beach "The biggest hazard on the beach is the sun," Pizzi reports. "Even on cloudy days, the sun's ultraviolet rays filter through, and you can get a really bad sunburn. Unfortunately, I hear people all the time say they can't go home without a sunburn—or no one will believe they came to Miami Beach!"

Theft   "Be careful of your belongings on the beach," Pizzi warns. "Don't take jewelry, billfolds, and large sums of cash to the beach. Cameras are generally okay if you don't take a long walk and leave them. Just take normal precautions with your valuables."

In the Water   Jellyfish, Pizzi says, top the list of hazards here. "Jellyfish can appear anytime, but are more common in the winter," he says. "Portuguese men-of-war, which are really beautiful creatures, are more common in the summer. We put out yellow warning flags to warn folks if they're in the water." If you get stung, use a pocketknife or credit card to carefully scrape the tentacle away from the skin. "Don't rub it," Pizzi warns. "Pull it off carefully, then treat it with vinegar. Better yet, if you get stung, go to a lifeguard for help."

Sea lice—actually, the spores of Portuguese men-of-war—are invisible creatures that cause an itchy rash best treated with cortisone lotions. The rash can last about a week. "It's also called 'swimmers' eruption,'" Pizzi adds. "It's pretty rare. But it's a good idea to avoid seaweed or anything else floating in the water, since the spores usually come into the beach on something else."

Rip tides, also called undertow, usually occur when easterly winds are blowing from 15 to 20 miles an hour, creating a break in an off-shore sandbar that sends water draining away from the beach. "If you get caught in a rip tide, even if you're a strong swimmer, don't fight it," Pizzi advises. "Swim parallel to the beach in the direction the water is pushing. Eventually, you'll break free. Remember that panic is the killer, and don't swim against a rip tide." When there's a rip tide, a red warning flag is posted at lifeguard stations. A red flag is a warning not to swim, although beaches are rarely closed and swimmers may choose to ignore the warning. Yellow flags mean caution; ask the lifeguard to tell you the specific hazard (jellyfish, rip tide, etc.).

Another hazard is stingrays, which bury themselves in the sand—and occasionally get stepped on by swimmers. "They have a barb on the end of their tails which isn't poisonous but is usually dirty, so infection is a problem," Pizzi says. "There's nothing you can do to avoid stepping on a stingray, but it's very rare."

Finally, what about everybody's favorite beach hazard—sharks? "Shark attacks are incredibly rare, not just in South Florida but all over the world," Pizzi reports. "But when we get a reported sighting, we send out a boat to investigate, get the Coast Guard to send up a helicopter, and clear the beach, if necessary. We check out all the reports."

Other Hazards   Sport concession areas (marked with buoys), getting lost (most beaches look the same and lots of children and adults manage to lose the location of their cars or possessions), snorkeling and diving (mark your location with a diving flag so you're not run over by a boat), and exceeding your physical limits when swimming. "A lot of people come here when it's winter at home, and they think they're in good physical shape—but they're not," Pizzi notes.

If You Need Help . . .

What should you do if you or another swimmer gets in trouble and needs help? "Try to float or tread water, remain calm, and don't exhaust yourself by screaming," Pizzi advises. "Wave for help and someone will be there soon." Tides cause the most problems for inexperienced ocean swimmers—and the lifeguards who rescue them. "People go out at low tide to play on the sandbars, then the tide comes in. Water that was four feet deep becomes six or seven feet deep," Pizzi explains. "Weak swimmers step into a hole and panic."

Pizzi emphasizes that the safest place to enjoy the beach is near one of the lifeguard stations. "It's always better to swim near a guard—even if it means leaving your oceanfront hotel and walking, driving, or taking public transportation," he says. "Lifeguards have first-aid kits, radios, and access to police and fire departments for any emergency."

Scuba Diving: Learning How

Every year, more than a million people travel to the Florida Keys to scuba dive at the only coral reef in the continental United States. Should you be one of them?

"Scuba diving is the most fun thing you can do outside of a bed," quips Captain Ed Sides, a master diver trainer who has instructed thousands of people how to dive safely over the last 20 years. "It's a wonderful, wonderful thing to do."

Intrigued? The requirements to become a certified scuba diver are minimal. You must be at least 12 years old, able to pass a swimming test, and fit enough to take on the rigors of handling and donning scuba gear in a rocking boat. "Diving is fun and relatively easy," Captain Sides says. "The hardest part is getting dressed out on the dive boat. Once you're in the water, you're nearly weightless. It's a lot easier than snorkeling."

How to Get Certified

To become a scuba diver, you need to be certified by an organization such as the Professional Association of Diving Instructors (PADI), the YMCA, or the National Association of Underwater Instructors (NAUI). Certification requires classroom work, passing a written final exam, "pool work," and two check-out dives with your instructor. Then you get a diving card that lets you rent equipment and dive anywhere in the world.

If your trip to South Florida is leisurely, you can become certified in three to four days. "I tell potential divers to buy the PADI dive manual and a dive table at a local dive shop and read it before they come down," Captain Sides says. "After they get to Key Largo, in two long morning sessions we can go through the text, watch some videotapes, take a few quizzes to make sure they're getting the information they need, and take the final exam." Next comes the pool work, where new divers learn how to assemble their gear, accomplish underwater rescue, clear their masks, and other skills necessary to master the sport. If there are no more than four students in the class, it usually takes a long afternoon to complete the session. The final step is two two-tank practice dives with the instructor. "We do all the little drills in the ocean that we learned in the pool," Captain Sides explains. "There are no surprises. After you've sucked four tanks of air, you're certified." Total cost? Around $300, which includes all equipment except a mask, fins, and snorkel—and anyone interested in diving should make this $60–120 investment for personal gear.

What if you're on a tighter schedule—and don't want to spend valuable time in South Florida sitting in a classroom and swimming in a pool? "Do everything but the check-out dive at home and get a transferal document from your instructor that states you've completed all your course work and pool work," Captain Sides says. "Then come here to do your check-out dives." The total cost to become certified, however, is usually higher that way, he adds. Another option is a "resort" diving course. Captain Sides explains: "I take you to a swimming pool and teach you the minimum things you need to know. Then I take you out on a dive boat, we jump in, and I stay with you for the whole dive. It gets you down there and shows you the experience." It's not cheap—prices range from $120 to about $175. But if you've got the money and want to find out whether or not scuba diving is for you, it's the way to go.

After You're Certified

After certification, how much does it cost to go diving? A typical price range is $35–50 for a two-tank trip—a half-day outing with two 60-minute dives, usually at two locations. A novice will also have to rent diving gear—a weight belt, two tanks, a regulator (the critical device that fits in your mouth and controls airflow from the air tank), and a buoyancy-control device (an inflatable vest usually called a "BCD"). Figure on another $32 a day.

Needless to say, if you've been bit by the diving bug and took the time and expense to get certified, it pays to start buying your own gear. The key component is the regulator, and list prices for quality units start around $600. "It's something you put in your mouth and something that your life depends on," Captain Sides notes. "It's a very personal piece of gear and the first thing you should buy. You can get good units on sale for around

$450." A good vest will cost around $300—and with the exception of mask, fins, and snorkel, that's all that most divers need to purchase. "Most people don't buy weight belts and tanks, because flying with them isn't a good idea," Captain Sides explains. "Unless, of course, you live next to the water or you have your own boat."

Is diving dangerous? "It's a very safe sport," the dive master responds. "But it also provides you with the opportunity to do horrible things to yourself. It's not unlike driving a car. So I take it seriously and make sure my students get good at what they do—and that they act responsibly. I drill it into people: you always dive with a buddy and always watch that person." His advice: Find a dive instructor who's certified by one of the major diving organizations, and make sure they have the same attitude toward safety.

DEEP-SEA FISHING

If the allure of battling the elements in a small boat and hooking the elusive Big One escapes you, it's time to bone up on your Hemingway. For a lot of visitors to South Florida, however, going to sea to do battle with glamour fish such as marlin, tuna, sailfish, or shark is a major attraction to visiting the Sunshine State. In fact, Florida is called the Sport Fishing Capital of the United States.

Trolling

The premier way of satisfying the primal urge to see a sailfish do an aerial rumba—eight feet above the water while hooked to the end of your line—is by charter boat, sometimes called trolling. Fifty-foot power boats leave once and twice daily with groups of six to eight anglers on full- or half-day trips from marinas up and down the South Florida coast and the Keys. A half-day charter averages around $350, and no experience is necessary. On the way out to the fishing grounds, the boat's mate baits the hooks, arranges the lines on outriggers on the side of the boat (to prevent individual lines from tangling), and talks to the customers about the vagaries of hooking the Big One. He also gives explicit instructions on what to do when a fish strikes.

Once all the lines are out and the boat is over the fishing grounds, the boat "trolls" at a slow speed until a fish is hooked. Depending on the bait, tackle, and depth of the hook, rods react differently when a fish strikes; it's up to the mate to spot the action, set the hook, and get the rod into the hands of a customer. The captain will slow the boat until the fish is landed—or cuts the line and escapes. In fact, with the declining population of most billfish such as marlin and sailfish, catch-and-release is the norm on most charter boats these days.

"It's a very passive type of fishing—you sit in the fighting chair and if a fish strikes, the mate sets the hook and passes the rod to the angler, who just has to work the reel," explains Captain Jeff Cardenas, who has guided deep-sea fishing trips in the Florida Keys for more than ten years. "For some people, it's very relaxing."

The goal of a fishing charter is to catch fish, and the captain will use his local knowledge of reefs, wrecks, currents, and weather to put the boat where he suspects the fish are. (He's also on the radio talking to other skippers doing the same thing.) The kind of fish you can expect to catch include mako shark, barracuda, bonita tuna, king mackerel, bluefin tuna, and wahoo. While the captain will move the boat from location to location in search of fish, there are no guarantees you'll come back from your trip with a trophy to grace your rec room wall.

Finding a Charter Boat

How do you select a charter boat? A referral, Captain Cardenas says, is your best bet. But first-time visitors without local contacts still have a chance of finding a charter boat with a crew that works hard and shows a good attitude.

Here's how: At least a day before you plan to go on a deep-sea charter, head for a marina around 5 p.m. and hang out. That's when the charter boats are returning from their afternoon and all-day runs. Killing time, watching the pelicans, and hanging out around the docks watching the post-trip action is a South Florida tradition—and your key to locating a good charter boat. As the boats pull in, happy or disgruntled customers (sometimes both) disembark. Depending on the success of the trip, the mate will unload a variety of fish for admiration by folks like you. (Note: If you're staying at a place with a kitchen, this is the time to buy some very fresh fish fillets.)

"Walk the docks and talk to the captains and mates," advises Captain Cardenas. Note which boats are bringing in big sport fish, ask about rates, and try to find a crew you're comfortable with. But before you select a charter boat and leave a deposit for the trip, Captain Cardenas suggests you do one more thing that can elevate your fishing charter from a passive experience to a really memorable event. "Make an arrangement with your captain that you'd like to set the hooks and release the fish," he says. "In other words, negotiate terms of the trip to enhance the experience. Otherwise, the mate hooks the fish and all you do is crank it in."

Drift Boats

Charter boats aren't your only deep-sea fishing alternative: Drift boats (also called party boats) are larger than charter boats and transport 30–40 anglers at a time out to an off-shore reef. Once there, the captain turns off the engine, the boat begins to drift in the current, and the fishing lines go over the side—often with amusing results, as the lines begin to cross.

"It's the least expensive way to deep-sea fish," Captain Cardenas points out. "You use a conventional rod and reel baited with squid or mullet for bottom fishing, throw the line over the side and wait for a bite. Most people who go out on drift boats are fishing for dinner." Not, he could have added, for trophy fish to hang on the wall. Species typically caught from a drift boat include redtail and yellowtail snapper, flounder, barracuda, grouper, and pompano.

You'll also get to know your neighbor as you stand elbow to elbow on the side of the large drift boat and pass your rods back and forth in an effort to untangle your lines. When things get really complicated, a crew member shows up to straighten it all out.

Just like a charter boat, drift boats have a crew that baits the customers' hooks and "gaffs" (spears) the catch after it's reeled in close to the boat. Beginners get plenty of help and advice—from both the crew and fellow party boaters—and tackle is available for rent on the boat. Bring your own rod and a typical three-and-a-half-hour drift boat excursion is $20; if you rent tackle, it's around $25.

A bad sign: a poker game starts up in the cabin of the drift boat, a sure indication that the fish aren't biting. "The fishing has declined a thousand percent over the last few years," moaned one glum fisherman between hands on a recent excursion out of Miami Beach. "It used to be that after an hour you caught your limit and were sick of reeling fish in."

Light-Tackle Fishing

In light-tackle fishing, a style popular in the Keys, a guide takes up to four anglers out in an open, 25-foot boat. Using LORAN coordinates (a long-range navigation system that allows a boat to reach a precise location), the guide will go anywhere from 10 to 70 miles off-shore looking for reefs and wrecks. Many guides take customers to their own "secret spots."

After reaching a promising location, the guide throws out chum (cut or ground bait) to attract fish: blackfin tuna, permit, cobia, and other hard-fighting species. "Light-tackle fishing offers good, fast action," says Captain Cardenas. "The fish come up right behind the boat and it doesn't take a high level of skill to land them. The captain baits the hook, the angler tosses the hook into the melee and hooks up." The total cost for an all-day trip is typically $400–450 for up to four anglers.

Sight Fishing

Sight fishing is another option, although technically it's not deep-sea fishing. Also called saltwater flats fishing, this type of angling calls for skill and patience. How it works: One or two customers and a guide in a 17-foot open boat are "poled"—pushed by the guide, who sits in an elevated chair with a long pole—through water that's only 18 inches deep (or shallower)

"This is what I get excited about," Captain Cardenas says. "Flats fishing takes place in a wonderful period of calm, wading birds, and clear water—

so you can see an incredible amount of sea life. The lack of a motor lets you approach all kinds of creatures." When a large predator such as a barracuda, bonefish, or permit is spotted—remember, this is called "sight" fishing—it's up to the angler to present the bait or fly to the fish. "You see them way in advance, so you stalk the fish," he explains. "It's primarily done with a fly rod and the guides are teachers, so it's fully participatory by the customer. It's immensely rewarding."

Sight fishing, however, isn't for anglers who judge a trip by the number of fish they catch. "There isn't a strong emphasis on catching a fish—it's more of a backcountry experience," Captain Cardenas explains. "And there's no killing for glory. The fish are so hard to catch, it seems to diminish the quality of the experience to whack them over the head. Most people practice catch and release."

But there can be plenty of action: "It's really exciting to see a barracuda on the flats," Captain Cardenas says. "It's a very aggressive fish, and shallow water is its territory. When you cast a fly in front of a barracuda, it charges. It's a very predatory moment happening right in front of your eyes as the fish jumps and does figure eights out of the water!" Typical costs for sight fishing trips are $350 for a full day and $250 for a half-day; no more than two anglers can split the cost because the boats are so small.

Seasons

In South Florida, charter and drift boats go out every day, and customers have a good chance of catching something at any time of year. But spring and fall offer better chances of landing a big fish—or at least seeing more action. May and June are excellent for tarpon, fish that are all muscle. As Captain Cardenas says, "Catch a 100-pound tarpon on a fly line and they go nuts." Guides are booked a year in advance during the tarpon season.

In general, better fishing occurs when the water temperature is above 72 degrees. In the winter, when the sea temperature drops below 70 degrees, the only thing that will usually bite is barracuda.

How to Judge a Fishing Trip

With four major styles of deep-sea fishing to choose from, anyone with the time, interest, and money can experience high-quality saltwater angling in South Florida, especially if you heed these final words of advice. "A lot of people get wrapped up in judging a fishing trip by the number of fish they caught," Captain Cardenas says. "That's not the way to do it, though. It's better to meet your own challenges and have a good time. The guy who caught 20 fish didn't necessarily have a better day. It's all in how you approach it. Like any sport, more involvement increases the enjoyment."

The Best of South Florida

Florida touring has long been associated with sun, water, and sports. Many such destinations are good; some are "the best." We've put together a purely subjective list of "bests" throughout South Florida. In some places, we've come up with more than one. For more information on each venue, see complete listings in each chapter.

Best Beaches

Hollywood Beach (Hollywood, Broward County)
Captiva Beach (Captiva, Lee Island Coast, Southwest Florida)
Crandon Park (Key Biscayne, Miami-Dade County)

Best Golf

The Breakers (Palm Beach, Palm Beach County)
Fiddler's Creek (Naples, Collier County, Southwest Florida)
Doral Country Club (Miami, Miami-Dade County)
PGA National Resort & Spa (Palm Beach Gardens,
    Palm Beach County)

Best Tennis

Delray Beach Tennis Center (Delray Beach, Palm Beach County)
Holiday Park (Fort Lauderdale, Broward County)
David Park (Hollywood, Broward County)

Best Diving

Artificial Reef program (Fort Lauderdale, Broward County)

Best Sport Fishing

Florida Keys
Miami Beach
Palm Beach County

Best Drift Fishing

Flamingo Fishing (Fort Lauderdale, Broward County)

Best Shelling

Captiva Island (Lee Island Coast, Southwest Florida)
Sanibel Island (Lee Island Coast, Southwest Florida)

Best Museum for Children

The Museum of Discovery & Science/Blockbuster IMAX 3D
    (Fort Lauderdale, Broward County)

Best Museums for Adults

Billie Swamp Safari and Ah-Tah-Thi-Ki Museum, Big Cypress Reservation
(west of Fort Lauderdale, Broward County)
Fort Myers Historical Museum (Fort Myers, Southwest Florida)
Norton Museum of Art (Palm Beach, Palm Beach County)

Best Museum for Fishermen

IGFA Fishing Hall of Fame & Museum (Dania Beach, Broward County)

Best Mode of Transportation

Water Taxi (Fort Lauderdale, Broward County)

Best Views of Nature

Babcock Wilderness Adventures (Punta Gorda, Lee Island Coast,
Southwest Florida)
J.N. "Ding" Darling National Wildlife Refuge (Sanibel Island,
Lee Island Coast, Southwest Florida)
Everglades Holiday Park (Fort Lauderdale, Broward County)
Anne Kolb Nature Center (Hollywood, Broward County)

Best View of Beautiful People

South Beach (Miami Beach, Miami-Dade County)

Best Dining Choices

Grill Room on Las Olas (Fort Lauderdale, Broward County)
Norman's (Coral Gables, Miami-Dade County)
Joe's Stone Crab (Miami Beach, Miami-Dade County)

Best Shopping

Sawgrass Mills (Sunrise, Broward County)
Fifth Avenue South (Naples, Southwest Florida)

Best Performing Arts Venues

Broward Theater of the Performing Arts (Fort Lauderdale, Broward County)
Philharmonic Center for the Arts (Naples, Southwest Florida)

Best Tree

Banyan tree at Thomas A. Edison Winter Home (Fort Myers,
Southwest Florida)

South Florida for Children

You'll find myriad opportunities for vacations with children throughout
the southern part of the Sunshine State. Designed to delight the kids, they

range from butterfly watching to hands-on science museums, from first-class zoos to a wonderful wooden roller coaster, from nature walks among hundreds of alligators, and beaches, beaches, beaches.

Most families with children visit South Florida during the summer months, when school is out—and the region is hot and humid. So, before starting off on a day of touring or a visit to the beach, parents should keep some things in mind.

Sunburn, Overheating, and Dehydration Due to South Florida's sub-tropical climate, parents with young children on a day's outing need to pay close attention to their kids. The most common problems of smaller children are sunburn, overheating and dehydration. Sunburn in young children can cause lifelong problems. Dr. Stuart Sobel, a Hollywood (Florida) board-certified dermatologist, says "Florida obviously has a lot of sunny, clear days. We don't have a lot of tall buildings that block out the sky, so there's a lot of ultraviolet light the comes at you from all over. If you can see blue sky, you can get burned." The doctor advises putting sunscreen on every morning before breakfast. Sweat, friction, or rain dilutes sunscreen, and it must be reapplied throughout the day.

Dr. Sobel also says that "[sun protection] numbering systems are about to be disbanded by the FDA," adding that what we considered 15 and above will be appropriate for medium skin and 30 and above for fair skin. "Don't forget to put sunscreen on neck, top of the shoulders, tops of feet, etc.," he says. He also says that any sunscreen should include the UVA blockers Parsol or Avobenzone, and he suggests products such as Solumbra, which are sun-proof, and ultraviolet-coated glasses. "Wear hats," he adds, "and be careful in the sun from about 11 a.m. to 3 p.m."

Don't count on keeping small children properly hydrated with soft drinks and water fountain stops. Long lines at popular attractions often make buying refreshments problematic, and water fountains are not always handy. What's more, excited children may not inform you or even realize that they're thirsty or overheated. We recommend renting a stroller for children six years old and under and carrying plastic water bottles.

The Beach Don't let kids swim alone. Don't leave kids alone on the beach. Practice the buddy system (we think that's good advice even for adults) and realize that it's easy to become disoriented in the water. Occasional riptides will be noted by lifeguards who warn of these hazards. For more information on the hazards of the beach and ocean swimming, see our section on swimming under "Considerations for Outdoor Recreation" (pages 21–23).

Blisters Blisters and sore feet are common for visitors of all ages, so wear comfortable, well-broken-in shoes or sandals. If you or your children are unusually susceptible to blisters, carry some precut Moleskin bandages; they offer the best possible protection, stick great, and won't sweat off. When you feel a hot spot, stop, air out your foot, and place a Moleskin over the area before a blister forms. Moleskin is available by name at all drugstores. Sometimes small children won't tell their parents about a developing blister until it's too late. We recommend inspecting the feet of preschoolers at least twice a day. White athletic socks absorb perspiration and might be your best bet.

Sunglasses   If you want your smaller children to wear sunglasses, it's a good idea to affix a strap or string to the frames so the glasses won't get lost and can hang from the child's neck while indoors. Remember, ultraviolet coating is advised.

Where to Go with Kids

The *Unofficial Guide* rating system for attractions includes an "appeal to different age groups" category indicating a range of appeal from one star (★), don't bother, up to five stars (★★★★★), not to be missed. To get you started, we've provided a list, county by county, of 30 attractions in South Florida most likely to appeal to children. These offer exposure to nature, a look at native or exotic wildlife, a sense of what Florida was like in its early days, or are museums designed purely with kids in mind.

Top Attractions for Kids

Palm Beach County
International Museum
  of Cartoon Art
Lion Country Safari

Broward County
Ah-Tah-Thi-Ki Museum
Butterfly World
Flamingo Gardens
Hurricane Wooden Roller
  Coaster
IGFA Fishing Hall of Fame
  & Museum
Museum of Discovery &
  Science/3D IMAX Theater
Young At Art Museum

Miami-Dade County
Biscayne National Park
Everglades National Park/Shark
  Valley Tram Tour
Gold Coast Railroad Museum
Historical Museum of South
  Florida
Metrozoo
Miami Museum of Science/
  Space Transit Planetarium
Monkey Jungle
Parrot Jungle and Gardens
Seaquarium
Weeks Air Museum

Top Attractions for Kids (continued)

Florida Keys
East Martello Museum
Fort Zachary Taylor State
  Historic Site
John Pennecamp Coral Reef State
  Park
Key West Aquarium
Natural History Museum of the
  Florida Keys

Collier County
Everglades City & Everglades
  National Park

Lee County
Babcock Wilderness Experience
Centennial Park
Imaginarium
Manatee Park
Thomas Edison/Henry Ford
  Winter Estates

How to Avoid Crime and Keep Safe in Public Places

CRIME IN SOUTH FLORIDA

You don't have to be a fan of *Miami Vice* reruns to know that Miami has a reputation for glamorous, over-the-top crime. Blame it on a lot of things: the city's geographical and (some say) moral position on the edge of the continent; a drug-smuggling industry that turns over as much as $12 billion a year; a proliferation of guns in the hands of its citizenry (the bloodiest shoot-out in FBI history took place in Miami, and Florida has *the* most liberal gun ownership laws in the country); a crush of immigrants fleeing dictatorial bad guys throughout Latin America (a situation which also spawned several racial disturbances in the last two decades); and rising crime against tourists. Inevitably you will ask yourself, Just how safe is Miami, anyway? Am I going to end up being another statistic?

The chances are slim. Crime statistics for all of South Florida—Miami-Dade included—are down. Way down. And savvy travelers should know that you don't take chances on vacation that you don't take at home. Do you wander about marginal areas of your home town late at night? Do you flash wads of bills or impressive jewelry without a second thought? We don't think so. We think most people are pretty circumspect about their behavior and eager to avoid becoming a victim. And we can't understand why that behavior should be altered just because sun and fun have been factored into the loop.

The fact is, most deadly violence that occurs anywhere today is either the result of domestic strife or a drug deal gone wrong. By steering clear of both situations, visitors can leave safely on the same airplane they came in on. Some experts even say that Miami is safer now than in the 1920s, when gangsters like Al Capone were muscling in on illegal nightclubs and casinos. A local historian notes that Miami's crime rate was three times higher per capita in 1925 than in the early 1980s, when the town earned its title as "Murder Capital USA." If that's true, bystanders have never been safer in South Florida.

Surviving Miami International Airport

And what about all the bad press a few years back about the killing of tourists leaving the Miami airport? The problem is simple: Miami International Airport is located in an economically distressed, high-crime neighborhood. And while the Airport Expressway whisks you the eight miles to Miami in about as many minutes (except during rush hour), getting to the expressway isn't so easy if your rental car agency is located on a side street outside the airport—and a lot of them are.

The solution? There are several, depending on your degree of concern about crime. You could choose a rental car company based on its easy access to the expressway instead of its rates. Or make sure you have a cellular phone. (A lot of Miami car rental agencies provide a car phone at no additional charge; you pay for the phone calls by the minute; they can also be rented.) Or take a taxi or shuttle van to your hotel and have your rental car delivered to you there.

Our opinion? We think most people overreacted to the spate of bad publicity Miami received in 1993 when nine foreign tourists were murdered in Florida. As tragic and frightening as these deaths are, that's nine unfortunate people killed out of the 20 million visitors who came to Florida that year. While the neighborhoods around the airport can be dangerous and confusing, signs to the expressway have been improved recently, and car rental agencies are providing detailed directions when they send you on your way.

In fact, car rental agencies take the crime threat *very* seriously. Today, all rental cars are virtually indistinguishable from private vehicles; they carry regular license plates and no stickers. Most car rental offices are equipped with TVs that continuously show videos instructing customers how to avoid becoming a crime victim; the offices also provide customers with detailed written information on avoiding crime.

More reassuring news: In 1995, more than 400 new directional highway signs were erected throughout Miami-Dade at a cost of nearly $3 million. The signs feature an orange sunburst logo and direct visitors toward major tourist areas. Finally, Miami-Dade has inaugurated a new police force, the Tourist Oriented Police Squad (TOPS), to patrol the airport area; look for the marked squad cars patrolling the roadways and neighborhoods surrounding MIA. In addition, the Tourist Robbery Abatement Program

(TRAP) assigns police officers to patrol areas frequented by tourists such as the airport, car rental parking lots, and nearby neighborhoods.

Area police departments, eager to help tourists and improve a poor image, offer the following advice:

- Don't read a road map at an intersection—it attracts people's attention.

- Go to a restaurant or well-lighted parking lot and read the map there.

- If you're bumped from behind by another car, it could be a bad guy trying to trick you into pulling over by staging a fake accident. Keep going.

- Another scam: Criminals will wave and point at your tires, acting like good samaritans who only want to warn you that one of your tires is bad. Their goal is to get you to stop and get out of your car—so that they can rob you, or worse.

- Use your imagination and you'll think of other methods that bad guys will use to set up unsuspecting tourists for a mugging. The key is to avoid becoming a victim by *not* pulling over on the side of the road, where you're most vulnerable. Drive to a safe, lighted area before stopping and leaving your car.

More Advice for Visitors

- Keep your luggage in the trunk. Bad guys look inside cars at traffic lights and if they see luggage, they know you're a tourist.

- At stoplights, leave room between you and the vehicle ahead. If someone approaches your car, you have room to make a U-turn.

- Do whatever it takes to avoid becoming a crime victim. If you have to run a red light to avoid someone who approaches you, do it.

- In parking lots, park near entryways to malls or shopping centers, or under bright lights.

- Always look in the rearview mirror and all around you. Crime can happen anywhere.

ROAD RAGE

A relatively new phenomenon, this can basically be described as the act of physically harming someone who may have cut you off, switched lanes, taken a parking place, etc. Most of us learned early on that controlling one's temper is a sign of maturity. Apparently, today's stresses, heavy traffic, and lousy drivers bring out a lot of immaturity. Cases on record include vulgar finger action, one driver reaching in and grabbing the sunglasses from another driver's face, and actual shootings.

Fortunately, it's not a common occurrence, but it does occur. Our best advice? Drive carefully and with uncommon courtesy. This is not a problem unique to South Florida. Overloaded highways, commuters who spend hours in their cars, fuel costs, and other challenges make it a universal situation. Again, drive with care—and courtesy. Signal lane changes or turns; don't let parking spaces turn you into an ogre. Drive with patience.

THE GOOD NEWS

The increased presence of the City of Miami police on the roads has, in fact, reduced crime: In late 1995, crimes against tourists dropped approximately 60 percent compared to the previous year. Visitor robberies decreased 80 percent between 1992 and 1996; a whopping 26 percent drop occurred between 1995 and 1996. As a result, we think Miami is no more dangerous than any other big U.S. city.

Similar statistics are available for other areas covered in this book: Broward, Collier, Lee, and Palm Beach Counties, as well as the Florida Keys. Crime is down, public awareness is up, and tourist communities are looking for visitors to come, enjoy, and go away happy. A tourist who's had to file a police report makes for bad public relations.

HAVING A PLAN

Random violence and street crime are facts of life in any large city. You've got to be cautious and alert and plan ahead. Police are rarely able to actually foil a crime in progress. When you are out and about, you must work under the assumption that you are on your own; if you run into trouble, it's unlikely that police or anyone else will be able to come to your rescue. You must give some advance thought to the ugly scenarios that might occur; consider both preventive measures that will keep you out of harm's way and an escape plan just in case.

Not being a victim of street crime is sort of a "survival of the fittest" thing. Just as a lion stalks the weakest member of the antelope herd, muggers and thieves target the easiest victims. Simply put, no matter where you are or what you are doing, you want potential felons to think of you as a bad risk.

On the Street   For starters, you always present less of an appealing target if you are with other people. Secondly, if you must be out alone, act alert and always have at least one of your arms and hands free. Felons gravitate toward preoccupied folks, the kind found plodding along staring at the sidewalk, with both arms encumbered by briefcases or packages. Visible jewelry (on either men or women) attracts the wrong kind of attention. Men, keep your billfolds in your *front* trouser or coat pocket, or in a fanny pack. Women, keep your purses tucked tightly under your arm; if you're wearing a jacket, put it on *over* your shoulder bag strap.

Here's another tip: carry two wallets, including one inexpensive one, carried in your hip pocket, containing about $20 in cash and some expired credit cards. This is the one you hand over if you're accosted. Your real credit cards and the bulk of whatever cash you have should be in either a money clip or a second wallet hidden elsewhere on your person. Women can carry a fake wallet in their purses and keep the real one in a pocket or money belt.

If You're Approached   Police will tell you that a criminal has the least amount of control over his intended victim during the first few moments of his initial approach. A good strategy, therefore, is to short-circuit the crime as quickly as possible. If a mugger starts by demanding your money, for instance, quickly take out your billfold (preferably your fake one), and hurl it as far as you can in one direction while you run shouting for help in the opposite direction. The odds are greatly in your favor that the criminal will prefer to collect your billfold rather than pursue you. If you hand over your wallet and just stand there, he will likely ask for your watch and jewelry next. If you're a woman, the longer you hang around, the greater your vulnerability to personal injury or rape.

Secondary Crime Scenes   Under no circumstances, police warn, should you *ever* allow yourself to be taken to another location—a "secondary crime scene," in police jargon. This move, they explain, provides the criminal more privacy and, consequently, more control. A mugger can rob you on the street very quickly and efficiently. If he tries to remove you to another location, whether by car or on foot, it is a certain indication that he has more in mind than robbery. Even if the thief has a gun or knife, your chances are infinitely better running away. If the criminal grabs your purse, let him have it. If he grabs your jacket, come out of it. Hanging onto your money or jacket is not worth getting mugged, sexually assaulted, or murdered.

Another maxim: never believe anything a criminal tells you, even if he's telling you something you desperately want to believe, for example, "I won't hurt you if you come with me." No matter how logical or benign he sounds, assume the worst. Always, *always,* break off contact as quickly as possible, even if that means running.

In Public Transport   When riding a bus, always take a seat as close to the driver as you can; never ride in the back. Likewise, on the subway or elevated train, sit near the driver's or attendant's compartment. These people have a phone and can summon help in the event of trouble.

In Cabs   While it's unlikely you'll need to hail a cab on the street in Miami or elsewhere in South Florida, you are somewhat vulnerable in the process if you do. Particularly after dusk, call a reliable cab company and stay inside while they dispatch a cab to your door. When your cab arrives, check the driver's certificate, which must, by law, be posted on the dashboard. Address the cabbie by his last name (Mr. Jones or whatever) or mention the number of his cab. This alerts the cab driver to the fact that you are going to remember him and/or his cab. Not only will this contribute to your safety, it will keep your cabbie from trying to run up the fare.

If you are comfortable reading maps, familiarize yourself with the most direct route to your destination ahead of time. If you can say, "South Beach via the Julia Tuttle Causeway, please," the driver is less likely to run up your fare by taking a circuitous route so he can charge you for extra mileage.

If you need to catch a cab at the train station or at one of the airports, always use the taxi queue. Taxis in the official queue are properly licensed and regulated. Never accept an offer for a cab or limo made by a stranger in the terminal or baggage claim area. At best, you will be significantly overcharged for the ride. At worst, you may be abducted.

Personal Attitude

While some areas of every city are more dangerous than others, never assume that any area is completely safe. Never let down your guard. You can be the victim of a crime and it can happen to you anywhere. If you go to a restaurant or nightspot, use valet parking or park in a well-lighted lot. Women leaving a restaurant or club alone should never be reluctant to ask to be escorted to their cars.

Never let your pride or sense of righteousness and indignation imperil your survival. This is especially difficult for many men, particularly when in the presence of women. It makes no difference whether you are approached by an aggressive drunk, an unbalanced street person, or an actual criminal, the rule is the same: forget your pride and break off contact as quickly as possible. Who cares whether the drunk insulted you, if everyone ends up back at the hotel safe and sound? When you wake up in the hospital with a concussion and your jaw wired shut, it's too late to decide that the drunk's filthy remark wasn't really all that important.

Criminals, junkies, some street people, and even some drunks play for keeps. They can attack with a bloodthirsty hostility and hellish abandon that is beyond the imagination of most people. Believe me, you are not in their league . . . nor do you want to be.

Self-Defense

In a situation where it is impossible to run, you'll need to be prepared to defend yourself. Most policemen insist that a gun or knife is not much use to the average person. More often than not, they say, the weapon will be turned against the victim. Additionally, concealed firearms and knives are illegal in most jurisdictions. The best self-defense device for the average person is Mace. Not only is it legal in most states, it's nonlethal and easy to use.

When you shop for Mace, look for two things: it should be able to fire about eight feet, and it should have a protector cap so it won't go off by mistake in your purse or pocket. Carefully read the directions that come with your device, paying particular attention to how it should be carried and stored, and how long the active ingredients will remain potent. Wearing a rubber glove, test-fire your Mace, making sure that you fire downwind.

When you are out about town, make sure your Mace is someplace easily accessible, say, attached to your keychain. If you are a woman and you keep your Mace on a keychain, avoid the habit of dropping your keys (and your Mace) into the bowels of your purse when you leave your hotel room or your car. *The Mace will not do you any good if you have to dig around in your purse for it.* Keep your keys and your Mace in your hand until you have safely reached your destination.

More Things to Avoid

When you do go out, walk with a minimum of two people whenever possible. If you have to walk alone, stay in well-lighted areas that have plenty of people around. And don't walk down alleys. It also helps not to look too much like a tourist when venturing away from beaches and other tourist areas. Don't wear a camera around your neck and don't gawk at buildings and unfold maps on the sidewalk—or thumb through guidebooks, including this one. Be careful about who you ask for directions. (When in doubt, shopkeepers are a good bet.) Don't count your money in public, and carry as little cash as possible. At public phones, if you must say your calling card number to make a long-distance call, don't say it loud enough for strangers around you to hear. And avoid public parks and beaches after dark.

Carjackings

With the recent surge in carjackings, drivers also need to take special precautions. Stay alert when driving in traffic and keep your doors locked, with the windows rolled up and the air conditioning on. Leave enough space to the car in front of you so that you're not blocked in and can make a U-turn if someone approaches your car and starts beating on your windshield. Store your purse or briefcase under your knees when you are driving, rather than on the seat beside you.

The Homeless

If you're not from a big city or haven't been to one in a while, you're in for a shock if you visit Miami. Near large public buildings in downtown Miami, you will see people sleeping in blankets and sleeping bags, their possessions piled up next to them.

Who Are These People? "Most are lifelong residents who are poor," responds Joan Alker, assistant director of the National Coalition for the Homeless, an advocacy group headquartered in Washington, D.C. "The people you see on the streets are primarily single men and women. A disproportionate number of them are minorities and people with disabilities—they're either mentally ill or substance abusers or have physical disabilities."

Are They a Threat to Visitors? "No," Alker says. "Studies show that homeless men have lower rates of conviction for violent crimes than the population at large. We know that murders aren't being committed by the homeless. I can't make a blanket statement, but most homeless people you see are no more likely to commit a violent crime than other people."

Should You Give the Homeless Money? "That's a personal decision," Alker says. "But if you can't, at least try to acknowledge their existence by looking them in the eye and saying, 'Sorry, no.'" While there's no way to tell if the guy with the Styrofoam cup asking for a handout is really destitute or just a con artist, no one can dispute that most of these people are what they claim to be: homeless.

Ways to Help It's really a matter for your own conscience. We confess to being both moved and annoyed by these unfortunate people; moved by their need and annoyed that we cannot enjoy any major city these days without running a gauntlet of begging men and women. In the final analysis, we found that it is easier on the conscience and spirit to get a couple of rolls of quarters at the bank and carry a pocket full of change at all times. The cost of giving those homeless who approach you a quarter really does not add up to all that much, and it is much better for the psyche to respond to their plight than to deny or ignore their presence.

There is a notion, perhaps valid in some cases, that money given to a homeless person generally goes toward the purchase of alcohol or other drugs. If this bothers you excessively, carry granola bars for distribution, or, alternatively, buy some inexpensive gift coupons that can be redeemed at a McDonald's or other fast-food restaurant for coffee or a sandwich.

We have found that a little kindness regarding the homeless goes a long way, and a few kind words delivered along with your quarter or granola bar brightens the day for both you and someone in need. We are not suggesting a lengthy conversation or prolonged involvement, but something simple like, "Sure, I can help a little bit. Take care of yourself, fella."

Those moved to get more involved in the nationwide problem of homelessness can send inquiries—or a check—to the National Coalition for the Homeless, 1612 K Street, NW, Suite 1004, Washington, D.C. 20006.

Keep It Brief Finally, don't play psychologist. All the people you encounter on the street are strangers. They may be harmless, or they may be dangerous. Either way, maintain distance and keep any contacts or encounters brief. Be prepared to handle street people in accordance with your principles, but mostly, just be prepared. If you have a junkie in your face wanting a handout, the last thing you want to do is pull out your wallet and thumb through the twenties looking for a one-dollar bill. As the sergeant used to say on *Hill Street Blues:* Be careful out there.

Things The Natives Already Know
CUSTOMS AND PROTOCOL

With its tropical climate and reputation as a vacation capital, South Florida takes casualness to extremes that can startle folks from colder, stuffier climes —and we're not referring to the profusion of topless bathers on South Beach.

Attire

It's hard not to think of a situation where shorts, a loud print shirt, and a straw hat wouldn't be appropriate—with the exception of a small number of exclusive restaurants and clubs that require jackets and ties (or more commonly, just jackets) for men and equally formal attire for women. Casual, cool, lightweight, and colorful clothing is the norm throughout South Florida. The usual outfit for men and women during the day is T-shirt and shorts. Silks, cottons, and linens—natural fibers—are the coolest, allowing the skin to breathe in hot, humid weather. We note both men's and women's clothing takes advantage of these fabrics.

But we must offer a word of caution for the business traveler. Professionals still opt for suits—a business-like demeanor is definitely called for in the elegant office buildings of downtown Miami, Fort Lauderdale, or on the Gulf Coast. Shirts and ties are as necessary for an important business meeting whether the temperature is 90 degrees or 9, and whether it takes place in New York City or Naples, Florida. It's a mistake to assume that Florida means a total lack of formality. Barely there tops or T-shirts with inappropriate messages won't work any better in South Florida boardrooms or banks than they do up north.

Nighttime is dressier. It's a time to glitz up and get out, and we've seen some wild-looking outfits on South Beach and more toned-down looks everywhere else. It's really a matter of taste. Casual is the operative mode of dress, but be aware that even in South Florida a jacket can be a necessity.

A formal notice: Although Chambers of Commerce won't always agree, Florida—even the most southern portions—occasionally suffers cold spells. A lightweight jacket, cotton sweaters, and long pants become the clothes of choice during December, January, and February. We also suggest some kind of rainproof jacket for a visit any time of the year.

Finally, no matter how hot or how humid—*everything* is air-conditioned. We go from air-conditioned homes (hotels) into air-conditioned cars, to air-conditioned shops, to air-conditioned restaurants, theaters, museums, etc. Unless you plan to hike ten miles a day, South Florida in the summer is no worse than New York, Omaha, or Pittsburgh in July and August.

Eating in Restaurants

South Florida has emerged as a kind of capital of Latin America and an international mixing bowl of cultures. This mix boasts an astounding variety of restaurants. In fact, the emergence of a new cuisine in town could be an indicator of political unrest somewhere in the world. The first thing new immigrants do when they hit Florida, it seems, is open a restaurant.

Again, casual is the byword when it comes to dining in most Florida restaurants. (If you are concerned, ask if there's a dress code.) Don't feel intimidated by unfamiliar menus or a waitstaff that doesn't speak English— many Latin restaurants offer menus in both Spanish and English, and you only need to point to place your order. (Just as many French restaurants offer bilingual menus. And during the season in Broward County, you will find many French-speakers.)

Early Birds   Not your typical aviary, South Florida restaurants are home to Early-Bird Specials. Translated, that means cheaper meals, served earlier than normal dining times and sometimes (but not always) made up of smaller portions. Often these meals are three courses, and diners can take home leftovers. Most restaurants run their Early Birds until 6 or 7 p.m., while some offer Early, Early Birds which are served somewhere around 3 or 4 p.m.

Tipping

Is the tip you normally leave at home appropriate in South Florida? The answer is yes. Just bear in mind that a tip is a reward for good service. Here are some guidelines:

Porters and Skycaps   A dollar a bag.

Cab Drivers   A lot depends on the service and courtesy. If the fare is less than $8, give the driver the change and a dollar. Example: If the fare is $4.50, give the cabbie fifty cents and a buck. If the fare is more than $8, give the driver the change and $2. If you are asking the cabbie to take you only a block or two, the fare will be small, but your tip should be large ($3–5) to make up for his wait in line and to partially compensate him for missing a better-paying fare. Add an extra dollar if the driver does a lot of luggage handling.

Parking Valets $2 is correct if the valet is courteous and demonstrates some hustle. A dollar will do if the service is just OK. Only pay when you check your car out, not when you leave it.

Bellmen   When a bellman greets you at your car with one of those rolling luggage carts and handles all of your bags, $5 is about right. The more luggage you carry yourself, of course, the less you should tip.

Waiters   Whether in a coffee shop, an upscale eatery, or ordering room service from the hotel kitchen, the standard gratuity ranges from 15 to 20% of the tab, before sales tax. At a buffet or brunch where you serve yourself, leave a dollar or two for the folks who bring your drinks. Some restaurants, however, are adopting the European custom of automatically adding a 15% gratuity to the bill, so check before leaving a cash tip.

Cocktail Waiters/Bartenders   In this case you tip by the round. For two people, a dollar a round; for more than two people, $2 a round. For a large group, use your judgment: Is everyone drinking beer, or is the order long and complicated? Tip accordingly.

Hotel Maids   On checking out, leave a dollar or two per day for each day of your stay, providing the service was good.

How to Look and Sound Like a Native

First, a definition: a South Florida native is anyone who has lived in town for five years or longer. In other words, this is an area of transients. As a result, visitors to Palm Beach or Naples, to Fort Myers or Miami, to Fort Lauderdale or Key West needn't feel concerned about not fitting in. Keep in mind that this region hosts millions of visitors a year from all over the world, and most leave wanting to return.

Yet, if it's important to you not to look like A Visitor on Holiday in the Sun and Fun Capital of North America, we offer the following tongue-in-cheek advice for Miami-Dade:

1. Pronounce the city's name "My-AM-uh," the way folks did when Miami was more Anglo than Latin. Problem is, a lot of natives may not understand what you're saying.

2. Never ever admit visiting the Everglades.

3. Be obsessive, if not maniacal, about the Dolphins, Panthers, Marlins, or the Heat.

4. Be drop-dead beautiful and strut your stuff on Ocean Drive in South Beach. An eye-catching option for ladies: Strap on a thong bikini and cruise through Lummus Park on in-line skates.

5. Sit alone at a sidewalk café on Ocean Drive in South Beach and engage in an intense conversation—on your cellular phone.

6. Men: For a night of clubbing on South Beach or Coconut Grove, sport an earring, ponytail, and gold Rolex while attired in a tux jacket, gaudy Bermuda shorts, and no socks.

7. For women on the town, it's ego-dressing: An orchid behind the ear, a low-cut blouse, a skirt slit up the thigh, or a silk nightgown; other options include anything in a bright floral pattern or leopard skin, or a tight leather miniskirt.

8. Leave the dog at home. A parrot perched on your shoulder or a boa constrictor draped over an arm is a sure indication you're not from Duluth.

9. Hire a hot-pink Rolls Royce and a driver and go clubbing on South Beach. Needless to say, as the hot wheels idle outside blocking traffic, you'll be making a statement.

10. Never eat green Key lime pie.

Okay, get the point? When in Rome (or a city in South Florida) do what the natives do and don't call attention to yourself.

PUBLICATIONS FOR VISITORS

The *Miami Herald* is Miami's only daily newspaper, while the *Fort Lauderdale Sun-Sentinel* does the job for Broward County. Both papers provide Friday editions with comprehensive information on entertainment, restaurants, nightclubs, happenings for kids, art reviews, and things going on around town. Try to grab a Friday edition before heading south.

Another source for listings is the weekly *New Times,* an alternative newspaper available free from street machines as well as from a wide variety of clubs, bars, and shops around town. It carries listings for both Miami-Dade and Broward Counties.

Other publications available at newsstands and hotel lobbies include *Metro Metro,* the area's main monthly magazine; *Ocean Drive,* a glossy South Miami Beach magazine that chronicles the comings and goings of celebrities and beautiful people; *South Beach,* a bimonthly with a more artistic slant on SoBe life; *City and Shore,* a new bimonthly; and *Travel Host,* a visitors' guide with information on shopping, dining, clubs, pay-per-view television, and maps.

In Palm Beach, it's the *Palm Beach Post.* Both the *Herald* and the *Sun-Sentinel* include the Palm Beach area in their weekly listings on Friday.

As for daily newspapers, in Fort Myers it's the *News-Press,* and in Naples it's the *Naples Daily News.* The area's magazines include *Florida Journal, Fort Myers Life, Gulfshore Life, Southwest Florida Business Magazine,* and *Times of the Islands/Shore and Island Living.*

RADIO

Aside from the usual babble of format rock, talk, easy listening, and country music stations, South Florida is home to a few radio stations that really stand out for high-quality broadcasting. Tune in to what hip locals listen to.

South Florida's High-Quality Radio Stations

South Florida:

Format	Frequency	Station
Jazz, Latin	88.9 FM	WDMA
Progressive rock, jazz, punk	90.5 FM	WVUM
Public radio	91.3 FM	WLRN
Classical, jazz	93.1 FM	WTMI

Southwest Florida:

Format	Frequency	Station
Rock	96.1	WRXK
Country Western	107.1	WCKT
Hip Hop	105.5	WBTT
Public radio	90.1	WGCU

TIPS FOR DISABLED VISITORS

Most public places in South Florida offer generally impressive facilities for disabled visitors, because a lot of buildings are recent structures built with wheelchair access in mind. Plus, many buses have lowering platforms that allow wheelchair-bound passengers to board.

Florida State law requires guide dogs to be permitted in all establishments. Also, motorists must yield to people with white canes and guide dogs.

Disability Parking

Out-of-state vehicles displaying disability parking permits/plates issued by another state are allowed to park in spaces designated for persons with disabilities.

Additional Information for Disabled Visitors

In Everglades National Park, all the walking trails are wheelchair accessible. Due to the passage of the Americans with Disabilities Act in 1990, the issue of access for folks with disabilities has gotten a higher profile in Miami. Even small Art Deco hotels in South Beach now offer elevators, ramps, and bathrooms with railings to make their rooms wheelchair-accessible.

In addition, there are a number of services in South Florida to serve the needs of disabled folks.

- The **Deaf Services Bureau** (Gables One Tower, 1320 South Dixie Highway, Suite 760, Coral Gables; (305) 668-4407 voice/TDD, fax (305) 668-4669) provides interpreter services, advocacy, information, personal counseling, special needs assistance, and a 24-hour crisis hotline: (305) 668-4694 (TDD). Open Monday, Tuesday, Thursday, and Friday, 9 a.m.–5 p.m.; Wednesday, 9 a.m.–noon.

■ The **Deaf Service Center of Southwest Florida** (12995 S. Cleveland Avenue, #1050, Fort Myers; (941) 936-3080, (941) 936-5535 TDD).

■ The **Florida Relay Service** (200 S. Biscayne Boulevard, Suite 600, Miami; (305) 579-8644 or (800) 955-8770; TDD is (800) 955-8771) serves as a liaison for deaf and hard-of-hearing visitors with TDDs who need to contact persons without TDD-equipped phones. Open 24 hours a day, seven days a week.

■ The **State of Florida Division of Blind Services** (401 NW 2nd Avenue, Suite S714, Miami, (305) 377-5339 and 2133 Winkler Avenue, Suite 410, Fort Myers, (941) 278-7130) provides services to visually impaired people.

■ Paraplegics and other physically disabled people needing referrals to services in the Miami area can contact the **Metro-Dade Disability Services and Independent Living** (D-SAIL) office located at 1335 NW 14th Street in Miami; (305) 547-5444.

■ The **Disability Affairs** section of the **Broward County Equal Opportunity Office** (115 S. Andrews Avenue, Fort Lauderdale; (954) 357-6500) is in accord with the ADA.

■ **Advocacy Center for Persons with Disabilities** (Broward County, (954) 967-1493).

■ **Disabilities Helpline** (Broward County, (954) 467-6333).

■ **Emergency Management** (Broward County, (954) 831-3916 and (954) 357-6402).

Transportation Services for the Disabled

In Palm Beach   Dial-A-Ride (phone (561) 689-2222).

In Broward   Paratransit (phone (954) 357-6794 or (954) 347-8400 for schedules and routes), **Tri Rail TDD** (phone (800) 273-7535).

In Southwest Florida   Good Wheels (10075 Bavaria Road, Fort Myers, phone (941) 433-500); **Help Link** (7275 Concourse Drive SW, Fort Myers, phone (941) 433-5000 or (941) 433-5154 TDD); **Alert Non-Emergency Transport** (phone (941) 565-3909); **Andres Medicar Service** (phone (941) 275-6050); **Comfort Service** (phone (941) 995-8313); **Elite**

Transportation (phone (941) 275-8726); **People in Motion** (phone (941) 489-4560); **Serenity Services** (phone (800) 924-0760 and (941) 433-4355); and **Sunshine Transportation** (phone (941) 489-3666).

BUGS

The area's subtropical climate regularly soaks South Florida in extended stretches of heat, rain, and humidity. Because South Florida rarely experiences freezing temperatures, the result is a plethora of insect activity year-round. For people from more temperate climes, often the biggest shock they receive on a visit to the area is the sight of *cockroaches*.

But visitors shouldn't be shocked or overly concerned about the bugs—because most sightings are brief glimpses at night as they scurry out of sight when a light is turned on. Unless you're staying at a ritzy resort that goes to the expense of protecting its guests from the sight of insects, you're bound to see an occasional roach during your stay in South Florida.

Relax.

"Just because you see roaches doesn't mean a place isn't clean," reports one longtime resident who says she's as freaked out by bugs as anyone from more temperate climes. "They're only active at night, they don't crawl on you, and they don't bite or make noise. The really good news is that roaches don't like people. But roaches are a part of Florida."

Another local insect with a notorious reputation—this one more well deserved—is the *mosquito*. But if your stay in South Florida revolves around the beach, mosquitoes aren't much of a problem: Ocean breezes keep the pesky critters at a minimal level year-round.

On the other hand, if your visit isn't centered on the beach, or if you plan to make some inland sojourns, get ready to be attacked by mosquitoes. The worst place of all for mosquitoes is the Everglades, which we recommend only visiting in the winter—and even then, it's a good idea to use insect repellent, which is readily available at retail outlets and visitor centers.

During the summer, many South Florida residents listen closely to local news broadcasts for reports of mosquito activity. Long, wet periods of rain often result in a predictable explosion in the mosquito population. If one is on the way, it's a good idea to reschedule any extended outdoor activities that you're planning away from the beach.

ENCEPHALITIS

Mosquitoes flourish during periods of summer rain. One particularly awful result of a heavy infestation of mosquitoes is encephalitis. It is not a common disease in Florida, and most summers see no cases reported. Rather, health officials advise taking precautions during periods of warmth and moisture. These precautions include:

- Avoid outdoor activities between dusk and dawn when mosquitoes are most active.

- If you must be outside at night, wear long pants and long-sleeved shirts, as well as insect repellent on exposed skin.

- Avoid water—especially standing water—at night.

BRING LOTS OF QUARTERS

After spending a day or two exploring South Florida by car, you'll discover this fact: Because of ubiquitous parking meters, you can't survive without quarters—lots of them. The demand for two-bit pieces is so intense, in fact, that some businesses in the Miami-Dade area charge each other $1 for a $20 roll of quarters. One shop owner on Miami Beach pointed out that the only places that drop the surcharges are banks and Publix food stores. Our advice: Buy a few rolls before hitting town, tuck them in a corner of your luggage, and generously resupply your pocket or purse with quarters each day.

A CUBAN COFFEE PRIMER

You'll see crowds huddling around an open window in front of the restaurants that line Calle Ocho in Little Havana and dot the rest of Miami. It's the café window, presenting the same aroma of Cuban coffee that hits you when you enter the MIA terminal and stays curled in your nostrils as you tour Miami. It's as ubiquitous as the palm trees.

In the mornings, workers stop by the windows for a Styrofoam cup of *cafe con leche,* espresso with steamed milk. In late afternoon, the men in their *guayaberas* (loose-fitting shirts) gather to talk politics and drink thimblefuls of black, sweetened espresso. Some of the local Anglos call it "jet fuel."

Here's a java glossary of *cafe Cubano* in ascending order of potency.

Cafe con leche—usually a morning drink. About one part coffee to four parts steamed whole milk. Usually served *con azucar* (with sugar) and very sweet. Ask for it *sin azucar* (without sugar) and add your own to taste. For more of a kick, ask for it *oscuro* (dark).

Cortadito—smaller than a *cafe con leche.* About one part espresso to two parts milk.

Colada—a cup of straight, hypersugared espresso served with about five plastic thimble-sized cups for sharing. Only the truly intestinally fortified would venture to drink one solo.

For gifts or to replicate *cafe Cubano* in your espresso machine at home, Cafe Bustelo and Cafe Pilon are two of the most popular brands of espresso and are available in almost all local supermarkets and stores; stock up before you leave South Florida.

¿HABLA ESPANOL?
A CRASH COURSE IN SPANISH FOR ANGLOS

Though many would say otherwise, the official language of South Florida *is* English. Most locals speak rudimentary English, although their native tongue often is Spanish. But it's possible, on rare occasions (say, your car breaks down or you're in a small shop or restaurant), to find yourself in a situation where there's no one around who speaks English. Of course, you'll have this book at hand.

If you find yourself trying out your rudimentary Spanish with a non-English speaker, keep these hints in mind: Speak slowly and clearly. Charades and hand gestures have been known to bridge language gaps. And the critical ingredient to cross-cultural communication is a sense of humor.

Hola. Como estas? (Oh-lah. Como es-tahs?) Hello. How are you?

Donde esta la playa? El aeropuerto? (Don-day es-tah lah ply-yah? El arrow-pwerto?) Where is the beach? The airport?

Es muy lejos? (Es moo-ey lay-hohs?) Is it very far?

Esta bien. (Es-tah bee-en.) Okay.

Quiero el cafe sin azucar, por favor. Quiero arroz con pollo y una cerveza. (Key-err-o el cah-fey seen azoo-car, pour fah-vor. Key-err-oh-rose cone poy-yo ee oon-a ser-vay-sah.) I would like a coffee without sugar, please. I'd like chicken with rice and a beer.

No puedo hablar espanol (No pway-doh ab-lar es-pan-nyol.) I can't speak Spanish.

No se. (No say.) I don't know.

Dime. (Dee-may.) Tell me.

Dame. (Dah-may.) Give me.

Gracias. (Grah-see-ahs.) Thank you.

Cuanto cuesta? (Kwan-toe kwes-tah?) How much is it?

DEFENSIVE DRIVING

We can't say it too many times. Driving in rush hour is always rife with problems. Okay, that's overstating the obvious, but specific roadways such as I-95 in Palm Beach, Broward or Miami-Dade, I-595 in Broward, I-75 to the Southwest Coast and Tamiami Trail between Fort Myers and Naples are heavily traveled highways at the best of times. During tourist seasons, at holidays, and during rush hour these can become a parking lot, and one accident can hold up traffic for hours. We can't stress too much that this is the time for caution and patience behind the wheel.

Part Two

Hotels

Deciding Where to Stay

LOCATION

Your main reason for visiting South Florida will help frame your choice of hotel. Your primary consideration should be location. Traffic is so bad in South Florida that you do not want to commute to your business or touring destination, or to the beach. While there are hotels all over South Florida—with some stuck in quite improbable places—we deal primarily with those hotels that are located in areas of concentrated tourist activity, business activity, or both.

Palm Beach County

Boca Raton A beautiful, safe, and accessible upscale resort area, Boca Raton offers many attractions as well as high-quality hotels and restaurants. Nestled east of the Florida Turnpike between Highway 798 and NW 51st Street, Boca Raton is convenient to many museums, theaters, and golf courses. The Boca Raton airport is less than five minutes northeast of the town center. For those traveling on a budget but still hoping to enjoy the glamour of Boca, a hotel just south in Deerfield or Hillsboro Beach would be a better choice.

West Palm Beach and Palm Beach West Palm Beach is more of a retail and business traveler–oriented place than Palm Beach. The hotels in West Palm service the Palm Beach International Airport, as well as the Dreher Park Zoo and the West Palm Beach Stadium. A short trip east lands you on the strip of land called Palm Beach, which is much more aristocratic (and expensive) than its western counterpart. Many high-ranking hotels and exquisite restaurants are located within this four-mile stretch of A1A. For the budget day-tripper, bicycle rental for a beautiful beachside excursion and a tour of the Flagler Museum are great ways to enjoy the area.

Palm Beach County Accommodations

1. Best Western University Inn
2. The Breakers Palm Beach
3. Canopy Palms Resort
4. Chesterfield Palm Beach
5. Colony Hotel & Cabana Club
6. Colony Palm Beach
7. Crowne Plaza West Palm Beach
8. Days Inn Oceanfront Resort
9. Days Inn Turnpike/Airport West
10. Delray Beach Marriott
11. DoubleTree Guest Suites Boca Raton
12. DoubleTree Hotel in the Gardens
13. Embassy Suites Boca Raton
14. Embassy Suites Palm Beach Gardens
15. Fairfield Inn & Suites
16. Four Seasons Resort Palm Beach
17. Hampton Inn West Palm Beach
18. Heart of Palm Beach Hotel
19. Hilton Palm Beach Airport
20. Hilton Singer Island Oceanfront Resort
21. Holiday Inn Boca Raton Town Center
22. Holiday Inn Express Downtown Boca Raton
23. Holiday Inn Highland Beach
24. Holiday Inn Palm Beach Airport
25. La Quinta West Palm Beach
26. Palm Beach Hawaiian Ocean Inn
27. Palm Beach Hilton Oceanfront
28. PGA National Resort
29. Radisson Bridge Resort of Boca Raton
30. Radisson Suite Hotel Boca Raton
31. Radisson Suite Inn Palm Beach Airport
32. Ramada Boca Raton
33. Ritz-Carlton Palm Beach
34. The Seagate
35. Sheraton Boca Raton Hotel
36. Sheraton Oceanfront North Palm Beach
37. Sheraton West Palm Beach
38. SpringHill Suites
39. Wright by the Sea

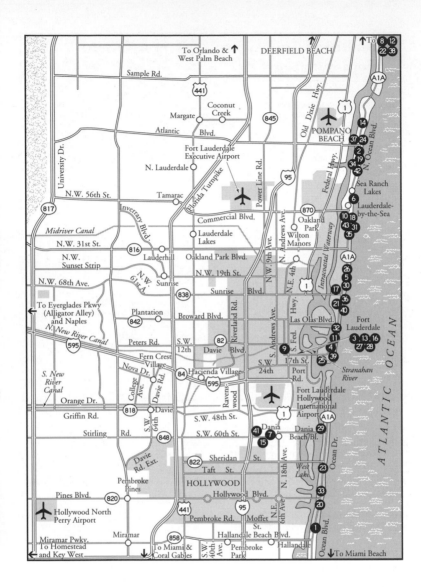

Broward County Accommodations

1. Ambassador Resort Hollywood Beach
2. Best Western Beachcomber
3. Best Western Marina Inn & Yacht Harbor
4. Best Western Oceanside Inn
5. Best Western Pelican Beach Resort
6. Clarion Lauderdale Beach Resort
7. Comfort Inn Fort Lauderdale Airport
8. Comfort Inn Oceanside
9. Comfort Suites Airport
10. Days Inn Fort Lauderdale
11. DoubleTree Hotel Fort Lauderdale Oceanfront
12. Embassy Suites Deerfield Beach Resort
13. Embassy Suites Fort Lauderdale
14. Four Points Sheraton Pompano Beach
15. Hampton Inn & Suites
16. Holiday Inn Express Port Everglades
17. Holiday Inn Fort Lauderdale Beach
18. Holiday Inn Lauderdale by the Sea
19. Holiday Inn Pompano Beach
20. Holiday Inn SunSpree Resort Hollywood Beach
21. Howard Johnson Ocean's Edge Fort Lauderdale
22. Howard Johnson Plaza Resort Deerfield Beach
23. Howard Johnson Plaza Resort Hollywood
24. Howard Johnson Plaza Resort Pompano Beach
25. Hyatt Regency Pier Sixty-Six
26. Ireland's Inn Beach Resort
27. Landmark Inn Airport
28. Marriott Fort Lauderdale Marina
29. Motel 6 Dania Beach
30. Ocean Hacienda Inn
31. Ocean Manor
32. Radisson Bahia Mar Beach Resort
33. Ramada Inn Hollywood Beach Resort Hotel
34. Ramada Inn Paradise Beach Resort
35. Ramada Plaza Beach Resort
36. Ramada Sea Club Resort
37. Sands Harbor Resort
38. Seabonay Beach Resort
39. Sheraton Yankee Clipper
40. Sheraton Yankee Trader
41. SpringHill Suites
42. Traders Ocean Resort
43. Travelodge Fort Lauderdale

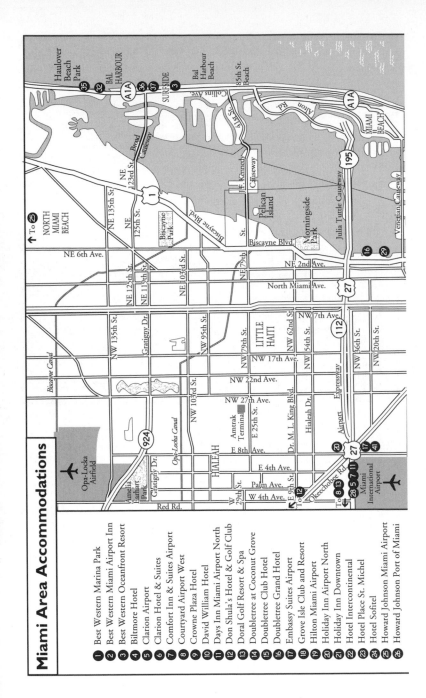

Miami Area Accommodations

1. Best Western Marina Park
2. Best Western Miami Airport Inn
3. Best Western Oceanfront Resort
4. Biltmore Hotel
5. Clarion Airport
6. Clarion Hotel & Suites
7. Comfort Inn & Suites Airport
8. Courtyard Airport West
9. Crowne Plaza Hotel
10. David William Hotel
11. Days Inn Miami Airport North
12. Don Shula's Hotel & Golf Club
13. Doral Golf Resort & Spa
14. Doubletree at Coconut Grove
15. Doubletree Club Hotel
16. Doubletree Grand Hotel
17. Embassy Suites Airport
18. Grove Isle Club and Resort
19. Hilton Miami Airport
20. Holiday Inn Airport North
21. Holiday Inn Downtown
22. Hotel Intercontinental
23. Hotel Place St. Michel
24. Hotel Sofitel
25. Howard Johnson Miami Airport
26. Howard Johnson Port of Miami

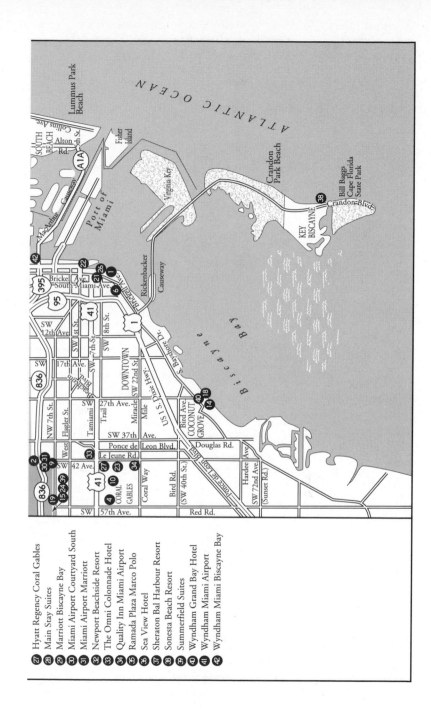

27 Hyatt Regency Coral Gables
28 Main Stay Suites
29 Marriott Biscayne Bay
30 Miami Airport Courtyard South
31 Miami Airport Marriott
32 Newport Beachside Resort
33 The Omni Colonnade Hotel
34 Quality Inn Miami Airport
35 Ramada Plaza Marco Polo
36 Sea View Hotel
37 Sheraton Bal Harbour Resort
38 Sonesta Beach Resort
39 Summerfield Suites
40 Wyndham Grand Bay Hotel
41 Wyndham Miami Airport
42 Wyndham Miami Biscayne Bay

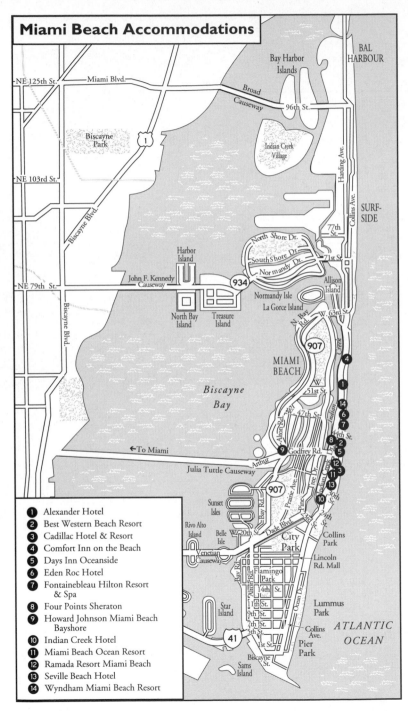

Miami Beach Accommodations

1 Alexander Hotel
2 Best Western Beach Resort
3 Cadillac Hotel & Resort
4 Comfort Inn on the Beach
5 Days Inn Oceanside
6 Eden Roc Hotel
7 Fontainebleau Hilton Resort & Spa
8 Four Points Sheraton
9 Howard Johnson Miami Beach Bayshore
10 Indian Creek Hotel
11 Miami Beach Ocean Resort
12 Ramada Resort Miami Beach
13 Seville Beach Hotel
14 Wyndham Miami Beach Resort

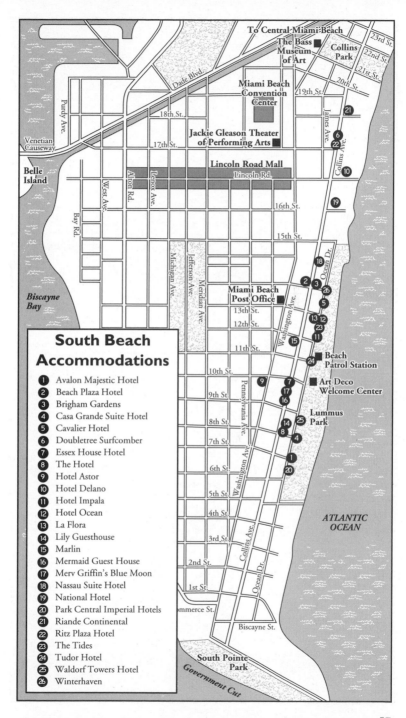

South Beach Accommodations

1. Avalon Majestic Hotel
2. Beach Plaza Hotel
3. Brigham Gardens
4. Casa Grande Suite Hotel
5. Cavalier Hotel
6. Doubletree Surfcomber
7. Essex House Hotel
8. The Hotel
9. Hotel Astor
10. Hotel Delano
11. Hotel Impala
12. Hotel Ocean
13. La Flora
14. Lily Guesthouse
15. Marlin
16. Mermaid Guest House
17. Merv Griffin's Blue Moon
18. Nassau Suite Hotel
19. National Hotel
20. Park Central Imperial Hotels
21. Riande Continental
22. Ritz Plaza Hotel
23. The Tides
24. Tudor Hotel
25. Waldorf Towers Hotel
26. Winterhaven

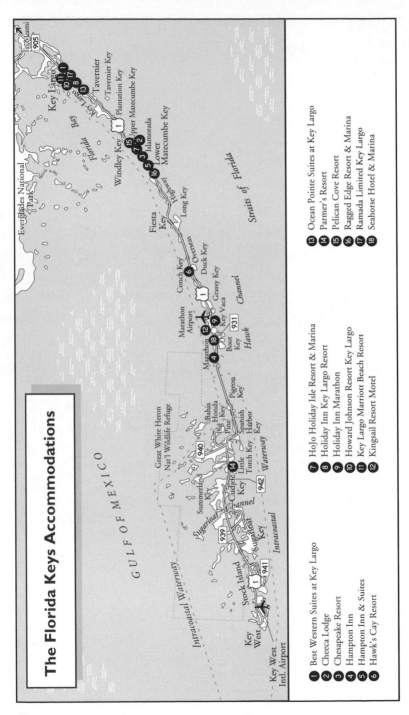

The Florida Keys Accommodations

1. Best Western Suites at Key Largo
2. Cheeca Lodge
3. Chesapeake Resort
4. Hampton Inn
5. Hampton Inn & Suites
6. Hawk's Cay Resort
7. HoJo Holiday Isle Resort & Marina
8. Holiday Inn Key Largo Resort
9. Holiday Inn Marathon
10. Howard Johnson Resort Key Largo
11. Key Largo Marriott Beach Resort
12. Kingsail Resort Motel
13. Ocean Pointe Suites at Key Largo
14. Parmer's Resort
15. Pelican Cove Resort
16. Ragged Edge Resort & Marina
17. Ramada Limited Key Largo
18. Seahorse Hotel & Marina

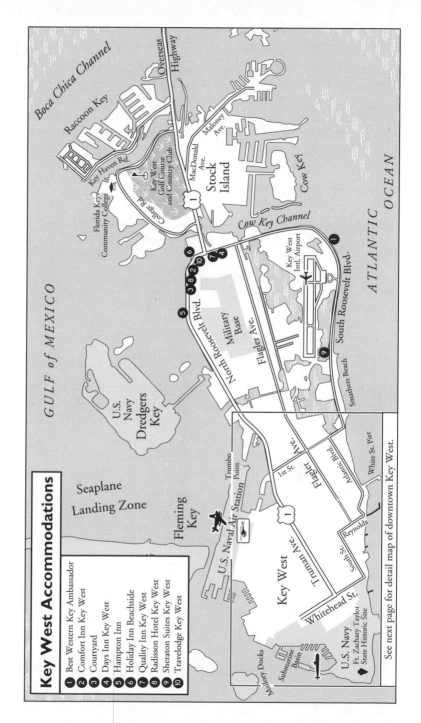

Key West Accommodations

1. Best Western Key Ambassador
2. Comfort Inn Key West
3. Courtyard
4. Days Inn Key West
5. Hampton Inn
6. Holiday Inn Beachside
7. Quality Inn Key West
8. Radisson Hotel Key West
9. Sheraton Suites Key West
10. Travelodge Key West

GULF of MEXICO

Boca Chica Channel

Raccoon Key

Overseas Highway

Key Haven Rd.

Florida Keys Community College

Key West Golf Course and Country Club

College Rd.

MacDonald Ave.

Maloney Ave.

Stock Island

Cow Key

Cow Key Channel

Key West Intl. Airport

North Roosevelt Blvd.

Military Base

Flagler Ave.

South Roosevelt Blvd.

Smathers Beach

ATLANTIC OCEAN

U.S. Navy Dredgers Key

Seaplane Landing Zone

Fleming Key

U.S. Naval Air Station

Trumbo Point

Key West

Truman Ave.

Whitehead St.

South St.

Reynolds

1st St.

Flagler Ave.

Atlantic Blvd.

White St. Pier

Mallory Docks

Submarine Basin

U.S. Navy Ft. Zachary Taylor State Historic Site

See next page for detail map of downtown Key West.

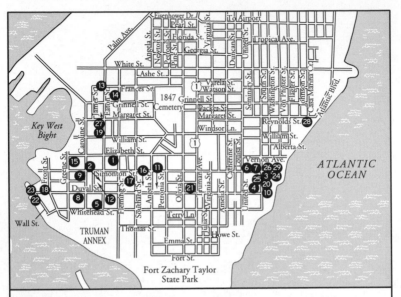

Downtown Key West
Accommodations

1. Ambrosia House
2. Artist House
3. Atlantic Shores Motel
4. Avalon Bed & Breakfast
5. Banyon Resort
6. Best Western Hibiscus Motel
7. Blue Marlin
8. Crowne Plaza La Concha
9. Curry Mansion Inn
10. Dewey House
11. Duval House
12. Eaton Lodge
13. Eaton Manor Guesthouse
14. Eden House
15. Garden House
16. Gardens Hotel
17. Heron House
18. Hyatt Key West Resort & Marina
19. Island City House Hotel
20. La Mer Hotel
21. La Te Da Hotel
22. Ocean Key Resort & Marina
23. Pier House
24. South Beach Oceanfront Motel
25. Southernmost Motel
26. Spanish Gardens
27. Westwinds
28. Wyndham Casa Marina Resort
29. Wyndham Reach Resort

Southwest Florida Accommodations

1. Barron River Motel and Villas
2. Bayview Bed & Breakfast
3. Beachouse Motel
4. Bokeelia Tarpon Inn
5. Bridge Water Inn
6. Captain's Table Motel
7. Everglades City Motel
8. Knoll's Court Motel

Note: See the following pages for accommodations in Fort Myers, Fort Myers Beach, Naples, Marco Island, and Sanibel and Captiva.

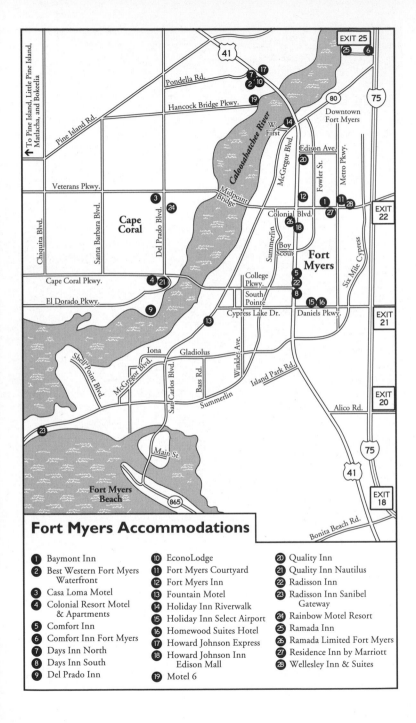

Fort Myers Accommodations

1. Baymont Inn
2. Best Western Fort Myers Waterfront
3. Casa Loma Motel
4. Colonial Resort Motel & Apartments
5. Comfort Inn
6. Comfort Inn Fort Myers
7. Days Inn North
8. Days Inn South
9. Del Prado Inn
10. EconoLodge
11. Fort Myers Courtyard
12. Fort Myers Inn
13. Fountain Motel
14. Holiday Inn Riverwalk
15. Holiday Inn Select Airport
16. Homewood Suites Hotel
17. Howard Johnson Express
18. Howard Johnson Inn Edison Mall
19. Motel 6
20. Quality Inn
21. Quality Inn Nautilus
22. Radisson Inn
23. Radisson Inn Sanibel Gateway
24. Rainbow Motel Resort
25. Ramada Inn
26. Ramada Limited Fort Myers
27. Residence Inn by Marriott
28. Wellesley Inn & Suites

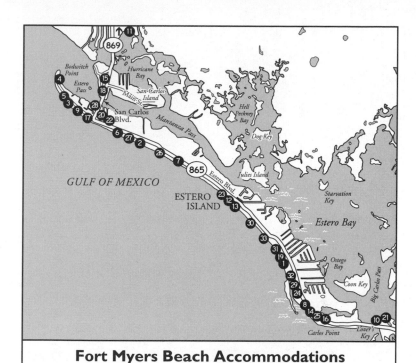

Fort Myers Beach Accommodations

1. The Beach House
2. Beacon Motel & Gift Shop
3. Best Western Beach Resort
4. Best Western Pink Shell Beach Resort
5. Casa Playa Beach Resort
6. Days Inn Island Beach Resort
7. DiamondHead All Suite Beach Resort
8. Dolphin Inn
9. Edison Beach House
10. GrandView All Suite Resort
11. GuestHouse Inn Mariner's Lodge
    & Marina
12. Gulf Echo Motel
13. Gulf Motel
14. Gullwing Beach Resort
15. Hidden Harbor Inn
16. Holiday Inn Fort Myers Beach

17. Howard Johnson Beachfront
18. Island Motel
19. Kahlua Beach Club
20. Lighthouse Island Resort
21. Lover's Key Beach Club
22. Matanzas Inn
23. Neptune Inn
24. Outrigger Beach Resort
25. Pointe Estero Resort
26. Quality Inn & Suites at the Lani Kai
27. Ramada Inn Beachfront
28. Rusty's Motel
29. Sandpiper Gulf Resort
30. Sandy Beach Hideaway
31. Ti Ki Resort
32. Tropical Inn Resort
33. The Wild Wave

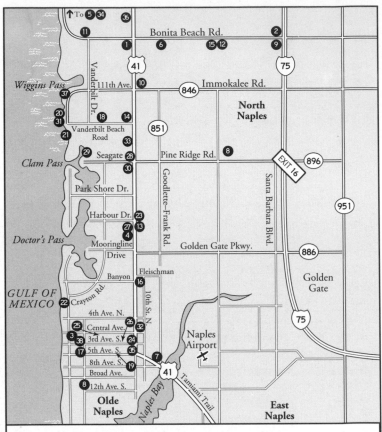

Naples Accommodations

1. Americinn Motel & Suites
2. Baymont Inn
3. Bel Mar Resort
4. Best Western Naples
5. Bonita Beach Resort Motel
6. Comfort Inn
7. Comfort Inn Downtown Naples
8. The Cottages of Naples
9. Days Inn
10. DoubleTree Guest Suites Naples
11. Flamingo Motel
12. Hampton Inn
13. Hampton Inn
14. Hilton Naples & Towers
15. Holiday Express Hotel & Suites
16. Holiday Inn Naples
17. Hotel Escalante
18. Inn at Pelican Bay
19. Inn on Fifth

20. La Playa Beach Resort
21. Lighthouse Inn
22. Naples Beach Hotel & Golf Club
23. Naples Courtyard by Marriott
24. Naples Hotel & Suites
25. Neptune Motel
26. Olde Naples Inn & Suites
27. Quality Inn Gulfcoast
28. Ramada Plaza Hotel
29. The Registry Resort
30. Residence Inn by Marriott
31. Ritz-Carlton Naples
32. Sea Court Hotel
33. Staybridge Suites by Holiday Inn
34. The Tradewinds
35. Trail's End Motel
36. Trianon Bonita Bay
37. Vanderbilt Beach Resort House
38. White Sands Resort Club

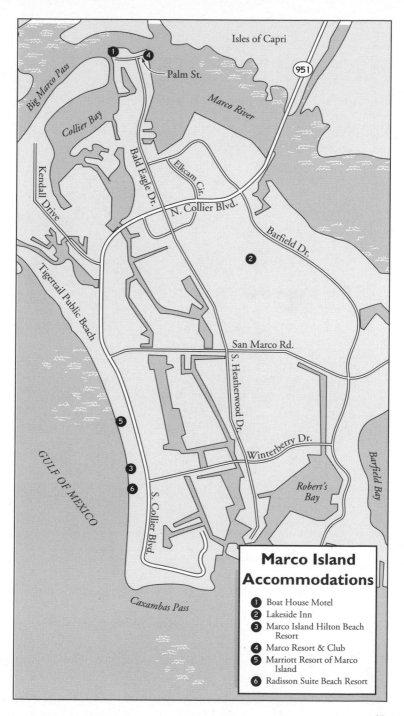

Isles of Capri

Big Marco Pass

951

Palm St.

Marco River

Collier Bay

Bald Eagle Dr.

Elkcam Cir.

Kendall Drive

N. Collier Blvd.

Barfield Dr.

2

San Marco Rd.

Tigertail Public Beach

S. Heatherwood Dr.

5

Winterberry Dr.

GULF OF MEXICO

3

6

Robert's Bay

Barfield Bay

S. Collier Blvd.

Caxambas Pass

Marco Island Accommodations

1 Boat House Motel
2 Lakeside Inn
3 Marco Island Hilton Beach Resort
4 Marco Resort & Club
5 Marriott Resort of Marco Island
6 Radisson Suite Beach Resort

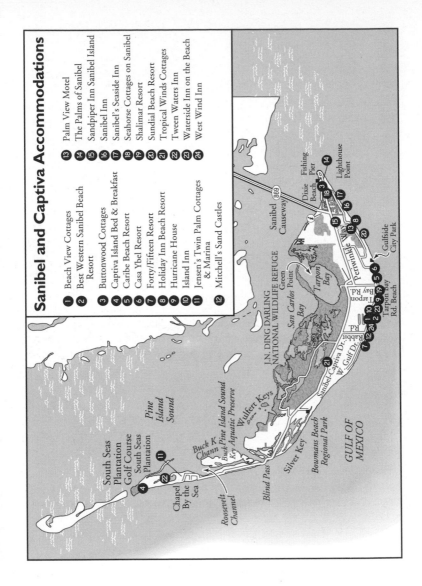

Sanibel and Captiva Accommodations

1. Beach View Cottages
2. Best Western Sanibel Beach Resort
3. Buttonwood Cottages
4. Captiva Island Bed & Breakfast
5. Caribe Beach Resort
6. Casa Ybel Resort
7. Forty/Fifteen Resort
8. Holiday Inn Beach Resort
9. Hurricane House
10. Island Inn
11. Jensen's Twin Palm Cottages & Marina
12. Mitchell's Sand Castles
13. Palm View Motel
14. The Palms of Sanibel
15. Sandpiper Inn Sanibel Island
16. Sanibel Inn
17. Sanibel's Seaside Inn
18. Seahorse Cottages on Sanibel
19. Shalimar Resort
20. Sundial Beach Resort
21. Tropical Winds Cottages
22. Tween Waters Inn
23. Waterside Inn on the Beach
24. West Wind Inn

Broward County

Hollywood and Dania Beach   Located north of Miami Beach and south of Fort Lauderdale, this area is generally not quite as overrun with beach-going tourists. Instead, the proximity to Fort Lauderdale/Hollywood International Airport as well as the Dania Jai Alai and numerous golf courses is the main draw here. Aside from walking along the beach, very little is accessible by foot.

Fort Lauderdale and Its Beaches   Clustered within the area surrounded by 17th Street Causeway, South Federal Highway, and East Las Olas Boulevard are numerous chain hotels. These service the Fort Lauderdale Convention Center and Fort Lauderdale/Hollywood International Airport. Pier 66, located across from the convention center, and Riverwalk on SW 6th Street are two tourist draws worth experiencing. The Center for Performing Arts, the Fort Lauderdale Museum of Art, and the Museum of Science and Discovery are located just North of Riverwalk on East Broward. North of Fort Lauderdale on A1A are the waterfront hotels of Fort Lauderdale Beach and Lauderdale-by-the-Sea. Both the restaurants and hotels in this area are generally overpriced for the quality of goods and services they offer. Access to these places is very good, with five causeways to the beach in a distance of less than five miles.

Miami-Dade County

Downtown Miami   Hotels in downtown Miami are close to the Port of Miami, the Orange Bowl, city government, the airport, and Miami's business and financial center. The Miami Beach Convention Center is a 15-minute commute under optimal traffic conditions. Downtown Miami is not particularly active after business hours, and the choice of restaurants and nightspots is decidedly limited compared to Miami Beach, Coral Gables, or Coconut Grove. Though downtown Miami is generally safe for visitors on foot, we recommend walking in groups or taking a cab after dark.

Miami International Airport Area   The airport is located inland just west of downtown Miami. Hotels situated near the airport are convenient to Coral Gables, downtown Miami, major expressways leading south to the Keys and north toward the Hialeah Race Track, Pro Player Stadium (home of the Miami Dolphins), and Fort Lauderdale. Commuting time from airport area hotels to Miami Beach or to the Miami Beach Convention Center is about 20 to 30 minutes if the traffic isn't bad. Accommodations near the airport are scattered around a 16-square-mile area criss-crossed by expressways. If you need to travel beyond your hotel, you will need a car or a cab.

Coral Gables Coral Gables is about two miles south of the airport, four miles southwest of downtown, and extends south to Biscayne Bay. A banking and trade center as well as one of Miami's nicest residential areas, Coral Gables is also home to the University of Miami and the Miracle Mile, one of Florida's best shopping venues. Likewise, many of Miami's finest restaurants are located in Coral Gables. Hotels in Coral Gables are convenient to the University of Miami, the airport, Coconut Grove and Biscayne Bay, and several attractions. Miami Beach and the Miami Beach Convention Center are a complicated 30- to 50-minute commute from Coral Gables. Downtown Coral Gables and the Miracle Mile are safe for pedestrians both day and evening, though normal safety precautions should be observed.

Coconut Grove Coconut Grove is an upscale bayside community framed on the west and south by Coral Gables. Coconut Grove is convenient to a number of southern Dade County attractions, including Parrot Jungle, Miami Seaquarium, Fairchild Tropical Garden, and Vizcaya. Key Biscayne and various Biscayne Bay marinas are also easily accessible from Coconut Grove. Miami Beach and the Miami Beach Convention Center are 30 to 50 minutes away via I-95 and I-195 or the MacArthur Causeway. Coconut Grove is considered safe for visitors on foot throughout the day and evening.

Miami Beach Miami Beach is situated on a barrier island roughly across upper Biscayne Bay from downtown Miami. Collins Avenue (also US A1A) is the main north-south thoroughfare. East-west thoroughfares are numbered streets, running from 1st Street in the south to 96th Street in the north. Contiguous with Miami Beach as you head north on Collins Avenue past the city limits (at 87th Street) is Surfside, followed by Bal Harbour, then Sunny Isles. Four causeways connect Miami Beach to the mainland. Hotels between 5th and 61st streets are about a half-hour drive from the Miami International Airport.

The Historic Art Deco District The Art Deco District, extending from 5th Street northward along the beach to 15th, represents Miami Beach at its finest. Hotels here are small, independently owned, and architecturally distinctive in the Deco/Caribbean style of Miami Beach's original tourist boom. Many of these hotels have been lovingly restored and provide a glimpse of a bygone era. The feel here is hot, sultry, and very active. Diners in open-air cafés watch an endless parade of in-line skaters, joggers, models, and young, hip nightclubbers. While parking is virtually nonexistent, dozens of restaurants and clubs are within easy walking distance—and so is the beach. The Miami Beach Convention Center is a 20- to 30-minute walk or 5- to 10-minute cab ride away. Hotel rooms in the Art Deco District may be smaller than you would find in a chain hotel. Though the baths are generally small and modest by modern standards, the guest rooms themselves are often beautifully appointed. If you opt to stay in this area, you will enjoy the quintessential Miami Beach experience. Be forewarned, however, that the Art Deco District is a party zone: clubs rock long into the night and quiet is sometimes hard to come by. The Art Deco District is well patrolled by the Miami Beach Police and is pretty safe both day and night, though you may have to contend with some panhandlers or hustlers.

Miami Beach North of the Historic Art Deco District to Arthur Godfrey Road (I-195) While the officially designated, historic Art Deco District runs from 5th to 15th Street, there are many hotels in the Art Deco style all the way up to 43rd Street. North of 15th, however, they tend to be larger hotels, and may or may not have been recently renovated. Development from 15th north to 43rd Street has been somewhat erratic, with little emphasis on artistic or historic preservation. Art Deco–era hotels in this area are sprinkled among more modern hotels, condominiums, and whole blocks of small retailers.

To muddy the water for travelers and travel agents, many hotels north of the designated historic district claim in their promotional literature, AAA guides, and the *Hotel & Travel Index* to be in the Art Deco District. If you want to stay in one of the small Art Deco hotels in the historic district, confirm that your hotel is located across from Lummus Park (beach front) or on Collins Avenue (one block west of the beach) between 5th and 15th streets.

Above 15th Street are many good hotels and quite a few rundown ones. This area is improving each year, however, by virtue of its close proximity to the Miami Beach Convention Center. Businesspeople staying at beach hotels between 15th and 23rd Streets are within a 5- to 12-minute walk of the Convention Center. For specific recommendations of hotels, check out our hotel ratings and rankings to find the nicest rooms and the best deals.

Miami Beach above the Art Deco District is safe days and evenings during business hours for visitors on foot. Those enjoying the local after-hours nightlife scene should walk in groups, drive, or take a cab between clubs.

Miami Beach North of Arthur Godfrey Road (I-195) to the John F. Kennedy Causeway Driving north on Collins Avenue from South Miami Beach, you cross Arthur Godfrey Road, also known as 41st Street. Running east-west, this road directly links Miami Beach to Miami via I-195, and dead-ends into Collins Avenue. Collins Avenue, north of Arthur Godfrey to the Kennedy Causeway (71st Street), is the home of Miami Beach's fabled hotel giants. Though many of the great hotels are gone and others have been renamed or replaced by skyward-stretching condominiums, the Fontainebleau and the Eden Roc, among others, still invite visitors to relive the zenith of Miami Beach's golden age.

Huge, commanding, and magnificent after 40 years, these hotels almost single-handedly saved this area of Miami Beach from decline. Sandwiched between the Intracoastal Waterway on the west and the Atlantic Ocean on the east, hotels here offer stunning views in all directions. Each of the great hotels offers elaborate swimming pools, landscaped gardens, meeting facilities, shopping arcades, and a variety of restaurants. They are, as intended, complete resorts. Today they cater more to business travelers and tour groups than to the individual tourist. But like the hotels of the Art Deco District, they offer a taste of a world past. If you elect to experience this slice of Florida history, you will be happier if you have a car. The nightlife and restaurants of South Miami Beach are a 10- to 30-minute drive away, depending on traffic. The Miami Beach Convention Center is 10 to 20 minutes by cab or convention-sponsored bus. The area is considered safe for pedestrians days and evenings.

Bal Harbour, 96th Street to the Haulover Bridge   This area along the ocean is an isolated bastion of affluence and beauty. Large, modern, well-maintained hotels alternate with equally imposing condominiums. The Bal Harbour Shops, one of the most diverse and tasteful shopping venues in the Southeast, is situated at the 96th Street end of the area. Nearby to the north is Haulover Park and Marina, featuring deep-sea fishing and kite flying as well as a nice beach. The airport is about 40 to 55 minutes away in light to moderate traffic. The Miami Beach Convention Center can be reached in about the same amount of time. Visitors on foot have little to fear.

Sunny Isles and North   Bal Harbour is the last community to the north on the barrier island of Miami Beach. From here, Collins Avenue (US A1A) crosses the Haulover Cut (connecting the Intracoastal Waterway and the Atlantic Ocean) and passes through Haulover Beach Park. Beyond the park is Sunny Isles and Golden Shores. This area was developed during the late '50s and early '60s and is characterized by small, motel-sized properties with exotic themes ranging from space travel to the Suez Canal. Once again, while there are some nice rooms to be had, many of the properties have seen better days. Plus, the area is pretty remote unless you are bound for the Calder Race Track or Pro Player Stadium. Walking is generally safe during day and evening business hours.

Gateway to the Keys

Homestead and Florida City have both come a long way from the vast destruction that they experienced in 1992 from Hurricane Andrew. What used to be a "stop-only-if-you-can't-stay-awake-long-enough-to-get-to-the-Keys" place is now a nice resting point, either for dinner or overnight in an inexpensive chain hotel. Either coming from Fort Myers or Naples on Highway 41 or from Miami on Highway One, the gateway cities are a bright spot on an otherwise lengthy and boring stretch of road.

The Keys

From Key Largo to Key West, expect everything that costs money to cost more here. Gas, food, and especially lodging are tremendously expensive. As in any resort area, off-season travel is absolutely the way to go here. Hotels are clustered in the more touristy areas, such as Islamorada and Key West. If time permits, don't miss swimming with the dolphins on Marathon Key; reservations must be made up to nine months in advance. Great food is available everywhere, from the hole-in-the-wall seafood shacks to the gourmet beachside establishments. As the price of hotels is truly astronomical, try the quaint bed-and-breakfasts located in Olde Key West as an alternative to the same-priced mediocre chain hotels that lure tourists. Also, keep in mind that the speed limit is strictly enforced throughout the Keys.

Southwest Florida

Fort Myers   Fort Myers is located west of Interstate 75 and mostly south of the Caloosahatchee River. Though tourists stop in Fort Myers to see Thomas Edison's and Henry Ford's estates, it is generally considered a city to be passed through en route to the beautiful beaches of Estero Island, Sanibel, and Captiva. There are accommodations clustered on all sides of the airport but very few anywhere else on the mainland. Fort Myers Beach is six miles of tourism—hotel upon hotel upon hotel. Quality here is directly related to money spent.

Marco Island   The largest of the Ten Thousand Islands of Southwest Florida, Marco Island has always been known for its beautiful, quiet beaches. With the opening of a new resort hotel in 2002, added to the two that have opened in the past two years, this previously affordable place is slowly becoming more and more exclusive. While on Marco Island, don't miss Briggs Nature Center on Shell Island Road or taking a trolley tour of the island.

Naples   From the pricey high-rise hotels on the beach to the more affordable downtown chains, Naples is the vacation town that has accommodations for everyone. The city is located 35 miles south of the Southwest Florida International Airport. The small Naples Municipal Airport is located just east of the Olde City, east of Naples Bay. As the beach is actually in Olde Naples, there are no barrier islands or causeways. Highway 41 changes names to 9th Street North while traveling south through Naples and changes again to Tamiami Trail at 5th Avenue South.

Sanibel and Captiva   If you are willing to spend the money for a good-quality, clean hotel room on Fort Myers Beach, take that same money and go to Sanibel. Even with the many hotels and resorts located here, the arrangement is such that the secluded nature of these beautiful beaches is protected. Crossing Sanibel Causeway leads to Periwinkle Way, which eventually turns into Sanibel-Captiva Road. Driving from the Causeway to the end of Captiva can take an incredibly long time due to traffic and slow speed limits. Don't expect to be entertained—Jet skis and parasailing are not allowed within 300 yards of the beaches. If you have kids (or if you consider yourself to still be one), dinner at the Bubble Room is a must.

MIAMI'S CONFUSING HOTEL SCENE

Over the years, Miami and Miami Beach have been through so many boom and bust cycles that the hotel scene tends to remain in constant flux. On the ocean, hotel development began in South Beach, the southernmost part of the barrier island known collectively as Miami Beach. Over the years, as Miami Beach's popularity spiraled, new hotel development worked its way north along the Atlantic coast in a seemingly unstoppable wave. At first times were good, and each new hotel was larger and grander than its older neighbors to the south.

Miami Beach reached its zenith in the late 1950s, when the Fontainebleau, Eden Roc, Diplomat, and Kennilworth were among the largest and most resplendent hotels in America. Their opulent, cathedral-sized lobbies, enormous swimming pools, and formal gardens signaled Miami's arrival as the preferred playground of the wealthy and influential.

As it turned out, the supply of luxury hotel rooms eventually outran demand, and the developers shifted their attention to the vacation needs of people of more modest means. A new crop of hotels sprang up along the coast north of Bal Harbour. These properties were smaller (glorified motels really) and employed fanciful themes to compete with their more established competitors to the south. Desert-themed hotels such as the Sands and the Dunes stationed a small caravan of fiberglass camels at their entrances. Other properties drew inspiration from the Sputnik satellite and space exploration craze of the time. Though faddish and outlandish, these smaller hotels prospered, along with the more established large hotels, throughout the 1960s.

During this period, South Beach, the cradle of Miami tourism, fell into decline. Unable to compete with the Fontainebleaus, Eden Rocs, and mod-theme hotels, the smaller inns at the southern end of Miami Beach became the permanent residences first of Jewish retirees from the northeast, and later of Cuban emigrés and refugees.

In the 1970s Walt Disney World opened near Orlando. At first, Disney's impact on Miami tourism was minimal, with motoring vacationers stopping at Disney World for a one-day visit before continuing south to Miami. With the opening of Epcot Center in 1982, however, South Florida tourism was changed forever. Walt Disney World had become a destination instead of merely a stopover. For South Florida and particularly Miami, it was as if a wall had been constructed in the center of the state, a Disney wall that blocked the flow of American tourists to destinations south of Orlando. Overbuilt and underfed, Miami tourism fell on hard times. Luxury hotels failed by the score or plugged along in a state of increasing disrepair. Tourists were supplanted by legions of retirees, and many of Miami's and Miami Beach's most notable hostelries were razed to make way for high-rise condominiums.

By the end of the 1980s, Miami had recovered some of its tourist base by targeting Latin Americans and Europeans. British and the German travelers especially were ready to initiate a love affair with Miami. In the early 1990s, the Miami Beach Convention Center expanded to become one of the largest and most well-designed meeting venues in the United States. This resurgence in tourism and convention traffic coincided with an upswing in commerce to trigger the most explosive growth seen in greater Miami since the 1950s.

In downtown Miami, Coral Gables, Coconut Grove, and around the airport, growth largely addressed the needs of business. Here, the presence of national chain hotels created a recognizable standard. Catering primarily to business travelers, hotels on the mainland kept pace with Miami's growing stature as the financial, trade, and transportation capital of the Caribbean. Across the bay in Miami Beach, however, it was (and is) a different story entirely.

In the boom of the late 1940s and the 1950s, Miami Beach's growth and development were at least geographically organized: there was a predictable march of new construction heading due north, right up the beach. Since those days, some hotels have survived, some have failed, others have been renovated or replaced entirely by high-rise condos. For the most part, there has been precious little discernible logic to all of this change.

To an outsider, particularly, it seems as if Miami and Miami Beach have evolved almost randomly since the mid-1960s. You'll find new luxury resorts sharing the same block with 1980s condominiums and ramshackle hotels from the 1940s. Properties of every conceivable size, and with vastly different clientele, populate the same stretch of oceanfront. In a half-mile stroll along Collins Avenue in Miami Beach, you will see small residential hotels with inhabitants clustered in lawn chairs on canvas-covered porches. Next door might be a recently restored Art Deco hotel with a sidewalk café, and across the street, a modern condominium tower.

The practical lesson to be derived from this bit of history is that Miami Beach is a pretty mixed-up place. If you want to find nice accommodations, you have to dig a little deeper than a hotel's ad promising "an established hotel right on the ocean in the heart of Miami Beach." Though dozens of hotels can truthfully make that claim, there are many among them you would not wish on your worst enemy.

Getting a Good Deal on a Room

High Season vs. Low Season

High season in South Florida is from Christmas through Easter. Additionally, some hotels observe a second high season from mid-June through mid-August, known as the family season. Room rates for many hotels are 25–50% higher during these times of year. September, October, November (excluding the Thanksgiving holiday), and the first two weeks of December are the best times for obtaining low rates. Be aware, though, that large conventions can drive rates up regardless of the season. Check with your destination city's convention and visitors bureau to make sure your visit does not fall during a big meeting or trade show.

Special Weekend Rates

While well-located hotels are tough for the budget-conscious, it's not impossible to get a good deal, at least relatively speaking. For starters, most downtown hotels that cater to business, government, and convention travelers offer special weekend discount rates that range from 15 to 40% below normal weekday rates. You can find out about weekend specials by calling the hotel or consulting your travel agent.

Getting Corporate Rates

Many hotels offer discounted corporate rates (5–20% off rack rates). Usually you do not need to work for a large company or have a special relationship with the hotel to obtain these rates. Simply call the hotel of your choice and ask for their corporate rates. Many hotels will guarantee you the discounted rate on the phone when you make your reservation. Others may make the rate conditional on your providing some sort of *bona fides,* for instance a fax on your company's letterhead requesting the rate or a company credit card or business card on check-in. Generally, the screening is not rigorous.

Half-Price Programs

The larger discounts on rooms (35–60%), in South Florida or anywhere else, are available through half-price hotel programs, often called travel clubs. Program operators contract with an individual hotel to provide rooms at deep discount, usually 50% off rack rate, on a "space available" basis. Space available, in practice, generally means that you can reserve a room at the discounted rate whenever the hotel expects to be at less than 80% occupancy. A little calendar-sleuthing to help you avoid city-wide conventions and special events will increase your chances of choosing a time for your visit when the discounts are available.

Most half-price programs charge an annual membership fee or directory subscription charge of $25–125. Once enrolled, you are mailed a membership card and a directory listing all the hotels participating in the program. Examining the directory, you will notice immediately that there are a lot of restrictions and exceptions. Some hotels, for instance, "black out" certain dates or times of year. Others may only offer the discount on certain days of the week, or require you to stay a certain number of nights. Still others may offer a much smaller discount than 50% off rack rate.

Some programs specialize in domestic travel, some specialize in international travel, and some do both. The more established operators offer members between 1,000 and 4,000 hotels to choose from in the United States. All of the programs have a heavy concentration of hotels in California and Florida, and most have a very limited selection of participating properties in New York City or Boston. Offerings in other cities and regions of the United States vary considerably. The programs with the largest selection of hotels in South Florida are *Encore, Travel America at Half Price (Entertainment Publications), International Travel Card,* and *Quest.*

Encore	(800) 638-0930
Entertainment Publications	(800) 285-5525
International Travel Card	(800) 342-0558
Quest	(800) 638-9819

One problem with half-price programs is that not all hotels offer a full 50% discount. Another slippery problem is the base rate against which the discount is applied. Some hotels figure the discount on an exaggerated rack rate that nobody would ever have to pay. A few participating hotels may deduct the discount from a supposed "superior" or "upgraded" room rate, even though the room you get is the hotel's standard accommodation. Though hard to pin down, the majority of participating properties base discounts on the published rate in the *Hotel & Travel Index* (a quarterly reference work used by travel agents) and work within the spirit of their agreement with the program operator. As a rule, if you travel several times a year, you will more than pay for your program membership in room rate savings.

A noteworthy addendum to this discussion is that deeply discounted rooms through half-price programs are not commissionable to travel agents. In practical terms this means that you must ordinarily make your own inquiry calls and reservations. If you travel frequently, however, and run a lot of business through your travel agent, he or she will probably do your legwork, lack of commission notwithstanding.

Preferred Rates

If you cannot book the hotel of your choice through a half-price program, you and your travel agent may have to search for a lesser discount, often called a "preferred rate." A preferred rate could be a discount made available to travel agents to stimulate their booking activity or a discount initiated to attract a certain class of traveler. Most preferred rates are promoted through travel industry publications and are often accessible only through an agent. We recommend sounding out your travel agent about possible deals. Be aware, however, that the rates shown on travel agents' computerized reservations systems are not always the lowest rates available. Zero in on a couple of hotels that fill your needs in terms of location and quality of accommodations, then have your travel agent call for the latest rates and specials. Hotel reps are almost always more responsive to travel agents because travel agents represent a source of additional business. There are certain specials that hotel reps will disclose only to travel agents. Travel agents also come in handy when the hotel you want is supposedly booked. A personal appeal from your agent to the hotel's director of sales and marketing will get you a room more than half the time.

Wholesalers, Consolidators, and Reservation Services

If you do not want to join a program or buy a discount directory, you can take advantage of the services of a wholesaler or consolidator. Wholesalers and consolidators buy rooms, or options on rooms (room blocks), from hotels at a low, negotiated rate. They then resell the rooms at a profit through travel agents, tour packagers, or directly to the public. Most wholesalers and consolidators have a provision for returning unsold rooms to participating hotels, but are disinclined to do so. The wholesaler's or consolidator's relationship with any hotel is predicated on volume. If they return rooms unsold, the hotel might not make as many rooms available to them the next time around. Thus, wholesalers and consolidators often offer rooms at bargain rates, anywhere from 15 to 50% off rack, occasionally sacrificing profit margin in the process, to avoid returning the rooms to the hotel unsold.

When wholesalers and consolidators deal directly with the public, they frequently represent themselves as "reservation services." When you call, you can ask for a rate quote for a particular hotel, or alternatively ask for their best available deal in the area where you prefer to stay. If there is a maximum amount you are willing to pay, say so. Chances are the service will find something that will work for you, even if they have to shave a dollar or two off their own profit. Sometimes you will have to pay for your room when you make your reservation using your credit card. Other times you will pay as usual, when you check out. Listed below are several services that frequently offer substantial discounts:

Budget Reservations	(800) 681-1993
Central Reservation Service	(800) 950-0232
Hotel Reservations Network	(800) 964-6835
Florida Hotel Network	(800) 538-3616

Exit Information Guide

A company called EIG (Exit Information Guide) publishes a book of discount coupons for bargain rates at hotels throughout the state of Florida. These books are available free of charge in many restaurants and motels along the main interstate highways leading to the Sunshine State. Since most folks make reservations prior to leaving home, picking up the coupon book en route does not help much. For $2 ($5 Canadian), however, EIG will mail you a copy (third class) before you make your reservations. If you call and use a credit card, EIG will send the guide first class for $3. Write or call:

Exit Information Guide
4205 NW 6th Street
Gainesville, FL 32609
(352) 371-3948

Condominium Deals

There are a large number of condo resorts and timeshares in South Florida that rent to vacationers for a week or even less. Bargains can be found, especially during off-peak periods. Reservations and information can be obtained from Condolink, (800) 733-4445.

The majority of area condos that rent to visitors also work with travel agents. In many cases the condo owners pay an enhanced commission to agents who rent the units for reduced consumer rates. It's worth a call to your travel agent.

HOW TO EVALUATE A TRAVEL PACKAGE

Hundreds of South Florida package vacations are offered to the public each year. Packages should be a win-win proposition for both the buyer and the seller. The buyer only has to make one phone call and deal with a single salesperson to set up the whole vacation: transportation, rental car, lodging, meals, attraction admissions, and even golf and tennis. The seller, likewise, only has to deal with the buyer once, eliminating the need for separate sales, confirmations, and billing. In addition to streamlining selling, processing, and administration, some packagers also buy airfares in bulk on contract like a broker playing the commodities market. Buying a large number of airfares in advance allows the packager to buy them at a significant savings from posted fares. The same practice is applied also to hotel rooms. Because selling vacation packages is an efficient way of doing business, and because the packager can often buy individual package components (airfare, lodging, etc.) in bulk at discount, savings in operating expenses realized by the seller are sometimes passed on to the buyer so that, in addition to convenience, the package is also an exceptional value. In any event, that is the way it is supposed to work.

All too often, in practice, the seller realizes all of the economies and passes nothing in the way of savings on to the buyer. In some instances, packages are loaded additionally with extras that cost the packager next to nothing, but that run the retail price of the package sky-high. As you might expect, the savings to be passed along to customers are basically nil.

When considering a package, first choose one that includes features you are sure to use. Whether you use all the features or not, you will most certainly pay for them. Second, if cost is a greater concern than convenience, make a few phone calls and see what the package would cost if you booked its individual components (airfare, rental car, lodging, etc.) on your own. If the package price is less than the à la carte cost, the package is a good deal. If the costs are about the same, the package is probably worth it for the convenience.

HELPING YOUR TRAVEL AGENT HELP YOU

When you call your travel agent, ask if he or she has been to your South Florida destination. First-hand experience means everything. If the answer is no, either find another agent or be prepared to give your travel agent a lot of direction. Do not accept any recommendations at face value. Check out the location and rates of any suggested hotel and make certain that the hotel is suited to your itinerary.

Because some travel agents are unfamiliar with South Florida, your agent may try to plug you into a tour operator's or wholesaler's preset package. This essentially allows the travel agent to set up your whole trip with a single phone call and still collect an 8–10% commission. The problem with this scenario is that most agents will place 90% of their South Florida business with only one or two wholesalers or tour operators. In other words, it's the line of least resistance for them, and not much choice for you.

Often, travel agents will use wholesalers who run packages in conjunction with airlines, like Delta's Dream Vacations or American's Fly-Away Vacations. Because of the wholesaler's exclusive relationship with the carrier, these trips are very easy for travel agents to book. However, they will probably be more expensive than a package offered by a high-volume wholesaler who works with a number of airlines in a primary South Florida market.

To help your travel agent get you the best possible deal, do the following:

1. Determine where you want to stay in South Florida and, if possible, choose a specific hotel. This can be accomplished by reviewing the hotel information provided in this guide and by writing or calling hotels that interest you.

2. Check out the South Florida travel ads in the Sunday travel section of your local newspaper and compare them to ads running in the newspapers of one of South Florida's key markets, i.e., New York, Philadelphia, or Boston. Often you will be able to find deals

advertised in these newspapers that beat the socks off anything offered in your local paper. The best source of all is the "Sunday Travel" section of the *New York Times*. See if you can find some packages that fit your plans and that include a hotel you like.

3. Call the wholesalers or tour operators whose ads you have collected. Ask any questions you might have concerning their packages, but do not book your trip with them directly.

4. Tell your travel agent about the packages you find and ask if he or she can get you something better. The packages in the paper will serve as a benchmark against which to compare alternatives proposed by your travel agent.

5. Choose from among the options uncovered by you and your travel agent. No matter which option you elect, have your travel agent book it. Even if you go with one of the packages in the newspaper, it will probably be commissionable (at no additional cost to you) and will provide the agent some return on the time invested on your behalf. Also, as a travel professional, your agent should be able to verify the quality and integrity of the package.

IF YOU MAKE YOUR OWN RESERVATION

As you poke around trying to find a good deal, there are several things you should know. First, always call the hotel in question as opposed to the hotel chain's national 800 number. Quite often, the reservationists at the national number are unaware of local specials. Always ask about specials before you inquire about corporate rates. Do not be reluctant to bargain. If you are buying a hotel's weekend package, for example, and want to extend your stay into the following week, you can often obtain at least the corporate rate for the extra days. Do your bargaining, however, before you check in, preferably when you make your reservations.

Hotels and Motels: Rated and Ranked
ROOM RATINGS

To separate properties according to the relative quality, tastefulness, state of repair, cleanliness, and size of their standard rooms, we have grouped hotels and motels into classifications denoted by stars. Star ratings in this guide apply to South Florida properties only, and do not necessarily correspond to ratings awarded by Mobil, AAA, or other travel critics. Because stars have little relevance when awarded in the absence of commonly recognized standards of comparison, we have tied our ratings to expected levels of quality established by specific American hotel corporations.

Hotel and Motel Toll-Free 800 Numbers

Best Western	(800) 528-1234 U.S. & Canada
	(800) 528-2222 TDD
	(Telecommunication Device for the Deaf)
Comfort Inn	(800) 228-5150 U.S.
Courtyard by Marriott	(800) 321-2211 U.S.
Days Inn	(800) 325-2525 U.S.
Doubletree	(800) 528-0444 U.S.
Econo Lodge	(800) 424-4777 U.S.
Embassy Suites	(800) 362-2779 U.S. & Canada
Fairfield Inn by Marriott	(800) 228-2800 U.S.
Doubletree Guest Suites	(800) 424-2900 U.S. & Canada
Hampton Inn	(800) 426-7866 U.S. & Canada
Hilton	(800) 445-8667 U.S.
	(800) 368-1133 TDD
Holiday Inn	(800) 465-4329 U.S. & Canada
Howard Johnson	(800) 654-2000 U.S. & Canada
	(800) 654-8442 TDD
Hyatt	(800) 233-1234 U.S. & Canada
Loews	(800) 223-0888 U.S. & Canada
Marriott	(800) 228-9290 U.S. & Canada
	(800) 228-7014 TDD
Quality Inn	(800) 228-5151 U.S. & Canada
Radisson	(800) 333-3333 U.S. & Canada
Ramada Inn	(800) 228-3838 U.S.
	(800) 228-3232 TDD
Residence Inn by Marriott	(800) 331-3131 U.S.
Sheraton	(800) 325-3535 U.S. & Canada
Wyndham	(800) 822-4200 U.S.

Star ratings apply to room quality only, and describe the property's standard accommodations. For most hotels and motels a "standard accommodation" is a hotel room with either one king bed or two queen beds. In an all-suite property, the standard accommodation is either a one- or two-room suite. In addition to standard accommodations, many hotels offer luxury rooms and special suites, which are not rated in this guide. Star ratings for rooms are assigned without regard to whether a property has restaurant(s), recreational facilities, entertainment, or other extras.

In addition to stars (which delineate broad categories), we also employ a numerical rating system. Our rating scale is 0 to 100, with 100 as the best possible rating, and zero (0) as the worst. Numerical ratings are presented to show the difference we perceive between one property and another. Rooms at the Lily Guesthouse, Ritz Plaza Hotel, and Essex House Hotel on Miami Beach are all rated as three and a half stars (★★★½). In the numerical ratings, the Lily Guesthouse is rated an 82, the Ritz Plaza Hotel an 81, and the Essex House Hotel a 77. This means that within the three-and-a-half-star category, the Lily Guesthouse and Ritz Plaza Hotel are comparable, and both have slightly nicer rooms than the Essex House Hotel.

Cost estimates are based on the hotel's published rack rates for standard rooms. Each "$" represents $50. Thus a cost symbol of "$$$" means a room (or suite) at that hotel will be about $150 a night.

HOW THE HOTELS COMPARE

Here is a hit parade of the nicest rooms in South Florida. We've focused strictly on room quality, and excluded any consideration of location, services, recreation, or amenities. In some instances, a one- or two-room suite can be had for the same price or less than that of a hotel room.

If you use subsequent editions of this guide, you will notice that many of the ratings and rankings change. We'll include new properties, as well as reflecting in our ratings such positive developments as guest room renovation or improved maintenance and housekeeping in hotels already listed. A failure to properly maintain guest rooms or a lapse in housekeeping standards can negatively affect the ratings.

Finally, before you begin to shop for a hotel, take a hard look at this letter we received from a couple in Hot Springs, Arkansas:

> *We canceled our room reservations to follow the advice in your book [and reserved a hotel highly ranked by the* Unofficial Guide*]. We wanted inexpensive, but clean and cheerful. We got inexpensive, but [also] dirty, grim, and depressing. I really felt disappointed in your advice*

and the room. It was the pits. That was the one real piece of information I needed from your book! The room spoiled the holiday for me . . .

Needless to say, this letter was as unsettling to us as the bad room was to our reader. After all, our integrity as travel journalists is based on the quality of the information we provide our readers. However, even with the best of intentions and the most conscientious research, we cannot inspect every room in every hotel. What we do, in statistical terms, is take a sample: we check out several rooms selected at random in each hotel and base our ratings on those rooms. The inspections are conducted anonymously and without the knowledge of the property's management. Although it's unusual, it is certainly possible that the rooms we randomly inspect are not representative of the majority of rooms at a particular hotel. Another possibility is that the rooms we inspect in a given hotel are representative, but that by bad luck a reader is assigned a room which is inferior. When we rechecked the hotel our reader disliked so intensely, we discovered our rating was correctly representative, but that he and his wife had unfortunately been assigned to one of a small number of threadbare rooms scheduled for renovation.

The key to avoiding disappointment is to do some advance snooping around. We recommend that you ask to be sent a photo of a hotel's standard guest room before you book, or at least get a copy of the hotel's promotional brochure. Be forewarned, however, that some hotel chains use the same guest room photo in their promotional literature for all hotels in the chain, and that the guest room in a specific property may not resemble the photo in the brochure. When you or your travel agent call, ask how old the property is and when the guest room you are being assigned was last renovated. If you arrive and are assigned a room inferior to that which you had been led to expect, demand to be moved to another room.

Room Star Ratings

★★★★★	*Superior Rooms*	Tasteful and luxurious by any standard
★★★★	*Extremely Nice Rooms*	What you would expect at a Hyatt Regency or Marriott
★★★	*Nice Rooms*	Holiday Inn or comparable quality
★★	*Adequate Rooms*	Clean, comfortable, and functional without frills (like a Motel 6)
★	*Super Budget*	

How the Hotels Compare in Palm Beach County

Hotel	Star Rating	Quality Rating	Cost ($=$50)	Phone
Boca Raton				
Radisson Suite Hotel	★★★★	87	$$$$+	(561) 483-3600
Sheraton Boca Raton Hotel	★★★★	86	$$$−	(561) 368-5252
Embassy Suites	★★★★	85	$$−	(561) 994-8200
DoubleTree Guest Suites	★★★★	85	$$−	(561) 997-9500
SpringHill Suites	★★★★	84	$$−	(561) 994-2107
Radisson Bridge Resort	★★★★	83	$$$+	(561) 368-9500
Holiday Inn Boca Raton Town Center	★★★½	76	$$−	(561) 368-5200
Best Western University Inn	★★½	60	$$−	(561) 395-5225
Ramada	★★½	59	$+	(561) 395-6850
Holiday Inn Express Downtown	★★½	57	$$−	(561) 395-7172
Delray Beach				
Delray Beach Marriott	★★★★	89	$$$−	(561) 274-3200
The Colony Hotel & Cabana Club	★★★½	79	$$$	(561) 276-4123
The Seagate	★★★½	77	$$$−	(561) 276-2421
Wright by the Sea	★★★	67	$$$−	(561) 278-3355
Highland Beach				
Holiday Inn	★★★½	77	$$+	(561) 278-6241
Manalapan				
The Ritz-Carlton Palm Beach	★★★★½	95	$$$$$$$−	(561) 533-6000
Palm Beach				
Four Seasons Resort	★★★★½	93	$$$$$$$−	(561) 582-2800
The Breakers	★★★★½	90	$$$$$$$+	(561) 655-6611
The Chesterfield	★★★★	87	$$$$−	(561) 659-5800
The Colony	★★★★	86	$$$+	(561) 655-5430
Palm Beach Hilton	★★★½	82	$$$$−	(561) 586-6542
Palm Beach Hawaiian Ocean Inn	★★½	60	$$$	(561) 582-5631
Fairfield Inn & Suites	★★½	57	$$−	(561) 582-2581
Heart of Palm Beach Hotel	★★½	57	$$$$−	(561) 655-5600
Palm Beach Gardens				
PGA National Resort	★★★★	88	$$$$$$−	(561) 627-2000
Embassy Suites	★★★★	85	$$$−	(561) 622-1000
DoubleTree Hotel in the Gardens	★★★★	83	$$+	(561) 622-2260

How the Hotels Compare in Palm Beach County (cont.)

Hotel	Star Rating	Quality Rating	Cost ($=$50)	Phone
Singer Island				
Hilton Singer Island Oceanfront Resort	★★★½	81	$$$–	(561) 848-3888
Canopy Palms Resort	★★★½	80	$$+	(561) 848-5502
Sheraton Oceanfront North Palm Beach	★★★	74	$$+	(561) 842-6171
Days Inn Oceanfront Resort	★★½	57	$$+	(561) 848-8661
West Palm Beach				
Sheraton	★★★½	82	$$+	(561) 833-1234
Hilton Palm Beach Airport	★★★½	80	$$–	(561) 684-9400
Crowne Plaza	★★★	66	$$$+	(561) 689-6400
Holiday Inn Palm Beach Airport	★★★	65	$+	(561) 659-3880
Radisson Suite Inn Palm Beach Airport	★★½	64	$$$–	(561) 689-6888
Hampton Inn	★★½	63	$$–	(561) 471-8700
Days Inn Turnpike/ Airport West	★★	54	$$–	(561) 686-6000
La Quinta	★★	52	$+	(561) 697-3388

How the Hotels Compare in Broward County

Hotel	Star Rating	Quality Rating	Cost ($=$50)	Phone
Dania Beach				
SpringHill Suites	★★★	73	$$+	(954) 920-9696
Motel 6 Dania Beach	★★	49	$–	(954) 921-5505
Deerfield Beach				
Embassy Suites Deerfield Beach Resort	★★★★	86	$$$$+	(954) 426-0478
Howard Johnson Plaza Resort	★★½	59	$$+	(954) 428-2850
Comfort Inn Oceanside	★★	55	$+	(954) 428-0650
Fort Lauderdale				
Hyatt Regency Pier Sixty-Six	★★★★	88	$$$$+	(954) 525-6666
Embassy Suites Fort Lauderdale	★★★★	87	$$$+	(954) 527-2700

How the Hotels Compare in Broward County (cont.)

Hotel	Star Rating	Quality Rating	Cost ($=$50)	Phone
Fort Lauderdale (continued)				
Marriott Fort Lauderdale Marina	★★★½	82	$$$+	(954) 463-4000
Ireland's Inn Beach Resort	★★★½	81	$$+	(954) 565-6661
Radisson Bahia Mar Beach Resort	★★★½	75	$$$	(954) 764-2233
Sheraton Yankee Trader	★★★½	75	$$	(954) 467-1111
Sheraton Yankee Clipper	★★★	73	$$+	(954) 524-5551
Holiday Inn Fort Lauderdale Beach	★★★	72	$$$−	(954) 563-5961
DoubleTree Hotel Fort Lauderdale Oceanfront	★★★	68	$$+	(954) 524-8733
Comfort Suites Airport	★★★	67	$$+	(954) 767-8700
Best Western Pelican Beach Resort	★★★	65	$$−	(954) 568-9431
Ocean Hacienda Inn	★★½	63	$$−	(954) 564-7800
Holiday Inn Lauderdale by the Sea	★★½	58	$+	(954) 776-1212
Days Inn Fort Lauderdale	★★½	57	$$+	(954) 563-2521
Best Western Oceanside Inn	★★½	56	$$$−	(954) 525-8115
Holiday Inn Express Port Everglades	★★½	56	$+	(954) 728-2577
Ocean Manor	★★½	56	$$−	(954) 566-7500
Ramada Plaza Beach Resort	★★½	56	$$−	(954) 565-6611
Best Western Marina Inn & Yacht Harbor	★★	54	$$$−	(954) 525-3484
Ramada Sea Club Resort	★★	54	$$−	(954) 564-3211
Landmark Inn Airport	★★	52	$+	(954) 525-5194
Travelodge Fort Lauderdale	★★	52	$$−	(954) 563-0660
Howard Johnson Ocean's Edge Fort Lauderdale	★★	49	$+	(954) 563-2451
Hillsboro Beach				
Seabonay Beach Resort	★★½	56	$+	(954) 427-2525
Hollywood				
Hampton Inn & Suites	★★½	64	$$+	(954) 922-0011
Comfort Inn Fort Lauderdale Airport	★★½	63	$+	(954) 922-1600

How the Hotels Compare in Broward County (cont.)

Hotel	Star Rating	Quality Rating	Cost ($=$50)	Phone
Hollywood (continued)				
Ambassador Resort Hollywood Beach	★★½	62	$+	(954) 458-1900
Hollywood Beach				
Holiday Inn SunSpree Resort Hollywood Beach	★★★	66	$$+	(954) 923-8700
Ramada Inn Hollywood Beach Resort Hotel	★★½	62	$$$–	(954) 921-0990
Howard Johnson Plaza Resort	★★½	61	$+	(954) 925-1411
Lauderdale-by-the-Sea				
Clarion Lauderdale Beach Resort	★★½	59	$$–	(954) 776-5660
Pompano Beach				
Four Points Sheraton Pompano Beach	★★★½	79	$$$–	(954) 782-5300
Holiday Inn Pompano Beach	★★★	70	$$–	(954) 941-7300
Traders Ocean Resort	★★½	58	$$–	(954) 941-8400
Ramada Inn Paradise Beach Resort	★★	55	$$–	(954) 785-3300
Best Western Beachcomber	★★	54	$$$–	(954) 941-7830
Howard Johnson Plaza Resort Pompano Beach	★★	53	$+	(954) 781-1300
Sands Harbor Resort	★★	53	$$$–	(954) 942-9100

How the Hotels Compare in Miami-Dade County

Hotel	Star Rating	Quality Rating	Cost ($=$50)	Phone
Bal Harbour				
Sheraton Bal Harbour Resort	★★★★½	90	$$$$$–	(305) 865-7511
Sea View Hotel	★★★★	89	$$$$$–	(305) 866-4441
Coconut Grove				
Grove Isle Club and Resort	★★★★★	97	$$$$$–	(305) 858-8300
Wyndham Grand Bay Hotel	★★★★½	92	$$$$$$+	(305) 858-9600
Doubletree at Coconut Grove	★★★★	83	$$$–	(305) 858-2500

How the Hotels Compare in Miami-Dade County (cont.)

Hotel	Star Rating	Quality Rating	Cost ($=$50)	Phone
Coral Gables				
The Omni Colonnade Hotel	★★★★½	94	$$$$+	(305) 441-2600
Biltmore Hotel	★★★★½	92	$$$$$$$+	(305) 445-1926
Hyatt Regency Coral Gables	★★★★½	91	$$$$$$$–	(305) 441-1234
Hotel Place St. Michel	★★★★½	90	$$$	(305) 444-1666
David William Hotel	★★★★	88	$$$+	(305) 445-7821
Florida City				
Hampton Inn Florida City	★★½	64	$$–	(305) 247-8883
Travelodge	★★½	64	$–	(305) 248-9777
Best Western Gateway to the Keys	★★½	63	$$–	(305) 246-5100
Fairway Inn	★★½	61	$+	(305) 248-4202
Comfort Inn	★★½	59	$+	(305) 248-4009
Key Biscayne				
Sonesta Beach Resort	★★★½	82	$$$$–	(305) 361-2021
Miami				
Hotel Intercontinental	★★★★½	94	$$$–	(305) 577-1000
Doral Golf Resort & Spa	★★★★	89	$$$$–	(305) 592-2000
Hotel Sofitel	★★★★	88	$$$$–	(305) 264-4888
Wyndham Miami Biscayne Bay	★★★★	88	$$$+	(305) 374-0000
Doubletree Grand Hotel	★★★★	86	$$$–	(305) 372-0313
Embassy Suites Airport	★★★★	86	$$+	(305) 634-5000
Hilton Miami Airport	★★★★	85	$$$+	(305) 262-1000
Marriott Biscayne Bay	★★★★	84	$$$+	(305) 374-3900
Clarion Hotel & Suites	★★★★	83	$+	(305) 374-5100
Miami Airport Marriott	★★★★	83	$$$+	(305) 649-5000
Summerfield Suites	★★★★	83	$$$–	(305) 269-1922
Doubletree Club Hotel	★★★½	82	$$+	(305) 266-0000
Wyndham Miami Airport	★★★½	82	$$–	(305) 871-3800
Miami Airport Courtyard South	★★★½	78	$$$–	(305) 642-8200
Crowne Plaza Hotel	★★★½	75	$$$	(305) 446-9000
Best Western Marina Park	★★★	70	$$–	(305) 371-4400
Holiday Inn Downtown	★★★	70	$$–	(305) 374-3000
Clarion Airport	★★★	67	$$–	(305) 871-1000

How the Hotels Compare in Miami-Dade County (cont.)

Hotel	Star Rating	Quality Rating	Cost ($=$50)	Phone
Miami (continued)				
Best Western Miami Airport Inn	★★½	64	$$+	(305) 871-2345
Howard Johnson Port of Miami	★★½	64	$+	(305) 358-3080
Howard Johnson Miami Airport	★★½	60	$+	(305) 945-2621
Quality Inn Miami Airport	★★	49	$$+	(305) 871-3230
Miami Beach				
Marlin	★★★★★	97	$$$$$$+	(305) 673-8770
The Tides	★★★★★	96	$$$$$$	(305) 604-5000
Casa Grande Suite Hotel	★★★★½	95	$$$$$+	(305) 672-7003
Hotel Ocean	★★★★½	94	$$$$	(305) 672-2579
Hotel Delano	★★★★½	93	$$$$$$$+	(305) 672-2000
Alexander Hotel	★★★★½	92	$$$$–	(305) 865-6500
Hotel Impala	★★★★½	92	$$$$+	(305) 673-2021
Hotel Astor	★★★★½	91	$$$$$$$$+	(305) 531-8081
Wyndham Miami Beach Resort	★★★★½	90	$$$$$	(305) 532-3600
Eden Roc Hotel	★★★★	89	$$$$–	(305) 531-0000
The Hotel	★★★★	89	$$$$$$+	(305) 531-2222
Winterhaven	★★★★	88	$$$$+	(305) 531-5571
La Flora	★★★★	86	$$$$–	(305) 531-3406
Merv Griffin's Blue Moon	★★★★	86	$$$–	(305) 673-2262
National Hotel	★★★★	85	$$$$$+	(305) 532-2311
Doubletree Surfcomber	★★★★	83	$$$+	(305) 532-7715
Newport Beachside Resort	★★★★	83	$$–	(305) 949-1300
Park Central Imperial Hotels	★★★★	83	$$$–	(305) 538-1611
Lily Guesthouse	★★★½	82	$$$+	(305) 535-9900
Ritz Plaza Hotel	★★★½	81	$$$$–	(305) 534-3500
Waldorf Towers Hotel	★★★½	81	$$+	(305) 531-7684
Cavalier Hotel	★★★½	80	$$$	(305) 604-5064
Fontainebleau Hilton Resort & Spa	★★★½	79	$$$+	(305) 538-2000

How the Hotels Compare in Miami-Dade County (cont.)

Hotel	Star Rating	Quality Rating	Cost ($=$50)	Phone
Miami Beach (continued)				
The Nassau Suite Hotel	★★★½	79	$$$–	(305) 534-2354
Essex House Hotel	★★★½	77	$$$+	(305) 534-2700
Four Points Sheraton	★★★	74	$$$–	(305) 531-7494
Avalon Majestic Hotel	★★★	72	$$+	(305) 538-0133
Indian Creek Hotel	★★★	72	$$$–	(305) 531-2727
Comfort Inn on the Beach	★★★	71	$$–	(305) 868-1200
Miami Beach Ocean Resort	★★★	68	$$$–	(305) 534-0505
Brigham Gardens	★★★	67	$$	(305) 531-1331
Mermaid Guest House	★★★	67	$$–	(305) 538-5324
Riande Continental	★★★	65	$$+	(305) 531-3503
Days Inn Oceanside	★★½	64	$$–	(305) 673-1513
Best Western Beach Resort	★★½	61	$$–	(305) 532-3311
Ramada Plaza Marco Polo	★★½	60	$+	(305) 932-2233
Tudor Hotel	★★½	60	$+	(305) 534-2934
Seville Beach Hotel	★★½	59	$$$–	(305) 532-2511
Best Western Oceanfront Resort	★★½	56	$$–	(305) 864-2232
Beach Plaza Hotel	★★	52	$+	(305) 531-6421
Cadillac Hotel & Resort	★★	52	$$+	(305) 531-3534
Ramada Resort Miami Beach	★★	52	$+	(305) 531-5771
Howard Johnson Miami Beach Bayshore	★★	50	$$–	(305) 532-4411
Miami Lakes				
Don Shula's Hotel & Golf Club	★★★★	85	$$+	(305) 821-1150
Miami Springs				
Courtyard Airport West	★★★½	76	$$$+	(305) 477-8118
Main Stay Suites	★★★	70	$$–	(305) 870-0448
Comfort Inn & Suites Airport	★★★	65	$+	(305) 871-6000
Holiday Inn Airport North	★★★	65	$$–	(305) 885-1941
Days Inn Miami Airport North	★★½	57	$+	(305) 888-3661

How the Hotels Compare in The Keys

Hotel	Star Rating	Quality Rating	Cost ($=$50)	Phone
Duck Key				
Hawk's Cay Resort	★★★★	87	$$$$	(305) 743-7000
Islamorada				
Cheeca Lodge	★★★★	85	$$$$$$$$+	(305) 664-4651
Hampton Inn & Suites	★★½	63	$$$–	(305) 664-0073
Pelican Cove Resort	★★½	63	$$+	(305) 664-4435
Chesapeake Resort	★★½	62	$$–	(305) 664-4662
Ragged Edge Resort & Marina	★★	55	$$–	(305) 852-5389
HoJo Holiday Isle Resort & Marina	★★	53	$$$$	(305) 664-2711
Key Largo				
Key Largo Marriott Beach Resort	★★★★	86	$$$$+	(305) 453-0000
Best Western Suites at Key Largo	★★★½	78	$$$+	(305) 451-5081
Ramada Limited	★★★	67	$$+	(305) 451-3939
Howard Johnson Resort Key Largo	★★½	63	$$$$–	(305) 451-1400
Ocean Pointe Suites at Key Largo	★★½	60	$$+	(305) 853-3000
Holiday Inn Key Largo	★★½	58	$$+	(305) 451-2121
Key West				
The Gardens Hotel	★★★★½	92	$$$+	(305) 294-2661
Heron House	★★★★½	91	$$$–	(305) 294-9227
Dewey House	★★★★½	90	$$$+	(305) 296-5611
Ocean Key Resort & Marina	★★★★	89	$$$$$$–	(305) 296-7701
Hyatt Key West Resort & Marina	★★★★	88	$$$$$–	(305) 296-9900
Pier House	★★★★	88	$$$$$$$–	(305) 296-4600
La Mer Hotel	★★★★	87	$$$	(305) 296-5611
Wyndham Casa Marina Resort	★★★★	86	$$$$+	(305) 296-3535
Avalon Bed & Breakfast	★★★★	84	$$$+	(305) 294-8233
Wyndham Reach Resort	★★★★	84	$$$$+	(305) 296-5000
Sheraton Suites Key West	★★★★	83	$$+	(305) 292-9800
Curry Mansion Inn	★★★½	82	$$$	(305) 294-5349

How the Hotels Compare in The Keys (cont.)

Hotel	Star Rating	Quality Rating	Cost ($=$50)	Phone
Key West (continued)				
Island City House Hotel	★★★½	82	$$$–	(305) 294-5702
South Beach Oceanfront Motel	★★★½	82	$$$+	(305) 296-5611
Crowne Plaza La Concha	★★★½	81	$$$+	(305) 296-2991
Ambrosia House	★★★½	79	$$$$–	(305) 294-5181
Duval House	★★★½	79	$$$$–	(305) 294-1666
The Artist House	★★★½	78	$$$+	(305) 296-3977
Eaton Lodge	★★★½	78	$$+	(305) 292-2170
La Te Da Hotel	★★★½	77	$$$$–	(305) 296-6706
Garden House	★★★½	76	$$$–	(305) 296-5368
Banyon Resort	★★★½	75	$$$+	(305) 296-7786
Eaton Manor Guesthouse	★★★	72	$$+	(305) 294-9870
Holiday Inn Beachside	★★★	67	$$$–	(305) 294-2571
Comfort Inn Key West	★★★	65	$$–	(305) 294-3773
Courtyard	★★★	65	$$+	(305) 294-5541
Best Western Key Ambassador	★★½	64	$$+	(305) 296-3500
Quality Inn Key West	★★½	64	$$–	(305) 294-6681
Radisson Hotel Key West	★★½	64	$$$–	(305) 294-5511
Days Inn Key West	★★½	63	$$–	(305) 294-3742
Hampton Inn	★★½	63	$$–	(305) 294-2917
Westwinds	★★½	63	$$–	(305) 296-4440
Southernmost Motel	★★½	62	$$+	(305) 296-6577
Travelodge Key West	★★½	60	$$+	(305) 296-7593
Best Western Hibiscus Motel	★★½	59	$$–	(305) 296-6711
Blue Marlin	★★½	57	$$–	(305) 294-2585
Spanish Gardens	★★	52	$+	(305) 294-1051
Eden House	★★	51	$$+	(305) 296-6868
Atlantic Shores Motel	★★	47	$$–	(305) 296-2491
Little Torch Key				
Parmer's Resort	★★½	59	$$+	(305) 872-2157
Marathon				
Hampton Inn	★★★	67	$$$–	(305) 743-9009
Holiday Inn Marathon	★★★	66	$$–	(305) 289-0222
Kingsail Resort Motel	★★	52	$+	(305) 743-5246
Seahorse Hotel & Marina	★★	50	$$–	(305) 743-6571

How the Hotels Compare in Southwest Florida

Hotel	Star Rating	Quality Rating	Cost ($=$50)	Phone
Bokeelia				
Bokeelia Tarpon Inn	★★★★	89	$$$$$$–	(941) 283-8961
Beachouse Motel	★★★	70	$$–	(941) 283-4303
Bonita Springs				
Trianon Bonita Bay	★★★★	88	$$+	(941) 948-4400
Comfort Inn	★★★	73	$$–	(941) 992-5001
Americinn Motel & Suites	★★★	71	$+	(941) 495-9255
The Tradewinds	★★★	68	$$$$$–	(941) 992-2111
Hampton Inn	★★★	67	$+	(941) 947-9393
Baymont Inn	★★★	66	$+	(941) 949-9400
Bonita Beach Resort Motel	★★★	65	$+	(941) 992-2137
Holiday Express Hotel & Suites	★★★	65	$+	(941) 948-0699
Flamingo Motel	★★	55	$+	(941) 992-7566
Days Inn	★★	54	$–	(941) 947-3366
Cape Coral				
Quality Inn Nautilus	★★★	66	$+	(941) 542-2121
Rainbow Motel Resort	★★½	64	$+	(941) 542-0061
Colonial Resort Motel & Apartments	★★½	63	$+	(941) 542-2149
Casa Loma Motel	★★½	58	$+	(941) 549-6000
Del Prado Inn	★★	53	$+	(941) 542-3151
Captiva				
Captiva Island Bed & Breakfast	★★★½	78	$$$–	(941) 395-0882
Tween Waters Inn	★★★	70	$$$+	(941) 472-5161
Jensen's Twin Palm Cottages & Marina	★★½	64	$$$–	(941) 472-5800
Everglades City				
Captain's Table Motel	★★★	67	$–	(941) 695-4211
Barron River Motel and Villas	★★½	59	$+	(941) 695-3591
Everglades City Motel	★½	42	$	(941) 695-4224
Fort Myers				
Residence Inn by Marriott	★★★★	84	$$–	(941) 936-0110
Holiday Inn Riverwalk	★★★½	82	$$$–	(941) 334-3434
Rock Lake Motel	★★★½	81	$+	(941) 693-2003

How the Hotels Compare in Southwest Florida (cont.)

Hotel	Star Rating	Quality Rating	Cost ($=$50)	Phone
Fort Myers (continued)				
Radisson Inn Sanibel Gateway	★★★½	80	$$–	(941) 466-1200
Ramada Inn	★★★½	79	$$–	(941) 337-0300
Fort Myers Courtyard	★★★½	77	$$–	(941) 275-8600
Homewood Suites Hotel	★★★½	77	$$$–	(941) 275-6000
Holiday Inn Select Airport	★★★	69	$$–	(941) 482-2900
Radisson Inn	★★★	68	$$+	(941) 936-4300
Ramada Limited Fort Myers	★★★	66	$$+	(941) 275-1111
Comfort Inn Fort Myers	★★★	65	$$–	(941) 694-9200
Quality Inn	★★½	64	$+	(941) 332-3232
Baymont Inn	★★½	62	$+	(941) 275-3500
Wellesley Inn & Suites	★★½	61	$+	(941) 278-3949
Comfort Inn	★★½	59	$+	(941) 936-3993
Howard Johnson Inn Edison Mall	★★½	59	$+	(941) 936-3229
Fort Myers Inn	★★½	57	$+	(941) 936-1959
Days Inn South	★★	52	$+	(941) 936-1311
Fountain Motel	★★	49	$+	(941) 481-0429
Fort Myers Beach				
Lover's Key Beach Club	★★★★½	93	$$+	(941) 765-1040
Gullwing Beach Resort	★★★★½	92	$$$–	(941) 765-4300
Pointe Estero Resort	★★★★½	91	$$+	(941) 765-1155
Edison Beach House	★★★★	89	$$+	(941) 463-1530
DiamondHead All Suite Beach Resort	★★★★	86	$$$+	(941) 765-7654
Best Western Beach Resort	★★★	71	$$$–	(941) 463-6000
Days Inn Island Beach Resort	★★★	71	$$	(941) 463-9759
GrandView All Suite Resort	★★★	71	$$+	(941) 765-4422
Best Western Pink Shell Beach Resort	★★★	70	$$	(941) 463-6181
GuestHouse Inn Mariner's Lodge & Marina	★★★	70	$+	(941) 466-9700
Ramada Inn Beachfront	★★★	70	$$	(941) 463-6158
Quality Inn & Suites at the Lani Kai	★★★	69	$$$–	(941) 463-3111
Howard Johnson Beachfront	★★★	68	$$–	(941) 463-9231
Lighthouse Island Resort	★★★	68	$$–	(941) 463-9392
The Wild Wave	★★★	68	$$–	(941) 463-8900

How the Hotels Compare in Southwest Florida (cont.)

Hotel	Star Rating	Quality Rating	Cost ($=$50)	Phone
Fort Myers Beach (continued)				
Casa Playa Beach Resort	★★★	66	$$–	(941) 765-0510
Neptune Inn	★★½	64	$$$–	(941) 463-6141
Holiday Inn Fort Myers Beach	★★½	63	$$–	(941) 463-5711
Hidden Harbor Inn	★★½	61	$$+	(941) 463-9382
Matanzas Inn	★★½	61	$$+	(941) 463-9258
Gulf Echo Motel	★★½	60	$$–	(941) 463-9193
Kahlua Beach Club	★★½	60	$$–	(941) 463-5751
Sandpiper Gulf Resort	★★½	60	$$–	(941) 463-5721
Rusty's Motel	★★½	59	$$+	(941) 463-4691
The Beach House	★★½	58	$$–	(941) 463-4004
Island Motel	★★½	58	$+	(941) 463-2381
Sandy Beach Hideaway	★★½	56	$$–	(941) 463-1080
Tropical Inn Resort	★★½	56	$$–	(941) 463-3124
Gulf Motel	★★	55	$$–	(941) 463-9247
Outrigger Beach Resort	★★	55	$$–	(941) 463-3131
Ti Ki Resort	★★	55	$+	(941) 463-9547
Beacon Motel & Gift Shop	★★	52	$$–	(941) 463-5264
Dolphin Inn	★★	50	$+	(941) 463-6049
Marco Island				
Marriott Resort of Marco Island	★★★★	85	$$$$–	(941) 394-2511
Marco Resort & Club	★★★★	84	$$–	(941) 394-2777
Marco Island Hilton Beach Resort	★★★½	82	$$$$–	(941) 394-5000
Radisson Suite Beach Resort	★★★½	78	$$$+	(941) 394-4100
Boat House Motel	★★½	59	$$	(941) 642-2400
Lakeside Inn	★★½	59	$$$–	(941) 394-1161
Matlacha				
Bayview Bed & Breakfast	★★★	68	$$$	(941) 283-7510
Bridge Water Inn	★★★	65	$$	(941) 283-2423
Knoll's Court Motel	★★½	59	$+	(941) 283-0616
Naples				
Ritz-Carlton Naples	★★★★½	93	$$$$$$	(941) 598-3300
Hotel Escalante	★★★★½	92	$$$$+	(941) 659-3466
The Registry Resort	★★★★½	90	$$$$–	(941) 597-3232
Inn on Fifth	★★★★	88	$$+	(941) 403-8777

How the Hotels Compare in Southwest Florida (cont.)

Hotel	Star Rating	Quality Rating	Cost ($=$50)	Phone
Naples (continued)				
DoubleTree Guest Suites Naples	★★★★	87	$$+	(941) 593-8733
La Playa Beach Resort	★★★★	87	$$$$$$–	(941) 597-3123
Hilton Naples & Towers	★★★★	85	$$$–	(941) 430-4900
The Cottages of Naples	★★★★	84	$$$$+	(941) 450-0776
Inn at Pelican Bay	★★★½	82	$$	(941) 597-8777
Ramada Plaza Hotel	★★★½	82	$$–	(941) 430-3500
Residence Inn by Marriott	★★★½	82	$$–	(941) 659-1300
Naples Beach Hotel & Golf Club	★★★½	81	$$$+	(941) 261-2222
Staybridge Suites by Holiday Inn	★★★½	81	$$+	(941) 643-8002
Naples Courtyard by Marriott	★★★½	77	$+	(941) 434-8700
Best Western Naples	★★★	74	$$–	(941) 261-1148
Holiday Inn Naples	★★★	71	$$$$	(941) 262-7146
Hampton Inn	★★★	69	$$	(941) 261-8000
Neptune Motel	★★★	67	$$	(941) 262-6126
Vanderbilt Beach Resort House	★★★	67	$$–	(941) 597-3144
White Sands Resort Club	★★★	66	$$–	(941) 261-4144
Bel Mar Resort	★★½	64	$$$$–	(941) 403-4747
Lighthouse Inn	★★½	64	$+	(941) 597-3345
Quality Inn Gulfcoast	★★½	62	$$$–	(941) 261-6046
Comfort Inn Downtown Naples	★★½	61	$$–	(941) 649-5800
Naples Hotel & Suites	★★	52	$+	(941) 262-6181
Sea Court Hotel	★★	52	$	(941) 435-9700
Trail's End Motel	★★	51	$–	(941) 262-6336
North Fort Myers				
Best Western Fort Myers Waterfront	★★★	73	$+	(941) 997-5511
Howard Johnson Express Inn	★★½	60	$+	(941) 656-4000
EconoLodge	★★	55	$–	(941) 995-0571
Days Inn North	★★	52	$+	(941) 995-0535
Motel 6	★★	50	$	(941) 656-5544

Hotel	Star Rating	Quality Rating	Cost ($=$50)	Phone
How the Hotels Compare in Southwest Florida (cont.)				
Sanibel				
Casa Ybel Resort	★★★★½	90	$$$$$+	(941) 472-3145
Hurricane House	★★★★	88	$$$$+	(941) 472-1696
Sundial Beach Resort	★★★★	88	$$$$+	(941) 472-4151
West Wind Inn	★★★★	83	$$$$−	(941) 472-1541
Sanibel Inn	★★★½	80	$$$+	(941) 472-3181
Caribe Beach Resort	★★★½	75	$$	(941) 472-1166
Waterside Inn on the Beach	★★★	73	$$$$−	(941) 472-1345
Best Western Sanibel Beach Resort	★★★	67	$$$−	(941) 472-1700
Holiday Inn Beach Resort	★★★	67	$$$−	(941) 472-4123
Tropical Winds Cottages	★★★	67	$$+	(941) 472-1765
Palm View Motel	★★★	65	$$$+	(941) 472-1606
Sandpiper Inn Sanibel Island	★★½	64	$$$+	(941) 472-1529
Shalimar Resort	★★½	64	$$$$+	(941) 472-1353
Mitchell's Sand Castles	★★½	63	$$+	(941) 472-1282
Island Inn	★★½	62	$$$$+	(941) 472-1561
Sanibel's Seaside Inn	★★½	61	$$$+	(941) 472-1400
Beach View Cottages	★★½	60	$$$+	(941) 472-1202
Buttonwood Cottages	★★½	60	$$$+	(941) 395-9061
Forty/Fifteen Resort	★★½	59	$+	(941) 472-1232
Seahorse Cottages on Sanibel	★★½	59	$$$$−	(941) 472-4262
The Palms of Sanibel	★★½	58	$$$−	(941) 395-1775

The Best Deals

Having listed the nicest rooms in town, let's reorder the list to rank the best combinations of quality and value in a room. As before, the rankings are made without consideration of location or the availability of restaurant(s), recreational facilities, entertainment, or amenities. Once again, each lodging property is awarded a value rating on a 0 to 100 scale. The higher the number, the better the value.

We recently had a reader complain to us that he had booked one of our top-ranked rooms in terms of value and had been very disappointed in the room. We noticed that the room the reader occupied had a quality rating of

★★½. We would remind you that the value ratings are intended to give you some sense of value received for dollars spent. A ★★½ room at $50 may have the same value rating as a ★★★★ room at $100, but that does not mean the rooms will be of comparable quality. Regardless of whether it's a good deal or not, a ★★½ room is still a ★★½ room.

Listed below are the best room buys for the money, regardless of location or star classification, based on averaged rack rates. Note that sometimes a suite can cost less than a hotel room.

The Top 10 Best Deals in Palm Beach County

Hotel	Star Rating	Quality Rating	Cost ($=$50)	Phone
1. SpringHill Suites	★★★★	84	$$–	(954) 994-2107
2. Embassy Suites Boca Raton	★★★★	85	$$–	(954) 994-8200
3. DoubleTree Guest Suites Boca Raton	★★★★	85	$$–	(954) 997-9500
4. Hilton Palm Beach Airport	★★★½	80	$$–	(954) 684-9400
5. DoubleTree Hotel in the Gardens	★★★★	83	$$+	(954) 622-2260
6. Holiday Inn Boca Raton Town Center	★★★½	76	$$–	(954) 368-5200
7. Embassy Suites Palm Beach Gardens	★★★★	85	$$$–	(954) 622-1000
8. Sheraton West Palm Beach	★★★½	82	$$+	(954) 833-1234
9. Sheraton Boca Raton Hotel	★★★★	86	$$$–	(954) 368-5252
10. Holiday Inn Highland Beach	★★★½	77	$$+	(954) 278-6241

The Top 10 Best Deals in Broward County

Hotel	Star Rating	Quality Rating	Cost ($=$50)	Phone
1. Sheraton Yankee Trader	★★★½	75	$$	(954) 467-1111
2. Holiday Inn Pompano Beach	★★★	70	$$–	(954) 941-7300
3. Howard Johnson Plaza Resort	★★½	61	$+	(954) 925-1411

The Top 10 Best Deals in Broward County (cont.)

Hotel	Star Rating	Quality Rating	Cost ($=$50)	Phone
4. Ireland's Inn Beach Resort	★★★½	81	$$+	(954) 565-6661
5. Comfort Inn Fort Lauderdale Airport	★★½	63	$+	(954) 922-1600
6. Ambassador Resort Hollywood Beach	★★½	62	$+	(954) 458-1900
7. Four Points Sheraton Pompano Beach	★★★½	79	$$$–	(954) 782-5300
8. Embassy Suites Ft. Lauderdale	★★★★	87	$$$+	(954) 527-2700
9. Best Western Pelican Beach	★★★	65	$$–	(954) 568-9431
10. Motel 6 Dania Beach	★★	49	$–	(954) 921-550

The Top 30 Best Deals in Miami-Dade County

Hotel	Star Rating	Quality Rating	Cost ($=$50)	Phone
1. Clarion Hotel & Suites	★★★★	83	$+	(305) 374-5100
2. Travelodge	★★½	64	$–	(305) 248-9777
3. Newport Beachside Resort	★★★★	83	$$–	(305) 949-1300
4. Wyndham Miami Airport	★★★½	82	$$–	(305) 871-3800
5. Embassy Suites Airport	★★★★	86	$$+	(305) 634-5000
6. Hotel Intercontinental	★★★★½	94	$$$–	(305) 577-1000
7. Don Shula's Hotel & Golf Club	★★★★	85	$$+	(305) 821-1150
8. Comfort Inn & Suites Airport	★★★	65	$+	(305) 871-6000
9. Best Western Marina Park	★★★	70	$$–	(305) 371-4400
10. Holiday Inn Downtown	★★★	70	$$–	(305) 374-3000
11. Hotel Place St. Michel	★★★★½	90	$$$	(305) 444-1666
12. Comfort Inn on the Beach	★★★	71	$$–	(305) 868-1200
13. Main Stay Suites	★★★	70	$$–	(305) 870-0448
14. Merv Griffin's Blue Moon	★★★★	86	$$$–	(305) 673-2262

The Top 30 Best Deals in Miami-Dade County (cont.)

Hotel	Star Rating	Quality Rating	Cost ($=$50)	Phone
15. Clarion Airport	★★★	67	$$–	(305) 871-1000
16. Park Central Imperial Hotels	★★★★	83	$$$–	(305) 538-1611
17. Doubletree Club Hotel	★★★½	82	$$+	(305) 266-0000
18. Waldorf Towers Hotel	★★★½	81	$$+	(305) 531-7684
19. Summerfield Suites	★★★★	83	$$$–	(305) 269-1922
20. Ramada Plaza Marco Polo	★★½	60	$+	(305) 932-2233
21. Doubletree Grand Hotel	★★★★	86	$$$–	(305) 372-0313
22. Holiday Inn Airport North	★★★	65	$$–	(305) 885-1941
23. Howard Johnson Miami Airport	★★½	60	$+	(305) 945-2621
24. Howard Johnson Port of Miami	★★½	64	$+	(305) 358-3080
25. Tudor Hotel	★★½	60	$+	(305) 534-2934
26. Mermaid Guest House	★★★	67	$$–	(305) 538-5324
27. Alexander Hotel	★★★★½	92	$$$$–	(305) 865-6500
28. Doubletree Coconut Grove	★★★★	83	$$$–	(305) 858-2500
29. David William Hotel	★★★★	88	$$$+	(305) 445-7821
30. Comfort Inn	★★½	59	$+	(305) 248-4009

The Top 20 Best Deals in The Keys

Hotel	Star Rating	Quality Rating	Cost ($=$50)	Phone
1. Heron House	★★★★½	91	$$$–	(305) 294-9227
2. Sheraton Suites Key West	★★★★	83	$$+	(305) 292-9800
3. The Gardens Hotel	★★★★½	92	$$$+	(305) 294-2661
4. Holiday Inn Marathon	★★★	66	$$–	(305) 289-0222
5. La Mer Hotel	★★★★	87	$$$	(305) 296-5611
6. Dewey House	★★★★½	90	$$$+	(305) 296-5611

The Top 20 Best Deals in The Keys (cont.)

Hotel	Star Rating	Quality Rating	Cost ($=$50)	Phone
7. Eaton Lodge	★★★½	78	$$+	(305) 292-2170
8. Island City House Hotel	★★★½	82	$$$−	(305) 294-5702
9. Avalon Bed & Breakfast	★★★★	84	$$$+	(305) 294-8233
10. Comfort Inn Key West	★★★	65	$$−	(305) 294-3773
11. Days Inn Key West	★★½	63	$$−	(305) 294-3742
12. Ramada Limited Key Largo	★★★	67	$$+	(305) 451-3939
13. Curry Mansion Inn	★★★½	82	$$$	(305) 294-5349
14. Spanish Gardens	★★	52	$+	(305) 294-1051
15. Westwinds	★★½	63	$$−	(305) 296-4440
16. Garden House	★★★½	76	$$$−	(305) 296-5368
17. Eaton Manor Guesthouse	★★★	72	$$+	(305) 294-9870
18. Crowne Plaza La Concha	★★★½	81	$$$+	(305) 296-2991
19. Hawk's Cay Resort	★★★★	87	$$$$	(305) 743-7000
20. Best Western Suites at Key Largo	★★★½	78	$$$+	(305) 451-5081

The Top 30 Best Deals in Southwest Florida

Hotel	Star Rating	Quality Rating	Cost ($=$50)	Phone
1. Rock Lake Motel	★★★½	81	$+	(941) 693-2003
2. Captain's Table Motel	★★★	67	$−	(941) 695-4211
3. Marco Resort & Club	★★★★	84	$$−	(941) 394-2777
4. Naples Courtyard by Marriott	★★★½	77	$+	(941) 434-8700
5. Pointe Estero Resort	★★★★½	91	$$+	(941) 765-1155
6. Ramada Plaza Hotel	★★★½	82	$$−	(941) 430-3500
7. Americinn Motel & Suites	★★★	71	$+	(941) 495-9255
8. Residence Inn by Marriott	★★★★	84	$$−	(941) 936-0110
9. Holiday Express Hotel & Suites	★★★	65	$+	(941) 948-0699
10. Lover's Key Beach Club	★★★★½	93	$$+	(941) 765-1040

The Top 30 Best Deals in Southwest Florida (cont.)

Hotel	Star Rating	Quality Rating	Cost ($=$50)	Phone
11 Bonita Beach Resort Motel	★★★	65	$+	(941) 992-2137
12. Radisson Inn Sanibel Gateway	★★★½	80	$$–	(941) 466-1200
13. Trianon Bonita Bay	★★★★	88	$$+	(941) 948-4400
14. DoubleTree Guest Suites Naples	★★★★	87	$$+	(941) 593-8733
15. Best Western Fort Myers Waterfront	★★★	73	$+	(941) 997-5511
16. Ramada Inn	★★★½	79	$$–	(941) 337-0300
17. Residence Inn by Marriott	★★★½	82	$$–	(941) 659-1300
18. Gullwing Beach Resort	★★★★½	92	$$$–	(941) 765-4300
19. GuestHouse Inn Mariner's Lodge & Marina	★★★	70	$+	(941) 466-9700
20. Fort Myers Courtyard	★★★½	77	$$–	(941) 275-8600
21. Hampton Inn	★★★	67	$+	(941) 947–9393
22. Inn at Pelican Bay	★★★½	82	$$	(941) 597-8777
23. Edison Beach House	★★★★	89	$$+	(941) 463-1530
24. Baymont Inn	★★★	66	$+	(941) 949-9400
25. Quality Inn Nautilus	★★★	66	$+	(941) 542-2121
26. Inn on Fifth	★★★★	88	$$+	(941) 403-8777
27. Rainbow Motel Resort	★★½	64	$+	(941) 542-0061
28. Staybridge Suites by Holiday Inn	★★★½	81	$$+	(941) 643-8002
29. Caribe Beach Resort	★★★½	75	$$	(941) 472-1166
30. Colonial Resort Motel & Apartments	★★½	63	$+	(941) 542-2149

Part Three

Palm Beach County

A Brief History

Palm Beach County is larger than the state of Delaware and is comprised of 37 municipalities and unincorporated areas. But most visitors are only interested in opulent Palm Beach and affluent Boca Raton.

The county's earliest known residents weren't tourists, but Seminole Indians. Then the region was claimed for Spain in 1513. When the new United States took over, the Seminoles resisted longer than any other North American tribe. The Seminole Indian Wars, fought from 1835 to 1842, ended Indian control of the area. That war's Federal commander, Colonel William Jenkins Worth, is commemorated in Lake Worth and Worth Avenue.

The county's oldest non-native settlement, Jupiter, was founded as a wartime fort in 1836. The Jupiter Lighthouse began operating in 1860 and continues to the present.

In the 1890s, visionary Henry Flagler, a founding partner of Standard Oil, built the Florida East Coast Railway system connecting the east coast of Florida from Jacksonville to Key West in order to open the state as a winter paradise. He also built two large hotels, The Royal Poinciana Hotel and The Breakers, plus his own winter home, Whitehall, now The Flagler Museum. The Town of Palm Beach, on a barrier beach, was incorporated in 1911. The area continued to grow as a fashionable winter retreat, and the number of workers and services meeting their needs escalated.

A legendary story tells of the African-American workers who toiled on Palm Beach so visitors might vacation. These workers lived in shacks on the beach. Developers wanted to use this land for their advantage but couldn't oust the settlers. Supposedly, a large tent was erected on the mainland in West Palm Beach and a huge party thrown for them, with food, drink, and entertainment. While they were enjoying themselves, a "mysterious" fire

Palm Beach County

ATTRACTIONS

1. Arthur R. Marshall Loxahatchee National Wildlife Refuge
2. Barry Aviation Florida
3. Blood's Hammock Groves
4. Boca Raton Museum of Art
5. Boomers
6. The Flagler Museum
7. Florida Crystal Sugar & Rice Tours
8. Gumbo Limbo Environmental Complex
9. Hoffman's Chocolate Shoppe & Gardens
10. International Museum of Cartoon Art
11. John D. MacArthur Beach State Park
12. Jonathan Dickinson State Park
13. Jupiter Inlet Lighthouse
14. Knollwood Groves
15. Lion Country Safari
16. Loxahatchee Everglades Tours
17. Morikami Museum and Japanese Gardens
18. Mounts Botanical Garden
19. Norton Museum of Art
20. Old School Square Cultural Arts Center
21. Palm Beach Groves
22. Palm Beach Kennel Club
23. Palm Beach Polo
24. Palm Beach Zoo at Dreher Park
25. Pan's Garden
26. Peanut Island Tour
27. Rapids Water Park
28. Red Reef Park
29. Roger Dean Stadium
30. South Florida Science Museum

(Legend continued on page 104.)

103

Palm Beach County (continued)

RESTAURANTS

- **31** Amici
- **32** Boston's on the Beach
- **33** Cafe Chardonnay
- **34** Cafe L'Europe
- **35** Cafe Protege
- **36** Cornell Cafe
- **37** East City Bistro
- **38** Echo
- **39** Eilat Cafe
- **40** Ellie's 50's Diner Cafe
- **41** Hamburger Heaven
- **42** John G's Restaurant
- **43** L'Anjou French Restaurant
- **44** L'Escalier at the Florentine Room
- **45** La Vielle Maison
- **46** Lucille's Bad to the Bone BBQ
- **47** Mark's at Mizner Park
- **48** Mark's at CityPlace
- **49** Max's Grille
- **50** Mississippi Sweets BBQ Co.
- **51** Pete's
- **52** The Restaurant
- **53** Souplantation & Sweet Tomatoes
- **54** Spoto's Oyster Bar
- **55** Storza Ristorante
- **56** Wolfie Cohen's Rascal House
- **57** Zemi

NIGHTCLUBS

- **58** Blue Anchor British Pub
- **59** Blue Martini
- **60** City Hall Bar & Grill
- **61** Dakotah 624
- **62** Leopard Lounge
- **63** The Liquid Room
- **64** Lulu's Place
- **65** Pete's

broke out, burning down the shacks. The workers were moved to new housing in West Palm Beach.

Today, Palm Beach's Ocean Boulevard is lined with millionaires' homes built by such gilded names as the Vanderbilts and the Whitneys. Perhaps the most recognizable is Donald Trump's place where it meets Southern Boulevard, formerly the 118-room mansion Mar-a-Lago built for cereal heiress Marjorie Merriweather Post. It's now a private club. Across the road is the gorgeous blue ocean. How do these elite snowbirds get there? Walkways have been built beneath the road (not for the commoners, these luxe walkways). But, because the beaches are public, there's nothing to stop anyone from entering the Palm Beach Municipal Beach—say, at the foot of Worth Avenue—and walking along the beach in either direction. Besides mansion-gazing, you might spot a celeb or two. Just don't expect to use any bathrooms!

Many of the stops along the railroad's route blossomed into full communities. For instance, Boca Raton was settled in 1896. It became noteworthy because of the foresight of architect Addison Mizner. His 100-room hotel, The Cloister, built in 1925, is now part of the world-renowned Boca Raton Resort and Club. The lobby retains the grand architectural elements and antiques. Unfortunately, visitors can't pop into the Boca Raton Resort and Club to glimpse the period's opulence unless they're registered guests or guests of those who are. However, you may view the amazing lobby of The Breakers in Palm Beach, and even dine there without being a registered guest (for big bucks, of course). Other buildings are characterized by the Mizner mixture of Mediterranean, Spanish, and Moorish influences and are found around town, called Mizner-this and Mizner-that. The buildings are usually painted in Boca pink—a calamine lotion tone.

Even though today many outsiders think all the residents are retired Northerners, it's not so (the nationally broadcast 2000 voter recount destroyed some of that myth). Palm Beach County has been a Southern-minded state for much of its history. While racism wasn't as blatant as in some other states, it nevertheless existed and was certainly apparent to those who were excluded or came in contact with it.

For instance, Barbara Chane of Lake Clark Shores moved to Florida with her New York–based family in 1946, when she was in second grade. Currently a sixth-grade teacher at Palm Beach Lakes Middle School, she recalls that her high-school-aged brother was riding on a bus when a uniformed African American soldier boarded, on crutches because of his missing leg. There was no vacant seat in the back—the colored section—and the driver said he couldn't sit up front although there was a vacant seat. Chane's brother spoke up, saying he should be given the (white-only) seat. The driver stopped and put them both off the bus. Chane also remembers when The Breakers Hotel didn't permit Jews as guests. Ironically, now many Jewish charities hold their major functions there. Chane's sister Anne Faivus was one year old when they arrived in Palm Beach County. Also of Lake Clark Shores, Faivus is a specialist in gifted education for Palm Beach County. She remembers that when she taught school here from 1965 to 1970, segregated white and colored schools still existed. They weren't integrated until 1971.

As for the social scene, the Everglades Club was notorious for its policy denying membership to blacks and Jews, who were not even welcome as guests for lunch or dinner. A legendary story reports that socialite C. Z. Guest brought cosmetics queen Estee Lauder for lunch. Even though Lauder denied her Jewishness at the time, Guest's tennis privileges were temporarily revoked as punishment. And in 1985, the late famed choreographer Jerome Robbins (who was also Jewish) cancelled a cocktail party at the club scheduled to honor the New York City Ballet when he learned of its exclusionary policy.

Today African Americans aren't seen often in other than service roles on tony Palm Beach, but they shop in the stores and eat in the restaurants. Hispanics have become more visible since 1992's Hurricane Andrew destroyed many of their homes in Dade County, prompting a northward flow. And Jewish families of industrial and financial giants now reside in some of the mansions. In fact, the Raymond F. Kravis Center for the Performing Arts is named for the philanthropic Jewish Kravis family.

Later, major headquarters for IBM in Boca and Motorola in Boynton Beach drew numerous young families to relocate to the area. Now Boca is an area of upscale manicured country clubs, condominiums, and elegant shops and restaurants catering to these full- and part-time residents, and it's pretty much built out. Boynton Beach has homes popping up on every piece of spare land. And Jupiter is the latest area to be experiencing huge growth. The most recent population figures for Palm Beach County (2000) count 1,062,400 residents, about 10 percent of which are winter residents.

Arriving

BY CAR

Most drivers enter Palm Beach County from the north, either via I-95 (with well-marked signage) from the Northeast or Florida's Turnpike (with its service plazas) from Orlando. Some visitors drive east from the Gulf Coast via Routes 70/710 (70 becomes 710), skirting north of Lake Okeechobee. But don't expect to see much of this second-largest freshwater lake in the country unless you leave the highway. The scenery consists of large sugar plantations with fields of waving sugar cane and not much else.

BY PLANE

Palm Beach International Airport (PBI), though still relatively small, just a few years ago was merely a stone building without air conditioning and only a few gateways. Today, it's a three-level modern facility with all the amenities of other large city airports, and it's serviced by most major airlines. The international status is primarily because of flights to the Bahamas, but the newest landing strip expansion and new direct highway connections from I-95 should lure more international airlines. Southwest Airlines, JetBlue, and Delta Express have just begun service. Rental car agencies have desks conveniently located in the luggage retrieval area. For more information, call (561) 471-7400.

BY TRAIN

Amtrak (the station is in a lovely old Spanish Renaissance–style building) is at 201 South Tamarind Avenue, West Palm Beach, near the Kravis Center and CityPlace, (561) 832-6169.

Tri-Rail is a commuter train service running among Miami-Dade, Broward, and Palm Beach Counties (phone (800) 874-7245), with stops in West Palm Beach, Delray Beach, and Boca Raton. Extra trains are added for major events, such as football games.

BY BUS

Greyhound Bus Lines has terminals in West Palm Beach (205 South Tamarind Avenue, (561) 833-8536) and Lake Worth (929 North Dixie Highway, (561) 588-5002).

Getting Around

DRIVING YOUR CAR

The main north-south arteries within the county are Florida's Turnpike and I-95. Although the turnpike usually provides smoother sailing, it's several miles west of the major Palm Beach County destinations. And the cost of using the turnpike is considerable, especially in the county's northern reaches. I-95 generally has more traffic, particularly trucks. And when an accident occurs (which happens daily), there's often terrible start-and-stop movement in the opposite direction, as myriad rubber-neckers brake to see the carnage. By all means avoid rush hours and use parallel roads such as Congress Avenue, Military Trail, and Jog Road/Powerline Road (*Note:* Jog Road/Powerline Road is inconsistently named one or both in different sections).

Construction is endemic, as lanes are added to handle the influx of 1,000 emigrants to Florida per day. And it's usually at the height of tourist season. A supposedly better connection from I-95 to Palm Beach International Airport seems to be taking longer to complete than the time it took to construct the airport. Try to avoid this section by using corollary roads such as Congress Avenue, Military Trail, or Route 1.

State Road A1A (stands for alternate 1A) offers a delightful, leisurely ride along the ocean, providing glimpses here and there of gorgeous beach vistas and millionaires' mansions. In some spots it narrows considerably, so visitors may watch the boat action on the Intracoastal Waterway and the seaside.

If you plan to park on a shopping street or at a public beach, remember to bring heaps of quarters for the meters.

BY BUS

Palm Tran (phone (561) 233-4287; www.co.palm-beach.fl.us/palmtran) operates a fleet of buses—each seats 42—throughout the county, with numerous stops. Schedules are available on the bus or at any county library (remember, every library is not county-operated and may be a city or village library). Fares cost $1.25 for adults or 60¢ for seniors age 60 and over, students, and disabled citizens (you must show a valid ID to receive the reduced fare); unlimited day passes are $3 or $2 reduced.

OTHER OPTIONS

Palm Beach Water Taxi (98 Lake Drive, Palm Beach Shores; (561) 683-8294 or (800) 446-4577) is the latest—and probably most pleasant—way to get around near the Intracoastal Waterway. Choose among guided tours or shuttle service to Clematis Street and waterfront restaurants.

A free trolley connects West Palm Beach's CityPlace and the Clematis Street district.

Gathering Information

For general tourist information, contact Palm Beach County Convention and Visitors Bureau (1555 Palm Beach Lakes Boulevard, Suite 204, West Palm Beach 33401; (561) 471-3995) or log on to www.palmbeachfl.com.

Summer offers savings on many fronts. Request the coupon book "$1,000 Worth of the Palm Beaches for Free" to save on many dining, shopping, sight-seeing, and sports attractions. Call (800) 554-PALM. Many hotels provide a seventh night free, while restaurants often reduce prices to attract customers while the tourist and snowbird seasons wind down.

The Beaches

Major hotels boast oceanfront beaches. The Boca Raton Resort and Club offers registered guests the beach at its Boca Beach Club property, but frequent trams and *Mizner's Dream,* a period boat, bring guests from other buildings. Hotel concierge desks provide the schedule.

Numerous strands dot the ocean side of State Road A1A, luring young families and retirees. Remember, always heed warnings of riptides and sea lice. The beaches listed below offer bathrooms and outside showers.

Boca Raton   The most popular Boca beaches include: the small **South Beach Pavilion** at Spanish River Boulevard, with free parking for just 17 cars; there's additional public parking on Palmetto Park Road. North up the road is the larger **Red Reef Park,** featuring picnic tables and barbecue grills; it's accessible from the parking lot on the west side of State Road A1A through three underground tunnels ($8 per car weekdays, $10 weekends and holidays). A little known fact is that free parking is available on Spanish River Boulevard, on both sides of the Intracoastal Bridge. This beach particularly draws the young singles set.

Delray Beach A long stretch of narrow beach is accessible north and south of Atlantic Avenue. Several eateries and beach supply shops are located on the west side of A1A. Bring lots of quarters for the parking meters.

Lake Worth At Lake Avenue, a large complex provides lovely beaches, a municipal pool, a children's playground, a fishing pier, fast-food restaurants, John G's (which has lines around the block at times—see the restaurant profile), and tourist-oriented shops. Parking here costs 25 cents per 15 minutes, with a maximum of 10 hours. Arrive early for the closest parking. The City of Lake Worth runs three complimentary trolleys to the pier, leaving every hour on the hour from the depot at Lake Avenue and H Street, at City Hall. Printed schedules are available at City Hall or call (561) 586-1720.

Jupiter South of Indiantown Road on State Road A1A, the huge complex at **Carlin Park** draws many families. Parking is complimentary. The 3,000-foot beach competes for attention with other activities, including a Little League baseball field, tennis courts, children's playground, and bocce and volleyball courts. There are picnic tables and grills. And the Lazy Loggerhead Cafe (call (561) 747-1134) is open for most meals daily, has patio and inside seating, and dishes up fast fare and more ambitious meals. It has won the "Best Casual Beach Restaurant" award in Palm Beach County designated by the *Palm Beach Post.*

For information on additional town beaches within Palm Beach County, call Boca Raton Parks and Recreation (phone (561) 393-7810); Delray Beach Parks and Recreation Department (phone (561) 243-7250); Jupiter Parks and Recreation (phone (561) 746-5134); and Palm Beach Gardens Parks and Recreation (phone (561) 775-8270).

Recreation

FITNESS CENTERS AND AEROBICS

Though many visitors will choose to pump up in their hotel's fitness center, some might enjoy mixing with locals who are similarly focused. One of the most popular spots, with locals and visitors, is **Ultima Fitness** (downtown at 400 Clematis Street, West Palm Beach; (561) 659-1724). It boasts 20,000 square feet that include 40 pieces of cardiovascular equipment (life fitness cross trainers, treadmills, recumbent and upright bikes, and Tetrix Stairmasters), Cybex machines, Hammer Strength and Strive machines, and free weights. There are 45 aerobics classes weekly, including kick boxing, plus yoga classes. Other attractions include dry saunas, on-site nursery care with a minimal charge ($3 per child up to two hours), and a health-food restaurant. Membership is $15 per day and $60 per week.

A hit with young, local professionals (because it's located near large business complexes) is **The Athletic Club Boca Raton** (1499 Yamato Road, Boca Raton, (561) 241-5088). This whopping facility—78,000 square feet—offers cardiovascular equipment (treadmills, bikes); indoor and outdoor pools; racquetball, handball, basketball, and squash courts; an indoor track; aerobics, spinning, and yoga classes; sauna, steam, and whirlpool; and a restaurant. Nonmembers may purchase a one-day pass for $23.50, five-day for $75, and ten-day for $135.

Gold's Gym & Aerobic Center, started in 1965 in California, has several branches in Palm Beach County: the Palm Beach Gardens facility (9840 Alternate A1A; (561) 694-6727) boasts more than 50 pieces of cardio equipment, including treadmills, bikes, and Stairmasters. It's open 24 hours daily; offers free day care for little ones, a sauna, adult and kids' karate, and a juice bar; and has personal trainers. Guests may have complimentary fat composition evaluations. Other locations include: 2121 Palm Beach Lakes Boulevard, West Palm Beach, (561) 471-8880; 11427 West Palmetto Park Road, Boca Raton, (561) 470-9494; and 499 NE Spanish River Boulevard, Boca Raton, (561) 362-6001. Call the other branches for individual equipment offered. Daily rates are $10, weekly rates $35.

Jim Woolard's World Gym (6832 Forest Hill Boulevard, West Palm Beach; (561) 966-4653) lures with Bodymasters, Hammer Strength, Nautilus, Hoist, Star Trek for cardio equipment, Life Cycle, Life Steps, and cross trainers. Rates for visitors are $10 daily, $30 weekly. Other branches with similar prices are at 4762 Congress Avenue, Boynton Beach, (561) 964-6676; 14550 South Military Trail, Delray Beach, (561) 638-9980; and 4430 North Lake Boulevard, Palm Beach Gardens, (561) 630-3933.

The **YMCA** (6631 Palmetto Circle South, Boca Raton; (561) 395-9622) offers reciprocal, complimentary use to members of other Ys; nonmembers may buy temporary memberships for $10 per day or $30 per week. The YMCA has Stairmasters, treadmills, cross trainers, saunas, free weights and machines, a pool, and day care ($3 per day). A new YMCA facility has opened at 9600 South Military Trail, Boynton Beach. Memers of Ys out of the area may use the facilities free for two weeks; they may take a week off and return for another two free weeks. Nonmembers may buy short-term memberships for $15 a day or $30 a week; there are also children's rates and family rates. For more information, call (561) 738-9622.

The **Jewish Community Center** (9801 Donna Klein Boulevard, Boca Raton; (561) 852-3200) offers six free visits to members of other JCCs. Daily guest passes cost $35 for up to five days or $8 for just one day. Equipment in the 80,000-square-foot athletic facility includes two University gyms, Precor EFX elliptical cross trainers, bikes, Stairmasters, Cybex machines, and a full free-weight facility; racquetball and basketball courts, aerobics classes, sauna and steam baths, and two pools are also available.

Other JCC locations are at 8500 Jog Road, Boynton Beach, (561) 740-9000 (they offer limited temporary membership to active members of other JCCs—five free visits, then $5 daily for up to nine visits) and 3151 North Military Trail, West Palm Beach, (561) 689-7700 (they provide five free visits for members of other JCCs and $5 per day for nonmembers).

WALKING AND RUNNING

The major parks offer trails for walking and running. An outstanding choice is the **Lake Trail** on Palm Beach. Few communities boast sidewalks, but large strips of A1A from Boca Raton's southern line (where it meets Deerfield Beach) to Delray Beach are paved. Many walkers do their morning treks in air-conditioned shopping malls, which open earlier than the stores. Most major strolling takes place in shopping venues, including Boca Raton's Mizner Park and West Palm Beach's CityPlace. And, of course, window shopping along Palm Beach's Worth Avenue is mandatory. The Athletic Club Boca Raton (1499 Yamato Road, Boca Raton; (561) 241-5088) boasts an indoor track. Those who run outside usually choose early morning or late afternoon; mid-day gets too hot.

HIKING

South Florida has no hills to hike, but several trails provide access to nature's unique wonders. One especially fine way to experience the Everglades is to hike any of the five trails at **Arthur R. Marshall Loxachatchee National Wildlife Refuge** (10216 Lee Road, Boynton Beach; (561) 734-8303). For more options, see the section on Walking and Running above.

TENNIS

South Florida's weather is ideal for year-round tennis playing, which is why so many former and upcoming champions relocate here. In Boca Raton, world-famous champion Chrissie Evert runs the **Evert Tennis Academy** at 10334 Diego Drive South; call (561) 488-2001 or (800) 417-3783. The complex boasts 9 hard courts, 12 clay courts, and 2 red clay courts. Adult lessons are given only on clay courts, 9–11:30 a.m., for $75 a session. Three days of lessons run $210, 5 days $325. The Junior Program costs $895 per month with board; nonboarding lessons are given 9–11:30 a.m. for $550 a week; 2:30–6:30 p.m. at $450 a week; and 4–6:30 p.m. at $225 week. Facilities are closed to the public unless taking lessons. Looking for a special gift? How about a fantasy clinic with Chrissie?

Also in Boca, **Patch Reef Park** (2000 Yamato Road; (561) 997-0881) has 17 lighted hard courts and is open 7:30 a.m.–10 p.m., closing Sunday at 6 p.m. Non–Palm Beach County residents pay $5.75 per person for one-and-a-half hours of play. Lessons are available. The **City of Boca Raton**

Memorial Park (271 NW Second Avenue; (561) 393-7978) is open 7:30 a.m.–10 p.m. The four hard courts and six clay courts are lighted. Nonresident adults pay $5 to play the clay courts for one hour before 2:30 or one-and-a-half hours after 2:30, $4.50 on the hard courts for one hour. Juniors pay $4 for clay, $3.50 for hard courts, with same time restrictions. Lessons are available. The **Boca Del Mar Tennis and Golf Club** (6202 Boca Del Mar Drive; (561) 392-8118) holds Junior clinics Monday, Wednesday, and Friday, 4:30–6:30 p.m. Nonmember rates for 1 day per week (4 classes) are $85; 2 days per week (8 classes) run $170; 3 days week (12 classes) are $255. Family discounts are also available.

Northward up the coast, the area's top tennis center is the **Delray Beach Tennis Center** (201 West Atlantic Avenue, Delray Beach; (561) 243-7360). Besides watching exciting professional matches, normal players may also call "game, set, and match" among 6 hard courts and 34 clay courts. Nonresidents pay $12 for one-and-a-half hours, children pay $8. There are adult and children's clinics and classes as well.

In Boynton, the **Boynton Beach Tennis Center** (3111 South Congress Avenue; (561) 742-6575) has 4 hard courts and 17 Har-Tru courts. Open to the public Monday–Friday, 8 a.m.–9 p.m.; Saturday and Sunday, 8 a.m.–dusk. Fees for one-and-a-half hours are $6 on clay courts and $2 on hard courts. Juniors under 18 cost $1 for one-and-a-half hours on any court. There's a $3 light fee per court at night.

The **City of West Palm Beach** has five courts open to the public daily 8 a.m.–8 p.m. at no charge. At the **South Olive Park Tennis Learning Center** (345 Summa Street; (561) 540-8831), Michael Baldwin runs a program of tennis lessons for Pee Wees through teens, adults, and seniors. Lessons are given mornings, afternoons, and evenings. This facility has four all-weather lighted courts.

Also operated by the city with no pay-for-play: **Gaines Park Tennis Court** (1501 Australian Avenue; (561) 659-0735) has six all-weather lighted courts; **Howard Park Tennis Club** (901 Lake Avenue; (561) 833-7100) offers five clay courts and two all-weather lighted courts; **Phipps Park** (4301 Dixie Highway; (561) 722-8702) has four all-weather lighted courts; and **Vedado Park** (3710 Paseo Andalusia; (561) 835-7035) has one unlighted all-weather court.

Farther north in Jupiter, the **Jupiter Bay Tennis Club** (353 US Highway One; (561) 744-9424) offers seven clay courts, three of them lighted; rates are $16 per person, $12 each with a friend for one-and-a-half hours. Clinics are conducted for juniors and adults.

North Palm Beach Tennis Club (951 US Highway One, North Palm Beach; (561) 626-6515) offers ten lighted clay courts; it's open 7 a.m.–9 p.m. The daily guest fee for nonresidents is $10 per adult, $3 for juniors. An adult clinic is available.

GOLF

Palm Beach lures duffers with a batch of facilities. Visitors probably won't find themselves teeing off alongside the rich and infamous—private courses flourish here—but everyone from beginners to club champions will find a course to meet their needs.

Atlantis Country Club

Established: 1972

Address: 190 Atlantis Boulevard, Atlantis 33462

Phone: (561) 968-1300

Status: Resort/semiprivate course

Tees: Championship: 6,610 yards, par 72, USGA 72.2, slope 137.
Men's: 6,060 yards, par 72, USGA 69.3, slope 130.
Ladies': 5,242 yards, par 72, USGA 67.6, slope 122.

Fees: In season, $77 per person, after 1 p.m. $67; reduced in summer.

Facilities: Dining room, driving range, snack bar, locker rooms, 24-room inn.

Comments: Soft spikes only. Although there's a misconception that Atlantis only has a private course, this one has been open to the public 25 years.

Belle Glade Golf Course

Established: 1989

Address: State Road 7, Belle Glade 33430

Phone: (561) 996-6605

Status: Public course

Tees: Championship: 6,558 yards, par 72, USGA 70.0, slope 116.
Men's: 6,044 yards, par 72, USGA 70.0, slope 116.
Ladies': 5,182 yards, par 72, USGA 69.8, slope 112.

Fees: $36 for 18 holes.

Facilities: Although it's a pretty bare-bones operation, Belle Glade does offer a driving range, practice tee, pro shop, and restaurant.

Comments: Popular course with locals.

Boca Raton Resort & Club (Resort Course)

Established: 1997

Address: 501 East Camino Real, Boca Raton 33432

Phone: (561) 395-3000

Status: Resort course

Tees: Championship: 6,253 yards, par 72, USGA 69.3, slope 128.

Men's: 5,902 yards, par 71, USGA 67.6, slope 124.

Ladies': 4,577 yards, par 71, USGA 64.3, slope 107.

Fees: $160 per person.

Facilities: Driving range, clubhouse, locker rooms, and restaurant will be completed November 2001.

Comments: Soft spikes only. Available only to registered guests and club members.

Boca Raton Resort & Club (Country Club Course)

Established: 1985

Address: 17751 Boca Club Boulevard, Boca Raton 33432

Phone: (561) 395-3000

Status: Resort/private course

Tees: Championship: 6,714 yards, par 72, USGA 73.0, slope 138.

Men's: 6,361 yards, par 72, USGA 71.1, slope 132.

Ladies': 5,776 yards, par 72, USGA 68.4, slope 121.

Fees: $100 per person.

Facilities: New clubhouse with pro shop, locker rooms, fitness center, restaurant, bar.

Comments: Soft spikes only. Available only to registered guests and club members.

Boca Raton Municipal Golf Course

Established: 1982

Address: 8111 Golf Course Road, Boca Raton 33434

Phone: (561) 483-6100 (Automated tee times)

Status: Public course

Tees: Championship: 6,514 yards, par 72, USGA 70.5, slope 126.

Men's: 6,115 yards, par 72, USGA 68.5, slope 119.

Ladies': 5,306 yards, par 72, USGA 69.8, slope 114.

Fees: Green fees only: 9 holes $23.75, 18 holes $37.25. With cart, 9 holes $34.50, 18 holes $50.

Facilities: Practice range, lockers, snack bar.

Comments: Soft spikes only.

Boca Dunes Golf & Country Club

Established: 1977

Address: 1400 Country Club Drive, Boca Raton 33428

Phone: (561) 451-1600

Status: Semiprivate course

Tees: Championship: 7,093 yards, par 72, USGA 73.1, slope 134.
Men's: 6,800 yards, par 72, USGA 72.2, slope 126.
Ladies': 5,743 yards, par 72, USGA 71.1, slope 121.

Fees: $59 with cart for 18 holes.

Facilities: Clubhouse, driving range, lockers, bar, grill.

Comments: Soft spikes only.

The Breakers Ocean Course

Established: 1897

Address: 1 South County Road, Palm Beach 33480

Phone: (561) 659-8407

Status: Private course

Tees: Championship: 6,167 yards, par 72, USGA 68.1, slope 127.
Men's: 5,765 yards, par 72, USGA 66.1, slope 127.
Ladies': 5,254 yards, par 72, USGA 69.0, slope 123.

Fees: $145 for 18 holes, $85 for nine holes; slight reduction in summer.

Facilities: New clubhouse, pro shop, small fitness center, restaurant, bar, putting green, driving range, golf academy.

Comments: Soft spikes only. Only hotel guests and members may play.

The Club at Winston Trails

Established: 1993

Address: 6101 Winston Trails Boulevard, Lake Worth 33463

Phone: (561) 439-3700

Status: Semiprivate course

Tees: Championship: 6,835 yards, par 72, USGA 73.0, slope 130.
Men's: 6,443 yards, par 72, USGA 71.1, slope 128.
Ladies': 5,405 yards, par 72, USGA 70.0, slope 119.

Fees: Monday–Friday, $49; weekends, $59 to 11 a.m., $52 after 11 a.m.; all fees include cart.

Facilities: Clubhouse, fitness center, restaurant, bar, snack bar.

Comments: A "cart girl" drives around selling drinks. Soft spikes only,

Delray Beach Golf Club

Established: 1923

Address: 2200 Highland Avenue, Delray Beach 33445

Phone: (561) 243-7380

Status: Public course

Tees: Championship: 6,907 yards, par 72, USGA 73.0, slope 126.
Men's: 6,360 yards, par 72, USGA 70.2 slope 119.

Ladies': 5,189 yards, par 72, USGA 69.8, slope 117.

Fees: $53.50 nonresidents; $33 Delray Beach residents.

Facilities: Clubhouse, restaurant, bar, lockers, driving range, pro shop.

Comments: Soft spikes only.

Golf Club of Jupiter

Established: 1980

Address: 1800 Central Boulevard, Jupiter 33458

Phone: (561) 747-6262

Status: Semiprivate course

Tees: Championship: 6,275 yards, par 70, USGA 69.9, slope 117.
Men's: 5,600 yards, par 71, USGA 67.4, slope 114.
Ladies': 5,150 yards, par 71, USGA 69.5, slope 118.

Fees: $55 7 a.m.–noon; $40 noon–3 p.m.; $20 after 3 p.m.

Facilities: Luncheonette, bar, lockers, putting green, club storage.

Comments: Course has an aqua range (over pond).

Lacuna Golf Club

Established: 1985

Address: 6400 Grand Lacuna Boulevard, Lake Worth 33460

Phone: (561) 433-3006

Status: Semiprivate course

Tees: Championship: 6,700 yards, par 71, USGA 70.4, slope 121.
Men's: 6,400 yards, par 71, USGA 69.7, slope 118.
Ladies': 5,119 yards, par 71, USGA 67.5, slope 111.

Fees: $35 all year.

Facilities: Restaurant, pro shop, putting green.

Comments: Popular course with locals year-round and with seasonal tourists in winter.

Lake Worth Municipal Golf Course

Established: 1980

Address: One 7th Avenue North, Lake Worth 33460

Phone: (561) 582-9713

Status: Public course

Tees: Championship: 6,120 yards, par 70, USGA 68.9, slope 119.
Men's: 5,600 yards, par 70, USGA 67.3, slope 115.
Ladies': 5,100 yards, par 70, USGA 69.5, slope 114.

Fees: In season, $42 including cart until noon, $32 without; after noon, $35 including cart, $28 without; after 2:30 p.m., $28 with cart, $23 without. In summer, $22 until 3 p.m., $16 after 3 p.m.

Facilities: Clubhouse, restaurant, lockers, pro shop, chipping area opening November 2001.

Comments: Yet another popular course with locals year-round and tourists in season.

The Links at Boynton Beach

Established: 1984

Address: 8020 Jog Road, Boynton Beach 33437

Phone: (561) 742-6500

Status: Public course

Tees: Championship: 6,231 yards, par 71, USGA 70.4, slope 132.
Men's: 5,801 yards, par 71, USGA 68.3, slope 124.
Ladies': 4,913 yards, par 65, USGA 64.9, slope 108.

Fees: $39 for 18 holes, including cart.

Facilities: Clubhouse, restaurant, driving range, practice green, putting and chipping greens, lockers.

Comments: Soft spikes only.

The Links at Polo Trace

Established: 1989

Address: 13397 Hagen Ranch Road, Delray Beach 33446

Phone: (561) 495-5301

Status: Semiprivate course

Tees: Championship: 7,084 yards, par 72, USGA 74.8, slope 139.
Men's: 6,684 yards, par 72, USGA 72.6, slope 133.
Ladies': 5,301 yards, par 72, USGA 71.6, slope 125.

Fees: $150 per person in season; after April 16, $135.

Facilities: Pro shop, locker rooms, restaurant, bar and lounge, driving range open to players that day only.

Comments: Soft spikes only.

Mizner Trail Golf Course

Established: 1972

Address: 22689 Camino Del Mar, Boca Raton 33433

Phone: (561) 392-7992

Status: Semiprivate course
   Championship: 6,800 yards, par 72, USGA 73.3, slope 135.
   Men's: 6,202 yards, par 72, USGA 70.1, slope 128.
   Ladies': 5,400 yards, par 72, USGA 69.7, slope 121.

Fees: Weekdays before 11 a.m., $65; after 11 a.m., $60; after 1 p.m., $55.
Weekends before 11 a.m., $80; after 11 a.m., $65; after 1 p.m., $55.

Facilities: Clubhouse, restaurant, bar, pro shop, putting green, driving
range, chipping green.

Comments: Soft spikes only.

North Palm Beach Country Club

Established: 1956

Address: 951 US Highway One, North Palm Beach 33408

Phone: (561) 691-3433

Status: Semipublic—a municipal course for members and nonmembers

Tees: Championship: 6,281 yards, par 72, USGA 69.9, slope 120.
   Men's: 5,781 yards, par 72, USGA 63.3, slope 113.
   Ladies': 5,033 yards, par 72, USGA 68.9, slope 114.

Fees: $62; off-season reduced rates.

Facilities: Clubhouse, restaurant, bar, lockers, putting green, driving
range.

Comments: Soft spikes only. For additional charge, golfers may use the
Olympic-sized pool and lighted tennis courts.

Palm Beach Gardens Golf Club

Established: 1991

Address: 11401 Northlake Boulevard, Palm Beach Gardens 33418

Phone: (561) 775-2556

Status: Public course

Tees: Championship: 6,500 yards, par 72, USGA 70.6, slope 128.
   Men's: 6,375 yards, par 72, USGA 68.7, slope 123.
   Ladies': 4,663 yards, par 72, USGA 66.0, slope 110.

Fees: $44 before noon, $37 noon–2 p.m., $23 after 2 p.m. Prices drop $5
after May 1st.

Facilities: Clubhouse, restaurant, bar, driving range.

Comments: Always busy—one of the region's most popular courses.

PGA National Golf Club (Champion Course)

Established: 1981

Address: 1000 Avenue of the Champions, Palm Beach Gardens 33418

Phone: (561) 627-1800

Status: Private

Tees: Championship: 7,022 yards, par 72, USGA 142, slope 74.7.
Men's: 6,367 yards, par 72, USGA 71.7, slope 133.
Ladies': 5,377 yards, par 72, USGA 71.1, slope 123.

Fees: $225 (18 holes), slight fee reduction in summer.

Facilities: Clubhouse, pro shop, lockers, restaurant, bar, nine putting greens, two driving ranges.

Comments: Must be a guest of the resort.

PGA National Golf Club (Estate Course)

Established: 1984

Address: 1000 Avenue of the Champions, Palm Beach Gardens 33418

Phone: (561) 627-1614

Tees: Championship: 6,694 yards, par 72, USGA 73.4, slope 138.
Men's: 6,122 yards, par 72, USGA 71.7, slope 132.
Ladies': 4,903 yards, par 72, USGA 68.4, slope 118.

Fees: $130 (18 holes), slight fee reduction in summer.

Facilities: Pro shop, driving range, putting green.

Comments: Must be guest of the resort.

PGA National Golf Club (Squire Course)

Established: 1981

Address: 1000 Avenue of the Champions, Palm Beach Gardens 33418

Phone: (561) 627-1800

Tees: Championship: 6,465 yards, par 72, USGA 71.3, slope 132.
Men's: 6,000 yards, par 72, USGA 69.9, slope 127.
Ladies': 4,982 yards, par 72, USGA 69.8, slope 123.

Fees: $225 (18 holes), slight fee reduction in summer.

Facilities: Clubhouse, pro shop, lockers, restaurant, bar, nine putting greens, two driving ranges.

Comments: Must be a guest of the resort.

PGA National Golf Club (Haig Course)

Established: 1980

Address: 1000 Avenue of the Champions, Palm Beach Gardens 33418

Phone: (561) 627-1800

Tees: Championship: 6,806 yards, par 72, USGA 73.5, slope 135.
Men's: 6,335 yards, par 72, USGA 71.3, slope 129.
Ladies': 5,645 yards, par 72, USGA 72.5, slope 121.

Fees: $225 (18 holes), slight fee reduction in summer.

Facilities: Clubhouse, pro shop, lockers, restaurant, bar, nine putting greens, two driving ranges.

Comments: Must be a guest of the resort.

PGA National Golf Club (General Course)

Established: 1984

Address: 1000 Avenue of the Champions, Palm Beach Gardens 33418

Phone: (561) 627-1800

Tees: Championship: 6,768 yards, par 72, USGA 72.6, slope 132.
   Men's: 6,219 yards, par 72, USGA 70.0, slope 125.
   Ladies': 5,324 yards, par 72, USGA 71.0, slope 122.

Fees: $225 (18 holes), slight fee reduction in summer.

Facilities: Clubhouse, pro shop, lockers, restaurant, bar, nine putting greens, two driving ranges.

Comments: Must be a guest of the resort.

Villa Delray Golf Club

Established: 1972

Address: 6200 Via Delray, Delray Beach 33484

Phone: (561) 498-1444

Status: Semiprivate course

Tees: Championship: 6,241 yards, par 71, USGA 71.0, slope 128.
   Men's: 5,959 yards, par 71, USGA 68.8, slope 126.
   Ladies': 5,236 yards, par 71, USGA 67.0, slope 119.

Fees: In season, $46 including cart, $39 without cart, $15 after 3 p.m.; in summer, $18 with cart, $15 after 3 p.m.

Facilities: Driving range, restaurant, pro shop, lockers, putting green, bag storage.

Comments: A full-service club catering to seniors.

The Village Golf Club

Established: 1980

Address: 122 Country Club Drive, Palm Beach 33480

Phone: (561) 793-1400

Status: Semiprivate course

Tees: Championship: 6,880 yards, par 72, USGA 73.3, slope 134.
   Men's: 6,464 yards, par 72, USGA 70.7, slope 128.
   Ladies': 5,455 yards, par 72, USGA 71.7, slope 126.

Fees: Weekdays, $50 before 1 p.m., $30 after 1 p.m.; weekends, $55 and

$35 respectively (all fees include golf cart). Florida residents get $5 off each price.

Facilities: Clubhouse, restaurant, bar, lockers, putting green, driving range, pro shop. Swimming pool and tennis are available.

Comments: Soft spikes only.

Westchester Golf & Country Club

Established: 1988

Address: 12250 Westchester Club Drive, Boynton Beach 33437

Phone: (561) 734-6300

Status: Semiprivate course

Tees: Championship: 6,772 yards, par 72, USGA 72.9, slope 137.
Men's: 6,000 yards, par 72, USGA 71.2, slope 130.
Ladies': 4,728 yards, par 72, USGA 69.7, slope 119.

Fees: Monday–Thursday, $49 before 1 p.m., $39 after 1 p.m.;
Friday–Sunday, $59 before 1 p.m., $49 after 1 p.m.

Facilities: Restaurant, driving range, locker room, 18-hole par 3.

Comments: Soft spikes only; three championship nine-hole courses

BICYCLING

For the most unique bicycling, visit the **Palm Beach Bicycle Trail Shop** (223 Sunrise Avenue, in Palm Beach Hotel, Palm Beach; (561) 659-4583). Rental rates are $7 per hour, $18 for the day. The shop is open Monday–Saturday, 9 a.m.–5:30 p.m.; Sunday, 10 a.m.–5 p.m. The business started here 28 years ago. Bikers cycle along the paved Lake Trail between millionaires' homes and the Intracoastal Waterway, spotting boats and dog-walkers along the way. The trail's south end starts at the Flagler Museum and continues for about one mile. Then, near the rental shop, it continues northward from Sunrise Avenue for another nine miles to Palm Beach Inlet. The shop also rents helmets and children's bikes. Guided tours, pointing out the famous residents' homes, are by reservation only.

An extremely popular trail is along State Road A1A (Ocean Boulevard) in Boca Raton and Highland Beach; bikers sometimes glimpse the ocean or Intracoastal. **Richwagen's Cycle Center** (217 East Atlantic Avenue, Delray Beach; (561) 243-2453) rents a variety of bikes, from single speeds and hybrids to tandem bikes and children's bikes. One of the most popular is the seven-speed cruiser, costing $8 per hour, $25 per day, or $45 per week. Open Monday–Friday, 9 a.m.–6 p.m.; Saturday, 9 a.m.–5 p.m.

Most large parks boast bicycle trails and bicycle racks, along with other athletic facilities and picnic areas. There are bicycle paths at **Carlin Park** in Jupiter (south of Indiantown Road on State Road A1A; (561) 746-5134);

John Prince Park (2700 6th Avenue South, Lake Worth; (561) 966-6600), which also offers a 1.2-mile fitness trail; and **Okeeheelee Park** (7715 Forest Hill Boulevard, West Palm Beach; (561) 966-6600), which also has a lighted water ski course. There are also bicycle trails at **Jonathan Dickinson State Park** (see Attractions, page 142).

CANOEING AND KAYAKING

A world of wildlife opens up to those who rent canoes and kayaks, which take them into shallow areas inaccessible to big boats. Check conditions before arriving, since a major three-year drought has forced some enterprises to temporarily cease operations.

Loxahatchee Canoe Rentals (10216 Lee Road, Boynton Beach; (561) 733-0192) rents canoes and kayaks at the Arthur R. Marshall Loxahatchee National Wildlife Refuge. Boaters will see sawgrass, swamp hibiscus, and arrowroot, plus alligators and ibis; if you're lucky, you may spot otters, storks, and white-tailed deer. Self-driven boats cost $20 each; three- to four-hour guided tours cost $25 per canoe and $30 per two-person kayak. Each canoe holds three to four people. Call for directions (it's somewhat hard to find) and to see if they're operating.

Canoes and kayaks are available for rent at the **Jupiter Outdoor Center** on the Intracoastal Waterway (18095 North State Road A1A, Jupiter; (561) 747-9666). Paddlers pass mangroves and may spot teems of birds, including great blue herons and osprey; you might even catch sight of Smoky the dolphin or manatees. Rates for singles run $20 the first hour, $15 for the second hour, and $45 for four hours. For doubles it's $30 for the first hour, $20 for the second hour, and $55 for four hours. The center also offers 50 guided tours. The most popular is the Saturday night tour, which focuses on stargazing and ends with a campfire (bring your own food and drink). Cost is $20 adults, $14 for children age 12 and under. Another guided tour is the four-hour Indian River Lagoon Kayak Adventure, which goes to the Nature Conservancy at Blowing Rock (admission included in price of $45 per adult, $35 per child); participants may see sea turtles and manatees.

Jonathan Dickinson State Park (US Highway 1, Jupiter; (561) 546-2771) also rents canoes and kayaks. Rowers paddle up the northwest fork of the Loxahatchee River. You may see little blue herons, greenback herons, osprey, and manatees (which are usually more plentiful in winter)—and maybe even an alligator. Loxahatchee means river of turtles, and you're likely to see peninsular cooters (a type of turtle). Canoes, which usually hold two adults and one small child, cost $10 for the first two hours and $4 each additional hour. Single kayaks rent for $15 for the first two hours and $6 each additional hour. Double kayaks go for $20 for the first two hours and $6 each additional hour.

SCUBA DIVING

Reef diving is tops here. The same coral reef that extends along Broward and Miami-Dade Counties is offshore here, except it's extremely deep off the Pam Beach coast. And there are artificial reefs made with all manner of sunken items, including (typically Palm Beach) a Rolls Royce.

To participate, contact the **Scuba Club** (4708 North Flagler Drive, West Palm Beach; (561) 844-2466 or (800) 835-2466). Join the two-hour trips aboard a 40-foot boat with equipment available for rent. Trips leave Tuesday–Friday, 10 a.m. and 2:30 p.m.; Saturday and Sunday, 9 a.m. and 2 p.m. Cost is $23 per person.

Another option is **Force-E Dive Centers,** family-owned since 1976 and with several locations: 877 Palmetto Park Road East, Boca Raton, (561) 368-0555; 7166 Beracassa Way, Boca Raton, (561) 395-4407; 660 Linton Boulevard, Delray Beach, (561) 276-0666; 12189 US Highway One, North Palm Beach, (561) 624-7136; and 155 East Blue Heron Boulevard, Riviera Beach, (561) 845-2333. Each center uses ten boats and operates daily (except when seas are rough). The most frequently requested trips down under are two-tank dives, which cost $40–45. Equipment is sold and rented, and Jacques Cousteau wannabees may take courses at these PADI five-star facilities.

American Dive Center (1888 NW 2nd Avenue, Boca Raton; (561) 393-0621) is a PADI outfit and provides anything to do with scuba diving: rentals, reef trips on seven boats, and lessons. They go out daily and charge $45–50 for the boat trip; equipment is separate.

SNORKELING

Force-E Dive Centers (see locations above under Scuba Diving) also offer snorkeling. The average price is $30 for four hours, depending on which boats are used and whether equipment is included or not. **American Dive Center** (1888 NW 2nd Avenue, Boca Raton; (561) 393-0621) is another option; they usually offer snorkeling trips on weekends. Cost is $35 for a four-hour trip.

SAILBOATS AND SAILING SCHOOLS

There are few sailboat rentals here because the Boca Inlet has become extremely difficult to navigate and it takes a long time to reach a better inlet. The major hotels still schedule sailings because their captains go through the inlet daily. **Fast Break Sailing Charters** (400 North Flagler Drive, West Palm Beach; (561) 659-4472) heads down through the Hillsboro Inlet. Its 41-foot-long classic boat has been in the Palm Beach area for 15 years. They schedule only private charters with one to six sailors; they won't join passengers from one group with another. A three-and-a-half-hour trip costs $300; a seven-hour trip costs $600 and includes lunch.

FISHING

Florida fishing licenses are always required, whether you drop a line off the nearest bridge or go out on a party boat. Licenses are available at sporting goods stores, tackle shops, and K-Marts. A saltwater license is $13.50 a year for Florida residents; it's $6.50 for three days and $16.50 for seven days for nonresidents. A freshwater fishing license is $13.50 a year.

Drift Boats

The Captain Bob, a 65-foot party boat docked at 200 East 13th Street, Riviera Beach (call (561) 842-8823) accepts individual fishermen twice daily. The four-hour sessions leave from the Port of Palm Beach Thursday–Tuesday, 8:30 a.m. and 1:30 p.m. Charges are $25 for adults and $20 for children age 12 and under (when accompanied by an adult). Price includes everything participants need to fish, including bait, rods, and fishing license. Closed on Wednesday.

The **B-Love Fleet** (314 East Ocean Avenue, Lantana; (561) 588-7612) offers two boats that take three four-hour trips daily. Prices include fishing license, bait, and tackle. Cost is $25 for adults and $18 for children age 12 and under. Seniors fish for $22 on day trips Monday–Friday. A six-hour trip costs $35.

The 72-foot-long *Sea Mist* (700 Casa Loma Boulevard, Boynton Beach; (561) 732-9974) also sails three times a day. Cost is $25 for adults, $18 for children age 12 and under, and $22 for seniors over age 65. Fees include everything you'll need for fishing: rods, reels, bait, tackle, and fishing license.

SPECTATOR SPORTS

Tennis

At the **Delray Beach Tennis Center** (201 West Atlantic Avenue, Delray Beach; (561) 243-7360) you can watch such exciting matches as the Citrix Tennis Championships and the Chris Evert Pro-Celebrity match under top-notch conditions at the center stadium court.

Golf

The **PGA Resort,** of course, is almost synonymous with golf. It's host to several national tours and holds Optimist, a junior golf tournament. Also at the PGA Resort, March sees the annual five-day PGA National Invitational Croquet Tournament, luring players from throughout the country. It's open to the public with free admission. Call (561) 627-2000 for more information on the PGA Resort. The **Boca Raton Resort and Club** (call (561) 395-3000) hosts the EMC^2 Skills Challenge on alternate years; in 2000 participants included Jack Nicklaus and Arnold Palmer.

Shopping

Among the numerous shopping opportunities in shop-til-you-drop Palm Beach County, a few are especially noteworthy. Locals and visitors alike will find the latest styles from Paris and Milan, as well as more reasonable duds for the masses. You may even find a bargain or two cast off from a socialite's closet.

STROLLING AND WINDOW SHOPPING

Worth Avenue on the island of Palm Beach is one of the country's most glamorous shopping streets; even natives of Beverly Hills say it's more beautiful than Rodeo Drive. Most buildings are only one or two stories high, and the architecture is Mizner-style Mediterranean, with blooming bougainvillea all about. There are street-side meters and valet parking at the eastern end near **Saks Fifth Avenue** (172 Worth Avenue, Palm Beach; (561) 694-9009). And don't miss the famous doggie watering trough outside **Phillips Galleries** at 318 Worth Avenue.

For world-class shoppers, Worth Avenue boasts such recognizable names as **Chanel, Armani, Cartier, Hermes, Brooks Brothers, Gucci,** and **Ungaro.** Along with antique and other collectibles shops are some long-standing icons, such as **Trillion** (315 Worth Avenue; (561) 832-3525), which has featured a splayed rainbow display of men's sweaters for 16 years; the individual garments are changed frequently to showcase different colors. Visitors shouldn't miss the opportunity to stroll down the "vias," small but charming alleyways with specialty boutiques and outdoor cafes. Here, for instance, is **Morgan Terry Hats** (5 Via DeMario; (561) 659-0771), a spot to find the absolutely perfect Palm Beach straw hat. The whimsical chapeaux range from about $130 to $200. A little-known fact is that Worth Avenue businesses often host unadvertised after-season sales—discreetly noted by tiny but tasteful signs in the window, of course. These sales start in April.

Mizner Park (407 Plaza Real, Boca Raton; (561) 362-0606) is a beautiful outdoor shopping area anchored by **Jacobson's** and filled with fashionable boutiques, galleries, and restaurants. A standout is **Liberties Fine Books, Music & Cafe** (309 Plaza Real, Boca Raton; (561) 368-1300)—a fabulous store that regularly hosts book signings by famed authors (open

Sunday–Thursday, 10 a.m.–11 p.m.; Friday and Saturday, 10 a.m.–1 a.m.). The charming and immaculate Mediterranean-style village also houses offices and residences.

In West Palm Beach, the city that developed to provide service for Palm Beach residents, the new **CityPlace** (Okeechobee Boulevard; (561) 366-1000) is a shopping/entertainment/dining/residential complex. Preserved in the 1926 Spanish Colonial Revival church is the **Harriet Himmel Gilman Theatre.** The theater features original details such as pecky cypress doors and beams and is used for cultural events. Outside at Palladium Plaza is a set of fountains, choreographed to provide watery displays announced by the church bell. Free outdoor concerts are held Friday and Saturday nights, which prompt some spontaneous dancing. There's no additional number for "The Harriet" (as it's now dubbed); for information, contact the CityPlace Information Line (700 South Rosemary Avenue, West Palm Beach; (561) 366 1000), which can also connect you to the following shops: **FAO Schwarz** (700 South Rosemary Avenue, West Palm Beach; (561) 835-0007) and **Ahava** (700 South Rosemary Avenue, West Palm Beach; (561) 833-6244).

The complex is not merely composed of a street or two; it incorporates several of the previous streets and includes sherbet-colored townhouses and apartments—embellished with wrought-iron railings and barrel-tiled roofs—reminiscent of a Riviera city. A complimentary trolley service connects with Clematis Street; it transports 40,000 people a month.

MALL SHOPPING

Local malls keep growing and growing, and they're especially crowded when the weather is rainy or cloudy. **Boynton Beach Mall** (801 North Congress Avenue, Boynton Beach; (561) 736-7900) appeals to both retirees and the younger set, offering 100-plus stores. It's looking perkier since the Simon Property Management Group took over, and it's anchored by Macy's, Burdines, Sears, Dillard's, and JC Penney.

Palm Beach Mall (1801 Palm Beach Lakes Boulevard, West Palm Beach; (561) 683-9186) draws a lot of locals with its 120 shops. Anchors are Burdines, Dillard's, JC Penney, Lord & Taylor, and Sears.

The Gardens of the Palm Beaches (3101 PGA Boulevard, Palm Beach Gardens; (561) 775-7750) is a lovely two-story mall with open, airy garden styling that's all bright and sunny. Among its 175 stores are anchors Macy's, Burdines, Sears, Bloomingdale's, and Saks Fifth Avenue.

Town Center at Boca Raton (6000 Glades Road, Boca Raton; (561) 368-6000). This upscale enclosed center has recently been expanded with even more glamorous shops for shopaholicss, now totaling 220. Anchors include Bloomingdale's, Saks Fifth Avenue, Burdines, Sears, Lord & Taylor, and Nordstrom. Valet parking is available.

SPECIALTY SHOPS

Antiques

Do you think all South Florida residents decorate their homes in modern pastels? Think again. You'll find a gaggle of antiques stores (about 43) located on **Antique Row,** on South Dixie Highway (two blocks north of Southern Boulevard) in West Palm Beach. Pop into any of the stores on the six-block stretch for a printed map—South Dixie Antique Row—showing locations and types of merchandise. **David Strasser Antiques** (3631 South Dixie Highway; (561) 833-7070) features 19th-century American and English furniture and porcelain. **Peter Werner, Ltd.** (3709 South Dixie Highway; (561) 832-0428) offers 18th- to 20th-century furnishings and paintings. **Boomerang Modern** (3301 South Dixie Highway; (561) 835-1865) specializes in mid-20th-century furnishings, glass, and ceramics. **Cassidy's Antiques** (3621 South Dixie Highway; (561) 832-8017) boasts museum-quality 17th- and 18th-century Spanish and Italian pieces.

Longtime names around tony Worth Avenue include **Christian Du Pont Antiques** (352 Peruvian Avenue, Palm Beach; (561) 655-7794), specializing in 17th- through 19th-century intricate French marquetry and sparkling crystal chandeliers, and **Yetta Olkes Antiques** (332 South County Road, Palm Beach; (561) 655-2800), which has been on the scene for about 20 years. She specializes in 19th- and 20th-century porcelains and small decorative objects, often sold or consigned by local people.

Art

Wally Findlay Galleries (165 Worth Avenue, Palm Beach; (561) 655-2090) has long been a bastion of fine art on Palm Beach. **Wentworth Galleries** has two locations representing international contemporary painters and sculptors: Town Center Mall (Boca Raton; (561) 338-0804) and the Gardens Mall (Palm Beach Gardens; (561) 624-0656). At **World Posters** (51 Glades Road, Boca Raton; (561) 750-1554), you'll find vintage posters from the 19th and 20th centuries, primarily French and Italian, plus Art Deco and Art Nouveau originals. Contemporary copies are also for sale.

Bait

Every overpass over the Intracoastal Waterway seems to hold a constant stream of anglers. Remember that anyone fishing, even off a bridge, needs a fishing license, except Florida residents who are fishing from land. Licenses are sold at tackle and bait stores and K-Marts. Fishing is a popular pastime in these parts, so most bait and tackle shops have been on board for decades.

Boynton Fisherman Supply (618 North Federal Highway, Boynton Beach; (561) 736-0568), a family-owned business for 18 years, carries fresh and saltwater bait and fishing tackle—lures, hooks, rods, and reels.

Perk's Bait & Tackle (307 North 4th Street, Lantana; (561) 582-3133) appeals to many who fish at the Boynton Beach Inlet. Family-owned for 55 years, it boasts everything for offshore fishing, whether in bay, ocean, or fresh water. They'll even make custom-made rods. Most of their customers are locals who fish year-round, but the best fishing is March–November.

Bargains

Long familiar to savvy New York shoppers of discounted ladies' clothing off the rack, **Loehmann's** has two locations (8903 Glades Road, Boca Raton, (561) 852-7111 and 4100 PGA Boulevard, Palm Beach Gardens, (561) 627-5575). Don't forget to pop into **The Back Room** for special occasion glam. Sales on swimwear and shoes begin in May, after season. Near Palm Beach's Worth Avenue awaits a high-class consignment shop, **Deja vu,** where shopaholics might find a cast-off glitzy gown formerly owned by a local celeb or society type. Maxie Barley, co-owner with her sister Marilyn Lanham, have been recycling duds from socialites who dare not wear the same outfit twice. The most popular items requested are Chanel designs; the shop sells bouclé suits for $500–1,000 that were originally $3,000. Savvy shoppers might save enough to pay for some outrageous dinners.

Bookstores

Barnes & Noble Booksellers (1400 Glades Road, Boca Raton, (561) 750-2134; 333 North Congress Avenue, Boynton Beach, (561) 374-5570; and 700 Rosemary Avenue, West Palm Beach, (561) 514-0811) offers books, a vast selection of magazines and out-of-town newspapers, and music (CDs, DVDs, and videos). They also host book clubs and have a cheerful section for youngsters (where they hold a preschool story time). There's a cafe for that caffeine jolt and some comfy upholstered chairs for reading. Best-sellers are usually offered at a 40% discount, and the bargain section proffers books at 30–40% reductions.

   Books-A-Million (1630 South Federal Highway, Delray Beach, (561) 243-3395; 2471 Okeechobee Boulevard, West Palm Beach, (561) 615-6917; and 6370 West Indiantown Road, Jupiter, (561) 743-8094) is a chain of retail books, newspapers, and magazines; each shop also features a cafe.

   Borders Books, Music & Cafe stores (9887 Glades Road, Boca Raton, (561) 833-5854; 525 North Congress Avenue, Boynton Beach, (561) 734-2021; and 1801 Palm Beach Lakes Boulevard, West Palm Beach, (561) 689-4112) are massive outposts of the chain, offering books, newspapers and magazines, CDs, DVDs, videos, and a cafe. They carry their own lists of best-sellers (not the *New York Times* list), whose titles are discounted

   Liberties Books (Mizner Park, Boca Raton; (561) 368-1300) is a happening place that offers books, CDs, a cafe, and lots of book readings and signings. It's open Sunday–Thursday, 9 a.m.–11 p.m. and Friday and Saturday, 9 a.m.–1:30 a.m.; off-season hours are somewhat reduced.

The **Albert Post Gallery** (809 Lucerne Avenue, Lake Worth; (561) 582-4477) offers books of vintage posters along with its antiques. And **The Bookworm** (4111 Lake Worth Road, Lake Worth; (561) 965-1900) has been here since 1966. Room after room opens up to reveal about 200,000 books—almost entirely used—and thousands of used magazines. (Owner Judith DeWitt says 99% of the books are used, but they must carry some new tomes for insurance purposes.)

Rand McNally Map & Travel Store (Palm Beach Gardens Mall; (561) 775-7602) not only has tons of travel books but also everything travelers could wish for, be they backpackers or armchair travelers: games (to keep the kids occupied on those endless car rides), maps, travel kits, luggage, electrical adapters, and mini pillboxes.

Ethnic Goods

Italian   Doris Italian Market & Bakery (9101 Lakeridge Boulevard, Boca Raton; (561) 482-0770). You'll want to mange here when you see the excellent Italian groceries, cheeses, top-grade olive oils, pastas, and sauces. The butcher carries high-grade Italian meats and fresh-frozen homemade dinners. At the bakery, you'll find popular Italian pastries, including baba au rhum, cannoli, and tiramisu cake, fresh-baked on the premises. At **King's Italian Market** (1900 North Military Trail, Boca Raton; (561) 368-2600) foodies find more than just the Italian angel. Choose from top-quality, exotic produce; goodies from the in-house bakery; the finest prime meats and name-brand deli items; dozens of varieties of cheeses; and 50 of King's gourmet prepared salads.

Jewish   Flakowitz Bake Shop (8202 Glades Road, Boca Raton; (561) 488-0900) is a Jewish bakery that exudes the smell of familiar breads like challah and pumpernickel rye, and pastries like apple strudel and skinny stuff. **Wolfie Cohen's Rascal House** (2006 Executive Center Drive, Boca Raton; (561) 982-8899)—besides being a sit-down restaurant—is the place to buy lox and corned beef. Their chopped liver isn't chopped liver, either.

Hispanic   Tulipan Bakery (704 Belvedere Road, West Palm Beach; (561) 832-6107) dispenses Hispanic baked goods—you'll shout "ole" for the guava pastries. They also offer prepared meat-filled pastries and Cuban sandwiches (filled with pork, ham, cheese, and pickles).

Fresh Fish

Unfortunately, fewer and fewer markets for fish and seafood remain onboard; many have closed their doors because the "product" has become scarce and therefore expensive. **Captain Frank's** (435 Boynton Beach Boulevard, Boynton Beach; (561) 732-3663) offers fresh fish and shellfish, bought directly from the fishing boat anglers or flown in from elsewhere (except king crab legs, which are frozen). Most of their customers are year-round locals, which says something for the store's power to please. They also offer a fisherman's catch of homemade goodies: crab cakes from Maryland blue crabs, lake cakes (the lobster meat shipped in fresh from Maine), and fish chowders.

Delray Seafoods (120 SE 4th Avenue, Delray Beach; (561) 278-3439) offers locally caught fresh fish such as dolphin (fish, not Flipper's relatives), grouper, and tuna and fresh fish flown in, including salmon and Chilean sea bass. Shellfish includes local blue crabs. The firm, located here since 1960, has connections with operators of fishing boats, who often sell directly to the store.

Fresh Produce and Fruit Shipping

The Blood family at **Blood's Hammock Groves** (4600 Linton Boulevard, Delray Beach; (561) 498-3400 or (800) 235-5188) has had 50 years' experience in the Florida citrus business. Customers can view the processing from the observation deck. Fresh-picked oranges, grapefruits, and pommelos (look like giant lemons) are sold, along with company-made marmalades and fruit baskets. A bakery sells scones and breads. They ship fruit and gourmet baskets. At **Knollwood Groves** (8053 Lawrence Road, Boynton Beach; (561) 734-4800 or (800) 222-9696) the initial trees were planted in 1930 by comedians Amos and Andy (of vaudeville and radio fame). Oranges and grapefruits are sold, plus other fresh produce and juice and fruit pies that are made on site. A tram ride takes visitors to see the groves and packing house and to watch an alligator show. Oranges and grapefruits are shipped according to their seasons (different fruits ripen at different times). Closed Sundays in summer.

The **West Palm Beach Green Market** (Narcissus Avenue and 2nd Street, West Palm Beach) is open Saturdays from late October to late April and offers free parking. The 60-plus vendors sell only Palm Beach County–grown fruits, vegetables, and plants (from palm trees to orchids), along with honey, cakes, and pastries made by five local bakeries. (No arts and crafts.)

Jewelry

Big spenders might head toward Palm Beach's elegant Worth Avenue for some jaw-dropping baubles at **Cartier Fine Jewelry** (214 Worth Avenue, Palm Beach; (561) 655-5913), **Tiffany & Co.** (259 Worth Avenue, Palm Beach; (561) 659-6090), or **Van Cleef and Arpels** (249 Worth Avenue, Palm Beach; (561) 655-6767). Those in search of more value than name head for **International Jewelers Exchange** (8221 Glades Road, Boca Raton; (561) 488-0648), which claims it's Florida's largest and oldest jewelry exchange. The complex houses 60 vendors displaying a glittering array of gold, gemstones, and pearls—just like New York's 47th Street. And all below retail. Open Tuesday–Saturday, 10 a.m.–5 p.m.; open daily from Thanksgiving to Christmas. Our favorite vendor is **ABS Gems,** where a registered gemologist knows the ropes.

Spas

Need to relax and beautify? Masseuses are just waiting to get their hands on you. The **PGA National Resort and Spa** (400 Avenue of the Champions, Palm Beach Gardens; (561) 627-2000) offers spa day programs to the public, as well as packages for registered guests. Costs for men's and women's half-day packages run $115–250; full-day packages are $255–435. With certain spa packages, daily guests may have access to the fitness facility as well. The **Ritz-Carlton Palm Beach** (100 South Ocean Boulevard, Palm Beach; (561) 533-6000) permits nonregistered guests to enjoy massage treatments for no charge beyond the massage itself. Additionally, half-day packages run $160–210 and full-day packages $290–340. During summer only, spa guests may use the pool or beach. The **Breakers Hotel** (One South County Road, Palm Beach; (561) 659-8480) offers nonregistered guests the opportunity to book a treatment in the spa (such as a facial or massage), which then includes access to all facilities except a cabana (i.e., the fitness center, four pools, and beach). Prices vary depending on the chosen treatment.

Swimwear

Swimland (Royal Palm Plaza [known in these parts as the Pink Plaza], 200 SE 1st Avenue, Boca Raton; (561) 395-4415) has racks and racks of teeny weeny bikinis and stunning Gottex outfits for ladies. Most women are sure to find something in their size. The shop features all the name brands, including Jantzen, Serena, and Gideon Oberson. Reduced-price sale begins before Memorial Day and ends shortly before Thanksgiving.

The high-action crowd heads to surfboard central at **Nomad Surf Shop** (4655 North Ocean Boulevard, Boynton Beach; (561) 272-2882). This surfers' heaven, which opened in 1968, features room after room of beachy togs such as Nomad clothing, Volcom clothing, and Quicksilver, for men and women. And, of course, they sell surfboards—even custom-made jobs. There's a sale the weekend before Memorial Day and a half-price sale the second week of October.

Toys

Kids ages 3 to 103 (the store's logo) will flip over the **Build-A-Bear Workshop** (Palm Beach Gardens Mall; (561) 630-7734). In this interactive store, customers start at the Dress-me Station and choose which outfits they want their teddy bear to wear—perhaps a basketball outfit or a bridal ensemble—next they add accessories such as shoes, hats, etc. Patrons then give their bear an air bath and go home with their self-styled teddy.

Used Yachts and Boats

Rybovich is an internationally known name for custom boats. Visitors are welcome at **Rybovich Spencer** (4200 North Flagler Drive, West Palm Beach; (561) 844-1800) and may join a free one-hour tour. Tours are held Thursdays at 4 p.m. (except during summer); guests must make reservations 24 hours ahead. They'll see the full-service marina and new sports fishermen (a type of boat) under construction; two boats are under construction at all times. They're all custom-made, each taking 18–24 months to complete. The yard also brokers used boats and offers full-service marina facilities.

To get a feel for what's available and the range of prices, pick up a copy of *Boat Trader*, a weekly black-and-white magazine that lists hundreds of photos and pertinent information; it's available at most convenience stores for $2.50. *Yacht Trader*, a sister publication, is also available for the same price in the same locations. Then steer to **HMY Yacht Sales** (2401 PGA Boulevard, Palm Beach Gardens; (561) 775-6000) for used yachts. It's currently berthing vessels from 31 to 105 feet. For something smaller, make your way to **Inflatable Experts** (155 East Blue Heron Boulevard, West Palm Beach; (561) 848-5588), which handles new inflatables such as Zodiacs and accepts used inflatables on trade-ins.

Wine and Gourmet foods

At **Chocolates by Mr. Roberts** (505 NE 20th Street, Boca Raton; (561) 392-3007), Heinz Robert Goldschneider, called Mr. Roberts because Henry Fonda adored his handmade chocolates when he was in New York, continues to turn out some two dozen varieties of handmade truffles—plus dipped chocolates and nuts—daily. The 70-something gentleman learned his techniques in Switzerland before emigrating to the United States. **Crown Wine & Spirits** has five branches (22191 Powerline Road, Boca Raton, (561) 391-6009; 3500 North Federal Highway, Boca Raton, (561) 392-6366; 737 South Federal Highway, Boca Raton, (561) 394-3828; 911 SE 6th Avenue, Delray Beach, (561) 278-2100; and 564 SE Woolbright Road, Boynton Beach, (561) 734-9463). They offer an array of liquors, chilled wines, and imported beer, plus gourmet cheeses and chocolates. Another option is **Good Life Wine Spirits & Gourmet** (1536 B South Federal Highway, Delray Beach; (561) 276-3838). At **Hampton Liquors** (257 Royal Poinciana Way, Palm Beach; (561) 832-8368), you might spot a bronzed and beautiful Palm Beacher. And **ABC Fine Wine &**

Spirits (1531 Boynton Beach Boulevard, Boynton Beach; (561) 732-0794) has a large range of alcohol, both wine and liquor. It boasts a wine cellar (actually a glassed-in area that's temperature- and humidity-controlled) and a wine vault, where customers may store their wines. It also offers imported cheeses and caviar and other gourmet goodies.

FLEA MARKETS

The **Delray Swap Shop & Flea Market** (2001 North Federal Highway, Delray Beach; (561) 276-4012) is a bargain-lovers paradise with 124 merchants indoors and 76 outdoors. Open Thursday–Monday, 9 a.m.– 4 p.m. Closed on Monday in summer.

At the **Uptown Downtown Flea Market & Outlet Mall** (5700 Okeechobee Boulevard, West Palm Beach; (561) 684-5700), approximately 200 merchants vie for sales in an enclosed mall. The outlet is open Monday–Thursday, 10 a.m.–6 p.m.; Friday and Saturday, 10 a.m.–8 p.m.; and Sunday, noon–6 p.m. The flea market is open Tuesday–Friday, 10 a.m.–5 p.m.; Saturday, 10 a.m.–6 p.m.; and Sunday, noon–6 p.m. Hours are reduced in the summer.

Attractions

Because of the wide range of Palm Beach County attractions, we've provided the following chart to help you prioritize your touring at a glance. Organized by category, in it you'll find the name, location, and author's rating from one star (skip it) to five stars (not to be missed). Some attractions, usually art galleries without permanent collections, weren't rated because exhibits change. Each attraction is individually profiled in detail later in this section. Most museum-type attractions offer group rates for ten or more people.

A Time-Saving Chart		
Name	City	Author's Rating
Amusement/Water Parks		
Boomers	Boca Raton	★★★
Rapids Water Park	West Palm Beach	★★
Aquariums/Nature Exhibits		
Gumbo Limbo Environmental Complex	Boca Raton	★★½
Lion Country Safari	Loxahatchee	★★★★½
Red Reef Park	Boca Raton	★★½

A Time-Saving Chart (continued)

Name	City	Author's Rating
Chocolate Factory		
Hoffman's Chocolate Shoppe & Gardens	Lake Worth	★★
Citrus Groves		
Blood's Hammock Groves	Delray Beach	★★½
Knollwood Groves	Boynton Beach	★★
Palm Beach Groves	Boynton Beach	★★½
Coast Guard Station Tour		
Peanut Island Tour	Phil Foster State Park	★★★
Cultural Center		
Old School Square Cultural Arts Center	Delray Beach	★★½
Gardens		
Mounts Botanical Garden	West Palm Beach	★★½
Pan's Garden	Palm Beach	★★½
Glider Ride		
Barry Aviation Florida	West Palm Beach	★
Industrial Tour		
Florida Crystal Sugar & Rice Tours	Boca Raton	★★½
Lighthouse		
Jupiter Inlet Lighthouse	Jupiter	★★½
Museums		
Boca Raton Museum of Art	Boca Raton	★★
The Flagler Museum	Palm Beach	★★★
International Museum of Cartoon Art	Boca Raton	★★½
Morikami Museum and Japanese Gardens	Delray Beach	★★★★
Norton Museum of Art	West Palm Beach	★★★
South Florida Science Museum	West Palm Beach	★★½
Parks and Refuges		
Arthur R. Marshall Loxahatchee National Wildlife Refuge	Boynton Beach	★★★
John D. MacArthur Beach State Park	North Palm Beach	★★★
Jonathan Dickinson State Park	Jupiter	★★½
Loxahatchee Everglades Tours	Boca Raton	★★★★

A Time-Saving Chart (continued)		
Name	City	Author's Rating
Sports Venues		
Palm Beach Kennel Club	West Palm Beach	★★★
Palm Beach Polo	Wellington	★★½
Roger Dean Stadium	Jupiter	★★★
Zoo		
Palm Beach Zoo at Dreher Park	West Palm Beach	★★★

ATTRACTION PROFILES

Arthur R. Marshall Loxahatchee National Wildlife Refuge

Type of Attraction: Everglades walking tours

Location: 10216 Lee Road, Boynton Beach 33437

Admission: $5 per vehicle

Hours: Refuge: daily, 6 a.m.–7 p.m.; Visitors Center: weekdays, 9 a.m.–4 p.m.; Saturday and Sunday, 9 a.m.– 4:30 p.m.; closed Monday and Tuesday, May–October.

Phone: (561) 734-8303

When to Go: Any time

Overall Appeal by Age Groups:

Pre-school	Grade School	Teens	Young Adults	Over 30	Seniors
★	★★★	★★★	★★★	★★★	★★★★

Author's Rating: ★★★

How Much Time to Allow: Two–four hours.

Description and Comments   The park includes 221 square miles of wetlands and fulfills most visitors' concept of what a swamp is like. Fascinating options include walking the boardwalk or four other trails through the marsh. Spot live alligators, cypress knees, and abundant bird life.

Touring Tips   Summer is very hot, and there's not much to see.

Other Things to Do Nearby   A short drive to the Morikami Museum immerses visitors in a different culture entirely.

Barry Aviation Florida

Type of Attraction: Glider rides

Location: 11600 Aviation Boulevard, West Palm Beach 33412

Admission: $75 for 20-minute flight, $199 for 60 minutes

Hours: Wednesday–Sunday, 9 a.m.–4 p.m.

Phone: (561) 624-3000

When to Go: On clear days, participants can see the beach. Weekends are most crowded, so weekdays permit more flexibility.

Special Comments: Participants must be over age 10, 14 to solo. Repeat customers include some over age 70.

Appeal by Age Groups:

Pre-school	Grade School	Teens	Young Adults	Over 30	Seniors
—	★	★★★	★★★	★★★	★★★

Author's Rating: ★

How Much Time to Allow: One–two hours

Description and Comments Want to feel like a bird? Flights leave from North County General Aviation Airport and go over the airport, sometimes toward the beach.

Touring Tips Appointments are necessary.

Other Things to Do Nearby Not a lot, since it's way out west toward the Everglades, but it's about a 15-minute drive to Palm Beach Gardens Mall.

Blood's Hammock Groves

Type of Attraction: Citrus groves

Location: Linton Boulevard, Delray Beach 33445

Admission: Free

Hours: 8:30 a. m.–5 p.m. daily; closed end of June–November 1st

Phone: (561) 498-3400

When to Go: Any time

Special Comments: Family-owned for 50 years.

Overall Appeal by Age Groups:

Pre-school	Grade School	Teens	Young Adults	Over 30	Seniors
★★	★★	★★	★★	★★½	★★½

Author's Rating: ★★½

How Much Time to Allow: One hour maximum

Description and Comments Watch as citrus fruit is cleaned and prepared for shipping. Sample fresh fruits and juices, which visitors buy since they taste so much better than those in a store.

Touring Tips   Can be interesting if you've never seen a citrus plant.

Other Things to Do Nearby   Morikami Museum.

Boca Raton Museum of Art

Type of Attraction: Art museum

Location: 501 Plaza Real, Mizner Park, Boca Raton 33432

Admission: Adults, $6; seniors, $4.50; students, $3; children under age 12 free (prices increase for special exhibits)

Hours: Tuesday, Thursday, and Saturday, 10 a.m.–5 p.m.; Wednesday and Friday, 10 a.m.–9 p.m.; Sunday, noon–5 p.m.

Phone: (561) 392-2500

When to Go: Any time

Special Comments: The museum moved in February, 2001 into newer, larger quarters—40,000 square feet—at Mizner Park.

Overall Appeal by Age Groups:

Pre-school	Grade School	Teens	Young Adults	Over 30	Seniors
—	★	★★	★★	★★	★★

Author's Rating: ★★

How Much Time to Allow: One–one-and-a-half hours

Description and Comments   This small museum boasts a few items representing well-known artists such as Matisse and Picasso, plus 19th- and 20th-century modern masters. Traveling exhibits included a recent 100-piece Picasso show, aboriginal art from Australia's western desert, and juried Florida artists. An upcoming exhibit mounts photographs of Jewish tombstones of the Pale. On the second floor, a permanent collection includes pre-Colombian and African works.

Touring Tips   The museum stages cultural events, such as music by the Boca Pops (a local orchestra) or a jazz quartet in the sculpture garden one Sunday each month.

Other Things to Do Nearby   International Museum of Cartoon Art and window shopping at Mizner Park.

Boomers

Type of Attraction: Amusement park

Location: Airport Road, Boca Raton 33431

Admission: $3.50 to indoor arcade and play center for children; $5.50 ticket for each ride or $21 for all-day ticket

Hours: Monday–Thursday, noon–10 p.m.; Friday and Saturday, 10 a.m.–midnight; Sunday, 10 a.m.–10 p.m.

Phone: (561) 347-1888

When to Go: Any time

Overall Appeal by Age Groups:

Pre-school	Grade School	Teens	Young Adults	Over 30	Seniors
★★★	★★★★	★★★½	★★	★★	★★

Author's Rating: ★★★

How Much Time to Allow: Two–four hours

Description and Comments   This park provides hours of activities for grand-parents entertaining their visiting grandchildren (parents too). Bumper boats, race track, two 18-hole miniature golf courses.

Touring Tips   Adults accompanying children must pay admission. Check out "10 buck Tuesdays."

Other Things to Do Nearby   Muvico Theater.

The Flagler Museum

Type of Attraction: Millionaire's winter mansion with priceless furnishings and collections

Location: Cocoanut Row and Whitehall Way, Palm Beach 33480

Admission: Adults $8; children ages 6–12 $3; children under age 6 free

Hours: Tuesday–Saturday, 10 a.m.–5 p.m.; Sunday, noon–5 p.m.

Phone: (561) 655-2833

When to Go: Any time

Special Comments: Tour the elaborate home and view traveling exhibits of the era.

Overall Appeal by Age Groups:

Pre-school	Grade School	Teens	Young Adults	Over 30	Seniors
—	★★	★★	★★½	★★★	★★★½

Author's Rating: ★★★

How Much Time to Allow: One–two hours

Description and Comments   Here's a peek at how the wealthy once win-tered. Henry Morrison Flagler, a founding partner with John D. Rockefeller of Standard Oil, built several of Florida's earliest grand hotels (including the Palm Beach Inn, later known as The Breakers). He bought and combined several railroad companies, so his Florida East Coast Railway opened the state for development as far as Key West. Flagler built this 55-room mansion, Whitehall, in 1902—in the Beaux-Arts style—as a wedding gift for his third wife. The *New York Herald* then called it . . . "grander and more magnificent than any other private dwelling in the world."

After the family left and before it was reopened as a museum (in 1960), the property opened as the Whitehall Hotel in 1925. Seniors may recall the radio broadcaster Gabriel Heatter; his daughter Maida Heatter, author of a half-dozen cookbooks, recalled that the family wintered here when she was a child. The building has now been air-conditioned to prevent further deterioration of woodwork and furnishings due to humidity.

Most visitors take the 45-minute guided tour which reveals the country's largest marble room during the Gilded Age, silk-covered walls, gilded period furnishings, Baccarat crystal chandeliers, and frescoed ceilings.

Touring Tips Indulge in the elegant Gilded Age Tea (lunch) from noon–3 p.m., when finger sandwiches (such as watercress and goat cheese) and pastries (including scones) are served on silver platters, within sight of the Intracoastal Waterway. Cost is $10 per person. Visitors may also step inside Flagler's original, private 1886 railcar, on which he traveled to Key West.

Other Things to Do Nearby Norton Museum, Kravis Center, Worth Avenue.

Florida Crystal Sugar & Rice Tours

Type of Attraction: Industrial tours
Location: NW 24th Way, Boca Raton 33431
Admission: Adults, $17; children ages 7–teens, $14. Children under age 7 not permitted
Hours: Call to schedule
Phone: (954) 346-5576 for information
When to Go: Tours are given four times a week in season, twice a week in summer.

Overall Appeal by Age Groups:

Pre-school	Grade School	Teens	Young Adults	Over 30	Seniors
—	★★★	★★★	★★½	★★½	★★★

Author's Rating: ★★½
How Much Time to Allow: Two hours

Description and Comments A one-hour tour of the Sem-chi rice mill and packaging plant and a half-hour tour of the Okeelanta sugar packaging plant. Visitors learn how sugar cane is pressed and the juice evaporated to make organic sugar; rice is grown here as a rotation crop and milled on-premises.

Touring Tips   Open for tours since 1996, the El Joy Tours firm specializes in group tours but accepts individuals.

Other Things to Do Nearby   Lion Country Safari.

Gumbo Limbo Environmental Complex

Type of Attraction: Saltwater aquariums and nature exhibits
Location: 1801 North Ocean Boulevard, Boca Raton 33432
Admission: Free
Hours: Monday–Saturday, 9 a.m. – 4 p.m.; Sunday, noon– 4 p.m.
Phone: (561) 338-1473
When to Go: Any time
Overall Appeal by Age Groups:

Pre-school	Grade School	Teens	Young Adults	Over 30	Seniors
★	★★	★★	★★	★★½	★★½

Author's Rating: ★★½
How Much Time to Allow: One–two hours

Description and Comments   Four indoor saltwater tanks hold turtles, sharks, stingrays, and more. Some displays feature baby sea turtles. There are also two outdoor boardwalk trials.

Touring Tips   Make reservations to join an organized turtle watch or walk. From May until August, female sea turtles lay and bury as many as 120 eggs. The mother turtle returns to the ocean, leaving the hatchlings to fend for themselves. About two months later, the baby turtles hatch, dig their way out of the nest, and begin their journey to the ocean.

Other Things to Do Nearby   Spend time at the beach.

Hoffman's Chocolate Shoppe & Gardens

Type of Attraction: Chocolate factory and gift shop
Location: 5190 Lake Worth Road, Lake Worth 33463
Admission: Free
Hours: Weekdays, 9 a.m.– 4:30 p.m.
Phone: (561) 967-2213 and (888) 281-8800
When to Go: Busiest times are around Christmas and Easter, so avoid them if you don't want to compete with lots of onlookers.
Overall Appeal by Age Groups:

Pre-school	Grade School	Teens	Young Adults	Over 30	Seniors
★★	★★★	★★	★★	★★	★★★

Author's Rating: ★★

How Much Time to Allow: One–two hours

Description and Comments Visitors may watch, through a window, chocolate goodies being hand-made. At Christmas time, a large outdoor display of lights, trains, and other exhibits excites little ones. The retail store offers outstanding chocolates and gift baskets.

Touring Tips Don't even think of coming into this establishment if you're on a strict diet!

Other Things to Do Nearby Enjoy your chocolate!

International Museum of Cartoon Art

Type of Attraction: Cartoon art museum

Location: 201 Plaza Real, Mizner Park, Boca Raton 33432

Admission: Adults, $6; seniors, $5; students with ID, $4; children ages 6–12, $3; children under age 6 free

Hours: Tuesday–Saturday, 10 a.m.–6 p.m.; Sunday, noon–6 p.m.; closed July 4th

Phone: (561) 391-2200

When to Go: Any time

Overall Appeal by Age Groups:

Pre-school	Grade School	Teens	Young Adults	Over 30	Seniors
★	★★	★★½	★★½	★★★	★★★

Author's Rating: ★★½

How Much Time to Allow: One–two hours

Description and Comments The museum features more than 100,000 original drawings and cartoon videos in permanent and changing exhibitions. Although not presented in as exciting a setting as visitors might wish, it nevertheless has repeat guests, particularly those with nostalgic affection for old cartoons.

Touring Tips Little ones enjoy the interactive Create-a-Toon Center, theater, family programming, and other special events. And, of course, the gift store.

Other Things to Do Nearby Boca Raton Museum of Art and Mizner Park.

John D. MacArthur Beach State Park

Type of Attraction: Natural habitat park and beach

Location: 10900 A1A, North Palm Beach 33408

Admission: $3.25 per vehicle with up to 8 passengers; additional passengers $1 each; admission includes guided tours; visitors may come and go during the same day.

Hours: 8 a.m.–sundown daily

Phone: (561) 624-6950

When to Go: When it's cooler, fewer bugs hang around.

Overall Appeal by Age Groups:

Pre-school	Grade School	Teens	Young Adults	Over 30	Seniors
★★★	★★★	★★★	★★★	★★★	★★★

Author's Rating: ★★★

How Much Time to Allow: Half day to full day

Description and Comments   The park covers 225 acres of uplands and 535 acres underwater, including marine hammocks and mangroves. Boardwalks allow exploration of this subtropical coastal habitat. The park also offers good access to the beach. Picnic tables and grills are available. Three types of turtles nest here in June and July.

Touring Tips   Visitors may put their own canoes (no motorboats) in water. They may also bring their own snorkeling equipment for observing the reef; dive flags are available for rental. Kayaks and bicycles may be rented. Volunteer-led walks take place weekdays at 10 a.m., sometimes on weekends at 10 a.m. and 1 p.m.; call for schedule. A nature center provides other information.

Other Things to Do Nearby   Take a sight-seeing boat ride at Phil Foster State Park.

Jonathan Dickinson State Park

Type of Attraction: Marine and mangrove life and campgrounds

Location: US Highway 1, Jupiter 33455

Admission: $3.25 per car (maximum 8 people), $1 per person on bicycle, bus, or foot. River tour fare (call (561) 746-1466), $12 adults, $7 children ages 6–12, children under age 6 free. Canoe rentals: $10 for 2 hours; $4 each additional hour.

Hours: Park open daily 8 a.m.–dusk. River tours depart daily at 9 a.m., 11 a.m., 1 p.m., and 3 p.m. Canoe rentals available 9 a.m.–3:30 p.m. Trapper Nelson's Interpretive Site closed Monday–Tuesday.

Phone: (561) 546-2771 (phone is extremely busy in season); for river tour and cabin rental information, call (561) 746-1466

When to Go: Any time

Special Comments: Call ahead because sometimes the river is too shallow for the boat to reach the station (it's tidal because the river goes to the ocean). Campgrounds are booked up to 11 months in advance.

Overall Appeal by Age Groups:

Pre-school	Grade School	Teens	Young Adults	Over 30	Seniors
★★	★★	★★	★★★	★★★	★★★

Author's Rating: ★★½

How Much Time to Allow: Two hours–all day

Description and Comments The park covers 12,000 acres, including the Loxahatchee River. Bald eagles, scrub jays, and sandhill cranes are among the birds thriving amid the park's native plant life, including red mangroves, sabal palms, and gumbo limbo trees. Several walking trails include 18 miles of the Florida Trail. Guided tours depart to Trapper Nelson's station, started in 1936 on the Loxahatchee River, accessible only by 40-passenger pontoon boat (no reservations taken). Nelson made scads of money trapping beavers and other animals, with which he bought enough land to include the park's territory and leave more than $1 million to his heirs. Visitors may join a ranger-led tour and walk through the log- and tin-roofed original buildings.

Touring Tips Visitors may roam on their own or take ranger-led trips. During very rainy periods, three types of mosquitoes can make visitors' lives miserable, especially at sunrise and sunset and in shady areas like hammocks. Though it's not as bad as in the Everglades, come prepared with insect repellant.

Other Things to Do Nearby Jupiter Inlet Lighthouse and the beach.

Jupiter Inlet Lighthouse

Type of Attraction: Lighthouse and lighthouse museum

Location: 805 North US Highway 1, Jupiter 33477

Admission: Adults, $5; seniors, $4; children ages 6–18, $3; children under 6 free

Hours: Tuesday–Friday, 10 a.m.–5 p.m.; Saturday and Sunday, noon–5 p.m.; closed Monday. Lighthouse tours are conducted Sunday, Tuesday, and Wednesday, 10 a.m.–5 p.m.

Phone: (561) 747-6639

When to Go: Weekdays host a lot of school classes and camp groups, so families and seniors are better off on weekends.

Special Comments: The county's oldest standing structure (completed in 1860).

Overall Appeal by Age Groups:

Pre-school	Grade School	Teens	Young Adults	Over 30	Seniors
★	★★	★★	★★	★★★	★★★

Author's Rating: ★★½

How Much Time to Allow: One–two hours

Description and Comments Guests may visit the museum in The Oil House, a building harboring artifacts such as musket balls and old photos of ships and lighthouse keepers. They can also climb inside the 105-foot-tall red brick lighthouse for excellent views.

Touring Tips To ascend the lighthouse, visitors must be at least four feet tall and in good health; they must also wear closed-back shoes.

Other Things to Do Nearby Jonathan Dickinson State Park.

Knollwood Groves

Type of Attraction: Tours of citrus groves

Location: 8053 Lawrence Road, Boynton Beach 33436

Admission: Free to watch; tram ride costs $1 per person (children under age 3 free); alligator-handling show costs $6 per adult, $4 for children ages 3–11, children under age 3 free.

Hours: Daily, 8:30 a.m.–5:30 p.m.; closed Sundays in July and August, plus Christmas, Easter, and Thanksgiving

Phone: (561) 734-4800

When to Go: Any time for tram ride; Saturday at 2 p.m. for alligator handling show

Special Comments: The gift shop not only sells juice but also wonderful homemade Key lime and coconut cream pie.

Overall Appeal by Age Groups:

Pre-school	Grade School	Teens	Young Adults	Over 30	Seniors
★★½	★★½	★★	★★	★★	★★½

Author's Rating: ★★

How Much Time to Allow: One–two hours

Description and Comments Visitors tour 30 acres of orange groves and a juice processing plant. The half-hour tram ride through the groves demonstrates how fruits are grown, while the one-and-a-half-hour show in the simulated Seminole village exhibits Native American life and culture. Little ones also enjoy seeing the live deer, rabbits, and three little pigs.

Touring Tips Tram rides leave every hour on the hour, 10 a.m.–4 p.m. The first trees were planted by Amos and Andy (of radio fame) in 1930.

Other Things to Do Nearby Not much besides visiting Boynton Beach Mall.

Lion Country Safari

Type of Attraction: Drive-through African "safari"

Location: 2003 Lion Country Safari Road, Loxahatchee 33470 (18 miles west of I-95 on Southern Boulevard)

Admission: Adults, $15.50; children and seniors, $10.50

Hours: Daily, 9:30 a.m.–5:30 p.m.; last car admitted 4:30 p.m.

Phone: (561) 793-1084

When to Go: Any time except following lunch, when the animals have just been fed; often they're napping or lethargic.

Special Comments: No pets or convertibles allowed; guests may rent appropriate vehicles if theirs don't qualify.

Overall Appeal by Age Groups:

Pre-school	Grade School	Teens	Young Adults	Over 30	Seniors
★★★½	★★★★½	★★½	★★½	★★★★	★★★½

Author's Rating: ★★★★½

How Much Time to Allow: One hour for drive-through safari only, but many families stay three hours.

Description and Comments More than 1,300 animals—including chimps and zebras—roam this cageless 500-acre drive-through zoo. It has been wowing guests since 1967. Kids of all ages are thrilled as hippopotamuses walk past their car, or a group of elephants surround a baby for protection when a feeding truck arrives. Kiddie rides, paddle boats, a walk-through section for smaller animals (stroller accessible), and miniature golf add further appeal; there's even a real, live elephant ride. Guests remain in their cars and slowly drive through seven habitats—such as Serengeti Plain and Lake Nakuru—of elephants, lions, ostriches, and other major animals.

Touring Tips Both a restaurant and picnic areas provide for lunches.

Other Things to Do Nearby Florida Crystal Sugar & Rice Tours.

Loxahatchee Everglades Tours

Type of Attraction: Airboat rides in the Everglades

Location: 15490 Loxahatchee Road, Boca Raton 33076

Admission: Adults, $30; teens ages 11–15, $15; children ages 6–10, $10; children age 5 and under free

Hours: Daily, 9 a.m.–5 p.m.; first tour is 9:30 a.m.; last tour is 4 p.m.; closed Thanksgiving, Christmas, and New Years Day

Phone: (561) 482-8026 and (800) 683-5873

When to Go: Any time

Special Comments: Probable alligator sightings

Overall Appeal by Age Groups:

Pre-school	Grade School	Teens	Young Adults	Over 30	Seniors
★	★★½	★★★	★★★	★★★★	★★★★½

Author's Rating: ★★★★

How Much Time to Allow: One hour; tour is six to eight miles long.

Description and Comments   The Everglades is a unique attraction world-wide. It's not choreographed by Disney, however, so viewings can't be guaranteed. Participants may see alligators swimming or nesting, nests of alligator babies, American bald eagles, and unusual tropical birds. They'll also learn about sawgrass, pickerel weed, and marsh flowers.

Touring Tips   Those with hearing problems and very young children might find the engine noise overpowering, even though participants are given earplugs.

Other Things to Do Nearby   The Coconut Cove Water Park, with fun for all ages, is located within South County Regional Park (11200 Park Access Road, Boca Raton; (561) 274-1140). It's located 3.5 miles west of the Florida Turnpike's Glades Road exit.

Morikami Museum and Japanese Gardens

Type of Attraction: Japanese culture and history, particularly as related to Palm Beach County

Location: 4000 Morikami Park Road, Delray Beach (off Jog Road south of Linton Boulevard) 33446

Admission: Adults, $7; seniors over age 65, $6; children ages 6–18 and college students, $4; children under age 6 free

Hours: Tuesday–Sunday, 10 a.m.–5 p.m.

Phone: (561) 495-0233

When to Go: Any time for serene places to ponder life

Special Comments: Special events are scheduled, such as the annual Hatsume Fair in February celebrating spring with bonsai exhibits, drum performances, and flower arranging; the Bon Festival in August honors ancestors.

Overall Appeal by Age Groups:

Pre-school	Grade School	Teens	Young Adults	Over 30	Seniors
★	★★★	★★	★★	★★★★	★★★★

Author's Rating: ★★★★

How Much Time to Allow: Two–four hours

Description and Comments This 200-acre park, honoring an early Japanese settlement here, lures visitors with six stunning and tranquil gardens, seven-eighths of a mile in length. There are nature trails, ponds, waterfalls, and a bonsai garden. The two museum buildings feature changing and permanent exhibitions, a 225-seat theater, a library, a Japanese tea ceremony, and a cafe.

Touring Tips The Children's Day Celebration (Kodomo no hi) in April provides fun for youngsters within a Japanese cultural context, including sessions in making origami and opportunities to participate onstage in Japanese folk stories.

Other Things to Do Nearby Check out the oranges and grapefruits at Blood's Hammock Groves or opt for additional natural flora and fauna at Arthur R. Marshall Loxahatchee National Wildlife Refuge. Also near Morikami is the recently opened American Orchid Society.

Mounts Botanical Garden

Type of Attraction: Gardens for learning and relaxation

Location: 531 West Military Trail, West Palm Beach 33415

Admission: Free (except during special events)

Hours: Monday–Saturday, 8:30 a.m.–4:30 p.m.; Sunday and holidays, 1–5 p.m.

Phone: (561) 233-1749

When to Go: Any time, but tours are conducted Saturday at 11 a.m. and Sunday at 2:30 p.m.

Overall Appeal by Age Groups:

Pre-school	Grade School	Teens	Young Adults	Over 30	Seniors
★	★★★	★★	★★	★★★	★★★★

Author's Rating: ★★½

How Much Time to Allow: One–three hours

Description and Comments   Begun as part of the Palm Beach County Cooperative Extension Service in 1954, plantings in the 14 acres have been continuously enhanced. Some exotic plants and trees are huge, such as the kapok and rainbow eucalyptus. Several gardens, such as the aromatic herb garden and citrus area, are meant to teach visitors about different types of plants. Enjoy lovely lakeside spots for sitting and contemplating nature. Unfortunately, many of the identification signs are broken or missing.

Touring Tips   Picnic tables are available.

Other Things to Do Nearby   If you're up for seeing animals after the flowers, stop at the Palm Beach Zoo at Dreher Park. South Florida Science Museum is another option.

Norton Museum of Art

Type of Attraction: Art museum
Location: 1451 South Olive Avenue, West Palm Beach 33401
Admission: Adults, $6; children ages 13–21, $2; children under age 13
   free. Traveling exhibits may raise the ante considerably.
Hours: Monday–Saturday, 10 a.m. –5 p.m.; Sunday, noon–5 p.m.
Phone: (561) 832-5196
When to Go: Any time
Special Comments: National traveling exhibitions, like the recent "The
   Triumph of French Painting," expand the permanent collections.
Overall Appeal by Age Groups:

Pre-school	Grade School	Teens	Young Adults	Over 30	Seniors
★	★★	★★	★★★	★★★	★★★½

Author's Rating: ★★★
How Much Time to Allow: Two–four hours

Description and Comments   This ever-expanding art museum boasts a permanent but small collection of gems, including works by Monet, Gauguin, Picasso, Cezanne, Bellows, O'Keeffe (whose sister lived in Palm Beach), Hopper, Shahn, and Pollock. Additionally, Chinese, pre-Colombian, and Southwest sections add interest. A children's learning center helps develop budding talents.

Touring Tips   Rent an audio tape for professional explanations of artworks. Free guided tours daily at 2 p.m. The museum store offers great gift items, including many that are geared to kids; free children's programs (with paid general admission) lure families on Sunday and sometimes other days.

Other Things to Do Nearby Flagler Museum.

Old School Square Cultural Arts Center

Type of Attraction: Cultural center
Location: 51 North Swinton Avenue, Delray Beach 33444
Admission: Adults, $3; children ages 6–12, $1; children under age 6 free
Hours: Cornell Museum: Tuesday–Saturday, 11 a.m.–4 p.m.; Sunday,
   1–4 p.m.
Phone: (561) 243-7922
When to Go: Any time
Overall Appeal by Age Groups:

Pre-school	Grade School	Teens	Young Adults	Over 30	Seniors
★	★★	★★	★★	★★★	★★★

Author's Rating: ★★½
How Much Time to Allow: One–three hours

Description and Comments The Cornell Museum offers exhibits of all media, such as paintings, sculpture, and photography. Traveling theatrical groups perform in the Crest Theatre.

Touring Tips It's possible to keep youngsters occupied if you schedule them for some of the courses; interactive programs appeal to little ones, while Saturday art classes are conducted for teens.

Other Things to Do Nearby Stroll along Delray's Atlantic Avenue, popping into art galleries or enjoying a cool drink at an outdoor cafe.

Palm Beach Groves

Type of Attraction: Citrus groves
Location: 7149 Lawrence Road, Boynton Beach 33436
Admission: Free
Hours: Daily, 8:30 a.m.–5:30 p.m.; closed Christmas and Thanksgiving
Phone: (561) 965-6699
When to Go: Any time
Special Comments: Bring a picnic lunch to enjoy on the grounds.
Overall Appeal by Age Groups:

Pre-school	Grade School	Teens	Young Adults	Over 30	Seniors
★★½	★★½	★★	★★	★★★	★★★

Author's Rating: ★★½
How Much Time to Allow: One–one-and-a-half hours

Description and Comments   Take the free, 20-minute tram ride through the citrus groves November–April, then watch the fruits being processed. There's also a 5–10-minute walk on a nature trail.

Touring Tips   Check out the 50-year-old sausage tree and the strolling peacocks.

Other Things to Do Nearby   Take an air-conditioned break at Boynton Beach Mall.

Palm Beach Kennel Club

Type of Attraction: Greyhound racing

Location: 1111 North Congress Avenue, West Palm Beach 33409

Admission: $.50 for first-floor general admission; $1 for second-floor general admission; kids free with adults

Hours: Monday, Wednesday, Friday, and Saturday, post times are 12:40 p.m. and 7:30 p.m.; Sunday, 1 p.m.

Phone: (561) 683-2222

When to Go: Any time

Overall Appeal by Age Groups:

Pre-school	Grade School	Teens	Young Adults	Over 30	Seniors
★★	★★	★★	★★★	★★★	★★★½

Author's Rating: ★★★

How Much Time to Allow: Three–four hours

Description and Comments   This is greyhound racing, where the dogs' needs are attended to by veterinarians. Guests may dine in the second-floor Paddock Restaurant while watching races or choose a more casual meal on the Terrace. A poker room and simulcast wagering also draw gamers.

Touring Tips   Dining in the Paddock Room requires reservations; no shorts or jeans permitted, and men must wear a collared shirt (jacket is optional).

Other Things to Do Nearby   It's about a 20-minute drive to the Palm Beach Zoo at Dreher Park and South Florida Science Museum.

Palm Beach Polo

Type of Attraction: Polo club with matches open to public

Location: 11809 Polo Club Road, Wellington 33414

Admission: General admission is $10; children age 12 and under free. Box seating is $16, $37, and $40, depending on location. Fieldside parking costs $44 for a carload.

Hours: Saturday, 3 p.m.

Phone: (561) 798-7000 or (561) 793-1440

When to Go: Any time

Overall Appeal by Age Groups:

Pre-school	Grade School	Teens	Young Adults	Over 30	Seniors
★	★★	★★★	★★★	★★★	★★★

Author's Rating: ★★½

How Much Time to Allow: Two hours

Description and Comments Polo matches are played by professionals and royals such as Britain's Prince Charles. It's a good place for celebrity viewing: Tommy Lee Jones, for example, visits often. It's fun watching the celebs go out on the field in their finery during halftime to "stomp the divots," pushing the upended clumps of grass back into place with their Gucci shoes.

Touring Tips Attire ranges from casual for general seating to elegant-hatted outfits in box seats.

Other Things to Do Nearby If polo isn't enough for you, and you're up for more animals, spend a few hours at Lion Country Safari.

Palm Beach Zoo at Dreher Park

Type of Attraction: Zoo

Location: 1301 Summit Boulevard, West Palm Beach 33405

Admission: Adults, $6; seniors, $5; children ages 3–12, $4; children under age 3 free

Hours: Daily, 9 a.m.–5 p.m.; closed Thanksgiving

Phone: (561) 547-WILD or (561) 533-0887

When to Go: Any time

Special Comments: Children's petting zoo and reptile exhibit are favorites.

Overall Appeal by Age Groups:

Pre-school	Grade School	Teens	Young Adults	Over 30	Seniors
★★★	★★★½	★★½	★★½	★★½	★★★

Author's Rating: ★★★

How Much Time to Allow: Two–four hours

Description and Comments Although it's small by zoo standards—23 acres—the park keeps youngsters amused and learning for hours. The tropical birds, kangaroos, and tigers have their favorite audiences, but all kids love the prairie dogs. The zoo is currently undergoing a major expansion.

Touring Tips Despite the lush plantings, it gets very hot; plan to bring or buy lots of liquids. Wheelchairs and strollers have easy access on the paved walks; strollers may also be rented.

Other Things to Do Nearby South Florida Science Museum.

Pan's Garden

Type of Attraction: Vestpocket garden off busy Worth Avenue
Location: 386 Hibiscus Avenue, Palm Beach
Admission: Free
Hours: Daily, 9 a.m.–5 p.m.; May 15–November 15, open Monday–
  Friday, 10 a.m. –2 p.m.
Phone: (561) 832-0731
When to Go: Any time
Overall Appeal by Age Groups:

Pre-school	Grade School	Teens	Young Adults	Over 30	Seniors
★	★★	★	★	★	★★

Author's Rating: ★★½
How Much Time to Allow: 15 minutes–one hour

Description and Comments This serene, lush garden and pond offer benches for resting weary feet and studying the flowers and birds.

Touring Tips Photography is allowed.

Other Things to Do Nearby Shop or window shop on Worth Avenue.

Peanut Island Tour

Type of Attraction: 45-minute tour of former Coast Guard station and
  site of bomb shelter during President Kennedy's term
Location: 55 Blue Heron Boulevard at Phil Foster State Park for water
  taxi to island
Admission: Water taxi sight-seeing ride and tour of island: adults, $15;
  seniors over age 60, $14; children ages 5–17, $13. Island tour only
  (many reach the island via private boats): adults, $7; seniors, $6; students age 5–17, $5; children under age 5 free
Hours: Water taxi leaves park every hour on the hour for the 15-minute
  ride and leaves Peanut Island every hour on the half hour. However, if
  enough passengers gather, they make extra runs.
Phone: (561) 662-1415; for water taxi, (561) 683-TAXI
When to Go: Mornings are cooler on the island, although there's often a
  breeze.

Special Comments: Wooden walks and rest rooms are available.

Overall Appeal by Age Groups:

Pre-school	Grade School	Teens	Young Adults	Over 30	Seniors
★★	★★	★★	★★★	★★★½	★★★

Author's Rating: ★★★

How Much Time to Allow: Two hours–all day

Description and Comments Most fascinating is a visit inside the bomb shelter, built in 1961 for President John F. Kennedy's safety in case of enemy attack. The man-made island was named Peanut Island because of the 1917 placement of a peanut oil storage facility here, but hurricanes and the 1929 stock market crash destroyed that.

Touring Tips Families often come to spend the day, but nostalgia seekers and history buffs come just for the sights. For disabled visitors, call ahead and transportation will be provided on the ferry boat rather than the water taxi.

Other Things to Do Nearby Many people picnic and spend time at the island's beach.

Rapids Water Park

Type of Attraction: Water theme park

Location: 6566 North Military Trail, West Palm Beach 33407

Admission: $24; children under age 2 free

Hours: Park opens at 10 a.m. and closes at sunset, which varies from 5 p.m.–8 p.m. Open daily March 17–April 22 and May 19–Labor Day; weekends only April 23–May 18.

Phone: (561) 842-8756

When to Go: Weekdays are least crowded.

Overall Appeal by Age Groups:

Pre-school	Grade School	Teens	Young Adults	Over 30	Seniors
★★	★★★	★★★	★★	★★	★★

Author's Rating: ★★

How Much Time to Allow: Four–five hours

Description and Comments All sorts of water-related amusements on 22 acres, including water slides, a wave pool, and rubber tube flumes.

Touring Tips Participants must wear bathing suits—cutoff jeans not permitted—but can not wear water shoes on the rides (must go barefoot).

Other Things to Do Nearby It's a ten-minute drive from Palm Beach Gardens Mall or CityPlace.

Red Reef Park

Type of Attraction: Marine life park

Location: 1400 Ocean Boulevard, Boca Raton 33432

Admission: Weekdays, $8 per vehicle; weekends and holidays $10 per vehicle

Hours: Daily, 8 a.m.–10 p.m.

Phone: (561) 393-7974

When to Go: Any time

Overall Appeal by Age Groups:

Pre-school	Grade School	Teens	Young Adults	Over 30	Seniors
★★	★★★	★★	★★	★★	★★★

Author's Rating: ★★½

How Much Time to Allow: Two hours–all day

Description and Comments   At this 39.7-acre City of Boca Raton park, visitors may look for sea turtles, ospreys, pelicans, and manatees in their natural habitat. The park extends from the Intracoastal Waterway to the Atlantic Ocean.

Touring Tips   Besides school groups, many European tourists come here—many Americans don't seem to know about it.

Other Things to Do Nearby   Stop at the free 15-acre Gumbo Limbo Nature Center across the street (phone (561) 338-1473) to see live snakes, fish, and turtles; there's a beehive with live bees behind glass. The nature center is open Monday–Saturday, 9 a.m.–4 p.m.; and Sunday, noon–4 p.m. If you just want to relax, bring a picnic lunch or play at the beach.

Roger Dean Stadium

Type of Attraction: Baseball spring training stadium

Location: 4751 Main Street, Jupiter 33458

Admission: $6–18 a ticket

Hours: Monday–Friday, 8:30 a.m.–6 p.m.

Phone: (561) 775-1818

When to Go: March 2nd–March 29th for spring training, April 6th–beginning of September for Jupiter Hammerheads games

Special Comments: Spring training home of the Montreal Expos, St. Louis Cardinals, and Florida State League Jupiter Hammerheads (Single A team of the Montreal Expos).

Overall Appeal by Age Groups:

Pre-school	Grade School	Teens	Young Adults	Over 30	Seniors
—	★★	★★★	★★★	★★★	★★★½

Author's Rating: ★★★

How Much Time to Allow: Five–six hours

Description and Comments   This new stadium plans to inaugurate baseball fantasy camps in the future. The Tommy Hutton Baseball Academy started in June 2001.

Touring Tips   This area is experiencing tremendous growth; a new shopping mall is under construction and should provide further entertainment.

Other Things to Do Nearby   Plan to spend a few hours at Jonathan Dickinson State Park.

South Florida Science Museum

Type of Attraction: Hands-on science museum

Location: 4801 Dreher Trail North, West Palm Beach 33405

Admission: Adults, $6; children, $4. Daily planetarium shows (1 p.m. and 2 p.m.) cost $2 additional; daily laser shows (3 p.m. and 4 p.m.) cost $4 additional.

Hours: Monday–Thursday, 10 a.m.–5 p.m.; Friday, 10 a.m.–10 p.m.; Saturday, 10 a.m.–6 p.m.; Sunday, noon–6 p.m.

Phone: (561) 832-1988

When to Go: Any time

Overall Appeal by Age Groups:

Pre-school	Grade School	Teens	Young Adults	Over 30	Seniors
★★	★★★	★★★	★★	★★	★★

Author's Rating: ★★½

How Much Time to Allow: One–four hours

Description and Comments   Although it's a small museum, imaginative exhibits on light, energy, the environment, and the space program keep youngsters occupied for hours. Hands-on exhibits include brain teasers and a live frog exhibit; there's also an outdoor science trail. You'll find family-oriented activities for all ages.

Touring Tips   Call for directions; it's hard to find the entrance otherwise.

Other Things to Do Nearby   Palm Beach Zoo at Dreher Park.

Dining and Restaurants

Dining out in Palm Beach County is an Olympic-class sport, so an abundance of eateries beckons. The most outstanding ingredients, preparations, and service are obviously labor intensive and therefore costly to produce. The result is that such dining rooms—many have been here for decades—are clustered in the affluent areas of Boca Raton and Palm Beach.

There's a preponderance of Italian restaurants and a noticeable lack of great seafood dining rooms. Oriental options beyond the omnipresent Chinese offerings have increased to include a cornucopia of Japanese, Thai, and even Vietnamese choices.

And the Florida-Caribbean and fusion styles have taken root, largely due to the efforts of two people. Restaurateur Dennis Max pioneered when he opened Cafe Max (now Darrel & Oliver's Cafe Maxx in Pompano), Max's Grille, and Max's Place—which later became Mark's Place (in North Miami Beach). The latter is now closed but continued to wow foodies for years when talented chef/restaurateur Mark Militello became the owner. Militello has achieved stylish culinary wonders at Mark's Las Olas, Mark's at the Park, and Mark's CityPlace. Frequent diners sometimes feel they need a scorecard to keep track of the changes.

Hispanic influence also appears more and more frequently, although many Cubans say they don't dine out on Cuban food because they get that at home. Perhaps that's why there's a lack of really upscale Cuban sites.

Another factor in the escalating professionalism in Palm Beach restaurants is that, increasingly, more of the chefs are graduates of culinary schools, including Johnson & Wales University in North Miami and the Florida Culinary Institute in West Palm Beach.

Many South Florida restaurants open and close faster than you can say, "Your table is ready." Some people who move here from elsewhere are semi-retired, and some think that because they like to eat in nice restaurants, they're able to open one of their own. Those that stick around usually have the training and financial backing needed to pay good help and keep them onboard through the summer doldrums, when business is down. A resulting bonus to customers—they'll frequently offer special summer rates to create some business and maintain their staffs.

Note that even in many of the most elegant places, gentlemen may wear a collared shirt sans jacket and tie, while ladies choose dressy casual duds; however, shorts and jeans are often frowned upon in these restaurants. Always check ahead when in doubt.

EXPLAINING THE RATINGS

We have developed detailed profiles for the restaurants we think are the best in the county. Each profile features an easily scanned heading that allows you, in just a second, to check out the restaurant's name, cuisine, star rating, cost, quality rating, and value rating.

Star Rating The star rating is an overall rating that evaluates the entire dining experience, including style, service, and ambience, in addition to the taste, presentation, and quality of the food. Five stars is the highest rating possible, meaning the place has the best of everything. Four-star restaurants are exceptional, and three-star restaurants are well above average. Two-star restaurants are good. One star is given to average restaurants that demonstrate an unusual capability in some area of specialization, for example, an otherwise forgettable place that has great corned beef.

Cost Below and to the left of the star rating is an expense category giving the general price range for a complete meal. A complete meal for our purposes consists of an entrée with vegetable or side dish, and choice of soup or salad. Appetizers, desserts, drinks, and tips are excluded. Categories and related prices are listed below.

Inexpensive	$14 or less per person
Moderate	$15 to $30 per person
Expensive	More than $30 per person

Quality Rating On the far right of each heading appears a number and a letter. The number is a food quality rating based on a scale of 0 to 100, with 100 being the best rating attainable. The quality rating is based expressly on the taste, freshness of ingredients, preparation, presentation, and creativity of food served. There is no consideration of price. If you are a person who wants the best food available and cost is not an issue, you need look no further than the quality ratings.

Value Rating If, on the other hand, you are looking for both quality and value, then you should check the value rating, expressed in letters. The value ratings are defined as follows:

A	Exception value, a real bargain
B	Good value
C	Fair value, you get exactly what you pay for
D	Somewhat overpriced
F	Significantly overpriced

Payment   We've listed the type of payment accepted at each restaurant using the following codes:

AMEX	American Express (Optima)
CB	Carte Blanche
D	Discover
DC	Diners Club
MC	MasterCard
VISA	Visa

About These Choices

We have chosen restaurants that, while we can't guarantee their staying power, have proven to operate successfully for some time. We've also selected restaurants with a following among local professionals, residents, and tourists. We have included a mix of restaurants that are well known and some that are low-profile, and in the process we have tried to provide something for everyone. Bon appetit!

The Best of Palm Beach County Restaurants

Restaurant/Type	Star Rating	Quality Rating	Value Rating	City
American				
Cafe Chardonnay	★★★½	90	B	Palm Beach Gardens
John G's Restaurant	★★★½	88	B	Lake Worth
Spoto's Oyster Bar	★★★½	88	C	West Palm Beach
Cafe Protégé	★★★½	87	A	West Palm Beach
Max's Grille	★★★½	85	B	Boca Raton
Pete's	★★★½	85	C	Boca Raton
Amici	★★★	85	C	Palm Beach
Hamburger Heaven	★★★	85	B	Palm Beach
Boston's on the Beach	★★½	85	B	Delray Beach
Lucille's Bad to the Bone BBQ	★★½	80	C	Boca Raton
Mississippi Sweets BBQ Co.	★★½	80	B	Boca Raton, Lake Worth
Ellie's 50's Diner	★★½	75	C	Delray Beach
Contemporary				
The Restaurant	★★★★★	98	A	Palm Beach
Mark's CityPlace	★★★★	94	B	West Palm Beach

The Best of Palm Beach County Restaurants (cont.)

Restaurant/Type	Star Rating	Quality Rating	Value Rating	City
East City Bistro	★★★★	88	C	Delray Beach
Zemi	★★★★	87	B	Boca Raton
Continental				
Cafe L'Europe	★★★★½	90	B	Palm Beach
Pete's	★★★½	85	C	Boca Raton
Deli				
Wolfie Cohen's Rascal House	★★★	83	C	Boca Raton
French				
L'Escalier at the Florentine Room	★★★★★	99	A	Palm Beach
La Vielle Maison	★★★★★	98	A	Boca Raton
L'Anjou French Restaurant	★★★½	85	C	Lake Worth
Italian				
Storza Ristorante	★★★	80	C	West Palm Beach
Japanese				
Cornell Cafe	★★★½	85	B	Delray Beach
Kosher dairy				
Eilat Café	★★	80	C	Boca Raton
Mediterranean				
Mark's at Mizner Park	★★★★	92	B	Boca Raton
Pan-Asian				
Echo	★★★★½	95	B	Palm Beach
Seafood				
John G's Restaurant	★★★½	88	B	Lake Worth
Spoto's Oyster Bar	★★★½	88	C	West Palm Beach
Boston's on the Beach	★★½	85	B	Delray Beach
Vegetarian				
Souplantation & Sweet Tomatoes	★★★	80	B	Boca Raton

AMICI   ★ ★ ★

Contemporary American	Moderate	QUALITY
		85

288 South County Road, Palm Beach
(561) 832-0301

	VALUE
	C

Reservations: Necessary for dinner
When to go: Any time
Entree range: $10.95–33.95
Payment: VISA, MC, AMEX, DC
Parking: Street
Bar: Full service

Wine selection: Good; $4–7 a glass
Dress: Business
Disabled access: Good
Customers: Professionals and ladies who
    lunch, singles, celebrities

Lunch: Daily, 11:30 a.m.–2:30 p.m.

Dinner: Daily, 5:30–11 p.m.

Menu recommendations: Upscale pizzas and salads are the rage at lunch, while diners at dinner may choose among grilled swordfish in olive sauce and grilled veal chop with garlic mashed potatoes and portabella mushrooms.

Comments: Currently in favor with the beautiful people, this room is contemporary European in flavor, featuring dark wooden furnishings and bare windows; the bar is a popular spot for young singles after work.

BOSTON'S ON THE BEACH   ★ ★ ½

Seafood/American	Moderate	QUALITY
		85

40 South Ocean Boulevard, Delray Beach
(561) 278-3364

	VALUE
	B

Reservations: Recommended on
    weekends
When to go: Any time
Entree range: $6.75–8.50; Upper Deck,
    $10.95–23.95
Payment: VISA, MC, AMEX, D, DC
Parking: Street and valet

Bar: Full service
Wine selection: Adequate; $2–4 a glass
Dress: Casual
Disabled access: Good; elevator to 2nd
    floor
Customers: Young locals, families,
    tourists

Open: Daily, 7 a.m. –2 a.m.

Menu recommendations: Heaping baskets of fish and chips or fried shrimp, or lobster and tuna salad; the Upper Deck offers linguine and clam sauce, yellowfin tuna with ginger vinaigrette, and grilled mahi-mahi.

Comments: This is what beach life is about. Across the street from Delray Beach's public beach, this eatery offers street-side casual meals under an awning and slightly more formal eats on the Upper Deck, where diners see the gorgeous ocean and smell the briny breeze. Live reggae music adds the right note on Monday nights.

CAFE CHARDONNAY ★★★½

Contemporary American	Expensive	QUALITY
		90

4533 PGA Boulevard, Palm Beach Gardens
(561) 627-2662

VALUE
B

Reservations: Required in season	**Bar:** Wine and beer
When to go: Any time	**Wine selection:** Excellent; $5–15 a glass
Entree range: $22–35	**Dress:** Upscale casual
Payment: VISA, MC, AMEX, D	**Disabled access:** First floor only
Parking: Lot	**Customers:** Young professionals, tourists

Lunch: Monday–Friday, 11:30 a.m. –2:30 p.m.

Dinner: Daily, 5:30–10 p.m.

Menu recommendations: Start with a pesto-crusted goat cheese tart with grilled eggplant, roasted portabella mushrooms, and marinated pepper, and follow with a rack of roasted Australian lamb enhanced by a rosemary-scented port reduction, accompanied by herbed mashed potatoes. Dessert might be warm, deep-dish apple pie on a bed of caramel sauce.

Comments: At this bilevel restaurant where modern paintings provide a sophisticated background, wine lovers often sit at the wine bar, choosing among 500 selections.

CAFE L'EUROPE ★★★★½

Continental	Expensive	QUALITY
		90

331 South County Road, Palm Beach
(561) 655-4020

VALUE
B

Reservations: Required	choices); $7.75–20.50 a glass
When to go: Any time	**Dress:** Jackets in dining room; casual in
Entree range: $21.75–35.75	bistro (menu same)
Payment: VISA, MC, AMEX, DC	**Disabled access:** Good
Parking: Valet	**Customers:** Internationals, celebrities,
Bar: Full service	winter residents
Wine selection: Outstanding (1,225	

Lunch: Tuesday–Saturday, noon–2:30 p.m. (closed Saturday in summer)

Dinner: Daily, 5:30–10 p.m.; closed Monday

Menu recommendations: A caviar bar appeals to old-time Palm Beachers. A starter might be fried sweetbreads with poached pear, followed by a grilled veal chop in a tarragon reduction served with potato-scallion cake or risotto with porcini mushrooms. Dessert may star a flourless chocolate cake swathed with praline, served with butter pecan ice cream.

Comments: Elegant dining room with swagged drapes and divine accoutrements. A pianist provides soft background music, while dancers enjoy the jazz quartet on Friday and Saturday nights.

CAFE PROTEGE	★★★½

		QUALITY
American/New World	Moderate	87
2400 Metrocentre Boulevard, West Palm Beach		VALUE
(561) 687-2433 or (800) 826-9986		A

Reservations: Suggested	Wine selection: Very good (150 different
When to go: Any time	wines); $4–7 a glass
Entree range: $15–27	Dress: Dressy casual
Payment: VISA, MC, AMEX	Disabled access: Good
Parking: Lot	Customers: Locals, winter residents
Bar: Full service	

Lunch: Monday–Friday, 11:30 a.m. –2 p.m., including a lunch buffet

Dinner: Tuesday–Saturday, 5:30–9:30 p.m.

Menu recommendations: Appetizers include garlicky sautéed broccoli rabe and roasted red peppers, teamed with fettuccini pasta tossed with Asiago cheese. Among the entrees are venison medallions, pan-seared with apples and baby carrots and glazed with applejack brandy, served with mashed red potatoes. Check out the "Sunset Madness Menu," a three-course dinner served for $25.

Comments: Students at the Florida Culinary Institute practice their skills here, but the results are highly professional. The background sparkles with large picture windows.

CORNELL CAFE   ★★★½

Japanese	Inexpensive	QUALITY
		85

Morikami Museum, 4000 Morikami Park Road
Delray Beach; (561) 495-0233 x219

VALUE
B

Reservations: Not accepted
When to go: Lunch only
Entree range: $5.95–11.95; sushi a la carte costs $2.50–3.50 for two pieces
Payment: Cash only
Parking: Lot
Bar: Wine and beer

Wine selection: Japanese wines; $3–6 a glass
Dress: Casual
Disabled access: Good
Customers: Attendees who visit the Japanese museum and gardens are joined by local professionals

Open: Tuesday–Sunday, 11 a.m. –3 p.m.

Menu recommendations: Sushi selections include the ever-popular tuna and California rolls, but aficionados choose the bento box, an artistically arranged lacquer box of chef's choices: perhaps vegetable dumplings, teriyaki salmon, and eggplant with garlic sauce.

Comments: Tables are set outdoors overlooking the serene Japanese gardens. Patrons may eat at this small restaurant without paying museum admission.

EAST CITY BISTRO   ★★★★

Contemporary/New World	Moderate	QUALITY
		88

777 East Atlantic Avenue, Delray Beach
(561) 266-0744

VALUE
C

Reservations: Suggested
When to go: Before 7 p.m. for dinner
Entree range: $7.95–22.95
Payment: VISA, MC, AMEX, D, DC
Parking: Street and lot

Bar: Full service
Wine selection: Excellent; $5–10 a glass
Dress: Casual
Disabled access: Good
Customers: Locals, professionals, families

Lunch: Monday–Friday, 11:30 a.m. –5 p.m.

Dinner: Sunday–Thursday, 5–10 p.m.; Friday and Saturday, 5 p.m.–midnight; closed Sunday in summer

Menu recommendations: Sautéed chicken breast with black beans and rice, macadamia-crusted yellowtail snapper, designer pizzas, and sandwiches. Do not pass "Go" without finishing with a white-and-dark chocolate brownie oozing with chocolate sauce, mated with vanilla ice cream.

Comments: Starkly dramatic background dishes up cutting-edge dishes, as created by Darrel Broek and CIA-trained chef Oliver Saucy of Pompano Beach's Cafe Maxx.

ECHO ★★★★½

Pan-Asian	Moderate	QUALITY
		95

230 Sunrise Avenue, Palm Beach
(561) 802-4222

VALUE
B

Reservations: Suggested	Wine selection: Very good; $8–21 a glass
When to go: Any time	Dress: Upscale dressy casual; shorts per-
Entree range: $16–30	mitted at porch tables
Payment: VISA, MC, AMEX, D, DC	Disabled access: Good
Parking: Valet and street	Customers: Young locals, professionals,
Bar: Full service	tourists, internationals

Dinner: Tuesday–Sunday, 5:30–10:15 p.m.

Menu recommendations: Exquisitely fresh sushi and sashimi are available by the piece. Outstanding interpretations include steamed sea bass with a soy and ginger glaze, pad Thai with chicken and shrimp, Peking duck for two, and Vietnamese roasted chicken with lemon grass–chili sauce. A "Sharing Menu" for a table for four at $60 per person provides an exotic Asian trip.

Comments: Stunning contemporary design that imparts Oriental flavor. The menu, which features Chinese, Japanese, Thai, and Vietnamese, is divided into five elements: wind, fire, water, earth, and flavor. The loud rock music, though, detracts from the experience.

EILAT CAFE ★★

Kosher dairy	Inexpensive	QUALITY
		80

6853 SW Eighteenth Street, Boca Raton
(561) 368-6880

VALUE
C

Reservations: Not accepted	Wine selection: None
When to go: Any time	Dress: Casual
Entree range: $9.95–16.95	Disabled access: Very good
Payment: VISA, MC, AMEX, D, DC	Customers: Seniors, Orthodox families,
Parking: Lot	winter residents
Bar: None	

Open: Monday–Thursday, 11 a.m.–9 p.m.; Friday, 11 a.m.–2 p.m.; Sunday, noon–9 p.m.; closed Saturday, but open after sundown in season

Menu recommendations: Israeli classics like hummus and falafel, plus gourmet pizzas, sesame-seared salmon with mesclun greens, and St. Peter's fish marsala with shiitake mushrooms.

Comments: This bright and airy restaurant offers dairy dishes for its observant Jewish clientele. Tables—sans tablecloths—are inside and on the patio.

ELLIE'S 50'S DINER CAFE ★★½

American	Inexpensive	QUALITY
		75

2410 North Federal Highway, Delray Beach	VALUE
(561) 276-1570	**C**

Reservations: Not accepted
When to go: Any time
Entree range: $3.57–12.97
Payment: Cash only
Parking: Lot
Bar: Wine and beer

Wine selection: House wine only, $3.97 a glass
Dress: Casual
Disabled access: Good
Customers: Seniors, tourists, winter residents

Open: Sunday–Thursday, 8 a.m.–9:30 p.m.; Friday and Saturday, 8 a.m.–10:30 p.m.

Menu recommendations: Old standard dishes with oldie names: "Misty" is a Philly cheese steak with onions, "Love me Tender" a sirloin hamburger, and "Tutti Fruiti" a fruit salad. But with a bow to those on this century's diets, healthier foods are also available.

Comments: Spot the pink 1958 Chevy outside and you're "in like Flynn." It's a nostalgia trip back to the fifties, with mica counters and jukebox selections.

HAMBURGER HEAVEN ★★★

American/Burgers	Inexpensive	QUALITY
		85

314 South County Road, Palm Beach	VALUE
(561) 655-5277	**B**

Reservations: Not accepted
When to go: Any time, especially in season to spot the somebodies
Entree range: $3.95–7.95
Payment: Cash only
Parking: Street

Bar: None
Wine selection: None
Dress: Casual
Disabled access: Good
Customers: Locals, internationals, construction workers, winter residents

Open: Monday–Saturday, 7:30 a.m.–8 p.m. in season, 7:30 a.m.–4 p.m. in summer

Menu recommendations: Huge platters of eggs and sausage served with grits, gigantic hamburgers and garden burgers, and "lite" offerings. Freshly baked blueberry pie is a must.

Comments: Although Worth Avenue is tres elegante, this spot has maintained its steel and mica decor since it started in 1945. Construction workers chow down beside society ladies.

JOHN G'S RESTAURANT   ★★★½

American/Seafood	Inexpensive	QUALITY 88
10 South Ocean Boulevard, Lake Worth (561) 585-9860		VALUE B

Reservations: Not accepted	Parking: Nearby lot
When to go: Off-season (September is	Bar: None
the quietest month); always before	Wine selection: None
9 a.m. for breakfast	Dress: Casual, beachwear
Entree range: $4.75–17.50	Disabled access: Fair
Payment: Cash only	Customers: Families, seniors, tourists

Open: Daily, 7 a.m.–3 p.m.

Menu recommendations: French toast is extraordinary here: three slices of "Texas bread" (unusually thick) with cinnamon and sliced almonds cooked into them. Jumbo shrimp in a crispy batter fried and served with fries, cole slaw—and corn fritters.

Comments: Bring along patience for waiting in line at this popular breakfast and lunch eatery at the Lake Worth public beach. Seafood is immaculately fresh—even including the usually frozen shrimp—and portions huge. Family owned since 1973, John G sometimes distributes complimentary chocolate-dipped fruit to those who wait.

L'ANJOU FRENCH RESTAURANT   ★★★½

French	Moderate	QUALITY 85
717 Lake Avenue, Lake Worth (561) 582-7666		VALUE C

Reservations: Required	Entree range: $16–24.50
When to go: Any time	Payment: VISA, MC, AMEX

Parking: Street

Bar: Full service

Wine selection: Good; $3–6 a glass

Dress: Casual

Disabled access: Good

Customers: Locals, tourists, winter
   residents

Dinner: Daily, 5–9 p.m.; closed Monday and Tuesday in summer and all of September

Menu recommendations: Très French dishes such as vichyssoise, boeuf Bourguignon, and veal with Grand Marnier sauce have been luring several generations of followers. There's always filet mignon and filet of sole for the less continental.

Comments: Family owned since 1976, this charmingly French Provençal spot on Lake Worth's regentrified Lake Avenue offers sidewalk tables or seating inside, beyond the lace curtains.

L'ESCALIER AT THE FLORENTINE ROOM ★★★★★	
French Very Expensive	**QUALITY** **99**
The Breakers Hotel, One South County Road, Palm Beach (561) 659-8480	**VALUE** **A**

Reservations: Recommended

When to go: When celebrating a special
   occasion or impressing an important
   client

Entree range: $32–40

Payment: VISA, MC, AMEX, D, DC

Parking: Valet

Bar: Full service

Wine selection: Exceptional (6,500 selections, up to an $1,800 bottle); $8–24 a
   glass

Dress: Dressy

Disabled access: Good

Customers: Young dot.com millionaires,
   internationals, celebrities, special-events
   celebrators

Dinner: Daily, 6–10 p.m.

Menu recommendations: Heavenly dishes start with a complimentary opener, possibly cranberry beignets with a duck and port sauce; include grilled beef tournedos and foie gras, served with a black truffle and wild mushroom reduction; or the Floribbean (Floridian/Caribbean) pan-roasted Maine lobster morsels in curried coconut sauce with caramelized banana slices. End with a vanilla crème brulee, the Tahitian element punctuated by lemon grass.

Comments: Formerly The Florentine, this regally appointed dining room under a 24-foot-high frescoed ceiling serves arguably the county's best-prepared and elegantly served meals. Under the creative skills of dining room chef Matthew Sobon, cuisine has soared in the last few years. Diners know they're in for something special when the bread server presents a basket of four whole loaves (perhaps French, sourdough, multi-grain, and cherry-chocolate), then slices the diner's choices. At the meal's finale, the cheese presentation of 18 varieties appears on a cart; the server then describes each, peppering the history with humorous anecdotes.

LA VIELLE MAISON   ★★★★★

French	Very Expensive	QUALITY
		98

770 E. Palmetto Park Road, Boca Raton	VALUE
(561) 391-6701	A

Reservations: Recommended
When to go: For important dates, business or personal
Entree range: $24–42
Payment: VISA, MC, AMEX, D, DC
Parking: Valet
Bar: Full service

Wine selection: Excellent; $6.50–12.75 a glass
Dress: Dressy casual; jackets in season
Disabled access: Good
Customers: Corporate types, internationals, well-heeled tourists, celebrators

Dinner: Daily, 6–10 p.m.

Menu recommendations: Sevruga caviar accompanied by blini; wild-mushroom ravioli in lemon grass–scented cream sauce punctuated with tiny clams; a trio of medallions, the lamb rosemary scented, the beef teamed with béarnaise sauce, and the veal with morel sauce; corn meal–crusted mahi mahi with a Provençal zucchini cake; the finale a lemon crepe soufflé accented with raspberry sauce (although many repeaters prefer their chocolate "bag.")

Comments: If you want to know what life was like for the very wealthy winter residents of yesteryear, dine at this romantic 1920s mansion. The 25-year-old restaurant's awash with Mediterranean influences such as Provençal furnishings and lush gardens with gurgling fountains. Loyal servers are knowledgeable without being haughty. Private rooms are available. Summer sees reduced prices.

LUCILLE'S BAD TO THE BONE BBQ   ★★½

Southern	Inexpensive	QUALITY
		80

3011 Yamato Road, Boca Raton	VALUE
(561) 997-9557	C

710 Linton Boulevard, Delray Beach
(561) 330-6705

Reservations: Not accepted	**Bar:** Wine and beer
When to go: Before 6 p.m. or after 7:45 p.m.	**Wine selection:** Fair
	Dress: Casual
Entree range: $4.95–10.95	**Disabled access:** Good
Payment: VISA, MC, AMEX	**Customers:** Young families, seniors,
Parking: Lot	experts on Southern roadhouse eats

Open: Daily, 11 a.m.–10 p.m.

Menu recommendations: Rotisserie-roasted chicken and St. Louis ribs are major choices, served with zippy barbecue sauce, baked sweet potato, and pecan pie. Downhomers can order catfish, while finicky kids can always choose hamburgers. Platters include several side dishes. Don't forget to order the black cow root beer float.

Comments: Decor in this fun spot is funky Dixie roadhouse, where farm implements such as watering troughs and washboards provide local color. The name reflects B.B. King's eponymous guitar, Lucille. All-you-can-eat ba-a-ad to the bone ribs draw bushels of regulars on Tuesday, but locals bring the youngsters on Wednesdays, when kids under 12 eat free; a clown keeps them busy by painting faces and making balloon animals.

MARK'S AT MIZNER PARK ★★★★

Mediterranean/Fusion	Very Expensive	QUALITY 92
344 Plaza Real, Boca Raton (561) 395-0770		VALUE B

Reservations: Accepted	**Wine selection:** Very good; $6.50–12 a glass
When to go: Any time	
Entree range: $14–31	**Dress:** Smart casual
Payment: VISA, AMEX, D, DC	**Disabled access:** Good
Parking: Valet and street	**Customers:** Young locals, professionals,
Bar: Full service	winter residents, tourists

Brunch: Sunday, 11:30 a.m.–3 p.m.

Lunch: Daily, 11:30 a.m.–3 p.m.

Dinner: Daily, 5 p.m.–midnight

Menu recommendations: Dishes that seem commonplace are taken to new heights with the Mark Militello touch: lobster and asparagus pizza, grilled chicken Caesar salad with focaccia croutons, pork chop stuffed with pignoli and spinach, duckling with mashed sweet potatoes and braised greens.

Comments: Militello, who started out with restaurateur Dennis Max and branched off with his own highly successful hotspots, created this popular eatery next to Max's Grille in Mizner Park. The interior is dramatically contemporary, featuring ultra-high booth backs, but many choose to sit and sup at outdoor tables, as in Europe. Locals often sit at the seven-seat chef's table to watch the culinary whizzes in action. Noise level is high, in keeping with the boundless excitement. Some feel it's high-priced, but they're often those who don't appreciate the intensified labor needed for perfect touches.

MARK'S CITYPLACE		★★★★
Contemporary/Fusion	Expensive	**QUALITY** 94
700 South Rosemary Avenue, West Palm Beach (561) 514-0770		**VALUE** B

Reservations: Necessary for dinner and for parties of five or more	Wine selection: Very good; $6.50–12 a glass
When to go: Any time	Dress: Dressy casual
Entree range: $14–32	Disabled access: Very good
Payment: VISA, MC, AMEX, DC	Customers: Professionals, upscale locals, internationals
Parking: Valet and garage	
Bar: Full service	

Open: Monday–Thursday, 11:30 a.m.–11 p.m.; Friday and Saturday, 11:30 a.m.–midnight; Sunday, 11:30 a.m.–10 p.m.

Menu recommendations: Grilled chicken pizza with sundried tomatoes and arugula, black peppercorn–crusted, seared yellowfin tuna with celeriac mash and haricots verte, crab makimono (roll) with mango, avocado, and cucumber. The fresh-made sorbets are heavenly.

Comments: The newest star (opened December 2000) in much-awarded Mark Militello's galaxy of cutting-edge fusion foods, this is a stunning theater of cuisine. Located on the second floor, it offers outdoor tables and indoor seating beneath dramatic custom-made lighting fixtures and a ceiling that looks like copper-toned crumpled paper—it actually notches down the noise level. A sushi bar features smart-looking glazed pottery serving pieces.

MAX'S GRILLE   ★★★½

American/Contemporary	Moderate	QUALITY
		85

404 Plaza Real, Boca Raton

(561) 368-0080

	VALUE
	B

Reservations: Necessary for six or more

When to go: Any time

Entree range: $12.95–29.95

Payment: VISA, MC, AMEX

Parking: Valet and street

Bar: Full service

Wine selection: Good; $5.95–10.95 a glass

Dress: Dressy casual; men may not wear sleeveless shirts.

Disabled access: Good

Customers: Families, tourists, professionals

Open: Daily, 11:30 a.m.–11 p.m.

Menu recommendations: Pasta with chicken, goat cheese, and sun-dried tomatoes; ginger-glazed salmon with basmati rice and stir-fried greens; braised lamb with parsnip puree.

Comments: Dennis Max, the restaurateur responsible for many of the area's culinary innovations (starting with Pompano Beach's Cafe Max), created this more casual spot in Mizner Park. Imaginative dishes are served within its dramatic, dark-wood interior or at tables for dining al fresco—and people-watching—at this European-style cafe with au courant Pacific rim influences. Waitstaff, however, seems to change frequently. The stylish bar sees plenty of action.

MISSISSIPPI SWEETS BBQ CO.   ★★½

Southern	Inexpensive	QUALITY
		80

2399 North Federal Highway, Boca Raton

(561) 394-6779

	VALUE
	B

6604 Hypoluxo Road, Lake Worth

(561) 432-8555

Reservations: Not accepted

When to go: Before 5:30 p.m. or after 8 p.m.

Entree range: $4.50–10.95

Payment: VISA, MC

Parking: Lot

Bar: Wine and beer

Wine selection: House wines only, $2–4 a glass

Dress: Casual

Disabled access: Fair

Customers: Young locals, seniors, winter residents

Open: Monday–Thursday, 11:30 a.m. –9:30 p.m.; Friday and Saturday, 11:30 a.m.–10 p.m.; Sunday, noon–10 p.m.

Menu recommendations: Pulled pork and barbecued chicken are featured, but most folks come for the baby-back ribs served with a sweet-tangy barbecue sauce. Best "side road" is Mississippi sweets—sweet potatoes sliced paper thin and deep-fried.

Comments: This tiny eatery usually has lines waiting outside. Decor recalls life in Mississippi, through pictures of fishing boats and the Delta Queen steamboat. Food arrives in baskets on vinyl tablecloths. Country music sings through the air.

PETE'S		★★★½

American/Continental	Expensive	QUALITY 85
7940 Glades Road, Boca Raton		VALUE C
(561) 487-1600 or (561) 883-6979 for reservations		

Reservations: Suggested	**Bar:** Full service
When to go: Any time; singles find many like-minded hopefuls at the bar at cocktail hour (especially Tuesday nights)	**Wine selection:** Good; $6.50–9.50 a glass
	Dress: Dressy casual
	Disabled access: Good
Entree range: $17.95–34.95	**Customers:** Winter residents, tourists, singles
Payment: VISA, MC, AMEX, D, DC	
Parking: Valet and lot	

Lunch: Daily, 11:30 a.m.–3 p.m.

Dinner: Daily, 4:30–10 p.m.

Menu recommendations: Numerous cuts of steak, grilled veal chop in creamy wine sauce with morel mushrooms, chicken scampi over linguine. And positively the "chips and chunks brownie cake."

Comments: A lovely setting beside a small lake brings serenity to the dining room. The bar, however, is the scene of frenetic singles' action. Live dance music plays nightly. Families also enjoy the setting, since a model train running along the ceiling height in some sections fascinates little ones. The Christmas display is over the top.

SOUPLANTATION & SWEET TOMATOES		★★★

Vegetarian/Salads	Inexpensive	QUALITY 80
7110 Beracasa Way, Boca Raton		VALUE B
(561) 750-3303		

Reservations: Not accepted
When to go: Any time
Entree range: $1.49–6.69
Payment: VISA, MC, AMEX, D, DC
Parking: Adjacent lot
Bar: None

Wine selection: None
Dress: Casual
Disabled access: Good
Customers: Families, local professionals, winter residents.

Open: Sunday–Thursday, 11 a.m.–9 p.m.; Friday and Saturday, 11 a.m.–10 p.m.

Menu recommendations: Chicken wonton salad, Caesar's salad, BLT salad are favorites; the pizza really stands up as well.

Comments: An enormous all-you-can-eat self-serve counter, constantly replenished with fresh fare, with sub-stations for pasta, pizza, soup, yogurt, fruit—all of which are included.

SPOTO'S OYSTER BAR ★★★½

American/Seafood	Moderate	QUALITY
		88
125 Datura Street, West Palm Beach		VALUE
(561) 835-1828		**C**

Reservations: Not accepted
When to go: Any time
Entree range: $12.50–25
Payment: VISA, MC, AMEX, D, DC
Parking: Lot and street
Bar: Full service, nine beers on tap

Wine selection: Good; $4.75–13.75 a glass
Dress: Casual
Disabled access: Fair
Customers: Young locals, tourists, winter residents

Open: Sunday–Wednesday, 11:30 a.m.–11 p.m.; Thursday–Saturday, 11:30 a.m.–midnight

Menu recommendations: Oyster varieties on the half shell, New England clam chowder, sesame tuna, chocolate silk pie.

Comments: This jumping spot around the corner from Clematis Street, near the Intracoastal Waterway, has a lively bar and tables inside the wood-paneled, brick-floored area and outside. Staff is extremely gracious.

STORZA RISTORANTE ★★★

Bistro/Italian	Moderate	QUALITY
		80
203 Clematis Street, West Palm Beach		VALUE
(561) 832-8819		**C**

Reservations: Recommended at night
When to go: Any time
Entree range: $9.95–20.95
Payment: VISA, MC, AMEX, D, DC
Parking: Street
Bar: Full service

Wine selection: Adequate; $3.50–6.50 a
  glass
Dress: Casual
Disabled access: Good
Customers: Tourists, families, young sin-
  gles, students

Lunch: Monday–Friday, 11:30 a.m.–2:30 p.m.

Dinner: Monday–Friday, 5–10 p.m.; Friday and Saturday, 5–11 p.m.

Menu recommendations: Appetizer tower: three tiers of appetizers, which might include carpaccio, braciola (thin-sliced baked meat) stuffed with mushrooms, and veal sausage; warm goat cheese salad with spinach and squares of breaded, fried cheese; linguini with white clam sauce.

Comments: The dark, woody interior recalls European bistros, with copper tabletops; outdoor tables beckon as well, where people-watching is an appetizer.

THE RESTAURANT ★★★★★

New World/Contemporary	Expensive	QUALITY 98
Four Seasons Resort, 2800 South Ocean Boulevard Palm Beach (561) 582-2800		VALUE A

Reservations: Required
When to go: When in an elegant mood
Entree range: $31–42
Payment: VISA, MC, AMEX, D, DC
Parking: Valet only
Bar: Full service
Wine selection: Exceptional (300 labels,

up to a $2,700 bottle); $7.50–11 a
  glass
Dress: Jackets required
Disabled access: Good
Customers: Winter residents, celebrities,
  young locals celebrating special events

Dinner: Tuesday–Sunday, 6–10 p.m.; closed Tuesday in off-season

Menu recommendations: Yellowfin tuna tartare and queen conch carpaccio embellished with North American caviar; macadamia-crusted rack of lamb, served with a boniato and pineapple mash; and the signature dessert, molten chocolate lava cake complemented by Jack Daniels ice cream. A daily vegetarian option also is available.

Comments: This gorgeously rich-looking restaurant, overlooking the ocean through floor-to-ceiling windows, has lots more than travertine and stunning fresh flower arrangements. For ten years, its cuisine has been created by CIA-trained executive chef Hubert Des Marais, who started here when it was the Ocean Grand Hotel. Chef Des Marais insists on the highest-quality ingredients, and he even grows most of the herbs himself. Southern U.S. and Caribbean flavors appear in new incarnations, lovingly presented and garnished.

WOLFIE COHEN'S RASCAL HOUSE ★★★

Deli	Inexpensive	QUALITY
		83

2006 Executive Center Drive, Boca Raton	VALUE
(561) 982-8899	**C**

Reservations: Not accepted
When to go: To avoid lines, come before 11 a.m. for lunch and before 6 p.m. for dinner.
Entree range: $6.50–14.95
Payment: VISA, MC, AMEX, D, DC
Parking: Lot

Bar: Full service
Wine selection: Good; $3.95–6 a glass
Dress: Casual
Disabled access: Good
Customers: Locals, tourists, winter residents

Open: Daily, 8 a.m.–11 p.m.

Menu recommendations: Pickled lox in cream sauce, corned beef sandwiches with potato salad, beef brisket with potato pancakes—all the old favorites, along with patty melts and shrimp parmigiana.

Comments: The food has the right New York Jewish deli flavor, and the complimentary baskets of delicious muffins, Danish, and rolls provide take-home tidbits for many regulars. The multiroomed restaurant is bright and airy, thanks to its former locale as California Pizza Kitchen. However, some silly glitches annoy patrons. It's a lack of attention to details, such as running short of coffee spoons for breakfast or providing steak knives for butter and cream cheese instead of spreading knives.

ZEMI ★★★★

Contemporary	Moderate	QUALITY
		87

5050 Town Center Circle (in Boca Center),	VALUE
Boca Raton (561) 391-7177	**B**

Reservations: Suggested
When to go: Any time
Entree range: $10–30
Payment: VISA, MC, AMEX, D, DC
Parking: Valet and lot
Bar: Full service

Wine selection: Good; $6–14 a glass
Dress: Smart casual
Disabled access: Good
Customers: Young professionals, singles, tourists

Lunch: Monday–Friday, 11:30 a.m.–2:30 p.m.

Dinner: Daily, 6–10:30 p.m.

Menu recommendations: Selections are cutting-edge: wild-mushroom pizza drizzled with truffle oil, grilled pork T-bone with garlicky mashed potatoes and pear compote, pan-roasted Chilean sea bass mated with rice paper rolls stuffed with stir-fried vegetables.

Comments: Chic and stylish—designer Ilan Weisbrod worked with world-renowned restaurant designer Adam Tihany—this hip place caters to a sophisticated crowd. Wooden floors and lacquered surfaces make it too loud for those sensitive to high noise levels.

Entertainment and Nightlife

THEATER AND OTHER CULTURAL PURSUITS

The state-of-the-art **Raymond F. Kravis Center for the Performing Arts** (701 Okeechobee Boulevard, West Palm Beach; (561) 833-8300 or (800) KRAVIS-1) is the major venue for touring Broadway shows; it's also home to the excellent Florida Philharmonic Orchestra (phone (800) 226-1812), the proclaimed Ballet Florida—Palm Beach's resident dance company for 20 years (phone (561) 659-2000 or (800) 0172), and the Palm Beach Opera (phone 561) 833-7888) until their new opera house is completed. The playhouse hosts touring performances by the Miami City Ballet. There are three performance venues: the 2,200 seat-Dreyfoos hall; the intimate 300-seat Rinker Playhouse; and the Gosman Amphitheatre, an outdoor theater that holds 1,400 people.

The **Royal Poinciana Playhouse** (70 Royal Poinciana Plaza, Palm Beach; (561) 833-0705) is a jewelbox of a theater, formerly Palm Beach's only stage for major productions. Limited by size and technical possibilities, it now showcases dramatic performances and one-man shows. The small **Carefree Theatre** (2000 South Dixie Highway, West Palm Beach; (561) 833-7305) hosts artsy films, concerts, and comedians, and still shows the Rocky Horror Picture Show (it's been drawing audiences for more than 50 years). The **Caldwell Theatre** (7873 North Federal Highway, Boca Raton; (561) 241-7432 or toll-free in Palm Beach and Broward Counties at (800) 930-6400) is a small playhouse spotlighting drama, comedy, play readings, and musical nostalgia programs such as the recent "Our Sinatra," featuring live musicians. Florida Atlantic University's huge auditorium (777 Glades Road, Boca Raton; (561) 297-3737) seats 2,500. Concerts include well-known names such as Jackie Mason, Steve Lawrence and Edye Gorme, and Peter, Paul, and Mary.

The country's first Muvico Theater, the **Muvico Palace** 20 (3200 Airport Road, Boca Raton; (561) 395-4695), opened in spring, 2000 and brought cinema viewing to new heights. There's a standard 20-screen movie house, but what's really unique is The Premier. Located on a balcony, audience members sit in spacious, plush love seats with tables alongside for holding nibbles and wine glasses during the movies. Complimentary valet parking is included. Premier patrons—over age 21—may dine before or after in the Bistro or Bar (reservations accepted for The Premier and Bistro). Cost is $15 per person after 4 p.m., $11 per person before 4 p.m. Parents or grandparents may use The Premier while leaving children in a supervised fanciful playroom at $5.50 per child (ages 3–8) before 6 p.m. and $8 per child after 6 p.m. At CityPlace the 20-screen **Muvico Parisian,** fashioned somewhat after the Paris Opera House, has recently opened. The Premier and playroom are the same as the Boca location, but there's no restaurant in this branch. This is now the site of the annual Palm Beach County International Film Festival held each April. The festival includes guest appearances by such stars as Sylvester Stallone, Tommy Lee Jones, Burt Reynolds, and Samuel L. Jackson. Awards are presented at the Kravis Center.

Little Palm Family Theatre (154 NW 16th Street, Boca Raton; (561) 394-0206) holds children's theatrical workshops for budding thespians and performances that provide a good introduction to the stage (held at Jan McArt's Royal Palm Festival Dinner Theater). Admission is $8 per person for performances, held Saturday at 9:15 a.m. and Sunday at 1 p.m., but call in case of changes. The theater is dark April 7–8 and the last two weeks of September.

Clematis by Night is celebrated every Thursday night on West Palm Beach's downtown Clematis Street. The street is closed to traffic; there are dozens of free concerts (5:30–9 p.m.), street performers, arts and crafts for sale, and a cornucopia of restaurants with sidewalk cafes offering nibbles. Pop into the whimsically painted green and yellow Sloan's, dating from 1945 (112 Clematis Street; (561) 833-3335). See Sloan's profile under Dining and Restaurants.

The ***Palm Beach Princess*** (777 East Port Road, Riviera Beach; (561) 447-2290), a 421-foot-long cruise ship, leaves the Port of Palm Beach twice daily, for five- to six-hour cruises to nowhere. Prices vary but include all food and live entertainment. Gambling costs, of course, are at your own expense. Free bus pickups add to the cruises' popularity.

The Best of Palm Beach County Clubs

Name	Cover	Cost	City
Bars			
Blue Anchor British Pub	None	Inexp	Delray Beach
Lulu's Place	None	Inexp	Delray Beach
Dance Clubs			
Dakotah 624	None	Mod	Delray Beach
The Liquid Room	$10	Mod	West Palm Beach
Gay Club			
Lulu's Place	None	Inexp	Delray Beach
Live Music			
Blue Martini	None	Exp	West Palm Beach
City Hall Bar & Grill	None	Mod	West Palm Beach
Dakotah 624	None	Mod	Delray Beach
Lounge			
Leopard Lounge	None	Mod	Palm Beach
Singles Bars			
Blue Martini	None	Exp	West Palm Beach
Pete's	None	Mod	Boca Raton

CLUB PROFILES

The big action primarily takes place in two areas: Delray Beach's Atlantic Avenue and West Palm Beach's Clematis Street. However, the new City-Place has a few new hotspots.

BLUE ANCHOR BRITISH PUB

Lively British pub
Who Goes There: Brits and their fanciers, mostly singles

804 East Atlantic Avenue, Delray Beach; (561) 272-7272

Cover: None
Minimum: None
Mixed drinks: During weekday happy
hour until 7 p.m.: $1.75, then $3.25–4.50
Wine: Happy hour $3, then $3.25–4

Beer: Happy hour $2.75, then $3.75–7.25; 17 draught beers on tap
Food available: Limey foods like shepherd's pie or fish and chips, but Yanks also find salads and burgers.
Hours: Daily, 11:30 a.m.–2 a.m.

What goes on: Live music holds the fort Wednesday–Sunday, including a Texas blues band, contemporary jazz, and classic R&B.

Comments: Known as a good neighborhood place (like the corner pub), the 1865-era facade of English oak and stained glass was imported from a pub called the Blue Anchor on London's Chancery Lane, off Fleet Street. The interior reeks of dark wood paneling and beams, antiques, and old ship models. Unfortunately, customers complain they often must push through the smoke of the puffers.

BLUE MARTINI

Newest singles hangout
Who Goes There: Professionals ages 25–late 40s

CityPlace, West Palm Beach; (561) 835-8601

Cover: None
Minimum: None
Mixed drinks: $5.75 and up
Martinis: $11 and up
Wine: $7 and up

Beer: $4.25 and up
Food available: Finger foods: shrimp cocktails, miniature pizzas, fruit, and cheese.
Hours: Sunday–Thursday, 4 p.m.–3 a.m.; Friday and Saturday, 1 p.m.–4 a.m.

What goes on: Live music, such as top-40 tunes, Wednesday–Sunday, 7:30–11:30 p.m.

Comments: The latest hotspot in the Palm Beaches. It's mahogany paneled and features a bar made from milky onyx, which is lit from beneath. Modern paintings dot the walls, and live trees provide greenery. Attire is semi-dressy: collared shirts are required for men, but khaki pants are acceptable; ladies often sport dressy pants suits. No hats, tennis shoes, or cut-offs; jackets not required.

CITY HALL BAR & GRILL

THE spot for all types, young and not so young
Who Goes There: Straight and gay

319 Clematis Street, West Palm Beach; (561) 802-1777

Cover: None
Minimum: None
Mixed drinks: $5.50 and up
Wine: $6 and up
Beer: $4.25 and up
Food available: Full restaurant with

American fare, including steaks, seafood, and hamburgers.
Hours: Sunday–Wednesday, 5 p.m.–midnight; Thursday–Saturday, 5 p.m.–2 a.m.

What goes on: Lots of loud music provided by DMX, ranging from jazz to swing to hip hop and all stops between, for listening not dancing.

Comments: Happy hour 4–7 p.m. provides $1 drink discounts, starting the action early. Don't expect a staid, governmental building; decor is contemporary and uses rich tones of burgundy and gold; the dark wood bar is backed by stained glass outlining liquor bottles. There are also two pool tables in the back. Dress is casual.

DAKOTAH 624

Restaurant-cum-nightclub at 11 p.m.
Who Goes There: 30–60-something single yuppies

270 East Atlantic Avenue, Delray Beach; (561) 274-6244

Cover: None
Minimum: None
Mixed drinks: $5 and up; martinis $7 and up
Wine: $6 and up
Beer:$4.75 and up
Food available: Full restaurant offers New

American cuisine utilizing local ingredients, such as macadamia-crusted dolphin, and often with a Southern influence.
Hours: Sunday, 4–11 p.m.; Monday–Wednesday, 4 p.m.–1 a.m.; Thursday–Saturday, 4 p.m.–2 a.m.

What goes on: One of three DJs spins Thursday–Saturday 11 p.m.–2 a.m. Blues and dance music is featured; sometimes one DJ plays top 40 selections on the sax.

Comments: The spot is decorated in warm tones of butterscotch and caramel, with trompe l'oeil swags and sconces. Dakotah claims to be the area's first establishment to have a martini bar (five years ago, says owner Renee Ratabaum); its popularity has grown and it now offers 75 different martini choices. The most popular is the traditional martini, although 12–15 olive choices are offered as enhancement. Nontraditional types choose chocolate martinis.

LEOPARD LOUNGE

Classic Palm Beach watering hole
Who Goes There: Palm Beachers, internationals, and celebrities, both
singles and couples: Rod Stewart, Ben Vereen, Andy Rooney, and
Lorenzo Lamas—even the Kennedy kids—have been spotted.

The Chesterfield Hotel, 363 Cocoanut Row, Palm Beach; (561) 659-5800

Cover: None
Minimum: $5
Mixed drinks: $6–8, martinis $9; check
out cognac and cigar menu: servings
run from "affordable" $8 for some
single-malt Scotch up to $125 for
Louis XIII by Remy Martin.
Wine: $6

Beer: $5–6
Food available: An adjacent dining room
serves steaks and nut-crusted fish; more
casual items are available in the lounge;
true to the hotel's British influence, fish
and chips are available.
Hours: Daily, 5 p.m.–1 a.m.

What goes on: A mix of couples and singles hit the dance floor—which
lights up as areas are trod upon—to the accompaniment of a pianist, classical guitarist, or vocalist nightly. A younger crowd hangs out during the
nightly happy hour (5–7 p.m.), when drinks are half-price and complimentary hors d'oeuvres are served.

Comments: Though the hotel is charmingly British-flavored, the Leopard
Lounge decor is, well, jungly. The carpet is leopard-spotted, as is the ceiling-
height border, although the hand-painted fresco spotlights sensual frolicking
nymphettes. No jeans or shorts are permitted, and jackets are suggested for
gentlemen. Young Palm Beach kids dress in preppy style; older guests—
many with trophy wives—are more dressed up, particularly in season. Much
later, the youngsters return. There's complimentary valet parking.

THE LIQUID ROOM

Dance club, regular clientele, straight and gay, who go for the music
Who Goes There: 25–35-year-old professionals, Palm Beachers

313 Clematis Street, West Palm Beach; (561) 655-2332

Cover: $10
Minimum: None
Mixed drinks: $7 and up
Wine: $6 and up
Beer: $4 and up
Food available: Food from neighboring

restaurants includes fish dips, cheeses,
skewered filet mignon bits, and
vegetables.
Hours: Thursday–Saturday, 10 p.m.–
4 a.m.

What goes on: Dark wood paneling and crystal chandeliers set the tone. There's a VIP Room for bottle service (meaning customers buy alcohol by the bottle).

Comments: Habitués praise the DJs who play house music to get them up on the dance floor. Strobe lights, bubble machines, and smoke machines add to the sizzle and pop.

LULU'S PLACE

Largely gay piano bar—straighter early in the evening
Who Goes There: During happy hour, 4–8 p.m., mostly 40–70-year-olds; later a younger crowd

640 East Atlantic Avenue, Delray Beach; (561) 278-4004

Cover: None
Minimum: None
Mixed drinks: $2.50 and up
Wine: $4 and up; during happy hour $2
Beer: $2–3
Food available: Connected to two restau-rants next door. Menus are available and food, such as hamburgers and salads, is brought in.
Hours: Sunday and Tuesday–Thursday, 4 p.m.–1 a.m.; Friday and Saturday, 4 p.m.–2 a.m.

What goes on: Taped music provides melodies during happy hour. At 8 p.m., it becomes a piano bar, with baby grands both inside and outside in the courtyard; sometimes a drummer provides percussion or a small band jazzes.

Comments: In this friendly, upscale place featuring trompe l'oeil columns and ivy and an oak bar, people often get up to perform with the pianist. Sometimes tables are moved around when people feel the need to dance. And TVs are everywhere—but aren't tuned to sports events.

PETE'S

One of the hottest singles' spots around
Who Goes There: Singles aged 35 and up, including attractively dressed Boca-type seniors

7940 Glades Road in Parkway Center, Boca Raton; (561) 487-1600

Cover: None
Minimum: None
Mixed drinks: $5.25–7
Wine: $6.50–9.50
Beer: $4.50–5

Food available: Full-scale restaurant attached with lakeside view serves American-continental food with strong Italian overtones; see Pete's profile under Dining and Restaurants.

Hours: Entertainment at bar area runs nightly, 9 p.m.–1 a.m., somewhat reduced in summer.

What goes on: Nightly live entertainment in the form of a combo (and sometimes a vocalist) performing adult contemporary and Top 40 music for dancing.

Comments: This lively "meat rack" hosts hundreds nightly, often with 300 guests on Saturday, Sunday, and Tuesday nights. Tuesday is ladies' night, when females receive gifts such as a bottle of wine, hair treatments, and even a $100 dinner at the attached restaurant. The recipe works: lots of permanent relationships result, with couples who met at Pete's returning to celebrate a 10th anniversary. Dress is upscale casual, with jackets suggested for men.

Part Four

Broward County

Introduction

Greater Fort Lauderdale, the area of Broward County visited by most tourists and business travelers, is also known as the "Venice of America" as well as the "Yachting Capital of the World." Fort Lauderdale has more than 300 miles of waterways. It is a universally recognized warm-weather destination, offering a variety of activities from cultural events to some outstanding golf courses.

If you have the impression that the area is a wonderland for water lovers, you are absolutely correct. Broward County stretches 23 miles along the Atlantic Ocean between Palm Beach County on the north and Miami-Dade County on the south. Broward's western boundary is 505,600 acres of Everglades (occupying about two-thirds of the county). In all, Broward County encompasses 1,197 square miles.

More than 1.5 million people live in Broward, with 150,000 in Fort Lauderdale, the county's largest municipality and the seat of government. Thirty municipalities make up Greater Fort Lauderdale. Oceanfront communities include Hallandale, Hollywood, Dania Beach, Fort Lauderdale, Lauderdale-By-The-Sea, Lighthouse Point, Pompano Beach, Hillsboro Beach, Sea Ranch Lakes, and Deerfield Beach. Dania Beach, a small community between Fort Lauderdale and Hollywood, was once the country's tomato capital. Located just south of Fort Lauderdale/Hollywood International Airport, Dania Beach is famous for its Antiques Row (along US 1) with a marvelous collection of antique jewelry, furniture, and housewares.

Divers who explore Greater Fort Lauderdale's artificial reefs will encounter a variety of sea life. Captain Jim Mims, owner of Ocean Diving in Pompano Beach, says Broward County's artificial reef program is achieving its goals of rebuilding and augmenting the underwater ecosystem and

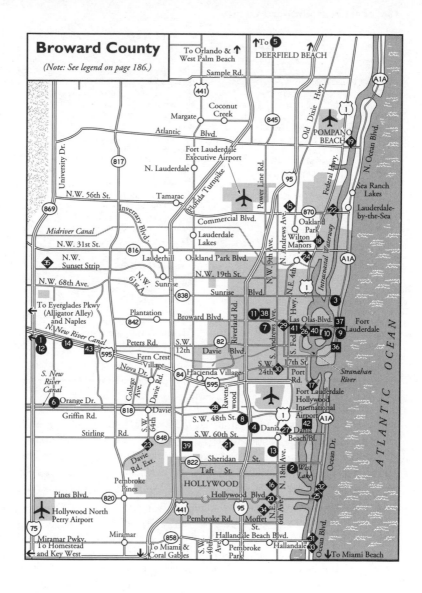

Broward County

(Note: See legend on page 186.)

To Orlando & West Palm Beach

To DEERFIELD BEACH

Sample Rd.

Margate

Coconut Creek

Atlantic Blvd.

Fort Lauderdale Executive Airport

N. Lauderdale

Tamarac

Commercial Blvd.

University Dr.

N.W. 56th St.

Midriver Canal

N.W. 31st St.

Lauderdale Lakes

Inverrary Blvd.

N.W. Sunset Strip

N.W. 68th Ave.

Lauderhill

Oakland Park Blvd.

N.W. 19th St.

Sunrise

Sunrise Blvd.

Plantation

Broward Blvd.

To Everglades Pkwy (Alligator Alley) and Naples

N. New River Canal

Peters Rd.

S.W. 12th

Davie Blvd.

S. New River Canal

Fern Crest Village

Nova Dr.

Orange Dr.

Hacienda Village

Griffin Rd.

Davie

Stirling Rd.

Ravenswood

S.W. 48th St.

Dania

Pembroke Pines

S.W. 60th St.

Sheridan St.

Taft St.

HOLLYWOOD

Pines Blvd.

Hollywood Blvd.

Hollywood North Perry Airport

Miramar Pkwy

To Homestead and Key West

Miramar

Pembroke Rd.

Moffet St.

Hallandale Beach Blvd.

To Miami & Coral Gables

Pembroke Park

Hallandale

Power Line Rd.

Old Dixie Hwy.

POMPANO BEACH

Federal Hwy.

N. Ocean Blvd.

Sea Ranch Lakes

Lauderdale-by-the-Sea

Oakland Park

Wilton Manors

Intracoastal Waterway

Riverland Rd.

N. Andrews Ave.

N.W. 9th Ave.

N.E. 4th

Las Olas Blvd.

Fort Lauderdale

S. Fed. Hwy.

Stranahan River

Port Rd.

Fort Lauderdale Hollywood International Airport

Ocean Dr.

Dania Beach/Bl.

West Lake

Ocean Blvd.

To Miami Beach

ATLANTIC OCEAN

Broward County

ATTRACTIONS

1. Ah-Tah-Thi-Ki Museum
2. Anne Kolb Nature Center
3. Bonnet House
4. Boomer's/Dania Beach Hurricane
5. Butterfly World
6. Flamingo Gardens
7. Fort Lauderdale Historical Museum
8. International Game Fish Association Fishing Hall of Fame & Museum
9. International Swimming Hall of Fame
10. Jungle Queen Riverboat
11. Museum of Discovery & Science/ Blockbuster IMAX 3D Theater
12. Sawgrass Recreation Park
13. South Florida Museum of Natural History
14. Young at Art

RESTAURANTS

15. Aruba Beach Café
16. Bavarian Village
17. Burt and Jack's
18. By Word of Mouth
19. Cafe Maxx
20. Christina Wan's
21. Deli Den
22. Eduardo de San Angel
23. Fulvio's
24. Gibby's Steaks & Seafood
25. Giorgio's
26. Grill Room on Las Olas
27. Islamorada Fish Company
28. Le Petit Café
29. Left Bank
30. Lester's Diner
31. Manero's Steakhouse
32. Oasis by the Sea
33. Padrino's
34. Try My Thai
35. Wolfgang Puck Grand Cafe

NIGHTCLUBS

36. Bahia Cabana
37. Cathode Ray Cocktail Lounge
38. Chili Pepper
39. Dinopetes
40. Howl at the Moon
41. O'Hara's Jazz Club
42. Tugboat Annie's
43. Uncle Funny's

renewing both the fish and coral life of the area. "It's now common to see angel fish, sergeant majors, sea turtles, octopus, butterflyfish, barracudas——even such large fish as sails and tuna. Many aspects of Greater Fort Lauderdale appeal to divers, whether they're exploring our underwater life or taking in the sights topside. The reef is a 20-minute boat trip, air service is frequent and economical, and there is much to do between dives."

Fort Lauderdale was a "Spring Break" destination for years, a place where young people partied around the clock and tourism honchos and hoteliers developed heartburn after wet T-shirt contests found their way to national television. At its heyday in 1985, Spring Break attracted more than 350,000 college students to the area, and it was definitely a Maalox Moment for locals. By 2000 the crowd of Spring Breakers was down to about 10,000, and tourists were arriving from the Northern and Midwest United States, Canada, Europe, and South America to enjoy the sun and fun as an adult and a family destination. Gay and lesbian travelers have also found the Fort Lauderdale area an attractive destination. These visitors, for the most part, are family-oriented and/or business travelers who enjoy the tropical climate and average year-round temperature of 77 degrees (23 Celsius). More than seven million tourists visited last year, the tenth year of steady increase.

Greater Fort Lauderdale boasts the second-highest hotel occupancy in the state (Orlando and the mighty mouse, Disney World rank number one). Nicki E. Grossman, president and CEO of the Greater Fort Lauderdale Convention & Visitors Bureau, says "the numbers tell the story. Greater Fort Lauderdale has more to offer its visitors and its citizens than a six-week binge with wall-to-wall people and bumper-to-bumper cars." She adds, "we expect visitor growth to increase." In recent years, there's been a boom in tourism, population, housing, job growth, and commercial real estate development, and $2 billion has been invested in tourism and recreation-relation programs in Greater Fort Lauderdale. Ground was broken in early 2001 for a $300 million Seminole Hard Rock Hotel & Resort, and the 1,000-room, 39-story Diplomat Resort will reopen summer 2001, while a four-star, $470 million Convention Center Hotel will open late in 2002.

A Brief History

Broward County was, for many years, a bedroom community for Miami workers. More suburban in setting, the area began to attract migrants from the Northeast and Midwest and former members of the military who had trained in the area during World War II. Many Georgians and Alabamans also settled in the region. While originally Broward was—like Miami Beach to the south—a community of retirees, current statistics indicate the average age of residents is now under 40.

The traditional pattern of migration to Florida's Southeast coast included a core group of people from the Northeast. Boston, New York, New Jersey, Philadelphia, Washington, D.C., and Baltimore retirees and families settled in communities along the Atlantic Ocean, primarily in Miami and Miami Beach. Although most Midwesterners opted for (and still choose) the Southwest Coast of Florida over the Southeast Coast, some chose the small-town feel of Broward County. Many of those migrating south were Jewish: some who had escaped from Hitler's Germany, some who had come out of concentration camps, and others who were first-generation American. All sought a better life and the promise of a fine climate and sunshine year-round.

Stuart Newman, founder and president of Stuart Newman Associates, a Miami public relations firm, was two years old when his parents moved from Chicago to Coral Gables in 1925. Two years later, the family moved up to Fort Lauderdale, where his father managed a shoe shop. His father, Abe, became the first president of Temple Emanuel, Fort Lauderdale's first synagogue, and he also became a member of a businessmen's group. When the group met at a beachfront hotel, Abe refused to attend because a sign out front said "no dogs or Jews allowed."

Of course, restrictions like those were lifted many years ago, and Fort Lauderdale has come a long way in 75 years. A hundred varieties of bagels are now available at dozens of bagel shops and delis throughout the area. More seriously, a rich Jewish cultural life supports some three dozen synagogues, Hebrew day schools, and Hebrew social service agencies throughout Broward County.

Today the area is also home to many Caribbean-basin immigrants who have settled in Fort Lauderdale's western suburbs, coming from island nations to seek that same "better life." After Hurricane Andrew struck South Dade County in 1992, many residents chose to move to Broward and begin anew. A large Hispanic population now resides in the county.

Broward County Today

So what do we have at the dawn of the new millennium? We have a vibrant community—including a business community that can hold its own with other centers in the South. Numerous residential villages dot the landscape from the ocean to the Everglades, and world-class shopping opportunities and cultural offerings range from Andrea Bocelli to Elton John.

Redevelopment and renewal projects—Broward's answer to the popularity of South Beach—have prompted a revitalized area in downtown Hollywood, with galleries and restaurants attracting people from as far away as South Miami and Palm Beach. Downtown Fort Lauderdale has become a center of fine dining opportunities, home to the Broward Center for the Performing Arts (and with it the Florida Philharmonic), and some outstanding museums. Realtors have rediscovered the popularity of these older communities with the addition of all the new amenities that have made them attractive to younger buyers. Finally, property values are somewhat lower in Broward than in Miami-Dade or Palm Beach.

And sports? Broward has 'em all! The state-of-the-art National Car Rental Center in Sunrise is home to the Florida Panthers hockey team. And just over the line in Miami-Dade is the home of Dolphins pro football and Florida Marlins pro baseball. The Fusion major league soccer team plays at Lockhart Stadium in Fort Lauderdale. Fort Lauderdale Stadium is where the Baltimore Orioles have their spring training season.

Where once the whole area seemed to close up shop in the summer months, today cultural offerings are on tap year-round at venues including Sunrise Musical Theater, Parker Playhouse, and Broward Center, where some of the world's best entertainers perform.

And whether you shop at Bloomingdale's or Saks, at Target or Nordstrom's, Broward has it all, as well as Sawgrass Mills, the country's largest outlet mall.

This mixed bag of shopping opportunities is reflected in housing as well. The county has an eclectic array of neighborhoods—some have million-dollar residences, while others offer more affordable homes. While the growth of the last several decades hasn't always included things like neighborhood parks or sufficient school buildings, Broward's quality-of-life ratio is improving all the time.

However, public transportation still leaves much to be desired, and Broward County residents drive everywhere (as traveling any cross-town road will reveal soon enough), but we think it's fairly easy to get around the area by car. Consider the county is bounded on one side by the Atlantic Ocean and the other by the Everglades. The northern boundary is Palm Beach County, while Miami-Dade marks the southern.

Arriving

While many travelers still choose to make the trek to Florida by automobile, most people fly into Broward County, to the Fort Lauderdale/Hollywood International Airport. In fact, many visitors going to Florida's Southwest Coast or Miami opt to fly into Fort Lauderdale/Hollywood International Airport because it's more user-friendly, and, specifically in the case of the Fort Myers area, airfares are often cheaper.

Some visitors arrive on cruise ships and spend a few days in the region. Port Everglades is just minutes away from the airport and is the second-largest cruise port in the world, serving more five-star cruise ships than any other port in the country. Among the lines serving Port Everglades are Celebrity, Costa, Crystal, Cunard, Discovery, Holland America, Princess, Radisson Seven Seas, Royal Caribbean, Royal Olympic, Seabourn, Sea-Escape, and Silversea.

Taxi service is available both at the airport and the cruise port.

By Plane

The bulk of Fort Lauderdale's tourism is made up of people who fly in from other parts of the world. The Fort Lauderdale/Hollywood International Airport is located between I-95 on the east and US 1 on the west, and between Griffin Road on the south and State Road 84 on the north. The airport is served by most major airlines, including the following domestic carriers: Air Canada, AirTran, America West, American, American Trans Air, Continental, Delta, Delta Express, JetBlue, MetroJet, Midway,

Midwest Express, Northwest, Southwest, Spirit, TWA, United, USAirways, USAirways Express. The airport is undergoing an expansion project that is estimated to cost about $1 billion by the year 2012, more than doubling the airport's passenger capacity from 11 million in 1996 to 25 million by 2015. It is a comfortable, easy-to-use airport, well marked and well lighted.

After leaving the airport, tourists work their way east to the Atlantic Ocean, west to the suburbs, north to Palm Beach, or south to Miami-Dade. While many local Fort Lauderdale-area hotels offer shuttle service from the airport (telephone hookups are available on the airport's lower level across from the baggage carousels), taxi service and rental cars are also available at the airport (car lots are nearby, but off the airport grounds). Rental cars serving the airport and cruise port are Alamo, Avis, Budget, Dollar, Enterprise, Hertz, National, Snappy, Thompson, Thrifty, and Value.

By Car

The most direct route to Fort Lauderdale Beach is to exit the airport onto US 1 North. Head *north* on US 1 (it is also called Federal Highway) to the 17th Street Causeway (which is also 17th Street). Turn right. This is one of the major beach-access roads, and traffic is always heavy. Drive carefully. You will pass over a bridge (which spans the Intracoastal Waterway). The road turns north at AIA.

If your destination is, for example, Hollywood Beach, Aventura, or North Miami Beach's strip of hotels, motels, and condos, take US 1 *south.* To reach Hollywood Beach, turn left onto Dania Beach Boulevard, passing Dania Jai Alai, and winding up on A1A. If you continue south on US 1 (be forewarned, you'll meet with heavy traffic), you will in fact pass the Aventura/Turnberry complex—and the Aventura mega-shopping mall with Bloomingdale's, Macy's, Sears, and JC Penney among the many stores. When you reach the Lehman Causeway (named for a former well-known and respected state legislator), turn left. You will be heading east toward the ocean. The view is merely spectacular, and traffic flows well most of the day. Don't let the fact that the highway is called 188th Street in Aventura and exits by the ocean at 192nd Street throw you. It just goes with the territory.

Because the traffic on US 1 can be stop and go, we offer an alternative to getting to Aventura or North Miami. Head south on US 1, turn left at Dania Beach Boulevard, and continue south on A1A. To return inland to Aventura, stay in the right-hand lane at Lehman Causeway (remember that it is 192nd Street) back to US 1 (Federal Highway).

If you're headed to the western area, follow the signs to I-595 and cut through Broward County to Cooper City, Sunrise, Plantation, or half a dozen other western suburbs. I-595 ultimately leads to I-75, the highway to Florida's Gulf Coast. You will pass community after community of townhomes, condominium apartments, and single-family dwellings. Many are country club communities and range from middle-class to extremely upwardly mobile. You will also pass an eclectic mix of strip malls.

An alternative to I-595 is to take an east-west road such as Griffin or Stirling west to Pine Island and head north to Sunrise, Plantation, etc.

South to Miami-Dade

Many people choose to fly into the Fort Lauderdale/Hollywood Airport rather than Miami International Airport because it is much more user-friendly. We, in fact, suggest you consider doing just that even if you have reservations in Miami or Miami Beach. Maybe either Coral Gables or Coconut Grove is your ultimate destination. In that case, follow the signs to I-595, then onto I-95 south.

BY BUS AND TRAIN

Greyhound Bus Lines and TriRail service Fort Lauderdale and Hollywood. Greyhound provides inter-city bus service. The main station is located at 515 NE Third Street, Fort Lauderdale; (954) 763-6551. More than 15 buses a day travel between Fort Lauderdale and Miami-Dade (many stop in Hollywood). Service starts at 7:50 a.m., and the last bus runs at 11:30 p.m. TriRail offers train service from Palm Beach County through Broward County and into Miami-Dade to Miami International Airport. Its main station is located at 205 South Andrews Avenue, Fort Lauderdale; (954) 357-8400 or (800) TriRail. TriRail runs frequently throughout the day but less often on weekends. Both the Greyhound and TriRail stations are in marginal areas of town but are patrolled regularly. Be careful and avoid traveling alone at night.

Getting Around

DRIVING YOUR CAR

Probably the best advice we can provide anyone choosing to rent a car and drive in South Florida (or anywhere, for that matter) is to request driving instructions from your hotel, motel, or host. Let them know where you will be picking up a car (Fort Lauderdale/Hollywood International Airport, Port Everglades, etc.) and get complete directions to the property.

Speed limits vary throughout South Florida: 30 mph is common in congested areas, around hotels, or heavily populated neighborhoods; 40 or 45 mph in others; and 65 or 70 mph on the Turnpike. Florida has a seat-belt law requiring everyone to be buckled up.

Many South Florida roadways have two names. US 1, for example, is also called Federal Highway. It runs from Maine down to Key West. When used in these pages, we've added the name of the nearest municipality.

Some cities, Fort Lauderdale, Dania Beach, Hallandale Beach, Pembroke Pines, for example, use a NW, NE, SW, SE pattern of street numbers from a core point in the city. Let's look at Fort Lauderdale. The intersection of Broward Boulevard and Andrews Avenue is effectively ground zero. North of Broward, addresses include "N" followed by an "E" or "W" denoting the direction east or west of Andrews. Streets, terraces, and courts generally run east and west. Avenues run north and south. This is not a hard and fast rule. Some streets run on an angle, start out east and west, then turn north or south. We suggest a good map as a traveling companion.

Broward County's major north-south arteries are: AIA, also called Ocean Drive (which runs along the Atlantic Ocean, except for a short run in Fort Lauderdale and Dania Beach where John U. Lloyd Beach State Recreation Area runs inland from the beach); US 1; I-95, a classic interstate with on-off ramps and the requisite fast-food outlets, gas stations, and strip malls; US 441 (also called State Road 7), a slow-going road lined with auto show-rooms, garages, chain restaurants, and seemingly perpetual construction; the Florida Turnpike, also called the Ronald Reagan Expressway; and University Drive, the major roadway toward suburbia and the towns west of Fort Lauderdale and Hollywood. East-west traffic is most heavy on I-595, a relatively new highway connecting the airport (and seaport) to the western suburbs. Major north-south arteries in western Broward include Pine Island Road, Nob Hill Road, Hiatus Road, and Flamingo Road. East-west streets that many tourists travel include:

Hallandale Beach Boulevard Also called State Road 858, from the Atlantic Ocean (at the east end) to University Drive (at the west) through Hallandale, Hollywood, and Miramar. In Miramar, the road becomes Miramar Parkway.

Hollywood Boulevard Also called State Road 820 to points west, from the Atlantic Ocean to the Everglades through Hollywood and Pembroke Pines. This becomes Pines Boulevard at University Drive.

Sheridan Street From the ocean to the Everglades, through Dania Beach, Hollywood, Cooper City, and Pembroke Pines. Oddly enough, it stays as Sheridan Street throughout.

Stirling Road Also called State Road 848. From US 1 west to the Everglades, through Dania Beach, Hollywood, Pembroke Lakes, Cooper City, and Davie.

Griffin Road   Also Called State Road 818. From US 1 west to the Everglades, through Dania Beach, Fort Lauderdale, Hollywood, Cooper City, and Davie, onward to Weston.

State Road 84   From Port Everglades, connects with I-595, toward Weston, through Fort Lauderdale.

Broward Boulevard   Also called State Road 842. West from US 1 to Pine Island Drive.

Sunrise Boulevard   Also called State Road 838. From the Atlantic Ocean west to Sawgrass Mills Mall, through Fort Lauderdale, Plantation, and Sunrise.

Oakland Park Boulevard   Also called State Road 816. From the ocean west through Fort Lauderdale and Sunrise.

Commercial Boulevard   Also called State Road 870, this road runs east and west from Ocean to Sunrise.

Pay Attention

Because you are most likely traveling new roadways, be very careful. Remember there are many other drivers unfamiliar with these highways. Just note the license plates on the cars you pass—New Jersey, Quebec, Ohio, Texas, New York, Indiana, Louisiana, Mississippi. They're all exploring new roads just as you are.

Use your turn signals. Stay in the left lane unless you are passing. One state, Virginia, recently passed a law requiring drivers to stay out of the left lane unless passing, and it makes great sense to us. Avoid a heavy hand on the horn—flash your high beams instead. Road rage is a fact of life today, and South Florida's tropical climate seems to exacerbate tempers. We suggest using hand signals that are socially acceptable, and avoiding all others. If another driver lets you into a line of traffic, signal your thanks. (Driving, like everything else mother told you, includes the use of "please" and "thank you.")

Most traffic accidents today seem to involve using cell phones while driving, speeding, or running red lights. Be cautious in all situations and keep your wits about you whenever you are behind the wheel.

PUBLIC TRANSPORTATION

Broward County Mass Transit offers bus service that works, though not especially well. There are more than 230 buses serving all of Broward (phone (954) 357-8400).

TriRail offers regularly scheduled train service between Palm Beach, Broward, and Miami-Dade Counties with stops throughout Broward (phone (800) 874-7245).

The Water Taxi of Fort Lauderdale is another mode of transportation that crisscrosses the Intracoastal Waterway on Fort Lauderdale's canals (phone (954) 728-8417). This a great way to get from one point to another and also a terrific way to get up close and personal with some of Fort Lauderdale's primo real estate.

Gathering Information

Greater Fort Lauderdale Convention & Visitors Bureau, 19850 Eller Drive, Suite 303, Fort Lauderdale, FL 33316; (800)-22-SUNNY x711 (in U.S. and Canada), and www.sunny.org on the web. A free CD-ROM with information about local dive sites is also available. There are numerous GFLCVB branch offices throughout the U.S. and elsewhere:

Alexandria (Washington, D.C.)
1800 Diagonal Road, Suite 130
Alexandria, VA 22314
(703) 684-0456; fax (703) 684-6848

Chicago
226 Homewood Avenue
Libertyville, IL 60048
(847) 247-9727; fax (847) 247-9728

Newport, RI
61 Homer Street
Newport, RI 02840
(401) 849-1515; fax (401) 849-1615

Canada
249 Cossack Court
Mississauga, Ontario L5B 4C2

(905) 276-6436; toll free (888) 834-4401; fax (905) 276-6488

Germany
Mangum Management GmbH
Herzogspitalstrasse 5
80331 Munich, Germany
011-49-89-23662133 or 011-49-89-2633210; fax 011-49-89-2604009

United Kingdom
Contact Travel Marketing Ltd.
21 Broadway
Maidenhead, Berks SL6 1NJ
011-44-1628 778863; fax 011-44-1628 676798

The Beaches

Washington-based Clean Beaches Council, the first national environmental beach certification in the United States, recently named Greater Fort Lauderdale beaches as Blue Wave Beaches—defined as safe, clean, and user-friendly beaches. Hollywood, Dania, Fort Lauderdale, Pompano, and Deerfield Beaches are the state's only beaches to qualify.

All beaches receiving the award have Blue Wave flags, public information kiosks, and beach-entrance boundary markers. Greater Fort Lauderdale has also been named one of the top diving destinations in the country.

Hollywood Beach is popular because of its Broadwalk (cq) running parallel to the ocean and dozens of little restaurants, many French in origin and geared to the French-Canadian tourists who winter in the area. It's a good family beach with many lifeguard stations.

Fort Lauderdale Beach is crowded, and images from *Where the Boys Are* are still around, but it's also another popular family favorite with plenty of lifeguard stations.

Deerfield Beach is much less crowded, but restaurants and cafes aren't as plentiful as along Hollywood or Fort Lauderdale Beaches.

Wherever you have beaches you have parking problems. Weekends are especially crowded, so we suggest metered parking or parking lots/garages. Don't try to park on the street. It could be a very costly day at the beach. Of course, if your hotel is on the ocean, walking to the beach is a nice option.

Recreation

FITNESS CENTERS AND AEROBICS

Many hotels today have air-conditioned state-of-the-art fitness centers and/or aerobics classes, eliminating the challenge of working out in the heat. Independent gym chains also have facilities that similarly allow you to feel the burn without burning up. If you can't work out in your hotel, here are some local options. **Gold's Gym Fitness and Aerobic Center** (1427 East Commercial Boulevard, Fort Lauderdale; (954) 491-8314) is a full service gym. Daily fees are $15. **Bally Total Fitness** (750 West Sunrise Boulevard, downtown Fort Lauderdale; (954) 764-8666) is another full service health club. Daily rates vary. Membership at other chain locations is honored here. **Club Body Tech** (1955 Harrison Street, Hollywood; (954) 929-2639) is a strictly local outfit with a day rate of $10. All of the above clubs are comparable in quality; just pick the location nearest you.

WALKING

Unlike New York, Chicago, or London, walking isn't popular in Broward. We don't see a lot of people walking to pick up a loaf of bread or their dry cleaning. This is strip-mall city, with mall after mall and parking lot after parking lot waiting for South Floridians to perform their errands.

However, those who want to walk for the aerobics involved can find a variety of venues: one of the prettiest is along the ocean on Hollywood Beach. The Hollywood Broadwalk (cq) runs north and south from just north of Sheridan Street to Washington Street, a distance of about four miles. Area high schools allow walkers to use their tracks when school is out. Many walkers opt to stroll through air-conditioned malls, and Broward Mall at University Drive and Broward Boulevard is a case in point. Many of the parks and attractions mentioned elsewhere also have nature trails.

RUNNING

Jogging tracks are available at **McTyre Park** (3501 SW 56th Avenue, Pembroke Park; (954) 964-0283); **North Broward Park** (4400 NE 18th Avenue, Pompano Beach; (954) 796-2195); **Brian Piccolo Park** (9501 Sheridan Street, Cooper City; (954) 437-2600); **Plantation Heritage Park** (1100 South Fig Tree Lane, Plantation; (954) 791-1025); and **Tradewinds** Park (3600 West Sample Road, Coconut Creek; (954) 968-3880).

TENNIS

If your hotel doesn't have tennis courts, don't worry, there are more than 550 public and private courts throughout Broward County. Consider the place where tennis champ Chris Evert did her thing, the **James Evert** (James is her dad) **Tennis Center** (701 NE 12th Avenue, Fort Lauderdale; (954) 828-5378) with 18 clay courts and 3 hard courts. Hours are Monday–Friday, 7:45 a.m.–9 p.m.; Saturday and Sunday, 7:45 a.m.–7 p.m. Fees are $3.50 for doubles and $4.50 for singles.

Free public courts in Fort Lauderdale can be found at **Bay View Park** (4400 Bay View Drive, between Oakland Park Boulevard and Sunrise Boulevard); **Hardy Park** (Andrews Avenue and SW 7th Street); and **Riverside Park** (500 SW 11th Avenue). All are open from 8 a.m. to dusk and operate on a first-come, first-served basis. For more information, call the Fort Lauderdale Parks and Recreation Department at (954) 828-5346.

Hollywood's **David Park Tennis Center** (510 North 33rd Court, Hollywood; (954) 967-4237) has nine clay and three hard courts. Fees are $6 per person all day; light fees are $1 for every 15 minutes of play at night. Hours are Monday–Thursday, 7:30 a.m.–9 p.m.; Friday, 7:30 a.m.–8 p.m.; Saturday and Sunday, 7:30 a.m.–5 p.m. Lessons are available.

Free courts are available 8 a.m.–8 p.m. at Hollywood's **Jefferson Park** (Jefferson Street between 15th and 16th Avenues; (954) 921-3404). Visitors can enjoy free play daily 8 a.m.–9 p.m. at Hallandale's **Peter Bluesten Park** (501 SE 1st Avenue, Hallandale; (954) 457-1457) and **Oreste Blake Johnson Park** (745 NW 9th Street, Hallandale; (954) 457-1453).

GOLF

Golf is a year-round, 24/7 pastime in South Florida. Although the "tourist" season starts somewhere after Thanksgiving and runs through Easter, golf courses are always busy. During the week, it's possible to get in on a game with no-shows. Weekends—when local residents hit the links—are busy year-round, and ensuring a morning reservation is difficult. Plan on teeing off before 1 p.m. so you're not racing the sun. Sunset occurs around 5 p.m. in the middle of winter, closer to 8:30 p.m. in the summer.

Courses throughout South Florida have been designed by some of the greatest golfers and best-known course designers, including Arnold Palmer, Pete Dye, and George and Tom Fazio. South Florida golf courses meet varying skill levels. Summer months in South Florida are hot and humid. Reserve an early morning or late afternoon tee time and avoid the links between 11 a.m. and 2 p.m. Greens fees are reduced at many courses during the off-season. Book in advance through your hotel. Some of the best courses in Broward are profiled below.

Bonaventure Country Club

Established: 1969

Address: 200 Bonaventure Boulevard, Weston 33326

Phone: (954) 389-2100

Status: Semiprivate/resort course, open to the public

Tees: West Course:
> Championship: 6,189 yards, par 70, USGA 71, slope 118.
> Men's: 5,730 yards, par 70, USGA 70, slope 116.
> Ladies': 4,993 yards, par 70, USGA 69.0, slope 114.

> East Course: (Includes seniors' tees)
> Championship: 7,011 yards, par 72, USGA 74.2, slope 132.
> Men's: 6,549 yards, par 72, USGA 72.5, slope 127.
> Ladies': 5,304 yards, par 72, USGA , 71.6, 122.
> Seniors': 5,688 years, par 72, USGA 68.3, slope 117.

Fees: Monday–Thursday, $70 for West, $80 for East. Weekend rates are $10 higher, cart included.

Facilities: Pro shop, restaurant and lounge, banquet facilities for 150, lessons, equipment rental.

Comments: Two popular 18-hole courses in good shape, used year-round by locals and guests at nearby Wyndham Resort and Spa, which some may remember as Bonaventure.

Club at Emerald Hills

Established: 1968

Address: 4100 North Hills Drive, Hollywood 33021

Phone: (954) 961-4000

Status: Semiprivate course

Tees: Championship: 7,117 yards, par 72 , USGA 74.6, slope 142.
> Men's: 6,733 yards, par 72, USGA 72, slope 137.
> Ladies': 5,032 yards, par 72, USGA 70.1, slope 116.

Fees: $100–150 top of the season, $50–75 low end.

Facilities: Catering services, restaurant, pro shop.

Comments: Course was completely redone in 2000 and is considered a top course; qualifying course for Honda and Doral tournaments.

Colony West Country Club

Established: 1970

Address: 6800 NW 88th Avenue (Pine Island Avenue), Tamarac 33321

Phone: (954) 721-7710

Status: Public Course

Tees: Championship: 7,312 yards, par 71, USGA 75.5, slope 146.
Men's: 6,875 yards, par 71, USGA 73.7, slope 142.
Ladies': 6,420 yards, par 71, USGA 71.7, slope 135.

Glades Course:
Men's: 4,207 yards, par 71, USGA 59.3, slope 89.
Ladies: 3,855, par 71, USGA 58.2, slope 84.

Fees: $75 plus tax, includes cart.

Facilities: Pro shop, restaurant, snack bar, banquet capacity for 250, outdoor area for parties.

Comments: Cart required on Championship course, golfers can walk Glades course.

Diplomat Resort Country Club & Spa

Established: 2000

Address: 501 Diplomat Parkway, Hollywood 33009

Phone: (954) 883-4444

Status: Resort course

Tees: Championship: 6,728 yards, par 72 , USGA 71.9, slope 136.
Men's: 6,392 yards, par 72, USGA 71.3, slope 129.
Ladies': 5,351 yards, par 72 , USGA 71.4, slope 119.

Fees: $150 per day, includes cart.

Facilities: Country club complex, two restaurants, 60 guest rooms, meeting space and yacht slips, pro shop, and two air-conditioned convenience stations.

Comments: This beautiful course, redesigned by golf architect Joe Lee, is state-of-the-art.

Hollywood Beach Golf and Country Club

Established: 1923

Address: 1600 Johnson Street, Hollywood 33020

Phone: (954) 927-1751

Status: Public

Tees: Championship: 6,336 yards, par 70, USGA 70, slope 117.
Men's: 6,024 yards, par 70, USGA 70, slope 117.
Ladies': 5,484 yards, par 70, USGA 70, slope 117.

Fees: Vary by season; $39 winter, $24 summer, lower after 12:30 p.m.

Facilities: Pro shop, clubhouse restaurant, 35-room full-service hotel, locker rooms, pool.

Comments: Designed by Donald Ross in 1925 and completely renovated in 1995, with ongoing program of upgrading. It's a golfing tradition, made even more important because little existed in Hollywood prior to the 1920s.

Orangebrook Golf Club

Established: Early 1950s

Address: 400 Entrada Street, Hollywood 33021

Phone: (954) 967-4653

Status: Public

Tees: West Course:
Championship: 6,380 yards, par 71, USGA 70.7, slope 122.
Men's: 5,877 yards, par 71, USGA 69.1, slope 118.
Ladies': 4,988 yards, par 71, USGA 71.7, slope 123.

East Course:
Championship: 6,545 yards, par 71, USGA 71.3, slope 120.
Men's: 6,066 yards, par 71, USGA 69, slope 114.
Ladies': 5,493 yards, par 71, USGA 71.5, slope 119.

Fees: Vary by season; about $35 high season, $20 low season; includes cart.

Facilities: Pro shop, restaurant, lessons available.

Comments: One of Hollywood's oldest, most popular courses, just one-half mile west of I-95.

Pompano Beach Municipal Golf Course

Established: 1967

Address: 1101 North Federal Highway, Pompano Beach 33062

Phone: (954) 786-4142

Status: Public

Tees: Pines:
Championship: 6,886 yards, par 72, USGA 72.7, slope 120.
Men's: 6,577 yards, par 72, USGA 70.6, slope 116.

Ladies: 5,748 yards, par 72, USGA 69.1, slope 113.

Palms:
Championship: 6,366 yards, par 71, USGA 69.8, slope 113.
Men's: 6,129, par 71, USGA 68.6, slope 111.
Ladies': 5,397 yards, par 71, USGA 67.8, slope 109.

Fees: $30 to walk and $42 to share cart; afternoons, $21.50 to walk, $33.50 to share cart; $3 more weekends and holidays.

Facilities: Driving range, practice greens, restaurant and bar, locker rooms and showers, pro shop and instruction.

Comments: A recent $2 million renovation has improved the course. Carts are not required. Pines course is long, and Palms course, with more doglegs, requires "position golf."

Tournament Players Club at Heron Bay

Established: 1996

Address: 11801 Heron Bay, Coral Springs 33076

Phone: (954) 796-2000

Status: Public

Tees: Championship: 7,258 yards, par 72, USGA 74.9, slope 133.
Men's: 6,782 yards, par 72, USGA 72.7, slope 128.
Ladies': 5,580 yards, par 72, USGA 67.0, slope 114.

Fees: $55–125, includes cart.

Facilities: Golf shop, full service restaurant and lounge, locker rooms, club and shoe rentals.

Comments: This course is the permanent home of the Honda Classic.

BICYCLING

Broward County, like most of Florida, is flat. Bicycling is best done along the ocean or on park bike paths. Heavy South Florida traffic doesn't lend itself to road biking. One of the best places for biking along the ocean is the Broadwalk in Hollywood, where **Bike Shack** (101 North Ocean Drive/A1A, Hollywood; (954) 925-2453) rents equipment. Rentals are $5, and bikers must be 18 and have a driver's license. Other bicycling options are the Fort Lauderdale Beach, where in-line skaters also do their thing, and through a variety of parks in Broward County. Helmets are compulsory.

Mountain bikers might want to check out **Quiet Waters Park** in Pompano Beach for a moderate to challenging 5.5-mile loop. For more details, contact Quiet Waters Park (401 South Powerline Road; (954) 360-1315). For other nearby off-road options, see *Mountain Bike! Florida* by Steve Jones (Menasha Ridge Press; (800) 243-0495).

HIKING

Nature Trails at **Anne Kolb Nature Park** at **West Lake Park** (751 Sheridan Street, Hollywood; (954) 926-2410) are mapped out for hikers. Canoe rentals are also available, and don't miss a narrated boat tour through mangrove swamps.

Hiking/jogging paths are available at other Broward County parks, such as **Brian Piccolo Park** (9501 Sheridan Street, Cooper City; (954) 437-2800); **Plantation Heritage Park** (1100 South Fig Tree Lane, Plantation; (954) 791-1025); **Quiet Waters Park** (401 South Powerline Road, Pompano Beach; (954) 360-1315); and **T.Y. Park** (3300 North Park Road, Hollywood; (954) 985-1980). Other Broward County parks offer a variety of other activities from horseshoes (**Easterlin Park,** 100 NW 36th Street, Oakland Park; (954) 938-0610) to a target range and pro shop (**Markham Park and Range,** 16001 West State Road 84, Sunrise; (954) 389-2000).

For complete Broward County Parks and Recreation Division activities, call (954) 357-8100 or (954) 587-2844 (TTY).

CANOEING AND KAYAKING

Canoeing is offered at **Hugh Taylor Birch State Park** (3109 East Sunrise Boulevard, Fort Lauderdale; (954) 564-4521) and **Tree Tops Park** (3900 SW 100th Avenue, Davie; (954) 370-3750). Both canoeing and kayaking are available at **West Lake Park/Anne Kolb Nature Center** (751 Sheridan Street, Hollywood; (954) 926-2410).

SWIMMING

Hotel pools are not unique to South Florida, so let's address Broward County's biggest attraction: the Atlantic Ocean. Most popular are **Hollywood Beach** and **Fort Lauderdale Beach.** In Hollywood, the action spreads north and south from the Johnson Street Parking Garage (although metered parking exists, it's only the early bird who gets it) or north from Hollywood's **North Beach Park** at Sheridan Street and the ocean. There's a small pocket park, **Charnow Park,** with picnic tables, a Vita course, and playground.

Fort Lauderdale Beach, about seven blocks south of Las Olas, is one of the state's most identifiable beaches. Again, parking is often at a premium. The area at the foot of Sunrise and A1A is nothing but sun, sand, and water, and if you don't need the picnic area or a playground, you'll love it.

For general information on swimming, see Part One, pages 21–23.

SCUBA DIVING

More than a million people a year travel to the Florida Keys to scuba dive at the only coral reef in the continental U.S., but artificial reefs also attract divers—and fish.

When the *Mercedes,* a 197-foot German freighter, was tossed upon a Palm Beach pool terrace in 1985, it was big news and a nuisance to the Palm Beach milieu. Today it lies in 97 feet of water, just a mile from the Fort Lauderdale beach, a habitat for myriad coral growth and other marine life. Legend tells that it even plays home to a barracuda so accustomed to divers, it reputedly can be hand-fed—if you dare. On very clear days, the *Mercedes* can actually be seen from the dive boat on the surface.

The *Mercedes* has helped position the Greater Fort Lauderdale area as one of the best wreck diving destinations in either the U.S. or the Caribbean. Coral growth begins right away on sunken ships, and fish come to feed. Other wrecks include the *Atria,* a 240-foot freighter lying in 112 feet of water, and the *Marriot,* a DC-4 airplane in 71 feet.

Divers in the area use more than 80 different sites between artificial reefs and the 23-mile-long, one and one-half to two-mile wide Fort Lauderdale Reef, which marks the northern end of the ancient living coral formation that runs from Palm Beach down past the Florida Keys.

For general information on diving certification, see Part One, pages 23–24. In Broward County, contact **Brownie's Third Lung** (1530 Cordova Road, Fort Lauderdale; (954) 524-2112). Fees are $40 for a four-hour, two-tank dive from a boat. Brownie's offers rental, air fills, and lessons. Similar prices prevail at **Scuba Network** (199 North Federal Highway, Deerfield Beach; (954) 422-9982) and at **South Florida Diving "Aquanaut"** (101 North Riverside Drive, Pompano Beach; (954) 783-2299).

Sample Reefs and Depths	
Suzannes Ledges	13–16 feet
Twin Ledges	30–45 feet
Copenhagen Wreck	15–30 feet
Tenneco Platforms	105–190 feet
Curry Reef	70–75 feet
Osborne Reef	60–75 feet
Dania EroJacks Reef	10–20 feet
Fishamerica	110–115 feet

FISHING

Drift fishing is popular with families. Usually the boat goes out for four hours at a time—generally in early morning, at noon, and occasionally at night. Hooks are baited, fish cleaned, and all the gear you need (poles, reels, tackle and bait) is supplied and covered in the cost. Some people call drift boats "party boats," but most of the 30 or 40 people who have paid to head out to sea are there to catch fish. Operators include **Helen S. Drift Fishing** (101 North Riverside Drive, #107, Pompano Beach; (954) 941-3209); **Sea Legs III** (5400 North Ocean Drive, Hollywood; (954) 923-2109); and **Flamingo Fishing** (801 Seabreeze Boulevard, in Bahia Mar Marina; (954) 462-9194). Rates average about $25 for adults and $15 for children.

Chartering a boat is a much more costly project, and recommendations include most any marina, such as Bahia Mar in Fort Lauderdale or Harbour Town in Dania Beach. Charters are more for dedicated fishers who go out for the entire day and are eager to go farther out to sea than drift boats. Knowledgeable fishers tell us that the best way to find a captain or a boat is to hang out at a marina around 5 or 5:30 p.m. and see what the boats are bringing back from their all-day or afternoon runs.

Glass-bottom boat cruises (A Admiral's Cruse Line, 801 Seabreeze Boulevard, Bahia Mar; (954) 522-2220), sail boat rentals (Palm Breeze Charter, Hillsboro Boulevard and the Intracoastal; (561) 368-3566), and even gambling cruises (SunCruz Casinos, 6024 North Ocean Drive, Hollywood; (954) 929-3800) are other means of shipping out.

MORE WATER SPORTS

There are water-skiing, windsurfing, and parasailing classes to choose from, not to mention sailboards and jet ski rentals. It is estimated that about 40,000 boats are registered in Fort Lauderdale. You can enjoy the water in many forms. Safety is important, and we heartily recommend three things: Don't try anything on the water if you can't swim, take the basic lessons required to head out on the briny, and never mix liquor with water sports.

SPECTATOR SPORTS

Once upon a time a visit to South Florida meant many a day at the beach. And that's about it. Today, there are many more options. One could conceivably vacation in Florida and never see the beach. One popular choice is watching major-league sports teams in action. And in the cases of the Florida Panthers and Miami Heat, both teams play in new, state-of-the-art arenas.

Pro Teams

The **Miami Dolphins,** the local AFC East football team, plays home games just over the Broward County line in Miami-Dade at Pro Player Stadium (2269 NW 199th Street, North Miami; (305) 620-2578). The stadium used to be called Joe Robbie Stadium, and many locals still use that name—he was the founder of the Dolphins and the owner when the team had its perfect season in 1972. Individual tickets range in price from $27 to $62, and they can be purchased at the stadium box office or via Ticketmaster (phone (954) 523-3309). Preseason games start in August. Check *The Miami Herald* or *Sun-Sentinel* for spring training times; some are open to the public.

The National League **Florida Marlins,** who won the 1997 World Series, also play at Pro Player Stadium. General admission tickets are $4–55 per seat. Call the stadium (phone (305) 620-2578), Ticketmaster (phone (954) 523-3309), or check *The Miami Herald* or *Sun-Sentinel* for game dates and additional information on obtaining tickets or special promotions.

The **Florida Panthers,** a National Hockey League team, made it to the Stanley Cup finals in their third season. They play in Sunrise at the National Car Rental Arena (2555 SW 137th Way, Sunrise). Individual tickets are available only through Ticketmaster (phone (954) 835-8326). Ticket prices range from $14 to $110.

The **Miami Heat,** the local NBA team, play at American Airlines Arena (601 Biscayne Boulevard, Miami). Ticket prices range from $5 to $200, available from Ticketmaster (phone (954) 835-8326).

The **Miami Fusion** (Lockhart Stadium, 2200 West Commercial Boulevard, Fort Lauderdale; (954) 717-2200) is a pro soccer team in the rough and tumble game picking up steam throughout the United States.

The **Baltimore Orioles** do their spring training at Fort Lauderdale Stadium (5301 NW 12th Avenue, Fort Lauderdale; (954) 776-1921). Tickets are $6–12.

THE BETTING SPORTS: HORSE RACES, GREYHOUNDS, HARNESS RACING, AND JAI ALAI

Pari-mutuel wagering, which enables winners to divide a pot after taking off a fee for management expenses, is a big-bucks business in Florida—despite a state lottery and an armada of gambling boats that ply the waters of the Gulf Stream and allow tourists and residents alike to play roulette, poker, blackjack, and craps.

Pari-mutuel betting is available at **Gulfstream Park Race Track, Hollywood Dog Track, Pompano Park Harness Racing,** and **Dania Jai Alai.** Both newspapers, *The Miami Herald* and *Sun-Sentinel,* print the entrants each day. Traditionally, thoroughbred horse racing and Florida have gone together hand in glove. Winter racing is on tap at Gulfstream Park (at US 1 and Hallandale Beach Boulevard, Hallandale; (954) 454-7000). For dog racing try Hollywood Greyhound Track (it's actually at 831 North Federal Highway in Hallandale; (954) 924-3200). Greyhounds are sleek animals that reach speeds of more than 40 miles an hour. The season runs through the end of May. Pompano Park Harness Racing (1800 Race Trace Road, Pompano Beach; (954) 972-2000) offers races through mid-April, Monday, Wednesday, Friday, and Saturday evenings

Jai Alai is a fast and furious game combining elements of lacrosse, tennis, and racquetball, played with a hard ball called a pelota and a cesta, a long, curved wicker basket. The Guinness record book says no ball travels faster than the pelota, which reaches speeds of over 180 mph. It is an exciting game. The local venue is Dania Jai Alai (301 East Dania Beach Boulevard; (954) 920-1511). Admission is free until 6 p.m. for simulcast and poker; box office is open Wednesday–Friday, 4–10 p.m.; Saturday, 11 a.m.–4 p.m.; and Tuesday, 11 a.m.–1 p.m.

Shopping

STROLLING AND WINDOW SHOPPING

One of the most delightful places to stroll and window shop is Fort Lauderdale's Las Olas Boulevard, a smart and sassy response to Rodeo Drive in Beverly Hills, Boulevard St. Germain in Paris, or Michigan Avenue in Chicago. It's where the savvy shopper finds cutting-edge fashion and boutiques, art galleries, charming restaurants, sidewalk cafes, and jazz houses. Las Olas is a class act.

Las Olas means "the waves" in Spanish, and it's definitely the wave of the past, present, and future for many South Florida shoppers. **Zola Keller** (818 East Las Olas Boulevard; (954) 462-3222) has clothed the area's best-dressed for years with outstanding women's wear from around the globe. Across the street, **Call of Africa's Native Vision Galleries** (807 East Las Olas Boulevard; (954) 767-8737) offers rare and exotic African art; and at **Maus & Hoffman** (800 East Las Olas Boulevard; (954) 463-1472) men's clothing appeals to shoppers from all over the world. **Genesis Fine Art** (803 East Las Olas Boulevard; (954) 467-6066) carries some interesting art forms. Paintings are the main attraction at Genesis, where landscapes and representational work are popular; you'll see watercolors, acrylics, and oils and modern and postmodern schools but few abstract works. A variety of gift shops and galleries—some funky, some fabulous—make Las Olas a great day's activity. Diverse eateries range from moderately priced to very expensive and offer many choices for resting one's footsies and packages.

The Shops & Restaurants of Downtown Hollywood (Hollywood Boulevard and Harrison Street; (954) 921-3016) make up one of those renovated downtown areas that are popping up all over the country. Old movie theaters reappear as restaurants, banks as shopping arcades . . . you know the drill. Hollywood has created a collection of clothing boutiques, art galleries and studios, and intimate cafes. Downtown Hollywood also has an array of nighttime live entertainment.

MALL SHOPPING

Sawgrass Mills

Statistics from the Travel Industry Association of America show outlet shopping malls are becoming major attractions for the country's travelers, with 39 percent of all travelers saying they visited a discount outlet mall in 1997. The grand Pooh-Bah of outlet malls, Sawgrass Mills, offers everything your little heart desires. We strongly recommend a visit to Sawgrass (12801 West Sunrise Boulevard, Sunrise; (954) 846-2300) just to ooh and aah at the size of it. Consider Saks Fifth Avenue and Neiman Marcus outlets, add Ann Taylor and Carter's children's wear, Levi Strauss, Benetton, Spiegel, American Tourister, Nine West, Joan & David, and DKNY, and you've got a trunkful of bargains. The values are there—it just takes some looking—and Sawgrass is not for those who are hit-and-run shoppers.

Sawgrass opened in 1992 and is considered a major tourist attraction. It is the world's largest discount and entertainment mall. The Oasis features a 300,000-square-foot entertainment area with more than 30 stores and restaurants. Surfers and surfer wannabes love the clothes and equipment, including surfboards, skateboards, swimwear, and beat gear at Ron Jon Surf Shop (phone (954) 846-1880), a two-year-old branch of the world's largest chain of surf shops—founded 64 years ago and respected by surfers from all over the world. Valet parking is available.

More Malls

Mall walkers are a 20th-century phenomenon especially appropriate to South Florida's tropical climate. Those who want to take a daily constitutional and do a mile or two can put on their walking shoes and head to the nearest mall and walk in air-conditioned comfort. And you can be sure that South Florida has almost as great a variety of malls as a variety of walkers.

In Broward there are several choices:

Galleria Mall (2414 East Sunrise Boulevard, Fort Lauderdale; (954) 564-1015) is one of those high-end malls with glitzy stores (Saks Fifth Avenue and Neiman Marcus), designer boutiques, and a huge parking garage—valet service is available. Also nearby, visit **Harmony Isle Gallery** (902 NE 19th Avenue, Fort Lauderdale; (954) 527-2880) and view work by local artists as well as national presentations, handmade jewelry, and other gift items and souvenirs.

Broward Mall in Plantation (Broward Boulevard and University Drive; (954) 473-8100) is home to Burdines (founded in 1898 and one of Florida's oldest department stores), Sears, Dillard's, JC Penney, and 120 smaller stores, plus a food court and Ruby Tuesday restaurant. Don't miss the fey San Francisco Music Box shop (near Dillards; (954) 452-9662) with an outstanding collection of charming musical gifts for everyone from Great Uncle Arthur to baby Jessica. This is classic suburban mall circa 1985, with every chain you can think of. Best thing about it? Four major department stores and plenty of parking.

Nearby, don't miss the **Fashion Mall at Plantation** (321 North University Drive; (954) 370-1884) anchored by Macy's and Lord & Taylor. There's a Sheraton Hotel and a restaurant in the complex, but the mall itself is really just another shoe/film/card shop mall. Unique is the Franklin Covey Store (phone (954) 723-0091), selling everything you need to keep your Palm Pilot straightened up and flying right. Franklin Covey obviously sells Palms, but it also carries all the accessories—and there are an amazing number of those.

Coral Springs is one of those upscale suburbs popular with the current spate of yuppies. Of course, the community has its own mall. **Coral Square Mall** (Atlantic Boulevard and University Drive; (954) 755-5550) has the major department stores: Burdines, Dillard's, JC Penney, Sears, many boutiques and chains, and one of the best candy stores around in Palm Beach Confections (phone (954) 748-0706).

Pines Boulevard (which starts out at the ocean as Hollywood Boulevard) is a textbook case of the move west—without John Wayne and covered wagons. Many of the shops that once graced the old **Hollywood Mall** (opened in the early 1960s, closed some 20 years later, and located about 10 miles east of the current hotspot) moved to the **Pembroke Lakes Mall** (11401 Pines Boulevard; (954) 436-3520). Typical mall fare: major stores, boutiques, chains, food court, and a huge parking lot.

In the heart of Fort Lauderdale's tourist hustle and bustle is **Southport Shopping Center** (SE 17th Street Causeway and Cordova Road, Fort Lauderdale; (954) 463-0520), with restaurants, a gym, card shop, supermarket, and drugstore geared to needs of visitors. **Carriage Clothiers, Ltd.** (1461 SE 17th Street Causeway, Fort Lauderdale; (954) 523-3545) carries a wide line of men's clothing and accessories; it's also near several major hotels and restaurants.

WHILE YOU ARE IN THE AREA

In nearby Sunrise, check out the baby stuff and children's wear at **Baby Love, Inc.** (8100 West Oakland Park Boulevard, Sunrise; (954) 741-2227). This warehouse-like store is simply the largest selection of kids' gear and clothing you can imagine. A paradise for expectant parents, new parents, and grandparents. Once the kid angle is covered, take a look at **Up, Up & Away** (829 North Nob Hill, Plantation; (954) 475-2002) with lots of artsy gift items, souvenirs, mementos, and charming ceramics.

The Plantation/Sunrise area seems at first glance to be made up of strip mall after strip mall. Culling the wheat from the chaff could be a full time job, but some exciting shops exist, and if time permits, they're worth the visit. There's a heavy concentration of children's clothing and toy stores, furniture and decorating shops, and chain after chain after chain.

SPECIALTY SHOPS

Antiques

While the tiny town of Dania Beach once stood in the spotlight as the tomato capital of the world, today it is best known for block after block of antique shops. These carry a lot of kitsch, but they also stock many fine items of antique glassware, furniture, jewelry, and more. Like Las Olas, this is a stroll-and-window-shop area, so take the time to explore some of the 250 shops.

One way to go about it is to visit the **Antique Center Mall of Dania** (3 North Federal Highway, Dania Beach; (954) 922-5467) with a selection including **Paula Schimmel's** antique and period jewelry, **Dick's Toys, E & F** antiques and collectibles, and **Madeleine France's 19th and 20th Century Past and Pleasure** perfume bottles, furniture, housewares, and gold. For antique art, try **Kodner Gallery** (45 South Federal Highway, Dania Beach; (954-925-2550), or try **Athena Gallery,** which buys antiques and estates (19 South Federal Highway, Dania Beach; (954) 921-7697); and visit **Attic Treasures** (32 North Federal Highway, Dania Beach; (954) 920-0280) with goodies from the first half of the 20th century. Remember, Federal Highway is also US 1.

Boat Gear

Whether it's a little dinghy or a world-class yacht, if you need something for your boat, try **Boat Owners Warehouse.** They carry more than 16,000 items, and they have locations at 311 SW 24th Street (State Road 84), Fort Lauderdale, (954) 522-7998; 750 East Sample Road, Pompano Beach, (954) 946-6930; and 1720 East Hallandale Beach Boulevard, Hallandale, (954) 457-5081.

Bookstores

The **Barnes & Noble** chain operates several free-standing mega-stores in Broward, complete with comfy chairs, couches, and coffee shops. The stores are a great place to go on a rainy day or a free afternoon, and sometimes children's story hours are scheduled to entertain the youngsters. Locations at 4170 Oakwood Boulevard, Hollywood, (954) 923-1738; 11820 Pines Boulevard, Pembroke Pines, (954) 441-1880; and 2700 University Drive, Coral Springs, (954) 344-6291. For autographed books, rare volumes, first editions, and CDs, try **Liberties Fine Books, Music, & Café** (888 Las Olas Boulevard, Fort Lauderdale; (954) 522-6789).

Cigar Stores

Tropical Republic (17 South Fort Lauderdale Beach Boulevard at Beach Place, Fort Lauderdale; (954) 753-8666) sells cigars from all over and carries a complete line of humidors and other smoking accoutrements. Don't inhale.

Fishing Gear

Outdoor World Bass Pro Shops (200 Gulf Stream Way, Dania Beach; (954) 929-7710) sells everything you need to be a fisher. The store also has an indoor archery range, gun range, restaurant, and all things fishy. Looking for a fish-print shirt for Uncle Jack? Boy, is this the place for you. Also on site is the Fishing Hall of Fame & Museum and a fresh-fish market, plus a four-story waterfall, aquarium, and trout pool.

Fruit Shipping

Mack's Groves (locations at 4405 North Ocean Drive, Lauderdale-by-the-Sea, (954) 776-0910 and 1180 North Federal Highway, Pompano Beach, (954) 941-4528 or (800) 327-3525) offer fresh citrus from South Florida's best groves. Marvel at fruit basket gift items to take home or ship while you enjoy the sunshine. **Publix** supermarkets (and they pretty much cover the state) also offer fresh-fruit shipping.

Jewelry

Across from the Galleria, visit **Daoud's Fine Jewelry** (2525 East Sunrise Boulevard, Fort Lauderdale; (954) 565-2734) for unique pieces, estate jewelry, and preowned Rolex watches. **Morningstar's** (2000 Hollywood Boulevard, Hollywood; (954) 923-2372) sells new and preowned pieces of jewelry. Stop by **Oakwood Jewelry Exchange** (2910 Oakwood Boulevard, Hollywood; (954) 923-1767) for a variety of silver and gold jewelry in a variety of price ranges. **Levinson Jewelers** (8139 West Broward Boulevard, Plantation; (955) 473-9700) is considered tops for fine jewelry.

Shoes

Birkenstock Footprints (491 East Sample Road, Pompano Beach; (954) 943-3041) has more than 400 colors and styles for adults and kids.

Swimwear

The latest (and briefest) swimwear on Fort Lauderdale or any beach is at **Swimland** (2571 East Sunrise Boulevard, Fort Lauderdale; (954) 561-2824) from Gottex, Anne Klein, Nautica, and all major names.

FLEA MARKETS

Two notable flea markets top the list of places where practically everything is for sale: **Festival Flea Market** (2900 West Sample Road, Pompano

Beach; (954) 979-4555) and **Swap Shop of Fort Lauderdale** (3291 West Sunrise Boulevard, Fort Lauderdale; (954) 791-7927). Festival Flea Market features upscale bargains, food court, and full service beauty salon. The Swap Shop features a circus, food court, and a carnival-like ambience with more than 2,000 vendors, and they offer shuttle bus service from hotels and downtown locations.

Attractions

A PERFECT DAY

Everyone's idea of perfection is different. Think about what elements you'd combine to make up a perfect day. For some, spending a day lounging on the beach with a good supply of sunscreen, a cooler of cold drinks, and a novel is enough. Others want to hit the links and play 18 holes before lunch. Some inveterate shoppers can't get enough charging through South Florida's malls, shopping centers, flea markets, or antique shops. The point is that you can create an utterly perfect day in Broward County whatever your interests may be. Below are a few of our recommendations.

A perfect day might begin with a sunrise walk along the four-mile Broadwalk on Hollywood Beach. Watch the sun come up over the ever-changing Atlantic Ocean, and stop for breakfast at one of a dozen or so beachfront restaurants, where the view is incredible and prices unbelievably low.

Then head over to the brand new spa at the Diplomat Resort & Country Club and reward yourself for that nice morning walk. This full-service, 30,000-square-foot spa offers massage, shiatsu, reflexology, mud and seaweed wraps, hydrotherapies, body scrubs, facials, and a variety of other services. Showers and a sauna will help refresh and restore, and the treatment will be totally hedonistic.

Relaxed and restored, climb back into the car and head west to Sawgrass Mills Mall and lunch at Wolfgang Puck's. Then stroll through the hundreds of stores for that ideal gift to take back home. Choose from Ann Taylor or Neiman Marcus, baby wear at Carter's, or jewelry at Exchange.

Packages tucked safely in your hotel room, plan on dinner at Giorgio's Mediterranean Restaurant (ask for a table on the deck and salivate at the posh boats—of all sizes and shapes—tying at your feet), saving time to catch a flick at the nearby Regal Oakwood Cinemas.

Or perhaps the outdoors hold more appeal for you and your family. Plan on heading up to Butterfly World in Tradewinds Park off Sample Road to see the largest live butterfly exhibit in the world. Wander through the three-acre rain forest. In the late morning, turn back south to Hillsboro Boulevard and the Intracoastal Waterway for a Palm Breeze sail on a 55-foot catamaran, scheduled daily at 12:45 p.m. (and booked ahead of time). That's a lot of sun for one day, so grab a late lunch, take a nap, then enjoy a gala dinner at the very romantic and luxe Burt and Jack's, where you can watch the moon shimmer on the water.

A final alternative might include a morning spent on the beach, followed by lunch at the Islamorada Fish Company in Dania Beach. Walk through the Bass Outdoor store, located in the same building, then head next door to the Fishing Hall of Fame & Museum, where virtual reality allows you to catch a marlin without getting wet. Make it a museum kind of day with a late-day visit to the Museum of Discovery & Science and dinner at one of the restaurants at nearby Las Olas River Front in Fort Lauderdale's Historic District.

WALKING TOURS

Broward County—actually, all of Florida—is not an area that lends itself to actual walking tours. It's hot, it's humid, and outside of parklands, few safe areas exist. Traffic in Florida is a challenge. On the other hand, Broward's parks feature nature trails that showcase local foliage and recreate some original wetlands. But aside from the Art Deco walk in South Beach on Miami Beach, formal organized walks with a guide just don't exist. Strolling Las Olas Boulevard or hoofing it on the beach take on new meaning in this case.

Because of the wide range of Broward County attractions, we've provided the following chart to help you prioritize your touring at a glance. Organized by category, in it you'll find the name, location, and author's rating from one star (skip it) to five stars (not to be missed). Some attractions, usually art galleries without permanent collections, weren't rated because exhibits change. Each attraction is individually profiled in detail later in this section. Most museum-type attractions offer group rates for ten or more people.

A Time-Saving Chart		
Name	City	Author's Rating
Amusement Park		
Boomers/Dania Beach Hurricane	Dania Beach	★★
Boat Ride		
Jungle Queen Riverboat	Fort Lauderdale	★★★★
Home Tour		
Bonnet House	Fort Lauderdale	★★
Museums		
Ah-Tah-Thi-Ki Museum	Seminole Big Cypress Reservation	★★★

A Time-Saving Chart (continued)		
Name	City	Author's Rating
Museums (continued)		
Fort Lauderdale Historical Museum	Fort Lauderdale	★★
Fishing Hall of Fame & Museum	Dania Beach	★★★
International Swimming Hall of Fame	Fort Lauderdale	★★
Museum of Discovery & Science/IMAX Theater	Fort Lauderdale	★★★★
South Florida Museum of Natural History	Dania Beach	★
Young at Art	Davie	★★
Nature Centers/Exhibits		
Anne Kolb Nature Center	Hollywood	★★★
Butterfly World	Coconut Creek	★★★
Parks and Refuges		
Flamingo Gardens	Fort Lauderdale	★★★
Sawgrass Recreation Park	N/A	★★

ATTRACTION PROFILES

Ah-Tah-Thi-Ki Museum

Type of Attraction: A unique perspective of the Seminole nation

Location: 17 miles north of Alligator Alley (I-75), Exit 14 on the Seminole Big Cypress Reservation

Admission: Adults, $6; seniors and students, $4; children under age 6 free

Hours: Tuesday–Sunday, 9 a.m.–5 p.m.

Phone: (863) 902-1113

When to Go: Mornings are the least busy

Special Comments: This is a great way to learn about some of the original Floridians and their many contributions to the region.

Overall Appeal by Age Group:

Pre-school	Grade School	Teens	Young Adults	Over 30	Seniors
★★★	★★★	★★★	★★	★★★★	★★★★

Author's Rating: ★★★

How Much Time to Allow: Two hours

Description and Comments   No traditional alligator wrestling (which most people associate with Seminoles), and that's the whole point of this museum—this is more about substance than form. A 17-minute orientation film and gallery, plus a mile-and-a-half walk through a Seminole village, impart that knowledge graciously and thoroughly. Don't miss the opportunity to watch Native American arts and crafts being constructed. The Seminoles continue to maintain a vibrant presence throughout the area, and new properties (including a Hard Rock Cafe Resort and Casino) are on the drawing board for the Seminole reservation in Hollywood; two ongoing Indian gaming halls in the county offer bingo and video poker 24 hours a day.

Touring Tips   Bring your own snacks and drinks. While food and drinks are not allowed inside, picnic tables are provided.

Other Things to Do Nearby   Complete your Native American indoctrination by visiting Billie Swamp Safari and Big Cypress Campground. These attractions lie in the middle of the Everglades, so come prepared and don't expect a strip mall on every corner, even though parts of Broward seem to be made up of exactly that.

Anne Kolb Nature Center

Type of Attraction: Nature Center, with canoe and kayak rentals
Location: 751 Sheridan Street, Hollywood 33020
Admission: Adults, $2; children under age 6 free
Hours: Daily, 9 a.m.–5 p.m.
Phone: (954) 926-2410
When to Go: Mornings or after 3 p.m.
Overall Appeal by Age Group:

Pre-school	Grade School	Teens	Young Adults	Over 30	Seniors
★★	★★★	★★★★	★★★★	★★★	★★★

Author's Rating: ★★★
How Much Time to Allow: Two hours

Description and Comments   The most recent addition to South Florida's tropical coastal ecosystems, Anne Kolb Nature Center and Marina encompasses more than 1,500 acres of mangrove wetlands and forest habitat. It's a beautiful environment with nature trails. You can take narrated boat tours, climb a five-story observation tower for a spectacular view of Southern Broward County, or bike, hike, or canoe through the wild. There's also a fishing pier nearby.

Touring Tips   Drink plenty of water and cover your head.

Other Things to Do Nearby   Visit Hollywood North Beach Park with its full facilities or head a few miles south to the refurbished Downtown Hollywood Historic area, with its galleries, boutiques, and many sidewalk cafes.

Bonnet House

Type of Attraction: Old Florida home

Location: 900 N. Birch Road, Fort Lauderdale 33301 (Sunrise Boulevard and A1A)

Admission: Adults, $9; seniors, $8; students ages 6–18, $7; children under age 6 free

Hours: Wednesday–Friday, 10 a.m.– 3 p.m. for house tours, but grounds are open until 4 p.m.; closed holidays and mid-August–September

Phone: (954) 563-5393

When to Go: When it opens or last tour, 1:30 p.m. Wednesday–Friday and 2:30 p.m. on Saturday and Sunday.

Special Comments: Don't miss the monkeys swinging through the banyan trees or the black swans in the pool. The house illustrates a lifestyle gone but not forgotten.

Overall Appeal by Age Group:

Pre-school	Grade School	Teens	Young Adults	Over 30	Seniors
★	★★	★★	★★	★★★	★★★★

Authors' Rating: ★★

How Much Time to Allow: Two Hours—guided tour lasts one-and-a-quarter hours

Description and Comments Great for history buffs who want to see what Old Florida was like. Built by painter Frederick Clay Bartlett, the 35-acre beachfront home is a turn-of-the-19th-century beauty. Imagine Edith Wharton with a tan and a southern accent.

Touring Tips More interesting to adults than kids, but young 'uns like the menagerie.

Other Things to Do Nearby A day at the beach is convenient—you're right there at the edge of the Atlantic. Or wander through nearby Beach Place, an eclectic strip mall/entertainment complex with various eateries, boutiques, and clubs.

Boomers/Dania Beach Hurricane

Type of Attraction: Amusement park

Location: 1500 NW First Street, Dania Beach 33304 (just east of I-95 between Griffin and Stirling Roads)

Admission: Per-ride basis, $4.50–6.25 each

Hours: Saturday–Thursday, 10 a.m.–2 a.m.

Phone: (954) 921-1411

When to Go: Any time

Special Comments: This was formerly Grand Prix Race-A-Rama

Overall Appeal by Age Group:

Pre-school	Grade School	Teens	Young Adults	Over 30	Seniors
★	★★	★★★	★★★★	★★★★	★★

Author's Rating: ★★

How Much Time to Allow: Two–three hours minimum

Description and Comments The new wooden roller coaster called the Hurricane is very popular with roller-coaster aficionados. It's the largest wooden roller coaster in the state and reaches speeds up to 60 mph—you can see it from I-95. Other than the Hurricane, this is a standard amusement park with midway rides and arcade games.

Touring Tips Go midweek rather than on the weekend and stick to morning or late afternoon. Mid-day is hot, hot, hot.

Other Things to Do Nearby Oakwood Plaza—only minutes away—has a variety of stores and a multiscreen theater.

Butterfly World

Type of Attraction: Butterfly exhibit and aviary

Location: 3600 West Sample Road, Coconut Creek 33319 (in Trade Winds Park, just west of the Florida Turnpike)

Admission: Adults, $12.95; children ages 4–12, $7.95; children under age 4 free

Hours: Monday–Saturday, 9 a.m.–5 p.m.; Sunday, 1 p.m.–5 p.m.

Phone: (954) 977-4400

When to Go: Early in the day when it's cooler

Special Comments: Museum/Insectarium and a three-acre rain forest paradise.

Overall Appeal by Age Group:

Pre-school	Grade School	Teens	Young Adults	Over 30	Seniors
★★	★★★	★★★	★★	★★★	★★★★

Author's Rating: ★★★

How Much Time to Allow: Two hours

Description and Comments This is a tour for the whole family—colorful, beautiful, tropical, and interesting. Little ones love the color, and older people enjoy the lush foliage.

Touring Tips   Wear a hat and drink water. Never underestimate the Florida sun.

Other Things to Do Nearby   Trade Winds Park is a pretty (and safe) area, so you might want to let the kids run free for a while before heading back to the hotel.

Flamingo Gardens

Type of Attraction: Botanical gardens and wildlife sanctuary
Location: 3750 Flamingo Road, David/Fort Lauderdale 33330
Admission: Adults, $12; children ages 4–11, $6; discounts for seniors and AAA members
Hours: Daily, 9:30 a.m.–5:30 p.m.; closed Monday in summer
Phone: (954) 473-2955
When to Go: Wildlife encounters at 12:30 p.m., 1:30 p.m., and 2:30 p.m. daily.

Overall Appeal by Age Group:

Pre-school	Grade School	Teens	Young Adults	Over 30	Seniors
★★	★★★	★★★	★★★	★★★★	★★★★★

Author's Rating: ★★★
How Much Time to Allow: Two–three hours

Description and Comments   Imagine everything from a subtropical rain forest to a free-flight aviary, nature trails, and wilderness animals, all coexisting on 60 acres of botanical gardens. The tram tour is a comfortable way to see everything, and kids seem to love it. The gardens are outstanding and offer a profusion of tropical flora. It's one of the prettiest sites in Broward.

Touring Tips   Take your time. Go early and explore the grounds.

Other Things to Do Nearby   You're close to Nova Southeastern University campus and the Sawgrass Mills Mall—all 270 stores, myriad restaurants, and movie theaters.

Fort Lauderdale Historical Museum

Type of Attraction: History Museum
Location: 231 SW 2nd Avenue, Fort Lauderdale 33301 (in the Arts and Science District)
Admission: Adults, $5; seniors and children, $3; children under age 6 free
Hours: Tuesday–Sunday, noon–5 p.m.
Phone: (954) 463-4431
When to Go: Any time

Overall Appeal by Age Group:

Pre-school	Grade School	Teens	Young Adults	Over 30	Seniors
★	★★	★★	★★	★★★	★★★

Author's Rating: ★★

How Much Time to Allow: Two hours

Description and Comments   If you don't know much about Fort Lauderdale's history or the Seminole Indians place in that history, this one's for you. You'll gain insight into the lives of early settlers who chose to make their home near the end of the Florida peninsula—near swamps and the Everglades—and built it into a thriving center. Life was often perilous for these settlers, and their history helps tourists appreciate the area's comfortable hotels and lovely beaches.

Touring Tips   Avoid school holidays.

Other Things to Do Nearby   Stroll along River Walk, visit Las Olas River Front, or consider the Discovery Center.

International Game Fish Association Fishing Hall of Fame & Museum

Type of Attraction: Museum focused on all phases of fishing

Location: 300 Gulf Stream Way, Dania Beach 33004

Admission: Call for current prices

Hours: Daily, 10 a.m.–6 p.m.; closed Thanksgiving and Christmas

Phone: (954) 922-4212

When to Go: Any time

Special Comments: Teaches respect for sea life and the importance of conserving and protecting our valuable natural aquatic resources.

Overall Appeal by Age Group:

Pre-school	Grade School	Teens	Young Adults	Over 30	Seniors
★★	★★	★★	★★★	★★★	★★★

Author's Rating: ★★★

How Much Time to Allow: Two hours

Description and Comments   The Tackle Gallery is interesting, and the collection of boats includes a 1933 "Wheeler," sister ship to Ernest Hemingway's Pilar. It's pretty much everything you ever wanted to know about fishing—and very well done.

Touring Tips   See the movie first; it's an excellent orientation for the museum.

Other Things to Do Nearby   Shop at Bass Pro Shops Outdoor World, or take a TriRail train ride from the station just down the way. And Oakwood Plaza is only five minutes away, but the Bass complex (and Islamorada Fish Factory restaurant) can keep you busy most of the day.

International Swimming Hall of Fame

Type of Attraction: Swimming memorabilia museum

Location: 1 Hall of Fame Drive, Fort Lauderdale 33316

Admission: Family, $5; seniors and students, $3

Hours: Monday–Friday, 9 a.m.–7 p.m.; Saturday and Sunday, 9 a.m.–
   5 p.m.

Phone: (954) 462-6536

When to Go: Any time

Overall Appeal by Age Group:

Pre-school	Grade School	Teens	Young Adults	Over 30	Seniors
★	★★	★★	★★★	★★★	★★★

Author's Rating: ★★

How Much Time to Allow: Minimum of one hour

Description and Comments   Anyone who has watched Olympic swimmers over the years will enjoy the museum. Look for lots of water-logged memorabilia featuring U.S. swimmers from Johnny Weismuller (an early "Tarzan" of film fame) to Mark Spitz (the Munich Olympics) and more contemporary swimmers such as Greg Louganis.

Touring Tips   Take it slow—there's a lot to see.

Other Things to Do Nearby   Swim at the pool, shop at the retail store, or take some time on the beach.

Jungle Queen Riverboat

Type of Attraction: Boat ride

Location: 801 Seabreeze Boulevard, Fort Lauderdale 33316

Admission: Adults, $13.25; children age 10 and under, $8.75

Hours: Sight-seeing cruises daily at 10 a.m. and 2 p.m., and a cruise down
   to Miami's Bayside Marketplace leaves at 9:15 a.m.

Phone: (954) 462-5596

When to Go: Any time

Special Comments: This is a "must-do" for first-timers.

Overall Appeal by Age Group:

Pre-school	Grade School	Teens	Young Adults	Over 30	Seniors
★	★★	★★★	★★★	★★★★	★★★★

Author's Rating: ★★★★

How Much Time to Allow: Two hours for the sight-seeing cruise

Description and Comments   This boat ride has been a Fort Lauderdale tradition for more than six decades. Even the locals take it. The daytime sight-seeing cruise is the best choice, and the accompanying live commentary is excellent.

Touring Tips   Sunscreen and a hat are essential, and don't forget a camera—you will be passing some of the prettiest (and most expensive) real estate in South Florida.

Other Things to Do Nearby   Catch a few more rays on the beach. It's a great area—everything looks like a picture postcard.

Museum of Discovery & Science/Blockbuster IMAX 3D Theater

Type of Attraction: Interactive museum and IMAX

Location: 401 SW Second Street, Fort Lauderdale 33312

Admission: Adults, $12.50; seniors and students, $11.50; children, $10.50; all prices include one IMAX feature

Hours: Monday–Saturday, 10 a.m.–5 p.m.; Sunday, noon–6 p.m.; closed Thanksgiving and Christmas

Phone: (954) 467-3367

When to Go: Any time

Special Comments: An outstanding museum—sure to be enjoyed by two-year-old Timmy or his great grandma Tessie.

Overall Appeal by Age Group:

Pre-school	Grade School	Teens	Young Adults	Over 30	Seniors
★★★	★★★	★★★	★★★★	★★★	★★★★

Author's Rating: ★★★★

How Much Time to Allow: At least three hours—more if you see the film

Description and Comments   A well-designed, hands-on, interactive facility with a five-story 3D IMAX theater.

Touring Tips   Take the little ones to the area designed for them first, then see the film before touring the rest of the museum.

Other Things to Do Nearby   Visit Las Olas River Front, stroll along River Walk, or stop in at the beautiful Museum of Art, host to many major international exhibits. There's a permanent collection featuring paintings by William Glackens and many 20th-century European and American pieces. The museum recently completed a $2.2 million renovation.

Sawgrass Recreation Park

Type of Attraction: National wilderness

Location: Turnpike or I-95 to I-595 west to I-75, north to US 27, then north two miles

Admission: Adults, $15; children, $7.50

Hours: Daily, 9 a.m.–5 p.m.

Phone: (800) 457-0788

When to Go: Any time

Overall Appeal by Age Group:

Pre-school	Grade School	Teens	Young Adults	Over 30	Seniors
★	★	★★	★★	★★★	★★★

Author's Rating: ★★

How Much Time to Allow: Two hours for all tours

Description and Comments   It's a long trek out here but worth it for a close look at the Everglades and extensive information on Seminole culture. Don't miss the alligator and reptile show. Sawgrass is an amazing example of nature at its most wild. Don't expect waterfalls and formal gardens.

Touring Tips   The airboat tour is really exciting.

Other Things to Do Nearby   Not much. You might want to opt for the indoors after that heavy dose of nature, so take I-595 to 136th Avenue (or Flamingo Road) and park it at Sawgrass Mills, with its game centers, restaurants, and shops.

South Florida Museum of Natural History (Formerly Graves Museum of Archeology and Natural History)

Type of Attraction: Museum

Location: 481 South Federal Highway, Dania Beach 33304

Admission: Adults, $9.95; seniors and students, $7; children ages 4–12, $6

Hours: Tuesday–Friday, 10 a.m.–4 p.m.; Saturday, 10 a.m.–6 p.m.; Sunday, noon–6 p.m.

Phone: (954) 925-7770

When to Go: Any time

Overall Appeal by Age Group:

Pre-school	Grade School	Teens	Young Adults	Over 30	Seniors
—	★★	★★	★★	★★★	★★★

Author's Rating: ★

How Much Time to Allow: No more than two hours

Description and Comments   South Florida's collection of early civilization artifacts. You'll see Peruvian miniature ceramics, textiles and metals, masks from Africa, Greek vases, an Egyptian tomb, and more.

Touring Tips   Some pieces are interesting, others just so-so. It's on the way to the Fort Lauderdale/Hollywood International Airport and might be a just-before-the-plane activity.

Other Things to Do Nearby   Antiques shopping in Dania Beach; Dania Jai Alai is also nearby

Young at Art

Type of Attraction: Children's museum and art center

Location: 11584 State Road 84, Davie 33325

Admission: Adults, $4; seniors, $3.50; children under age 2 free

Hours: Monday–Saturday, 10 a.m–5 p.m.; Sunday, noon–5 p.m.

Phone: (954) 424-0085

When to Go: Any time

Overall Appeal by Age Groups:

Pre-school	Grade School	Teens	Young Adults	Over 30	Seniors
★★	★★★	★	★	★	★★

Author's Rating: ★★

How Much Time to Allow: One–two hours

Description and Comments   Especially great for young children and children who have shown interest in any kind of art. Kids can learn computer art, build sculptures, attend art classes, and explore their imagination and creativity. Many hands-on activities are available.

Touring Tips   Take kids when they are most active—after a nap is ideal.

Other Things to Do Nearby   A variety of malls are nearby, as is the campus of Nova Southeastern University. Or drive through the town of Davie, a small western-influenced community with horse ranches and an annual rodeo.

Dining and Restaurants

Broward County has become home to some of Florida's most outstanding restaurants, meeting the needs of both well-traveled visitors and locals who simply enjoy good food. At the new millennium, sophisticated diners, comfortable with a variety of cuisines, have found special places to conduct power lunches and dinners, celebrate anniversaries and birthdays, and have intimate, romantic dinners for two.

Competition keeps restaurateurs on their toes, and while new eateries regularly open throughout the county, many popular restaurants have been in business for years. It's not unusual for second-generation diners to enjoy the same meals their parents did in the 1950s and 1960s. Broward County today is a much more cosmopolitan community than existed in the middle of the 20th century, and today's restaurants feature Chinese, Cuban, French, Greek, Italian, Mediterranean/Middle Eastern, Mexican, Peruvian, and Vietnamese.

Darrel & Oliver's Café Maxx in Pompano Beach, a top-of-the-line restaurant, is one of the new breed. The award-winning Café Maxx features a regional Floridian/Caribbean menu (sometimes called "Floribbean"), utilizing fruits and vegetables as well as local seafood. In addition to this exciting and innovative cuisine, Café Maxx is also famous for fine steaks.

A GASTRONOMIC GLOSSARY

Broward County, comics will tell you, is also home to the "early-bird special," a discounted menu usually offered before 6 p.m. or 7 p.m. Comedians seem to find something hilarious about "early birds," but remember, they get the worm—and early bird diners are people who probably don't get indigestion from eating late at night.

Some eateries offer "early, early-bird specials" between 3 p.m. and 5 p.m. And no matter whether you find that concept ridiculous or sublime, these specials are always a good value. Many retirees prefer to dine early, and some young families actually choose the same option. It makes sense. Portions are relatively good sized, and generally a salad, potato, and dessert are included in the early-bird price. Often the same offerings are $3–5 more later in the evening. "Doggie bags" are also part of the local restaurant vocabulary. Whether a foil-wrapped, sculpted swan, a white Styrofoam box, or a standard-issue plastic bag, most restaurants will offer to package leftovers for another meal—or for Fido.

CASUAL DRESS

Very few South Florida restaurants require a shirt and tie. Many professionals come straight to dinner in their suits and ties, but as a rule of thumb, a sports jacket and open-collared shirt for men and nice pants suit for women work well. Casual dress does not translate to shorts, rubber sandals, and T-shirts. Casual daytime wear may include a nice pair of shorts or a shorts outfit for women. No one wants to dine next to someone dressed to cut the lawn or fix the washing machine. Jeans fall into that marginal "gray" area of good taste, but jeans and a nice shirt or collared T-shirt make the cut. Jeans and a T-shirt with tasteless advertising are simply in bad taste.

When we say "dressy casual" we're talking about nice slacks and open-collared shirt, perhaps (but not necessarily) a sport jacket for men and business wear or pants suits for women. Dressy casual is also called "resort" or "cruise" wear.

EXPLAINING THE RATINGS

We have developed detailed profiles for the restaurants we think are the best in the county. Each profile features an easily scanned heading that allows you, in just a second, to check out the restaurant's name, cuisine, star rating, cost, quality rating, and value rating.

Star Rating　The star rating is an overall rating that evaluates the entire dining experience, including style, service, and ambience, in addition to the taste, presentation, and quality of the food. Five stars is the highest rating possible, meaning the place has the best of everything. Four-star restaurants are exceptional and three-star restaurants are well above average. Two-star restaurants are good. One star is given to average restaurants that demonstrate an unusual capability in some area of specialization, for example, an otherwise forgettable place that has great corned beef.

Cost　Below and to the left of the star rating is an expense category giving the general price range for a complete meal. A complete meal for our purposes consists of an entrée with vegetable or side dish, and choice of soup or salad. Appetizers, desserts, drinks, and tips are excluded. Categories and related prices are listed below.

Inexpensive	$14 or less per person
Moderate	$15 to $30 per person
Expensive	More than $30 per person

Quality Rating　On the far right of each heading appears a number and a letter. The number is a food quality rating based on a scale of 0 to 100, with 100 being the best rating attainable. The quality rating is based expressly on the taste, freshness of ingredients, preparation, presentation, and creativity of food served. There is no consideration of price. If you are a person who wants the best food available and cost is not an issue, you need look no further than the quality ratings.

Value Rating If, on the other hand, you are looking for both quality and value, then you should check the value rating, expressed in letters. The value ratings are defined as follows:

A   Exception value, a real bargain
B   Good value
C   Fair value, you get exactly what you pay for
D   Somewhat overpriced
F   Significantly overpriced

Payment We've listed the type of payment accepted at each restaurant using the following codes:

AMEX   American Express (Optima)
CB   Carte Blanche
D   Discover
DC   Diners Club
MC   MasterCard
VISA   Visa

ABOUT THESE CHOICES

We have chosen restaurants that, while we can't guarantee their staying power, have proven to operate successfully for some time. We've also selected restaurants with a following among local professionals, residents, and tourists whose travel plans include a trip, for example, to Burt and Jack's for an intimate romantic dinner for two, to Deli Den for an over-stuffed corned beef sandwich, or to Eduardo de San Angel for their famous crispy duck. We have included a mix of restaurants that are well known and some that are low-profile, and in the process we have tried to provide something for everyone. Bon appetit!

The Best of Broward County Restaurants

Restaurant/Type	Star Rating	Quality Rating	Value Rating	City
American				
Gibby's Steaks & Seafood	★★★	91	B	Fort Lauderdale
Wolfgang Puck Grand Cafe	★★★	88	B	Sunrise
Lester's Diner	★	80	A	Fort Lauderdale
Asian				
Christina Wan's	★★★	80	A	Hollywood
Caribbean				
Aruba Beach Café	★★★	85	B	Fort Lauderdale

The Best of Broward County Restaurants (cont.)

Restaurant/Type	Star Rating	Quality Rating	Value Rating	City
Cuban				
Padrino's	★★	84	B	Hallandale
Deli				
Deli Den	★	85	A	Fort Lauderdale
Floridian				
Cafe Maxx	★★★½	91	F	Pompano Beach
French				
Left Bank	★★★½	90	D	Fort Lauderdale
Le Petit Café	★★★	86	B	Dania Beach
German				
Bavarian Village	★★★	89	B	Hollywood
Greek				
Oasis by the Sea	★	80	C	Hollywood
Italian				
Fulvio's	★★★	89	C	Davie
Mediterranean				
Giorgio's	★★★	90	C	Hollywood
Mexican				
Eduardo de San Angel	★★★	88	C	Fort Lauderdale
New American				
By Word of Mouth	★★★★	90	D	Fort Lauderdale
Seafood				
Islamorada Fish Company	★★★	90	B	Dania Beach
Steak				
Grill Room on Las Olas	★★★★	95	D	Fort Lauderdale
Burt and Jack's	★★★★	93	D	Port Everglades
Manero's Steakhouse	★★★	91	B	Hallandale
Thai				
Try My Thai	★★	86	C	Hollywood

ARUBA BEACH CAFE ★★★

| Caribbean | Moderate | QUALITY |
| | | 85 |

One Commercial Boulevard, Fort Lauderdale
(954)-776-0001

VALUE
B

Reservations: Not necessary
When to go: Weekdays for lunch or
dinner—most crowded on weekends
Entree range: $12–20
Payment: VISA, MC, AMEX, DC, D
Parking: Valet or meter
Bar: Two full-service bars

Wine selection: Good; $19–39 bottle,
$5–7.50 by the glass
Dress: Casual
Disabled access: Yes
Customers: Located on the beach; expect
families and young people, but mature
diners like the pretty setting as well.

Open: Daily, 11 a.m–11 p.m. (bar open until 2 a.m.)

Breakfast: Sunday, 8:30 a.m.–noon

Menu recommendations: Seafood in various forms—pasta, blackened, coconut shrimp—plus steaks, salads, and burgers.

Comments: Great spot to watch the sun set.

BAVARIAN VILLAGE ★★★

| German | Moderate | QUALITY |
| | | 89 |

1401 N. Federal Highway, Hollywood
(954) 922-7321

VALUE
B

Reservations: Recommended on
weekends
When to go: Dinner
Entree range: $15–30
Payment: MC, VISA, AMEX, D, DC
Parking: Large lot
Bar: Full service

Wine selection: Large selection of fine
wine; bottles from $25, $5–6.50 by the
glass
Dress: Dressy casual
Disabled access: Yes
Customers: Young, old, in-between—all
who enjoy ethnic dining

Lunch: Sunday, noon–4 p.m.

Dinner: Monday–Thursday and Sunday, 4–10 p.m.; Friday and Saturday, 4–11p.m

Menu recommendations: Roast duck, roast goose, crispy potato pancakes; if you like red cabbage or heavy meals of any kind, this one's for you.

Comments: Oom-pah-pah music and decor straight out of the Black Forest. It's a vast room that must resemble mad King Ludwig's hunting lodge.

BURT AND JACK'S ★★★★

Steaks	Expensive	QUALITY
		93

Berth 23, Port Everglades	VALUE
(954) 522-5225	**D**

Reservations: Recommended
When to go: Dinner
Entree range: $25–50
Payment: MC, VISA, AMEX, DC, D
Parking: Valet only
Bar: Full service
Wine selection: Vast list; bottles start at

$20; $4.50–15 by the glass
Dress: Dressy
Disabled access: Yes
Customers: Elegant men and women celebrating something special, on an expense account, or looking for one of the area's most romantic restaurants.

Dinner: Sunday–Thursday, 5–10 p.m.; Friday and Saturday, 5–11:30 p.m.

Menu recommendations: Best filet mignon in town, lobsters so big they almost hop on the table, and other fresh seafood. Triple Layer Chocolate Cake is worth all the calories!

Comments: Rich decor, beautiful surroundings in Port Everglades, and excellent food and service make this a primo destination for that special meal.

BY WORD OF MOUTH ★★★★

New American	Expensive	QUALITY
		90

3200 NE 12th Avenue, Fort Lauderdale	VALUE
(954) 564-3663	**D**

Reservations: Recommended
When to go: Early evenings
Entree range: $17–37
Payment: VISA, MC, AMEX, D, DC
Parking: Convenient, on street
Bar: Beer and wine

Wine selection: Moderate; $22–55 bottle, $6–12.50 by the glass
Dress: Dressy casual
Disabled access: Yes
Customers: Yuppies, locals out to celebrate, discerning diners

Lunch: Monday–Friday, 11 a.m.–3 p.m.

Dinner: Wednesday–Saturday, 5–10 p.m.

Menu recommendations: Fresh Hawaiian fish, including monchong fillet, uhu fish, lobster lasagna, and pepper-crusted beef tenderloin, and more traditional favorites. Chocolate Decadence is just that.

Comments: Owner Ellen Cirillo has created—and maintained—an intimate restaurant with an open kitchen and varying menu. She also does a big catering business and runs a bakery at the same site.

CAFE MAXX   ★★★½

Floridian	Very Expensive	QUALITY
		91

2601 East Atlantic Boulevard, Pompano Beach
(954) 782-0606

	VALUE
	F

Reservations: Recommended
When to go: Weeknights are much less crowded, but always busy
Entree range: $19–40
Payment: VISA, MC, AMEX, D, DC
Parking: Valet

Bar: Beer and wine
Wine selection: Large; $25–800 bottle, $7–13 by the glass
Dress: Dressy casual
Disabled access: Yes
Customers: Upscale crowd of all ages

Dinner: Sunday–Thursday, 5:30–10:30 p.m.; Friday and Saturday, 5:30–11 p.m.

Menu recommendations: Filet mignon, shrimp dishes, and grilled salmon are popular and beautifully presented, and the crème brulee is as good as any in France.

Comments: A few years ago this restaurant won many gourmet awards; it's now living off its past reputation. It is overpriced and always noisy. Food isn't bad these days; it's just more commercial and hasn't won awards for a while. Service is too casual for prices paid. Ask for a table away from the cramped doorway/hostess station.

CHRISTINA WAN'S   ★★★

Asian	Moderate	QUALITY
		80

2031 Hollywood Boulevard, Hollywood
(954) 923-1688

	VALUE
	A

Reservations: Recommended on weekends
Entree range: $12–19
Payment: MC, VISA, D, DC
Parking: On street and nearby municipal lots
Bar: Beer and wine
Wine selection: Limited; $12–30 bottle, $3.50–6 by the glass

Dress: Casual
Disabled access: Yes
Customers: Many who have been dining at Wan family restaurants for years; downtown workers and suburban couples and families who like good Chinese food

Open: Tuesday–Thursday, 11:30 a.m.–10 p.m.; Friday and Saturday, 11:30 a.m.–10:30 p.m.; Sunday, 4–10 p.m.

Menu recommendations: Mandarin, Szechuan, and Cantonese menus. Chicken and cashews as spicy as you want, garlic eggplant you won't soon forget.

Comments: Combination dinners are served before 7 p.m. and are a great value. Good veggie menu as well. Service is excellent, but Sunday evenings are wild as families do their Sunday night outing: Babies cry, school-age kids wrestle, and older folks rant about getting a table in time for the early bird. The family-owned staff juggle things well.

DELI DEN		★

		QUALITY
Delicatessen	Inexpensive	**85**

	VALUE
2889 Stirling Road, Fort Lauderdale	**A**
(954) 961-4070	

Reservations: Not necessary
When to go: Any time
Entree range: $7–13
Payment: MC, VISA, AMEX
Parking: Large lot
Bar: Wine

Wine selection: Small, $2.25 by the glass
Dress: Casual
Disabled access: Yes
Customers: Workers, tennis and golf players, families, tourists

Open: Daily, 8 a.m.–10 p.m.

Menu recommendations: Great corned beef and pastrami sandwiches, requisite pickles and cole slaw, potato pancakes. Matzoh ball chicken soup like great aunt Bessie used to make.

Comments: A big, barn-like restaurant in a shopping center, there's no decor to speak of, but food and smells are just like coming home— whether home is in Brooklyn, New Orleans, or the Wild, Wild West. The same wait staff has worked there for years.

EDUARDO DE SAN ANGEL		★★★

		QUALITY
Mexican	Moderate	**88**

	VALUE
2822 East Commercial Boulevard,	**C**
Fort Lauderdale; (954) 772-4731	

Reservations: Recommended for weekends
When to go: Weeknights
Entree range: $12–15
Payment: MC, VISA, AMEX, DC
Parking: Shopping center plaza

Bar: Beer and wine
Wine selection: Large; $25–80 bottles, $7–13 by the glass
Dress: Casual
Disabled access: Yes
Customers: Upscale

Lunch: Monday–Friday, 11 a.m.–3 p.m.
Dinner: Monday–Saturday, 5:30–10:30 p.m.

Menu recommendations: Gourmet Mexican menu includes crisply roasted duck with sauce (the recipe is more than 200 years old) made with pumpkin seeds and green chiles. Garlic shrimp are also spectacular.

Comments: This romantic restaurant has been designed to look like a small hacienda.

FULVIO'S ★★★

Italian	Moderate	QUALITY
		89

4148 SW 64th Avenue, Davie	VALUE
(954) 583-3666	C

Reservations: Recommended
When to go: Midweek
Entree range: $15–25
Payment: VISA, MC, AMEX, DC, D
Parking: Street
Bar: Full service
Wine selection: More than 100 wines;
$17.95–80 bottles, $4.95–8.95 by the glass
Dress: Dressy casual
Disabled access: Yes
Customers: Suburbanites, families, tourists

Dinner: Sunday and Tuesday–Thursday, 5–10 p.m.; Friday and Saturday, 5–11 p.m.; closed Monday

Menu recommendations: Stuffed chicken (which locals call the chicken ball), stuffed shrimp and shrimp Fulvio—both stuffed with vegetables, bread crumbs, and cheese. Unlimited house salad is fresh and tasty.

Comments: A longtime favorite with locals. Expect white tablecloths and personalized service.

GIBBY'S STEAKS & SEAFOOD ★★★

American	Moderate	QUALITY
		91

2900 NE 12th Terrace, Fort Lauderdale	VALUE
(954) 565-2929	B

Reservations: Suggested
When to go: After 7:30 p.m.
Entree range: $16–33
Payment: VISA, MC, AMEX, D, DC
Parking: Valet
Bar: Full service
Wine selection: Good; $22–55 bottle, $6–12.50 by the glass
Dress: Dressy casual
Disabled access: Yes
Customers: Retirees, families

Dinner: Daily, 5–10 p.m.

Menu recommendations: Salmon, filet mignon, and roast duck are big favorites, as well as lobster and stone crabs in season. House salad dressing is a garlicky mix you won't quickly forget.

Comments: Salad, potato, and dessert included. Textbook steakhouse decor.

GIORGIO'S		★★★
Mediterranean	Expensive	**QUALITY** 90
606 North Ocean Drive, Hollywood (954) 929-7030		**VALUE** C

Reservations: Recommended	Bar: Full service
When to go: Dinner; go early or mid-week, as weekends are noisy, crowded, and service gets a bit spotty.	Wine selection: Huge selection; $19–200 bottle, $5.75–9.75 by the glass
	Dress: Dressy casual
Entree range: $19–40	Disabled access: Yes
Payment: VISA, MC, AMEX, D	Customers: Glitzy models, beautiful
Parking: Valet	people, retirees and tourists

Brunch: Sunday, 11 a.m.–3 p.m.

Dinner: Monday–Friday, 4 p.m.–midnight (becomes nightclub after midnight on Friday); Saturday, 4 p.m.–1 a.m.

Menu recommendations: Grilled snapper is marvelous, and avgolemono (Greek lemon soup) is a big seller.

Comments: Patio, dining room, and outside deck on the Intracoastal Waterway offer same menu in different settings. Music gets louder as the hour gets later. Discounted menu items are available 4–5:30 p.m.

GRILL ROOM ON LAS OLAS		★★★★
Steakhouse	Very Expensive	**QUALITY** 95
620 East Las Olas Boulevard, Fort Lauderdale; (954) 467-2555		**VALUE** D

Reservations: Recommended	$20–1,500 bottles, $4 and up by glass
When to go: During the week	Dress: Dressy; jackets preferred for men
Entree range: $20–50	Disabled access: Yes
Payment: VISA, MC, AMEX, D	Customers: Expense account diners, cele-brants, and those who love fine service
Parking: Valet only	and good food
Bar: Full service	
Wine selection: Many choices;	

Dinner: Monday–Thursday, 6–10 p.m.; Friday and Saturday, 6–11 p.m.; closed Sunday

Menu recommendations: Chateaubriand, New York strip steak, veal chop, lobster, and fresh fish.

Comments: Wonderful ambiance, gracious service and preparation. Located in the charming Riverside Hotel on Fort Lauderdale's exciting Las Olas Boulevard. Patio dining also available with same menu.

ISLAMORADA FISH COMPANY		★★★
		QUALITY
Seafood	Moderate	**90**
		VALUE
220 Gulfstream Way, Dania Beach		**B**
(954) 927-7737		

Reservations: Not necessary	bottles, $4–6 by the glass
When to go: Lunch or dinner	**Dress:** Casual
Entree range: $15–30	**Disabled access:** Yes
Payment: VISA, MC, D, AMEX	**Customers:** Workers on lunch break,
Parking: Plenty of spaces in huge lot	tourists, locals, and shoppers who fre-
Bar: Full service	quent the cavernous Bass Pro Shop
Wine selection: 20 choices; $20–80	

Open: Daily, 11 a.m.–10 p.m.

Menu recommendations: Stone crabs as good as that famous place in Miami Beach; fresh fish broiled, grilled, blackened, or fried; and a superb Key lime pie.

Comments: Located in the Bass Pro Shop at Johnny Morris' Outdoor World, the restaurant offers patio dining, the Marlin Room (a clubby sort of eatery), and a large dining room.

LE PETIT CAFÉ		★★★
		QUALITY
French	Moderate	**86**
		VALUE
3308 Griffin Road, Dania Beach		**B**
(954) 967-9912		

Reservations: Recommended on	**Payment:** MC, VISA
weekends	**Parking:** Available
When to go: Dinner	**Bar:** Beer and wine

Wine selection: Fair; $17–20 bottle,
  $3.25 by the glass
Dress: Casual

Disabled access: Yes
Customers: Workers at lunchtime; locals
  and tourists at dinner

Lunch: Tuesday–Friday, 11:30 a.m.–2:30 p.m.

Dinner: Tuesday–Sunday, 4:30–10 p.m.

Menu recommendations: Crepes with chicken, mushrooms, and cheese; wonderful fish dishes. Dessert crepes are also super. A cup of onion soup, a crepe, and a salade verte make a marvelous meal.

Comments: A little bit of France in South Florida. Glass-topped tables with linen napery, flowers, and music, but the restaurant is small and tables a bit close together. Excellent service and food help to compensate.

LEFT BANK		★★★½
French	Very Expensive	**QUALITY** **90**
214 S. Federal Highway, Fort Lauderdale (954) 462-5376		**VALUE** **D**

Reservations: Recommended
When to go: Weeknights or late on
  weekends
Entree range: $20–35
Payment: VISA, MC, AMEX, D, DC
Parking: Valet and lot
Bar: Beer and wine

Wine selection: Award-winning selection;
  $30 and up bottle, $5 and up by the
  glass
Dress: Dressy
Disabled access: Yes
Customers: Yuppies

Dinner: Daily, 5:30 p.m.–between 9:30 and 10 p.m., depending on how busy they are

Menu recommendations: Fresh seafood and changing menu with lamb, beef, and fish dishes always available. Filet mignon and New York steaks are tops, but the fish dishes are light, delightfully presented, and all in all quite wonderful. Veal New York is a mélange of flavors (veal, onions, and prosciutto) and a memorable dining experience.

Comments: Very romantic setting and excellent service, but pricey. This could be a charming boite in Paris, but it's right near the heart of Fort Lauderdale's theater center.

LESTER'S DINER   ★

American	Inexpensive	QUALITY
		80

150 State Road 84, Fort Lauderdale
(954) 525-5641

	VALUE
	A

Reservations: No
When to go: Any time
Entree range: $5–12
Payment: VISA, MC, AMEX, D, DC
Parking: Plenty
Bar: None

Wine selection: None
Dress: Casual
Disabled access: Yes
Customers: Truckers, tourists on their
   way to the nearby airport, families,
   workers on their lunch breaks

Open: Daily, 24 hours

Menu recommendations: Omelets, burgers, and sandwiches diner-style.

Comments: Little or no atmosphere, but good comfort food and fast service. A Fort Lauderdale tradition. Lester's is a cavernous 1950s-style diner with food to match. Soups are filling and taste like homemade, sandwiches are large enough for two, and desserts are big enough for three or four to share. Daily specials are a great value.

MANERO'S STEAKHOUSE   ★★★

Steakhouse	Moderate/Expensive	QUALITY
		91

2600 East Hallandale Beach Boulevard,
Hallandale; (954) 456-1000

	VALUE
	B

Reservations: Recommended for parties
   of six or more
When to go: Early
Entree range: $20–40
Payment: VISA, MC, AMEX, D
Parking: Valet and lot
Bar: Full service
Wine selection: About 40 choices;

$20–250 bottle, $4–6.25 by the glass
Dress: Casual
Disabled access: Yes
Customers: Track devotees when nearby
   Gulfstream Race Course is running;
   couples, families, and retirees who opt
   for the early-bird specials

Lunch: Monday–Friday, 11:30 a.m.–3:30 p.m.

Dinner: Monday–Thursday, 4–9:30 p.m.; Friday, 4–10 p.m.; Saturday and Sunday, 4:30–10 p.m.

Menu recommendations: Steaks to write home about, excellent broiled scrod, and a refillable gorgonzola cheese salad that has kept diners coming back for years.

Comments: Steakhouse decor, in the same location—operated by the same family—since 1953. Decor hasn't really changed much since then. Photos of sports stars line the walls, and seemingly most of the sports world has visited.

OASIS BY THE SEA		★

Greek	Inexpensive	QUALITY 80
1211 North Surf Road, Hollywood (954) 922-4800		VALUE C

Reservations: No
When to go: Any time
Entree range: $6–12
Payment: VISA, MC
Parking: On side streets
Bar: Beer and wine
Wine selection: $16–17 bottle, $4.99 half-bottle, $3.50 by the glass
Dress: Casual; not all (male) diners wear shirts
Disabled access: Yes, access from the Broadwalk (cq)
Customers: Beach enthusiasts, tourists, families, locals out for a stroll

Open: 9 a.m. until; closing time varies

Menu recommendations: Gyros, burgers, Greek salads, spanikopita, hummus, baba ghanoush—typical Greek specialties.

Comments: Beachfront restaurant, sort of a shack where it's perfectly okay to come in a bathing suit with a towel wrapped around your shoulders. Sand on the floor is expected, and there's always a holiday atmosphere.

PADRINO'S		★ ★

Cuban	Moderate	QUALITY 84
2500 East Hallandale Beach Boulevard, Hallandale (954) 456-4550		VALUE B

Reservations: Not accepted
When to go: Lunch or dinner
Entree range: $10–15
Payment: VISA, MC, AMEX, D
Parking: Street
Bar: Beer and wine
Wine selection: Limited; $15–23 bottle, $3.75–5.50 by the glass
Dress: Casual
Disabled access: Yes
Customers: Families and couples of all ages

Open: Sunday, noon–10 p.m.; Tuesday–Thursday, 11:20 a.m.–10 p.m.; Friday, 11:30 a.m.–10:30 p.m.; Saturday, noon–10:30 p.m.; closed Monday

Menu recommendations: Ropa viejo (shredded beef in a piquant tomato sauce) is popular, and shrimp in garlic sauce is muy bueno.

Comments: Cuban restaurants are not a novelty in South Florida, and Padrino's is one of the best in the moderate price range. Decor is pleasant, service fairly good, but music tends to be a bit loud. When the place is busy (and it often is), the noise level is unpleasant.

TRY MY THAI		★★

		QUALITY
Thai	Moderate	**86**
		VALUE
2003 Harrison Street, Hollywood		**C**
(954) 926-5585		

1507 North Federal Highway, Fort Lauderdale
(954) 630-0030

Reservations: Suggested for larger parties
When to go: Weeknights, early dinners
Entree range: $9–16
Payment: VISA, MC, AMEX, D, DC
Parking: Public lots, street
Bar: Beer and wine

Wine selection: Small list; $16–26 bottle, $5.50–6.50 by the glass
Dress: Casual
Disabled access: Yes
Customers: Suits, office workers at lunch; locals, tourists for dinner

Lunch: Monday–Friday, 11 a.m.–2:30 p.m.

Dinner: Daily, 5–10:30 p.m. (Fort Lauderdale closed Monday)

Menu recommendations: Holy Cow, a spicy mix of Thai basil, chili, and beef; Forever Shrimp, with shrimp, ginger, and vegetables; topped off with Thai donuts or Banana Surprise—slices of banana in crispy shells, deep fried, and sprinkled with honey and sesame seeds.

Comments: Decorated with ties—yes, "ties"—in a variety of colors, fabrics, and styles.

WOLFGANG PUCK GRAND CAFE		★★★

		QUALITY
American	Moderate	**88**
		VALUE
2610 Sawgrass Mills Circle, Sunrise		**B**
(954) 846-8668		

Reservations: Recommended for parties of seven of more
When to go: Early

Entree range: $7.95–16.95
Payment: VISA, MC, AMEX, DC
Parking: Large mall lot, plus valet service

Bar: Full service
Wine selection: Limited; $20–30 bottle, $7–12 by the glass
Dress: Casual
Disabled access: Yes
Customers: Yuppies, young families, retirees

Open: Monday–Thursday, 11:30 a.m.–11 p.m.; Friday and Saturday, 11:30 a.m.–midnight; Sunday, 11:30 a.m.–10 p.m.; open 30 minutes additionally each night with sushi and pizza menu only

Menu recommendations: Tortilla soup is spicy, pepperoni pizza with fresh tomatoes excellent, and wiener schnitzel the best this side of Austria. Salads and burgers are king-sized, and desserts are designed to sabotage any diet—especially the dark chocolate crème brûlée.

Comments: Like Wolfgang Puck's world-famous Spago, his Café exemplifies his "life, love, eat" logo. A popular spot—always busy.

Entertainment and Nightlife

Entertainment and nightlife in Broward County translates to a lot of bright lights, great music, and great clubs. If you're looking for the outrageous, the really hot stuff lies south. It's South Beach that makes the tabloids, movies, and television shows. But while Miami is a mega-club town, that doesn't put Broward completely in the shade. Not at all—the local club scene is just not as glitzy, loud, or notorious. The choices for nighttime entertainment in Greater Fort Lauderdale are plentiful. Broward has supper and jazz clubs, comedy and gay clubs, and strip clubs. There are bingo rooms and nightly casino cruises. Expect top-drawer symphonies, dance companies, performances from Andrea Bocelli to Bette Midler, from James Taylor to Riverdance, from Mozart to Eminem—at some time during the year, that proverbial something for everyone is on stage somewhere in Broward County. Broward residents are largely refugees from major northern cities and for the most part are well traveled. They expect culture with a capital "C" and talk about Lincoln Center and Kennedy Center, Civic Theater, Broadway, and what they've seen on stage in London. They are savvy about entertainment, and this demanding audience gets what it wants.

While Fort Lauderdale—until the 1990s—was known primarily as a spring break hangout, it has made giant strides in these last few years and now appeals to visitors of all ages. We note that membership in the Fort Lauderdale Philharmonic Society is huge, most touring companies sell out, a short winter run of the controversial *The Vagina Monologues* completely sold out, and both Jackie Mason and Dame Edna attracted great crowds to their unique brands of comedy. Because of the huge success of its winter production, *The Vagina Monologues* are scheduled to return during summer.

Broward's venues range from the National Car Rental Center to Broward Theater for the Performing Arts, from Parker Playhouse to War Memorial Auditorium, and from Sunrise Musical Theater to Bailey Hall on the Broward Community Center Campus. Nightly, weekly, and monthly schedules are available each Friday in *The Miami Herald* or *The Sun-Sentinel*, in *Miami Metro* magazine, *Ocean Drive*, and *City & Shore*. *Where, Travel Host*, and other publications available in hotels generally offer an overview.

THEATER AND OTHER CULTURAL PURSUITS

Francine Mason of the Greater Fort Lauderdale Convention & Visitors Bureau notes a recent study by the National Endowment for the Arts found that attendance at Greater Fort Lauderdale's cultural events—opera, dance, theater, symphony and jazz concerts—was higher than Chicago, Philadelphia, and Pittsburgh. Tickets sell quickly throughout the county to a variety of performances. There's an endless market for culture among the many retirees from major northern cities, young professionals and their families, and tourists. Whether you prefer opera or the Back Street Boys, rap or heavy-duty feminist theater, chances are it will have appeared on stage in Broward at some point during the year.

The Broward number for Ticketmaster is (954) 523-3309; they sell tickets for the Broward Center, National Car Rental Center, Sunrise Musical Theater, Parker Playhouse, and other venues.

THE NIGHTCLUB CONNECTION

Clubs come, clubs go. Popular one season, they may be shuttered the next. Live music clubs open all the time, and they range from country to rock and roll and from jazz to gospel. Most of the action is found along Fort Lauderdale Beach, Las Olas, or in downtown Hollywood's historic district.

The Miami area is filled with Latin dance clubs. Fort Lauderdale has far fewer, but **Café Samba** (350 East Las Olas Boulevard, Fort Lauderdale; (954) 468-2000) has a Latin beat nightly. One of Fort Lauderdale's primo nightclubs/tourist attraction/supper clubs is **Mai Kai Polynesian Restaurant and Dinner Show** (3599 North Federal Highway, Fort Lauderdale; (954) 566-9533). For more than three decades, the hula show—featuring fire twirlers and dancers from Tahiti and Samoa, as well as Hawaii—has told stories via carefully choreographed movements complemented by the songs, music, costumes, and artifacts of the islands. The setting for this long-running Polynesian show is a tropical garden.

Stop by **Casablanca Café** (3049 Alhambra, between Las Olas and Sunrise, Fort Lauderdale; (954) 764-3500) for food from the Mediterranean and live music. Irish tunes and a thick brogue are on tap at **Maguire's Hill**

#17 (535 North Andrews Avenue, Fort Lauderdale; (954) 764-4453), with live music Thursday–Sunday; and **Dicey Riley's** (217 SW Third Street, Fort Lauderdale; (954) 524-2202), a pub with blues and Irish music nightly. The joint is jumpin' at **Sushi Blues** (1836 South Young Circle, Hollywood; (954) 929-9560), with dinner at 6 p.m. and live music Thursday–Saturday. Even more blues can be had Wednesday–Sunday at **Twocan Blue** (Aruba Beach, One Commercial Boulevard, Lauderdale-by-the-Sea; (954) 776-0001) and at **Christopher's** (2857 East Oakland Park Boulevard, Fort Lauderdale; (954) 561-2136).

THE GAY SCENE

Out & About, a major gay and lesbian travel newsletter, has named Fort Lauderdale's **Royal Palms Resort** as one of the top gay accommodations in the United States. "The gay and lesbian travel industry is estimated to be a $25 billion market. Last year alone, more than 670,000 gay and lesbian travelers visited Greater Fort Lauderdale and spent approximately $570 million," says Richard Gray, owner of the Royal Palms.

Greater Fort Lauderdale has more than 100 gay-owned establishments, including hotels, bars, clubs, and restaurants, plus the second-largest Metropolitan Community Church congregation in the country, a Gay & Lesbian Community Center (phone (954) 563-9500), and three gay and lesbian publications: *HotSpots!* magazine (phone (954) 928-1862); *Scoop* (phone (954) 561-9707), and *The Express* (phone (954) 568-1880).

Many gay-friendly restaurants and clubs are located in Wilton Manors or nearby Fort Lauderdale. Recommended restaurants include **Chardees** (2209 Wilton Drive, Wilton Manors; (954) 563-1800), **Courtyard Café** (2211 Wilton Drive, Wilton Manors; (954) 563-2499), **Hi-Life Café** (3000 North Federal Highway, Fort Lauderdale; (954) 563-1395), and **Storks** (2505 NE 15th Avenue, Fort Lauderdale; (954) 567-3220). Bars and clubs include **Cathode Ray** (1307 East Las Olas Boulevard, Fort Lauderdale; (954) 462-8611), **Georgie's Alibi** (2266 Wilton Drive, Wilton Manors; (954) 565-2526), and **Tropics** (2004 Wilton Drive, Wilton Manors; (954) 537-6000). Action starts late and includes a variety of theme nights.

FAMILY ENTERTAINMENT

Gameworks (Sawgrass Mills, in the Oasis, 2608 Sawgrass Mills Circle, Sunrise; (954) 845-8740) is a state-of-the-art game room, full-service restaurant, and bar created by film honcho Steven Spielberg. It appeals equally to families, young couples, and singles. **Dave & Buster's** (3000 Oakwood Boulevard, Hollywood; (954) 923-5505) is a video game mecca attracting kids of all ages.

Boomer's Dania Beach (1801 NW First Street, Dania Beach; (954) 921-1411) offers go-kart racing, mini golf, and video games. **Beach Place** (17 South Atlantic Boulevard, Fort Lauderdale; (954) 764-3460) is a food and open-air entertainment complex, with five restaurants and four night-clubs—all in a courtyard atmosphere. A similar complex can be found at **Las Olas River Front** (300 SW First Avenue, Fort Lauderdale; (954) 522-1899) in the Fort Lauderdale Historic District.

The Best of Broward County Clubs

Name	Cover	Cost	City
Comedy Club			
Uncle Funny's	$7–10	Mod	Davie
Dance Club			
Tugboat Annie's	None	Mod	Dania Beach
Gay Club			
Cathode Ray Cocktail Lounge	None	Mod	Fort Lauderdale
Jazz Club			
O'Hara's Jazz Club	None	Exp	Fort Lauderdale
Live Music			
Bahia Cabana	None	Mod	Fort Lauderdale
Chili Pepper	$5	Mod	Fort Lauderdale
Dinopetes	None	Inexp	Hollywood
Piano Bar			
Howl at the Moon	Sunday: $5 locals, $10 tourists	Mod	Fort Lauderdale

CLUB PROFILES

BAHIA CABANA

Outdoor bar featuring pop music
Who Goes There: Young people, college students, yuppies who fondly remember spring break, tourists

3001 Harbor Drive, Fort Lauderdale, behind the Bahia Cabana Beach Resort (954) 524-1555

Cover: None
Minimum: None
Mixed drinks: $4–5
Wine: $3 and up
Beer: $3.25–3.50 (imports)

Food available: Full menu available, but lots of sandwiches and burgers
Hours: Sunday–Thursday, 7 a.m.–2 a.m.; Friday and Saturday, 7 a.m.–3 a.m.

What goes on: Great outdoor bar and biergarten with a wonderful view of the yacht harbor and either a DJ or live music nightly.

Comments: This is a Fort Lauderdale tradition—a kind of coming-of-age bar for locals—and the nightly action appeals to laid-back tourists of all ages. T-shirts and shorts are the most common outfit for guys and gals, but you'll run into a couple of suits who come by after work as well.

CATHODE RAY COCKTAIL LOUNGE

Gay and lesbian lounge
Who Goes There: Men and men, women and women, some mixed clientele—packs of pretty people; typical ages 25–30

1307 East Las Olas Boulevard, Fort Lauderdale; (954) 462-0291

Cover: None
Minimum: None
Mixed drinks: $4.25; half-price happy hour
Wine: $5

Beer: $3.25–3.75
Food available: Light fare, hamburgers, pizza, tuna nachos
Hours: Daily, 2 p.m.–2 a.m.

What goes on: Tourists and locals alike enjoy the chance to chat each other up, and dancers can do their thing to everything but rap music (okay, there's a lot of disco, but the 1970s weren't all bad). Non-dancers can watch music videos or enjoy the sports bar, while a piano bar appeals to all. Don't expect wild things, but theme nights bring out those with a bit more sense of adventure.

Comments: Everyone seems to have a good time. Cathode Ray has been around a long while.

CHILI PEPPER

A real hotspot with multiple stages in a warehouse venue
Who Goes There: Club and college kids, tourists, locals out for a night on the town

200 West Broward Boulevard, Fort Lauderdale; (954) 525-5996

Cover: $5

Minimum: None

Mixed drinks: $5

Wine: $5

Beer: $5

Food available: None

Hours: Wednesday–Sunday, 9 p.m.–
4 a.m.

What goes on: Popular Fort Lauderdale bar with outdoor stage for concerts, indoor DJ, balcony seating, and a variety of music and styles. SUTRA, a separate, more upscale area, is a bottle club for older guests.

Comments: It's a scene. Weekends are crazed and like someone's idea of what a noisy, loud, smoky club should be.

DINOPETES

I don't care what people say, rock 'n' roll is here to stay
Who Goes There: Young people, tourists, casino crowd from across the street

4221 North State Road Seven (also called US 441), Hollywood
(954) 966-4441

Cover: None

Minimum: Two drinks (unless you're eating dinner)

Mixed drinks: $4; half-price happy hour

Wine: $2.50–4

Beer: $2–2.75

Food available: Restaurant menu specializing in steak and lobster dinners for around $10

Hours: Monday–Saturday, 4 p.m. until;
closed Sunday

What goes on: Basically rock 'n' roll, but swing music and karaoke are on tap on specific nights.

Comments: Neighborhood bar meets rock, and the music is the best thing to come out of it. The owners are musicians with their own following and friends, so the place can really rock. Swing music on Wednesday nights brings its own kind of groupies—and older versions of rock 'n' roll enthusiasts. Monday and Thursday nights feature karaoke.

HOWL AT THE MOON

Dueling piano bars and sing-a-longs
Who Goes There: Tourists and locals who enjoy Beach Place or the area

17 South Atlantic Boulevard, Fort Lauderdale (on the third floor of Beach Place)
(954) 522-5054

Cover: Sundays, $5 for locals, $10 for out-of-towners
Minimum: Varies
Mixed drinks: $4–6.50
Wine: $4–6.50
Beer: $4–6.50
Food available: Finger food, appetizer-like

items including chicken fingers and conch fritters from Sloppy Joe's menu (adjacent eatery, a branch of the famous Key West bar founded in 1931 by Ernest Hemingway)
Hours: Sunday–Thursday, 7 a.m.–2 a.m.; Friday and Saturday, 7 a.m.–4 a.m.

What goes on: Dueling pianos play everything from classic rock to pop favorites, show tunes, current hits, classic rock, and country—basically anything that the crowd can sing along to—and they do so with passion. It's a good-time crowd, and the music is fairly good.

Comments: Parking can be difficult, and during the winter season crowds are pretty thick at Beach Place.

O'HARA'S JAZZ CLUB

Jazz club
Who Goes There: Jazz devotees of all ages, including yuppies and their parents and visiting musicians

722 East Las Olas Boulevard, Fort Lauderdale; (954) 524-1764

Cover: None
Minimum: Two drinks per set
Mixed drinks: $6–15
Wine: $5.25 and up
Beer: $4.25 and up

Food available: Light menu of appetizers, salads, and sandwiches
Hours: Sunday–Thursday, 11 a.m.– 2 a.m.; Friday and Saturday, 11 a.m.– 3 a.m.

What goes on: O'Hara's has become a tradition with jazz fans of all ages. Good live music starts nightly at 9 p.m., and crowds on the weekend can be huge.

Comments: O'Hara's has a second location in Hollywood (1902 Hollywood Boulevard; (954) 925-2555), which is larger and features the same live jazz and R&B. The Hollywood branch is open 5 p.m.–2 a.m. daily.

TUGBOAT ANNIE'S

Dance club and nightclub
Who Goes There: Young people who like the outdoors (it's right on the Intracoastal) and loud music, society folks who like to mingle with down-home bubbas; sometimes they're together

815 NE Third Street, Dania Beach (in Harbour Town Marina); (954) 925-3399

Cover: None
Minimum: None
Mixed drinks: $4–5
Wine: $3 and up
Beer: Varies

Food available: Pizza, seafood, raw bar,
and super burgers
Hours: Monday–Thursday, 11 a.m.–10
p.m.; Friday–Sunday, 11 a.m.–midnight

What goes on: Local bands perform nightly, offering a variety of music: Wednesday, it's steel drums; Thursday, a male vocalist performs; Friday, it's reggae; Saturday, blues and classic rock.

Comments: This is an out-of-the-way nightspot where anything goes. Picture tacky plastic tables and chairs with music that is often quite good (with food to match) and a tropical setting that is really what Florida nights are all about. When the music wails, and the moon shines, and the liquor flows, it's magic. Plenty of parking.

UNCLE FUNNY'S

Comedy club
Who Goes There: Folks who like to laugh, aged 18–85

9160 State Road 84, Davie; (954) 474-5653

Cover: $7–10
Minimum: Two drinks
Mixed drinks: $4.50–5
Wine: $3 and up
Beer: $3.25 and up
Food available: Full menu from Joe's
Sports Bar and Grill next door includes

wraps, grilled chicken sandwiches,
steaks, seafood
Hours: One show Wednesday, Thursday,
and Sunday at 8 p.m.; two shows Friday
at 8:30 p.m. and 11 p.m.; and three
shows on Saturday at 7 p.m., 9 p.m.,
and 11 p.m.

What goes on: Comics from around the country perform 90–105-minute shows, and the same performers appear every six to eight months, so there's a following of sorts. Singles, couples, and party groups all coexist in a fun environment. The 7 p.m. Saturday show is smoke-free.

Comments: This is a typical comedy club with an adjoining sports bar, so karaoke is available and all the big games are televised—if laughter isn't enough activity for you. They say it's the best medicine. No parking problems, and that's pretty funny.

Part Five

Miami-Dade County

The Capital of the Caribbean

Mention Miami and most folks are hit with a flood of impressions:

- Broad beaches, white sand, palm trees, and a stunning and intoxicatingly beautiful city by the sea.

- Candy-colored Art Deco palaces shimmering in the hot sun, and sidewalks jammed with slim-hipped Euro boys and girls, gorgeous fashion models with portfolios tucked under their arms, and Lycra-clad Rollerbladers.

- Guns and cocaine, Al Capone, and Miami Vice: a city awash in illegal money that proudly wears its reputation for crime and violence like a cheap perfume.

Vivid impressions, all, and totally in sync with this chamber-of-commerce message: Miami is the sun-and-fun capital of the universe, a jet-setter's paradise with a bad-boy reputation, a sun-drenched escape from the winter cold.

All of which is true. Yet Miami is something else.

It's a city of two million where more people speak Spanish than English; a multicultural collage and ethnic grab bag; the new capital of Latin America, full of banks and financial institutions; one of the premier convention sites in the United States; *the* place to go for millions of well-heeled Latin American and European tourists.

To put it another way: For Americans, Miami is an international destination that doesn't require a passport.

Yet, to unprepared travelers, Miami's Hispanic soul can come as a shock. From the moment they deplane at Miami International Airport, these unwary vacationers and business travelers are confronted with a confusing

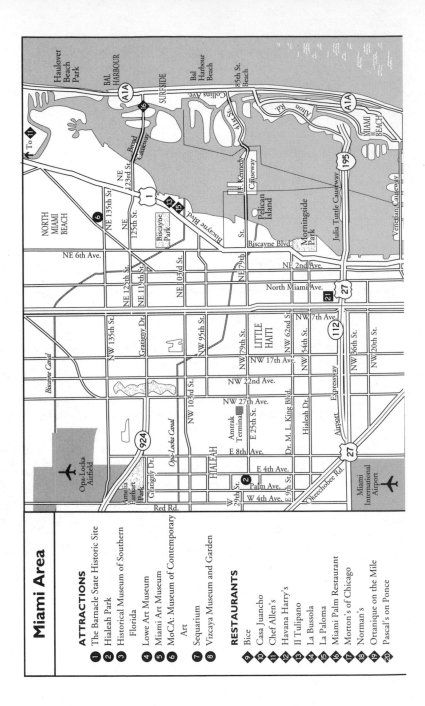

Miami Area

ATTRACTIONS

1. The Barnacle State Historic Site
2. Hialeah Park
3. Historical Museum of Southern Florida
4. Lowe Art Museum
5. Miami Art Museum
6. MoCA: Museum of Contemporary Art
7. Sequarium
8. Vizcaya Museum and Garden

RESTAURANTS

9. Bice
10. Casa Juancho
11. Chef Allen's
12. Havana Harry's
13. Il Tulipano
14. La Bussola
15. La Paloma
16. Miami Palm Restaurant
17. Morton's of Chicago
18. Norman's
19. Oranique on the Mile
20. Pascal's on Ponce

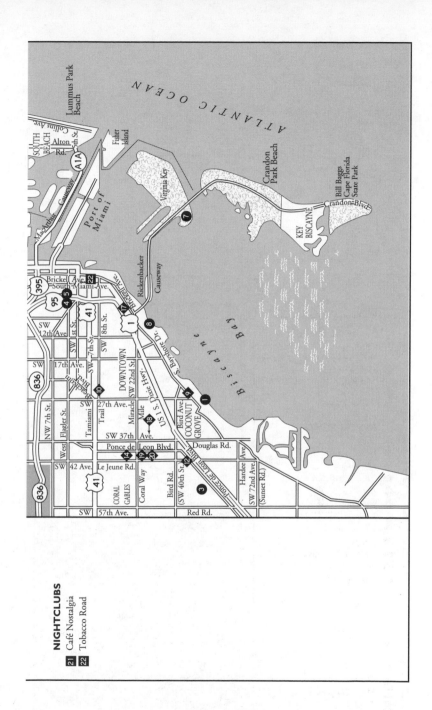

ATLANTIC OCEAN

Lummus Park Beach

Collins Ave.

SOUTH BEACH
Alton Rd.
A1A 5th St.

Fisher Island

MacArthur Causeway

Port of Miami

Virginia Key

Crandon Park Beach

Bill Baggs Cape Florida State Park

Crandon Blvd.

KEY BISCAYNE

7

Brickell Ave.
South Miami Ave.
22
395
95 4 5
41
SW 1st St.
SW 8th St.
SW 12th Ave.
SW 7th St.

Rickenbacker Causeway

Biscayne Bay

1
8

SW 17th Ave.

Bird Rd.

DOWNTOWN
SW 22nd St.

SW 27th Ave.
10

836

NW 7th St.
Flagler St.

Tamiami Trail

S. Bayshore Dr.

US 1 S. Dixie Hwy.

9
1

Bird Ave.

COCONUT GROVE

Mdle
Ave.
18
Miracle

Ponce de Leon Blvd.
Douglas Rd.

West

SW 42 Ave.
Le Jeune Rd.
21
19 20
14

Ponce de Leon Blvd.

Hardee Ave.

41

CORAL GABLES

Coral Way

Bird Rd.

(SW 40th St.)
12

3

SW 72nd Ave.

(Sunset Rd.)

836

SW 57th Ave.
Red Rd.

NIGHTCLUBS
21 Café Nostalgia
22 Tobacco Road

Miami Beach

ATTRACTIONS
1. Holocaust Memorial of Miami Beach
2. The Jewish Museum of Florida
3. The Wolfsonian

RESTAURANTS
4. Astor Place
5. Blue Door at Delano
6. China Grill
7. The Forge/Jimmy'z
8. Joe Allen
9. Joe's Stone Crab Restaurant
10. Nemo
11. Pacific Time
12. Red Square
13. Smith & Wollensky
14. Tuscan Steak
15. 1220 at the Tides

NIGHTCLUBS
16. Bash
17. The Clevelander Bar
18. Club Tropigala
19. Crobar
20. Jimmy'z
21. The Living Room at the Strand
22. Mac's Club Deuce
23. Twist

South Miami–Dade County

ATTRACTIONS

1. Biscayne National Park
2. Fairchild Tropical Garden
3. Gold Coast Railroad Museum
4. Metrozoo
5. Monkey Jungle
6. Parrot Jungle and Gardens
7. Weeks Air Museum

Babel of foreign languages, the pungent odors of cigars and *cafe Cubano,* the highly charged hustle and bustle that says "we're not in Kansas anymore." For visitors like these, Miami isn't really a city—it's a discordant clash of cultures that's best ignored in the rush to safe harbor at a beach or convention hall.

These folks are missing a lot of what this city has to offer: the chance to luxuriate in a warm, vibrant, and gregarious Latin culture, and the opportunity to experience an exotic metropolis where news from Havana, Caracas, or Bogotá can overshadow the latest scandal in Washington.

The unfamiliarity of the Latin culture to most Americans *does* make Miami intimidating to many visitors—especially if you step off the plane expecting to find a "normal" U.S. city.

It doesn't have to be this way for you.

In this section, you'll find suggestions for things to do that reveal the essence of this young, vibrant, and uninhibited city. In addition, you'll discover why Miami is described with words such as *sensual, spicy,* and *seductive.*

We give visitors explicit directions on how to visit Little Havana; where to sample the best in Cuban, Haitian, and Caribbean cuisine; where you can walk down streets and hear Spanish, Creole, Yiddish, Russian, and German spoken within a single block. We'll introduce you to a culture that's outspoken and unrestrained, offering visitors a taste of a vivid street life like no other city in North America.

A Brief History

For an American city, Miami is unique: the majority of the population is Hispanic and the city vibrates with an entrepreneurial spirit that drives Miami's breathtakingly—and, in traffic, nerve-wrackingly—frenetic pace. Dominated by Cuban entrepreneurs, Hispanic-owned businesses set the high-pitched corporate rhythm of Miami.

The Cubans' fast-paced commercial spirit is embodied in everything from family-owned grocery stores to huge corporations and banks. The roots of this hard-charging business community go back to the first Cuban refugees fleeing the Castro regime in the late 1950s—people from the entrepreneurial and professional classes who often arrived penniless but brought with them the skills and drive to become successfully self-employed in the United States.

They came to the right place. Historically, the success of the hard-working new immigrants fits a Miami pattern of boom and bust that began not very long ago. After all, the city was founded only a century ago on a long-shot business gamble that paid off. Through the decades that followed, Miami's history was a roller-coaster ride of dizzying successes and precipitous declines.

A Woman with a Dream

While South Florida's mild winters had been attracting visitors from the north for years in the mid- and late 1800s, it took an idea from a woman from Cleveland named Julia Tuttle to create the city of Miami. After settling on the north bank of the Miami River in 1891, Tuttle began to plan her city—and worked to find a railroad magnate who would extend a line south to the tip of the Florida peninsula.

Henry M. Flagler was one of the railroad men Tuttle tried to entice. His line reached Palm Beach in 1893, but he said he wasn't interested in extending it another 66 miles to tiny Miami. That is, until the winter of 1894–95.

A killer freeze struck Florida that winter and destroyed most of the valuable citrus fruit crops—but the cold didn't extend as far south as Miami, where the orange blossoms continued to bloom. The legend is that Tuttle sent a simple, eloquent message to Flagler as a final plea to extend his railroad line—a single orange blossom. Whether the legend is true or not, Flagler changed his mind and the line to Miami was completed on April 15, 1896. All 300 residents of Miami turned out to greet the locomotive—and a new era.

The Early Twentieth Century

The pace of development started to pick up. Within a few months a newspaper rolled off the press, local citizens voted to incorporate the town, streets were laid out, and churches and schools were established. The city was already promoting itself as "America's sun porch."

A modest boom resulted in the early years of the twentieth century. Swamps were drained, marking the beginning of the demise of the Everglades; Government Cut—the future Port of Miami—was dug across the lower end of Miami Beach to improve access to Miami's harbor; and Flagler extended his railroad farther south to Key West in 1912.

Thousands of people made the move south to take advantage of the year-round warmth and sunshine of Miami. In 1915, the citizens of Miami Beach voted to incorporate and elected a mayor, J. N. Lummus. The south end of the island already boasted several casinos, and holiday hotels began sprouting up.

The Roaring Twenties

Then the Roaring Twenties arrived, along with developers who carved up nearby farmland into subdivisions. The city's population doubled between 1920 and 1923. Soon, Miami's growth turned into a feeding frenzy as dozens of new communities sprang up. It was also the era of Prohibition—and rum-runners had a field day along South Florida's impossible-to-patrol coast. Mobsters moved in and operated with virtual immunity from the law. The city's reputation as a place teetering on both the moral and geographical edge of America had begun.

Miami in the early 1920s was real-estate crazy. Prices spiraled as property changed hands once, twice, three times. But most of the profits were on paper. Toward the end of 1925 the bottom began to fall out of the boom, sales at Coral Gables began to decline, and railroads announced an embargo of all but essential freight so they could repair their tracks, cutting off the supply of building materials.

The Pendulum Swings

But it took an act of nature to deliver a near-knockout blow. A hurricane struck on September 17, 1926, killing more than 100 people and leaving Miami in chaos. Houses were smashed, businesses were destroyed, boats were thrown onto dry land. National headlines screamed, "Miami Is Wiped Out!"—which was nearly the case.

Over the next few years, Miami's population fled northward. Local leaders went bankrupt. But it wasn't all bad news: Some money came to Miami from outsiders who purchased Hialeah racetrack, the city's aviation industry was born, and airports were built. During the Great Depression, Greynolds and Matheson Hammock Parks were constructed by the Civilian Conservation Corps.

Slowly, tourism began to pick up in the 1930s, especially in Miami Beach, where new, "modern" hotels and apartments proliferated on Collins Avenue. Northerners swarmed south again to escape cold winters—and the Depression. More than 500 Art Deco structures were built and tourists flocked to "futuristic" Miami Beach.

War . . . and Another Boom

The recovery didn't last long, however. The Japanese bombing of Pearl Harbor in 1941 and the U.S. declaration of war killed tourism. Nor did it help when a German U-boat torpedoed a tanker in full view of the Florida coast in February 1942. The city's hotels were empty.

That is, until the soldiers came to be trained in the warm climate of South Florida. By the end of 1942 the military had turned 147 hotels into barracks and many hotels into temporary hospitals for wounded soldiers. GIs trained on Miami Beach and German prisoners of war were interned at camps in suburban Kendall and Homestead.

After the war, thousands of former soldiers returned to South Florida with their families, became students on the GI Bill, and crowded the University of Miami. There was a new housing boom in Miami. Farms were transformed into suburbs, and by the end of the 1950s the population of Greater Miami was nearing one million. The future of Miami looked good.

A Revolution Revolutionizes Miami

But it was to change radically after Fidel Castro deposed Cuban dictator Fulgencio Batista in 1959. After Castro declared himself a socialist, confiscated property, and nationalized many island businesses, thousands of Cubans left Havana every day—many with nothing more than the clothes they wore. Most of them came to Miami. Almost overnight, entire neighborhoods filled with people speaking only Spanish.

After the failed, CIA-led Bay of Pigs invasion of Cuba in 1961 (many exiled leaders still believe they were betrayed by the United States) and the Cuban missile crisis of 1962 (in which Russia agreed to remove its missiles in return for a U.S. promise not to invade Cuba), it looked like the Cubans were in Miami to stay. Over the years, thousands of political refugees fled Cuba on "freedom flights" to Miami, expanding the city's Hispanic population base. By 1973, the Cuban population of Miami had swelled to 300,000.

In the 1960s and 1970s, another wave of immigrants moved to Miami: Jewish retirees from the north. By 1975, 300,000 Jews lived in Greater Miami, making the city's Jewish community second only to New York's in size. Most are concentrated in Miami Beach, and today the city serves as the de facto capital for retired American Jews during the winter months.

Ethnic Tension and the White Powder Trade

Miami, alas, is no melting pot. Urban renewal and hard-charging Cubans were squeezing out—and putting the economic squeeze on—Miami's African American community as many jobs were taken by recent immigrants. In 1968, Miami had its first race riot when Liberty City exploded just when Richard Nixon was giving his acceptance speech at the Republican National Convention in Miami Beach.

In the 1970s, drugs began playing a big role in Miami as big money poured into the city to satisfy America's demand for illegal narcotics. Yet, at the same time, the legitimate business community prospered; the Cuban community, no longer made up of penniless refugees, thrived and ran successful businesses throughout Miami.

Although a recession in the early 1970s was a setback, Miami was booming again at the end of the decade. The city had turned into an international banking center as money flowed in from Latin America, rapid transit construction was under way, and the downtown area was being revitalized.

Then, more setbacks. In 1980, more blacks and disadvantaged Miamians rioted after a Tampa jury acquitted a white policeman of murdering a black man, Arthur McDuffie. Haitian "boat people" were landing almost daily on South Florida beaches. Then Fidel Castro announced that anyone who wanted to leave Cuba could do so—and Miami Cubans sailed to Mariel Harbor in Cuba to help them. They were forced to bring back some unwanted passengers as well: criminals and inmates of Cuba's prisons and mental institutions. The city struggled under 125,000 new "Marielito" refugees, many of them undesirables who tarnished the city's reputation.

A lot of the new refugees settled in South Beach, further driving the neighborhood of 1930s hotels and apartments even closer to the brink of slumdom; Miamians avoided the neighborhood at night. Some Anglo residents of Miami were fed up and many cars sported bumper stickers that read: "Will the last American leaving Miami please bring the flag?" A variation of "white flight" had set in, and Anglo residents began to leave Miami, often heading north to Broward County and beyond.

The early 1980s were turbulent years in Miami. Drug dealers pumped more than $10 billion into the economy and the sale of handguns soared—as did the city's murder rate. In 1981, 621 people died violent deaths in Dade County, and Miami earned a national reputation as Murder Capital USA.

Miami Vice and a Jet-Set Destination

But just as with every other crisis that preceded this one, Miami bounced back. A new building boom started downtown. Next, the city's image improved dramatically in 1984 when *Miami Vice* premiered on national television and revealed a city steeped in glamorous danger and lush, tropical beauty. In 1985, the city elected its first Cuban-born mayor, Xavier Suarez. The new Bayside Marketplace attracted tourists and shoppers to downtown, and the Pope paid a visit in September 1987.

In the late 1980s South Beach made a spectacular comeback. Hundreds of millions of dollars were spent renovating the Art Deco hotels and apartment buildings built in the 1930s. Inhabited in the 1970s and early 1980s by Jewish retirees from colder climates, today these whimsical buildings are home to hotels, artists' lofts, chi-chi restaurants, oceanfront cafés, art galleries, and theaters. Jet-set celebrities such as Madonna, Robert De Niro, Cher, Cameron Diaz, and Sharon Stone are South Beach regulars. Today, instead of a place to avoid, South Beach is a place to be seen.

More Crime . . . and Tourists Are the Targets

Although Miami is an increasingly popular destination for tourists from outside the United States (especially South America and Europe), some well-publicized murders put a crimp in the city's tourist business. In 1993, nine foreign tourists were murdered in Florida, including a German visitor who was shot in his car after leaving Miami International Airport—as he was reading directions on how to avoid crime in Miami. In December 1993, tourism was down 7.6 percent compared to the previous December.

Miami has cleaned up its act somewhat—as we go to press, crime is down, even against tourists who continue to besiege the city in the winter.

But there are other problems that won't go away any time soon: Miami is a complicated city beset with serious social problems. Ethnic divisions between Anglos, Cubans, Haitians, Central Americans, and African Americans are often appallingly clear. Riots and violent expressions of rage have been a staple of Miami's civic life since the 1960s.

Compounding the problems are nonstop waves of immigration that began with Cubans in the late 1950s, continued with Nicaraguans in the 1970s and 1980s, and in the 1990s brought Haitians escaping economic deprivation and repression.

Miami on the Rebound

Travel industry experts say that in spite of the problems, Miami's and Florida's futures as tourist destinations look rosy: South Americans are a rapidly expanding market for Florida tourism, and safety and security in the state far surpasses that of most Latin American countries. Meanwhile, police and tourism agencies are beefing up police patrols around Miami International Airport (MIA), installing better highway signs, stripping rental cars of identifying markings, and implementing awareness campaigns to help visitors avoid becoming crime statistics. These and other visitor safety programs have reduced crimes against tourists by about 60 percent, and in 2000, FBI statistics dropped Miami from sixth to tenth place of the most crime-plagued cities in the United States. In 1999, Miami tourism authorities reported that 9.8 million overnight tourists visited Miami—and 55 percent were international. Today, it's one of the hottest travel destinations in the world.

Miami Neighborhoods

Many of Miami's neighborhoods are officially cities on their own, and each has a distinctive background and character. Most can be explored on foot, but a car is still indispensable to get from one neighborhood to another. Keep in mind that the character of a neighborhood can change rapidly in sprawling Miami, making it all too easy to stray into hostile territory.

The following list of Miami's most popular neighborhoods (all of which are safe for exploration by visitors on foot, except where noted) starts in South Miami Beach, continues north along the ocean to Sunny Isles, crosses Biscayne Bay to North Miami and Aventura, and turns south to Little Haiti, downtown, Coral Gables, and other towns and neighborhoods in south Dade County.

SOUTH BEACH

Created 50 years ago as a place for Northerners to escape cold winters and the Great Depression, South Miami Beach (usually called South Beach or

SoBe) is a 23-block area on the southern tip of Miami Beach. The architecture is intentionally whimsical—a collage of Art Deco, streamlined moderne, and Spanish Mediterranean–revival styles adapted to the South Florida climate. Over the decades, the old neighborhood has had its ups and downs, but today, South Beach is very much on a roll.

A preservation movement that began in the 1970s has resulted in a kaleidoscope of restored old buildings—mostly hotels, also some apartment buildings, restaurants, and condos—in lollipop colors, as well as streets filled with fashion models pouty young Europeans, international photographers, spandexed fitness fanatics, and a few retirees hanging on as prices keep going up.

South Beach is also a popular stop with the jet set. Singer Gloria Estefan and her hubby own a restaurant on Ocean Avenue (Lario's), Academy Award–winner Robert De Niro's apartment takes up the entire floor of an Art Deco apartment building, and the late fashion designer Gianni Versace spent $8 million to renovate the oceanfront, circa-1930 Mediterranean Revival villa on Ocean Drive (where he was murdered in July 1997). No wonder a group of major magazine editors dubbed South Beach the "American Riviera."

It's also a neighborhood with some problems, many of which soon become apparent to visitors. On weekends, traffic slows to a crawl, and finding a place to park induces heartburn. While South Beach has a reputation for being safe, car break-ins are a problem. Don't leave anything of value in your car. Finally, keep this in mind: Many Miami residents who own a car routinely take a taxi to South Beach for an evening on the town. Parking, they say, is too much of a hassle.

Thinking of renting a room? Accommodations tend toward the funky, with rooms and amenities right out of the 1950s. (Don't assume that a South Beach hotel's nifty, recently renovated Art Deco exterior is an indication that the rooms got a face-lift, too.) The nightclub and street scene goes on all night, seven nights a week: light sleepers, beware.

Everyone who visits Miami, however, should come to South Beach at least once. If the constant procession of hardbodies, neo-hippies, permatanned geriatrics, punk rockers, and portfolio-carrying fashionistas isn't enough to keep you entertained, then SoBe's eclectic spread of boutiques, outdoor cafés, nightclubs, art galleries, restaurants, and bookstores will.

And don't miss an evening stroll down Ocean Drive, where the best Art Deco architecture faces the sea and the beautiful people strut their stuff; walk down the street side for up-close, elbow-to-elbow people-watching, then cruise back on the Lummus Park (ocean) side for the best views of the architecture.

CENTRAL MIAMI BEACH

While the architecture of South Beach is rooted in the 1930s, the mile-long stretch of Miami Beach above 21st Street has its feet firmly planted in the 1950s. Outrageous, ostentatious hotels loom over the beach and Collins Avenue—and the most outré is the Fontainebleau Hilton, at 4441 Collins Avenue, a curving mass of 1950s kitsch.

Across Collins Avenue and Indian Creek is where Miami Beach's wealthiest residents live. Drive, stroll, or rent a bike to view exclusive homes along pine tree–lined roads such as Alton Road, Pine Tree Drive, Bay Drive, and La Gorce Drive. Famous names residing in the neighborhood include Julio Iglesias, Cher, and Sylvester Stallone. Boat cruises of Biscayne Bay are available at the marina across from the Eden Roc Hotel.

Some folks are confused by Miami Beach's strange mix of commercial properties—hotels, restaurants, bars, grocery stores, travel agencies, etc. —and residential properties—mostly large condominium and apartment buildings sprinkled throughout the town. And it does create a problem for some short-time visitors who are stymied in their search for, say, a restaurant or bar within walking distance of their hotel, which is surrounded by anonymous-looking apartment buildings. The reason for the odd mixture—odd for a resort town, anyway—is that Miami Beach is a year-round working city, not just a vacation mecca.

NORTH OF MIAMI BEACH

North of the procession of glitzy 1950s hotels in central Miami Beach a lot of the scenery gets uninspiring. Yet, for many people, that's okay: This stretch of Miami Beach is almost a purer Florida that lets up on the unrelenting trendiness to the south.

The communities of Surfside, Bal Harbour, and Sunny Isles are respectively dominated by Jewish and Canadian tourists and retirees, rich people living in an exclusive enclave, and middle-of-the-road tourists who don't know any better—or only care about easy access to the beach. With their seemingly endless succession of high-rise buildings, these neighborhoods comprise what's often called the "condo corner" of Miami.

Yet these communities offer a comfortable, low-key ambience that contrasts to the high-octane pulse of South Beach. Some bright spots along this stretch of US A1A are the North Shore State Recreation Area (between 91st and 95th streets; reputed to be one of the few places in Miami Beach to officially allow topless bathing—although our sharp reporters note that European women tend to ignore local conventions and doff their tops all along Miami Beach's shoreline); Haulover Beach Park (featuring uncrowded beaches—including a nude beach—a marina, kayak rentals, and a great place to fly kites); and Bal Harbour Shops, full of expensive designer stores as tony as any on Rodeo Drive.

Located at the northern end of Miami Beach, Sunny Isles offers folks out for a drive a throwback to American culture in the 1950s: a busy commercial strip along Collins Avenue filled with hotels and motels with "theme" motifs. Enjoy the whimsy before the chain hotels take over and homogenize the view.

Wolfie Cohen's Rascal House, a restaurant and sandwich shop in Sunny Isles, is considered by many to be one of Miami Beach's quintessential monuments to eating (along with Joe's Stone Crab in South Beach).

NORTH MIAMI

Communities east of Biscayne Bay (across from Miami Beach) and north toward Broward County include the bland, the luxurious and the truly dangerous. Yet scattered around are a few worthwhile destinations, some of them world-famous: Hialeah Park (and 400 pink flamingos), Opa-Locka (an economically depressed neighborhood filled with restored, Moorish-influenced architecture that was founded by real estate genius and aviation pioneer Glenn Curtiss in the 1920s), and Miami Jai-Alai. Not so famous, but still worth seeing, are places such as the Ancient Spanish Monastery and the new, 23,000-square-foot Museum of Contemporary Art.

This also is where you find major sporting venues such as Calder Race Track (horse racing), Pro Player (formerly Joe Robbie) Stadium (home of the Miami Dolphins), and the Golf Club of Miami.

Incorporated in 1995, Aventura is an upscale residential and shopping mecca featuring high-rises, luxurious single-family homes, and lush tropical landscaping that hugs the Broward County line. The booming enclave of 23,000 residents on the Intercoastal Waterway is a magnet for young families, retirees, and single professionals. While the 4.3-mile Don Soffer Aventura Fitness Trail is a major attraction for fitness buffs who like to strut their stuff, the town's major attraction is the gargantuan Aventura Mall, the biggest shopping venue in the Miami area. With over 250 stores anchored by Lord & Taylor, Bloomingdale's, JC Penney, and Macy's, Aventura Mall provides unlimited opportunities to give your credit cards a deserved workout.

Turnberry Isle Resort & Club, also located in Aventura, is Miami's most exclusive resort, featuring two golf courses, a new $10 million spa, two tennis centers, a full-service marina and several top-rated restaurants. The Mediterranean-styled resort—voted one of the world's best in a poll of *Conde Nast Traveler* readers—boasts a European-trained staff that averages out to three for each room. (Luckily, a service charge is added to all package rates to relieve guests of the hassle of tipping.) Each oversized room includes three-line phones, two TVs, a fax, safe, Jacuzzi, and private balcony. Two-night package deals start at just over $100 per person in the summer months; multiply that figure by three for the winter. For reservations, call (800) 327-7028.

LITTLE HAITI

Immigrants from Haiti are a major ethnic group in Miami, and a visit to Little Haiti gives visitors a chance to encounter this rich Caribbean culture. Yet the neighborhood's name promises more than it can deliver: this is no well-defined Chinatown or Little Italy but an amorphous community with few architectural features to make it stand out from the rest of sprawling Miami.

The best bet for first-time visitors is the Caribbean Marketplace (5927 NE 2nd Avenue). The open-air marketplace was designed to resemble the Iron Market in Port-au-Prince and houses food booths, record stores, tropical clothing, and Haitian arts and crafts. During the day, visits to the neighborhood are safe, but unfortunately we can't recommend visiting the area at night.

DOWNTOWN MIAMI

Downtown Miami, easily identifiable by its distinctive skyline of modern high-rises, is the small nerve center of this vibrant city. On weekdays in the morning through the early afternoon, streets are jammed with sidewalk vendors, dazed-looking tourists, professionals in suits, and street people. They're all a part of a surging throng of humanity that contributes to Miami's sophisticated character and international ambience.

Relaxing, it's not. Streets are lined with countless cut-rate shops hawking electronics, luggage, jewelry, and clothes. Mini shopping malls, exotic eateries offering Brazilian fare, small Cuban cafés (stop in for a quick *cafe Cubano* when the street scene gets overpowering and your energy level needs a boost), and a few honest-to-God tourist attractions (the Metro-Dade Cultural Center is the best) make downtown a must-see place for visitors.

Just make sure you visit in the morning or during lunch; by midafternoon, the crowds are gone. And don't even think about coming downtown at night: it's dead.

SOUTH OF DOWNTOWN MIAMI/BRICKELL AVENUE

Running from the Miami River (the southern border of downtown) to Coconut Grove along Brickell Avenue is the largest group of international banks in the United States—a parade of high-rises perched among sculpture-filled piazzas, fountains, and lush South Florida foliage. The collection of banks is partially the result of political instability throughout

Latin America in the late 1970s. Miami became a safe haven for corporate money and a new corporate banking center.

A little farther along Brickell Avenue is a collection of impressive high-rise condominiums. The buildings, home to many seasonal Latin American visitors with bucks and mostly done in bold primary colors, are immediately identifiable to fans of *Miami Vice*. The most famous is the Atlantis, a truly outrageous piece of architecture: A gaping square hole in the center of the building includes a palm tree, Jacuzzi, and a red spiral staircase.

LITTLE HAVANA

The impact of Cubans on Miami over the last three decades is incalculable; they are unquestionably the largest and most visible ethnic group in the city. However, the streets of Little Havana (located a few miles west of downtown) don't offer visitors much to see. In fact, the name "Little Havana" is misleading; while the words suggest a self-contained, ethnic enclave such as the Chinatown or Little Italy found in many large American cities, the reality is an amorphous neighborhood without strict boundaries that doesn't look a whole lot different from other parts of Miami.

Yet this neighborhood *does* offer visitors a taste of another culture, such as old men in *guayaberas* (billowing cotton shirts) playing dominoes in the park, exotic restaurants, and sights and sounds that are distinctly Cuban. You'll also see plenty of examples of what locals call "Spanglish": signs and billboards that charmingly mix English and Spanish, like one motel's boast, "Open 24 Horas."

The best place for a stroll in Little Havana is Calle Ocho (pronounced KAH-yeh OH-cho, Spanish for 8th Street), where streetside counters sell *café Cubano* (thimble-sized cups of sweet, highly charged Cuban coffee that Anglos call "jet fuel"), and the odor of cigars being rolled and baking bread fills the air. Our advice: Visit Little Havana for lunch or dinner at Versailles Restaurant (3555 SW 8th Street; (305) 444-0240). Hours: Sunday–Thursday, 8 a.m.–2 a.m.; Friday, 8 a.m.–3:30 a.m.; and Saturday, 8 a.m.–4:30 a.m. It offers great Cuban fare, it's cheap, easy to find, and parking is easy. Versailles is a Little Havana institution that shouldn't be missed.

CORAL GABLES

One of America's first planned communities, Coral Gables is a fascinating town filled with gorgeous, Mediterranean-style homes, manicured lawns, and lush foliage. The layout of the place, however, resembles a maze, with street names in Spanish written on small white stones at ground level that are hard to read. As a result, it's easy to get lost. Yet this classy old neighborhood, where many of Miami's most successful citizens live, is perfect for exploration by foot or bicycle.

Intriguing sights to be discovered on an informal tour of Coral Gables include the Venetian Pool, a freshwater coral rock lagoon called the best swimming hole in the world (bring a swimsuit, a towel, and five bucks); the Biltmore Hotel, fabulously restored after decades of neglect; and the Miracle Mile, a four-block stretch of expensive shops and boutiques where you can warm up your credit cards. Take a peek inside the recently restored Omni Colonnade Hotel; the rotunda is beautiful and the lobby features lots of cool marble. The building was the former office of George Merrick, the man who built Coral Gables.

COCONUT GROVE

To natives, it's "The Grove." Miami's former Bohemian quarter today is a mix of expensive shops, trendy bars and restaurants, and decidedly upscale galleries and boutiques: think of it as a bit of California trendiness gone astray. Although not as outrageous as South Beach, Coconut Grove offers people-watchers another outstanding opportunity to sit at an outdoor café and watch fashion magazine victims strut their stuff, in-line skaters weave through bumper-to-bumper traffic, and hip-looking cops ride by on mountain bikes.

Shoppers can browse in New Age bookstores, lingerie shops (including the ubiquitous Victoria's Secret), a surfboard boutique, a Harley-Davidson dealership, and flower shops. CocoWalk, a multilevel mall done in pink and beige, features a courtyard with live music on evenings and weekends.

KEY BISCAYNE

Unless you've got a yacht, the only way to reach this beautiful island is via the Rickenbacker Causeway ($1 toll). Once there, you'll see how well-off Miamians live their plush lifestyles off the beaten track.

Yet there's more to Key Biscayne than ogling the rich: The island features some of the best beaches in the Miami area—and most of them are open to the public. Seaquarium, Miami's sea mammal emporium, is located on Virginia Key, the island the causeway crosses before reaching Key Biscayne. On the five-mile-long causeway, visitors can pull over, park their cars, and rent sailboards and jet skis for zooming around the placid waters of Biscayne Bay. A note for those who travel with their pets: These are the only beaches in the Miami area that allow dogs.

Two state parks are located on the island. On the tip is Bill Baggs Cape Florida State Park, devastated by Hurricane Andrew in 1992. We're glad to report the foliage in the 406-acre park is recovering from its beating. Yet we recommend Crandon Park, with its wide, open beaches, as a better bet for visitors. Pack a lunch and swimming gear for a day at a Key Biscayne beach.

KENDALL AND PERRINE

Continuing south, Dade County gets less and less interesting, yet a few attractions are worth the drive. The premier tourist destination is Metrozoo, still a world-class zoo even after the devastation wrought by Hurricane Andrew in 1992. Other nearby attractions will appeal to train and airplane buffs, respectively: the Gold Coast Railroad Museum and the Weeks Air Museum.

HOMESTEAD AND FLORIDA CITY

Neither of these southern Dade County towns are neighborhoods worth exploring by short-term visitors, but both serve as jumping-off points for three areas that shouldn't be missed if you've got the time: Everglades and Biscayne National Parks, and the Florida Keys. Nearby attractions include Monkey Jungle, the Coral Castle, and the Fruit and Spice Park.

Arriving

BY CAR

Most people who drive to Miami arrive on I-95, which begins south of downtown and continues north along the Atlantic seaboard all the way to Maine; it's the major north-south expressway on the East Coast. Another major route for visitors traveling by car is Florida's Turnpike, a toll highway that starts near Orlando and Walt Disney World, runs down the center of the Florida peninsula, then heads east to Fort Pierce on the Atlantic coast; from there the turnpike parallels I-95 south to Miami. The Homestead Extension of Florida's Turnpike skirts Greater Miami to the west. It's the route to take if you're headed to the Keys.

Another major highway, I-75, funnels motorists to Miami from Naples, Fort Myers, St. Petersburg, Tampa, and other points along Florida's west coast. It's better known by another name: the Everglade Parkway. US 41, also called the Tamiami Trail and Alligator Alley, connects Miami and the Everglades to the west.

US 1 is the stoplight-laden road that I-95 and Florida's Turnpike replaced, but the old highway is still intact, and is a diversion from boring highway driving if you're not in a hurry. Though it's not a practical route for visitors on a tight schedule (traffic lights, shopping centers, and congestion often slow traffic to a crawl, and the road is rated as one of the most unpleasant driving experiences in South Florida), US 1 still affords glimpses of beaches, palm trees, occasional Florida kitsch, and plenty of strip shopping centers.

US A1A, the alternate Route 1, is an even better alternative for folks weary of interstates—and even slower. Much of this venerable old highway runs directly along the beach. Hint: for visitors who fly into Fort Lauderdale/Hollywood International Airport and are headed to Miami Beach, A1A is the way to go . . . if you're not in a rush.

If you're driving north to Miami from the Keys on US 1, take Florida's Turnpike, Homestead Extension in Florida City; US 1 between here and Miami is often unpredictably congested. Then take Route 874 north (the Don Shula Expressway) to Route 826 north (the Palmetto Expressway); next, go east on the Dolphin Expressway (Route 836), which goes past Miami International Airport and links up with I-95 near downtown Miami. It may sound complicated, but it's much faster.

The Penalty for Getting Lost: More on Driving around Miami

Greater Miami is a sprawling metropolis crisscrossed by busy expressways passing through neighborhoods that can change character from gentrified to seedy within a block. Sooner or later most visitors fall victim to Miami's infuriating lack of street signs and inadequate highway signs and find themselves taking an unplanned detour. Since you'll be hard put to forget all the bad publicity you've heard about Miami as you frantically drive along unfamiliar streets in search of an interstate ramp, it can be a very scary experience.

How concerned about safety should you be on an unplanned detour?

"Some neighborhoods look grim but aren't necessarily unsafe," reports one Miami native who regularly drives through some of the city's worst areas without incident. "But the lack of visual clues, especially to Anglo visitors not used to different cultures, makes it hard to discern if a neighborhood is truly 'dangerous' or just different. To a lost tourist, a house with a yard full of junk might look threatening in Miami—but the same house could be considered 'charming' if it were in Jamaica."

In addition, many visitors aren't prepared for the sharp contrasts that exist between trendy places near the beach and economically disadvantaged neighborhoods west of Biscayne Boulevard in Miami. Don't be fooled; the difference in safety may not be as wide as you think (both areas are relatively safe).

Yet our advice is to stay in areas that you know are safe (granted, that's not very helpful advice if you're lost) and not to wander around the city. "Neighborhoods change radically, and areas with crack and prostitution exist next to areas being renovated," our friend adds. "Check with one of the police vans stationed around the city or someone you know before wandering into an area that you don't know."

If you *do* get lost, it helps to think positive. Remember that during daylight you are much safer than at night, and if you avoid looking like a lost tourist, you're less likely to become a crime statistic. And remember that property values around interstates fall—and it shows. The streets that you're frantically driving on as you try to find that entrance ramp back to the highway may look bad, but they're not necessarily the most dangerous areas in the city.

BY PLANE

Virtually all foreign visitors flying into Miami must fly into Miami International Airport. Domestic flyers, however, have a choice: Fort Lauderdale/ Hollywood International Airport, a smaller facility, is a viable option and worth considering. It's only 30 minutes north of downtown Miami, close to I-95, and convenient for folks headed to Miami Beach because you can skip the major highways by taking US A1A south.

Miami International Airport (MIA)   MIA is the ninth-largest airport in the United States, and number three in the number of international passengers it handles. More airline companies fly into MIA (100) than to any other airport in the country, averaging more than 1,400 take-offs/landings a day. MIA has service to every major city in Latin America and the Caribbean, as well as connections to Europe and the Middle East. All told, MIA makes connections to 176 cities on 5 continents; more than 33 million passengers fly in and out of MIA each year.

MIA boasts 120 aircraft gates and 8 concourses; anticipating more growth, the Dade County–owned facility embarked on a $5.4 billion expansion program scheduled to be completed in 2007. Improvements will include increasing the number of gates to nearly 140, adding 3 new passenger concourses, upgrading baggage handling systems, and doubling the amount of retail space. But the place is already huge: the second-floor departure level of the horseshoe-shaped terminal is jammed with boutiques, bookstores, a hotel (with 260 rooms), bars, gift shops, restaurants, and a culturally diverse flow of people from around the world.

In spite of its size, however, MIA is an easy airport to navigate. From your gate, follow signs to the baggage area on the lower level; bus, taxi, SuperShuttle service, passenger car pickup, and rental car limos are outside the door. Directly across the street is a multilevel garage for short-term parking. If you're faced with a long walk between terminals, take the elevator to Level 3, where a "horizontal escalator" will save wear and tear on your feet.

Fort Lauderdale/Hollywood International Airport   This is a small, modern, easy-to-get-around facility only minutes off I-95. While not as convenient for Miami-bound travelers as its big brother to the south, this airport offers peace of mind to visitors who are anxious about safety when they drive to and from Miami International Airport. For more information, see pages 189–190 in the chapter on Broward County.

By Train

Amtrak operates a small, modern terminal located near Hialeah Park, northwest of downtown Miami. It's not very convenient if your destination is the beach or downtown Miami—and it's in a neighborhood that's not very safe.

If you're not being picked up by someone with a car, however, you're not out of luck: a Metrorail station (call (305) 770-3131 for transit information) is about eight blocks away. Outside the terminal, board Metrobus "L," which takes you to the elevated-train station; the fare is $1.25 plus $.25 for a transfer to the above-ground train. Check the bulletin board inside the train station for current bus, Metrorail, Metrobus, and driving information.

The terminal is located at 8303 NW 37th Avenue; for recorded arrival and departure information, call Amtrak at (800) 872-7245. For ticket prices and reservations, call (305) 835-1222. To reach the station by car from I-95, take NW 79th Street west to NW 37th Avenue and turn right; the station is a few blocks north where the street dead-ends. Signs will help direct you.

The Port of Miami

Miami is the "Cruise Capital of the World," with more than three million passengers a year sailing from the Port of Miami, the home of 17 cruise ships—the world's largest year-round fleet. Cruise passengers can choose from the world's most popular ports of call on sea vacations ranging from three-and-four-day excursions to voyages up to 11 days in length.

Destinations include exotic ports in the Caribbean, South America, the coastal resorts of Mexico, the Bahamas, and Key West. Year-round, passengers enjoy tropical weather virtually from the start of their voyages—a big attraction for vacationers from northern climates and a key to Miami's leadership in the cruise industry.

For cruise passengers flying into Miami International Airport who booked a cruise with airfare included, getting to the ship is easy: representatives from cruise ship operators, holding signs, greet passengers as they enter the passenger terminal. Luggage is transferred automatically to the ship and passengers board motorcoaches for the quick trip (less than 30 minutes) to the dock. Your luggage is later delivered to staterooms aboard ship.

If you booked your own flight to Miami, don't expect to be greeted by an official from the cruise line. Instead, proceed to the lower level, pick up your luggage, step outside, and take a cab to the Port of Miami. Taxi rates are $12–16 for up to five passengers.

If you're driving, the Port of Miami is easy to find: it's located on Dodge Island in Biscayne Bay between Miami and Miami Beach, and can be reached from Miami via Port Boulevard. From I-95, take Exit 3 to downtown and follow signs to Biscayne Boulevard; Port Boulevard is next to Bayside Marketplace. From I-395 (Exit 5 east on I-95, toward Miami Beach), take the Biscayne Boulevard south exit to downtown and follow signs to the Port of Miami. Parking is located in front of the terminals for $10 a day, payable prior to embarking. Have your cruise tickets handy and drop off your luggage at the terminal before parking your car; the luggage will be sent to your cabin.

The Port of Miami has 12 recently renovated, air-conditioned cruise passenger terminals that are wheelchair-accessible and feature duty-free shopping, ground-level customs clearance, and easy access to cars, buses, and taxis. In addition, the terminals are color-coded and marked with the name of the ship, which makes it easy for folks driving to the port to find the right one. Long-term parking is across from the terminals; luggage handed over to porters at the terminal entrances will be delivered to your stateroom. Unfortunately, due to an increase in terrorism in the past few years, security measures have been adopted that prevent noncruising visitors from boarding the cruise ships before they sail.

Note: Folks who drive to the Port of Miami or who booked their own airfare and aren't whisked to their ship in a bus can take advantage of a wider range of duty-free goods at Miami Duty Free (MDF), a clean, uncluttered shop located at 125 NE 8th Street in downtown Miami. Just present your cruise or flight ticket to the security guard, select and pay for your goods, and MDF will deliver them to your plane or ship on the day of departure. Items include liquor, perfumes, Wedgwood china, Waterford crystal, and Rolex watches, all at prices 20–40 percent below retail. Salespeople at MDF speak seven languages; the shop is open 10 a.m. to 6 p.m. daily. For more information, call (305) 377-0104.

Getting Around

THE MAJOR HIGHWAYS

Immediately south of downtown, I-95 ends and merges with US 1, also called South Dixie Highway. US 1 swings southwest along Biscayne Bay through congested suburbs that include the cities of Coral Gables, Coconut Grove, Kendall, South Miami, Perrine, Cutler Ridge, and Homestead. South Dixie Highway is infamous for its seemingly endless number of traffic lights and horrendous traffic jams.

Forming Greater Miami's western border is Florida's Turnpike, Homestead Extension. Folks heading south from Miami and Miami Beach to visit southern Dade County's attractions—or to tour the Florida Keys and Biscayne, and Everglades National Parks—should skip US 1 and take Route 836 (the Dolphin Expressway) to Florida's Turnpike and head south toward Homestead on this toll road; for more on driving around Miami, read on.

Other major highways that visitors to Miami need to know about are:

- Route 112, the Airport Expressway (a toll road that links Miami International Airport with I-95 and Miami Beach)

- Route 836 (the major east-west link connecting Florida's Turnpike, MIA, I-95, downtown Miami, and South Miami Beach)

- Route 826, the Palmetto Expressway (a major commuter route that runs north to south between MIA and Florida's Turnpike before heading east to I-95 in North Miami)

- Route 874, the Don Shula Expressway (which links the Palmetto Expressway and Florida's Turnpike in South Miami)

DRIVING YOUR CAR

Getting Out of Miami International Airport

Due to a flurry of bad publicity in late 1993, most visitors on their first visit to Miami International Airport are more concerned about personal safety after they leave the airport than they are in the air. While we think Miami's bad reputation for visitor safety is largely undeserved, there is cause for concern at MIA: the airport is located about eight miles west of downtown Miami in a confusing, economically depressed, and crime-ridden area.

If it were simply a matter of leaving the airport by car and jumping on the freeway, there would be no problem . . . and there isn't one if you're being picked up by a friend or business colleague, if you take public transportation or the SuperShuttle, or if you're being picked up by a cruise ship company and being whisked to the dock in a motor coach.

The problem is when you rent a car. Most of the rental car agencies are located outside the airport proper . . . and that's where the confusion begins. Poor highway signs and a landscape with few landmarks (at least to out-of-town visitors) compound the problem of finding your way out of a car rental agency. Our advice: When you rent your car, get a map and explicit directions from the car rental agency clerk to the closest highway that leads to your final destination (the rental agencies, you'll discover, take the threat of violence against visitors very seriously). And read "How to Avoid Crime and Keep Safe in Public Places" on pages 33–39 for advice on how to avoid being an easy mark for crooks as you drive around Miami. And hang on to the rental car agency map: When returning your car, it will come in handy on the confusing and poorly signed roadways around MIA.

I-95

It's not just another superhighway. Interstate 95, which starts below downtown and goes north all the way to Maine, is the Big Enchilada of expressways in car-crazy Miami. The north-south route connects all the major highways in South Florida . . . and when traffic isn't backed up ten miles by construction delays or an accident, travelers can breeze from Coconut Grove in the south to North Miami, the airport, and Miami Beach in minutes. When I-95 is working right, getting around Miami is a breeze.

The problem, as you've probably gathered, is that I-95 frequently *doesn't* work right. Construction delays, poor signage, confusing detours, and a peculiar mix of drivers indigenous to South Florida can induce soaring blood pressure and moments of pure terror—even in experienced drivers who routinely handle the frustrations of driving in other big American cites. The solution for first-time visitors is to study a road map carefully before venturing out, check the *Miami Herald* for a listing of construction delays and lane closures (often scheduled at night, causing backups that rival rush-hour traffic snarls), avoid driving in rush-hour traffic, and drive very defensively. And keep in mind that I-95 passes through some pretty rough territory.

Causeways to Miami Beach

The city of Miami Beach is on a barrier island across Biscayne Bay from Miami. Getting on and off the island means crossing long bridges, called causeways, that link the island to the mainland. You've got a number of choices to make.

Getting to South Beach   The best-known link between Miami and its sister city across the bay is the *MacArthur Causeway.* This toll-free (but not drawbridge-free) road provides a high-speed link between downtown Miami and South Beach (the southern end of Miami Beach). From downtown, the MacArthur Causeway is easy to find. Take Biscayne Boulevard (US 1) north a few blocks past Bayside Marketplace and bear right onto the multilane highway that crosses the bridge. (A landmark: the ugly, orange *Miami Herald* building anchors the causeway to the mainland on the left.) From I-95, take I-395 (Exit 5 east), which puts you directly on the MacArthur Causeway to Miami Beach.

Along the way you cross Watson Island (the future home of Parrot Jungle), pass the Port of Miami on the right, and pass Palm and Star islands on the left. When you reach Miami Beach, 5th Street and the Art Deco District are straight ahead; bear left onto Alton Road if your destination is farther north and you want to miss the congestion of Collins Avenue (Miami Beach's main drag); bear right to reach the Miami Beach Marina, South Pointe Park, and Joe's Stone Crab.

One final note: the return trip from Miami Beach to Miami at night offers one of the most impressive and beautiful cityscapes in the world—especially on weekends when cruise ships lit up like Christmas trees are framed by multicolored high-rises in the background.

Getting to Mid-Miami Beach The **Julia Tuttle Causeway** (I-195) is the main link between I-95, Biscayne Boulevard, and mid-Miami Beach; it's definitely the route to take if you want to avoid the congestion of downtown Miami and the almost 'round-the-clock insanity of South Beach. It's also a straight shot from MIA; Route 112, the Airport Expressway, changes route numbers when it crosses I-95 and becomes I-195 as it heads east over the Julia Tuttle Causeway toward Miami Beach.

The causeway drops you off at 41st Street (Arthur Godfrey Road) on Miami Beach; continue straight to Indian Creek Road and turn right if you're going south. If you're headed north, turn left on Collins Avenue (US A1A). The Julia Tuttle Causeway is a very convenient and usually uncongested way to get on and off Miami Beach, and the one the *Unofficial Guide* research team used the most (we roomed on Miami Beach). Although the view of Miami's skyline is good from the Julia Tuttle Causeway, it isn't as impressive as the MacArthur Causeway's up-close, heart-stopping panorama of cruise ships and high-rises.

Farther north, the **John F. Kennedy Causeway** (Route 934) connects NE 79th Street in Miami with 71st Street in Miami Beach (surprise: the street-numbering systems in the two cities are close, but don't quite match). While this is a good route to take if you're traveling to or from Biscayne Boulevard and Miami Beach, it's not a good choice for hooking up with (or leaving) I-95. Getting on and off the interstate from 79th Street in Miami is confusing at best—and it's a grim-looking neighborhood that most out-of-town visitors would rather avoid. Take the Julia Tuttle Causeway instead.

Getting to Miami Beach North The **Broad Causeway** (NE 123rd Street) links North Miami to Surfside and Bal Harbour at 96th Street on Miami Beach. It passes through a congested downtown shopping district on the mainland, then crosses northern Biscayne Bay before reaching Bay Harbor Islands and Miami Beach. Due to the traffic lights and congestion along NE 125th Avenue on the mainland side, it's not a fast way to reach I-95 from Miami Beach.

Farther north, the **Sunny Isle Causeway** (Route 826) connects NE 163rd Street in North Miami Beach (which, confusingly enough, is on the mainland) to Sunny Isles on Miami Beach around 170th Street. It's a major route to and from Haulover Beach Park, the Oleta River State Recreation Area, and Florida International University's Bay Vista campus. The

William Lehman Causeway (Route 856), just below the Broward County line, connects Biscayne Boulevard in North Miami Beach to 192nd Street on Miami Beach. Neither of these two causeways are major routes for out-of-town visitors.

An Alternative Route to South Beach There's one other route to Miami Beach we need to mention: the **Venetian Causeway,** the original bridge that linked the two cities. It's located just north of the MacArthur Causeway, and is a narrow, two-lane bridge that crosses several artificial islands in Biscayne Bay. While not a particularly convenient route (the MacArthur Causeway is usually faster), it's a pretty drive, a great bicycling or jogging route, and worth exploring if you have the time. The Venetian Causeway is also the route to take during rush hour when traffic is backed up for miles on the MacArthur Causeway.

The Miami side of the Venetian Causeway is tucked in behind condos and shopping malls just north of the *Miami Herald* building; it can be tough to find the first time. The Miami Beach side connects drivers with Dade Boulevard, just above the Lincoln Road Mall. Turn right on Washington Avenue to reach South Beach; go straight along Dade Boulevard to Collins Avenue.

Parking

Miami is a city that forces people to use their cars: public transportation is limited and the city is too spread out to make walking convenient. With all those cars in circulation, a question becomes obvious very quickly, especially on a trip to South Beach or Coconut Grove on a Saturday night: where do you park the car?

The answer is also obvious: you don't—take a cab, the alternative used by many Miami residents out for a night on the town.

TAXIS, SHUTTLES, AND PUBLIC TRANSPORTATION
Taxis

With a population highly dependent on private cars for getting around, Miami isn't a great town for hailing cabs. If you need one, a phone call is your best bet.

Taxis are usually plentiful outside the terminals at Miami International Airport; the rate is $1.75 a mile. Expect to pay about $18 for a trip from the airport to downtown and $23 to Coconut Grove. Flat-rate fares are available to Miami Beach south of 63rd Street ($22–24), Miami Beach between 67th Street and 87th Terrace ($29), Miami Beach between 87th Terrace and Haulover Park ($34), Miami Beach between Haulover Park and the Broward County line ($41), and Key Biscayne ($31). Trips to other destinations in and around Miami can range from $25 on up.

Popular Cab Companies	
Metro	(305) 888-8888
Super Yellow	(305) 885-1111
Tropical	(305) 945-1025
Yellow	(305) 444-4444

SuperShuttle

Another alternative for getting out of MIA without your own car or ride from a friend is **SuperShuttle,** a van service that can accommodate up to 11 passengers at a clip. It operates 7 days a week, 24 hours a day, and fares are lower than taxis. Rates begin around $9.50 per person (free for children age three and under) for downtown hotels, $10 for Coral Gables, $11 for South Beach, and $12 for mid–Miami Beach destinations. Call (305) 871-2000 the day before your return flight to arrange a ride back to the airport; keep in mind the shuttle typically makes two additional stops before heading to MIA, so schedule your pickup time accordingly.

Buses and Public Transportation

Miami, like a lot of large cities, jumped on the mass-transit bandwagon and built an elevated train system (in lieu of a subway, an engineering no-no in South Florida due to the region's high water table, which also rules out basements) and a downtown "People Mover." Yet the fledgling systems have a long way to go before native Miamians—and visitors to the area—can abandon their cars and rely on public transportation to get around. Our advice to visitors is to come in your own car or rent one after you reach Miami.

Metrorail, Miami's futuristic, above-ground train system, is a 21-mile-long, one-line system that runs from Hialeah in northwest Miami south through downtown to Kendall, a suburb southwest of the city. It's clean and modern, but really doesn't go where most visitors want to be—Miami Beach and the airport being two prime examples.

Moreover, the limited system hasn't really caught on with the local clientele (many of whom refer to the system as "MetroSnail"—the trains run about every 20 minutes). While Metrorail was once burdened with an unsafe reputation, security guards have since cleaned up most of the crime. Still, the line passes through some neighborhoods that visitors should avoid.

On the other hand, a ride on downtown's **Metromover**—called the "People Mover" by almost everyone—should be on every visitor's list of things to do on a Miami visit. It's really neat: a Disneyesque, automated monorail scoots people around downtown, treating them to spectacular views of the city, Biscayne Bay, and, off in the distance, the Atlantic Ocean. The system has recently been expanded with two out-and-back connections (in spite of their names, they're not "loops") to the Brickell Avenue business district to the south (Brickell Loop) and to the Omni Hotel to the north (Omni Loop). It's a very practical, clean, and safe system for getting around downtown Miami. Plus, it's air-conditioned.

Priced at a quarter a trip, the "People Mover" is the best tourist bargain in South Florida—and it hooks up with the Metrorail system. But unless you're staying downtown and don't plan to venture to other parts of Miami, this small transportation system won't replace your need for a car.

Miami's **Metrobus** system operates throughout Dade County, serving about 200,000 riders a day on 70 routes. Most of the lines radiate out of downtown Miami and run at least twice per hour between 6 a.m. and 7 p.m. weekdays, less often on weekends. The bus system is also the only public transportation in Miami Beach. Our advice: Short-term visitors should stick to their cars and leave the complicated, relatively slow bus system to commuters.

Visitors can cruise South Beach on the **ElectroWave,** Florida's first electric shuttle system. Shuttles stop every 6 to 11 minutes at 38 designated stops on Washington Avenue between 16th Street and South Pointe Drive and along Collins Avenue between 16th Street and Dade Boulevard. The mini-buses seat up to 22 passengers with wraparound seating and air-conditioning, and will allow visitors more convenient access between municipal parking lots and local hot spots. The shuttle operates 20 hours a day every day of the year. The fare is cheap, too: a quarter each way.

Gathering Information

For additional information on entertainment, sight-seeing, maps, shopping, dining, and lodging in Greater Miami, call or write the Visitor Service Center at the Greater Miami Convention and Visitors Bureau (701 Brickell Avenue, Suite 2700, Miami, Florida 33131; (800) 933-8448 or (305) 539-3034).

Ask for a free copy of *Greater Miami & The Beaches Vacation Planner,* a biannual publication with nearly 200 pages of information, including basic stuff such as post office locations, annual rainfall, language services, colleges and universities, hospitals, and real estate agents.

If you need specific information, ask for it when you call or write. For example, if you're planning on staying in a hotel or motel away from traditional tourist haunts and need to know if it's in a safe neighborhood, the folks at the Visitor Service Center can help.

WHERE TO FIND TOURIST INFORMATION IN MIAMI

If you're short on maps or need more information on sight-seeing, restaurants, hotels, shopping, or things to do in the Greater Miami area, there are several places to stop and pick up maps and brochures:

- at the Miami Beach Chamber of Commerce at 333 41st Street, Miami Beach; (305) 672-1270. Hours: Monday–Friday, 9 a.m.– 5 p.m.

- at the Coconut Grove Chamber of Commerce, 2820 McFarlane Road, Coconut Grove; (305) 444-7270. Hours: Monday–Friday, 9 a.m.–5 p.m.

- at the Sunny Isles Visitor Information Center, 17070 Collins Avenue, Suite 266B, at the Milam's Supermarket shopping center; (305) 947-5826. Hours: Monday–Friday, 9 a.m.–2 p.m.

- at the Greater Homestead/Florida City Chamber of Commerce, 43 North Krome Avenue in Homestead; (305) 247-2332 (Miami), (800) 388-9669 (Florida and U.S.). Hours: Monday–Friday, 8:30 a.m.–5 p.m.

- at Sears, Aventura Mall, 19505 Biscayne Boulevard, Aventura; (305) 937-7562. Hours: Monday–Saturday, 9:30 a.m.–9 p.m.; Sunday, 11 a.m.–6 p.m.

- at Sears, Coral Gables, 3655 SW 22nd Street (Coral Way at Douglas Road), Coral Gables; (305) 460-3400. Hours: Monday–Saturday, 9:30 a.m.–9 p.m.; Sunday, 11 a.m.–6 p.m.

- at Sears, Miami International Mall, 1625 NW 107th Street, Miami; (305) 470-7863. Hours: Monday–Saturday, 10 a.m.–9 p.m.; Sunday, 11 a.m.–6 p.m.

- at Sears, Westland Mall, 1625 W. 49th Street, Hialeah; (305) 364-3800. Hours: Monday–Saturday, 10 a.m.–9 p.m.; Sunday, noon–6 p.m.

- at Miami International Airport; there is a Tourist/Information Center on Level 2, Concourse E, across from the hotel; it's open 24 hours a day.

Finally, check the Greater Miami Convention and Visitors Bureau at 701 Brickell Avenue, Suite 2700. It's not particularly convenient for visitors who just want to pick up a map, but the view from these 27th-floor offices is spectacular. Park in the basement of the building—and don't forget to have your parking ticket stamped before you leave.

Visiting Miami on Business:
Not All Visitors Are Headed to the Beach

While most of the 10 million visitors a year who flock to Miami come to bask in the tropical sun, to enjoy the Latin culture, and to see and be seen in South Beach, not everybody has an itinerary centered around leisure-time activities. In fact, in 1996, more than three million visitors came to Miami for conventions and business.

In many ways, the problems facing business visitors on their first trip to Miami don't differ much from the problems of folks in town on a vacation. People visiting on business need to locate a hotel that's convenient, want to avoid the city's worst traffic hassles, and want to know the locations of Miami's best restaurants. We can help.

As for our recommendations on seeing South Florida's many attractions—who knows? Maybe you'll find the time to squeeze a morning or an afternoon out of your busy schedule, grab this book, and spend a few hours exploring some of the places that draw the other nine million or so visitors to Miami each year.

The Miami area is home to two major convention centers. The massive, million-square-foot **Miami Beach Convention Center** is South Florida's

---

Other Convention Venues

Other convention sites that draw national conventions include:

- Miami Convention Center in downtown Miami: 37 meeting rooms and the 28,000-square-foot Riverfront Hall

- adjacent Hyatt Regency Miami: 80,000 square feet of meeting and banquet rooms and the 12,000-square-foot Regency Ballroom

- Radisson Centre near Miami International Airport: 120,000 square feet of meeting, exhibition, and banquet space

- Doral Ocean Beach Resort in Miami Beach: 45,000 square feet of meeting space

- Doral Resort and Country Club in Miami: 75,000 square feet of meeting and banquet facilities

- Fontainebleau Hilton in Miami Beach: 190,000 square feet of meeting and exhibit space

- Sheraton Bal Harbour in north Miami Beach: 70,000 square feet of meeting and conference rooms

major exhibition venue. The smaller **Coconut Grove Convention Center,** located in the hip neighborhood south of downtown Miami, specializes in consumer-oriented exhibitions such as home shows, health and fitness expos, and gun and knife shows.

THE MIAMI BEACH CONVENTION CENTER

Expanded and renovated in 1990 at a cost of more than $92 million, the Miami Beach Convention Center is South Florida's premier convention locale. The 1.1-million-square-foot center is one of the best designed and modern facilities for conventions in the United States and can handle up to four conventions at a time.

Spanning four city blocks near Miami Beach's Art Deco District, the center is only minutes from the beach and great restaurants, and it's less than a half-hour from Miami International Airport (allow more time during rush hour). The center is located on Washington Avenue between 17th Street and Dade Boulevard; unfortunately, although it's a massive building, it's not visible from Miami Beach's main drag, Collins Avenue.

With all of its meeting rooms on one level, the center's main floor, with 500,000 square feet, either can be configured as a vast, centralized facility with four points of access or can be subdivided into four separate halls of approximately 125,000 square feet each. A skywalk with lounges, bars, and meeting rooms spans the halls, giving convention-goers a bird's-eye view of the space.

Surrounding the exhibit area are 70 separate meeting rooms for a total of 145,000 square feet of flexible space. All are fully carpeted and divided by soundproof walls. The meeting rooms can accommodate as few as 100 or as many as 2,000 convention-goers.

The exhibit areas and meeting rooms are well marked and easy to find. Parking around the center, however, is difficult; the 800-space lot adjacent to the center fills up quickly. We suggest you take advantage of hotel shuttle buses or take a cab during large conventions.

If you must drive and the lot is full, head for the 2,000-space parking garage on 17th Street (a block south toward the Lincoln Road Mall); trying to find street parking within walking distance is frustrating at best. For more information on the Miami Beach Convention Center, call (305) 673-7311.

On a happier note, places to dine around the Miami Beach Convention Center are plentiful; head down Washington Avenue into the heart of South Beach, where a wide range of high-quality eateries, bistros, and fast-food venues are close by. In addition, Lincoln Road Mall, a block south of the convention center between 16th and 17th streets, is another nearby destination with a wide range of trendy restaurants, bars, and shops.

ElectroWave, a new mini-bus service, makes a stop near the convention center on Washington Avenue and provides easy transportation south into the Art Deco District; the electric buses run about every six to 11 minutes, 20 hours a day. Now more than ever, making an escape from the exhibit floor for a quick bite or for a quiet meal with clients is easy.

THE COCONUT GROVE CONVENTION CENTER

Located south of downtown Miami at 2700 Bayshore Drive in the trendy enclave of Coconut Grove, this 150,000-square-foot hall was completely renovated and expanded in 1989 and accommodates shows of up to 18,000 attendees. It's in a striking location on the shores of Biscayne Bay, features a backdrop of sailboats in the nearby marina, and is located only 10 minutes from downtown Miami and less than half an hour from Miami International Airport.

The main hall is divisible into five halls measuring from 7,000 to 50,000 square feet and features an eight-window ticket booth. Two 30-foot-wide doors roll up to ceiling height at the north and south ends of the hall to enable easy access for service vehicles and exhibitors. All the exhibition space is on the ground level, making it easy to roll or carry equipment through the doors from the parking lot. In addition, two concession stands are located in the main hall and a full-service restaurant is located on the premises. A 1,000-plus-car parking lot surrounds the hall. For more information on the Coconut Grove Convention Center, call (305) 579-3310.

The Beaches

"Life is a beach": you heard it here first. For many visitors, South Florida is strictly a beach destination—and no wonder. With more than ten miles of wide, sandy, palm tree–studded beaches, Miami Beach is a sun-worshiper's paradise. All the beach is open to the public and staffed by lifeguards during daylight hours from 1st to 14th streets; at 21st, 35th, 46th, 52nd, 64th streets; and at North Shore State Recreation Area and Haulover Beach Park.

WHERE TO PUT THE CAR

Parking is one consideration when choosing a beach location to spend a few hours or the day. The farther south along Miami Beach you go, the harder it is to find a place to leave the car; on weekends, it can be nearly impossible unless you arrive early. Along Miami Beach, metered public parking lots, beach access, and rest rooms are provided along Collins Avenue at these locations:

Miami Beach Public Parking Lot, Beach Access, and Rest Room Locations
1st Street (at Washington Avenue, South Pointe Park)
6th to 14th streets, Lummus Park
21st Street
35th Street
46th Street (next to the Eden Roc Hotel)
53rd Street
64th Street
73rd Street (across from the North Shore Community Center)
79th to 87th streets (North Shore State Recreation Area)
93rd Street (Surfside)
96th Street (Bal Harbour)
108th Street (Haulover Park)
167th Street (next to the Holiday Inn)

WHO GOES WHERE?

The beaches of Miami Beach can also be broken down by the kinds of folks who congregate at them.

South Beach, especially 10th through 12th streets, is topless, while gays tend to favor the beach around 18th Street. South Beach also attracts Germans, Italians, the young and the restless, Eurotrash, and glitterati from the world over.

The War Zone is the old name for the tip of land below 5th Street down to Government Cut (the shipping channel leading to the Port of Miami). Just a few years ago this was mostly surfer turf, but the neighborhood is undergoing rapid change as the Art Deco District trendiness pushes south. Yet the Zone boasts a higher percentage of ungentrified residents than the rest of South Beach. There's a park on the oceanside between 2nd and 3rd streets where folks gather at sunup for tai chi.

Families, on the other hand, tend to flock to the 20s, 30s, and 40s—and north. A wooden boardwalk extends from the 20s to the 50s behind many of the huge hotels that line the beach; you'll see a wide array of people strolling and jogging.

Miami Beach is a city of many different communities featuring a wide range of ethnic groups. For example, mid-Miami Beach, centered around 41st Street, is the city's commercial strip and has one of the largest concentrations of Lubovitch Jews in the state.

Farther north, Surfside attracts an older population and is also a popular destination for Canadian and Scandinavian tourists. The epicenter of Canadian tourism is Hollywood, Florida, just over the line in Broward County. For folks looking to sunbathe in the raw, **Haulover Beach Park** (just past Bal Harbour) has a "clothing optional" (nude) section along its more than one-mile length. It's a beautiful park that features a marina and plenty of parking.

Sunny Isles, located above Haulover Beach, has a lovely park beach with sea grape trees and sand dunes (which are about as high above sea level as you'll get in Miami). It's a popular spot for families.

BEYOND MIAMI BEACH

Miami Beach, however, isn't your only beach option. Key Biscayne's **Crandon Park** offers miles of wide, white Atlantic Ocean beach and no parking problems; it's a popular destination for families and picnickers.

For swimming, windsurfing, or jet skiing in the shallow, placid waters of Biscayne Bay, pull over on the Rickenbacker Causeway that connects Key Biscayne to the mainland. It's a popular beach destination for local residents that features shade trees and picnic tables close to the water. And it's okay to bring the dog.

In North Miami Beach (which, confusingly enough, is a suburb of Miami located on the mainland), the **Oleta River State Recreation Area** has a small, sandy, man-made beach on the shores of Biscayne Bay and the Intracoastal Waterway. It's an oasis of quiet surrounded by condos. South of Coral Gables and east of the Miami suburb of Kendall, **Matheson Hammock Park** offers a small beach on Biscayne Bay with a terrific view of the Miami skyline.

Recreation

FITNESS CENTERS AND AEROBICS

Many Miami fitness centers are co-ed and accept daily or short-term memberships. The **Olympia Gym & Fitness Center,** located at 20335 Biscayne Boulevard in North Miami Beach, features two free-weight areas, fixed weights, Stairmasters, and aerobics classes. Daily membership is $15. Call (305) 932-3500 for more information.

The **Downtown Athletic Club** at 200 South Biscayne Boulevard (on the 15th floor of the Southeast Financial Building) boasts a 32,000-

square-foot facility that includes free weights, exercise bikes, treadmills, an indoor track, a basketball court, a whirlpool, and racquetball courts. The daily rate is $16. Members qualify for two and a half hours of free parking a day while working out; for more information, call (305) 358-9988.

Gold's Gym of Coral Gables at 3737 SW 8th Street offers free and fixed weights, Stairmasters, Lifecycles, and a treadmill. Membership is $12 a day and $30 a week; call (305) 445-5161 for more information.

On South Beach, **Iron Works** at 1676 Alton Road offers memberships for $10 a day, $25 for three days, and $56 a week. Facilities include a complete gym (with both free and fixed weights) and aerobic studios, but no sauna or whirlpool. For more information, call (305) 531-4743.

WALKING

By and large, Miami is as car crazy as any other large American city— maybe a bit more. When an errand requires a trip of two or three blocks or longer, most residents reach for their car keys. As a result, Miami isn't a very friendly city for strolling or walking. Folks looking for a place to stretch their legs may have to drive to get there.

There is, however, one great walking destination in Dade County: **Miami Beach.** From sunup to sundown, the sparkling white beach is a great place for a long walk or a leisurely stroll. (After the sun sets, stay off the beach— it's not safe after dark.) From 21st Street to 51st Street, the wooden **boardwalk** behind the hotels is a favorite destination for all kinds of people.

For a more structured walking tour that's also informative and fun, take the **Art Deco walking tour** of South Miami Beach, which starts every Saturday morning at 10:30 a.m. and every Thursday at 6:30 p.m. The cost is $10 (tax deductible), and the tour lasts 90 minutes. It begins at the Art Deco Welcome Center at the Ocean Front Auditorium located at 1001 Ocean Drive; reservations aren't required.

On the mainland, **Coconut Grove** and **Coral Gables** are good places to stretch your legs. For a longer walk, take the paved **bicycle path** that follows Biscayne Bay south along Bayshore Drive, Main Highway, Ingraham Highway, and Old Cutler Road.

In Coral Gables, start walking from the Miracle Mile west toward City Hall. The neighborhood gets really lush; energetic strollers can view famous landmarks such as the Merrick House (the former home of Coral Gables' founder), the ritzy Colonnade Hotel, the Venetian Pool, and the Biltmore Hotel.

For spectacular views of Biscayne Bay and downtown Miami, take a long walk along the **Rickenbacker Causeway,** which connects the mainland with Key Biscayne. Although it costs $8 to get in, **Fairchild Tropical Garden** is filled with paths that make for excellent walking.

Farther from Miami, **Everglades National Park** offers unlimited opportunities for walks—at least, during the winter months when the mosquitoes won't eat you alive. **Shark Valley,** about 35 miles west of Miami on Route 41, has a long, wide, paved path that makes a 15-mile loop into the glades, as well as a short nature path near the visitor center.

Near the park's southern entrance outside Florida City, strollers can choose from a wide number of paved and wooden pathways that show off the best of the glades' unique topography, flora, and wildlife.

RUNNING

On Miami Beach, the **boardwalk** between 21st and 51st Streets, as well as anywhere along the beach itself, offers the best—and safest—running surfaces. Above 30th Street, the beach gets narrow and it's often hard to find a packed track through the sand (unless you don't mind getting your feet wet near the surf where the sand is packed down by the waves). North of North Shore State Recreation Area (between 79th and 87th streets), a path runs parallel to the beach behind the narrow boardwalk toward Bal Harbour; its wide, packed surface is excellent for running.

On the mainland, the best destination for runners and joggers is the **bike path** that starts in Coconut Grove and continues south along Biscayne Bay; watch out for cyclists and cars as you cross the many intersections along the route. **Coral Gables** offers plenty of shaded, low-traffic back streets for serious joggers. The **Rickenbacker Causeway** to Key Biscayne has a path—and great views—that's excellent for a run that can reach marathon lengths if you continue around the island.

TENNIS

If you're not staying in a posh hotel or resort that offers free tennis, you're not entirely out of luck: the area abounds with plenty of public tennis courts.

The premier public tennis facility in the Miami area may be **The Tennis Center at Crandon Park** on Key Biscayne (phone (305) 365-2300), which offers 17 hard courts, 8 clay courts, and 2 grass courts. Hourly rates during the day for hard courts are $3 per person/per hour and $6 per person/per hour for clay. At night, only the hard courts are lighted; the rate is $5 per person/per hour. Advance reservations are accepted.

The Key Biscayne Tennis Association at 6702 Crandon Boulevard has seven clay and two hard courts that can be rented up to two days in advance. The courts are open 8 a.m. to 9 p.m. Monday through Thursday; until 6 p.m. Friday through Sunday; rates are $6 per person/per hour; only two clay courts and the two hard courts have lights. Call (305) 361-5263 for more information.

On Miami Beach, **Flamingo Park Center** at 1000 12th Street has 19 clay courts, all lighted for night play. The daytime rate is $5.33 per couple/per hour; at night, it's $6.40 per couple/per hour. Reservations for that day only may be made in person, not by phone. Call (305) 673-7761 for more information.

Farther up the beach in Surfside, the **A&M Tennis/Surfside Tennis Center and Pro Shop** at 88th Street and Collins Avenue features three hard courts and a fully staffed pro shop. Hours are 10:30 a.m. to 9 p.m. Monday through Friday, 9 a.m. to 5 p.m. on Saturday, and 9 a.m. to 5 p.m. on Sunday. The fee is $3 per person/per hour ($3.75 at night); reservations are accepted and the staff will find you a playing partner if you need one. Lessons and programs are available. Call (305) 866-5176 for more information.

In addition, the City of Miami and the Metro-Dade County Park and Recreation Department operate more than 250 tennis courts between them. Court locations include popular visitor destinations such as **Haulover Park** and **North Shore Park** (Miami Beach), **Peacock Park** (Coconut Grove), **Tamiami Park** (next to Florida International University), and **Tropical Park** (at the Palmetto Expressway).

GOLF

The peak season for golf in South Florida is Thanksgiving through mid-April. Midmornings are the most popular tee time and usually require reservations made well in advance. During the week, singles can frequently catch up with a game because of no-shows. Weekends, when local residents hit the links, are always busy (regardless of season), and getting a morning reservation is difficult. Plan on teeing off before 1 p.m. so you're not racing the sun, which sets around 5 p.m. in midwinter.

The summer months are ferociously hot and humid, so reserve a tee time either before 9 a.m. or after 4 p.m. to play nine holes; avoid the links between 1 and 3 p.m. In addition, afternoon thunderstorms frequently roll across Dade County. Greens fees, however, are reduced at many courses during the off-season.

Vacationers should reserve tee times when booking their hotels; some hotels block off tee times at nearby courses for their guests. During the summer, many golf courses offer discounts to local residents. Reservations at two municipal courses (Biltmore and Grenada) can be secured up to 24 hours in advance at no charge by calling the service at (305) 669-9500 on a touch-tone phone. Golfers on extended stays in Dade County might consider subscribing to the service to secure preferred times further in advance; the fee is $37 a year.

Biltmore Golf Course

Established: 1926

Address: 1210 Anastasia Avenue, Coral Gables 33134

Phone: (305) 460-5364

Status: Municipal course

Tees: Championship: 6,624 yards, par 71, USGA 71.5, slope 119.
Men's: 6,213 yards, par 71, USGA 69.7, slope 116.
Ladies': 5,600 yards, par 71, USGA 73.3, slope 122.

Fees: Daily, $76; twilight (after 2 p.m.), $48; includes cart; $9 (9 holes).

Facilities: Clubhouse, full-service pro shop with custom club-building and club repair capabilities, restaurant, locker rooms, driving range, putting greens, sand trap area, lessons from pros, tennis courts, Biltmore Hotel.

Comments: Redesigned in 1992, the Biltmore Golf Course is in excellent shape. Today, the course hosts the Coral Gables Open and the Orange Bowl International Junior Golf Championship.

City of Miami Springs Country Club

Established: 1923

Address: 650 Curtiss Parkway, Miami Springs 33166

Phone: (305) 863-0980

Status: Public course

Tees: Championship: 6,800 yards, par 71, USGA 72.7, slope 120.
Men's: 6,500 yards, par 71, USGA 72.9, slope 116.
Ladies': 5,700 yards, par 72, USGA 72.9, slope 122.

Fees: Weekdays, $20 after noon; weekends, $30 before noon, $25 after noon. Includes cart.

Facilities: Pro shop, restaurant, banquet facility for up to 700, lounge, lighted driving range, lessons from pros.

Comments: The Country Club in Miami Springs was opened by the City of Miami in 1923. The 18-hole championship par 71 course features challenging sand traps and a tropical ambience throughout its 6,741 yards. Home of the original Miami Open from 1925 until 1955, Miami Springs is now the annual host of the prestigious North-South Tournament. Less than five minutes from Miami International Airport and area hotels, Miami Springs has become a favorite among business travelers in Miami. With its low seasonal rates and extensive facilities, the manicured championship course welcomes visitors to Miami's tropical world of golf.

Doral Resort & Country Club

Established: 1961

Address: 4000 NW 87th Avenue, Miami 33178
Silver Course Clubhouse: 5001 NW 104th Avenue

Phone: (305) 592-2000

Status: Resort course

Tees: Course One (The Blue Monster)
Championship: 7,125 yards, par 72, USGA 74.5, slope 130.
Men's: 6,701 yards, par 72, USGA 72.2, slope 125.
Ladies': 5,392 yards, par 72, USGA 73, slope 124.

Course Two (The Gold Course)
Championship: 6,602 yards, par 70, USGA 73.3, slope 129.
Men's: 6,209 yards, par 70, USGA 70.7, slope 124.
Ladies': 5,179 yards, par 70, USGA 71.4, slope 123.

Course Three (The Red Course)
Championship: 6,146 yards, par 70, USGA 70.2, slope 121.
Men's: 6,058 yards, par 70, USGA 69.9, slope 118.
Ladies': 5,096 yards, par 70, USGA 70.6, slope 118.

Course Four (The White Course)
Championship: 7,171 yards, par 72, USGA 72.3, slope 128.
Men's: 6,085 yards, par 72, USGA 68.4, slope 113.
Ladies': 5,026 yards, par 72, USGA 70.7, slope 130.

Course Five (The Silver Course)
Championship: 6,557 yards, par 71, USGA 72.5, slope 131
Men's: 6,197 yards, par 71, USGA 70.9, slope 128.
Ladies': 4,738 yards, par 71, USGA 67.1, slope 117.

Course Six (The Green Course)
Nine holes: 1,085 yards, par 3.

Fees: In season (December 22–May 3): hotel guests—Blue course, $225;
White course, $225; Red course, $180; Gold course, $195; Silver course,
$195. Nonguests—Blue course, $250; White course, $250; Red course,
$200; Gold course, $225; Silver course, $225. Green course, $25 all the
time for all guests. Greens fees are significantly lower off-season.

Facilities: One of the world's largest pro shops, driving range, four putting
greens, world-class Doral Spa, on-course snack bar, three full service
restaurants, 15-court tennis facility, Doral golf learning center with Jim
McLean, caddies available, fishing in the course lakes. The clubhouse for

the Silver Course was under renovation at press time. The new facilities will be extensive.

Comments: The home of the famous Doral "Blue Monster" and the Doral-Ryder Open. This is one of the premier golf courses in the country. The Gold Course has recently been redesigned by Raymond Floyd (original designer of the "Blue Monster"). With the tropical Miami climate and four championship courses, this Florida destination is one that should not be missed by the avid golfer. Serene lakes and Cypress trees line the fairways of this wonderful setting, as you challenge the "Blue Monster."

Fontainebleau Golf Club

Established: 1970

Address: 9603 Fontainebleau Boulevard, Miami 33172

Phone: (305) 221-5181

Status: Public course

Tees: Course One (East)
Championship: 7,005 yards, par 72, USGA 73.3, slope 122.
Men's: 6,647 yards, par 72, USGA 71.6, slope 117.
Ladies': 5,586 yards, par 72, USGA 71.5, slope 119.

Course Two (West)
Championship: 6,944 yards, par 72, USGA 72.5, slope 120.
Men's: 6,650 yards, par 72, USGA 71.2, slope 118.
Ladies': 5,565 yards, par 72, USGA 71, slope 118.

Fees: For two people. Winter: weekdays, $50 ($40 after noon); weekends, $60 ($46 after noon). Call for summer rates. Includes cart fee.

Facilities: 36-hole championship course, driving range, snack bar, pro shop, lessons from PGA professional.

Comments: Mark Mahanna design.

Golf Club of Miami

Established: 1990

Address: 6801 Miami Gardens Drive, Miami 33015

Phone: (305) 829-8449

Status: Public course

Tees: Course One (West)
Championship: 7,017 yards, par 72, USGA 74, slope 132.
Men's: 6,139 yards, par 72, USGA 72, slope 128.
Ladies': 5,298 yards, par 72, USGA 70.1, slope 124.

Course Two (East)
Championship: 6,473 yards, par 70, USGA 70.3, slope 124.
Men's: 5,855 yards, par 70, USGA 69.8, slope 120.
Ladies': 5,025 yards, par 70, USGA 68.8, slope 118.

Fees: In season (December–April 15): weekdays, $55; weekends, $75. Off-season (April 16–December): $22–55. Rates include cart and green fees. Twilight fees are available. All fees subject to 6.5 percent Florida tax.

Facilities: Two grass driving ranges (one lighted), two pro shops, on-course beverage service, lessons from PGA professionals, Turn Key tournament operation, full service restaurant, banquet room, men's and women's locker rooms.

Comments: South Florida's premier public golf facility. Site of former National Airlines Open, the 1991 Senior PGA Tour National Qualifying School, and Regional USGA events such as the Mid-AM qualifier.

Hollywood Golf Hotel

Established: 1930

Address: 1600 Johnson Street, Hollywood 33020

Phone: (954) 927-1751

Status: Public course

Tees: Championship: 6,336 yards, par 70, USGA 69.7, slope 117.
Men's: 6,024 yards, par 70, USGA 68.5, slope 114.
Ladies': 5,484 yards, par 70, USGA 71.5, slope 112.

Fees: Winter, $35; summer, $26. Includes cart.

Facilities: Pro shop, clubhouse restaurant, 35-room full service hotel, locker rooms, pool.

Comments: Famous Florida club designed by Donald Ross in 1930. It was completely renovated in 1995.

International Links of Miami
(Formerly the Melreese Golf Course)

Established: 1960

Address: 1802 NW 37th Avenue, Miami 33125

Phone: (305) 633-4583

Status: Public course

Tees: Championship: 7,173 yards, par 71, USGA 73.7, slope 128.
Men's: 6,613 yards, par 71, USGA 71.1, slope 123.
Ladies': 5,534 yards, par 71, USGA 72.4, slope 122.

Fees: $98 before 3 p.m.; $30 after 3 p.m.; includes cart.

Facilities: Pro shop, restaurant/lounge, banquet facility for up to 200, lighted driving range, lessons from pros, rental equipment.

Comments: International Links of Miami is an outstanding 18-hole championship par 71 course with 14 holes bordering the water. It is rated as one of the finest municipal golf courses in the country. International Links has hosted the Ladies' PGA, Public Links Qualifying, the National Clergymen's Tournament, the National Baseball Players' Tournament, and the Regional Handicapped Tournament.

Miami National Golf Club
(Formerly the Kendale Lakes Golf Course)

Established: 1970

Address: 6401 Kendale Lakes Drive, Miami 33183

Phone: (305) 382-3930

Status: Semiprivate course

Tees: Marlin Course
Blue Tees: 3,359/3,334 yards, par 36.
White Tees: 3,120 yards, par 36.
Red Tees: 2,743 yards, par 37.

Dolphin Course
Blue Tees: 3,319 yards, par 36.
White Tees: 3,060 yards, par 36.
Red Tees: 2,579 yards, par 36.

Barracuda Course
Blue Tees: 3,360 yards, par 36.
White Tees: 3,092 yards, par 36.
Red Tees: 2,702 yards, par 37.

Fees: Winter: $39–45; $35–45 after 10 a.m.; $20–25 after 2 p.m. Cart fee: $20 weekdays; $30 weekends. Call for summer rates.

Facilities: Three championship 9-hole courses, 40-stall driving range (lighted), 12-court tennis facility (6 lighted), 2 Olympic-size pools, infant wading pool, swimming lessons from professionals, men's and women's locker rooms, banquet facility, and grill bar.

Comments: Miami National Golf Club was built in 1970 and is considered one of the best courses in Greater Miami. It was remodeled after Hurricane Andrew, with $2 million going to repair the clubhouse and golf course. It has been host to several LPGA tour events and PGA qualifiers for the Doral-Ryder Open and the Honda Classic.

Miami Shores Country Club

Established: 1937

Address: 10000 Biscayne Boulevard, Miami Shores 33138

Phone: (305) 795-2366

Status: Public course

Tees: Championship: 6,373 yards, par 71, USGA 70.6, slope 120.
Men's: 6,096 yards, par 71, USGA 69.1, slope 116.
Ladies': 5,442 yards, par 72, USGA 71.3, slope 121.

Fees: Winter, $75; includes cart.

Facilities: Clubhouse with three banquet rooms seating up to 450, pool, tennis courts, pro shop, lighted driving range, golf school, men's and women's locker rooms, spacious lounge area available for lunch and dinner.

Comments: Miami Shores is one of the oldest clubs in Miami. It is characterized by elevated tees and greens that are small and well bunkered.

BICYCLING

First, the good news: Dade County is flat.

And the bad? With its congestion and a decentralized layout that makes devising a long ride problematic, Miami is not a very bike-friendly town. Road riders out for a long-distance spin must often negotiate bumper-to-bumper traffic, share the road with rude drivers, and deal with the city's infuriating lack of street signs.

Nor are fat-tired cyclists immune to the problem of finding problem-free riding in South Florida: Unless you're into beach riding (which is *very* hard on equipment), mountain bikers will find little off-road cycling—and certainly no mountains.

In the summer, cyclists should keep a wary eye peeled for approaching afternoon thunderstorms, which can be fearsome. During the summer months' extreme heat and humidity, try to confine long rides to the early morning hours or risk heat exhaustion; carry plenty of water and take sunblock along for the ride. Away from breezes on the beach, mosquitoes can be a problem when you're not pedaling. On the other hand, the winter months offer excellent cycling conditions.

Where to Rent a Bike

Mountain bikes and beach cruisers are available for rental at **Miami Beach Bicycle Center,** 601 5th Street (at Washington Street, phone (305) 674-0150). Rental rates start at $20 per day or $70 per week. **Grove Cycles** at 3226 Grand Avenue in Coconut Grove (phone (305) 444-5415) rents beach cruisers, tandems, and in-line skates. Beach cruisers rent for $5.50 an hour, $15 a day, and $25 for 24 hours; tandems rent for $10 an hour and $45 a day; in-line skates rent for $5.50 an hour, $15 a day, and $25 for 24 hours; the price includes protective padding. Helmets rent for $1 an hour or $3 a day; children 15 years old and younger receive free helmet rental. **Mangrove Cycles** at 260 Crandon Boulevard on Key Biscayne (phone (305) 361-5555) rents one-speed bikes for $7 for 2 hours, $10 a day, and $35 a week; mountain bikes rent for $12 for 2 hours, $18 a day, and $45 a week. The shop is open every day 10 a.m. to 6 p.m. but is closed on Mondays.

Road Riding

For eye-pleasing scenery and enough tree cover to ward off the effects of the subtropical sun, most riders head for **Coconut Grove.** The streets are pretty, dense foliage such as bougainvillea and hibiscus keep the worst of the sun's effects at bay, and the area's eclectic architecture entertains the eye.

For a longer spin on skinny tires, follow the **bike path** south along Bayshore Drive, Main Highway, Ingraham Highway, and Old Cutler Road—although most serious riders will want to stay off the path and ride in traffic: the paved path is often broken up by tree roots and is better suited for fat tires and one-speed rental bikes. Figure on turning back around 152nd Street (Coral Reef Drive). From this point south, the foliage is sparse as the greenery continues to recover from Hurricane Andrew.

For a more energetic ride—and the biggest climb in Dade County— take the **Rickenbacker Causeway** to Key Biscayne. The climb to the top of the bridge offers stunning views, and a ride around the island is long enough to provide a real workout. You can still spot damage from Hurricane Andrew at the southern end of the island, but the foliage is starting to come back. A ride to and around Key Biscayne remains a Sunday morning favorite with area roadies.

Mountain Biking

Local hammerheads report that all is not lost in mountainless Dade County—although the good riding that's available emphasizes handling over aerobics.

The premier off-road destination is just over the line in Broward County: **Markham County Park** (phone (954) 389-2000), located near the intersection of I-75 and I-59, west of Fort Lauderdale. The park features whoop-de-whoops along single-track trails, jeep roads, real hills in the woods, and lots of black, sticky mud guaranteed to keep intermediate and advanced riders entertained for hours. There's a $1 entrance fee to the park on weekends and holidays.

Dade County offers three smaller destinations for mountain bikers looking for an off-road ramble. **Amelia Earhart Park** in Hialeah, while not offering any trails as difficult as those found in Markham County Park, has some nice single-track through woods, open fields, soft sand, and mud. **Greynolds Park,** off West Dixie Highway in North Miami Beach, has a 1.6-mile course that local riders like to jam around. **Haulover Park** offers three short rides in the woods that are fun to explore—but avoid riding through the field or you'll be picking thorns out of your inner tubes. **Oleta River State Recreation Area** (across from Sunny Isles in North Miami; (305) 919-1846) is constructing off-road paths for mountain bikers and offers an extensive system of dirt roads worth exploring. Admission to the area is $4 per vehicle. While there's no additional charge to ride the trails, helmets are required. For more details on some of these and other off-road rides in southeast Florida, pick up a copy of *Mountain Bike! Florida* by Steve Jones (Menasha Ridge Press).

HIKING

For unspoiled wilderness rambles by foot, hikers must first jump in their cars and drive west to Everglades National Park—but only during the winter months. Clouds of mosquitoes make spring, summer, and fall visits to the Everglades unthinkable.

Shark Valley, about a 90-minute drive from downtown Miami, offers a 15-mile paved walkway to an observation tower; admittedly, this a long trek for all but the most ardent walkers. But a shorter, out-and-back hike still offers glimpses of wildlife and views of the Everglades' unique fauna and topography. There's also a short, unpaved nature trail near the visitor center.

For a more varied look at the Everglades, head toward Homestead and the park's southern entrance leading to Flamingo. While it's a longer drive, it's still a manageable day trip, and you will leave with a much better sense of what the subtle Everglades are all about. A number of paved and elevated wooden pathways that radiate from the road to Flamingo lead visitors to hammocks (small islands of elevated land), views of the sawgrass prairie, and tropical jungles.

Once armed with heavy boots and experienced in using a compass and topographic map, savvy hikers can strike out on their own across the glades during the winter months (which is also the dry season; don't try this during the summer). The rewards include sightings of wildlife and a unique view of the sawgrass prairie that most visitors miss. Pull over anywhere along the road, and head off toward a hammock. Park rangers at the main visitor center near the entrance can offer advice and suggestions for exploring.

SWIMMING

The Miami area features two well-known swimming destinations: the *Atlantic Ocean* and *Biscayne Bay.* Miami Beach offers 10 miles of sandy white beaches along the ocean from South Pointe Park in South Beach north to Sunny Isles Beach at 192nd Street.

If you're not staying at a hotel close to the beaches, public beaches with metered parking, bathrooms, and outside showers are available along Route A1A (Collins Avenue) in Miami Beach at: 1st Street and Washington Avenue (South Pointe Park); 3rd Street; 6th to 14th streets (Lummus Park); 21st Street; 35th Street; 46th Street (next to the Eden Roc Hotel); 53rd Street; 64th Street; 73rd Street (across from the North Shore Community Center); 79th to 87th streets (North Shore State Recreation Area); 93rd Street (Surfside; a very small lot across Collins Avenue from the beach); 96th Street (another small lot); and a small lot next to the Holiday Inn on 167th Street (Sunny Isles) that charges $3.50 to park your car.

Other options for ocean swimming include **Haulover Beach** (just north of Bal Harbour between 163rd and 192nd streets; $3 per car), **Crandon Park** on Key Biscayne ($3.50 per car; $1 toll on the Rickenbacker Causeway), and **Bill Baggs Cape Florida State Park** (also on Key Biscayne; $3.50 per car). Haulover is renowned for its "clothing optional" (nude) area on the north end of the beach; Crandon Park is popular with families.

The clear waters of Biscayne Bay are shallow and usually calm; the most popular beaches are along the Rickenbacker Causeway. Picnic tables, shade trees, and no restrictions on pets make these beaches extremely popular with local residents; the waters are also popular with windsurfers (the beach after the first bridge on the causeway is informally called **Windsurfer Beach**).

If you're looking for a nonsaltwater experience, but your hotel doesn't have a pool, the **Venetian Pool** at 2701 DeSoto Boulevard in Coral Gables (phone (305) 460-5356) should be on your itinerary. Originally excavated to supply limestone for early Coral Gables homes, this large, coral-rock, outdoor pool offers a tropical lagoon–like setting, with caves, waterfalls, and stone bridges. In winter, the pool is open Tuesday–Sunday 10 a.m.–4:30 p.m.; closed Mondays; call for summer hours. Admission for adults is $5; children ages 12 and under are admitted for $2, and no children under age 3 are permitted. A new cafe offers a full luncheon menu.

For information on swimming hazards, see Part One, pages 21–23.

CANOEING AND KAYAKING

Visitors to Miami can rent canoes and kayaks to explore the backwaters of Biscayne Bay. The visual rewards range from close-up views of gorgeous waterfront estates to glimpses of Everglades-worthy wilderness located in Miami's backyard.

While 854-acre **Oleta River State Recreation Area** is virtually surrounded by high-rises, visitors can rent canoes and explore the quiet waters that surround the park—and possibly sight a manatee. Admission to the park is $4 per car (up to 8 people); canoe and paddleboat rentals are $12 per hour. One-person kayaks rent for $12 per hour. A $20 deposit and a driver's license are also required. Boat rentals are available weekdays, noon–5 p.m.; and weekends, 9 a.m.–5 p.m. The park is located off Sunny Isles Boulevard between Miami Beach and the mainland (North Miami Beach). For more information, call (305) 919-1846.

At Haulover Beach Park, the **Urban Trails Kayak Company** offers guided and unguided tours of the Oleta River area and its mangrove-shrouded waterways and uninhabited islands. That's not all: to the south, kayakers can explore the man-made backwaters and sumptuous estates bordering Biscayne Bay. Guided group tours ($45 per person) are by appointment; self-guided trips can start anytime. One-person kayak rental rates are $8 an hour, $20 for a half-day, and $25 a full day. Tandem (two-person) kayaks are $12 an hour, $30 a half-day, and $35 all day; no paddling experience required. Call (305) 947-1302 for more information.

Some of the world's most extensive mangrove forests can be explored by canoe at **Biscayne National Park,** near Florida City in southern Dade County. Canoe rentals are available 9 a.m.–4:30 p.m. for $8 an hour, $22 a half-day, and $32 a full day; the price includes paddles and life jackets. Folks with their own canoes can launch for free. Call (305) 230-1100 for more information.

SCUBA DIVING

For more experienced certified divers, Miami is a destination that offers a chance to explore an extensive line of natural reefs that parallels the entire length of Dade County. Miami is also home to one of the largest artificial reef programs in the world.

It started in 1972 with the sinking of the *Biscayne,* a 120-foot-long freighter that formerly hauled bananas from South America. The ship was the first of many wrecks (including barges, tugboats, naval vessels, and private yachts) that have been sunk for the enjoyment of sport divers. While the shallowest reefs near Miami are 30 feet down, wreck diving starts at 35 feet and goes down to about 130 feet. Private dive boats can lead visiting divers on tours of the wrecks and reefs, including night dives.

Up the coast in Sunny Isles, the **Diving Locker** offers a three-and-a-half-hour, two-dive trip every morning and afternoon, weather permitting. The cost, including tanks and weights, is $45. Most trips visit a wreck and a shallow reef. In addition, the shop offers a certification course (four-day private course is $350) and a one-hour introduction to scuba diving ($45, pool only). For more information and to schedule a dive trip, call (305) 947-6025.

Also in Sunny Isles is **H2O Scuba,** which offers four-hour, two-tank dive trips at 8:30 a.m. and 1 p.m. on weekends and at noon on weekdays;

the cost is $48 per person without equipment, $58 with two tanks, and $85 with all equipment. A certification course is $239. For more information, call H2O at (305) 956-3483.

SNORKELING

The closest place to Miami with reefs close enough to the surface for snorkelers to enjoy is **Biscayne National Park,** an underwater park located a few miles east of Florida City in southern Dade County; it's about an hour's drive from downtown Miami. Unlike scuba diving, which requires participants to be certified before they can dive, the requirements for snorkeling are minimal. You only need the ability to swim and a desire to see aquatic life up close.

At Biscayne National Park, three-hour snorkeling trips (two hours of travel, one hour exploring the reef) leave daily at 1:30 p.m., weather permitting; the cost is $29.95 per person and includes all the equipment you need. Call (305) 230-1100 to make a reservation. See our write-up on Biscayne National Park (page 312) for more information.

If you can't make it to Biscayne National Park, you're not completely out of luck. There's a small reef located off Miami Beach between 3rd and 6th streets in South Beach. The reef is 70 yards offshore and 16 feet down. Check with a lifeguard for the exact location and be sure to take out a diving flag to warn boaters that you're swimming in the area.

SAILBOATS AND SAILING SCHOOLS

To set sail on the calm, shallow waters of Biscayne Bay, head for **Sailboats of Key Biscayne,** located in the Crandon Park Marina on Key Biscayne. Catalina 22-footers rent for $35 an hour and $110 a half-day; each additional hour is $20; Catalina 25-foot, J-24, and Hunter 23-foot sailboats rent for $35 an hour, $110 for a half day, and $170 for a full day. Bareboat (no crew) charters on sailboats from 30 to 54 feet are also available. For more information, call (305) 361-0328; if there's no answer, call (305) 279-7424.

Never sailed? Then sign up for a 10-hour sailing course offered at Sailboats of Key Biscayne that will turn you into a certified skipper. There's no classroom time—all instruction is on the water—and graduates of the course qualify for a 15 percent discount on boat rentals. The cost of the private, one-on-one course is $250; add $100 for a spouse or friend for one-on-two instruction. After completing the course, graduates are qualified to rent a cruising sailboat and embark on an overnight sailing trip.

More options: **Dinner Key** in Coconut Grove is another nearby destination well known for sailboat rentals and sailing lessons, and is a good jumping off point for sailing Biscayne Bay.

SPECTATOR SPORTS

More well known as a tropical paradise, Miami is also a great sports destination. South Florida probably got its big start in sports when the opening of the railroad made it possible for major league baseball teams to come south for spring training. Next, the construction of the Orange Bowl brought in top-level college and professional football teams. To take full advantage of this cornucopia of team sports, check the *Miami Herald's* sports section for a daily listing of local games.

Pro Teams

Leading the list of attractions is the AFC East **Miami Dolphins** football team, which packs 'em in every season at Pro Player Stadium (formerly Joe Robbie Stadium). Successful? You bet—the Dolphins have played in the Super Bowl five times and in 1972 achieved everlasting glory with the only all-win, no-tie season in NFL history. The season is from August through December; ticket prices range from $24 to $130 and are available from the stadium box office or Ticketmaster at (954) 523-3309. The stadium is located at 2269 NW 199th Street in North Miami; phone (305) 620-2578 for more information.

Pro Player Stadium, which hosted its second Super Bowl in 1995, also hosts the annual **Blockbuster Bowl** football championship. It's also home to the newest addition to baseball's National League, the **Florida Marlins,** the 1997 World Series champs. General admission tickets for Marlins games range from $2 to $125. Call the stadium at (305) 626-7400 for home game dates and additional information on obtaining tickets.

The Miami Arena, located at 721 NW 1st Avenue in downtown Miami, hosts the **Miami Heat,** an NBA team offering fast-paced basketball action. The squad debuted in 1988 and recently completed a trip to the NBA's Eastern Conference Finals. Ticket prices are $15–135. Call (305) 577-HEAT for ticket information. The 15,000-seat Miami Arena is also home to the National Hockey League's **Florida Panthers,** who made an incredible run to the Stanley Cup finals in just their third season. Ticket prices are $14–100. For information, ticket prices, and dates for home hockey games, call (954) 835-7000.

Amateur Sports

Top-flight collegiate sports teams in South Florida include the **University of Miami Hurricanes** football, baseball, and basketball teams. Hurricanes football is played at the famous Orange Bowl from September through November; get a seat high up in the stands and you'll get a great view of Miami while watching exciting gridiron action: The team has won three national championships in the last decade. The stadium is located at 1400

NW 4th Street, west of downtown. Tickets are $18 and $22. For tickets to any Hurricane events, call (305) 284-CANE or (800) GO-CANES. For game information, call (305) 284-CANE.

The University of Miami Hurricanes baseball team plays about 50 home games a year at Mark Light Stadium on the school's Coral Gables campus. The season lasts from February to May, with both day and evening games on the schedule. Tickets are $5 for adults and $3 for children and seniors. The University of Miami basketball squad plays at the Miami Arena, 701 Arena Boulevard in downtown Miami. Tickets are $9 to $18. For more information on Hurricanes baseball and basketball, call (305) 284-2263.

Florida International University's **Golden Panthers** field a wide range of teams. Basketball is played November through March at the Golden Panther Arena, SW 8th Street and 112th Avenue in Miami. The baseball season is January through May; home games are played at the University Park Complex, SW 8th Street and 112th Avenue. Golden Panthers soccer is played September through November at the University Park Complex. For schedules, call (305) 348-4263.

Car Racing and Pro Tennis

The **Grand Prix of Miami** is South Florida's premier auto racing event. Each spring, international drivers compete at speeds of more than 100 mph at Metro-Dade Homestead Motorsports Complex in Homestead. Tickets for three days of racing action range from $40 to $200. For ticket information call the Homestead-Miami Speedway ticket office at (305)-230-RACE

To see the best in top-notch international tennis competition, don't miss the **Ericson Open,** held for two weeks each March at the International Tennis Center, 7300 Crandon Boulevard, Key Biscayne, in a new, 7,500-seat stadium. The event draws more than 200,000 spectators and is broadcast live each year to more than 30 countries as top players compete for more than $4.5 million in prize money. Call (305) 446-2200 or (800) 725-5472 for dates and ticket information.

The Betting Sports:
Horse Races, Greyhounds, and Jai Alai

Puppies and ponies and jai alai: South Florida is home to several sports that permit pari-mutuel wagering, the type of gambling where you bet against other bettors, not the house. For folks who can restrain themselves from wagering, the activities can be fun and inexpensive.

Note: While no one under age 18 may bet in Florida, children may accompany adults to horse races, greyhound races, and jai alai.

Thoroughbred Horse Racing   For more than 50 years Florida has been a center of thoroughbred horse racing. Classy **Hialeah Park** (2200 East 4th

Avenue, Hialeah; phone (305) 885-8000) trades racing dates with **Gulfstream Park** for winter racing. Gulfstream is located just over the Broward County line in Hallandale on US 1; phone (305) 931-RACE **Calder Race Course's** weatherproof track permits racing during the rainy summer; it's located at 21001 NW 27th Avenue, near I-95 near the Dade-Broward border. The phone number is (305) 625-1311. To see where the ponies are running during your visit, check the sports section of the *Miami Herald.*

Dog Racing   Greyhounds reach speeds of more than 40 miles an hour; you can see the action at two tracks in the Miami area. Like horse racing, the venue rotates throughout the year, so check the *Miami Herald* before heading out. Racing starts around 7:30 p.m. six nights a week; several days during the week feature matinees starting at 12:30 p.m.

The **Flagler Greyhound Track** is located at 401 NW 38th Court near Seventh Street and 37th Avenue, southeast of Miami International Airport; the phone number is (305) 649-3000. In Broward County, the **Hollywood Greyhound Track** is located on US 1 a mile east of I-95, just over the county line in Hallandale; phone (954) 924-3200 from Dade County.

Jai Alai   For an unusual experience that recalls the Damon Runyun–esque days of early Miami, make a trip to the **Miami Jai Alai Fronton,** located at 3500 NW 37th Avenue, near Miami International Airport (phone (305) 633-6400). The crowd looks like it stepped out of the pages of a John Steinbeck novel and the atmosphere is redolent with the pungent smell of cigars and beer. A fronton, by the way, is the 176-foot-long court where jai alai (pronounced "high lie") is played; Miami's, built in 1926, is the oldest in the United States.

Don't forget to watch the action behind the big screen as teams compete in the world's fastest sport, a Basque game dating from the 15th century that's a cross between lacrosse, tennis, and racquetball. The hard ball (called a *pelota*) flung and caught in a long, curved wicker basket (a *cesta*) has been clocked at 180 mph. Teams of two or four compete and the first team to score seven points wins.

You can bet on a team to win or on the order in which teams finish. It's all utterly confusing to first-time visitors—yet fascinating to watch. Admission is $1; the first game is at 7 p.m. five nights a week. Matinees are on Monday, Wednesday, Friday, and Saturday, noon to 5 p.m.

Shopping

STROLLING AND WINDOW SHOPPING

Downtown   Downtown Miami, a curious blend of Art Deco architecture and modern monoliths, contains a wondrous mix of shops, many owned and operated by second- and third-generation Latin families. As with most downtown metropolitan areas, the streets meander, but it's entirely possible to find everything you'll need by staying on the main drag, West Flagler, with a few side-street excursions. A word of caution: Most of what you've read about Miami is probably true, so wear sensible shoes, keep your jewelry in the hotel safe, and be home before the sun sets. You'll be fine.

Jewelry is really downtown Miami's main lure. For the real thing, visit the venerable **Seybold Building** (37 East Flagler Street; (305) 374-7922), chock-full of jewelers and some wholesalers who sell rough stones and gold and silver by the ounce. Small electronics stores are scattered about everywhere, with a deal or two to be found, but as far as returning your purchase should you change your mind, you'd be better off at Radio Shack.

South Beach   The current hotspot of South Florida, as well as much of the world, South Beach is a fine destination for shopping on foot. While the entire district spans a mere 17 blocks, with trendy boutiques and quaint galleries in unlikely places such as hotel lobbies, there are certain streets the *au courant* shopper will not want to miss:

Lincoln Road runs from the Ocean to the Bay, with nine blocks of shopping. In the 1940s, Lincoln Road was a chi-chi strip of elite retail stores, including Bonwit Teller, Saks Fifth Avenue, and Lillie Rubin. Today, like everything else on South Beach, it's hip. With a nod to New York's SoHo, Lincoln Road is a revamped, open-air, pedestrian mall that is home to artists, boutiques both funky and chic, chains store such as **Pottery Barn** (1045 Lincoln Road; (786) 276-8889) and sidewalk cafés. Don't overlook the side streets, which are scattered with worthwhile stores, salons, and cafés one block north and south of Lincoln Road. **Gerald Stevens' Flowers & Flowers** (925 Lincoln Road; (305) 534-1633) has the best blooms in Miami, plus intriguing gift items such as rose-scented beeswax candles and bitter orange potpourri. **Brownes Apothecary** (841 Lincoln Road; (305) 532-8703) offers a comprehensive selection of toiletries and up-to-the-minute beauty items, from old-fashioned hair pomade to lavender-scented soapstones; its Some Like it Hot salon in the rear is handy for an impromptu manicure or blow-dry. Just want a T-shirt to take back home? Try **Ete** (530 Lincoln Road; (305) 672-3265) for a witty, quality "T," as well as casual Miami chic. Stop by **Pink Palm Co.** (737 Lincoln Road; (305) 538-8373) for an unusual greeting card or colorful gift item. For designer clothing, try **En Avance** (734 Lincoln Road; (305) 534-0337), **Base** (939 Lincoln Road; (305) 531-4982), and **24 Collection** (744 Lincoln Road; (305) 673-2455). We like **Senzatempo** (1655 Meridian Avenue; (305) 534-5588) for its fascinating selection of vintage watches, furniture, and home accessories, as well as **Wick** (1661 Michigan; (305) 538-7022) which has an excellent assortment of candles, home and body aromatherapy products, and inexpensive gifts for friends back home. **Real.life.basic** (643 Lincoln Road; (305) 604-

1984) has everything the chic kitchen requires, from sushi-making kits to retro-inspired barware. Want to rent a video? Go where in-the-know locals and visiting celebs do—**New Concept Video** (749 Lincoln Road; (305) 674-1111) where you can find new releases as well as cult classics; great selection of magazines and groovy CDs, too. Need a quick bite? Try **David's Cafe II** (1654 Meridian Avenue, one block north of Lincoln Road; (305) 672-8707) for inexpensive Cuban food; **Rosinella** (525 Lincoln Road; (305) 672-8777) for down-home Italian lunches and dinners without the glitz; and the **Van Dyke Cafe** (846 Lincoln Road; (305) 534-3600)— Lincoln Road's answer to the renowned News Café—a perennial favorite for casual dining and people-watching in a sidewalk café setting. Love a good old-fashioned flea market? Many visitors try scheduling their trips around the semi-weekly Lincoln Road Antiques and Collectibles Market, held along the intersection of Lincoln Road and Drexel Avenue the second and last Sunday of each month from October to late May.

Espanola Way intersects Washington Avenue and is situated between 14th and 15th streets. This quaint block of shops includes adorable gift and vintage boutiques, as well as avant-garde art galleries. **South Beach Makeup** (439 Espanola Way; (305) 538-0805) carries a plethora of makeup as well as the Kiehl's line of products; and check out **Espanola Way Art Center** (409 Espanola Way; (305) 672-5305), where the resident artists always have several intriguing projects on display. On Sundays during tourist season, Espanola Way turns into a street fair-cum-block party, with vendors selling everything from handmade candles to vintage bric-a-brac.

Washington Avenue is South Beach's main commercial artery and is brimming with upscale boutiques, trendy restaurants, and the occasional hardware store. Some can't-miss stops are **My Uncle Deco Shop** (1570 Washington Avenue; (305) 534-4834) for preworn Levis and other gear favored by models and locals and **Betsey Johnson** (805 Washington Avenue; (305) 673-0023) for up-to-the-microminute fashion for young women.

Ocean Drive, at once scenic and chaotic, is fine for people-watching while sipping overpriced cappuccino, but as far as serious shopping is concerned, you're better off searching out the small boutiques located along its side streets. One block west is the Collins Avenue fashion district, a three-block stretch (from 6th to 9th Streets) littered with national boutiques including **Nicole Miller** (656 Collins Avenue; (305) 535-2200), **Banana Republic** (800 Collins Avenue; (305) 674-7079) and the **Gap** (673 Collins Avenue; (305) 531-6503).

Alton Road South Beach's quietest retail street is getting increasingly popular as rents in other areas skyrocket. Music buffs will want to check out **Revolution Records** (1620-A Alton Road; (305) 673-6464) for new and used CDs, cassettes, and hard-to-find LPs. Also on Alton Road, which could be considered Washington Avenue–by-the-bay (the street is just east of Biscayne Bay): **Spiaggia** (1624 Alton Road; (305) 538-7949) for an eclectic and ever-changing offering of new and vintage home decor; and **Alton Road Nursery** (1239 Alton Road; (305) 532-7939) for a fantastic collection of not only plants but also glorious antiques that the owner accumulates on her travels.

Coral Gables   A picturesque business-cum-residential area, Coral Gables contains one of Miami's most historic shopping areas, Miracle Mile. This four-block stretch of outdoor shopping (don't neglect the side streets) contains more than 150 boutiques, with something to satisfy everyone's taste level and budget. The area is probably the safest in Miami, as well as the best manicured. Favorite destinations include **Leather World** (339 Miracle Mile; (305) 446-7888), for all types of small leather goods imaginable; **Luminaire** (2331 Ponce de Leon Boulevard, (305) 448-7367), for contemporary furnishings and accessories; and **Books & Books** (265 Aragon Avenue; (305) 442-4408), Miami's favorite independently owned bookstore.

Coconut Grove   Miami's hotspot hippie village of the 1970s, Coconut Grove has retained its anti-establishment charm while continuing to attract young sophisticates. Follow narrow sidewalks down the shady streets and browse the afternoon away. Our favorites include **Ios** (3109 Commodore Plaza; (305) 442-7166), offering sleek hip-chick attire, and **Silvia Tcherassi** (3403 Main Highway; (305) 447-4540), which features the elegant and modern clothing of its Colombian designer-owner. Need a last-minute manicure, blow-out, or makeup application before dinner? Head to **Allure Express Salon** (3405 Main Highway; (305) 461-0020) for exceptional work at reasonable prices.

MALL SHOPPING

If it's a big, generic mall you want, Miami's got plenty. **Dadeland** and **Aventura** malls will do just fine, located respectively at 7535 North Kendall Drive (phone (305) 665-6226) and 19501 Biscayne Boulevard #450, North Miami Beach (phone (305) 935-1110). But it's that Miami flavor you crave, right? Okay, we know just where to send you.

Bal Harbour Shops, 9700 Collins Avenue, Bal Harbour; (305) 866-0311. If the thought of a $3,000 knit day dress doesn't send you into convulsions, you'll feel right at home at Bal Harbour Shops. A charming, two-floor mall with valet parking (self-parking by the hour is also available), a fleet of security guards, and French cafés serving $35 pasta entrees, Bal Harbour Shops is Miami's toniest mall. Offerings include Tiffany, Gucci, Chanel, Prada, Hugo Boss, Hermes, Saks Fifth Avenue, Neiman Marcus, Ferragamo, and Versace. For the label-conscious, this is paradise found.

Bayside Marketplace, 401 Biscayne Boulevard (NE 4th–NE 9th streets), Miami; (305) 577-3344. Fun for the whole family, the tropical, indoor/

outdoor Bayside is like an international carnival with stores. The lower level is teeming with stalls offering ethnic wares and cute (if largely useless) merchandise such as Flintstones coffee mugs and beach rafts in the image of the Venus de Milo. National chain stores include Brookstone, Victoria's Secret, The Limited, and The Gap. Great for gifts: the Disney Store, which stocks everything from Mickey Mouse silk boxer shorts to *101 Dalmatians* charm bracelets. Naturalists will appreciate Art by God, which carries oversized crystals to put on display at home, as well as zebra-skin rugs made from farm-raised herds. Just minutes from downtown Miami, Bayside is easy to find, safe, and clean, with plenty of sheltered, if slightly costly, parking.

CocoWalk, 3015 Grand Avenue, Coconut Grove; (305) 444-0777. Resembling a big Mediterranean birthday cake, CocoWalk is Miami's newest and most comprehensive shopping-cum-entertainment complex. Smack in the middle of Coconut Grove, the two-layer mall contains everything the Generation X mall rat craves: music, tapas, loud bands, a multiscreen cinema, and a Gap. Plus, grown-up choices including Victoria's Secret, JW Cooper for western wear, and a good bookstore.

The Falls, US 1 and SW 136th Street, Miami; (305) 255-4570. Probably Miami's most beautiful mall, The Falls is tropical and serene, with lots of wood, waterfalls, and leafy foliage. Bloomingdales is the big draw, but there are also 60 specialty and national boutiques, including Polo/Ralph Lauren, Banana Republic, Crate and Barrel, Pottery Barn, and Ann Taylor.

SPECIALTY SHOPS

Antiques

You'll find the greatest concentration of antique stores on NW 27th Street, directly west of South Dixie Highway (an extension of US 1). Whether it's a delicate fauteuil chair or a replacement chandelier crystal you need, chances are you'll find it. We like **Southern Fine Arts** (3070 SW 38th Avenue; (305) 446-1641) for rarefied artifacts, fossils, and unique, antiquated furnishings, such as a tapestry-covered 17th-century footstool. **Corinthian Antiques** (2741 SW 27th Avenue; (305) 854-6068), which carries a mix of American English and continental collectibles, is your best bet for shopping the Queen Anne circuit.

North of town, you'll find an inconspicuous strip mall littered with back-to-back antiques and collectibles stores on the 1600 block of 123th Street (just west of the traffic light at Biscayne Boulevard; it is on the south side of the street). One of our recent sprees yielded a minivan-full of cool stuff, from a golf-leafed writing desk from the mid-1960s to a shell-encrusted wall mirror. Be sure to check out **Mr. Bill's Antiques & Floral Emporium** (1662 NE 123rd Street; (305) 899-9924), where the eclectic contents of estate sales come in weekly.

Art

In addition to Miami's rejuventated Design District, Coral Gables, South Beach, and Bay Harbor Islands are your key areas for art. On the first Friday of every month, an air-conditioned minibus takes art lovers for a free tour of the Coral Gables galleries. There's no RSVP; just show up in the early evening hours at one of the galleries, such as **Artspace/Virginia Miller Galleries** (169 Madeira Avenue; (305) 444-4493). This area has a fine concentration of American and Latin American paintings.

On the trendy side, Lincoln Road on South Beach is a mini art row of sorts. Local artists, some of whom attract international recognition, are located next to well-established Miami art specialists, including **Barbara Gillman** (5582 NE Fourth Court; (305) 759-9155) and artist Romero Britto, whose gallery, **Britto Central** (818 Lincoln Road; (305) 531-8821), attracts high-profile collectors including Arnold Schwarzenegger and Marisa Tomei. Lincoln Road's Gallery Walk is held the second Saturday of the month, 6–10 p.m.

Bargains

If it's labels like Armani and Moschino that entice you, we recommend **Loehmann's Plaza** (2855 NE 187th Street; (305) 932-0520) in North Miami. This location consistently carries the best selection of designer wear at the lowest prices. The tireless bargain shopper could easily get addicted to **Sawgrass Mills** (12801 West Sunrise Boulevard, Sunrise; (800) 356-4557) and the newer **Dolphin Mall** (NW 12th Street, Miami; (305) 365-7446), both mega-discount designer malls.

In the gourmet food division, one of our secrets is **Alterman's Country Store** (12805 NW LeJeune Road, Opa-locka; (305) 688-3571 x1209), which sells undamaged high-end foodstuffs at a fraction of the retail cost. A friend of ours recently found a five-pound box of Godiva chocolates (retail: approximately $100) for $40. Revered goodies like imported cheeses and Maine lobsters turn up now and then. Expect a hit-or-miss inventory.

Bookstores

Any bookworm will tell you that everyone's favorite bookstore in Miami is **Books & Books** (two locations: 933 Lincoln Road, South Beach, (305) 532-3222; and 265 Aragon, Coral Gables, (305) 442-4408). A close second is **Borders Books & Music** (three locations: 9205 South Dixie Highway, Miami, (305) 665-8800; 3390 Mary Street, Coconut Grove, (305) 447-1655; and 19925 Biscayne Boulevard, Aventura, (305) 935-0027), which, like Books & Books, features meet-the-author readings and signings. For out-of-town news periodicals, try **Worldwide News** (1629 NE 163rd Street; (305) 940-4090) or **Joe's News** (1559 Sunset Drive, Coral

Gables; (305) 661-2020). **Lambda Passages,** a gay bookstore, has a good selection of biographies, history, and art books (7545 Biscayne Boulevard, Miami; (305) 754-6900).

Cigars

Stogie aficionados will appreciate **Mike's Cigars** (1030 Cane Concourse, Miami Beach; (305) 866-2277), which carries more than 300 brands from all over the globe. Also worthy: The **News Cafe Store and Restaurant** on trendy Ocean Drive (800 Ocean Drive; (305) 538-6397), which is open 7 days, 24 hours—a real plus for the all-night set.

Designer Clothing

If you can't find it in Bal Harbour Shops (see "Malls"), chances are it doesn't exist. Do check out, however, the **Versace Jeans Couture Boutique** in South Beach (755 Washington Avenue; (305) 532-5993) for casual wear and home items such as china and lavish $700 silk throw pillows; **Magazine** (180 8th Street, South Beach; (305) 538-2704), specializing in cutting-edge European fashion for women and men; and **En Avance** (734 Lincoln Road, Miami Beach; (305) 534-0337) for some of the hippest labels around, including Paola Fruni, Theory, and the new Samsonite clothing line.

Ethnic Goods

You might as well go to Bayside Marketplace, where you can find clothing and items from places as diverse as Jamaica, Africa, and India. The Caribbean Marketplace in Miami's Little Haiti district is interesting, but not so safe. **Island Trading Co.,** in the lobby of the Netherland Hotel (1332 Ocean Drive, South Beach; (305) 673-6300), is your answer for one-of-a-kind items collected from various locales around the world; everything from hand-woven tablecloths to crystal earrings and leather knapsacks. In the same vein is **World Resources** (two locations: 719 Lincoln Road, (305) 535-8987; and in the Miami Design District at 56 NE 40th Street, (305) 576-8799), where the selection includes exotic woods fashioned into furniture and other decorative arts.

Fresh Fish

Seafood is one of Miami's most reliable meals, and the waters around the city teem with more than 60 varieties of commercial fish that you can eventually find parked on a restaurant plate next to a lemon wedge. Some of the most popular saltwater catches are grouper, snapper, mahi mahi, mullet, trout, pompano, and redfish.

To buy fresh fish, avoid supermarket fish counters; most of their goods have been frozen. Instead, opt for fish fresh off the boat at some of the docks around the city when fishermen come in with their day's haul. The best time to buy is late afternoon when all the fishing boats have returned.

On Key Biscayne, the boat docks next to Sunday's restaurant are usually lined with fishermen from about 3 p.m. The docks are easy to spot on this narrow island. They're on the left at about the midway point.

If you can't make it to the docks and still want to buy fresh fish, head to **Joe's Stone Crab Takeaway** (11 Washington Avenue, Miami Beach; (305) 673-4611) for stone crabs during the season, from mid-October to mid-May.

Fruit Shipping

What's a trip to Florida without a box of rosy oranges and grapefruit to ship back home? **Norman Brothers Produce** (7621 SW 87th Avenue, South Miami; (305) 274-9363) will ship anything you wish from their amazing array of culinary exotica, which includes obscurities such as the dwarfed doughnut apple. Then there's always our favorite standby, **Publix** (numerous locations throughout Miami), which will do the shipping honors for you in season, November through February.

Jewelry

Besides downtown Miami, the **International Jeweler's Exchange** in North Miami (18861 Biscayne Boulevard, behind Loehmann's Plaza; (305) 935-1471) will fill the bill. Fifty stalls are stocked with gold, pearls, and diamonds. Open Monday–Saturday, 10 a.m.–6 p.m., with extended holiday hours.

Swimwear

Finding a good swimsuit in Miami should be the least of your worries. **Alice's Day Off** (5900 Sunset Drive, South Miami; (305) 284-0301), **Swim n' Sport** (many locations, including The Falls and Bal Harbour Shops), and **Ritchie Swimwear** (160 8th Street, Miami Beach; (305) 538-0201) are among the many fine options.

Tropical Furniture

To accommodate and adapt to the humidity and relentless sunshine of Miami, furniture is often made of rattan, wicker, or light woods. In many of the Art Deco hotels on South Miami Beach, 1950s-style furniture—with its whimsy and clean lines—decorates rooms and lobbies. Miami is a furniture-producing mecca, though the most outstanding and truly local is tropical and vintage furniture. Shipping should present no problem, but be sure to verify with your furniture dealer and remember to insure your purchase. Be sure to check out Miami's up-and-coming Design District—located two blocks west of Biscayne Boulevard at 36th Street—for a concentration of unique showrooms.

Rattan Shack (9840 NW 77th Avenue, Hialeah Gardens; (305) 823-9800) is a vast place off the Palmetto Expressway with rattan and wicker furniture for indoors and outdoors. **J & J Rattan** (4652 SW 72nd Avenue, Miami; (305) 666-7503) is another large warehouse exclusively selling rattan and wicker couches, dining sets, and chairs.

Wine and Gourmet Foods

Whether you're browsing for a new imported mustard or in search of the definitive California cabernet sauvignon, chances are you'll find it at **Epicure Market** (1656 Alton Road; (305) 672-1861), where the local elite shop for foodstuffs, as well as the freshest of produce, tempting bakery items, and old-fashioned Jewish deli fare. **Stephan's Gourmet Market & Cafe** (1430 Washington Avenue; (305) 674-1760), a gourmet Italian deli with a second-floor café, carries a great selection of cheeses, wines, and champagnes, plus prettily packaged candies, nuts, and the like.

If you're a hard-core Italian food and wine fan, you'll spend hours at **Laurenzo's,** an Italian/American market and wine emporium (16385 West Dixie Highway, North Miami; (305) 945-6381). The award-winning wine department features wines from Bordeaux, Burgundy, Spain, California, and Italy, among other regions, as well as more than 40 weekly in-store wine specials. Another fine choice—where you can also sit down for dinner in the landscaped courtyard—is **Stephan's Gourmet Deli** (2 NE 40th Street in the Miami Design District; (305) 571-4070).

The stone crab is more than a seafood specialty in Miami—it's an obsession, almost. You can share this kingliest of crustaceans with friends back home—for a price. **Joe's Stone Crab Takeaway** will ship the iced crabs to the doorstep of your choice by the following morning (call (800) 780-2722).

Sight-Seeing Tips and Tours

Residents of Miami are proud of their city and quick to point out that it has much more to offer than just great beaches, dazzling white light, and a famous downtown skyline. College and professional sports, art shows, street festivals, museums, film festivals, a book fair, a world-class zoo, and some fascinating attractions showcasing this subtropical paradise's flora and fauna make Miami a city well worth exploring, even if it means tearing yourself away from the beach for a day.

SPECIALIZED TOURS

A number of local companies offer specialized tours of Miami and Miami Beach, usually in comfortable, air-conditioned motor coaches; trained tour guides provide the narration. In addition to bus tours—which take visitors to popular tourist areas such as South Beach, Coconut Grove, Brickell

Avenue, Coral Gables, Little Havana, and downtown Miami—many of the guided tours are all-day or multi-day affairs that go to destinations well outside of Miami: the Florida Keys and Key West, the Bahamas, the Everglades, and Walt Disney World. Here's a run-down of some tours that are a little different. Most of the tours require advanced reservations and a deposit; most tour buses can pick you up and drop you off at your Miami or Miami Beach hotel.

Flamingo Tours offers daily narrated bus trips to Key West that pick you up at your Miami Beach hotel at 7 a.m. and bring you back around 11 p.m. The tour includes a breakfast stop at Key Largo, a brief stop at the Seven Mile Bridge, and an afternoon exploring Key West. Activities include visits to the Hemingway House, Mel Fisher's Treasure Exhibit, and a glass-bottom-boat ride. On the return trip, the bus stops in Islamorada. The price per person is $59; $25 for children ages 3–11. Other tours offered by Flamingo include one-day motor-coach trips to Walt Disney World on Sunday, Monday, and Wednesday ($99 for adults and $85 for children ages 3–9) and a city bus tour of Miami that also stops at Parrot Jungle ($43 for adults and $25 for children ages 3–11, including admission). For more information, call Flamingo Tours at (305) 948-3822.

In addition to an all-day bus tour to Key West, **Miami Nice Excursions** offers bus tours to the Everglades on Tuesday and Saturday, narrated in English and German. The tours stop at the Everglades Alligator Farm near Florida City and include an airboat ride. The bus leaves at 9 a.m. and returns at 5 p.m.; $45 for adults and $29 for children ages 3–9. Call (305) 949-9180 for more information.

On Tuesday and Saturday, **Miami Nice** leads a popular combination bus tour to the Everglades and the Gulf Coast that picks you up at your Miami Beach hotel around 8 a.m. and drops you off at 7 p.m. Tickets are $49 for adults and $29 for children ages 3 to 9. On Tuesdays the tour company offers one-day excursions to Walt Disney World, Epcot, Universal Studios, or Disney MGM Studios in Orlando. The "Disney Blitz" leaves Miami Beach at 6 a.m. and returns around midnight. The motor-coach trip costs $99 for adults and $70 for children ages 3 to 9; the price includes the entrance fee to one of the parks.

Deco Tours of South Beach offers a wide range of tours, including city-wide and shopping tours led by owner Dona Zemo. The most popular tour is the Art Deco Walking Tour, the official tour of the Miami Beach Chamber of Commerce (MBCC). The tour is available Monday through Friday. The cost of the two-hour tour is $15 per person; wear comfortable shoes. Call (305) 531-4465 for more information.

TOURING ON YOUR OWN: OUR FAVORITE ITINERARIES

If you've taken a guided tour of the city and you're looking for a less packaged experience, or if you've only limited time to sight-see and want to experience the flavor of Miami, here are some suggested itineraries, along with some advice to get you into a South Florida state of mind.

Rent a convertible (c'mon, this *is* Miami), set the FM dial to some pulsating Latin rhythms, and crank up the volume. Wear your bathing suit beneath your clothes. Wear comfortable walking shoes. Carry only as much money as you'll need for the day. Pretend that you live like this every day of the year.

For a one-day hit of Miami-ness:

1. Breakfast at Parrot Jungle in South Miami.
2. Meander through Coral Gables in the early morning. Stop at the Biltmore Hotel and have a club soda. Drive by the Venetian Pool.
3. Visit Vizcaya.
4. On to The Grove for a stroll and some shopping.
5. Lunch at a Cuban restaurant on Calle Ocho. Order arroz con pollo, cafe con leche, and flan at La Carreta, Versailles, or Casablanca.
6. Head over to South Beach for a few hours of strolling, sunning, and beaching.
7. Enjoy a late-afternoon cafecito.
8. Back to the hotel for a shower and a nap.
9. Dinner at an oceanside restaurant on South Beach.
10. Dancing, nightclubbing on South Beach.

If you have two days, make this day two:

1. Breakfast at an oceanside café on South Beach.
2. Take a walking tour of the Art Deco District or rent a bike and explore the area.
3. Head downtown at lunchtime, the time when it is liveliest. Take the "People Mover" as it loops around Miami and offers great city views.
4. Eat lunch at one of the many crowded, but cheap, Cuban, Brazilian, or other ethnic eateries found throughout downtown. Wash it down with a caffeine-charged *cafe Cubano*.
5. On to Key Biscayne for an afternoon of windsurfing.

6. Head back downtown to take the Heritage of Miami sunset cruise from behind Bayside Marketplace and see the city at dusk from a sailboat.

7. A late-night dinner at one of the many restaurants that dot Coral Gables.

If your stay in Miami is longer than a couple of days, try to include the following not-to-be-missed attractions on your itinerary: Fairchild Tropical Garden, Metrozoo, Hialeah Park, the Historical Museum of Southern Florida, the Lowe Art Museum, snorkeling at Biscayne National Park or John Pennecamp Coral Reef State Park, a bike ride down Old Cutler Road, and a day trip to the Everglades and/or the Keys.

MIAMI FOR CHILDREN

Although places like South Beach are definitely adult (some would suggest R-rated) in their appeal and the hustle and bustle of downtown will appeal only to adults and older children, Miami and its environs offer plenty to do for youngsters. Attractions include a world-class zoo, a marine-mammal emporium, a science museum designed for young folk, and some private "jungles" that will delight the kids.

Miami's Top Ten Attractions for Kids
Biscayne National Park
Everglades National Park/Shark Valley Tram Tour
Gold Coast Railroad Museum
Historical Museum of South Florida
Metrozoo
Miami Museum of Science/Space Transit Planetarium
Monkey Jungle
Parrot Jungle and Gardens
Seaquarium
Weeks Air Museum

SIGHT-SEEING CRUISES

One of the best ways to see sun-dappled Miami is from a ship, and the cruise boats that depart from downtown Miami and the marina across from the Fontainebleau Hilton on Miami Beach give visitors a chance to see the town's most spectacular sights the way they ought to be seen: from the water. Most tours are narrated in English and Spanish, and snacks and beverages are sold on board.

From Bayside, the new, two-story shopping mall by the water in downtown Miami, several large, air-conditioned tour boats leave on the hour to whisk visitors on one-hour excursions around placid Biscayne Bay. Tours generally leave every hour, starting at 11 a.m. until about 5:30 p.m. weekdays, and continuing until midnight on weekends. Ticket prices average $14–30 for adults and $7–20 for children ages 12 and under.

The sights include dazzling high-rise buildings downtown and the most conspicuous landmark on the water: the 65-foot Fender Stratocaster guitar rotating above the Hard Rock Cafe; its reported cost was a cool half-million dollars. Other sights on the cruise include the spiraling metal structure in Bayfront Park that's a monument to the crew of the space shuttle Challenger, and tugboats, freighters, and cruise ships tied up at the Port of Miami.

Next, the tour boats swing by Fisher Island, an exclusive community of high-rise condos that can only be reached by boat or helicopter, and Miami Beach. After passing under the MacArthur Causeway connecting Miami Beach and the mainland, a number of artificial islands is next, including the aptly named Star Island and Millionaires Row. Your guide will point out the former homes of Liz Taylor, Don Johnson and Melanie Griffith, Al Capone, and other Miami notables—it seems the elusiveness of fame and the high cost of real estate dictates who stays and who leaves Star Island— and the current home of mega-star Gloria Estefan.

After passing the Henry Flagler Monument and Palm Island, the tour boats swing back under the Venetian Causeway and complete their circuit of Biscayne Bay. It's a fun trip—and very scenic.

SAILING ABOARD A TALL SHIP ON BISCAYNE BAY

For the nautically inclined, a sure bet is a two-hour cruise on Biscayne Bay aboard the *Heritage of Miami II,* an 85-foot topsail schooner. Once out on the placid waters of the bay, the engine goes off, the wind fills the sails . . . and the hustle and bustle of hectic Miami drops away. If the weather cooperates, the skipper lets passengers take the helm for a few minutes while under sail.

Two-hour sails depart at 1:30 p.m. and 4 p.m.; a one-hour trip leaves at 6:30 p.m. All sails depart daily from Bayside Marketplace in downtown Miami. The cost is $15 for adults and $10 for children under age 12. One-hour sails depart on Friday, Saturday, and Sunday at various times. Call ahead for specific schedules on weekends. Prices are $10 per person. Our advice: In the winter, sign up for the 4 p.m. sail, which turns into a sunset cruise. For more information, call (305) 442-9697.

GREAT VIEWS

If stunning panoramas turn you on, you've come to the right place: Miami offers visitors a wide array of great views to gladden the eye and quicken the pulse. Here are some of the *Unofficial Guide* research team's favorites.

Cruise Ships and High-Rises   On a Friday, Saturday, or Sunday night, make the drive from Miami Beach to downtown Miami on the MacArthur Causeway and you're in for a treat: a magnificent panorama of glittering cruise ships tied up at the Port of Miami. The backdrop is another stunner: the knock-your-socks-off Miami skyline lit up like a Christmas tree. Many people consider it the most spectacular urban cityscape in the United States. Try to spot the CenTrust Building, a circular high-rise that changes color on command.

Downtown from a Slightly Different Angle   Another great view of downtown is from the Rickenbacker Causeway to Key Biscayne. Park on the left side of the causeway. By the way, this is one of Miami's most popular make-out spots.

Art Deco   Everyone loves the Art Deco District in South Beach. But for an unusual—and spectacular—view of the candy-colored architecture, try this: at sundown, put on a swimsuit, wade out into the surf until you're neck deep . . . and turn around. (Just don't inhale any salt water when you gasp at the view.) This is a popular diversion with hip Miami residents for beating the summer heat and cooling down for a torrid South Beach evening.

The "People Mover"   It's a fun, automated transportation system that scoots people around a 26-block chunk of downtown and provides a spectacular, bird's-eye view of the city, Biscayne Bay, and the Atlantic Ocean. The new Omni Loop provides an excellent view of Government Cut and the Port of Miami. A ride on the People Mover only costs a quarter.

From a Boat Miami is married to the water, and much of the beauty of the city is best seen from a boat. Downtown high-rises, Bayfront Park, and the Port of Miami all take on a different, and beautiful, perspective when seen from the water. For more information on boat tours of the harbor and Biscayne Bay, see page 307.

The Everglades   Although it's about an hour's drive west to Everglades National Park on Route 41, followed by a seven-mile tram or bicycle ride, your reward is one of the best views in South Florida, from the Shark Valley Observation Tower. The view from the top of the 50-foot tower (easily accessible from a ramp) stretches from horizon to horizon across stunning wilderness scenery. Directly below you lies a jungle scene featuring a wide array of bird life, huge fish, and giant turtles moving through the water.

Coral Way   One of the most scenic drives in the city—aside from elevated superhighways where drivers really shouldn't let themselves be distracted by the view—is Coral Way (SW 24th Street), a broad avenue stretching from Coral Gables to Biscayne Bay below downtown. Start at the Miracle Mile and drive east; on the left at Douglas Road is the thoroughly spaced-out-looking Miracle Center, designed by Arquitectonica.

A Bird's-Eye View of Miami   Stop by the Greater Miami Convention & Visitor Bureau's main office, located at 701 Brickell Avenue, Suite 2700, during regular business hours, pick up a free map, and check out the panoramic view of downtown Miami, the Miami River, Biscayne Bay, the Port of Miami, and the Atlantic Ocean from the office windows. Park in the basement of the high-rise, get your parking ticket validated, and parking is free.

Sunrise   Make it a point to get up early one morning to view the sunrise over the ocean. Better yet, stay up all night and greet the rising sun.

Sunset   From Key Biscayne, The Rusty Pelican Restaurant on the tip of the island has spectacular sunset views of downtown Miami. Also, from Miami Beach, sunsets over Biscayne Bay are a treat.

Cruise Ships and Freighters Navigating Government Cut   See the action from South Pointe Park on the southern tip of Miami Beach. The 38-foot-deep channel means even the largest cruise and container ships can steam in and out of the Port of Miami. Fridays and Sundays are your best bets.

SCENIC DRIVES

Driving is one of America's favorite pastimes, and because a car is a necessity for visitors in Miami, we've included a list of scenic and unusual routes for folks who like to jump in the car and go for a spin. Just don't leave during rush hour (7–9 a.m. and 3:30–6:30 p.m., weekdays).

One of the most memorable sights in Miami is the view of the city at night from the MacArthur Causeway—especially at night, when cruise ships are tied up at the Port of Miami (see above, "Great Views"). Farther north on Miami Beach's Collins Avenue in the 40s is the stunning trompe l'oeil mural that greets drivers as they drive north toward the Fontainebleau Hilton. The huge painting "fools the eye" by "revealing" the curving, glitzy hotel that actually sits behind the brick wall. Continue north along US A1A as far as you want; cruising this venerable old highway is a South Florida tradition.

South of downtown, near the Rickenbacker Causeway, Vizcaya, and the Miami Museum of Science, take Bayshore Drive for a long, relaxing drive through Coconut Grove, Coral Gables, and points south. As you meander along Main Highway, Ingraham Highway, and Old Cutler Road, you'll pass some of the lushest tropical scenery in the Miami area, beautiful homes, and glimpses of sparkling Biscayne Bay. The best way to do this drive is to take a map and not worry about getting lost. A perfect destination—and a real treat for outdoors lovers—is Fairchild Tropical Garden; Parrot Jungle is another. A good turning-back point is Coral Reef Drive (SW 152nd Street). That's where the damage from Hurricane Andrew—a noticeable decrease in foliage—starts to appear.

For a look at what all of South Florida used to look like, go west on Route 41 toward the Everglades. (In Miami, just west of downtown, Route 41 is 8th Street, Calle Ocho, and cuts through the heart of Little Havana.) After you get past Florida's Turnpike, you'll start to see natural flora and an astounding amount of bird life in the canals along the side of the road. Past the Shark Valley entrance to Everglades National Park is Big Cypress National Preserve; the scenery is lush and you pass several Native American villages on the road.

Attractions

Miami is an exotic resort, a sports town, a shopping town, a jet-set destination, all located in a lush tropical climate. But that's not all—Miami-Dade County provides visitors with a potpourri of attractions that show off its human and natural history, flora and fauna, art collections, unique landscapes, and, last but not least, its penchant for the kitschy and commercial.

Because of the wide range of Miami-Dade attractions, we've provided the following chart to help you prioritize your touring at a glance. In it, you'll find the name, location, and author's rating from one star (skip it) to five stars (not to be missed). Some attractions, usually art galleries without permanent collections, weren't rated because exhibits change. Each attraction is individually profiled later in this section. Most museum-type attractions offer group rates for ten or more people.

A Time-Saving Chart		
Name	City	Author's Rating
Aquarium		
Seaquarium	Miami	★★
Gardens		
Fairchild Tropical Garden	Miami	★★★★½
Vizcaya Museum and Garden	Miami	mansion: ★★★; gardens: ★★★★★

A Time-Saving Chart (continued)		
Name	City	Author's Rating
Home Tours		
The Barnacle State Historic Site	Coconut Grove	★★
Vizcaya Museum and Garden	Miami	mansion ★★★; gardens ★★★★★
Memorial		
Holocaust Memorial of Miami Beach	Miami Beach	★★★★
Museums		
Gold Coast Railroad Museum	Miami	★★½
Historical Museum of Southern Florida	Miami	★★★★
The Jewish Museum of Florida	Miami Beach	★★
Lowe Art Museum	Coral Gables	★★★★
Miami Art Museum	Miami	n/a
MoCA: Museum of Contemporary Art	North Miami	★★★½
Weeks Air Museum	Miami	★★½
The Wolfsonian	Miami Beach	★★★
Parks		
Biscayne National Park	Between Miami and Homestead	★★★★
Hialeah Park	Hialeah	★★★
Zoos/Animal Exhibits		
Metrozoo	Miami	★★★★★
Monkey Jungle	Miami	★★★½
Parrot Jungle and Gardens	Miami	★★★★½

ATTRACTION PROFILES

The Barnacle State Historic Site

Type of Attraction: The oldest home in Dade County (1891); a panoramic view of Biscayne Bay; an oasis of beauty and calm in hectic Coconut Grove. House tours are guided only; tours of the grounds are self-guided.

Location: In Coconut Grove; 3485 Main Highway

Admission: $1

Hours: Friday–Sunday, 9 a.m.– 4 p.m.; closed Monday–Thursday and Thanksgiving, Christmas, and New Year's Days

Phone: (305) 448-9445

When to Go: Any time

Special Comments: Pets are allowed on the grounds but must be kept on a leash.

Overall Appeal by Age Group:

Pre-school	Grade School	Teens	Young Adults	Over 30	Seniors
★	★½	★½	★★	★★	★★½

Author's Rating: A real find for history buffs and folks interested in how the landed gentry lived in South Florida a century ago. It's also a terrific picnic spot with a drop-dead view of Biscayne Bay. ★★

How Much Time to Allow: An hour or so for the building tour; or however long it takes to recharge your batteries after a morning of shopping or people-watching in the Grove.

Description and Comments   Early 20th-century yacht designer and wrecker (a person who earns a living by salvaging ships that run aground) Ralph Middleton Munroe first visited South Florida in 1877 and returned in 1886 to purchase 40 acres facing Biscayne Bay. In 1891, he built his home, called the "Barnacle," a one-story structure raised off the ground on wood pilings with a central room octagonal in shape. Today, visitors can tour the unique house filled with nautical touches; the building provides a glimpse of a way of life that no longer exists. Outside, a tropical hardwood "hammock" (or forest) isolates the grounds from busy Main Highway, giving way to a view that has attracted neighbors such as Sylvester Stallone and Madonna.

Touring Tips   Guided house tours are free and conducted at 10 a.m., 11:30 a.m., 1 p.m., and 2:30 p.m., Friday through Sunday; meet on the porch of the main house. Tours are limited to the first ten people who show up, so try to arrive a few minutes early. Bring a picnic lunch.

Other Things to Do Nearby   The Grove is second only to South Beach for world-class people-watching, shopping, and dining. If the Barnacle whetted your appetite for more outdoor splendor on the shores of Biscayne Bay, continue south on Main Highway a few miles to Fairchild Tropical Garden.

Biscayne National Park

Type of Attraction: More than 180,000 acres of underwater reefs, islands, and the closest coral reef snorkeling to Miami. Guided and self-guided tours.

Location: The Convoy Point Visitor Center, the only part of the park accessible by car, is about 25 miles south of Miami and six miles east of US 1 and Homestead. From the Florida Turnpike Extension, take SW 328th Street (North Canal Drive) to the park entrance on the left.

Admission: Free. A park concession offers three-hour glass-bottom-boat tours of the bay and reef. The cost is $19.95 for adults and $12.95 for children ages 12 and under; the trips leave at 10 a.m. daily. Three-hour snorkeling trips to the reef are $29.95 per person and include all equipment; the boat leaves at 10 a.m. and 1 p.m. daily. Two-tank scuba dives for certified divers are offered at 8:30 a.m. and 1 p.m. on weekends only; the cost is $44.95. Advance reservations for the boat tour and the snorkel trip are strongly advised; reservations are required for the scuba dives. Canoe rentals are $8 an hour, and kayak rentals are $16 an hour; prices include paddles and life jackets.

Hours: Visitor center: daily, 8:30 a.m.–5 p.m.

Phone: (305) 230-7275; for reservations for snorkel, scuba, and boat trips, call (305) 230-1100

When to Go: Any time, weather permitting. While mosquitoes and other biting insects are present year-round, their populations are lowest from January to April. Around holiday weekends, call at least three days in advance for a reservation for a boat tour or diving trip. While reservations usually aren't necessary at other times, call ahead to make sure a boat trip isn't canceled due to a chartered event.

Special Comments: Because the park is almost completely underwater, visitors are at the mercy of the weather; tours and canoe rentals are sometimes canceled in windy conditions. If the air is cold, snorkelers can rent wet suits. Boat schedules change seasonally, so it's always a good idea to call first.

Overall Appeal by Age Group:

Pre-school	Grade School	Teens	Young Adults	Over 30	Seniors
★★	★★★	★★★	★★★½	★★★★	★★★★

Author's Rating: Viewing a coral reef through a face mask or glass-bottomed boat sure beats looking at fish through glass in an aquarium.
★★★★

How Much Time to Allow: Half a day or longer

Description and Comments Clear blue water, a bright yellow sun, dark green woodlands, coral reefs, and islands combine to create a subtropical paradise only an hour or so from hectic Miami. Unlike most parks, however, Biscayne is dominated by water—and enjoying it requires renting a canoe or taking a boat excursion.

The top attraction for most folks is snorkeling the coral reefs. Brilliantly colored tropical fish such as stoplight parrotfish, finger garlic sponge, goose-head scorpionfish, and peppermint goby populate the shallow-water reefs drenched in sunlight. A reef explorer outfitted in mask, snorkel, flippers, and a life vest can spend hours drifting lazily in the waters above the reefs while watching a procession of astounding marine life.

Touring Tips   Call at least a day ahead of time to make reservations for a boat trip. Exploring the reefs is best on calm, sunny days. Unless you're an experienced snorkeler or diver, go on the group trip, which is run by experts who provide plenty of hand-holding for novices. Canoes are available for rent for exploring the mangrove shoreline along the mainland. Fishermen can try their luck for saltwater fish from the jetty; stop at the visitor center for regulations and in Homestead for fishing licenses. The new visitor center is attractive and has a few small displays on bay ecology, local history, and Hurricane Andrew.

Other Things to Do Nearby   The Everglades National Park is due west of Homestead. If you haven't had your fill of Florida tourist schlock yet, stop by the Coral Castle, just north of Homestead on US 1. You'll also find a nearly endless selection of fast-food joints along the venerable old highway.

Fairchild Tropical Garden

Type of Attraction: 83 beautifully landscaped acres containing plants from tropical regions around the world. Guided and self-guided tours.

Location: 10901 Old Cutler Road, Miami; south of Coconut Grove on Old Cutler Road

Admission: $8; children under age 12 free; includes a narrated, 30-minute, open-air tram tour of the garden

Hours: Park: daily, 9:30 a.m.–4:30 p.m.; closed Christmas Day. *Rainforest Café:* Tuesday–Sunday, 11 a.m.–2 p.m.; closed Monday

Phone: (305) 667-1651

When to Go: Any time, but avoid hot and humid summer afternoons. In the fall, winter, and spring, the late afternoon sun lights the foliage with a rich, red glow. While the park is seldom crowded, fewer people visit during the week than on weekends.

Special Comments: The expanded Garden Shop sells tropical gardening books, plants, and unique gifts. The free tram tour leaves on the hour.

Overall Appeal by Age Group:

Pre-school	Grade School	Teens	Young Adults	Over 30	Seniors
★	★½	★★	★★★	★★★½	★★★★

Author's Rating: This manicured park filled with lush palms and exotic trees and dotted with man-made lakes is a knockout. ★★★★½

How Much Time to Allow: At least two hours; half a day or more for a leisurely exploration

Description and Comments   Fairchild Tropical Garden is the largest tropical botanical garden in the United States; its mission is education, scientific research, and display. The grounds and plant life are stunning, in spite of the beating they took from Hurricane Andrew in 1992. You don't have to be a certified tree hugger to appreciate the beauty and tranquility found here.

Touring Tips   After taking the tram tour, go back to areas pointed out by the guide that interest you. For example, Cycad Circle features the same plants that dinosaurs munched 300 million years ago. The 1939 Gate House has been restored and is now a historical museum with permanent exhibits on plant exploration. Sandwiches, drinks, and snacks are available at the snack bar, where you can eat under a huge sapodilla tree (weekends only). If you bring your own food, picnic next door at Matheson Hammock Park.

Other Things to Do Nearby   Parrot Jungle is right around the corner; Coconut Grove is loaded with places to eat, drink, and shop. Matheson Hammock Park features a beach, marina, and a terrific view of downtown Miami.

Gold Coast Railroad Museum

Type of Attraction: A museum featuring steam and diesel locomotives, as well as a presidential railroad car. Guided and self-guided tours.

Location: South of Miami near the entrance to Metrozoo. Take the Florida Turnpike Extension to SW 152nd Street and follow signs to Metrozoo.

Admission: Adults, $5; children ages 3–12, $3

Hours: Monday–Friday, 11 a.m.–3 p.m.; Saturday and Sunday, 11 a.m.–4 p.m.

Phone: (305) 253-0063 or (888) 608-7246

When to Go: Any time except hot, humid summer afternoons

Special Comments: The new railroad shed and museum shop are now open. (The original shed took a direct hit from Hurricane Andrew in 1992.)

Overall Appeal by Age Group:

Pre-school	Grade School	Teens	Young Adults	Over 30	Seniors
★★★	★★★★	★★	★★½	★★	★★

Author's Rating: A must-see for railroad buffs and kids; ★★½

How Much Time to Allow: One hour

Description and Comments   This complex of Navy blimp hangars destroyed in a 1945 hurricane rose again to become a railroad museum—only to be wiped out by another hurricane in 1992. The things are now back in shape, and visitors can check out an array of historic railroad cars (including one used by former Presidents Roosevelt, Truman, Eisenhower, and Reagan) and memorabilia.

Touring Tips   The Gold Coast Railroad Museum is a nice diversion before or after visiting Metrozoo, which is right next door. On weekends at 1 p.m. and 3 p.m., rides on the museum's two-foot-gauge railroad are offered; the cost is $2 additional per person. Rides last 15–20 minutes.

Other Things to Do Nearby   Metrozoo, Monkey Jungle, the Weeks Air Museum, and a wide selection of fast-food restaurants are all close.

Hialeah Park

Type of Attraction: Gorgeous grounds, a racetrack listed on the National Register of Historic Places, and a flock of 400 pink flamingos. A self-guided tour.

Location: 2200 East Fourth Avenue (at 22nd Street) in the north Miami neighborhood of Hialeah. From I-95, take the 79th Street exit west to 4th Street and turn left. Then turn left on 22nd Street; the entrance is on the right. Bear right and park your car near the clubhouse.

Admission: $4

Hours: Monday–Friday, 9 a.m.–5 p.m. Call ahead for racing dates. Most weekends feature public events such as flea markets.

Phone: (305) 885-8000

When to Go: Any time. Races, however, are only held three months a year, rotating between spring, fall, and winter.

Special Comments: Bring binoculars; the flamingos are in the track's infield.

Overall Appeal by Age Group:

Pre-school	Grade School	Teens	Young Adults	Over 30	Seniors
★	★½	★★	★★½	★★½	★★★

Author's Rating: Stately, old-world elegance; ★★★

How Much Time to Allow: 30 minutes off-season; half a day during the racing season

Description and Comments   The best way to visit this world-famous thoroughbred racetrack is to go when the ponies are running. But if you're in town when the ponies are racing at another track, the gorgeous coral clubhouse and stands, along with the flock of pink birds, is worth a stop. Most facilities such as bars and restaurants, however, will be closed.

Touring Tips On quiet mornings during the middle of the week, you've got the whole place to yourself. Behind the clubhouse, look for trainers working with racehorses. When racing is in progress, Hialeah is a great breakfast stop.

Other Things to Do Nearby Opa-locka, a planned community that fell on hard times but is experiencing a comeback, is north of Hialeah Park and features some outrageous Moorish-style architecture; it's worth a peek, but we don't recommend visiting on foot. For another dose of old Miami, stop by Miami Jai Alai, near the airport.

Historical Museum of Southern Florida

Type of Attraction: 10,000 years of Florida history on display. A self-guided tour.

Location: 101 West Flagler Street in downtown Miami, in the Metro-Dade Cultural Center. Take the "People Mover" to the Government Center station.

Admission: Adults, $5; children ages 6–12, $2; children under age 6 free

Hours: Monday–Saturday, 10 a.m.–5 p.m.; Thursday, 10 a.m.–9 p.m.; Sunday, noon–5 p.m.

Phone: (305) 375-1492

When to Go: Any time

Special Comments: Discounted parking is available at Cultural Center Parking, 50 NW 2nd Avenue and at Metro-Dade County Garage, 140 West Flagler Street. Have your parking ticket validated at the admission desk.

Overall Appeal by Age Group:

Pre-school	Grade School	Teens	Young Adults	Over 30	Seniors
★★	★★★★	★★★½	★★★★	★★★★	★★★★

Author's Rating: A spiffy museum that will entertain and educate both kids and adults; ★★★★

How Much Time to Allow: One–two hours

Description and Comments With lots of interactive displays (some feature earphones that let you hear jungle sounds, others are big enough to walk through), this sparkling, well-designed museum is a lot of fun. Visitors can discover the Florida that existed before the tourists came—even before people ever set foot in South Florida. The museum also emphasizes the rich cultural diversity of modern Florida's multiethnic population, ranging from Hispanic theater to Jewish heritage.

Touring Tips   Kids really like the various colonial-era cannons in the historical exhibits. They'll also like climbing aboard an old 1920s trolley car. The Indies Company, the museum's gift shop, offers a wide range of items that reflect South Florida and the Caribbean, including a large assortment of old poster reproductions.

Other Things to Do Nearby   Couple your visit to the Historical Museum of South Florida with a stop at the Miami Art Museum, across the plaza. If you've never boarded the "People Mover," Miami's automated downtown transportation system, do it now: It's the best 25 cent investment you'll ever make.

Holocaust Memorial of Miami Beach

Type of Attraction: A memorial to the six million Jews killed in the Holocaust. A self-guided tour.

Location: Dade Boulevard and Meridian Avenue (near the Miami Beach Convention Center) in Miami Beach

Admission: Free

Hours: Daily, 9 a.m.–9 p.m.

Phone: (305) 538-1663

When to Go: Any time

Special Comments: While this is a hard area to find parking (especially if a convention is taking place), reserved street parking is available on Meridian Avenue for Holocaust Memorial visitors *only.*

Overall Appeal by Age Group:

Pre-school	Grade School	Teens	Young Adults	Over 30	Seniors
★	★★	★★½	★★★	★★★★	★★★★½

Author's Rating: A moving experience; ★★★★

How Much Time to Allow: One hour

Description and Comments   Dedicated in 1990 in a ceremony that featured Nobel Prize laureate Elie Wiesel, the Holocaust Memorial utilizes contrasting elements to deliver an emotional punch: bright Jerusalem stone, somber black granite, the stillness of a reflecting pool, the backdrop of an azure sky, and a stunning, 42-foot sculpture of a giant outstretched arm (tattooed with a number from Auschwitz) rising up from the earth. Miami Beach is home to one of the world's largest populations of Holocaust survivors.

Touring Tips   There's more to the memorial than just the dramatic sculpture that seems to rise from the reflecting pool—but you must get out of your car to experience it. Black granite panels contain a concise history of the Holocaust plus pictorial representations, text, and maps. After walking through an enclosed, shrinelike space and a narrow passage, the visitor is greeted with a stunning sight: a circular plaza surrounded by shining black granite that mirrors the 42-foot bronze sculpture.

Other Things to Do Nearby   The Wolfsonian and the Jewish Museum of Florida are both nearby in South Beach.

The Jewish Museum of Florida

Type of Attraction: 230 years of Florida Jewish life on display in a 1936 Art Deco–style building. Guided and self-guided tours.

Location: In South Beach; 301 Washington Avenue

Admission: Adults, $5; seniors and students, $4; $10 for families; admission is free on Saturday

Hours: Tuesday–Sunday, 10 a.m.–5 p.m.; closed Monday, Jewish holidays, and major holidays (except Christmas)

Phone: (305) 672-5044

When to Go: Any time

Special Comments: The neighborhood around this former Orthodox synagogue (which predates the Art Deco District a few blocks north) is rapidly changing as developers move in; enjoy the ambience before high-rise condos take over.

Overall Appeal by Age Group:

Pre-school	Grade School	Teens	Young Adults	Over 30	Seniors
★	★★	★★½	★★½	★★½	★★★

Author's Rating: A narrow yet interesting slice of South Florida history; a beautiful interior that's worth a peek; ★★

How Much Time to Allow: One hour

Description and Comments   This recently restored Art Deco building once served as Miami Beach's first Orthodox synagogue. Today visitors can enjoy nearly 80 stained glass windows, a copper dome, the marble bimah (Torah reading platform), and many Art Deco features such as chandeliers and sconces. Arranged on the slanted floor (a design feature that made it easier for the rabbi to be heard by the congregation) is a collection of temporary exhibits on Jewish life and culture in Florida, as well as nearly 300 years of Jewish history in the Sunshine State. Visitors are sure to find something of interest, and the spacious, light-filled interior is a treat.

Touring Tips   For a more meaningful visit, hook up with one of the museum's trained docents (museum guides), who can explain the layout and make a few suggestions on what to see as you browse. Don't miss the

15-minute video that explains the museum's restoration and mission. And look for the window sponsored by notorious gangster Meyer Lansky (it's on the right as you enter the main room). "He was a member of the synagogue," explained my docent, with a smile and a shrug.

Other Things to Do Nearby   Drive south and turn right onto Biscayne Street to reach Joe's Stone Crab, the most famous (and crowded) restaurant in South Florida (open mid-October through mid-May). Watch huge freighters and cruise ships on their way to and from the Port of Miami at South Pointe Park. Explore the Art Deco District, which starts above 5th Street, two blocks north.

Lowe Art Museum

Type of Attraction: A diverse art collection ranging from antiquities to Renaissance, traditional, contemporary, and non-Western works. A self-guided tour.

Location: Just off US 1 on the Coral Gables campus of the University of Miami; two blocks north of the University Metrorail Station

Admission: Adults, $5; seniors and students, $3; children under age 12 free. Slightly higher fees are sometimes charged for special shows.

Hours: Tuesday, Wednesday, Friday, and Saturday, 10 a.m.–5 p.m.; Thursday, noon–7 p.m.; Sunday, noon–5 p.m.; closed Monday

Phone: (305) 284-3535

When to Go: Any time

Special Comments: A 10,000-foot expansion was recently completed.

Overall Appeal by Age Group:

Pre-school	Grade School	Teens	Young Adults	Over 30	Seniors
★	★★	★★½	★★★	★★★½	★★★

Author's Rating: A little bit of everything in bite-sized chunks that don't overwhelm; the best art museum in the Miami area. ★★★★

How Much Time to Allow: At least an hour; if the special exhibitions grab you, figure a half-day.

Description and Comments   The oldest visual arts institution in Dade County boasts a collection of 7,000 works of art in its permanent collection, including Baroque art, paintings by Spanish masters such as El Greco, and works by modern artists such as Warhol, Lichtenstein, and Hanson. The Lowe also features several special exhibitions each year, further varying the kind of art you'll see on any visit. The museum also emphasizes non-Western art, with exhibits of Southwestern Indian art, Latin American art, Guatemalan textiles, and pre-Columbian objects. For art lovers, the Lowe is a real find.

Touring Tips   The Lowe Museum of Art is all on one floor, which makes it an easy destination to tour for elderly and disabled folks. The museum store offers unusual gifts, art books, museum publications, and cards for sale.

Other Things to Do Nearby   Coconut Grove is a great place for eating, drinking, shopping, and people-watching. The Venetian Pool in Coral Gables is a classy swimming hole; Parrot Jungle and Fairchild Tropical Garden are two of the Miami area's best tourist destinations.

Metro-Dade Cultural Center

This downtown conglomeration of attractions consists of the Historical Museum of Southern Florida (page 317), the Miami Art Museum (below), and a branch of the Dade County public library.

Miami Art Museum (formerly Center for the Fine Arts)

Type of Attraction: An art gallery that features constantly changing exhibitions of a wide range of art from around the world. A self-guided tour.

Location: 101 West Flagler Street, in the Metro-Dade Cultural Center in downtown Miami. Take the "People Mover" to the Government Center station.

Admission: Adults, $5; seniors and students, $2.50; children ages 6–12 free; free on Sunday and the second Saturday of the month

Hours: Tuesday–Friday, 10 a.m.–5 p.m.; Saturday and Sunday, noon– 5 p.m.; Thursday, noon–9 p.m.; closed Monday

Phone: (305) 375-1700

When to Go: Any time

Special Comments: Judging from the exhibit of drawings from the British Museum recently on display, the Miami Art Museum is a gallery that emphasizes high-quality art and hosts national touring shows. Discounted parking is available at Cultural Center Parking, 50 NW 2nd Avenue and at Metro-Dade County Garage, 140 West Flagler Street. For free parking, validate your parking ticket at the admission desk.

Overall Appeal Comment: Because the museum has no permanent collection and exhibits are constantly changing, it's not possible to rate the gallery by age group.

Author's Rating: Again, it's not possible to rate this museum. But it's a comfortable, large gallery that should be on any art lover's itinerary. The shows are consistently professional and well attended.

How Much Time to Allow: One–two hours

Description and Comments   This is a logical place to visit before or after seeing the Historical Museum of South Florida, located across the plaza. It's a large, airy gallery with exhibits on two floors. Stop at the admission desk to find out what's on display during your visit, or check Friday's edition of the *Miami Herald.*

Other Things to Do Nearby   The Miami Art Museum is paired with the Historical Museum of South Florida; Metrorail's "People Mover" makes the rest of downtown Miami easy to get to.

Metrozoo

Type of Attraction: A "new-style" zoo that features cageless animals that roam on plots of land surrounded by moats. Guided and self-guided tours.

Location: South of Miami. Take the Florida Turnpike Extension to the SW 152nd Street exit and follow the signs to the entrance.

Admission: Adults, $8; children ages 3–12, $4

Hours: Daily, 9:30 a.m.–5:30 p.m.

Phone: (305) 251-0400 for a recorded message; (305) 251-0401 for more information

When to Go: With much of its lush, shady foliage ripped out by Hurricane Andrew in 1992, it's imperative that visitors avoid touring the zoo on sweltering summer afternoons. "You'll die here midday in July and August," a zoo employee reports. Come before 10 a.m. or after 3:30 p.m. to beat the worst of the heat. Saturday, predictably enough, is the most crowded day, while Sunday morning is usually a quiet time to see the zoo. Keep in mind, too, that animals are most active early in the morning and late in the day.

Special Comments: At Ecology Theatre in the Children's Zoo, handlers bring out a variety of animals for close-up views. Hedgehogs usually steal the shows, which are free and held at 11 a.m., 1 p.m., and 3 p.m. Kids will love the petting zoo. Chimps and gorillas—the most popular exhibits—are fed at 2 p.m.

Overall Appeal by Age Group:

Pre-school	Grade School	Teens	Young Adults	Over 30	Seniors
★★★★★	★★★★★	★★★★	★★★★	★★★★	★★★★

Author's Rating: It's no surprise that this is rated by experts as one of the best zoos in the world. And no cages mean that people who normally hate zoos may love this one. ★★★★★

How Much Time to Allow: At least two hours—although that's enough time to induce heat stroke on a sweltering summer afternoon.

Description and Comments   Metrozoo was clobbered by Hurricane Andrew, and the worst blow was the total destruction of Wings of Asia, Metrozoo's world-class bird exhibit, now scheduled to be rebuilt and opened in 2002. But don't let that deter you from making a visit. The zoo's monorail service is again making a complete loop of the park, and more than 7,000 trees have been planted since the hurricane. New additions since the hurricane include a meerkat exhibit in the children's zoo and an educational court with interactive zoological exhibits.

Touring Tips Take the free Zoofari Monorail, which makes a complete loop of Metrozoo. The round trip takes 20 to 25 minutes. Then either get off at station 1 and begin walking toward station 2 or continue on the train to station 4 (the last stop) and walk back toward the zoo entrance. Along the way you'll pass outdoor exhibits featuring gorillas, chimpanzees, elephants, Himalayan black bears, a white Bengal tiger, and other exotic animals. They're all uncaged—and appear a lot more content than animals behind bars in other zoos. Some exhibits feature "viewing caves" that let you view animals through plate-glass windows on their side of the moat.

Folks who would like to avoid the stairs or long ramps leading to the monorail stations—or who just don't feel like walking—can take a narrated tram tour ($2). You'll also see some behind-the-scenes areas such as the animal hospital.

Keep in mind that while Southern Florida's semitropical climate makes it possible to build a cageless zoo, it also means that visitors are at the mercy of the weather. Try to plan your day accordingly; Metrozoo doesn't issue rain passes.

Other Things to Do Nearby The Gold Coast Railroad Museum is located outside of the entrance of Metrozoo. Other nearby attractions include the Weeks Air Museum and, closer to Miami, Parrot Jungle and the Fairchild Tropical Garden. But if you've done justice to Metrozoo, you'll be too tired for more sight-seeing.

MoCA: Museum of Contemporary Art

Type of Attraction: The only art museum in Miami solely dedicated to modern art. A self-guided tour.

Location: 770 NE 125th Street, North Miami. From Miami Beach, take the Broad Causeway at 96th Street, which becomes NE 125th Street. MoCA is on the left.

Admission: Adults, $5; seniors and students, $3; children under age 12 free

Hours: Tuesday–Saturday, 11 a.m.–5 p.m.; Sunday, noon–5 p.m.; closed Monday

Phone: (305) 893-6211

When to Go: Any time

Special Comments: All on one level. Docent-led tours are available on weekends.

Overall Appeal by Age Group: Because the gallery changes its exhibits regularly, use these general ratings as a guide.

Pre-school	Grade School	Teens	Young Adults	Over 30	Seniors
★	★	★★	★★★½	★★★½	★★½

Author's Rating: Never a dull moment in Miami's newest museum; a gem; ★★★½

How Much Time to Allow: One hour

Description and Comments After moving from cramped quarters and undergoing a name change, MoCA is still basically a one-room exhibition hall. But the room's a heck of a lot bigger, allowing MoCA to stage larger shows of cutting-edge contemporary art. Expect to be flabbergasted (or, at least, amused) by whatever is on display during your visit to Miami. Films, lectures, artists' talks, and excursions are also offered at MoCA.

Touring Tips The gift shop features handcrafted jewelry and other one-of-a-kind items.

Other Things to Do Nearby The Museum of Contemporary Art is located in North Miami, infamous for its lack of tourist attractions. The posh shops of Bal Harbour are directly across the Broad Causeway; turn right on NE 123rd Street to get there. One of Miami's best sushi joints is Tani Guchi's Place, a few miles east in a strip shopping center just west of the Broad Causeway (2224 NE 123rd Street; (305) 892-6744).

Monkey Jungle

Type of Attraction: A primate zoo where visitors walk in screened walkways that pass through large "habitats" (actually, larger cages) that feature a wide variety of monkeys. A self-guided tour.

Location: 14805 SW 216th Street (Hainlin Mill Drive), about 20 miles south of Miami. Take the Florida Turnpike Extension to Exit 11 (SW 216th Street) west and drive 3 miles to the entrance on the right.

Admission: Adults, $13.50; seniors, $10.50; children ages 4–12, $8; children age 3 and under free

Hours: Daily, 9:30 a.m.–5 p.m.; ticket office closes at 4 p.m.

Phone: (305) 235-1611

When to Go: Avoid the hottest times of the day by arriving by 10 a.m. or just before 4 p.m. Crowds are lighter during the week than on weekends.

Special Comments: Don't forget mosquito repellent; visitors are outside the entire time. If it rains, pick up a rain pass at the entrance.

Overall Appeal by Age Group:

Pre-school	Grade School	Teens	Young Adults	Over 30	Seniors
★★★★★	★★★★★	★★★★	★★★	★★★	★★★

Author's Rating: A lot of fun—and it's okay to feed the primates; ★★★½

How Much Time to Allow: One hour; two hours if you want to catch all the shows

Description and Comments Gibbons, spider monkeys, orangutans, a gorilla, chimpanzees, and more are close at hand as you walk through screened walkways that wind through a tropical forest. While not all the monkeys roam free—a lot of them reside in large cages located along the walkways— many primates can be seen when you pass through the larger jungle habi-tat. Founded in the 1930s, Monkey Jungle is a slice of pre-Disney Florida that most visitors shouldn't miss.

Touring Tips Bring quarters; monkey food dispensers that resemble bubble-gum machines are located along the walkways. Four different shows featur-ing swimming monkeys, a gorilla, twin chimpanzees, and orangutans start at 10 a.m. and run continuously at 45-minute intervals.

Other Things to Do Nearby Coral Castle, Metrozoo, the Weeks Air Museum, and the Gold Coast Railroad Museum are nearby. For something different—and a little less touristy—stop by the Fruit & Spice Park on SW 248th Street, about five miles away.

Parrot Jungle and Gardens

Type of Attraction: A bird sanctuary and botanical gardens that also include trained bird shows, a flock of pink flamingos, and wildlife shows. A self-guided tour.

Location: 11000 SW 57th Avenue (South Red Road), about 11 miles south of downtown Miami. Take I-95 south until it turns into US 1, then turn left on SW 57th Avenue; the entrance is on the right.

Admission: Adults, $14.95; children ages 3–12, $9.95

Hours: Daily, 9:30 a.m.–6 p.m.

Phone: (305) 666-7834

When to Go: Weekends are usually very crowded, so try to arrive before 2 p.m. to beat the worst of the crowds. Monday through Wednesday are the least crowded days.

Special Comments: Parrot Jungle is scheduled to move and reopen on 18.6 acres on the north side of Watson Island (the first island on the way to Miami Beach on the MacArthur Causeway) in 2003. While that's a more convenient location, it's hard to imagine all this tropical lushness being recreated in a new spot—which is all the more reason to make the trip to South Miami and visit this venerable Miami tourist site in its old digs, which will remain open until the new $46 million park debuts. When you do visit the existing Parrot Jungle, expect to get lost (well, disoriented) as you wander through this lush tropical paradise.

Overall Appeal by Age Group:

Pre-school	Grade School	Teens	Young Adults	Over 30	Seniors
★★★★★	★★★★★	★★★★½	★★★★	★★★★	★★★★

Author's Rating: What a hoot—or, better yet, screech; don't miss it; ★★★★½

How Much Time to Allow: Two hours if you want to catch all the shows

Description and Comments You'll find a lot more than a zillion parrots (actually, about 2,000) at Parrot Jungle. Alligators, gibbons, pink flamingos, tortoises, a children's playground, a petting zoo, and a Miccosukee Indian display are waiting to be discovered in this lush tropical garden. Fortunately, winding paths disperse the crowds that flock to this place throughout its 12 acres. Along the way you'll see more than 1,100 varieties of birds and more than 1,000 types of plants. It's a great park and a real Florida classic.

Touring Tips Don't miss the trained bird show in the Parrot Bowl Amphitheater: macaws and cockatoos ride bikes, drive trucks, and race chariots. Watch trainers work with young birds in the Baby Bird Training Area, and see non-avian Florida wildlife in the Jungle Theater. In the Bird Posing Area, get your picture taken with a macaw perched on your head; there's no charge.

Other Things to Do Nearby Fairchild Tropical Garden will restore your sense of tranquility after touring the Parrot Jungle on a crowded day; Coconut Grove features eateries, bars, shops, and great people-watching. The Lowe Art Museum is on the Coral Gables campus of the University of Miami, just off US 1.

Seaquarium

Type of Attraction: A tropical marine aquarium. A self-guided tour.

Location: 4400 Rickenbacker Causeway (on Virginia Key between Key Biscayne and Miami)

Admission: Adults, $22.95 plus tax; children ages 3–9, $17.95 plus tax; children under age 3 free. Parking is $3 and the causeway toll is $1.

Hours: Daily, 9:30 a.m.–6 p.m.; ticket office closes at 4:30 p.m.

Phone: (305) 361-5705

When to Go: During the high tourist season (Christmas through April), try to arrive at 9:30 a.m. You can catch all of the shows by 1:30 p.m. and miss most of the crowds. Monday is the slowest day of the week; the throngs peak on the weekend.

Special Comments: Kids will love the frolicking dolphins in the Flipper Show. Don't sit too close to the water during the shows or you'll get soaked by a diving dolphin or killer whale.

Overall Appeal by Age Group:

Pre-school	Grade School	Teens	Young Adults	Over 30	Seniors
★★★★★	★★★★★	★★★★	★★★½	★★½	★★★

Author's Rating: Very expensive—and a bit worn around the edges. And now you have to pay to park! ★★

How Much Time to Allow: Four hours to see all of the shows; two hours to see one or two shows and catch the exhibits that interest you.

Description and Comments Unquestionably, the hottest attraction at this South Florida tourist mainstay is Lolita, Seaquarium's killer whale. It's an adrenaline rush you don't want to miss when this 20-foot-long behemoth goes airborne—and lands with a splash that drenches the first ten rows of spectators. Plan your visit around the Killer Whale Show, usually offered twice daily. Call ahead for the schedule.

Other performances at Seaquarium include the "Flipper" Show, a reef aquarium presentation, the Top Deck Dolphin Show, the Golden Dome Sea Lion Show, and a shark presentation. There's also a rain forest, a sealife touch pool, a wildlife habitat, a crocodile exhibit, and a tropical aquarium to view between shows.

The Seaquarium shows are slick and well orchestrated. But like the disco music played during the performances, this marine-life park struck us as a little worn . . . and outdated. (It's almost 40 years old.) And following the recent dose of consciousness-raising from the film *Free Willy* (and its sequels), a lot of folks may feel a twinge of guilt as they watch these magnificent—but captive—animals.

Touring Tips Plan your visit to Seaquarium so that you eat lunch before or after your visit: the food for sale in the aquarium is overpriced. Don't miss a manatee presentation, usually scheduled twice daily: It may be your only opportunity to see these docile, endangered mammals. A staffer talks about the manatees' plight and feeds them. You may also get to see a manatee do a "trick"—roll over on its back for the trainer. Then go see the "Flipper" Show for more action.

Other Things to Do Nearby Key Biscayne has plenty of places to eat and great beaches too. Back on the mainland, Vizcaya, a fabulous estate and gardens, is near the entrance to the Rickenbacker Causeway. The Lowe Museum of Art in Coral Gables is an excellent art museum.

Vizcaya Museum and Garden

Type of Attraction: A magnificent 16th-century Italian Renaissance–style villa and formal gardens built by the cofounder of International Harvester. Guided and self-guided tours.

Location: 3251 South Miami Avenue, Miami; near the Rickenbacker Causeway and across from the Miami Museum of Science

Admission: Adults, $10; children ages 6–12, $5; f children age 5 and under, free

Hours: Daily, 9:30 a.m.–5 p.m.. The ticket booth closes at 4:30 p.m., and the gardens close at 5:30 p.m.

Phone: (305) 250-9133

When to Go: Vizcaya is rarely mobbed. To beat the crowds in the high tourist season (Christmas through April), try to arrive soon after the gates open in the morning.

Special Comments: The mansion is beautifully decorated for the holidays in December.

Overall Appeal by Age Group:

Pre-school	Grade School	Teens	Young Adults	Over 30	Seniors
★	★★	★★½	★★★	★★★½	★★★★

Author's Rating: The mansion: Robber-baron decadence in a stunning setting on Biscayne Bay—so-so art; ★★★ The gardens: fabulous; ★★★★★

How Much Time to Allow: Two hours

Description and Comments   Chicago industrialist James Deering built his winter home on the shores of Biscayne Bay in 1916, an era when the fabulously rich weren't shy about showing off their wealth. Vizcaya's 34 rooms are loaded with period furniture, textiles, sculpture, and paintings from the 15th century through the early 19th century. The effect is that of a great country estate that's been continuously occupied for 400 years.

Most visitors go on a guided tour of the first floor that lasts 45 minutes. (If no tour guides are available, you're given a guidebook and turned loose.) Highlights of the magnificent rooms include a rug that Christopher Columbus stood on, an ornate telephone booth (check out the early example of a dial telephone), and dramatic carved ceilings and patterned marble floors. The house also has some eccentricities: Mr. Deering didn't like doors slamming from the continuous breeze off the bay, so many doors were hung at off-angles so they would close slowly. The breeze is not as much of a problem today: the proliferation of high-rise condos on Biscayne Bay blocks much of the wind.

Touring Tips After the guided tour, explore the second-floor bedrooms on your own. Then stroll the ten-acre formal gardens, which feature spectacular views of Biscayne Bay. The Great Stone Barge in front of Vizcaya's East Facade acts as a breakwater and creates a harbor for small boats.

Other Things to Do Nearby Seaquarium and Key Biscayne are on the other side of the Rickenbacker Causeway; Coconut Grove is the place to go if you're hungry. The Lowe Museum of Art is on the campus of the University of Miami in Coral Gables, just off US 1.

Weeks Air Museum

Type of Attraction: A museum dedicated to the preservation and restoration of aircraft from the beginning of flight through World War II. A self-guided tour.

Location: Kendall-Tamiami Airport in Southwest Miami (on SW 137th Avenue, a few miles northwest of Metrozoo)

Admission: Adults, $9.95; seniors, $6.95; children ages 4–12, $5.95; children age 3 and under free

Hours: Daily, 10 a.m. to 5 p.m.

Phone: (305) 233-5197

When to Go: Any time

Special Comments: As restoration continues from the clobbering the museum took from Hurricane Andrew in 1992, more aircraft and exhibits will be added. An interesting note: The goal of the museum is to restore most of the planes on display to flying condition.

Overall Appeal by Age Group:

Pre-school	Grade School	Teens	Young Adults	Over 30	Seniors
★	★★★	★★½	★★½	★★½	★★★½

Author's Rating: A small, attractive museum that will appeal to aviation and World War II history buffs—and those old enough to fondly recall the Swing Era; ★★½

How Much Time to Allow: One hour

Description and Comments The big attractions here are full-sized, mostly World War II–era fighting aircraft that we've all seen in the movies—such as the huge Grumman F6F-3 Hellcat fighter that helped U.S. forces gain air superiority over Japan in the Pacific half a century ago. On the other end of the scale is the P-51 fighter, built for the European theater of war. While surprisingly small compared to the Hellcat, this sleek-looking warbird had the range to go "all the way" in its mission of protecting Allied bombers on their way to targets deep in Europe. Other fascinating airplanes on display include the Tempest (a British fighter bomber with a top speed of 440 mph), an A-26 Invader (a twin-engine bomber; steps leading up to the cockpit let visitors peek inside), and a German Messerschmidt ME-108 fighter.

Touring Tips   Don't miss the exhibits on the Tuskegee Airmen, the all-black 99th Fighter squadron that fought with distinction in Africa, Sicily, and Europe. The well-stocked gift shops feature a wide selection of goodies that will appeal to aviation buffs, including model kits of World War II aircraft, prints, T-shirts, goatskin bomber jackets, and aviation-themed postcards.

Other Things to Do Nearby   Metrozoo and the Gold Coast Railroad Museum are only minutes away. For something to eat, go out the main entrance of the airport and drive either north or south on SW 137th Avenue for a wide selection of fast-food eateries.

The Wolfsonian

Type of Attraction: A museum of design dedicated to the art, architecture, design, and cultural history of the period 1885 to 1945. A self-guided tour.

Location: In South Beach; 1001 Washington Avenue

Admission: Adults, $5; seniors, adult students (with ID), and children ages 6–12, $3.50; free to all Thursday, 6–9 p.m.

Hours: Tuesday, Wednesday, Friday, and Saturday, 11 a.m.–6 p.m.; Thursday, 11 a.m.–9 p.m.; Sunday, noon–5 p.m.; closed Mondays, the Fourth of July, and Thanksgiving, Christmas, and New Year's Days

Phone: (305) 531-1001

When to Go: Any time

Special Comments: Park the kids at the beach; the Wolfsonian will bore smaller children silly. Because this place just oozes with European sophistication, to really fit in guys should wear a tweed jacket with leather elbow patches, smoke a pipe, and mutter approvingly in Italian as they move from exhibit to exhibit. Gals may want to opt for the New York "Fashion Nun" look: all black.

Overall Appeal by Age Group:

Pre-school	Grade School	Teens	Young Adults	Over 30	Seniors
—	★	★½	★★	★★★	★★★½

Author's Rating: Design plus art equals Art Deco . . . and who could imagine a more appropriate location for a museum like this than South Beach? A drawback: an off-putting "high-brow" atmosphere. ★★★

How Much Time to Allow: One–two hours

Description and Comments South Beach is all about surfaces: tanned bodies, thong bikinis, pastel-colored Art Deco hotels, models, and Eurotrash and tourists elbow to elbow on Ocean Drive. At the Wolfsonian, however, visitors get a chance to delve beneath the surfaces and ponder the meanings that lurk within everyday things such as furniture, household items, model trains, posters, and a zillion other objects taken from a collection of more than 70,000 decorative items dating from 1885 to 1945. Major themes in the changing exhibits focus on how design trends function as agents of modernity, how design works as a key element in reform movements, and how design elements are incorporated as vehicles of both advertising and political propaganda. Wear your thinking cap.

Temporary and semi-permanent exhibits are housed in a spiffed-up, former storage building restored to its 1920s, Mediterranean-style elegance. Most of the building is used for storing the collection; the surprisingly small exhibit spaces are located on the fifth, sixth, and seventh floors. Who collected all this stuff? Mitchell Wolfson Jr., an heir to a fortune made in the movie theater business.

Touring Tips Take the elevator up to the seventh-floor exhibit area and work your way down.

Other Things to Do Nearby Great (and not-so-great) restaurants line Washington Avenue, along with a wide array of shops. Lincoln Road Mall is six blocks north; frenetic Ocean Drive (and the ocean) is two blocks east. Watch out for weaving Rollerbladers.

Dining and Restaurants

That Miami and its environs is an "eating out" area is reflected in the number of restaurants it sustains. In Dade County alone there are more than 6,000 restaurants, with upwards of 6,000 more in adjoining Broward and Palm Beach counties. There are more restaurants per resident in Florida than anywhere else in the country. Most of them are "good"—or else they would not survive the competition—and a surprising number are very good and excellent.

With its diverse population—more than 60 percent of Miami's residents are Hispanic, mixed with sizable Haitian, Jamaican, Indian, and Asian communities—it follows that the eateries are as diverse as the population, making for a lively and exciting restaurant scene.

Because it continues to be an area with a growing population and some of the most favorable weather in the country, Miami seems to draw a continuing stream of young chefs—many of them graduates of U.S. culinary schools, which have proliferated in this area during the past decade.

The most exciting, innovative, and truly native trend in culinary development, comes from the young and talented American chefs who are creating a distinct new "Florida" cuisine, sometimes referred to as "Florida-Caribbean," "Floribbean," or "New World" cooking. By any name, this style of cooking continues to capture the interest of food writers, not only from around this country, but from other countries as well. These local chefs are combining and adapting the culinary styles of neighboring Caribbean countries with products that are native to the tropics, a fact that has encouraged the growth of numerous specialty farms in South Florida. These small farmers, along with individual local fishermen, bring their harvests directly to the back doors of these young restaurateurs who insist on products so fresh that dewdrops still glisten on them.

Thus, Miami restaurants boast a profusion of exotic foods unique to Florida, such as plantains, papaya, mangoes, hot chili peppers, malanga, yucca, and other exotic fruits and vegetables. In the pages of the dining profiles that follow, the specializations of various restaurants will be evident.

THE BUSINESS SCENE

In the Coral Gables section of Miami, home of some of Miami's finest restaurants, professionals pour into upscale restaurants in a flood. Influenced in part by the Hispanic population, as well as the concentration of businesses here, lunch is often a leisurely affair, designed for conducting business while enjoying fine food. Other similar areas are Coconut Grove and the Brickell areas.

SOUTH BEACH

For the past five years, South Beach's revitalized Art Deco District has been highly publicized and glorified around the world—with some justification. It is indeed glitzy, strange, and bizarre, bursting with locals and internationals in indescribable fashions. In addition to the familiar faces of movie stars, models, photographers, celebrities, and wannabes abound.

Along this strip called South Beach, restaurants pop up and disappear faster than the quick tropical showers. A hot new bar or restaurant will draw the trendies one week, only to be stone cold dead the next. On weekends, the sight-seer can scarcely make his or her way through the throngs of sidewalk diners. Most South Beach restaurants have outdoor terraces or porches, placing tables and chairs on the sidewalk for the overflow. This is a "see and be seen" scene.

Parking on the beach is difficult day and night. Even if you find a space near the restaurant of your choice, a valet parking attendant is apt to rush up before you leave the car, informing you that it will cost you $12 and sometimes $18 for the privilege. Prices vary. There may be free parking available if you look hard enough, (beware of the parking areas reserved for residents only) but chances are that the space you find will be at least several blocks away.

Be forewarned that nearly every restaurant on Ocean Drive, adds a 15–18 percent gratuity to your bill. If you are ignorant of this practice and add another 15 percent, don't expect to be informed of your error.

ETHNIC DINING

Because of its ethnic diversity and appeal to world tourism, Miami harbors a wide variety of restaurants, including a plethora of Cuban restaurants, many of them in what is called "Little Havana." Most are dedicated to serving traditional Cuban food, with rice and black beans, plantains, and yucca almost always accompanying the entrees. Additionally, however, there is an emerging number of "new" Cuban restaurants offering lighter twists on the traditional. Foremost among them are Havana Harry's and Yuca restaurants.

Perhaps the most popular, and some of the best, of the ethnic restaurants are Italian. Both in Coral Gables and on South Beach, good Italian restaurants abound. Among the best are Osteria del Teatro and Tuscan Steak in South Beach, La Bussola and Caffe Abbracci in Coral Gables. In North Miami there's Il Tulipano, arguably the best Italian restaurant in Dade County.

Among other ethnic groups represented are French, Thai, Indian, Greek, Middle Eastern, Japanese, Vietnamese, and Chinese. Several Chinese restaurants in the area specialize in dim sum, including the prominent and elaborate Tropical Chinese Restaurant. Peruvian, Argentinean, Mexican, Brazilian, and Nicaraguan restaurants also are to be found, though in lesser numbers.

Both the Hispanic and American populations of Miami are partial to steak and other red meats. European tourists, not able to eat beef in their countries (mad cow disease) and long aware of the high quality of American beef, seek out our steak houses. Among the classier and more expensive of these are The Palm, Smith & Wollensky, and Tuscan Steak, all beloved by the rich and sometimes famous.

Steak notwithstanding, the question most often asked by tourists of concierges is, "Can you give me the name of a good seafood restaurant?" Quite natural, since Miami floats like an island between the Gulf waters and the ocean. Although there are one or two outstanding specialty seafood restaurants, such as Joe's Stone Crab, restaurants like Nemo, Chef Allen's, Blue Door at Delano, and 1220 at The Tides usually have their fish delivered to the kitchen door on a daily basis, ensuring impeccable freshness. The tourist will find no lack of restaurants that serve local fish in tropical South Florida.

It's O.K. to Be Casual

There has been, during the past decade, a decided trend toward informality in restaurant decor, service style, and dress requirements. Most tourists, winter residents, and even locals come to this tropical area to relax and do not relish dressing formally. Therefore the dress code is lenient. Less than a handful of restaurants require a jacket.

Some lovely restaurants that offer formal, professional service and fine wines remain and continue to be popular. One of them is La Paloma, a Swiss-American restaurant on Biscayne Boulevard. It features ornate surroundings, top-notch service, and generally modest prices. Even so, a jacket is not required.

Outdoor Dining

Strangely enough, there was little outdoor dining in Miami and South Florida until the 1980s. There were waterfront restaurants that offered dining on the porch or terrace, but as the natives mumbled, "Only tourists would go out in that hot sun."

All that has changed since the local lifestyle became more and more informal. Everyone, it seems, including residents, now wants to eat outdoors, humidity notwithstanding. Many new restaurants are built to offer outdoor dining, and older restaurants are scrambling to do the same.

Breakfast

Usually, tourists eat breakfast in their hotels and are not searching for breakfast spots. There are a few places, however, that draw both locals and tourists on a continuing basis.

On South Beach, News Cafe and Van Dyke attract more people than there are seating spaces. The Rascal House, on North Miami Beach, has been the most steadily popular and busy restaurant through the years. It is a landmark worth visiting if you like deli-style food. Some of the better and more interesting breakfast spots to pop up lately are in recently renovated hotels such as Delano, The Tides, and Astor, all in South Beach.

Then, of course, there are the bagel houses. Among the most popular in Dade County are The Bagel Emporium in Coral Gables and Bagels & Co. in North Miami on Biscayne Boulevard.

Landmark Restaurants

There are few true landmark restaurants in South Florida, perhaps because of its youth, and because some places, on their way to becoming legends, simply closed their doors.

Perhaps the best-known legend in the Miami area is Joe's Stone Crab on South Beach, which opened some 80 years ago, when Miami was in its infancy. It attracts both local residents and tourists, hundreds of them daily. The restaurant is closed during the summer months.

Its single attraction is stone crabs, a delicious shellfish available in surrounding waters, and one sold in nearly every other restaurant in South Florida during the season. Somehow, they seem to taste better at Joe's, maybe because of all the celebrities here. Beginning in the days of J. Edgar Hoover and Walter Winchell, and continuing the tradition today with movie stars, sports figures, and power brokers, sooner or later, everyone goes to Joe's Stone Crab.

Equally phenomenal is the Rascal House, a deli-style restaurant that opened in the 1950s and, it is said, feeds some 5,000 people a day during the season. This is easy to believe when you view the long lines forever waiting to get in. Surprisingly, the waits are never long. The restaurant is a model of efficiency; its waitresses are remarkably good and in a half-hour you'll be munching on the gratis pickles and beets.

HOTEL DINING

At the turn of the century, Miami hotels harbored some of its best restaurants. This changed in the 1950s and 1960s as many hotels, particularly those catering to tourists, downgraded their restaurants to what resembled fast-food outlets. But this downward trend was reversed in the late 1970s and early 1980s, when the focus on good and exciting food became prominent again. Many hotels scrambled to open fine restaurants once more, hiring talented chefs to run their kitchens. The best of these today are the Blue Door at the Delano; 1220 at The Tides; Astor Place at The Astor, Bice at the Wyndham Grand Bay Hotel, and the newest jewel: Azul at the Mandarin Oriental

GOOD AND GETTING BETTER

Because of the importance of tourism, Miami has always offered many good restaurants. But until very recently, its culinary scene was never considered in the same league with San Francisco, New Orleans, and New York.

In the past decade, however, Florida chefs have emerged as among the most touted in the country. This is due largely to the tremendous influx of Cubans and other Hispanics to the area and the availability of their exotic products, flavors, and spices, traces of which now can be found in most Miami restaurants—including Italian and French.

Pioneers in the development of this new and richly flavorful cuisine are Norman Van Aken of Norman's, Mark Militello of Mark's Las Olas, Allen Susser of Chef Allen's, Robbin Haas of Baleen, Cindy Hutson of Ortanique on the Mile, and Pascal Oudin at Pascal's on Ponce (Oudin recently opened his own restaurant and has gone back to his roots, French cooking). The essence of their inspired cooking has fanned out to influence young chefs in restaurants throughout South Florida. These chefs in turn have influenced other ethnic chefs to follow suit, thus improving the quality of independent restaurants throughout the area.

The restaurants described here are among the best in the various cuisine categories, and they are the most recommended restaurants in Miami. Local residents as well as tourists frequent most of the restaurants listed in this guide. In the sweltering summer, tourism dies in South Florida, and unless restaurants attract a substantial local trade, they too die. Thus you can be sure the restaurants listed are not just "tourist traps."

Altogether, though there remain a good percentage of mediocre restaurants, the dining in Miami has never been more diverse and exciting.

EXPLAINING THE RATINGS

We have developed detailed profiles for the restaurants we think are the best in the County. Each profile features an easily scanned heading that allows you, in just a second, to check out the restaurant's name, cuisine, star rating, cost, quality rating, and value rating.

Star Rating   The star rating is an overall rating that evaluates the entire dining experience, including style, service, and ambience, in addition to the taste, presentation, and quality of the food. Five stars is the highest rating possible, meaning the place has the best of everything. Four-star restaurants are exceptional and three-star restaurants are well above average. Two-star restaurants are good. One star is given to average restaurants that demonstrate an unusual capability in some area of specialization, for example, an otherwise forgettable place that has great corned beef.

Cost   Below and to the left of the star rating is an expense category giving the general price range for a complete meal. A complete meal for our purposes consists of an entree with vegetable or side dish, and choice of soup or salad. Appetizers, desserts, drinks, and tips are excluded. Categories and related prices are listed below.

Inexpensive	$14 or less per person
Moderate	$15 to $30 per person
Expensive	More than $30 per person

Quality Rating   On the far right of each heading appears a number and a letter. The number is a food quality rating based on a scale of 0 to 100, with 100 being the best rating attainable. The quality rating is based expressly on the taste, freshness of ingredients, preparation, presentation, and creativity of food served. There is no consideration of price. If you are a person who wants the best food available and cost is not an issue, you need look no further than the quality ratings.

Value Rating   If, on the other hand, you are looking for both quality and value, then you should check the value rating, expressed in letters. The value ratings are defined as follows:

A   Exception value, a real bargain
B   Good value
C   Fair value, you get exactly what you pay for
D   Somewhat overpriced
F   Significantly overpriced

Payment   We've listed the type of payment accepted at each restaurant using the following codes:

AMEX   American Express (Optima)
CB   Carte Blanche
D   Discover
DC   Diners Club
MC   MasterCard
VISA   Visa

ABOUT THESE CHOICES

Because restaurants are opening and closing all the time in Miami, we have tried to confine our list to establishments with a proven track record over a fairly long period of time. Those newer or changed establishments that demonstrate staying power and consistency will be profiled in subsequent editions. Also, the list is highly selective. If we leave out a particular place it does not necessarily mean that restaurant is not good, but only that it was not ranked among the best in its genre. Detailed profiles of each restaurant follow in alphabetical order.

The Best of Miami–Area Restaurants

Restaurant/Type	Star Rating	Quality Rating	Value Rating	City
American				
The Forge/Jimmy'z	★★★½	92	B	Miami Beach
Joe Allen	★★½	80	A	Miami Beach
Continental				
La Paloma	★★	85	A	Miami
Cuban				
Havana Harry's	★★★	89	B	Coral Gables

The Best Miami-Area Restaurants (continued)

Restaurant/Type	Star Rating	Quality Rating	Value Rating	City
Florida-Caribbean				
Ortanique on the Mile	★★★★	95	C	Coral Gables
Astor Place	★★★½	90	B	Miami Beach
French				
Pascal's on Ponce	★★★★	96	B	Coral Gables
Blue Door at Delano	★★★★	94	C	Miami Beach
Italian				
Il Tulipano	★★★½	92	B	Miami
Tuscan Steak	★★★½	92	B	Miami Beach
La Bussola	★★★½	89	B	Coral Gables
BICE	★★★	86	C	Miami
New American				
Nemo	★★★★	94	B	Miami Beach
New Florida				
Chef Allen's	★★★★	96	B	Miami
New World				
Norman's	★★★★½	98	B	Coral Gables
Pacific Rim				
Pacific Time	★★★★	92	C	Miami Beach
Pan Asian				
China Grill	★★★½	90	C	Miami Beach
Progressive American				
Red Square	★★★★	92	B	Miami Beach
1220 at The Tides	★★★½	90	B	Miami Beach
Seafood				
Joe's Stone Crab	★★★	90	B	Miami Beach
Spanish				
Casa Juancho	★★½	80	C	Miami
Steak				
Miami Palm	★★★½	94	C	Bay Harbor Island
Morton's of Chicago	★★★½	92	B	Miami
Tuscan Steak	★★★½	92	B	Miami Beach
Smith & Wollensky	★★★½	90	C	Miami Beach

ASTOR PLACE ★★★½

		QUALITY
Florida-Caribbean	Expensive	90
		VALUE
956 Washington Avenue (Astor Hotel), Miami Beach; (305) 672-7217		C

Reservations: Accepted
When to go: Early
Entree range: $26–36
Payment: AMEX, VISA, MC, DC
Parking: Valet
Bar: Full service
Wine selection: Outstanding from Cali-

fornia and Europe; $35–1,200 bottles,
$8–16 by the glass
Dress: Casual
Disabled access: Good
Customers: Young residents, tourists,
professionals

Breakfast: Monday–Saturday, 7:30–11 a.m.

Brunch: Sunday, noon–2:30 p.m.

Lunch: Monday–Saturday, 11:30 a.m.–2:30 p.m.

Dinner: Monday–Thursday and Sunday, 7–11 p.m.; Friday and Saturday, 7 p.m.–midnight

Menu recommendations: Blue corn-crusted leg of duck confit cakes with mango slaw and fresh berry demi-glace; wild mushroom pancake "shortstack" drizzled with balsamic syrup; my foie gras " liver and onions," truffled potatoes, balsamic caramelized shallots; herb-scented rotisserie roasted Bell and Evans chicken, corn sauce, truffled mashed potatoes and baby vegetable ragout; Astor surf and turf; rack of lamb, mustard-herb crum crusted, creamy Yukon mashed potatoes; wasabi skillet seared tuna steak, rock shrimp stir fried jasmine rice, cashews, wakame and sprout salad, pineapple ponzu.

Comments: Original Executive chef Johnny Vinczencz is back and things could not be better. His bold Caribbean Cowboy cuisine results in food both richly flavorful and artistic in presentation.

BICE ★★★

		QUALITY
Italian	Expensive	86
		VALUE
2669 South Bayshore Drive (at Wyndham Grand Bay Hotel), Miami; (305) 860-0960		C

Reservations: Recommended
When to go: Any time
Entree range: $ 24–$35
Payment: AMEX, VISA, MC, DC

Parking: Valet
Bar: Full service
Wine selection: Good California and Italian; $18–760 bottles, $6–10 by the glass

Dress: Casual/business

Disable access: Good

Customers: Hotel guests, community leaders, locals

Breakfast: Daily, 7–11:30 a.m.

Lunch: Daily, 11:30 a.m.–3 p.m.

Dinner: Daily, 6–10:30 p.m.

Menu recommendations: Deep fried baby squid, zucchini, eggplant, and peppers with tartar and spicy tomato sauces; home-marinated salmon with Belgium endives, strawberries; homemade veal ravioli; homemade gnocchi gorgonzola; classic Tuscan seafood soup with snapper, sea scallops, shrimp, mussels, clams, monkfish and Maine lobster; veal ossobuco braised with vegetables and fresh herbs, saffron risotto; 12-ounce veal chop "Milabes style" with arugula and cherry tomato salad; veal scaloppine with marsala sauce, broccili rabe, and mashed potatoes.

Comments: This upscale international chain of restaurants assures the traveler consistency and quality away from home. Fresh and impeccably produced pastas are a specialty of the house. Once the best hotel in town, the now Wyndham Grand Bay still remains as classic as the cuisine at Bice.

BLUE DOOR AT DELANO		★★★★
French	Very Expensive	**QUALITY** 94
1685 Collins Avenue (Delano Hotel), Miami Beach; (305) 674-6400		**VALUE** C

Reservations: Recommended

When to go: Any time

Entree range: $25–46

Payment: AMEX, VISA, MC, DC

Parking: Valet

Bar: Full service

Wine selection: Extensive champagne list; well-selected American and French wines; $30–950 bottles, $7–15 by the glass

Dress: Casual/business

Disabled access: Good

Customers: Young locals, the "in" crowd, wealthy tourists, celebrities

Breakfast: Daily, 7–11 a.m.

Lunch: Daily, 11:30 a.m.–3 p.m.; all-day menu until 7 p.m.

Dinner: Daily, 7 p.m.–midnight

Menu recommendations: Thon-Thon, black and blue tuna with marinated daikon in lime juice; foie gras burger; big raviole, jumbo ravioli filled with taro mousseline and white truffle oil; loup cajou, Chilean sea bass in a brown butter sauce with cashew nuts, garlic, lime, and fresh herbs, served with fresh hearts of palm.

Comments: A walk through the long lobby of the well-hyped Delano takes the visitor past white, gauzy draperies defining seating alcoves with chinchilla throws covering uniquely fashioned chaises. Eventually one reaches the all-white restaurant, and this is a setting one must see to believe. It is a magnet to celebrities and large crowds. Consulting chef Claude Troisgros seasonally re-creates the menu, and the prompt and friendly waitstaff make dining here a pleasure.

CASA JUANCHO ★★½

Spanish	Moderate	QUALITY
		80
2436 SW 8th Street, Miami		VALUE
(305) 642-2452		C

Reservations: Accepted
When to go: Early
Entree range: $14–40
Payment: VISA, AMEX, MC, DC
Parking: Valet
Bar: Full service
Wine selection: Extensive selection of

Spanish, South American, and Italian
wines; $18–24 bottles, $4.88–5.75 by
the glass
Dress: Casual/business
Disabled access: Good
Customers: Hispanic locals, professionals,
internationals

Open: Sunday–Thursday, noon–midnight; Friday and Saturday, noon–1 a.m.

Menu recommendations: Spanish roast peppers stuffed with codfish mousse; baby eels in spicy garlic sauce; garlic soup Castillian-style; chilled whole two-pound Florida lobster with two salsas; grilled snapper fillet over flaming oak logs splashed with fiery garlic and vinegar sauce; rabbit cured in sherry and baked with thyme and creamy brown sauce.

Comments: A popular, Spanish-style themed dining spot for active members of the Hispanic community. The mood at night is festive, and the various rooms are crowded. One sees a wonderful slice of Hispanic life.

CHEF ALLEN'S ★★★★

New Florida	Expensive	QUALITY
		96
19088 NE 29th Avenue, Miami		VALUE
(305) 935-2900		B

Reservations: Accepted
When to go: Early
Entree range: $24.95–38.95
Payment: VISA, AMEX, MC, DC
Parking: Adjoining lot
Bar: Full service

Wine selection: Extensive selection of top Americans; a treat of a list; $45–1,200 bottles, $8–14 by the glass

Dress: Informal, business

Disabled access: Good

Customers: Locals, tourists, internationals

Dinner: Sunday–Friday, 6–10:30 p.m.; Saturday, 6–11 p.m.

Menu recommendations: A tasting menu of five courses for $75. Bahamian lobster and crab cakes with tropical fruit chutney and vanilla beurre blanc; yellowfin tuna tartar with sevruga caviar and bloody mary spiked with Grey Goose; Chai tea–cured salmon gravlax with cucumber raita; telecherry pepper seared French foie gras, crisp pancetta, candied onion, brioche toast and mango jam; Tribeca veal chop, white beans, wild mushroom ragout, and double mustard sauce; pistachio crusted black grouper, fricassee of rock shrimp, mango, leeks and coconut rum; crab-crusted mahi mahi, spiny lobster risotto, haricot verts and smoked tomato butter.

Comments: Operating in a stylish, contemporary setting, Chef Allen is one of the most daring interpreters of bold New American cuisine, embellishing his dishes with Florida-Caribbean tastes, flavors, and ingredients. Chef Allen is one of the most respected chefs in South Florida.

CHINA GRILL   ★★★½

Pan Asian	Expensive	QUALITY
		90
404 Washington Avenue, Miami Beach		VALUE
(305) 534-2211		**C**

Reservations: Accepted, necessary

When to go: Early

Entree range: $18.50–49

Payment: AMEX, VISA, MC, DC

Parking: Valet

Bar: Full service

Wine selection: Fair selection from

around the world; $30–290 bottles; $7–18 by the glass

Dress: Casual to dressy

Disabled access: Good

Customers: Locals, professionals, celebrities, tourists

Open: Monday–Friday, 11:45 a.m.–6 p.m.; Sunday–Thursday, 6 p.m.–midnight; Friday and Saturday, 6 p.m.–1 a.m.

Menu recommendations: Broccoli rabe dumplings; crackling calamari salad; Peking duckling salad; sashimi tempura with wasabi champagne cream, lobster pancakes; oriental BBQ salmon; wild mushroom profusion pasta with sake-Madeira cream sauce.

Comments: The "world cuisine" is delicious and as extraordinarily beautiful as the setting. Though prices are not inexpensive, portions are enormous and are meant to be shared family-style. There's a separate VIP area for celebrities and stars, with gold-threaded draperies that may be drawn for privacy. Ordinary folk are equally welcome.

THE FORGE/JIMMY'Z   ★★★½

American	Expensive	QUALITY
		92
432 41st Street, Miami Beach		VALUE
(305)-534-4536		B

Reservations: Accepted	Wine selection: The best in Miami; out-
When to go: Any time	standing American and French vintages;
Entree range: $19.95–90	$30 bottles, $8 by the glass
Payment: VISA, MC, AMEX, D	Dress: Business attire/casual elegant
Parking: Valet	Disabled access: Yes
Bar: Full service	Customers: Well-heeled locals, tourists

Dinner: Sunday–Thursday, 6–11 p.m.; Friday and Saturday, 6 p.m.– midnight

Menu recommendations: Chilled jumbo shrimp; shrimp marlin; petrossian smoked salmon; yellow fin tuna tartare; The Forge's chopped salad; The Forge's "Super Steak," voted the number one steak in America by *Wine Spectator* magazine; prime rib; snapper cashew; duck cassis; rack of lamb; chocolate soufflé.

Comments: The Forge, an institution in dining, is one of Miami's most complete and reliable dinning experiences. With the opening of Jimmy'z, an adjacent restaurant and disco, The Forge expands to attract all nightlife owls. Chef Kal is the genius who creates the high volume and extensive menu.

HAVANA HARRY'S   ★★★

Cuban	Inexpensive/Moderate	QUALITY
		89
4612 Le Jeune Road, Coral Gables		VALUE
(305) 661-2622		B .

Reservations: Not required	Payment: VISA, AMEX, MC, DC
When to go: Early	Parking: Self park in adjacent lot
Entree range: $8.95–24.95	Bar: Full service

Wine selection: Moderate; $17–120
  bottles, $4.50–7 by the glass
Dress: Casual, a family place

Disabled access: Good
Customers: Professionals, locals

Open: Monday–Thursday, 11 a.m.–10 p.m.; Friday, 11 a.m.–11 p.m.; Saturday, noon–11 p.m.; Sunday, noon–10:30 p.m.

Menu recommendations: Malanga Cream; tostones rellenos, stuffed green plantains with beef, seafood, or a combination; fried pork chunks, caldo Gallego, a Galitian specialty soup; Harry's chicken, grilled and topped with avocado sauce, cream and cheddar cheese served with white rice, black beans and sweet plantains; Caribbean shrimp, grilled with mango sauce; salmon with tamarind sauce covered with sesame seeds, served with mashed potatoes and mariquitas; Springtime snapper, broiled covered with crab and avocado sauce, served with the usual black beans and white rice with sweet plantains.

Comments: Many feared that with the move to a bigger location, Havana Harry's quality and popularity would decline. On the contrary, this place has never been so busy, and the food is better than ever. This is a honest family-run operation where everyone shares responsibilities. Without a doubt, the best Cuban food in Miami.

IL TULIPANO ★★★½

		QUALITY
Italian	Expensive	**92**
11052 Biscayne Boulevard, Miami		VALUE
(305) 893-4811		**B**

Reservations: Accepted
When to go: Early
Entree range: $15–25
Payment: VISA, AMEX, MC, DC
Parking: Valet
Bar: Full service
Wine selection: One of the best Italian

and French wine lists; $24–500 bottles,
  $7–12 by the glass
Dress: Business, casual-elegant
Disabled access: Good
Customers: Professionals, locals, tourists,
  celebrities

Dinner: Monday–Thursday, 6–11 p.m.; Friday and Saturday, 6 p.m.–midnight; closed Sunday

Menu recommendations: Large, tricolored roasted peppers bathed in olive oil and balsamic vinegar; cloudlike agnolotti impannate; risotto verde with baby asparagus spears; enormous Mediterranean red prawns with olive oil, garlic, and thyme; veal cutlet Valdostana with prosciutto, fontina cheese, and fresh tomato sauce; leg of lamb.

Comments: Now owned and managed by seasoned restaurateur Ron Wayne, Il Tulipano runs better then ever. Though the previous owner, Filipo Il Grande, paid special attention to VIPs, Ron shows no favoritism and treats everyone like a VIP; his personality has brought a new and different level of friendliness.

JOE ALLEN ★★½

		QUALITY
American	Moderate	**80**
1787 Purdy Avenue, Miami Beach		VALUE
(305) 531-7007		**A**

Reservations: Accepted 1 week in advance
When to go: Any time
Entree range: $8.50–24
Payment: VISA, MC
Parking: Ample metered parking
Bar: Full service

Wine selection: Small but satisfactory;
   $20–45 bottles, $6–12 by the glass
Dress: Casual
Disabled access: Good
Customers: Locals, tourists

Brunch: Saturday, noon–4 p.m.; Sunday, noon–3:30 p.m.

Lunch: Monday–Friday, noon–4 p.m.

Dinner: Daily, 4 p.m.–midnight; bar open until 2 a.m., Friday and Saturday

Menu recommendations: Gazpacho Andaluzas with spicy croutons; arugula salad with grilled portobello mushrooms, roasted red peppers and gorgonzola dressing; great hamburgers with french fries; pizzas include the traditional Margherita and five more; grilled New York sirloin steak with french fries; sautéed calf's liver with mashed potatoes and sautéed spinach; meatloaf with mashed potatoes.

Comments: Legendary restaurateur Joe Allen, owner and operator of a string of successful namesake establishments—including the original location in the heart of New York's theater district—brings his signature style of informal dining to South Florida. The price and value are great, and the service is as friendly as it gets.

JOE'S STONE CRAB RESTAURANT   ★★★

Seafood	Moderate/Expensive	QUALITY
		90

11 Washington Avenue, Miami Beach	VALUE
(305) 673-0365	C

Reservations: Not accepted
When to go: Early
Entree range: $5–60
Payment: VISA, AMEX, MC, DC
Parking: Valet
Bar: Full service
Wine selection: An adequate but small selection of wines from California and Europe
Dress: Casual
Disabled access: Good
Customers: Tourists from around the world, locals

Lunch: Tuesday–Sunday, 11:30 a.m.–2 p.m.

Dinner: Sunday–Thursday, 5–10 p.m.; Friday and Saturday, 5–11 p.m.

Menu recommendations: Though other restaurants serve stone crabs, none seem to taste quite like those at Joe's. Nearly essential accompaniments are the generous plates of hash browns and coleslaw. Also try fried soft-shell crabs; blue crab cakes; sautéed fillet of sole; ginger salmon; fried or grilled pompano, swordfish, or grouper; New York sirloin or broiled lamb chops for non-fish eaters.

Comments: South Florida's most popular and famous restaurant, it's open from mid-October to mid-May. A must for tourists and a hang out for locals, Joe's is busy, a bit noisy, but always an exciting experience. Owned and operated by the original owner's granddaughter, Joan Sawitz Bass, Joe's luster never diminishes.

LA BUSSOLA   ★★★½

Italian	Moderate/Expensive	QUALITY
		89

264 Giralda Avenue, Coral Gables	VALUE
(305) 445-8783	B

Reservations: Accepted
When to go: Early
Entree range: $14–25
Payment: VISA, AMEX, MC, DC
Parking: Nearby lot, street, valet for dinner
Bar: Full service
Wine selection: Excellent Italian wines; $30–500 bottles, $8–15 by the glass
Dress: Casual, business
Disabled access: Good
Customers: Professionals, internationals, tourists, locals

Lunch: Monday–Friday, noon–3 p.m.

Dinner: Sunday–Thursday, 6–11 p.m.; Friday and Saturday, 6–11:30 p.m.

Menu recommendations: Julienne of roasted peppers with grilled jumbo shrimp; broiled jumbo sea scallops with orange sauce and mint-marinated artichokes; mixed grill of wild mushrooms, wilted spinach, and roasted pine nuts; spinach and cheese ravioli with fresh thyme and white truffle sauce; Bistecca alla fiorentina with herbs and olive oil; mushroom-crusted baked red snapper with thyme Chardonnay sauce; grilled veal chop.

Comments: This stunning restaurant is lively and busy both at lunch and dinner, yet service remains impeccable and caring. It exemplifies high-style Italian cooking. Owner Elizabeth Giordano is acknowledged as operating one of the finest Italian restaurants in the Miami area.

LA PALOMA ★★½

Continental/Swiss	Moderate	QUALITY 85
10999 Biscayne Boulevard, Miami (305) 891-0505		VALUE A

Reservations: Accepted	**Wine selection:** Basic but well rounded;
When to go: Early or late	$24-plus bottles, $4.50 by the glass
Entree range: $13.95–29.95	**Dress:** Casual, business
Payment: VISA, AMEX, MC, DC	**Disabled access:** Good
Parking: Valet	**Customers:** Locals, tourists, winter
Bar: Full service	residents

Lunch: Monday–Friday, 11:30 a.m.–3 p.m.

Dinner: Monday–Friday, 5 p.m.–midnight; Saturday and Sunday, 4 p.m.– midnight

Menu recommendations: Oysters Rockefeller; coquille St. Jacques; escargot Bourguignonne; chicken Kiev; duckling with orange sauce; steak au poivre; jumbo grilled veal chop with wild mushrooms; fillet of sole with capers, lemon, scallions, and fresh tomato dice; Wiener schnitzel; Grilled rack of lamb à la diable. Entrees are accompanied by house salad and a mix of vegetables.

Comments: La Paloma is all about the way things used to be, transporting the diner to the salons of "The Age of Innocence." This restaurant never wavers from offering its version of Swiss food, which includes the influences of French, Italian, and German cuisine.

MIAMI PALM RESTAURANT   ★★★½

		QUALITY
Steak	Expensive	**94**
		VALUE
9650 East Bay Harbor Drive, Bay Harbor Island		**C**
(305) 868-7256		

Reservations: Accepted
When to go: Early
Entree range: $16–30; lobster, market price
Payment: VISA, AMEX, MC, DC
Parking: Valet
Bar: Full service

Wine selection: Good American reds to match their aged steaks; $30–600 bottles, $7–11 by the glass
Dress: Informal, business
Disabled access: Good
Customers: Professionals, tourists, internationals, locals

Dinner: Monday–Thursday, 5–10 p.m.; Friday–Sunday, 5–11 p.m.

Menu recommendations: The Palm is a steakhouse, specializing in big prime steaks. Another specialty is the lobster, never less than four pounds; also veal Milanese and sautéed shrimp. Side dishes, all of them à la carte, are excellent and enough for two. Among them are french fried onions, creamed spinach, hash browns, and cottage fries.

Comments: This is a restaurant to visit when you have an irresistible urge for a big steak or lobster, with no concern for cost.

MORTON'S OF CHICAGO   ★★★½

		QUALITY
Steakhouse	Expensive	**92**
		VALUE
1200 Brickell Avenue, Miami		**B**
(305) 400-9990		

Reservations: Accepted
When to go: Early
Entree range: $19–35
Payment: VISA, MC, AMEX
Parking: Valet
Bar: Full service

Wine selection: Excellent American, European, and New World wines; $35–1,300 bottles, $8–15 by the glass
Dress: Business attire
Disabled access: Yes
Customers: Professionals, locals, tourists

Lunch: Monday–Friday, 11:30 a.m.–2:30 p.m.

Dinner: Monday–Saturday, 5:30–11 p.m.; Sunday, 5–10 p.m.

Menu recommendations: All of it is USDA prime-aged grain-fed steaks; smoked Pacific salmon; fresh lump crabmeat cocktail; sautéed wild mushrooms; double filet mignon with béarnaise sauce; porterhouse steak; New York strip steak; domestic rib lamb chops; broiled Block Island swordfish steak; special-fed, farm-raised salmon; whole Maine lobster; sautéed fresh spinach and mushrooms.

Comments: This is one of the most reliable and best steakhouses to open in the Miami area. Service is some of the best in town, if not the best. This is one of 38 Morton's locations nationwide.

NEMO ★★★★

New American	Moderate/Expensive	**QUALITY** 94
100 Collins Avenue, Miami Beach (305) 532-4550		**VALUE** B

Reservations: Accepted
When to go: Early
Entree range: $23–33
Payment: AMEX, VISA, MC, DC
Parking: Valet
Bar: Full service
Wine selection: Well-studied and com-
pact selection; excellent for it's size; $22–450 bottles, $8–18 by the glass
Dress: Casual
Disabled access: Good
Customers: Young locals, tourists, area professionals

Brunch: Sunday, noon–4 p.m.

Lunch: Monday–Friday, noon–3 p.m.

Dinner: Monday–Saturday, 7 p.m.–midnight; Sunday, 6–11 p.m.

Menu recommendations: Polenta fries (a must); garlic- and ginger-cured salmon rolls with tobiko caviar and wasabi mayo; crispy prawns with spicy salsa cruda and mesclun greens; sautéed mahi mahi with sautéed asparagus and orange-basil citronette; spicy pork loin with caramelized onions and papaya relish; grilled swordfish with ragout of white beans, tomato, and broccoli rabe; curried lentil stew with sweet caramelized onions and wilted greens.

Comments: Chef Michael Schwartz, once a chef at Wolfgang Puck's Chinois and a partner of New York restaurateur Myles Chevitz, applies a fusion of culinary techniques to his cooking in an unusual and pleasant atmosphere that can best be described as "South Beach casual."

NORMAN'S ★★★★½

		QUALITY
New World	Expensive	**98**

	VALUE
21 Almeria Avenue, Coral Gables	**B**
(305) 446-6767	

Reservations: Accepted	Wine selection: Very good; $29–750
When to go: Early	bottles, $7–13 by the glass
Entree range: $30–40	Dress: Casual, business
Payment: AMEX, VISA, MC, DC	Disabled access: Good
Parking: Valet	Customers: Locals, business leaders,
Bar: Full service	tourists

Dinner: Monday–Thursday, 6–10:30 p.m.; Friday and Saturday, 6–11 p.m.; closed Sunday

Menu recommendations: Foie gras wafers on Cuban breads "shortstack" with exotic fruits caramel; jerked chicken skewer on pigeon pea salsa; bacalao fritters with ancho–black olive aioli; yucca-stuffed shrimp with sour orange mojo, greens, and tartar salsa; rum- and pepper-painted grouper on mango-habanero mojo with boniato-plantain mash en poblano; palomilla strip steak au poivre with cabrales crema, blistered bell peppers, stacked sweet tater torta, and West Indian pumpkin.

Comments: Norman Van Aken is considered one of the country's finest and most inventive chefs, the forerunner in the development of Florida's New World cuisine. Often called a Picasso in the kitchen, he sets a stylish, sophisticated, and unique tone with both his cuisine and restaurant setting.

ORTANIQUE ON THE MILE ★★★★

		QUALITY
Florida-Caribbean	Expensive	**95**

	VALUE
278 Miracle Mile (next to the Actor's Playhouse),	**C**
Coral Gables; (305) 446-7710	

Reservations: Accepted	European, and New World wines;
When to go: Early	unusual finds and values; $30–400
Entree range: $14–33	bottles, $7–10 by the glass
Payment: VISA, MC, AMEX	Dress: Casual
Parking: Valet	Disabled access: Good
Bar: Full service	Customers: Young residents, profession-
Wine selection: Well-selected American,	als, tourists

Lunch: Monday–Friday, 11:30 a.m.–2:30 pm

Dinner: Monday–Saturday, 6 p.m.–11 p.m.; Sunday, 5:30–9:30 p.m.

Menu recommendations: Tropical mango and fresh hearts of palm salad; assorted Caribbean ceviches: Caicos Island conch ceviche; Ceviche del mar, button mushroom ceviche; jerk tuna tataki with mango papaya relish; roasted cumin and coriander encrusted mahi mahi on spicy tomato eggplant; pan seared Bahamian black grouper marinated in teriyaki with Ortanique orange liqueur and Bacardi limon sauce; filet mignon au poivre with shiitake mushrooms, port wine sauce and chef's mashed potatoes.

Comments: Named as one of the "Best New Restaurants" by *Esquire* magazine in 1999, Chef Cindy Hutson and Ortanique have only received the highest accolades from food critics and the public.

PACIFIC TIME		★★★★

Pacific Rim	Moderate/Expensive	QUALITY 92
915 Lincoln Road, Miami Beach (305) 534-5979		VALUE C

Reservations: Accepted; recommended on weekends
When to go: Early
Entree range: $19.50–34
Payment: VISA, AMEX, MC, DC
Parking: Adjoining lot
Bar: Full service

Wine selection: Outstanding California wines; great by the glass choices; $28-plus bottles, $7–15 by the glass
Dress: Casual
Disabled access: Good
Customers: Locals, tourists, internationals

Dinner: Sunday–Thursday, 6–11 p.m.; Friday and Saturday, 6 p.m.–midnight

Menu recommendations: Grilled giant squid with local Asian greens and hot-and-sour vinaigrette; pan-seared Hudson Valley foie gras with California port, red, and plum wines over organic; wok-sautéed local yellowfin tuna with sushi bar flavors, roasted sesame rice, avocado, and fresh Malpeque oyster sauce; whole ginger-stuffed Florida yellowtail snapper tempura with steamed ribbon vegetables and sizzling fish dipping sauce; shiitake-grilled certified Angus beef with Indochine spices, shiitake mushrooms, bok choy, sugar snaps, sweet saké, and baked Idaho fingerling potatoes.

Comments: Owner Jonathan Eismann came to this pleasant, pastel-toned setting by way of Manhattan's China Grill. He combines his Oriental skills with the tastes of the Caribbean with fascinating results and artistic presentations.

PASCAL'S ON PONCE ★★★★

French	Moderate/Expensive	QUALITY
		96
2611 Ponce de Leon Boulevard, Coral Gables		VALUE
(305) 444-2024		**B**

Reservations: Highly recommended
When to go: Early
Entree range: $16.95–25.95
Payment: VISA, MC, AMEX
Parking: Valet and self parking
Bar: Beer and wine

Wine selection: Small but carefully selected with top, affordable buys; $25–192 bottles, $6.50–11.50 by the glass
Dress: Casual/dressy
Disabled access: Yes
Customers: Locals, tourists

Lunch: Monday–Friday, 11:30 a.m.–2:30 pm

Dinner: Monday–Thursday, 6–10:30 p.m.; Friday and Saturday, 6–11 p.m.

Menu recommendations: Lobster bisque with quenelles flavored with brandy; pan-seared lump crab cake with roasted pepper butter; braised baby artichoke heart "Barigoule"; sautéed yellow fin tuna tournedos, pommes puree, and green peppercorn sauce; tenderloin sautéed with snails, wild mushrooms, and garlic with bordelaise sauce; mustard crusted rack of lamb, potato boulangere, and stuffed Mediterranean vegetables; court-bouillon steamed Atlantic salmon, blanquette of shrimp, and scallops with saurelle cream.

Comments: 1995 *Food & Wine Magazine's* one of the best new chefs in the country and hailed by *Esquire Magazine* as one of the "Best New Restaurants in America 2000," Pascal and his wife Ann-Louise have a solid success in their 50-seat, one-year-old restaurant. After many years of working for others, Pascal is now cooking the most simple and impeccable French cuisine in Miami at his very own place.

RED SQUARE ★★★★

Progressive American	Expensive	QUALITY
		92
411 Washington Avenue, Miami Beach		VALUE
(305) 672-0200		**B**

Reservations: Accepted
When to go: Early
Entree range: $20–35
Payment: VISA, MC, AMEX
Parking: Valet
Bar: Full service

Wine selection: Adequate; $35–180 bottles, $7–10 by the glass
Dress: Casual/dressy
Disabled access: Yes
Customers: Locals, tourists

Dinner: Tuesday–Thursday, 7 p.m.–midnight.; Friday and Saturday, 7 p.m.–2 a.m.

Menu recommendations: Smothered Blinis with beurre blanc and American caviar; crab & corn cakes with Beluga lentil salsa; warm foie gras salad; chilled seafood martini; Siberian nachos; rack of lamb with goat cheese potato piroshkies; herb-roasted Bell & Evans chicken with smoked mozzarella polenta cake; filet mignon with Roquefort butter, Maine lobster and black truffle fettuccine.

Comments: Another one of China Grill Management's highly sophisticated but comfortable concepts, Red Square is intimate, plush, and very red. Known for its bar and lounge atmosphere, Red Square serves some of the best food in town. Still a secret for some, those who have discovered the passionate culinary soul of chef Barbara Scott come back weekend after weekend.

SMITH & WOLLENSKY ★★★½

		QUALITY
Steakhouse	Expensive	**90**

	VALUE
1 Washington Avenue in South Pointe Park, Miami Beach; (305) 673-2800	**C**

Reservations: Accepted
When to go: Early
Entree range: $25–45
Payment: VISA, MC, AMEX
Parking: Valet
Bar: Full service
Wine selection: One of the best and most user-friendly wine lists in town; rare vintages; $24–1,300 bottles, $9–15 by the glass
Dress: Casual
Disabled access: Yes
Customers: Professionals, locals, tourists

Open: Monday–Saturday, noon–2 a.m.; Sunday, noon–11:30 p.m.

Menu recommendations: Lobster cocktail; Salmon Pastrami; Crackling pork shank with firecracker apple sauce; angry lobster; filet mignon; sirloin steak; prime rib; lamb chops, mustard-crusted tuna; veal NY/Milan; veal chops; creamed spinach; hash browns.

Comments: Named "the quintessential New York steakhouse" by *Gourmet* magazine, almost every table has a view of the water, and the restaurant's temperature-controlled aging room assure Miami diners the same quality of prime beef aging that made the New York restaurant known all over the world.

TUSCAN STEAK ★★★½

Italian Steakhouse Expensive	QUALITY
	92

433 Washington Avenue, Miami Beach	VALUE
(305) 534-2233	B

Reservations: Accepted
When to go: Early
Entree range: $40–60
Payment: VISA, MC, AMEX
Parking: Valet
Bar: Full service
Wine selection: Upscale yet affordable

Italians concentrating on Super Tuscans;
$30–500 bottles, 7.50–12.50 by the
glass
Dress: Casual
Disabled access: Good
Customers: Young residents, professionals,
tourists

Dinner: Sunday–Thursday, 6 p.m.–midnight; Friday and Saturday, 6 p.m.–1 a.m.

Menu recommendations: White truffle garlic bread; assorted antipasto from the antipasto bar; gnocchi gorgonzola; three-mushroom risotto with Alba white truffle oil; filet mignon gorgonzola with Barolo sauce; Tuscan Steak's famous Florentine T-bone steak with roasted garlic puree; whole grilled Tuscan-style country chicken with sage; grilled whole yellowtail snapper with braised garlic, thyme, and lime essence; amaretto-infused mashed sweet potatoes

Comments: This new endeavor from the China Grill Management Group has become one of Miami Beach's best concepts to export to New York and London. The sophisticated interiors in warm, dark wood tones set the stage for this family-style Florentine grill that serves large portions of Tuscan cuisine with Florida accents.

1220 AT THE TIDES ★★★½

Progressive American Expensive	QUALITY
	90

1220 Ocean Drive, Miami Beach	VALUE
(305) 604-5000	C

Reservations: Accepted
When to go: Early
Entree range: $25–33
Payment: VISA, MC, AMEX
Parking: Valet
Bar: Full service
Wine selection: Outstanding values on

French and California wines; $22–200
bottles, $7.50–12 by the glass
Dress: Casual
Disabled access: Good
Customers: Young residents, professionals,
tourists

Dinner: Sunday–Thursday, 7–10:30 p.m.; Friday and Saturday, 7–11 p.m.

Menu recommendations: Island princess conch tempura, fennel citrus salad, ginger vinaigrette; blue prawn risotto, black trumpet mushrooms, curry essence; spinach gnocchi, Texas gulf crab, asparagus, grana parmesan cream; spa lobster tail, green beans, vanilla corn vinaigrette; pink snapper with lavender-basil risotto, roasted beet coulis, citrus essence; butter-poached Maine lobster, carrot-saffron vanilla broth; citrus glazed sea bass, plantain mash, banana ketchup.

Comments: Located inside the tallest and most elegant Art Deco hotel to grace Ocean Drive is the understated but casually luxurious 1220 at The Tides. New executive chef Roger Ruch portrays his eclectic culinary style that includes classical French, Southeast Asian, Pacific Rim, and American cuisine, focusing on clean, clear flavors and appearances.

Entertainment and Nightlife

Miami is a city that never sleeps, even when the sun comes up. Whether it's because the residents and visitors of this dynamic city are easily bored or easily amused is a toss-up. The fact is, Miami's social side is like a multifaceted theme park, full of wondrous amusements for all ages that bring out the child in everyone.

There are enough worthwhile diversions in Miami to literally keep people busy around the clock, which could explain the city's extreme fondness for *colada,* the Cuban espresso coffee so eye-opening it is doled out in thimble-size cups. There are parties, then after-parties, and then after-hour parties, which start at the hour most good suburbanites are already in the carpool lane.

Miami is one of those spicy, late-night towns where the diversity of expression is reflected in the ethnic eclecticism of its community. The melting pot image is not quite right for Miami. It is more like a human paella.

There are supper clubs, coffeehouses, dance companies, symphonies, drag shows, discos, strip joints, comedy clubs, concert halls, jazz boites, gay clubs, gallery walks, and rock pubs to suit every taste, and then some. It's only a matter of finding the time. Miami nightlife can be divided into three basic categories: theater and other cultural pursuits; live jazz, Latin, R&B, or rock music; and the restaurant-cum-disco scene. Noteworthy establishments are described in the following pages. After that, we list individual club profiles of the best places Miami has to offer. For those venues with live music, we advise calling ahead for scheduling information and reservations.

Nightly, weekly, and monthly schedules of live music clubs, theatrical productions, and special events are printed in the *Miami Herald's* Weekend section on Friday as well as community newspapers, including *Entertainment News & Views, New Times,* and *The Sunpost,* and free local hip sheets such as *Street, Wire,* and *Ego Trip.*

THEATER AND OTHER CULTURAL PURSUITS

The performing arts world in Miami boasts a broad array of offerings, from legitimate local theater to national touring companies. Tickets tend to be reasonably priced for evenings and events, and the venues run the gamut from offbeat playhouses to grander locales, such as the renovated **Jackie Gleason Theater** (1700 Washington Avenue, Miami Beach; (305) 673-7300), the site of touring Broadway productions and national ballet companies. Miamians take full advantage of the cultural possibilities, so make every effort to investigate ticket availability early.

Quality theater abounds. The **Coconut Grove Playhouse** (3500 Main Highway, Coconut Grove; (305) 442-4000) is a popular venue for national tours, such as "Death of a Salesman," starring Hal Holbrook. You'll find more intimate theater in the Playhouse's Encore Room, (305) 442-4000. For local talent and productions with an edge, **New Theater** (65 Almeria Avenue, Coral Gables; (305) 443-5909) offers first-class production values with a sense of the avant garde, under the direction of Rafael de Acha.

Classical music spills out from a number of renowned concert halls and associations. The highly acclaimed **New World Symphony** (541 Lincoln Road, Miami Beach; ticket office: (305) 673-3331) is the country's largest training orchestra and offers a wide range of concerts, including a Sunday afternoon series. The **Concert Association of Florida (CAF)** (offices at 555 17th Street, Miami Beach; (305) 532-3491) has been Miami's foremost presenter of symphonies, ballets, and opera divas for the past 35 years. CAF concerts are held at various venues throughout Miami.

The dance divine can be caught at the **Miami City Ballet** (performances at the Jackie Gleason Theater, 1700 Washington Avenue, Miami Beach; call (305) 532-4880 for tickets) under the inspired artistic direction of Edward Villella. For fluid moves, try the **Momentum Dance Company** at La Salle High School (3601 South Miami Avenue, Coconut Grove; (305) 858-7002).

For a more modern approach to the performing arts, **Miami Light Project** (at various venues; call (305) 576-4350) imports the freshest talents in the worlds of dance, music, and theater.

Once a year, for ten days in February, the Miami Film Society presents the **Miami International Film Festival.** An internationally acclaimed event that showcases brilliant filmmaking from around the world, the festival has featured many avant-garde directors, including new-wave Spanish filmmaker Pedro Almodovar, who was introduced to American audiences at the festival in 1984 with his film *Dark Habits*. **The Miami Beach Film Society** (presentations at various venues on Miami Beach; call the hotline at (305) 673-4567) feeds South Beach's hunger for the unusual with special cinema-themed events The propaganda arts–themed **Wolfsonian Museum** (1001 Washington Avenue, Miami Beach; call (305) 531-1001) features exhibitions and screenings of movie classics such as Fritz Lang's *Metropolis*.

LIVE ENTERTAINMENT: CAFÉ CLUBS AND CONCERT CLUBS

Miami offers not only the unusual small concert clubs, but also the café-cum-club, and these are some of the best nightlife bets in the area. Restaurants that feature live performances of salsa, jazz, and just about everything else run rampant. Impromptu dancing on tabletops is not uncommon. Local, regional, and less mainstream national talent can be found every night, all over Dade county. Miami being Miami, the Latin music is unbeatable, and the Latin jazz is among the best in the world. **Yuca** (501 Lincoln Road, Miami Beach; (305) 532-9822), a restaurant whose name is not only a popular root vegetable used in Cuban cuisine but also an acronym for its clientele (Young Urban Cuban Americans), serves up Latin vocalists in its upstairs concert space.

In the café club category, **Monty's Raw Bar** (2550 South Bayshore Drive, Coconut Grove; (305) 856-3992) is an oasis of fun with calypso and reggae throughout the week and weekends, right on the waterfront. **John Martin's** (253 Miracle Mile, Coral Gables; (305) 445-3777) features fantastic and hard-to-find Irish music on Saturdays and Sundays. The intimate upstairs space at the **Van Dyke Café** (846 Lincoln Road, Miami Beach; (305) 534-3600) offers live jazz nightly in a candlelit setting. **Satchmo Blues Bar & Grill** (60 Merrick Way, Coral Gables; (305) 774-1883) is a music lover's venue that varies its live jazz line-up weekly. **Café Iguana** (8505 Mills Drive, Miami; (305) 274-4948) sheds its modern disco duds on Sundays with a wild Western Night, featuring food, music, and costume contests with a country flair; line dance lessons start at 6 p.m. **Taurus** (3540 Main Highway, Coconut Grove; (305) 443-5553), in the heart of Coconut Grove, showcases blues talent and more in its terraced locale, Tuesday through Saturday. Also in the Grove is the **Improv Comedy Club and Cafe** (3390 Mary Street, Coconut Grove; (305) 441-8200), where you can catch stand-up acts every night of the week while enjoying a drink or dinner. On weekends, the tropically appointed **Cardozo Cafe**— within the Cardozo Hotel, which is owned by Gloria and Emilio Estefan—turns into a disco until 2 or 3 in the morning (1300 Ocean Drive, Miami Beach; (305) 695-2822). **Globe Café & Bar** (377 Alhambra Circle, Coral Gables; (305) 445-3555) features live jazz on Thursdays and is home to a very popular happy hour on Fridays. A trendy alternative is **Power Studios** (3701 NE Second Avenue, Miami; (305) 576-1336), a multimedia art, entertainment, and dining complex.

In South Beach, check out **Mango's Tropical Cafe** (900 Ocean Drive; (305) 673-4422), **Clevelander Hotel** (1020 Ocean Drive; (305) 531-3485), and **I Paparazzi** (940 Ocean Drive; (305) 531-3500). At the exotic restaurant-lounge **Tantra** (1445 Pennsylvania Avenue, Miami Beach; (305) 672-4765), diners can have a taste of fabulosity with their meal (the place is swarming with models, trendies, and movie stars on any given night); of special note is the Sod Lounge with the tented banquettes and fresh grass floor. In a similar vein, **Touch** (910 Lincoln Road; (305) 532-8003) serves up glamour and belly dancing with its $34 entrees. At the "it" spot **Pearl** (at Penrod's Beach Club, One Ocean Drive; (305) 673-1575), the modern orange-and-white interior and round champagne bar are a suitable backdrop for the restaurant-lounge's fashion-y crowd.

Concert clubs in Miami feature an eclectic and diverse line-up. **Tobacco Road** (626 South Miami Avenue, Miami; (305) 374-1198) is undeniably lively, and even holds the title of being Miami's oldest club. The nightly live music ranges from Latin jazz to rock and R&B. Hardcore rock fans will appreciate **Churchill's Hideway** (5501 NE 2nd Avenue, Miami; (305) 757-1807), an English-themed rock 'n' roll pub showcasing local bands and serving traditional pub grub. For live jazz and R&B in a dimly lit boite, check out **Jazid** (1342 Washington Avenue; (305) 673-9372), which offers cabaret acts downstairs and billiards upstairs. For live Latin music with dancing, **Café Nostalgia** (432 41st Street, Miami Beach; (305) 604-9895)—located next door to the esteemed Forge restaurant—is a must-go.

THE NIGHTCLUB CONNECTION

Now that Miami (and particularly South Beach) is one of the nightclub capitals of the world, celebrities mingle with models and the uncommonly beautiful dance with boys-and-girls-next-door. Club life is always volatile, so keep your ears open for news on the hot clubs du soire. The scene shifts and regroups constantly. Our advice is ask your servers at dinner what they recommend that evening. Miami's wait staff—many of whom are models and actors, at least on South Beach—is extremely well informed on life in the demimonde. Whenever possible, call ahead for information on theme nights and specials.

Most of the action, of course, is on South Beach. Fortunately, most clubs are concentrated along Washington Avenue, South Beach's main commercial artery. While there are very few clubs per se on famed Ocean Drive or the seven-block, shopping-cum-dining stretch of Lincoln Road, there are numerous restaurants with sidewalk seating that feature a jazz or blues vocalist. A sprightly walk along the oceanfront strip reading the menus and sidewalk marquees will give you all the info you need. The nightclub circuit is unpredictable at best, with new developers taking over spaces at a moment's notice, so there's a good chance that your favorite dance club last year is now a parking lot, or will be soon. Since most of the area nightclubs don't get going until at least 11 p.m., an afternoon nap (or, as locals call it, a disco coma) is advised. Once refreshed, venture out to one of the many options. **320** (320 Lincoln Road, Miami Beach; (305) 672-2882), a two-story dance club with a 1970s-meets-millennium aesthetic, is a favorite late-night choice for local trendoids. **Bash** (655 Washington Avenue, Miami Beach; (305) 538-2274) is a dance club that attracts celebs and trendies; reggae is played in the outdoor garden bar. **Crobar** (1445 Washington Avenue, Miami Beach; (305) 531-5027) caters to the trendier-than-thou crowd, offering a complexly designed, industrial dance club that features a myriad of bars, VIP rooms, and balcony seating areas that overlook the strobe-lit dance floor. **Level** (1235 Washington Avenue, Miami Beach; (305) 532-1525) is a three-floor dance club of mammoth proportion that features international DJs and live shows. **The Living Room at the Strand** (671 Washington Avenue, Miami Beach; (305) 532 2340) is a Euro-flavored, upscale lounge—plenty of models and celebs, with the *de rigueur* attitude from the doormen who guard the velvet ropes. **Shadow Lounge** (1532 Washington Avenue, Miami Beach; (305) 531-9411) is South Beach's only big club without the big-club attitude; two levels provide plenty of niches for roaming. The lounge **Goddess** (681 Washington Avenue; Miami Beach; (305) 531-2717)—owned by the Tantra restaurant guys—is a bastion of chic, adorned with kamasutra art. When it's so late you don't think you can stay awake another second, the crowd is just sauntering in at **Club Space** (142 NE 11th Street, Miami; (305) 375-0001), downtown Miami's hot after-hours club.

For salsa, the unanimous choice is **Starfish** (1427 West Avenue, Miami Beach; (305) 673-1717), where the dance floor is packed every weekend from 9 p.m. with sultry young people moving to the Latino groove; if you're salsa-impaired, the club gives lessons on Mondays and Wednesdays at 7 and 8 p.m. for $8 an hour, and features gay salsa night on Tuesdays.

In Coconut Grove, you'll find **Bar 609** (3342 Virginia Street, Coconut Grove; (305) 444-6096), booming with Top 40 music and a mix of locals, University of Miami students, and visitors.

On a less wholesome note, there are the clubs where the charm is measured by how much skin is showing. Most of these clubs are concentrated on Biscayne Boulevard, just north of 163rd Street. **Madonna** (1527 Washington Avenue, Miami Beach; (305) 534-2000) is slick and stocked with lovely ladies, including centerfold celebs. **Deja Vu** (2004 Collins Avenue, Miami Beach; (305) 538-5526) offers a most interesting menu—hundreds of beautiful girls and three ugly ones.

THE GAY SCENE

Miami, especially South Beach, has been described as a gay mecca. Its active and involved gay community is evident on many levels. From lawyers to drag divas, the crowds congregate in a variety of bars and clubs. Endless theme offerings at these clubs include boys' nights, women's nights, drag shows, strip shows, and many things you might not have ever heard of. South Beach serves as a central spot for much of Miami's gay society. An always-happening boite is **Twist** (1057 Washington Avenue, Miami Beach; (305) 538-9478), whose two floors of bar space make it perfect for late-night gossip and cocktails. **Salvation** (1771 West Avenue, Miami Beach; (305) 673-6508), a large club known for its high-energy Saturday night party, caters to a crowd that considers dancing integral to survival. **Score** (727 Lincoln Road, Miami Beach; (305) 535-1111) is much more casual, even featuring café tables set up along Lincoln Road, which the bar-cum-club fronts. Several of South Beach's big clubs also feature gay nights, including Fridays at Level and Sundays at Crobar. And off the Beach, the action continues at a number of clubs. **Cactus** (2041 Biscayne Boulevard, Miami; (305) 438-0662) is a favorite locals bar where watching a drag show and shooting pool are both options. **Ozone** (6620 SW 57th Avenue; (305) 667-2888) draws devotees from all over Miami with excellent dance music, nightly specials, and a powerful pace.

FOR THE ENTIRE FAMILY

Dave and Buster's in the Dolphin Mall (11481 NW 12th Street, Miami; (305) 468-1555) is Miami's newest family-oriented entertainment complex, with 65,000 square feet of fun, including an American-themed restaurant, virtual reality game room with bar, billiards room featuring 13 world-class billiard tables, and a 30,000-square-foot entertainment room holding every video game imaginable. Parents can enjoy an alcoholic beverage while racing on motorcycle games as the kids challenge each other on the snowboard machines.

The Best of Miami–Area Clubs

Name	Cover	Cost	City
Bars			
Café Nostalgia	$15	Exp	Miami
Mac's Club Deuce	None	Inexp	Miami Beach
Dance Clubs			
Bash	$10–15; Tuesday, none	Mod	Miami Beach

The Best of Miami–Area Clubs			
Name	Cover	Cost	City

Dance Clubs (continued)

Café Nostalgia	$15	Exp	Miami
Crobar	$10–25	Exp	Miami Beach
Jimmy'z	$15 (waived for members)	Exp	Miami Beach

Gay Club

Twist	None	Mod	Miami Beach

Live Music

The Clevelander Bar	None	Mod	Miami Beach
Tobacco Road	Usually $5–6, weekends only	Inexp	Miami

Lounge

The Living Room at the Strand	$20	Exp	Miami Beach

Supper Club

Club Tropigala	Show only, $20; dinner & show, prices vary	Mod	Miami Beach

CLUB PROFILES

BASH

Euro dance club with bohemian streak
Who Goes There: 23–40; well-heeled straight couples, NFL players on vacation, reggae fans, celeb friends of owners Sean Penn and Mick Hucknall

655 Washington Avenue, Miami Beach; (305) 538-BASH

Cover: $10–15; Tuesday, none	Beer: $5
Minimum: None	Food available: None
Mixed drinks: $5–6	Hours: Tuesday–Saturday, 10 p.m.–
Wine: $5	5 a.m.; Sunday, 11 p.m.–5 a.m.

What goes on: Smoky, dark, and sexy, Bash has all the energy of a really good private party. It's not about the decor, because one barely remembers the black velvet banquettes or undulating steel bar (too dark inside) or the sexy cocktail servers (everyone on South Beach looks like a model, anyhow). It might have something to do with the celeb owners who, when in town, have been known to travel in an entourage that includes filmmaker Oliver Stone and actors Dennis Hopper and Johnny Depp—the ultimate PR weapon for a hot club.

Comments: Partner Mick Hucknall of the English rock group Simply Red has described Bash as being "three clubs in one," and rightly so. The main room has a smallish, eternally packed dance floor pumping Euro/house music at unearthly decibels and three VIP lounges. The long, narrow bar is separated by structural columns and is demimonde unto itself. In the back, the outdoor patio serves as an island-themed escape valve, where couples with happy feet bounce to reggae, salsa, and the Gipsy Kings. Better wear a designer outfit, unless you care to show the doorman six forms of ID; no running shoes, even if they're by Gaultier; jackets for men are strongly recommended on weekends.

CAFÉ NOSTALGIA

Miami version of a Cuban nightclub of yore
Who Goes There: 25–45; an international and artistic Latin crowd

432 41st Street, Miami; (305) 538-8533

Cover: $15, which gets you into both Café Nostalgia and The Courtyard	**Mixed drinks:** $7–9
Minimum: None unless you are sitting at one of the cocktail tables during cabaret hours, when there is a 2 drink minimum per person	**Wine:** $7 and up; bottle service available
	Beer: $4.50–5.50
	Food available: All-night tapas menu
	Hours: Wednesday–Saturday, 9 p.m.–5 a.m.; call for events schedule

What goes on: Many will reminisce about the heyday of Havana, even those born after the fall of Cuba. In Miami, it's all luscious legend and remembrance of things past, and Café Nostalgia is appropriately named. People come for comfort, entertainment, or to dance madly to live Afro-Cuban bands that take the stage at 10:30 p.m. If you can't manage to fudge some odd version of salsa or merengue, just wiggle in your seat and smile a lot. Every night, Latin bands play several sets interspersed with a DJ to keep people dancing. Most individuals sit at cocktail tables or crowd around one of the two bars, if they aren't on the dance floor salsaing to the music. The newest addition to the club is The Courtyard, an outdoor bar and dance area in between The Forge and Café Nostalgia, featuring a DJ spinning the latest in dance and international music.

Comments: All nightclubs once looked like this—tiny tables, dark corners, intimate lighting, and an inviting bar. Cuban songsters from the 1950s are featured in original campy videos on an overhead screen. Spanish is by far the language of choice among patrons and staff, but feel free to order your drinks in English. There is an extensive list of wines and liquors by the bottle. Café Nostalgia is a mix of modern and elegant cabaret decor, with Cuban artwork adorning the walls. Outside in The Courtyard, classic Colonial Cuban decor meets Morocco color schemes. Dress is casual chic: *Miami Vice* meets the 1990s for the men with dark jackets, jeans, and cellular phones; tight things with a touch of glitter for the girls' cocktail dresses.

THE CLEVELANDER BAR

Oceanfront hotel bar, gym, and outdoor nightspot
Who Goes There: 21–45; restless youth, locals, European tourists, Causeway crawlers, bikini babes

1020 Ocean Drive, Miami Beach; (305) 531-3485

Cover: None	Food available: Full menu until 3 a.m.,
Minimum: None	from burgers to surf 'n' turf; live lob-
Mixed drinks: $4–5	ster tank
Wine: $4–5.75	Hours: Bars: daily, 11 a.m.–5 a.m.
Beer: $3.50–4.50	

What goes on: The 1990s version of Beach Blanket Bingo, with scantily clad babes and bronzed hunks parading around the pool/bar of this popular oceanfront hotel. Live bands nightly and omnipresent DJs keep the rambunctious spirit going. Needless to say, this is prime cruising territory.

Comments: Smack on trendy Ocean Drive, this outdoor bar is studded with palm trees and cartoonish, Jetsonian obelisks. Ten TVs inside and out ensure you'll never miss a music video or major sporting event, not that you won't get distracted by the onslaught of physical beauty on display. The glass-enclosed gym, appropriately suspended above the stage and dance floor, stays open till 11 p.m. Less active types can always shoot a game of pool on one of the four tables located inside and out. You'll see all forms of beachwear, from bikinis with sarongs to shorts and sandals; on a breezy night, Levis; this is one place where less is more. Weekday happy hour, 5–7 p.m., with two-for-one drinks.

CLUB TROPIGALA

1950s Havana-inspired supper club and salsa parlor
Who Goes There: 21–60; Latins who know how to dance, stylemongers, tourists, condo groups, locals with a sense of adventure

4441 Collins Avenue (Fontainebleau Hilton Resort and Spa),
Miami Beach; (305) 538-2000

Cover: Show only, $20; dinner and show, prices vary

Minimum: None

Mixed drinks: $5.25−9

Wine: $4.75−7

Beer: $3−6

Food available: Full menu; continental standards

Hours: Showtimes: Wednesday, Thursday, and Sunday, 8:30 p.m.; Friday and Saturday, 8 and 10 p.m.; dancing until the wee hours

What goes on: This world-renowned supper club draws an eclectic crowd of all ages and looks, from discerning trendies who think it's the ultimate in camp, to older Latin couples who've made it their Saturday night tradition for years. Thirty performers and special acts, plus a 10-piece orchestra for dancing.

Comments: It's right out of the Jungle Book, with extravagant tropical murals, palm fronds, bamboo, waterfalls, and color-enhanced dancing fountains. The truly huge room is successfully tiered for greater intimacy. What's really amazing is that every seat is filled. Men should wear jackets, while ladies' dress is semiformal.

CROBAR

Trendier-than-thou dance club for the hipnoise

Who Goes There: Celebrities, models, locals, and beautiful people with plenty of lunch money; on Sunday's gay night, shirtless go-go boys and bewigged gender illusionists jockey for space on the dance floor

1445 Washington Avenue, Miami Beach; (305) 531-5027

Cover: $10−25, depending on the night

Minimum: None, except at tables where there is a two-bottle minimum

Mixed drinks: $8−9

Food available: None

Hours: Thursday–Monday, 10 p.m.–5 a.m.

What goes on: The scene doesn't get much trendier in South Beach, especially on weekends. On Mondays, the locals party Back Door Bamby is full tilt till the wee hours. Expect to wait in line, as this branch of the award-winning Chicago club is the perennial favorite of visiting celebrities and local hipsters. Guest DJs from around the country can often be found spinning the latest house music.

Comments: Industrial-chic architects have transformed the historic Art Deco Cameo Theater into a complex, voyeuristic space with a futuristic feel. There is plenty of tucked-away seating within its two levels so that you'll never feel spied upon, plus a large strobe-lit dance floor and requisite VIP room.

JIMMY'Z

Euro disco/trance, disco, Top 40
Who Goes There: 21–50; Fellini-esque mix of models, Euroboys in crested blazers, celebs, upscale barflies, young women with bionic décolleté

432 41st Street, Miami Beach; (305) 604-9798

Cover: $15 (waived for members)
Minimum: None
Mixed drinks: $8–10
Wine: $7.50
Beer: $6

Food available: Memorable gourmet cuisine in a private dining room
Hours: Tuesday–Saturday, 10 p.m.–5 a.m.

What goes on: Regine Choukroun, the legendary Queen of the Night, is the impresario of the club, which caters to the junior jetset. There are theme nights galore, from Tuesday jazz nights with combos and full Latin bands to whimsical soirees named for exotic destinations the average Joe will never get to but the privileged know first-hand. Wednesday is alarmingly popular, with a loyal contingent for the weekly disco night, as well as spill-over from the adjoining luxury restaurant, the Forge.

Comments: Sophisticated yet full of character—like Regine herself—Jimmy'z doesn't lack for color. There are red walls, gilt-edged mirrors, a chandelier as large as a Subaru in the Champagne Jazz Room, a bed done up in rich jewel tones by one of the bars, and an extravagant walk-in humidor that houses the VIP stogies of celebs. Concerning attire, the wilder the better for this crowd.

THE LIVING ROOM AT THE STRAND

Euro-flavored lounge with dancing, dining, and (much) posing
Who Goes There: Sprite models with deeply tanned playboys; urban sophisticates from 20 to 40; visiting celebs and rock stars after their Miami concert gigs

671 Washington Avenue, Miami Beach; (305) 532-2340

Cover: $20
Minimum: None
Mixed drinks: $6 and up
Wine: $6 and up; bottle service available

Beer: $4 and up
Food available: None
Hours: Thursday–Sunday, 10 p.m.–4 a.m.

What goes on: Dancing, necking, and champagne-consumption among beautiful, attitudinal, and somewhat reckless types who care not what tomorrow brings. The young are gorgeous and know it, the aged are beautiful and paid for it, so everyone's basically happy, if rather clannish, preferring that you keep to your side of the double banquette, thank you very much.

Comments: As its name implies, the spacious club is plush and overstuffed, with cozy velvet couches. The catch, though, is that you have to buy a bottle (vodka or champagne are typical) in order to qualify to sit in one, and it doesn't come cheap, starting at $80. The lighting is mercifully dim, which, with the rampant hedonism in this crowd, could be a very good thing. Wearing Gucci, Prada, or Chanel will cut down the risk of your having to wait in line, an unfortunate (and unfortunately very common) occurrence here. And don't even think of wearing non-designer denim unless you happen to be very good-looking or very famous.

MAC'S CLUB DEUCE

Oldest, least pretentious locals bar on South Beach
Who Goes There: Hip and not-so-hip locals, pool junkies, barflies, tattooed bikers, drag queens, film crews, unfazed normal folk, New Yorkers

222 14th Street, Miami Beach; (305) 673-9537

Cover: None	Food available: Miniature pizzas, pickled
Minimum: None	eggs
Mixed drinks: $2.50–4.50	Hours: Daily, 8 a.m.–5 a.m.—365 days
Wine: $3	a year
Beer: $2.50–3.25	

What goes on: A neo–Fellini-esque documentary waiting to happen. Since 1926, the constant stream of nightcrawlers taking their place at the wraparound bar has served as the main attraction. The best training a novice barfly could get.

Comments: Wouldn't win any design awards, but then, it's not that kind of place. Assorted neon beer signs dot the walls; a worn pool table sits off to a corner. A decently stocked juke box and cigarette machine get lots of use. The big-screen TV is the only trace of modernism. Smoky and dim, but not so dark that you can't see the elements around you, which is a good thing. Dress is inexplicably casual, although we once saw a woman wearing a pink taffeta pea coat.

TOBACCO ROAD

Noted Miami institution, neighborhood bar featuring live music/concert venue/home of annual blues festival
Who Goes There: 21–45; hep cats, rockers, bikers, modern bohemians

626 South Miami Avenue, Miami; (305) 374-1198

Cover: Usually $5–6, weekends only	Food available: Lunch and dinner in the
Minimum: None	American vein: steaks, burgers, chicken
Mixed drinks: $3.25–3.75	wings, and nachos, plus daily specials
Wine: $3.25	Hours: Daily, 11:30 a.m.–5 a.m.;
Beer: $2.75–3.25	kitchen is open until 2 a.m.

What goes on: A Miami hot spot since 1912, this New Orleans–type bar is the city's oldest, and holds Miami's first liquor license. Perennially popular with locals, Tobacco Road was among the first to showcase local and national blues acts. The theme nights are among the best: Monday night is blues jam; Wednesday, live jazz. Once a year, in October, the bar sponsors a Blues Fest, showcasing 20 bands in the rear parking area.

Comments: Charmingly quaint, the wooden frame structure has the feel of a roadhouse. There are two stories, each with a stage. Often, both stages are in use simultaneously. Outside, the wooden deck patio is shaded by a huge oak tree; thatched tiki-style huts and colored patio lights complete the bohemian picture. Rags range from tuxedoes to Harley gear—anything goes. Weekday happy hour is 5–8 p.m. with $1–2 appetizer plates.

TWIST

Party palace just for the boys
Who Goes There: 21–45; the young, tan, and built—your basic gay Greek gods

1057 Washington Avenue, Miami Beach; (305) 538-9478

Cover: None	Beer: $4 and up
Minimum: None	Food available: None
Mixed drinks: $4 and up	Hours: Daily, 1 p.m.–5 a.m.
Wine: $5 and up	

What goes on: Twist yourself into a quiet corner or contort yourself on the dance floor. Twist offers a number of very different atmospheres to suit your mood. Very popular with locals, this relatively long-standing gay bar/club satisfies a wide variety of tastes. Depending on the area you select, it can be a place for a romantic drink on a first date or a spot to let loose to throbbing music on the packed dance floor. And, of course, this being Florida, there's an outdoor deck bar that makes you realize Key West is only several hours away. Essentially, all kinds of people go for all kinds of reasons.

Comments: There's chrome and leather and some strong wall colorations—but, frankly you won't remember much about the decor because it will be packed to the gills. You'll probably have too much fun, too. Nonetheless, don't end your experience at the first-level bar, which is where the chatty locals hang out with flippant (but cute) bartenders and overhead videos. Venture up the staircase, and you can scam drinks, play pool, or dance before heading outside to the terrace. Attire is South Beach casual—jeans, T-shirts (frequently removed), or more exotic apparel announcing availability such as a scrap of leather.

Part Six

The Florida Keys

Introduction

Say the words "Florida Keys," and most folks think of black-and-white images of Humphrey Bogart in *Key Largo* weathering a hurricane in an old clapboard house with a nasty Edward G. Robinson. Or maybe they picture a robust Ernest Hemingway imbibing at Sloppy Joe's and penning yet another masterpiece in his study. Others flash on ex-hippies and artists reliving the late 1960s in laid-back Key West.

Alas, most of these romantic images come from a never-ending flow of fiction, film, and public-relations hype. Today's reality is that the Keys are a tourist, diving, and sportfishing mecca that draws over a million visitors each year. It's been more than a decade, locals say, since the Keys' earthy, rum-soaked sleaziness was largely pushed aside by restoration, revitalization, and the good intentions of the tourist industry.

THE END OF THE ROAD

But dig a little deeper into the Keys' mystique and you'll find a hard-to-ignore fact: this is, after all, the end of the road—literally. US 1 stretches for more than 100 miles beyond the tip of mainland South Florida, linking a string of islands that form a natural barrier between the Atlantic Ocean and the Gulf of Mexico that ends up closer to Cuba than to the U.S. mainland.

While the PR copy overstates the romance, intrigue, and hipness to be found in the Keys, there are remnants of an end-of-the-road feel—in Key West, anyway. Here you'll find a sense of escape into the exotic, a feeling that your next step might be the jungles of South America, or the equally exotic world of different attitudes, some of which might not be happily tolerated on the mainland. While the Keys are increasingly touristy and

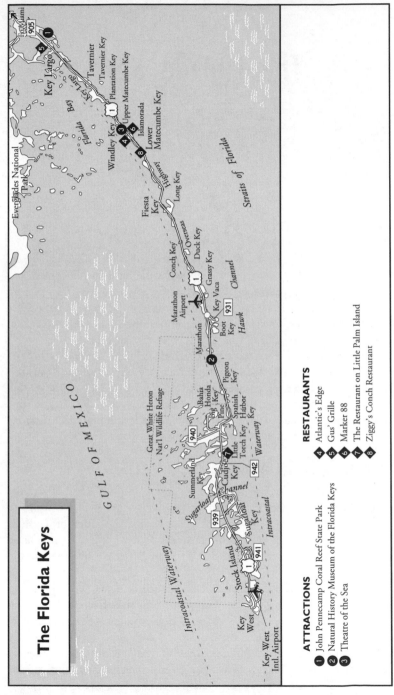

The Florida Keys

ATTRACTIONS

1. John Pennecamp Coral Reef State Park
2. Natural History Museum of the Florida Keys
3. Theatre of the Sea

RESTAURANTS

4. Atlantic's Edge
5. Gus' Grille
6. Marker 88
7. The Restaurant on Little Palm Island
8. Ziggy's Conch Restaurant

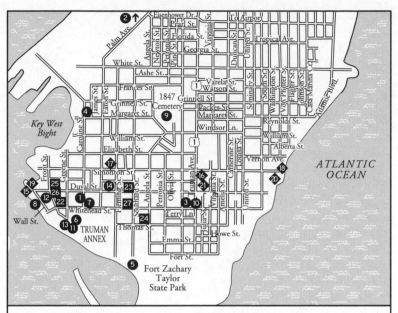

Key West

ATTRACTIONS

1. Audubon House & Tropical Gardens
2. East Martello Museum
3. Ernest Hemingway Home & Museum
4. Flagler Station Over-Sea
   Railway Historeum
5. Fort Zachary Taylor State Historic Site
6. Harry S Truman Little White
   House Museum
7. Jessie Porter's Heritage House and
   Robert Frost Cottage
8. Key West Aquarium
9. Key West Cemetery
10. Key West Lighthouse Museum
11. The Key West Museum of Art
    and History
12. Key West's Shipwreck Historeum
13. Mel Fisher's Treasure Exhibit
14. Ripley's Odditorium

RESTAURANTS

15. Bagatelle
16. Café Des Artistes
17. Café Marquesa
18. Louie's Backyard
19. Pier House Restaurant
20. Shula's on the Beach
21. Square One

NIGHTCLUBS

22. Captain Tony's
23. Epoch
24. Green Parrot Bar
25. Rick's/Durty Harry's
    Entertainment Complex
26. Sloppy Joe's Bar
27. Wax

overdeveloped, they still afford a comfortable abode for misfits and dropouts, artists and writers, gays and lesbians, and anyone else not in lockstep with the conventional American dream.

A GEOGRAPHIC OVERVIEW

Physically, the Florida Keys are a 150-mile chain of islands made of fossilized coral rock. In the 18th and 19th centuries, pirates buried treasure here, fortunes were made scavenging sea wrecks on the reef, and smugglers and slave traders plied their trades, finding cover in the lush, dark hardwood hammocks located on the islands.

A few miles offshore lies the jungle of the sea, the coral reef. Thousands of sea plants and animals thrive in and around the coral reef in water anywhere from 10 to 60 feet deep. The cracks and holes in the reef provide protection or homes for all types of marine animals. The variety of life on display makes for a moving kaleidoscope of colors and shapes—and a wonderland for divers and snorkelers. The living, slow-growing reef is very fragile, however, and visitors must be careful not to stand on, sit on, or touch the coral, because it will die. Doing so, by the way, almost always results in a painful scratch.

EARLY HISTORY

Not long after Christopher Columbus set foot in the New World in 1492, Spanish explorers Ponce de Leon and Antonio de Herrera were the first Europeans to sight the Florida Keys, on May 15, 1513. Over the next few centuries, pirates were the only Europeans to visit the string of islands.

Key West was not settled until 1822, and development in the rest of the Keys came even later. Early settlers farmed productive groves of Key limes, tamarind, and breadfruit. In the Lower Keys, pineapple farms flourished, and a large pineapple processing factory supplied canned pineapple to most of the eastern United States.

The real money, however, was in salvaging cargo from ships sunk on nearby reefs. As a result of the efforts of the "wreckers," Key West became the wealthiest U.S. city in the early years of the American republic. Later, sponge fishermen developed a thriving market for the high-quality sponges harvested in the waters off Key West. Later still, cigar makers from Cuba built factories in the city.

DECADES OF BOOM AND BUST

Henry Flagler, the associate of John D. Rockefeller who opened up the east coast of Florida at the end of the 19th century with his railroad, extended his tracks to the Keys in 1905. The Overseas Railroad—also called "Flagler's

Folly"—was an incredible engineering feat for its time. The greatest technical achievement was the Seven Mile Bridge, which links Marathon to the Lower Keys. The railroad reached Key West in 1912 and wealthy visitors took the train to vacation here.

The Depression years were bleak in the Keys, and Key West declared bankruptcy in 1934. More bad luck: While Flagler's bridges took everything Mother Nature threw their way, the Labor Day hurricane of 1935 tore up the railroad; the bridges later were adapted for roadways. In 1938, the Overseas Railroad became the Overseas Highway.

The new road opened up hope for the renewal of tourism, but World War II intervened. During the war, the opening of a submarine base in Key West started an economic revival, as boosted by the development of a commercial shrimp industry. Ernest Hemingway and other notable writers and artists called Key West home—at least some of the year—and enhanced its reputation as a mecca for creative types. The most recent, tourist-fueled economic upswing began in the early 1980s—and, judging by the size of the crowds on Duval Street, it shows no signs of letting up.

Why Go to the Florida Keys?

The Florida Keys are the primary vacation destination for about 1.5 million people who visit South Florida each year. Most, but not all, are outdoorsy people who come to enjoy the islands' unique location between two large bodies of water: the Atlantic Ocean and the Gulf of Mexico. The mingling of these waters results in a fantastic array of marine life—and world-class sportfishing. Some visitors come to dive and snorkel in gin-clear waters and view the only coral reef in the continental United States. Others explore the Keys' unusual and beautiful backcountry that is full of birds and marine life. Finally, Key West is a popular tourist destination that draws over a million visitors each year.

One reason *not* to come to the Keys is to savor miles and miles of gleaming white beaches: There's no naturally occurring sand. It takes waves to make sand, and the offshore reef eliminates the surf action.

DAY-TRIPPING TO THE KEYS

For folks on a visit to Miami who can spare a day or two out of their schedule, the Keys offer a dramatic—and usually appreciated—contrast to the high-octane pace of hot, hot, hot Miami. The Upper Keys aren't much more than an hour's drive away from the city. Most folks who take a day trip to the Keys don't get below the Upper Keys; if you only have a day yet *must* visit Key West, we suggest taking a bus tour. See the section on specialized tours, page 378, for information on commercial tours to Key West.

When to Visit

The tourist season in the Florida Keys roughly mirrors that of Miami and the rest of South Florida. The winter season begins in mid-November and ends around Easter; both Christmas and Easter are periods when hotels, motels, restaurants, and other tourist-dependent facilities are jammed.

While the summer months are off-season, keep in mind that the Keys are a popular destination for many South Florida residents seeking relief from the intense heat and humidity; the Keys are typically 10 degrees cooler than Miami and much breezier. As a result, a lot of native Floridians crowd US 1 on Friday afternoons and evenings during the summer for a weekend escape; most of them return on the following Sunday evening. Out-of-state visitors should try to avoid the weekend traffic crushes.

The summer months are also increasingly popular with foreign visitors, especially those from Asia and Germany. Increasingly, Key West's popularity as a port of destination on minicruises out of Miami and Fort Lauderdale is resulting in many people returning to the town for a summer vacation.

Summer visitors discover that rooms are cheaper and Key West is less crowded. A note to anglers: While migrating tarpon swim past the Keys April through June, don't expect to find a fishing guide who's available; they're booked at least a year in advance—unless you get lucky and there's a cancellation.

Locals say the best months to visit the Keys are September and October: the weather is warm, crowds are nonexistent and lodging is cheaper.

How to Get More Information before Your Trip

For additional information on Key West and the Florida Keys, call (800) FLA-KEYS. If you're planning on visiting Key West, for example, you can get an accommodations guide listing hotels, motels, bed-and-breakfasts, rental properties, and real estate agents. All the information is free.

Arriving

By Plane

While both Key West (at the end of the string of islands) and Marathon (located in the Middle Keys) have small commercial airports, most folks headed to the Keys by air arrive at Miami International Airport, rent a car, and drive to their final destination.

A glance at a map shows why: MIA is located west of Miami near Route 836, a major east-west highway that connects with Florida's Turnpike Homestead Extension. You can literally be in the Upper Keys within an hour after landing at MIA—if you didn't check any baggage and the line at the rental car agency is short. If your final destination is Key West, figure on about a three-hour drive from the airport, or longer if it's a Friday afternoon.

For folks concerned about Miami's reputation for crime against tourists, we have good news: getting to the Keys from MIA takes you *away* from high-crime areas, not through them. At the rental car agency, get explicit driving directions. Most people will take LeJeune Road south to Route 836 west. After you get on Route 836, it's about six miles to Florida's Turnpike. Take it south to Homestead, another 12 miles or so.

CONTINUING TO THE KEYS BY CAR

From the end of Florida's Turnpike at Florida City, **US 1** heads south toward the tip of Florida through stands of tangled mangrove and thick trees; Mile Marker 127, just south of Homestead, counts down to Mile Marker 00 in Key West.

Say good-bye to four-lane expressways: US 1 is a mostly two-lane road as it heads over land and water on its way to Key West. Traffic on the narrow road can be a bear, especially around weekends and holidays, when many South Floridians and tourists head for Key West and other points along the way. During the winter, avoid driving to the Keys on Friday afternoons and evenings, and on Sunday evenings. The traffic is usually horrendous and multihour backups are routine.

And don't think that off-season is any better. That's when Miami residents and other South Floridians descend on the Keys by the thousands to escape the heat and humidity that bakes Miami in the summer. Try to leave on Friday morning and return on Monday to beat the worst of the weekend traffic.

After passing Florida City, you can make a more dramatic entrance to the Keys than ho-hum US 1 by hanging a left onto **Card Sound Road** (Route 905A). You'll miss most of the tourist traffic heading south and the toll bridge over Card Sound offers a great view of undeveloped Key Largo and Florida Bay. Savor the view—farther south on Key Largo, the commercialism is rampant.

DRIVING SOUTH TOWARD KEY WEST: THE UPPER KEYS

After merging back with US 1 (now also called the Overseas Highway), continue south on to **Key Largo.** The name is pure hype: The eponymous, late 1940s flick starring Bogart and Robinson wasn't filmed here. The local flacks changed the name of the island from Rock Harbor to Key Largo to cash in on the publicity generated by the movie.

More tenuous links with Tinseltown are on tap at the local Holiday Inn, where the original *African Queen,* the small, steam-powered boat used in the film of the same name starring Bogie and Katharine Hepburn, is on display in the hotel's marina (when it's not on promotional tours). Needless to say, that movie wasn't made here either—it was filmed in England and Africa.

Welcome to Suburbia

From US 1, don't expect a whole lot in the way of legendary Keys' ambience. Key Largo is close enough to Homestead and the southern 'burbs of Miami to serve as a bedroom community to the city, and strip malls, restaurants, gas stations, and fast-food joints line the highway. To find anything interesting to see, you've got to get off the island.

Luckily, that's easy to do. **John Pennecamp Coral Reef State Park,** located at Mile Marker 102.5, offers visitors an easy escape to snorkeling, diving, and glass-bottom-boat trips. In addition, a small sandy beach (a rare commodity in the Keys) and a visitor center make this unusual park a worthwhile stop. (See page 391 for more information.) The park is also a major draw for the million-plus divers who come to Key Largo each year, making it the "Diving Capital of the U.S."

Another snorkeling option is **Key Largo Undersea Park,** an acre-wide enclosed lagoon where snorkelers can swim with more than 100 marine species. Other attractions include an underwater hotel, a working undersea marine research center, marine archaeology experiments, and an underwater art studio. First-time snorkelers get expert supervision, extensive pre-swim instruction, and enjoy the placid waters of the inshore lagoon. The park is open daily from 9 a.m. to 3 p.m.; admission is free and self-guided tours are $10 (which includes use of a mask, snorkel, fins, and life vest). The rate for a family of four is $35. Scuba diving in the lagoon costs $25 for a one-tank dive without equipment, and $45 per person with all equipment. For directions and more information, call (305) 451-2353.

Tavernier is the next town traversed as you continue south on US 1. **Harry Harris Park,** located on the left at Mile Marker 92.5, is a county park offering a sandy beach, a tidal pool, barbecue pits, picnic tables, a playground—and an excuse to pull over and relax.

Past Tavernier is a 20-mile stretch of islands collectively known as Islamorada (pronounced EYE-la-ma-RAHD-a), which touts itself as the "Sportfishing Capital of the World." Indeed, this is big-time deep-sea fishing country, as the many marinas and bait-and-tackle shops along the road attest; folks with other interests should keep driving south. An exception: As with all the Keys, the snorkeling and diving at offshore reefs is excellent. Stop in any dive shop along the highway for more details.

Theatre of the Sea, a fish-and-sea-mammal emporium at Mile Marker 84.5, is the second-oldest marine park in the world. Sea lions, dolphins, glass-bottom-boat tours, saltwater aquariums, and ongoing shows make this a worthwhile stop, especially for kids. See the profile on page 399 for more information.

Long Key State Recreational Area, at Mile Marker 68.5, offers canoe rentals, camping, and another excuse to get out of the car, smell the salt air, and unwind. Two nature trails on boardwalks offer views of mangrove forests and tropical hammocks.

THE MIDDLE KEYS

South of Long Key are the Middle Keys, about halfway to Key West. Views of water on both sides of the highway start to appear and you get the feeling that you're actually off the North American continent and out to sea. The next town is Marathon, the second-largest community in the Keys; it even has an airport. While the waters offshore are a big draw with the fishing and boating crowd, the town itself doesn't exude a lot of personality.

But there are some worthwhile stops. At the **Dolphin Research Center,** a nonprofit, educational facility located at Mile Marker 59, visitors can spend time with researchers and dolphins; one-hour, guided walking tours are offered five times daily. Tickets are $12.50 for adults, $10 for seniors age 55 and older, and $7.50 for children ages 4–12. No reservations are required; for more information, call (305) 289-1121.

The Natural History Museum of the Florida Keys at Mile Marker 50.5 is a small museum offering exhibits on the history, geology, and biology of the Keys; there's also a short nature trail and a children's museum. (For more information, see page 397.) For a quick dip, **Sombrero Beach,** off the Overseas Highway at Mile Marker 50, is a family beach on the ocean with a small grassy park and picnic tables.

Next is the **Seven Mile Bridge** connecting Marathon to the Lower Keys, built in the early 1980s at a cost of $45 million. To the right is the original bridge, built by Henry Flagler for his Overseas Railroad in the early years of the twentieth century. The fine structure took all the weather the Keys could throw its way, but the infamous Labor Day hurricane of 1935 destroyed the railroad and the bridge was converted into a highway. Now it's a fishing and jogging pier *par excellence.*

THE LOWER KEYS

Entering the Lower Keys is like stepping back in time; it's easy to imagine that the rest of the Keys, now so commercial, must have looked like this 30 years ago. These islands are heavily wooded, primarily residential, and decidedly noncommercial.

The Lower Keys are where you find **Bahia Honda State Recreation Area,** located at Mile Marker 37 and one of the loveliest spots in the Keys. Attractions in the 300-acre park include a nationally ranked white sand beach, nature trails, plentiful bird life, snorkeling, and diving. It's a popular day-trip destination for Key Westers—or Conchs (pronounced "conks"), as they're called—with a yen for the feel of sand between their toes.

Big Pine Key is home to canine-sized Key deer, an endangered species under federal protection since 1952; the miniature white-tailed deer are only found on Big Pine Key and 16 surrounding keys. The **Key Deer National Wildlife Refuge** is the only wildlife refuge in the Keys accessible without taking a boat ride; your best chances to see the deer are in the early morning, late afternoon, or early evening. Take Key Deer Boulevard to Watson Boulevard to pick up information at the refuge headquarters, open Monday–Friday, 8 a.m.–5 p.m.

Looe Key National Marine Sanctuary, a five-square-mile area of submerged reef six miles southwest of Big Pine Key, is considered the best reef in the Keys for snorkeling, diving, fishing, and boating. Its gin-clear waters reveal underwater sights such as brain coral, tall coral pillars rising toward the surface, and other interesting formations. To visit the reef, make arrangements at any dive shop.

Key West

As US 1 enters Key West, a sign for the far right lane reads: "Right Lane Go At All Times." Follow these directions and North Roosevelt Boulevard leads to Duval Street and Old Town Key West, full of bars, restaurants, hotels, bed and breakfasts, museums, galleries, blocks of charming old homes, and congested, narrow streets.

If you ignore the sign above and go left as you enter Key West you'll pass Houseboat Row, the Atlantic Ocean, snazzy resorts, Key West International Airport, Southernmost Point, and then Old Town.

TAKING AN ORIENTATION TOUR

If you're a first-time visitor, you might want to get oriented before you drive right into town. Park at the Welcome Center near the intersection of US 1 and North Roosevelt Boulevard and sign up for the next **Conch Tour Train:** an open-air, narrated "trolley"—really an open-air bus—that transports visitors around Key West and gives them an overview of the town.

Is it corny? You bet. The train's "engine" is a diesel-powered truck disguised as a locomotive, and even has a whistle. But the 90-minute tour is fun and informative.

With its rich, complicated history, Key West can be difficult for first-time visitors to grasp. A ride on the Conch Tour Train can help you understand why this city was once the wealthiest per capita in the United States, show that it once was the largest producer of natural sponges and cigars, explain its roles during the Civil War and the Cuban missile crisis of 1962, and reveal insights into why people such as John James Audubon, Ernest Hemingway, Harry Truman, Tennessee Williams, and Robert Frost came to identify with Key West.

You'll also gain some insight into the ups and downs this town of 30,000 people has endured over the centuries—from the boom years of the wreckers in the early 1800s to the depths of the Great Depression of the 1930s (the city declared bankruptcy in 1934), to its attempted secession from the United States in the 1980s. The tour will also help you understand the town's physical layout and show you attractions that you can go back and visit later on your own.

The Conch Tour Train leaves every 30 minutes from 9 a.m. to 4:30 p.m. daily. You can board at the Roosevelt Boulevard location or in Old Town's Mallory Square. Tickets are $18 for adults and $9 for children ages 4–12. Passengers can disembark in Old Town, wander around or get lunch, and catch the next "train" 30 minutes later. Call (305) 294-5161 for more information.

Another option for a guided tour is **Old Town Trolley,** open-air buses that shuttle visitors on a 90-minute, narrated tour of Key West. Unlike the Conch Tour Train, passengers can depart at any of 12 marked stops on the tour route and reboard another trolley later; many hotels are on the route. The tours depart every 30 minutes from 8:55 a.m. to 4:30 p.m. from Mallory Square. The tour is $18 for adults and $9 for children ages 5–12. For more information, call (305) 296-6688.

OLD TOWN KEY WEST

Compact **Old Town,** a square mile of restored houses that makes up the heart of Key West, is best viewed on foot or by bicycle. While main avenues such as **Duval Street** are frequently jammed with tourists, the side streets still ooze with the peculiar Key West charm that's made the town famous. As the many bike rental shops attest, Key West is a very bicycle-friendly town. Do yourself a favor and don't attempt driving a car down the narrow streets; walk or ride a bike.

While there's little evidence of anything but unbridled tourist schlock on the main drags, the residential streets frequently reveal glimpses of the anarchic spirit of its residents—even if it's only the sound of Bob Dylan's "Blonde on Blonde" blasting from a hippie crash pad at nine in the morning. And much of the architecture is beautiful, iconoclastic, and fun to look at.

Boom Town

Key West's tolerant spirit has fueled its latest economic revival: the town has become a mecca for gay people. The large population of homosexuals in Key West has given support to restoration efforts, pushed up the price of real estate, and given the town a solid economic boost.

Today's main tourist strip is the once-seedy Duval Street, renovated with well-manicured boutiques, T-shirt shops, bars, T-shirt shops, restaurants, T-shirt shops, galleries, beachwear shops, and other essentials to vacationing tourists. (For God's sake, do your duty and buy a T-shirt!) For folks unfamiliar with the layout of Old Town, Duval Street serves as an anchor as it cuts a swath across the island from the Gulf of Mexico to the Atlantic Ocean.

A Daily Celebration

On the Gulf end of Duval Street is **Mallory Square,** famous for its daily sunset celebration. The "square" is in fact a cramped old concrete wharf that hosts a mini street festival late each afternoon. During high tourist season (between Christmas and Easter), it's shoulder-to-shoulder along the dock with tourists, cruise ship passengers, and street vendors selling anything from fruit-and-yogurt shakes to "Southernmost" falafels.

Key West–style free entertainment includes a troupe of trained cats (most impressive), a bowling ball juggler, an escape artist, innumerable Dylan clones strumming guitars, and the "Southernmost Bag Piper" (least impressive). You'll have trouble seeing any of this, though, because of the throngs.

For folks expecting a re-creation of Haight-Ashbury during the mid-1960s, Mallory Square is a letdown: no hippies pass joints to toast the setting sun, and no bohemian types pass around a bottle of rum to mark the end of another day. Our feeling is that this famous "ritual" is touristy and overrated . . . at least when the crowds are overpowering.

CRUISE SHIPS

Speaking of crowds: Keep an eye peeled for huge cruise ships docked at the foot of Whitehead Street, near Mallory Square. Not that you'll have any trouble seeing them—the bigger ships tower over the docks and look like they could accommodate the entire population of Key West. The presence of one or more of the big ships could mean even bigger crowds along Duval and Whitehead streets, so try to tour away from the dock area until the ships leave. Restaurants, however, aren't usually affected: many of the cruise passengers return to their ships for meals.

BEYOND THE HYPE

On the Atlantic side of Duval Street—actually, a block over on parallel Whitehead Street—is **Southernmost Point,** another example of Key West hype. A huge buoy perched on land and a placard mark the most southern point in the continental United States. But, as any schoolchild will readily point out, the land continues south a few yards to the water's edge—the **real** southernmost point. Still, you can't deny the draw of this otherwise undistinguished place: it's usually packed with tourists getting their picture taken in front of the buoy.

Behind the tourist schlock and commercialization, Key West still retains enough of its quixotic past to charm visitors. Our advice: To really enjoy Key West, get off Duval Street, wander its back roads, visit its unique and interesting museums, get a handle on its rich and unusual history. Stop at an outdoor café for a two-hour lunch and hang out in bars that don't have T-shirt shops on the premises (which rules out Sloppy Joe's and Jimmy Buffett's Margaritaville, two very touristy places). Slow the pace, give it a chance, and you'll soon discover Key West's charms.

Outdoor Recreation

If you start to grow a little restless from lounging around bars and restaurants and moseying around museums, remember that Key West is, geographically speaking, in a unique position: between the Atlantic Ocean and the Gulf of Mexico. For outdoor enthusiasts, there's a wealth of things to do and see, including world-class snorkeling and scuba diving, deep-sea fishing, sight fishing, and exploring the Dry Tortugas and Fort Jefferson, a 19th-century coastal fortification 70 miles west of Key West that's only accessible by boat or sea plane.

"We're on the seam of two huge bodies of water and tremendous tidal forces and flows of water wash across the Keys twice daily," explains Capt. Jeff Cardenas, a retired fishing guide and owner of the Saltwater Angler, a custom fishing rod, tackle, and outdoors shop in Key West. "The result is wonderful feeding and breeding grounds for aquatic wildlife—and a tremendous water clarity. Key West is where the land runs out and the ocean takes over."

Anglers looking for some recommendations for reputable guides and fishing boat charters available at Key West marinas can stop by the **Saltwater Angler** at the Hilton Resort and Marina, 243 Front Street, and talk to Captain Cardenas, who spent 10 years guiding flats fishermen in the Keys before opening his custom rod shop. He's an expert on the outdoors around Key West and happy to offer advice. The phone number is (800) 223-1629 or (305) 296-0700. You'll also find a discussion on the hows, whys, and wheres of South Florida sportfishing in "Deep-Sea Fishing" in Part One: Planning Your Visit to South Florida.

Seaplanes of Key West offers full- and half-day flights to Fort Jefferson and the Dry Tortugas that include coolers, ice, sodas, and snorkeling gear—all you need to bring is a towel and a camera. The 70-mile flight is 40 minutes each way; the plane flies at low altitude so passengers can view the clear waters, shipwrecks, and marine life. You spend two hours on the island. Four-hour trips leave at 8 a.m. and noon daily; prices are $179 for adults, $129 for children ages 7–12, and $99 for children ages 2–6. Full-day trips are $305 for adults, $225 for children ages 7–12, and $170 for children ages 2–6. For reservations, call (800) 950-2359.

Another option for visiting Fort Jefferson and the Dry Tortugas is the **Fort Jefferson Ferry,** which sails out of Lands End Marina (251 Margaret Street in Key West) for full-day excursions. The 100-foot *Yankee Freedom II* boasts a large, air-conditioned salon with a chef's galley, a large sundeck, and freshwater showers for swimmers, snorkelers, and divers. The ferry departs daily at 8 a.m. and returns at 5:30 p.m.; it's three hours each way, and visitors can enjoy about four hours on the island (including a complete tour of the fort). The price for the all-day trip is $95 for adults, $85 for seniors age 62 and older, and $60 for children age 16 and under. For schedule and booking information call (800) 634-0939 or (305) 294-7009.

EXPLORING THE BACKCOUNTRY

Bill Keogh of **Big Pine Kayak Adventures** in Big Pine Key has guided visitors for 18 years on kayak trips to the Keys' backcountry. No experience is necessary to paddle the calm, shallow waters in stable, easy-to-paddle sea kayaks on tours that emphasize seeing wildlife. On the trip you'll view birds, animals, and marine life in Great White Heron and Key Deer wildlife refuges; snorkeling is another popular option on the tours. Trips are $49 per person and last about four hours; tour times vary. A guide, equipment, instruction, and a snack are provided. Big Pine Key is 30 miles from Key West. Big Pine Kayak Adventures is based at Old Wooden Bridge Fishing Camp adjacent to No Name Key Bridge. For a sailing eco-adventure, try a trip on a 26-foot catamaran that takes visitors and their kayaks into shallow-water areas; half-day and overnight trips start at $200 for parties of six or less. For more information or to make a reservation, call (305) 872-2896.

BOAT TOURS, ETC.

The *MV Discovery,* a glass-bottom boat with an underwater viewing room that puts you at eye level with marine life, offers trips at 10:30 a.m., 1:30 p.m., and (in winter) sunset. Tickets for the two-hour trip are $20 for adults and $15 for children (plus tax); kids sail free on the first trip of the day. The ship is located at the Lands End Marina, 251 Margaret Street in Key West. For more information, call (800) 262-0099 or (305) 293-0099.

WHERE TO DIVE

A seemingly limitless number of kiosks and dive shops in Key West offer half-day snorkeling and diving trips to the reef. Shop around for the best price and most convenient departure time. If you have your own gear, you can snorkel right from the beach at Fort Zachary Taylor State Historic Site, located in the Truman Annex at Whitehead and Southard streets in Old Town Key West.

Certified scuba divers, however, can dive anywhere on their own. The Keys offer both beginning and experienced divers plenty of great scenery in protected waters that are relatively shallow (60 feet deep and less). It's the site of the only living coral barrier reef in North American continental waters: giant brain coral grows up to six feet in height; elkhorn corals are six to ten feet high; and mountainous star coral grows to five feet or more across and up to ten feet high. There's lots to see and explore.

Popular dive sites include **John Pennecamp Coral Reef State Park** in Key Largo (see page 391 for more information), **Looe Key National Marine Sanctuary** (near Big Pine Key in the Lower Keys), and the **Marquesas** (22 miles west of Key West). Dive shops are located all along US 1 and throughout Key West.

Attractions

While most visitors to the Florida Keys are outdoor enthusiasts who come to enjoy a unique, subtropical area between the Gulf of Mexico and the Atlantic Ocean, there's more to do on this string of islands than just fish, dive, snorkel, or explore the backcountry. The Keys, and especially Key West, offer many interesting attractions that are worth the time and effort to visit.

Because of the wide range of attractions in the Keys, we've provided the following chart to help you prioritize your touring at a glance. Organized by category, in it you'll find the name, location, and author's rating from one star (skip it) to five stars (not to be missed). Some attractions, usually art galleries without permanent collections, weren't rated because exhibits change. Each attraction is individually profiled in detail later in this section. Most museum-type attractions offer group rates for ten or more people.

A Time-Saving Chart		
Name	City	Author's Rating
Aquarium		
Key West Aquarium	Key West	★★½
Cemetery		
Key West Cemetery	Key West	★★★
Funhouse		
Ripley's Odditorium	Key West	★★
Historic Site		
Fort Zachary Taylor State Historic Site	Key West	★★★★

A Time-Saving Chart (continued)

Name	City	Author's Rating
Home and Garden Tours		
Audubon House & Tropical Gardens	Key West	★★★
Ernest Hemingway Home & Museum	Key West	★★★★
Harry S Truman Little White House Museum	Key West	★★½
Jessie Porter's Heritage House & Robert Frost Cottage	Key West	★★★★½
Lighthouse		
Key West Lighthouse Museum	Key West	★★★★
Museums		
East Martello Museum	Key West	★★★
Flagler Station Over-Sea Railway Historeum	Key West	★★★★
The Key West Museum of Art and History	Key West	★★★½
Key West's Shipwreck Historeum	Key West	★★★★
Mel Fisher's Treasure Exhibit	Key West	★★½
Natural History Museum of the Florida Keys	Marathon	★★½
Parks		
John Pennecamp Coral Reef State Park	Key Largo	★★★★★
Theatre of the Sea	Islamorada	★★★½

ATTRACTION PROFILES

Audubon House & Tropical Gardens

Type of Attraction: The restored home of an early 19th-century Key West harbor pilot and wrecker. A self-guided tour.

Location: Whitehead and Greene streets in downtown Key West

Admission: Adults, $8.50; students, $5; children ages 6–12, $3.50

Hours: Daily, 9:30 a.m–5 p.m.

Phone: (877) 281-2473 (toll free) or (305) 294-2116

When to Go: Any time

Special Comments: You must climb three sets of stairs; the second-floor gallery of Audubon porcelains is air-conditioned.

Overall Appeal by Age Group:

Pre-school	Grade School	Teens	Young Adults	Over 30	Seniors
★	★½	★★	★★½	★★★	★★★½

Author's Rating: A beautifully restored house and gardens; ★★★

How Much Time to Allow: One hour

Description and Comments Captain George H. Geiger was an early Key West harbor pilot and wrecker who, like many Key West residents, made a fortune salvaging cargo from ships wrecked on the Florida Reef. Captain Geiger and his heirs lived in this house for more than 120 years, but in 1958 the deteriorating structure was slated for demolition. Through the efforts of local conservationists, the house was saved and restored, decorated with exquisite period pieces collected in Europe, and dedicated as a museum commemorating the Key West visits of painter and ornithologist John James Audubon. The restoration of the house inaugurated a movement that saved many historically significant Key West buildings.

Touring Tips Don't miss the children's room on the third floor; two pairs of 19th-century roller skates look like forerunners of in-line skates popular today. Outside, orchid-filled trees evoke the wealthy, cosmopolitan lifestyle of early Key West residents. Check out the duplex outhouse in the corner of the garden.

Other Things to Do Nearby Jessie Porter's Heritage House, the Harry S Truman Little White House, the Wreckers' Museum House, and Mel Fisher's Treasure Exhibit are all within a few blocks.

East Martello Museum

Type of Attraction: A Civil War fort converted to an eclectic museum. A self-guided tour.

Location: 3501 South Roosevelt Boulevard, Key West, near the airport

Admission: Adults, $6; students, $4; children under age 6 free

Hours: Daily, 9 a.m.–5 p.m.; closed Christmas day

Phone: (305) 296-3913

When to Go: Any time

Special Comments: The climb up the lookout tower requires negotiating a steep spiral staircase.

Overall Appeal by Age Group:

Pre-school	Grade School	Teens	Young Adults	Over 30	Seniors
★★★★	★★★★	★★★½	★★★	★★★	★★★

Author's Rating: A bizarre museum with a little bit of everything; ★★★
How Much Time to Allow: One–two hours

Description and Comments   It might be easier to catalog what you *won't* find here, but we'll give it a try. The low brick ceilings and arches of this old fort house a horse-drawn hearse and wicker casket (circa 1873), ship models, exhibits on Native Americans, Civil War and Spanish American War military artifacts, a hotel safe, "junkyard" art, a deep-sea diver's air suit and a wooden air pump, and a crude raft used by Cubans to escape the Castro regime. Ankle biters can play in the "junior museum"—a tiny house that adults must stoop to enter—located on the well-manicured grounds. There's also an art museum that features temporary exhibits.

Touring Tips   On the way up the spiral staircase leading to the lookout tower, stop to view an exhibit of odd and whimsical "junkyard" art by Stanley Papio.

Other Things to Do Nearby   The Atlantic Ocean is directly across Roosevelt Boulevard.

Ernest Hemingway Home & Museum

Type of Attraction: The house and gardens of Nobel Prize–winning author
   Ernest Hemingway. Guided and self-guided tours.
Location: 907 Whitehead Street, Key West
Admission: Adults, $8; children ages 6–12, $5
Hours: Daily, 9 a.m.–5 p.m.
Phone: (305) 294-1575
When to Go: In the morning during hot weather; the house isn't air-
   conditioned.
Special Comments: Hemingway loved cats and about 40 of their alleged
   descendants (some with six or seven toes per foot) lounge around the
   one-acre grounds; yet some experts dispute the local legend that says
   these cats are the descendants of the great writer's pets. Either way,
   folks not fond of (or allergic to) felines, beware. Visitors must climb
   two sets of steep stairs on the tour.
Overall Appeal by Age Group:

Pre-school	Grade School	Teens	Young Adults	Over 30	Seniors
★	★★	★★½	★★★	★★★½	★★★★

Author's Rating: An interesting slice of American literary history; ★★★★
How Much Time to Allow: One hour

Description and Comments   Ernest Hemingway owned this Spanish-Colonial house, built in 1870, from 1931 until his death in 1961. In his study in the loft of his pool house, he wrote some of his most famous novels and short stories, including *A Farewell to Arms,* "The Snows of Kilimanjaro," and *For Whom the Bell Tolls.* The spacious mansion gives visitors a glimpse into genteel life in the 1930s. Much (but not all) of the furniture and memorabilia on display belonged to Hemingway.

Touring Tips Don't skip the optional 30-minute guided tour; the tour leaders are witty, literate, and tell great stories about the writer, whom many critics consider the greatest American author. The 65-foot, saltwater swimming pool was the first built in Key West; part of the cats' water fountain located between the house and the pool is a urinal rescued by the writer from Sloppy Joe's Bar.

Other Things to Do Nearby The Key West Lighthouse Museum is across the street.

Flagler Station Over-Sea Railway Historeum

Type of Attraction: Concise collection of memorabilia, documents, and video footage and documentaries pertaining to the construction of the over-sea railway.

Location: 901 Caroline Street, Key West

Admission: Adults, $5; children age 12 and under, $2.50

Hours: Daily, 9 a.m.–5 p.m.

Phone: (305) 295-3562

When to Go: Any time

Special Comments: Two of the three films have limited seating/viewing areas, and since it doesn't matter which order they are viewed, choose based on which screen you can see best.

Overall Appeal by Age Group:

Pre-school	Grade School	Teens	Young Adults	Over 30	Seniors
★½	★★	★★	★★★½	★★★★	★★★★

Author's Rating: Good films tout an interesting piece of not-so-widely-known history; ★★★★

How Much Time to Allow: 45 minutes

Description and Comments This small collection of clothing, contracts, photos, building materials, and other bits of history are accented by three highly enjoyable and informative films about Henry Flagler's goal to build the first railway from Miami to Key West. The first film is 13½ minutes long and runs continuously—it makes the most sense to see it from the beginning, but you can pick it up at any time and watch through the loop. It takes four minutes to rewind between showings, so it is relatively easy to catch it at the beginning. The film, entitled "The Day the Train Arrived," is about Flagler's personal drive and the actual building of the railway. The second film, "The Seven-Mile Bridge," lasts 3½ minutes and is a quick synopsis of bridge and railroad construction—especially as it related to this specific project. The last film, "A Trip down the Florida Keys," is an 8 ½-minute narrative of life in the Keys before and after construction of the railway.

Touring Tips The Historeum is a nice stroll down Caroline Street, just a few blocks from the hustle and bustle of Duval. As the exhibit is actually outside on the back porch area of the enclosed, air-conditioned gift shop, it would be wiser to head here as a wind-down aspect of the day—around 3 p.m. or so.

Other Things to Do Nearby Walk back down to Duval Street and have a cocktail or window shop until sunset; then head over to Mallory Square.

Fort Zachary Taylor State Historic Site

Type of Attraction: A partially restored Civil War fort and museum; the best beach in Key West. Guided and self-guided tours.

Location: Southard Street (in the Truman Annex), Key West

Admission: $4 per carload; $1 for pedestrians and bicyclists

Hours: Daily, 8 a.m.–sundown

Phone: (305) 292-6713

When to Go: Any time, but it's elbow to elbow on the beach on weekends.

Special Comments: Free guided tours of the fort are offered at noon and 2 p.m., daily.

Overall Appeal by Age Group:

Pre-school	Grade School	Teens	Young Adults	Over 30	Seniors
★★★★★	★★★★★	★★★★	★★★★	★★★★	★★★★

Author's Rating: A triple hit: a neat fort, interesting history, and a beach you can snorkel from; ★★★★

How Much Time to Allow: Half a day: Allow 30 minutes to an hour to tour the fort, spend the afternoon on the beach, then catch the best view of the sunset in Key West.

Description and Comments For 145 years, Fort Zachary Taylor defended the harbor of Key West. During the Civil War, it was one of four Union forts in Confederate territory that never fell into Southern hands. As a result, hundreds of cannons trained on the nearby shipping lanes kept ships bottled up in Key West throughout the Civil War. The workmanship of the exquisite brickwork throughout the fort couldn't be duplicated today.

Touring Tips Don't miss the 30-minute guided tour of the fort, which gives visitors a quick education on the evolution of seacoast fortification through the 19th and 20th centuries. You'll also hear some interesting anecdotes from the park ranger who leads the tour. For example: Many ten-inch cannons were so loud that local merchants demanded a 15-minute warning before practice firing so they could rush home and open their windows; the concussion of the big guns could shatter the glass!

There's also a great view of the Gulf of Mexico from the top of the fort. The ocean beach is made of coral and is great for swimming, snorkeling, and sunbathing; the west side of the park offers anglers a wide variety of saltwater fish (a Florida fishing license is required). Shaded picnic areas, tables, grills, several outdoor showers, and a bathhouse are available to visitors.

Other Things to Do Nearby The Harry S Truman Little White House is on the grounds of the adjacent Truman Annex.

Harry S Truman Little White House Museum

Type of Attraction: The restored vacation home of President Harry Truman. A guided tour.

Location: 111 Front Street (one block up Caroline Street through the presidential gates), Key West

Admission: Adults, $8; children age 12 and under, $4 for.

Hours: Daily, 9 a.m.– 4:30 p.m. Guided tours leave every 15 minutes or so.

Phone: (305) 294-9911

When to Go: Any time

Special Comments: Visitors must negotiate a set of steep stairs on the tour.

Overall Appeal by Age Group:

Pre-school	Grade School	Teens	Young Adults	Over 30	Seniors
★	★½	★½	★★	★★★	★★★★★

Author's Rating: A nostalgia trip for folks old enough to remember "Give 'Em Hell" Harry; ★★½

How Much Time to Allow: One hour

Description and Comments President Harry Truman spent 175 vacation days during his presidency (1945–53) at this house in Key West. Today the building is completely redone to posh 1949 standards, although most of the furnishings aren't original. One exception is the custom-made mahogany poker table. The guide tells visitors that while Truman disapproved of gambling in the White House, poker playing with "the boys" was a major form of relaxation for the president when he was vacationing in Key West.

Touring Tips The tour begins with a 10-minute video that evokes the Truman era and primes visitors for the tour. The guides offer interesting tidbits about Truman's personal life when vacationing in Key West. For example, Bess Truman didn't often accompany her husband because she preferred their home in Independence, Missouri. Don't miss the gift shop, which sells aprons inscribed, you guessed it, "If you can't stand the heat, get out of the kitchen."

Other Things to Do Nearby Mel Fisher's Treasure Museum, the Key West Aquarium, and the Audubon House are all close.

Jessie Porter's Heritage House and Robert Frost Cottage

Type of Attraction: An 1830s sea captain's home full of literary memorabilia and antique furnishings from the China Trade. A guided tour.

Location: 410 Caroline Street, Key West

Admission: Adults, $6; seniors, $5; students, $3; children under age 12 free

Hours: Monday–Saturday, 10 a.m.–5 p.m.; Sunday, 11 a.m.–4 p.m.; closed Christmas day

Phone: (305) 296-3573

When to Go: Any time

Special Comments: Unlike many old Key West homes open to visitors, this residence never needed restoration; it's exactly as its owner left it after her death in 1972.

Overall Appeal by Age Group:

Pre-school	Grade School	Teens	Young Adults	Over 30	Seniors
★	★½	★★	★★★	★★★½	★★★★

Author's Rating: Fascinating stuff—don't miss it; ★★★★½

How Much Time to Allow: 30 minutes

Description and Comments Jessie Porter, a granddaughter of one of Key West's founders, was a friend to famous writers such as Ernest Hemingway, Tennessee Williams, and Robert Frost. In addition to photos of a few of America's great literary stars and some original manuscripts, this old house is filled with priceless artifacts, unique furnishings, musical instruments, exquisite silk kimonos . . . the list goes on and on. In the backyard is a small cottage where poet Robert Frost spent many winters. While it's not open to the public, the tour guide plays a tape of Frost reading one of his poems.

Touring Tips Look for the marijuana leaves imprinted in the handmade tiles around the fireplace. The freshwater well outside the front door was used by Native Americans as early as the 12th century.

Other Things to Do Nearby   The Audubon House, the Harry S Truman Little White House, and the Wreckers' Museum are all close.

John Pennecamp Coral Reef State Park

Type of Attraction: A 178-square-mile underwater park featuring snorkeling tours, scuba diving trips, and glass-bottom-boat trips.

Location: On US 1 at Mile Marker 102.5, Key Largo (about a 90-minute drive south of Miami)

Admission: The entrance fee to the park is $2.50 per car and driver, $5 for two, and 50 cents per additional person up to eight people. Snorkeling tours are $25.95 plus tax for adults and $20.95 plus tax for children under age 18. Tours leave at 9 a.m., noon, and 3 p.m. Mask, snorkel, and fins rental is an additional $5 (you keep the snorkel).

Four-hour guided scuba trips are $39 per person and leave at 9:30 a.m. and 1:30 p.m. Rental of two air tanks for two one-hour dives is $14.

Four-hour sailing and snorkeling trips on a 38-foot catamaran are $31.95 for adults and $26.95 for children under age 18 and leave at 9 a.m. and 1:30 p.m. Mask, snorkel, and fins rental is an additional $5 (you keep the snorkel).

Two-and-a-half-hour glass-bottom-boat tours on the new *Spirit of Pennecamp* cost $18 plus tax for adults and $10 for children under age 12 and depart at 9:15 a.m., 12:15 p.m., and 3 p.m.

Hours: Daily, 8 a.m.–sunset

Phone: (305) 451-1621

When to Go: Any time, to visit the park. For diving and snorkeling trips to the reef, on weekends during the winter, reservations should be made several weeks in advance; call at least a day ahead of time during the week to reserve a spot.

Special Comments: All trips are subject to weather conditions and a minimum number of paying customers. Only certified divers can go on the scuba trips; anybody who can swim can go on a snorkeling tour. Complete rental and instruction are available for scuba diving. Full certification takes three days and costs $450 (assuming more than one person is in the class; see pages 23–25 for more information on becoming certified); a "resort" course that lets you dive with an instructor or dive master takes a full day and costs $160. For more information on diving courses, call the dive center at (305) 451-6322.

Overall Appeal by Age Group:

Pre-school	Grade School	Teens	Young Adults	Over 30	Seniors
★★★★	★★★★	★★★★	★★★★★	★★★★★	★★★★★

Author's Rating: Find out why Key Largo is the dive capital of the United States; ★★★★★

How Much Time to Allow: Half a day or longer

Description and Comments   The 78 miles of living coral reef in this park are only a small portion of one of the most beautiful reef systems in the world. But because it's all underwater, the best way to see it is . . . underwater. Unless you can't swim, we recommend taking the snorkel tour. After the 30-minute boat ride to the reef, it's over the side for up-close views of a fantastic array of aquatic life. The boat crew gives plenty of coaching to novices and a 10-minute minicourse on how to snorkel. All snorkelers must wear inflatable life vests, which are provided.

Touring Tips   If swimming with the fishes doesn't appeal or nonswimmers are in your party, take the two-and-a-half-hour, glass-bottom-boat tour. Other facilities in the park include hiking trails, a small swimming beach, an aquarium, canoe rentals, and a visitor center featuring ecological displays on Keys flora and fauna. Good news: The park recently added a new—and larger—bath house with freshwater showers.

Other Things to Do Nearby   Theater of the Sea is 18 miles south in Islamorada. Key Largo is very commercial and has plenty of places to eat, sleep, and shop.

Key West Aquarium

Type of Attraction: An old-fashioned aquarium featuring sea life from both the Atlantic and the Gulf of Mexico. Guided and self-guided tours.

Location: 1 Whitehead Street, Key West

Admission: Adults, $8; children ages 4–12, $4; children under age 3 free. Tickets are good for two days.

Hours: Daily, 10 a.m.–6 p.m.; guided tours and feedings at 11 a.m., 1 p.m., 3 p.m., and 4:30 p.m.

Phone: (305) 296-2051

When to Go: Any time

Special Comments: If you're on a short visit to Key West, spend your valuable touring time elsewhere and come back on a later visit.

Overall Appeal by Age Group:

Pre-school	Grade School	Teens	Young Adults	Over 30	Seniors
★★★★★	★★★★	★★★½	★★★	★★½	★★

Author's Rating: Great for the kiddies, but otherwise a bit ho-hum; ★★½

How Much Time to Allow: One hour

Description and Comments   This aquarium is small but comfortable, and will especially please younger children. At the touch tank, kids can handle conch, starfish, and crabs. You'll probably never get closer to a shark unless you hook one.

Touring Tips   This is a browsing kind of place with long rows of fish tanks at eye level to stroll past. The moray eels are especially creepy, and you'll see many specimens of smaller sharks such as lemon, blacktip, and bonnethead.

Other Things to Do Nearby   You're in the heart of downtown Key West: Mel Fisher's Treasure Exhibit, the Audubon House, and Mallory Square are within a few blocks' walk.

Key West Cemetery

Type of Attraction: The final resting place of many prominent—and unusual—Key West residents. Guided and self-guided tours.

Location: The main gate is at Margaret and Angela streets, Key West

Admission: Free

Hours: Daily, 7 a.m.–sunset

Phone: (305) 292-8170

When to Go: Any time, but avoid the middle of the day in hot weather.

Special Comments: Although all the residents are buried above ground, it's not a ghoulish place.

Overall Appeal by Age Group:

Pre-school	Grade School	Teens	Young Adults	Over 30	Seniors
★	★	★★	★★★	★★★	★★★

Author's Rating: A wacky side of Key West that's managed to avoid the rest of the island's rampant commercialism; ★★★

How Much Time to Allow: One hour, although it could take most of the day to explore the entire 25 acres.

Description and Comments   A high water table and tough coral rock explains the unusual burial practices in this corner of paradise—everyone here is "buried" above ground. As a result, the cemetery is filled with coffin-shaped tombs, many of them stacked on top of one another like mortuary condominiums. In addition, pets are often interred next to their owners.

Touring Tips   Guided tours depart the main gate Tuesday and Thursday mornings at 9:30 a.m.; the cost is $10 per person. The most inspired headstone inscription in the cemetery may be that of a famous Key West hypochondriac, Mrs. B. P. Roberts: "I told you I was sick."

Other Things to Do Nearby The cemetery is on the edge of Old Town Key West; explore some of the quiet, shaded streets lined with charming houses that range from shacks to Victorian masterpieces. Some are lovingly restored, while others look as if they haven't been touched since Hemingway lived here. Look in the yards for concrete cisterns, which were once the chief source of fresh water on the island.

Key West Lighthouse Museum

Type of Attraction: An 1848 lighthouse and a museum that tells the story of lighthouses in the Florida Keys. A self-guided tour.

Location: 938 Whitehead Street, Key West

Admission: Adults, $8; children ages 6–12, $4

Hours: Daily, 9 a.m.–5 p.m.; closed Christmas Day

Phone: (305) 294-0012

When to Go: Any time

Special Comments: Folks who aren't in shape or don't like heights should skip the climb to the top of the 90-foot lighthouse.

Overall Appeal by Age Group:

Pre-school	Grade School	Teens	Young Adults	Over 30	Seniors
★★	★★★★	★★★★	★★★★	★★★★	★★★

Author's Rating: A great view and interesting history; ★★★★

How Much Time to Allow: One hour

Description and Comments Next to doing "12-ounce curls" (drinking beer) at Sloppy Joe's, a climb to the top of the lighthouse is the most rewarding workout in Key West. The 88 steps to the top lead to an impressive view of the Atlantic Ocean, the Gulf of Mexico, and cruise ships docked in the harbor.

Touring Tips The nearby museum (formerly the Keeper's Quarters when this was an operating lighthouse) is small, dark, cool, and filled with fascinating artifacts from the days when the big light atop the tower guided navigators through the treacherous waters outside Key West.

Other Things to Do Nearby Hemingway House is directly across Whitehead Street.

The Key West Museum of Art and History

Type of Attraction: A small collection of permanent and traveling works located in the beautifully restored Custom House in the heart of old Key West.

Location: 281 Front Street, Key West

Admission: Adults, $6; seniors and locals, $5; children ages 7–17, $4; children age 6 and under free

Hours: Daily, 9 a.m.–5 p.m.

Phone: (305) 295-6616

When to Go: Any time

Special Comments: Be sure to bring the kids—they'll love Stanley Papio's "Junkyard Art."

Overall Appeal by Age Group:

Pre-school	Grade School	Teens	Young Adults	Over 30	Seniors
★★★	★★★	★★★	★★★★	★★★★	★★★

Author's Rating: Beautiful architecture housing varied and interesting works; ★★★½

How Much Time to Allow: One hour

Description and Comments   The Key West Museum of Art and History at the Custom House has several permanent exhibits. These include a room dedicated to (and funded by) Wilhelmina Harvey, who calls herself Key West's most famous political celebrity. You can also find the work of Stanley Papio, sculptor of amusing characters from all sorts of scrap metal junk, and the woodcarvings of local artist Mario Sanchez. He creates intricately carved three-dimensional scenes representing different aspects of life in Key West in a folk art style. Additionally, the permanent collection of art and history of Key West, including the history and restoration of the Custom House will be completed by fall 2001. This will also include pieces of the past permanent exhibit "The *U.S.S. Maine*" as it relates to the history of Key West.

Touring Tips   As the Custom House is a relatively small arena for art display, look for art in places you wouldn't expect—leading to the third floor office area, on the walls and floors behind the volunteers' posts and down the hallway to the restrooms—to name a few.

Other Things to Do Nearby   Include a pass through the Custom House during Duval Street/Mallory Square sight-seeing. It is right in the middle of everything and is much easier to access on foot than trying to park nearby.

Key West's Shipwreck Historeum

Type of Attraction: A replica of an 1856 Key West wreckers warehouse where skits, films, laser technology, and actual artifacts combine to present a picture of 19th-century Key West life and how the wrecking profession influenced the island's society. A self-guided tour.

Location: 1 Whitehead Street at Mallory Square, Key West

Admission: Adults, $8; children ages 4–12, $4; children under age 4 free

Hours: Daily, 9:45 a.m.– 4:45 p.m.; shows begin 15 minutes before and after the hour

Phone: (305) 292-8990

When to Go: Any time

Special Comments: The Historeum is not wheelchair accessible. You must descend several stairs to where the movie is shown, and the museum tour involves several flights of stairs. The lookout tower provides an incredible view of the historic district and the barrier reef, but it requires visitors to climb nine flights of stairs. Those afraid of heights might want to skip this part of the attraction.

Overall Appeal by Age Group:

Pre-school	Grade School	Teens	Young Adults	Over 30	Seniors
★½	★ ★½	★★★	★★★★	★★★★	★★★★

Author's Rating: Talented actors, interesting history, and impressive booty; ★★★★

How Much Time to Allow: About 45 minutes for the entire tour

Description and Comments   Drift back in time as Asa Tift, a famous 19th-century Key West wrecker, greets you in his warehouse as a potential crew member. Listen to the story of how Key West became the "richest city in the U.S.A." when the vessel *Isaac Allerton* sank in 1856. A 20-minute video depicts the life of the wreckers and their fight to save lives and precious cargo from ships doomed by the dangerous reefs. Much of the story is told through comments and stories from some of Key West's prominent figures of the time.

Touring Tips   The *Isaac Allerton* was the richest shipwreck in our history, and the self-guided museum tour displays a multitude of impressive artifacts—the ship was headed for New Orleans loaded with expensive and precious items intended to decorate the Customs House. Asa Tift seems busy at work in the room where you begin the museum tour, but he will be happy to stop and answer any questions you might have. The actor playing Tift will make it worth your time to stop and chat—our guide was loaded with interesting Key West tidbits. Don't forget about Tift's Wreckers Lookout, which marks the end of the tour. If you're up for the climb, you will be rewarded with a spectacular view.

Other Things to Do Nearby   You're in the heart of Mallory Square and only a few blocks' walk from the Aquarium, the Audubon House, and Mel Fisher's Treasure Exhibit.

Mel Fisher's Treasure Exhibit

Type of Attraction: A display of treasure recovered from two Spanish galleons sunk off Key West in a 1622 hurricane. A self-guided tour.

Location: 200 Greene Street, Key West

Admission: Adults, $6.50; children ages 6–12, $3; AAA and AARP discounts available

Hours: Daily, 9:30 a.m.–5:30 p.m. The last video presentation is at 4:30 p.m.

Phone: (305) 294-2633

When to Go: Any time

Special Comments: Don't expect to find any mention of the raging dispute between Fisher and the government over who owns what. The gift shop is full of tacky stuff like paper pirate hats and eye patches for the kids.

Overall Appeal by Age Group:

Pre-school	Grade School	Teens	Young Adults	Over 30	Seniors
★★★	★★★★	★★★★	★★★½	★★★	★★★½

Author's Rating: Impressive booty, a small exhibit, and plenty of self-promotional schlock; ★★½

How Much Time to Allow: One hour

Description and Comments   Ever dreamed of finding a trove of treasure worth millions? Well, Mel Fisher, the best-known salvager in the Keys, did—and bars of solid silver, a solid gold dinner plate, pieces of eight in a cedar chest, and cannons and sailors' artifacts from the 17th century are among the items on display in this small museum. Exhibits also explain how modern treasure hunters find the ancient wrecks and bring the loot up from the bottom of the sea. Yet the relentless self-promotion and commercialism of this private museum—not to mention its small size—are a letdown.

Touring Tips   The *Margarita,* part of a fleet of ships sailing from Havana, Cuba, in 1622 and sunk during a hurricane during its passage to Spain, was discovered in 1980. But it wasn't until 1985, when Fisher located the hull structure and the main cargo of the fleet's flagship *Nuestra Senora de Atocha,* that the bulk of the treasure was found; a 20-minute video tells the story.

Other Things to Do Nearby   The Key West Aquarium, the Harry S Truman Little White House, and the Audubon House are all within a few blocks.

Natural History Museum of the Florida Keys

Type of Attraction: A child-friendly museum emphasizing the natural history and ecology of the Florida Keys. A self-guided tour.

Location: On US 1 at Mile Marker 50.5, Marathon

Admission: Adults, $7.50; seniors, $6; students, $4; children age 6 and under free

Hours: Monday–Saturday, 9 a.m.–5 p.m.; Sunday, noon–5 p.m., Sunday

Phone: (305) 743-9100

When to Go: Any time

Special Comments: Don't forget mosquito repellent before walking the quarter-mile nature trail.

Overall Appeal by Age Group:

Pre-school	Grade School	Teens	Young Adults	Over 30	Seniors
★★★★	★★★★★	★★★	★★½	★★½	★★½

Author's Rating: A small, spanking-new museum geared for children, who will love it; ★★½

How Much Time to Allow: One–two hours

Description and Comments A small, new, and tasteful museum with exhibits on ancient Indians, pirates, wreckers, and the railroaders who built the rail line to Key West. Kids will like the re-creation of an underwater cave, as well as the 15,000-gallon saltwater lagoon, and tanks featuring spiny lobsters, an iguana, and a parrot. A separate children's museum features touch tanks that lets kids handle spiny sea urchins and other creatures, and a corner with books and a chair for reading.

Touring Tips The nature trail leads to a rare tropical palm hammock, home to some uncommon and unusual plants.

Other Things to Do Nearby Seven Mile Bridge, one of the engineering marvels of the world when it was completed in 1910, is a few miles south. Farther south at Mile Marker 37, Bahia Honda State Park offers weary travelers a real sand beach (rare in the Keys), a nature trail, and a respite from the highway.

Ripley's Odditorium

Type of Attraction: A carnival funhouse for youngsters and loony adults featuring exhibits from "Ripley's Believe It or Not." A self-guided tour.

Location: 527 Duval Street, Key West

Admission: Adults, $10.95 plus tax; children ages 4–10, $8.95 plus tax

Hours: Daily, 9 a.m.–11 p.m.

Phone: (305) 293-9686

When to Go: Any time

Special Comments: A number of exhibits are right out of a roadside carnival, so be ready for unsettling special effects—both optical and physical—such as wobbly decks and lunging "sharks."

Overall Appeal by Age Group:

Pre-school	Grade School	Teens	Young Adults	Over 30	Seniors
★★	★★★★	★★★★★	★★★	★★	★½

Author's Rating: Tacky, tasteless, and often hilarious—expensive, too; ★★

How Much Time to Allow: One hour for adults, two to three hours for youngsters

Description and Comments   Is it really Ripley, returned from the dead, who materializes at his desk and invites visitors to explore his museum? Or is it a "hologram" of an actor who looks vaguely like Christopher Walken wearing a smoking jacket? Who cares?

Join in the fun on an exploration of this ridiculous—and funny— "museum." You'll find oddities of questionable authenticity ("shrunken" heads), endlessly repeating film clips of human bizarreness (a guy blowing up a balloon through his eye), grainy film clips with corny narration of New Guinea natives chowing down on grubs and a roast crocodile (gross!), lots of juvenile sex teasers (walk by in one direction, you get a glimpse of a naked lady's backside, but walk by in the other direction and she's gone). It's all corny, seedy, and often quite funny.

Touring Tips   Some people—opera lovers and their ilk—might offer this touring advice: Don't. In reality, this is a perfect rainy day kind of place. You don't have to be a kid to enjoy this wacky place, but having one along would certainly increase the fun. And don't ask yourself what any of this has to do with Key West.

Other Things to Do Nearby   Buy a T-shirt: Duval Street must offer more T-shirts for sale than any other place in the universe. Knock down a you-know-what at Jimmy Buffett's Margaritaville (across the street) or stretch your legs for a stroll to the Southernmost Point; hang a left as you leave Ripley's. Is the sun low in the sky? Then head for Mallory Square and the sunset celebration; it's to the right.

Theatre of the Sea

Type of Attraction: A marine park offering continuous shows featuring sea lions and dolphins, "bottomless" boat rides, snorkeling trips, an aquarium, and opportunities to swim with dolphins.

Location: On US 1 at Mile Marker 84.5, in Islamorada

Admission: Adults, $17.25; children ages 3–12, $10.75; children under age 3 free. Group rates are available. Price of admission does not include the Dolphin Swim, boat rides, or snorkeling trips.

Hours: 9:30 a.m. to 4 p.m.

Phone: (305) 664-2431

When to Go: Any time

Special Comments: If you are interested in taking a dip with the dolphins, call ahead for reservations. Also note that this is your only opportunity to swim at the park.

Overall Appeal by Age Group:

Pre-school	Grade School	Teens	Young Adults	Over 30	Seniors
★★★	★★★½	★★★	★★★	★★★	★★★½

Author's Rating: ★★★½

How Much Time to Allow: At least 2½ hours; half a day for leisurely exploration

Description and Comments   Established in 1946, Theater of the Sea is the world's second-oldest marine park. Here, you can explore the surroundings of the deep in a natural lagoon setting. Activities such as bottomless-boat rides, aquatic shows, and lagoon tours will entertain guests of all ages, as well as educate them about marine life. Children are especially drawn to the touch tank, where they can pet a shark or kiss a sea lion. Also, children of all ages are invited to take part in the shows.

Touring Tips   To escape the crowds and the heat, the best time to go is early in the morning during the week. Show up at 8:30 a.m. for a four-hour snorkeling trip and 13-mile boat cruise. The boat leaves the dock at 9 a.m. daily; the cost is $55 for adults and $33 for children ages 6–12. Snorkeling equipment can be rented. There is also an afternoon trip; plan to arrive by 1 p.m.

Other Things to Do Nearby   The Tiki Bar is right next door. Adults can refresh themselves with a cocktail and a little Calypso music, while the kids play in the pool. Float and jet ski rentals are also available.

Dining and Restaurants

Key West is the southernmost tropical city in the continental United States as well as one of the warmest year-around spots in the country. The people of the Conch Republic extend to over 100 miles north of Key West in a row of small villages spanning all the way to South Miami, but the best restaurants begin to appear south of mile marker 90, with Marker 88 being one of the first and better known in the Islamorada area.

The island of Key West, where most of the restaurants concentrate, offers a treat for the masses that travel down to relax and explore the wild sights that make Key West so unique. Nightly, locals and tourists take the stroll down Duval Street to Mallory Square to witness the sunset celebration. The restaurants listed in this section are proven to be the best and have been in business for many years. Also, the average check for dinner in the Keys (with the exception of Little Palm Island) is the lowest in South Florida.

Explaining the Ratings

We have developed detailed profiles for the restaurants we think are the best in the county. Each profile features an easily scanned heading that allows you, in just a second, to check out the restaurant's name, cuisine, star rating, cost, quality rating, and value rating.

Star Rating   The star rating is an overall rating that evaluates the entire dining experience, including style, service, and ambience, in addition to the taste, presentation, and quality of the food. Five stars is the highest rating possible, meaning the place has the best of everything. Four-star restaurants are exceptional and three-star restaurants are well above average. Two-star restaurants are good. One star is given to average restaurants that demonstrate an unusual capability in some area of specialization, for example, an otherwise forgettable place that has great corned beef.

Cost   Below and to the left of the star rating is an expense category giving the general price range for a complete meal. A complete meal for our purposes consists of an entrée with vegetable or side dish, and choice of soup or salad. Appetizers, desserts, drinks, and tips are excluded. Categories and related prices are listed below.

Inexpensive	$14 or less per person
Moderate	$15 to $30 per person
Expensive	More than $30 per person

Quality Rating   On the far right of each heading appears a number and a letter. The number is a food quality rating based on a scale of 0 to 100, with 100 being the best rating attainable. The quality rating is based expressly on the taste, freshness of ingredients, preparation, presentation, and creativity of food served. There is no consideration of price. If you are a person who wants the best food available and cost is not an issue, you need look no further than the quality ratings.

Value Rating   If, on the other hand, you are looking for both quality and value, then you should check the value rating, expressed in letters. The value ratings are defined as follows:

A   Exception value, a real bargain
B   Good value
C   Fair value, you get exactly what you pay for
D   Somewhat overpriced
F   Significantly overpriced

Payment   We've listed the type of payment accepted at each restaurant using the following codes:

AMEX	American Express (Optima)
CB	Carte Blanche
D	Discover
DC	Diners Club
MC	MasterCard
VISA	Visa

ABOUT THESE CHOICES

We have chosen restaurants that, while we can't guarantee their staying power, have proven to operate successfully for some time. We've also selected restaurants with a following among local professionals, residents, and tourists. We have included a mix of restaurants that are well known and some that are low-profile, and in the process we have tried to provide something for everyone. Bon appetit!

The Best of The Keys Restaurants				
Restaurant/Type	Star Rating	Quality Rating	Value Rating	City
American				
Café Marquesa	★★★½	94	B	Key West
The Restaurant on Little Palm Island	★★★½	92	D	Little Torch Key
Square One	★★★½	90	C	Key West
Louie's Backyard	★★★	84	C	Key West
Ziggy's Conch Restaurant	★★½	77	C	Islamorada
Caribbean				
The Restaurant on Little Palm Island	★★★½	92	D	Little Torch Key
Square One	★★★½	90	C	Key West
Pier House Restaurant	★★★	88	C	Key West
Gus' Grille	★★★	86	B	Key Largo

The Best of The Keys Restaurants (cont.)

Restaurant/Type	Star Rating	Quality Rating	Value Rating	City
Caribbean (continued)				
Louie's Backyard	★★★	84	C	Key West
Marker 88	★★★	80	B	Islamorada
Continental				
Marker 88	★★★	80	B	Islamorada
Florida-Caribbean				
Bagatelle	★★★	80	C	Key West
French				
Café Des Artistes	★★★	83	C	Key West
New American				
Atlantic's Edge	★★★½	91	C	Islamorada
Pier House Restaurant	★★★	88	C	Key West
Gus' Grille	★★★	86	B	Key Largo
Steakhouse				
Shula's on the Beach	★★★½	90	C	Key West

ATLANTIC'S EDGE   ★★★½

New American/Caribbean	Expensive	QUALITY
		91

Overseas Highway US 1, Mile Marker 81 (Cheeca Lodge),
Islamorada; (305) 664-4651

VALUE: C

Reservations: Accepted	**Wine selection:** Good selections from all
When to go: Any time	over the world; $24–160 bottles, $6–9
Entree range: $19–32	by the glass
Payment: VISA, AMEX, MC, DC	**Dress:** Casual
Parking: Valet	**Disabled access:** Good
Bar: Full service	**Customers:** Tourists, locals

Menu recommendations: Indian river blue crab cake with tossed mesclun greens and sweet basil salsa; Caribbean mojo duck tostones, golden pineapple, Hudson Valley foie gras and Peruvian lime essence; Key lime–marinated local seafood ceviche, crimson onions, roasted corn, and

Jamaican sweet potatoes; wild west rubbed beef tenderloin, crispy yuca, Kentucky king beans and guava glaze; purple-sage-and-rosemary–marinated mixed grill, yukon gold potatoes, wild mushrooms and lemon thyme essence; onion-crusted yellow tail snapper, spicy pickled beets, crisp arugula and jumbo lump blue crab.

Comments: The most formal dining room in the best resort in Islamorada is Atlantic's Edge. Inhabited primarily by the hotel guests, it is also frequented by local area fishermen and many drivers to the Keys, lured daily by the interesting food and relaxing ambience.

BAGATELLE ★★★

Florida-Caribbean	Moderate/Expensive	QUALITY 80
115 Duval Street, Key West (305) 296-6609		VALUE C

Reservations: Accepted
When to go: Any time
Entree range: $15.95–23.95
Payment: VISA, AMEX, MC, DC
Parking: Nearby lots
Bar: Full service

Wine selection: Good French and American wines; $18–180 bottles, $5.50–7.50 by the glass
Dress: Casual
Disabled access: Adequate
Customers: Tourists, locals

Lunch: Daily, 11:30 a.m.–3 p.m.; light menu, 3–4 p.m.

Dinner: Daily, 5:30–10 p.m.

Menu recommendations: Conch ceviche marinated with lime juice, cilantro, and Scotch bonnet peppers; escargot Martinique in puff pastry with mushrooms and shallots in brandy crème sauce; grilled jumbo shrimp with garlic herb butter over pasta; pan-fried snapper; macadamia-crusted fish sautéed with mango butter sauce.

Comments: This choice house in Old Town Key West is classic revival in style and has had a rich history of owners. Dining on the verandas alone is a nostalgic regress into a historic past.

CAFÉ DES ARTISTES ★★★

French	Expensive	QUALITY 83
1007 Simonton Street, Key West (305) 294-7100		VALUE C

Reservations: Accepted
When to go: Any time

Entree range: $23.95–29.95
Payment: VISA, AMEX, MC

Parking: Nearby
Bar: Full service
Wine selection: Mostly French;
$32–1,500 bottles, $7.50–11.75 by

the glass
Dress: Casual
Disabled access: Good
Customers: Tourists, internationals, locals

Dinner: Daily, 6–11 p.m.

Menu recommendations: Terrine of grilled eggplant with tomato and citrus vinaigrette; terrine of duck liver with port and truffles with lentil vinaigrette; yellowtail sautéed with shrimp and scallops in lemon butter; lobster flambéed in cognac with shrimp in saffron butter, mango, and basil; roast half-duckling with fresh raspberry sauce.

Comments: This restaurant, said to have been built by one of the Al Capone gang in 1934, offers an opportunity—rare in the Keys—to dine elegantly on French food that (due to the influence of its surroundings) contains interesting Caribbean nuances.

CAFÉ MARQUESA		★★★★

Contemporary American	Expensive	QUALITY
		94
600 Fleming Street, Key West		VALUE
(305) 292-1919		B

Reservations: Recommended
When to go: Early
Entree range: $24–36
Payment: VISA, AMEX, MC, DC, D
Bar: Full service
Wine selection: Very good and well

compiled; $28–300 bottles,
$6.50–12.50 by the glass
Dress: Casual, business
Disabled access: Good
Customers: Tourists, locals, and
internationals

Dinner: Daily, 7–11 p.m. (summer); 6–11 p.m. (winter)

Menu recommendations: Feta and pine nut–crusted rack of lamb with rosemary natural demi-glace, polenta and eggplant caponata; peppercorn-dusted, seared yellowfin tuna with saffron risotto and melange of roasted vegetables and spinach pesto; vegetarian delight of Asian vegetables with grilled basil sauce and black Thai rice. All bread and desserts are made on premises.

Comments: One of Key West's most popular restaurants to celebrate a special occasion because it's regarded the best. Situated in the charming, well-appointed Marquesa Hotel, the open kitchen is set behind a giant trompe l'oeil wall painting of a kitchen scene. Large mahogany framed mirrors give diners a larger perspective on this small 50-seat dining room.

GUS' GRILLE ★★★

New American/Caribbean	Moderate/Expensive	QUALITY 86
103800 Overseas Highway (Key Largo Bay Beach Resort), Key Largo; (305) 453-0000		VALUE B

Reservations: Accepted
When to go: Any time
Entree range: $14.50–21.50
Payment: VISA, AMEX, MC, DC, D
Bar: Full service

Wine selection: Very moderate; $20–125 bottles, $4.50–7 by the glass
Dress: Casual, business
Disabled access: Good
Customers: Tourists, internationals

Dinner: Daily, 7:30–11 p.m.

Menu recommendations: Bahamian conch chowder; lump crab cake; chicken chili quesadilla; paella with saffron risotto; pecan-crusted yellowtail snapper, pan-sautéed with Frangelica reduction and potatoes; Florida spiny lobster sautéed with saffron cream.

Comments: This resort was built immediately after Hurricane Andrew, and it's one of the loveliest in the Upper Keys. The restaurant focuses on Caribbean-style cooking, using the abundance of fresh fish available there.

LOUIE'S BACKYARD ★★★

American/Caribbean	Moderate/Expensive	QUALITY 84
700 Waddell Street, Key West (305) 294-1061		VALUE C

Reservations: Accepted
When to go: Early
Entree range: $25–29.50
Payment: VISA, AMEX, MC, DC
Parking: Alongside restaurant
Bar: Full service

Wine selection: A fair mostly American selection; $20–100 bottles, $5–30 by the glass
Dress: Casual
Disabled access: Good
Customers: Tourists, locals, internationals

Brunch: Sunday, 11:30 a.m.–3 p.m.

Lunch: Monday–Saturday, 11:30 a.m.–3 p.m.

Dinner: Daily, 6–10:30 p.m.

Menu recommendations: Crisp fried cracked conch with red pepper jelly and pickled ginger slaw; Bahamian conch chowder with bird pepper hot sauce salad; pan-seared shrimp and chorizo with whiskey corn cream and corn muffins; pan-cooked Atlantic salmon with sweet soy, wakame salad, shiitake mushrooms, and spinach; grilled tamarind-glazed Key West shrimp, roasted yam barbecue sauce, and cayenne-dusted plantain chips; grilled black angus steak with Rioja wine sauce.

Comments: Nestled among a profusion of tropical foliage, flowering bougainvillea, and hibiscus, the restaurant looks out on a dockside dining deck that sits on the sandy beach. This is a popular, attractive restaurant that typifies the laid-back Key West character.

MARKER 88   ★★★

Continental/Caribbean	Moderate/Expensive	QUALITY
		80

	VALUE
Overseas Highway US 1, Mile Marker 88; Islamorada (305) 852-9315 or (305) 852-5503	B

Reservations: Accepted
When to go: Early
Entree range: $16.95–28.95
Payment: VISA, AMEX, MC, DC, CB, D
Parking: Alongside building
Bar: Full service
Wine selection: Well rounded from Cali-
fornia and Europe; $18–380 bottles, $4.25–6.75 by the glass
Dress: Casual
Disabled access: Good
Customers: Tourists, locals, fishermen, celebrities

Dinner: Tuesday–Sunday, 5–11 p.m.; closed Monday

Menu recommendations: Conch ceviche with red onions and sweet-and-sour sauce; oysters Moscow topped with caviar and creamy horseradish; Cuban black bean soup; conch steak; yellowtail, snapper, grouper, dolphin, or pompano prepared many ways, including fried, sautéed meunière, broiled, poached, grilled, Grenoblaise, and blackened; shrimp Milanesa with angel hair pasta; Apalachicola soft-shell crabs fried, meunière, or with garlic butter; veal Wiener schnitzel.

Comments: Almost every famous person who has visited the Keys has also visited Marker 88, a rustic, weathered building which overlooks the Florida Bay. An interesting mix of dishes, from conch fritters to such long-time French classics as rack of lamb Provençale, is available here in an area free of urban clutter.

PIER HOUSE RESTAURANT   ★★★

New American/Caribbean Moderate/Expensive	QUALITY
	88

One Duval Street (Pier House Hotel), Key West	VALUE
(305) 296-4600	C

Reservations: Accepted
When to go: Any time
Entree range: $25–33
Payment: VISA, AMEX, MC, DC, D
Parking: Adjoining lot
Bar: Full service
Wine selection: Well-rounded with wines
from around the world; $24–300
bottles, $6–11 by the glass
Dress: Casual
Disabled access: Good
Customers: Tourists, winter residents,
celebrities

Brunch: Sunday, 11 a.m.–2 p.m.

Dinner: Daily, 5–10:30 p.m.

Menu recommendations: Sautéed Gulf shrimp with olives, tomato, lemon oil, mustard, and basil; lobster salad with avocado and grapefruit; conch eggrolls with vegetable slaw and hot mustard sauce; terrine of salmon and scallops with tomato crème fraiche coulis; breast of chicken with roasted corn cakes, sautéed spinach and ginger lemon sauce; pan-seared grouper with baby leeks confit; baked Florida lobster with marinated plantains and vegetables; grilled veal chops with portobello mushrooms and rosemary and sage demi-glace.

Comments: Located in Key West's most famous hotel, the Pier House Restaurant is one of the area's best. Stylish and popular, the restaurant and its Havana dock are a hub of activity and conviviality, particularly during the winter season.

THE RESTAURANT ON LITLE PALM ISLAND ★★★½

New American/Caribbean Moderate/Expensive	QUALITY
	92

Overseas Highway US 1, Mile Marker 28.5	VALUE
Little Torch Key; (305) 872-2551	D

Reservations: Required
When to go: Any time
Entree range: $25–32
Payment: VISA, AMEX, MC, DC
Parking: At reception area
Bar: Full service
Wine selection: Good; $25–300 bottles,
$8–25 by the glass
Dress: Casual
Disabled access: Adequate
Customers: Professionals, tourists,
celebrities

Breakfast: Daily, 7:30–10 a.m.

Brunch: Sunday, 11:30 a.m.–2:30 p.m.

Lunch: Daily, 11:30 a.m.–2:30 p.m.

Dinner: Daily, 6:30–10 p.m.

Menu recommendations: Lobster Martini, chili spiced chilled lobster, cucumber slaw, sweet hot pineapple jasmine rice; mushroom gateau, wild mushrooms, duck confit and foie gras duxelle, ginger scallion crepes, roast corn truffle cream; lobster fettuccine with tarragon vanilla emulsion; caviar selection; pan seared yellow snapper and red lobster dumplings, watermelon relish, tamarind pineapple jus; Adam's crab cakes, jumbo lump crab, pints of asparagus, tomato truffle salad, coulis of leek saffron-chive butter; Riesling chicken, roasted, wild mushrooms, white grapes and pancetta, tarragon Riesling sauce.

Comments: Located on a hidden island—a 30-mile drive from Key West and a 20-minute boat ride provided by the management—the resort's restaurant building sits amid a profusion of tropical plants. A Robbin Haas restaurant concept with a menu executed by chef Adam Votaw. This site has long been an exclusive retreat for the rich and famous, including an occasional president.

SHULA'S ON THE BEACH ★★★½

Steakhouse	Moderate/Expensive	QUALITY
		90
1435 Simonton Street (Reach Resort), Key West		VALUE
(305) 296-5000		C

Reservations: Accepted
When to go: Any time
Entree range: $20.95–33.95
Payment: VISA, AMEX, MC, DC
Parking: Valet
Bar: Full service

Wine selection: Good, mostly American; $23–140 bottles, $6–9 by the glass
Dress: Casual
Disabled access: Good
Customers: Tourists, locals

Lunch: Monday–Friday, noon–2:30 p.m.

Dinner: Sunday–Thursday, 6–10:30 p.m.; Friday and Saturday, 6–11 p.m.

Menu recommendations: Oysters Rockefeller; lobster bisque; BBQ shrimp stuffed with fresh basil wrapped in applewood bacon; certified Angus beef selections include 16-ounce New York strip, 12-ounce filet mignon, 24-ounce porterhouse steak, and 22-ounce cowboy steak; gigantic lobsters; and steak Mary Anne—two 5-ounce filet mignons with a creamy peppercorn sauce.

Comments: This lovely retreat offers a perfect getaway setting now with the addition of Shula's on the Beach. Excellent service and fine china and crystal add to the elegance of the decor, while huge cuts of meat and larger-than-life lobsters can be savored while watching the sunset far in the distance.

SQUARE ONE		★★★½

American/ Caribbean	Moderate/Expensive	QUALITY 90
1075 Duval Street at Duval Square, Key West (305) 296-4300		VALUE C

Reservations: Recommended	Wine selection: Good down to earth wine
When to go: Any time	list; $18–250 bottles, $4.50–6.50 by
Entree range: $18.95–28.95	the glass
Payment: VISA, AMEX, MC	Dress: Casual
Parking: Self parking in the streets	Disabled access: Good
Bar: Full service	Customers: Tourists, winter residents

Dinner: Daily, 6–10:30 p.m.

Menu recommendations: Salade camembert, mixed greens with fried camembert, sherry walnut vinaigrette; steak tartare, freshly ground beef tenderloin with condiments; grilled Caribbean-marinated pork tenderloin with saffron risotto and banana guava chutney; roast honey lacquered white duck breast and leg confit, native orange and Grand Marnier glaze; sautéed Key West pink shrimp with roasted pepper sauce; pecan-crusted native snapper served with Cuban bananas and key lime rum butter; Caribbean paella, baked lobster, shrimp, clams, chicken and Andouille sausage simmered in Caribbean herbs, yellow rice, and spicy saffron broth.

Comments: One of Key West locals' favorite for tropical gourmet fare in a friendly and relaxed atmosphere. Owner Michael Stewart created this restaurant with just the right amount of elegance for a casual area like the Keys.

ZIGGY'S CONCH RESTAURANT ★★½

		QUALITY
American	Moderate	**77**

	VALUE
Overseas Highway US 1, Mile Marker 83, Islamorada (305) 664-3391	**C**

Reservations: Accepted	Bar: Full service
When to go: Early, weeknights	Wine selection: Adequate
Entree range: $11–25	Dress: Casual
Payment: VISA, AMEX, MC, D	Disabled access: Good
Parking: Alongside building	Customers: Tourists, locals

Dinner: Daily, 5:30–10:30 p.m.

Menu recommendations: Conch chowder; raw conch salad marinated in lime juice with peppers and onions; conch fritters; cracked conch; oysters prepared five ways; any native fish prepared fried, broiled, meunière, amandine, or Lorenzo, lemon butter, béarnaise sauce and baked with crabmeat stuffing; lobster imperial; fried shrimp; fried oysters; clams casino; Florida lobster curry; grilled strip steak.

Comments: Open since 1962, Ziggy's original chef was French, a fact that continues to be reflected in the menu. The present executive chef has been there for over 30 years and continues the French touches. Fresh, native fish, however, is the main attraction here.

Entertainment and Nightlife

In Key West, where laid-back bars—many of which feature a combination of reggae and karaoke—rule over the flashy disco scene favored in Miami, some of the more popular haunts include the open-air **Schooner Wharf Bar** (202 Williams Street; (305) 292-9520), open 8 a.m.–4 a.m. with live music Thursday–Saturday. The **Green Parrot Bar** (see profile below) is another good choice for a little piece of Key West, with prime people-watching. The Sunday evening tea dance at the **Atlantic Shores Motel** (510 South Street; (305) 296-2491), a sixteen-year institution, features a disco overlooking the pier and a largely gay clientele. **Oak Beach Inn** (227 Duval Street; (305) 292-7828) boasts Key West's only oxygen bar, as well as nightly entertainment, DJs, and karaoke. Martini bars such as **Wax** (422 Appelrouth Lane; (305) 2296-6667) and cocktail lounges such as **Virgilio's** (Appelrouth Lane; (305) 296-8118) offer an alternative to the traditional Margaritaville scene.

The Best of the Keys Clubs			
Name	Cover	Cost	City
Adult Entertainment			
Rick's/Durty Harry's Entertainment Complex	None	Mod	Key West
Bars			
Captain Tony's	None	Inexp	Key West
Green Parrot Bar	None	Inexp	Key West
Sloppy Joe's Bar	None, except special events	Inexp	Key West
Dance Clubs			
Epoch	$3–8	Mod	Key West
Rick's/Durty Harry's Entertainment Complex	None	Mod	Key West
Wax	None	Mod	Key West
Karaoke			
Rick's/Durty Harry's Entertainment Complex	None	Mod	Key West
Live Music			
Captain Tony's	None	Inexp	Key West
Rick's/Durty Harry's Entertainment Complex	None	Mod	Key West
Lounge			
Wax	None	Mod	Key West

CLUB PROFILES

CAPTAIN TONY'S

Local watering hole with eclectic live music
Who Goes There: 25–40; locals and tourists, spring breakers

428 Greene Street, Key West; (305) 294-1838

Cover: None
Minimum: None
Mixed drinks: $3–5
Wine: $3.50

Beer: $2–3.25
Food available: None
Hours: Monday–Saturday, 10 a.m.–2
a.m.; Sunday, noon–2 a.m.

What goes on: This is one of the Keys' legendary bars, owned since the 1960s by local character Captain Tony, who is 77, has been married seven times, has 13 children, and was even elected mayor (1988–91). Captain Tony, who originally came to the Keys as a fisherman in the 1940s, occasionally drops by the bar, amusing patrons with incredible stories, such as how he used to give Jimmy Buffett $10 a day, plus all he could drink. In case Captain Tony doesn't show, there are live musical acts daily, starting in the afternoons. Music is truly eclectic, ranging from Nirvana to the Top 40 hits of the 1950s. In case you experience déjà vu, the bar site is the former location of the original Sloppy Joe's, before it moved to Duval Street.

Comments: An amusing hodgepodge of bar patrons past, with mementos stuffed everywhere. Wall-to-wall business cards, musical instruments, license plates, celebrity bar stools, a plane propeller, and even a bra dangling from the ceiling. Folklore has it that the bar's tip bell was stolen from an old Key West fire truck by none other than Hemingway himself, according to Captain Tony. You can wear cut-offs and flip flops, but shoes and shirts are requested at night. Try the house pirate's punch, a gin/rum/fruit-juice concoction served in a 22-ounce souvenir jug.

EPOCH

Dance club for those who are all about the music
Who Goes There: Hip 25-to-35-year-old locals in Key West casual garb; tourists who've had their fill of karaoke; DJ groupies; techno music fans

623 Duvall Street, Key West; (305) 296-8521

Cover: Friday, $3 general admission or $6
for all-you-can-drink draft beer; Saturday, $8 general admission
Minimum: None
Mixed drinks: $4

Wine: $4–6
Beer: $3–3.50
Food available: None
Hours: Tuesday–Friday, 7 p.m.–4 a.m.;
Saturday, 10 p.m.–4 a.m.

What goes on: Dancing, and lots of it. The main floor plays a mix of hip-hop, dance, R&B and reggae, while upstairs features techno music for the hardcore. Guest DJs from around the country are regularly featured. Special events include live salsa bands and the exhibitionistic bubble boxing. Saturday night is pure mayhem; the place is packed by midnight.

Comments: Imagine a spruced-up warehouse with a mega-sound system. The two-level club is spartanly furnished: exposed beams, cement floors, seven bars, and a 70,000-watt light show—the essentials to gyrate with abandon. Don't expect overstuffed banquettes or cute cocktail tables— they don't exist.

GREEN PARROT BAR

Key West's oldest bar
Who Goes There: 21–75; locals, tourists, New Yorkers escaping the rat race

601 Whitehead Street, Key West; (305) 294-6133

Cover: None	Food available: Standard Tex-Mex fare
Minimum: None	from the Gato Gordo restaurant next
Mixed drinks: $3–3.50	door
Wine: $2.75	Hours: Monday–Saturday, 10 a.m.–4
Beer: $1.50–2.75	a.m.; Sunday, noon–4 a.m.

What goes on: Open since 1890, this popular bar features live entertainment every Saturday with reggae, rock, and blues from 10 p.m. to 2 a.m. Once a month, poetry slams liven up Sundays with open readings. Occasionally, single acts perform on Saturday afternoons. Several years back, the bar's propensity for attracting the most eligible bachelors in town was noted in *Playboy* magazine.

Comments: This is an open-air bar, known to display bold (if not quality) art, with the outside walls covered in various themes (i.e., sports, slice-of-life, Jamaica). Two pool tables, two deluxe pinball machines, three dart boards, and an eclectically stocked jukebox add to the bar's breezy, laid-back charm. Dress is Key West casual. Happy hour: 4–7 p.m., 7 days a week, with $2.25 mixed drinks, $1 draft, and $1.50 domestic beer.

RICK'S/DURTY HARRY'S ENTERTAINMENT COMPLEX

Long-running Key West dance/comedy/karaoke/live music/adult entertainment venue
Who Goes There: A cross-section of Key West humanity, 20- to whatever-somethings, college-aged karaokeaholics, thirsty tourists

200 Duval Street, Key West; (305) 296-4890

Cover: None
Minimum: None
Mixed drinks: $3.25
Wine: $3.75–5.25

Beer: $2.75
Food available: Peanuts
Hours: Monday–Saturday, 11 a.m.– 4
a.m.; Sunday, noon– 4 a.m.

What goes on: You'll never be bored in this five-bars-in-one entertainment complex, which features live performers daily 3–11 p.m. in Durty Harry's Bar; karaoke at Rick's downstairs bar from 11 p.m. to closing; dancing with three bars and an open deck upstairs at Rick's upstairs bar; adult entertainment with two stages, a bar, and a private dance floor at the 21-and-older Red Garter Saloon; and al fresco cocktailing at the Tree Bar, which fronts Duval Street. Local comedian/musician Steven Neil performs Thursday through Monday evenings. Music offerings are typically reggae and rock.

Comments: New rustic. Dark wood bars–the one in the Tree Bar is so massive it spans the entire length of the space–and dim lighting pretty much sum up the decor, which relies on the local color for aesthetics.

SLOPPY JOE'S BAR

Famous and infamous Key West watering hole that Ernest (Poppa) Hemingway used to call home
Who Goes There: A mix of humanity, from local barflies to Midwestern tourists

201 Duval Street, Key West; (305) 294-5717

Cover: None, unless it's a special event
Minimum: None
Mixed drinks: $3.75–5.50
Wine: $3.25

Beer: $2.75–3.50
Food available: Light menu
Hours: Monday–Saturday, 9 a.m.– 4 a.m.;
Sunday, noon– 4 a.m.

What goes on: Famed for being the local watering hole of Ernest Hemingway, this bar has gained a following with both locals and the international tourist crowd. The Hemingway Days Festival, which originated at the bar in 1981, has now become a world-renowned week-long event. The bar continues to host the outrageous Hemingway Look-A-Like Contest in mid-July. Entertainment goes on all day and night, with a varied selection of country duets, rock, and blues vocalists.

Comments: Everything about the bar reads "sit back, relax, and have fun." There is an enormous amount of memorabilia on Hemingway and George

Russell (Hemingway's friend and owner of the bar). The original long, curving bar, ceiling fans, and jalousie doors open on busy Duval Street. Note the Depression-era mural of Russell, Hemingway, and Skinner. Check out the constant drink specials, including the bar's Pop Double, Hemingway Hammer, and Key Lime shooter, priced from $2.25–6.

WAX

Citified, clubby lounge o' the moment
Who Goes There: 25–35, hip out-of-towners and locals, both gay and straight, looking for a little bit of urban decorum (or not) in relaxed Key West

422 Appelrouth Lane, Key West; (305) 296-6667

Cover: None	Beer: $2.75–3.50
Minimum: None	Food available: None
Mixed drinks: $5	Hours: Monday–Sunday, 9 p.m.–4 a.m.
Wine: $5–6.50	

What goes on: Evenings start on a relatively mellow note at this two-year-old establishment, with well-dressed patrons sipping cocktails and over-sized martinis. The scene gradually progresses into a frenzied nightclub, with self-liberated souls dancing on banquettes and every other available surface. Local DJs spin house music every night, with national DJs making guest appearances when in the area.

Comments: This urban cocktail-lounge-meets-dance-club is tiny but packs in 250 people on a weekend night. Chinese red–lacquered walls, plush red velvet benches, and steel tables and bar give Wax the look of a sleekly modern bordello. An outside courtyard bar in the back provides relief for those needing to escape the chaos and remember they are indeed in tropical Key West.

Part Seven

Southwest Florida

Introduction

Southwest Florida, the destination on the Gulf of Mexico that most people know best as Fort Myers and Naples, has grown rapidly in recent years as northerners discover the area and its wonderful beaches. More laid-back than its cousins along the Atlantic Coast, Southwest Florida doesn't offer a lot of glitz. It is more like the Old South meets the Old West with great resorts. Peak season is January through April, and reservations are essential throughout the area during those months.

Eco-Tourism

Southwest Florida's eco-tourism is a big draw. Consider the following outstanding examples of unspoiled wetlands offering a glimpse of Florida in pristine condition:

J. N. "Ding" Darling National Wildlife Refuge, Sanibel Island

Sanibel-Captiva Nature Conservation

Calusa Nature Center and Planetarium, Fort Myers

Lovers Key State Recreation Area, Black Island, just south of Fort Myers Beach

Matanzas Pass Wilderness Preserve, Estero Island

Mound Key, accessible only by boat from Estero Island

Babcock Wilderness Adventures, North Fort Myers

Corkscrew Swamp Sanctuary, Bonita Springs

Everglades National Park and Big Cypress Swam, home of the National Audubon Society, are a short day-trip from anywhere in the region.

Southwest Florida

ATTRACTIONS

❶ Cayo Costa State Park

❷ Useppa Museum

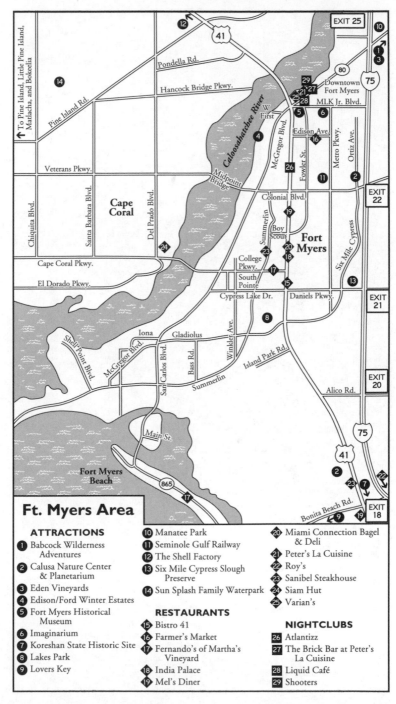

Ft. Myers Area

ATTRACTIONS

1. Babcock Wilderness Adventures
2. Calusa Nature Center & Planetarium
3. Eden Vineyards
4. Edison/Ford Winter Estates
5. Fort Myers Historical Museum
6. Imaginarium
7. Koreshan State Historic Site
8. Lakes Park
9. Lovers Key
10. Manatee Park
11. Seminole Gulf Railway
12. The Shell Factory
13. Six Mile Cypress Slough Preserve
14. Sun Splash Family Waterpark

RESTAURANTS

15. Bistro 41
16. Farmer's Market
17. Fernando's of Martha's Vineyard
18. India Palace
19. Mel's Diner
20. Miami Connection Bagel & Deli
21. Peter's La Cuisine
22. Roy's
23. Sanibel Steakhouse
24. Siam Hut
25. Varian's

NIGHTCLUBS

26. Atlantizz
27. The Brick Bar at Peter's La Cuisine
28. Liquid Café
29. Shooters

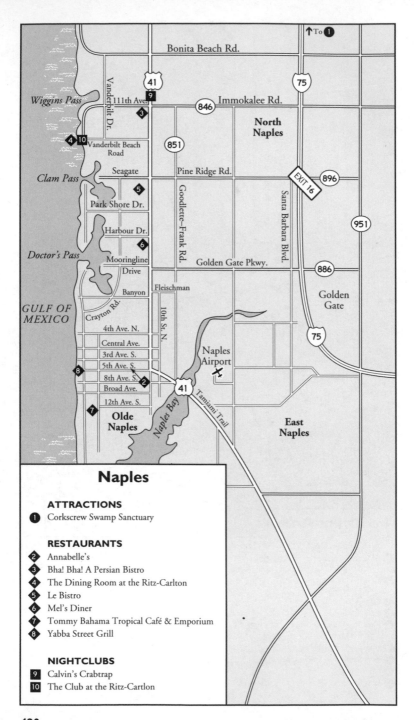

Naples

ATTRACTIONS
1 Corkscrew Swamp Sanctuary

RESTAURANTS
2 Annabelle's
3 Bha! Bha! A Persian Bistro
4 The Dining Room at the Ritz-Carlton
5 Le Bistro
6 Mel's Diner
7 Tommy Bahama Tropical Café & Emporium
8 Yabba Street Grill

NIGHTCLUBS
9 Calvin's Crabtrap
10 The Club at the Ritz-Cartlon

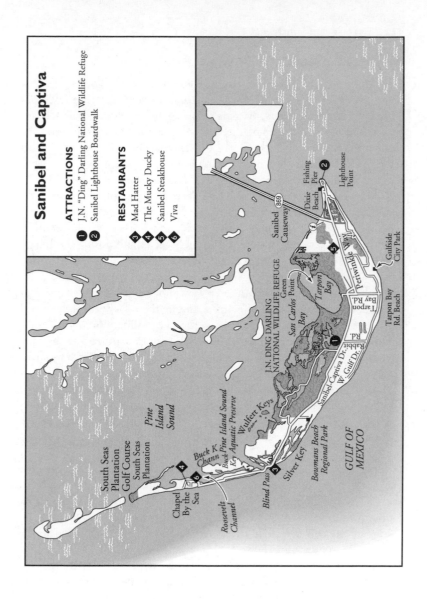

Sanibel and Captiva

ATTRACTIONS

1. J.N. "Ding" Darling National Wildlife Refuge
2. Sanibel Lighthouse Boardwalk

RESTAURANTS

3. Mad Hatter
4. The Mucky Ducky
5. Sanibel Steakhouse
6. Viva

Pine Island Sound

South Seas Plantation Golf Course
South Seas Plantation

Buck Key
Buck Pine Island Sound
Key Aquatic Preserve
Chann

Roosevelt Channel

Chapel By the Sea

Blind Pass Rd.

Silver Key

Wulfert Keys

J.N. DING DARLING NATIONAL WILDLIFE REFUGE

Green Point

San Carlos Bay

Tarpon Bay

Sanibel-Captiva Dr.
W. Gulf Dr.

Bowmans Beach Regional Park

GULF OF MEXICO

Rabbit Rd.

Tarpon Bay Rd.

Tarpon Bay Rd. Beach

Periwinkle Way

Gulfside City Park

Dixie Beach

Fishing Pier

Lighthouse Point

Sanibel Causeway

869

A Brief History

Stan Mulford, the official historian and volunteer at the Fort Myers Historical Museum, says Fort Myers, located on the Caloosahatchee River, has a history tied strongly to Native Americans, Spanish colonials, and Cubans who fished the rich waters of the Gulf of Mexico (which leads into the Caloosahatchee). One such Cuban fisherman, Manuel Gonzalez, sailed from Spain for Cuba looking for fishing grounds. He missed the island nation and settled in the Fort Myers area, later moving on to Key West.

Southwest Florida's ties to Cuba are deep. For example, cattle was sold and shipped to Cuba from Lee County from 1868 to 1878. When the rebellion between Cuba and Spain ceased, the price of cattle dropped. Boundaries of reservations were deliberately set inland during the Indian wars to prevent fishing and trading with Cubans who sold arms to the Indians.

Mulford says that in 1839 the area was home to little more than alligators, a few bears, and Cuban fishermen, among them Gonzalez, who fished off the barrier islands. Two years later, the U.S. military built a fort near the mouth of the Caloosahatchee River to supply another fort that had been hit badly by a hurricane. Eventually the new fort was named for Lieutenant Colonel Abraham Charles Myers, an Army quartermaster.

Fort Myers shipped 20 boxcars of fruit a day during the picking season, and had a nationwide reputation as a center for citrus. The historic freeze that struck Florida in 1894 prompted a discovery that citrus in the Caloosahatchee region was available, and prices soared to as much as $200 for fruit from one tree.

This was also a time when running livestock on the open range was another industry of the region. Cuba purchased Central Florida Cattle in the 1860s, and Fort Myers was the last leg on the journey over the water. Herds were driven to Punta Rassa, the shipping center. Jacob Summerlin, "king" of the cowmen built a causeway connecting the mainland to the island of Punta Rassa in 1868.

During World War II there were more military personnel than residents in the Fort Myers area. And many of those service men and women chose to return to the area and set up their post-war homes.

Today, the region is popular with tourists who enjoy the varied history and the natural beauty of the Lee Island Coast. An early tourist was the inventor Thomas A. Edison, who came to Fort Myers on doctor's orders after a rainy and cold spell in St. Augustine sent him scurrying for sunshine and warmth during the winter of 1884–1885. He spent 46 winters in Lee County, enjoying the mild climate and encouraging friends such as Henry Ford and Harvey Firestone to come and visit.

Southwest Florida Destinations

LEE ISLAND COAST

Sometimes hyperbole is right on target. Fort Myers' title of "Florida's tropical island getaway" is most accurate. The current population of Fort Myers alone is 500,000, approximately 150,000 more than in 1990. One of the state's prime growth areas, the city welcomed close to two million tourists in 1999, and growth continues as new hotels, shopping centers, and condominium complexes pop up overnight.

The area has long been a magnet for retirees from the Midwest who choose sunny skies, white sand beaches, and the wondrous waters of the Gulf of Mexico over nasty winters ruled by wind chill factors and driveways knee-deep in snow. Today, visitors come from all over the world to enjoy this beautiful "last frontier" of South Florida.

The Lee Island Coast is the area of Southwest Florida between Naples and Sarasota and includes such popular tourist destinations as Sanibel Island, Captiva Island, Fort Myers Beach on Estero Island, Bonita Springs and Beaches, Fort Myers, Pine Island, Cape Coral, Lehigh Acres, Boca Grande on Gasparilla Island, North Fort Myers, Cabbage Key, Useppa Island, Cayo Costa State Island Preserve, and North Captiva Island—a total of 652,000 acres of total land area, 590 miles of shoreline, 50 miles of beaches, and over 100 barrier and coastal islands in the Gulf of Mexico.

Each area making up the Lee Island Coast has its own personality. The islands are even more laid-back than the mainland, and a couple of them are uninhabited. A visit (by boat) conjures images of Robinson Crusoe and provides an up-close-and-personal view of the beauty, serenity, and charm of a deserted tropical island.

TROPICAL ISLAND GETAWAYS

At one time, the only way to get to tiny Sanibel or Captiva Islands was by boat or ferry. Today, a three-mile-long causeway connects the islands to the mainland.

Sanibel offers world-class shelling opportunities with some 200 varieties found on the beach. The posture one assumes looking for shells has been named the "Sanibel Stoop," and dedicated shellers have been known to attach flashlights to their heads to try to be the first on the beach after an especially high or low tide and capture an especially exotic prize shell.

Captiva's charm is its isolation and outstanding natural beauty. The late Anne Morrow Lindbergh wrote her best-selling memoir *A Gift From the Sea* on the island.

Fort Myers Beach is considered one of the "world's safest beaches" because of its gently sloping shoreline and powdered-sugar-like soft sand. During winter months, the area is home port for a large shrimp and fishing fleet.

Lesser-known North Captiva and Cayo Costa Island Preserve are often deserted and feature tempting coastlines and great shelling. Shelling guides offer excursions to these islands because competition is much less fierce than on Captiva or Sanibel.

Cabbage Key is a big-bucks destination. Mystery writer Mary Roberts Rinehart helped her son build a home here in 1938. That home is now a cozy six-room inn. The dining room is papered in thousands of autographed dollar bills worth about $30,000 today. Legend has it that the custom began when a thirsty fisherman left his bill taped to the wall, insuring a cold drink the next time he stopped by. Now, most visitors leave a green calling card.

NAPLES AND MARCO ISLAND

Naples is minutes south of Fort Myers in Collier County. It has always appealed to wealthy tourists and residents who look for fine dining, cultural events, and posh shopping opportunities. Naples is also called the "Golf Capital of America," and 1.5 million visitors spent $590 million there last year. The Collier County region is considered one of the fastest growing in the country.

The city was surveyed, plotted, and lots were sold beginning in 1887. (The area that was the primo central commercial district at the dawn of the 20th century is today a revitalized shopping and dining area.) Debt brought further development to a screeching halt until Memphis-born millionaire Barron Gift Collier used his fortune to introduce paved roads, electricity, and other conveniences to the town in the 1920s. Collier County was incorporated in 1923. Five years later, Collier completed the Tamiami Trail (connecting Miami-Dade County with the state's west coast), and the potential of an agricultural and tourist industry was first explored. Development took off after World War II, and in the 1950s began in earnest. Major hotels, such as the Ritz-Carlton in Naples, came into the region in the late 1980s.

Naples is more than just a material girl. Eleven miles of beach and nature preserves line the Gulf of Mexico. Two local beaches—Clam Pass and Delnor-Wiggins—have been rated in the Top 20 National Beaches Survey compiled by Dr. Stephen Leatherman, professor and director of the Laboratory for Coastal Research and International Hurricane Center at Florida International University, Miami. With more than 50 fine golf courses, the Naples area attracts serious golfers as well as those who enjoy eco-tourism, fishing, nature preserves, and parks.

Marco Island is the largest of Florida's Ten Thousand Islands, sometimes described as the Western Gateway to the Florida Everglades. Another golfer's delight, Marco has also established a reputation as an angler's paradise. Backwater fishing is a popular pastime.

Arriving

By Car

Many people choose to drive to Southwest Florida from their northern homes. Others head to the Gulf Coast from visits to other Florida cities. From Palm Beach, for example, take the Florida Turnpike (also known as the Ronald Reagan Expressway) south to US 595/Alligator Alley, or the Sawgrass Expressway to I-75 North, then straight into Fort Myers. I-75 South from the Tampa Bay area is a major roadway into the Fort Myers area. This latter route is the road most often taken from the Midwest, a primary source of area tourism.

Miami's Tamiami Trail (US 41) leads into Fort Myers and Naples. I-75 and US 41 are major north-south arteries into the region, and Alligator Alley and US 41 east of Naples are the key east-west highways.

Sample Distances and Drive Times to Naples

Because Florida is such a long state—and the destinations in this book lie at the southern end of the peninsula—many people tie in a trip to South Florida or the Southwest Coast with visits to other parts of the state. You have to pass through (or near) Tampa, Orlando, or Jacksonville, so why not stop?

Daytona Beach	243 miles (Five hours drive time)
Jacksonville	348 miles (Six hours dive time)
Miami	110 miles (Two hours drive time)
Orlando	189 miles (Four hours drive time)
Tampa	134 miles (Three hours drive)

By Plane

The major airport in Southwest Florida is aptly called **Southwest Florida International Airport** and is located approximately one mile east of Exit 21 off I-75. Based at Southwest Florida are Air Canada, Air Tran, Air Transat, America West, American, American Eagle, American Trans Air, Balair-CTA, Canada 3000 Airlines, Cape Air, Condor German Airlines,

Continental/Continental Connection, Delta, Delta Express, JetBlue, LTU, Midwest Express, Northwest/KLM, Pro Air, Spirit Airlines, Sun Country, TWA, United Airlines, and US Air. To reach Marco Island and the Everglades from the airport, take I-75 South to Exit 15. To reach Naples, take I-75 south to Exit 15, 16, or 17.

Visitor Services Centers are located near the baggage claim areas at the airport to help travelers with questions regarding attractions, accommodations, beaches, and parks. German is spoken at the center in the LTU International Airway Terminal. For more information, call (941) 768-1000.

Naples Municipal Airport offers commuter and direct flights, private charters, and regularly scheduled flights to the Florida Keys, Key West, and Miami. For more information, call (941) 543-0733. **Marco Island Executive Airport** offers commuter and charter flights to and from nearby international airports. For more information, call (941) 394-3355.

Taxi and limousine services are available at the airports. Taxi fares to beach resorts are about $40 from Southwest Florida International Airport and about $20 from Naples Municipal Airport. Fares from Miami International Airport run to $150.

Rental car companies include: Alamo, Avis, Budget, Cape Coral, CarTemps, Dollar, Enterprise, Hertz, National, Ro-Lin, and Thrifty. Reservations are not required for taxis and limos. Travelers simply make arrangements upon arrival at the ground transportation booth located in the median between the airport terminal and the parking lot.

Getting Around

TRAFFIC

Probably the best advice we can provide anyone choosing to rent a car and drive in Southwest Florida (or anywhere, for that matter) is to request driving instructions from your hotel, motel, or host. Let them know where you will be picking up a car and get complete directions to the property.

Speed limits vary throughout South Florida: 30 mph is common in congested areas, around hotels, or heavily populated neighborhoods; 40 or 45 mph in others, and 65 or 70 mph on the Turnpike and on I-75. Florida has a seat-belt law, requiring everyone to be buckled up, and a recently passed state law requires that children under age eight be in booster seats as well.

MAJOR ROADWAYS

US 41 (also known as the Tamiami Trail) is a major highway running east-west from Miami. It's a two-lane road through much of the route. While this highway is picturesque, it takes about three hours to get from Miami to Naples on the Tamiami.

At Naples, US 41 runs north and south between Naples and Fort Myers. It is very slow going and heavily traveled. For many years, this was the *only* highway connecting the east and west coasts. Construction along US 41 is pandemic. Although I-75, which also runs north-south from Naples, was built to handle the overflow and speed traffic through Collier and Lee Counties, it doesn't do the job. Rush hours can find both major roadways clogged.

FORT MYERS AND SURROUNDING AREAS

US 41 and I-75 carry the bulk of the north-south traffic in the area (they also lead northwest to the Tampa Bay area). East-west streets vary in the amount of traffic; a series of one-way streets in downtown Fort Myers tend to confuse visitors, but signage is clear if you pay attention.

The Caloosahatchee and Edison Bridges span the Caloosahatchee River, and State Road 80 (also called Palm Beach Road) parallels the curve of the bay. State Road 80 accesses I-75 at Exit 25.

The major routes to Fort Myers Beach and Sanibel and Captiva Islands are across McGregor Boulevard or Summerlin Road. Both roads lead to the Summerlin Bridge. You can also take San Carlos and Estero Boulevards to Fort Myers Beach; Estero Boulevard, also called State Road 865, also leads to Bonita Beach.

However, if you don't want the hassle of parking, consider other means of getting around the area:

- Bike rentals are available all across the islands, and customers are provided with a detailed map and highlighted waypoints. We suggest **Bike Route, Inc.** (2330 Palm Ridge Road, Sanibel Island; (941) 472-1955); **Billy's Rentals** (1470 Periwinkle Way, Sanibel Island; (941) 472-5248); **Finnimore's Cycle Shop** (2353 Periwinkle Way, Sanibel Island; (941) 372-5577); and **Trikes, Bikes, & Mowers, Inc.** (3451-53 Fowler Street, Fort Myers; (941) 936-1851).

- Trolley tours are also popular and provide guides with knowledge of the region. **Adventure in Paradise Trolley** picks up visitors for a narrated two-hour tour at 11 a.m. at the Sanibel and Captiva Islands Chamber of Commerce (1159 Causeway Road, Sanibel; (941) 472-1080). Cost is $15 adults, $12 children, and children under 3 ride free. Another trolley ride costs only 25 cents and runs up and down Estero Boulevard the length of Fort Myers Beach. This trolley serves only as transportation, providing no narration or sight-seeing, but it may be better than trying to park along the beach.

- **Lee Tran** buses and trolleys offer transportation to Bonita Beach Park on Little Hickory Island, leaving from the K-Mart store at Bonita Beach Road and US 41 in Bonita Springs. Cost is 25 cents.

- Captiva offers cruises to Cabbage Key and Useppa Islands, as well as shelling cruises and a late-afternoon cruise to view dolphin and wildlife. For more information, contact **Captiva Cruises** (11401 Andy Rosse Lane, Captiva Island; (941) 472-5300) or **Captiva Kayak and Wildside Adventures** (11401 Andy Rosse Lane, Captiva Island; (941) 395-2925).

NAPLES AND MARCO ISLAND

Three exits from I-75 reach Naples: Exit 15 is Golden Gate, a main Naples exit; Exit 16, Pine Ridge Road, leads directly to US 41; and Exit 17, Immokalee Road, leads to North Naples to the west and the National Audubon Society's famed Corkscrew Swamp Sanctuary to the East. Corkscrew is 18 miles northeast of Naples. To get to Marco Island, take Exit 15 (Golden Gate) off I-75 and head south on Collier Boulevard for 20 miles.

The Naples/Marco Island area is smaller than Fort Myers, and a turn to the west takes you to the beaches as well as hotels, restaurants, and local attractions. Naples has a special charm—it's more intimate and pricey than it's larger neighbor but has the same wonderful beaches.

Naples' Third Street South is a remnant of the town's old central commercial district. Third Street is at the western edge of Fifth Avenue South, Naples' Main Street. It is the heart of old Naples, and legend has it that Charles and Anne Morrow Lindbergh often landed their plane on a strip at the corner of Fifth Avenue and Third Street to have Sunday lunch at the Naples Hotel. Today, Third Street South sits on the National Register of Historic Places and is home to more than 100 shops, galleries, outdoor cafes, and restaurants.

Marco Island is a serene outpost on the Gulf of Mexico where many vacationers choose to get around by bicycle or trolley. You can get there via FL 951/Isle of Capri Road. Day cruises leave from Marco Island to Key West (Key West Shuttle, 1079 Bald Eagle Drive #3, Marco Island; (941) 394-7979).

These counties and municipalities are well aware they are tourist destinations, and every road is clearly marked with signs.

PUBLIC TRANSPORTATION

LeeTran offers local bus service Monday–Saturday from 5:30 a.m. to 9:45 p.m. and limited service to the beach on Sunday from 6 a.m. to 9:45 p.m. LeeTran also offers airport service hourly 6 a.m.–10 p.m. to a transfer point at Daniels Parkway and U.S. 41 with connections to other routes. Fare is $1 adults, 50¢ seniors and disabled citizens, and free for children

---

LeeTran Ticket Outlet Locations

LeeTran Administration Building: 10715 East Airport Road
Lee County Administration Office: Monroe and 2nd Streets
Edison Community College: Student Services Building
Cape Coral City Hall: Country Club at Nicholas
Cape Coral McCrory's: Leonard at Cape Coral Parkway

---

under 42 inches tall. For more information on LeeTran, call (941) 275-8726 or check the web at **www.lee-county.com/leetran.**

Gathering Information

General Florida information is available from FLAUSA in a variety of sources: (888) 7FLA-USA; **www.flausa.com;** Visit Florida Headquarters, P.O. 1100, Tallahassee, FL 32302-1100. Vacation guides are available for domestic and international visitors, including a version for the United States, the United Kingdom, and versions in German, French, and Spanish.

Southwest Florida Information

Lee County Alliance of the Arts
10091 McGregor Boulevard
Fort Myers, FL 33919
(941) 939-2787

Lee Island Coast Visitor and
   Convention Bureau
2180 West First Street, Suite 100
Fort Myers, FL 33901
(800) 237-6444 or
   (941) 338-3500
www.leeislandcoast.com

Marco Chamber of Commerce
1102 North Collier Boulevard
Marco Island, FL 34145
(941) 394-7549
chamber@marco-island-
   florida.com

Marco Island Everglades
(800) 785-8252

Greater Naples, Marco Island,
   and The Everglades
Tourism Alliance of Collier
   County
5395 Park Central Court
Naples, FL 34109
(941) 597-8001
www.marcoislandeverglades.com
www.classicflorida.com

Southwest Florida Hispanic
   Chamber of Commerce
3343 Palm Beach Boulevard
Fort Myers, FL 33916
(941) 334-3190

The Beaches

Southwest Florida is best known for three things: a wide variety of eco-tourism opportunities, myriad golf and tennis opportunities, and outstanding sugar-sand beaches along the turquoise Gulf of Mexico. It's Florida's laid-back coast, an ideal vacation destination as well as a great place to live.

Below we list some of the most outstanding beaches in Southwest Florida.

FORT MYERS AREA

Bowman's Beach, Sanibel Island   This is a city-operated beach that has picnic areas and showers. Parking is available.

Sanibel Lighthouse, Sanibel Island   The beach at this 100-year-old lighthouse offers picnic facilities and pier fishing.

Turner Beach   Big-time shelling area between Sanibel and Captiva Islands. Foot showers and handicapped parking and rest rooms are available. This is one of the most popular beaches and parking is limited. If you've ever heard the expression "Sanibel Stoop," this is where it originated, with dedicated shellers looking for the best.

Gulfside Park, Sanibel Island   Located off Casa Ybel Road on Sanibel Island, the beach offers swimming, picnicking, showers, and rest rooms.

Lovers Key State Recreation Area   Between Fort Myers Beach and Bonita Beach, the state's newest park offers 2.5 miles of white sand beaches, shelling, swimming, bridge-top and back-bay fishing, bird-watching, and more. Entry fee is $2 per person, two–eight people in one vehicle $4, walk-ins and bicyclists $1 per person.

Bowditch Point Regional Park, Estero Island   A 17-acre park designed to provide a total day at the beach. Free parking at Main Street, or ride the trolley for 25 cents; handicapped parking is available inside the park.

Lakes Regional Park   This park at 7330 Gladiolus Drive in Fort Myers consists of 279 acres of Florida foliage and summertime fresh-water swimming. Other water sports and picnic tables are also available. Expect a $2 per person fee to ride the miniature train. Parking is 75 cents per hour, $3 maximum per day.

Bonita Beach Park, Bonita Springs   A full-service beach with plenty of parking. Alternatively, you can park at the Big K at Bonita Beach Road and US 41 in Bonita Springs and take the bus or trolley for 25 cents.

Cayo Costa Island State Preserve   Between North Captiva and Boca Grande; (941) 964-0375. This is a secluded island accessible by boat only with unique plants that are purportedly the same as they were 500 years ago. (That's not documented, but this is an uninhabited park and a little-known hideaway.)

NAPLES AND MARCO ISLAND

Delnor-Wiggins State Recreational Area   Just north of Naples, Delnor-Wiggins is called "an unspoiled beach" by Dr. Stephen Leatherman (also called "Dr. Beach"), author of *America's Best Beaches* and professor and director of the Laboratory for Coastal Research and International Hurricane Center at Florida International University. He says the sand has a unique white color and is made up of whole shells. Sea oats, sea grapes, and cabbage palms dot the sand dunes.

Clam Pass   Another outstanding natural Naples beach that's rated highly by Dr. Leatherman, who evaluates the qualities of sand and water. Leatherman says this beach at the south end of Naples has "gentle waves and a shallow, sandy bottom," making it a good place to take children.

Marco Island   Marco Island's broad beaches are all of the white sand variety and offer some excellent shelling varieties—some 400 in all. Shellers say the choices are great and include fighting conchs, cockles, and lion's paw.

Recreation

Recreation is the name of the game in Southwest Florida. The area is best known for its golf courses, and those who know say that on the Lee Island Coast alone (the Fort Myers area) a golfer can play 18 holes per day, seven days a week, and would not play the same hole twice for nearly two months. The number is somewhere around 125 courses in the Fort Myers–Naples region, considered to have more golf holes per capita than anywhere in the world. In less than ten years, 47 courses have opened in Lee (Fort Myers) and Collier (Naples) Counties.

Courses for every skill level—from less difficult "executive" courses to championship courses—seem to be around every corner. And while rates are higher (and courses busier) during the high season months of January through April, off-season golfing is a wonderfully kept secret. You can play entire courses in half the time.

Tennis, fishing, swimming, and oh-so-many water sports are also available throughout the area. Picnic grounds and bike trails, nature walks, and birding areas are all on the menu. It's an area that truly offers something for everyone, which accounts for its growing population.

FITNESS CENTERS

Most of today's new hotels offer a fitness center. It may have only two or three treadmills and a lifecycle machine, or you might find state-of-the-art cardiovascular equipment geared to keep you buff. And many hotels do not charge for the use of their fitness equipment. If your hotel doesn't offer a fitness program, here are some other options: **Wellness Center** (300 Goodlette Road, Naples; (941) 436-6770) costs $10 a day; **YMCA of Collier County** (5450 YMCA Road, Naples; (941) 597-3148) costs $8 a day; **Fitness on the Move** (13010 Metro Parkway, Fort Myers; (941) 561-1177) costs $10.60 a day; and **Asylum Fitness Club** (13211 McGregor Boulevard, Fort Myers; (941) 437-3488) costs $12 a day.

WALKING

Park and wildlife preserves offer boardwalks and walking/hiking trails. See Attractions in this chapter for profiles on **J.N. "Ding" Darling National Wildlife Refuge, Corkscrew Swamp Sanctuary, Lakes Regional Park,** and others. Also notable for walking, hiking, or running are **Mackle Park** (1361 Andalusia Terrace, Marco Island; (941) 642-0575) and **Briggs Nature Center** (401 Shell Island Road, Naples; (941) 775-8569). And the many miles of white sand beaches also offer a beautiful natural backdrop for walks along the beach. In Naples, for example, the most popular walking area is directly on the beach, but there's also a popular four-and-a-half-mile walk along the North Loop of Gulfshore Road from Admiral Ty Point to Seagate Drive that draws countless hoofers.

TENNIS

Tennis, like golf, is a year-round affair in Southwest Florida. Consider that many residents are northern transplants who seek sun and fun and have the opportunity to play golf and tennis all year. The area is a paradise to those who have shoveled snow, bundled up children, and fought the elements for years. And while golfers might argue the point, tennis is a big-bucks business all along the Gulf Coast.

Sanibel Harbour Resort & Spa has a 5,550-seat stadium court with eight lighted clay courts. Tennis greats like Pete Sampras, John McEnroe, Jimmy Connors, and Andre Agassi have all played here. Agassi says, "It's the prettiest place I've played in the United States, that's for sure. The only thing is, I don't know if we will be able to get away from the beauty to play tennis! Playing may be a bit hot, but it is worth it because when you're done, you can go swimming in the pool or at the beach. It's ideal."

Sundial Beach & Tennis Resort and **Sanibel Harbour Resort & Spa** on Sanibel Island offer outstanding beachfront tennis facilities, both clay and hard lighted courts. **South Seas Resort & Yacht Harbour** has 21 laykold courts (seven lighted for night play) and has been honored by trade magazines for outstanding facilities.

Marco Island is another tennis haven. **Racquet Club of Marco Island** (1275 San Marco Road; (941) 394-5454) and the **Hilton, Marriott,** and **Radisson** Hotels all have tennis facilities available for tourists and locals. Local public courts in Fort Myers include **Alva Community Center** (21471 North River Road, Alva; (941) 728-2587), **Bay Oaks Recreation Center** (2731 Oak Street, Fort Myers Beach; (941) 765-4222), **Boca Grande Community Center** (131 First Street West, Boca Grande; (941) 964-4492), **Hancock Park** (1526 Oak Drive, Fort Myers; (941) 656-7748), **Judd Park** (1297 Driftwood Drive, North Fort Myers; (941) 656-5138), **Olga Community Center/Park** (2325 South Olga Drive, Fort Myers; (941) 694-6355), and **Waterway Estates Park** (5820 Poetry Lane, North Fort Myers; (941) 656-5138).

GOLF

The Lee Island Coast alone has almost 80 golf courses at last count—more golf holes per capita that anywhere else in the country. The National Golf Foundation says Southwest Florida scores highly in the number of potential golfers per 18 holes of golf—Fort Myers is ranked number five nationally. It is one of the country's most popular golfing centers, with facilities for duffers and pros alike. And while seasonal crowds make tee times tough, Southwest Florida is wonderful in the off season, and in high season try to play at odd times of the day: late afternoon (which is ideal in summer) or early morning. Additionally, off-season golf is more affordable as well as accessible.

Rich Lamb, director of golf at Eastwood Golf Course and the Fort Myers Country Club, both in Fort Myers, says "it's a great place to be whether you're a golfer or not. Price-wise, it's outstanding. Whatever you can afford, you'll find something in your range. The climate is ideal and there are many courses to choose from."

These include the 6,400-yard, par-72 **Eastwood course,** which has been ranked among the top 50 public courses in the nation by golf publications for many years. It is one of three municipal courses on the Lee Island Coast, the others being the 6,1000-yard, par-71 **Fort Myers Country Club,** a course more than 84 years old and designed for walkers; and the 6,623-yard, par-72 **Coral Oaks Course** in Cape Coral. Many courses in the area are practically on the shores of the Gulf of Mexico and provide some of the most scenic rounds in the country.

Naples has about 50 golf courses and has been called the "Golf Capital of the World," while Marco Island is another popular area for golfers.

Alden Pines Country Club

Established: 1980
Address: 14261 Clubhouse Drive, Bokeelia 33922

Phone: (941) 283-2179

Status: Public course

Tees: Championship: 5,600 yards, par 71, USGA 65.4, slope 136.
Men's: 5,130 yards, par 71, USGA 65.2, slope 116.
Ladies': 4,500 yards, par 71, USGA 64.4, slope 116.

Fees: High-season rates are $37 before 11:30 a.m. including cart rental.
Rates drop later in the day and in low season.

Facilities: Snack bar, bar, club rental, GPS on each cart.

Comments: Gorgeous course with paved cart paths. Alligators and wildlife share the fairways. The greens, nurtured by brackish water, are beautiful to behold.

Bay Beach Golf Club

Established: 1975

Address: 7401 Estero Boulevard, Fort Myers Beach 33905

Phone: (941) 463-2064

Status: Public course

Tees: Men's: 3,091 yards, par 61, USGA 57.4, slope 99.
Ladies': 2,632 yards, par 61, USGA 48, slope 99.

Fees: Vary by season; run about $23 for 18 holes, without cart rental.

Facilities: Snack bar.

Comments: On lovely and serene Estero Island, Bay Beach, one of the area's oldest courses, is set in one of the prettiest beach communities in Florida. Cart rental extra.

Beachview Golf Course

Established: 1974

Address: 1100 Parkview Drive, Sanibel 33957

Phone: (941) 472-2626

Status: Public course

Tees: Championship: 6,320 yards, par 71, USGA 70.8, slope 127.
Men's: 5,838 yards, par 71, USGA 67.8, slope 118.
Ladies': 4,937 yards, par 71, USGA 67.6, slope 116.

Fees: Vary by season and time of day; early morning fees are $65, later in the day, $95. Prices plummet to $35 in the later afternoon. All prices include cart.

Facilities: Pro shop, restaurant, lockers.

Comments: This pretty course, located one block from the Gulf of Mexico, is dotted with little ponds and lakes and provides one of the most natural golf settings in the country.

Burnt Store Marina & Country Club

Established: 1982

Address: 5000 Burnt Store Road, Punta Gorda 33955

Phone: (941) 637-1577

Status: Semiprivate course; 27-hole course (Pelican and Heron courses combined below)

Tees: Championship: 3,990 yards, par 60, USGA 61.4, slope 112.
Men's: 3,542 yards, par 60, USGA 60.0, slope 105.
Ladies': 3,118 yards, par 60, USGA 60.9, slope 107.

Fees: $28–40, including cart.

Facilities: Driving range, snack bar (beer and wine only), rental clubs.

Comments: Right on Charlotte Harbor, in a gated community of homes and condos.

Country Creek Country Club

Established: 1989

Address: 21131 Country Creek Drive, Estero 33928

Phone: (941) 947-3840

Status: Semiprivate course

Tees: Championship: 3,871 yards, par 61, USGA 60.3, slope 102.
Men's: 3,462 yards, par 61, USGA 58.3, slope 97.
Ladies': 2,531 yards, par 61, USGA 55.3, slope 86.

Fees: $37, including cart rental, in high season; $16 before 11 a.m., $11 after 11 a.m. in off-season.

Facilities: Pro shop (lessons available), lockers, restaurant.

Comments: An executive course designed by Gordon Lewis and set in one of many new golf communities.

Dunes Golf & Tennis Club

Established: 1973

Address: 949 Sandcastle Road, Sanibel 33957

Phone: (941) 472-3355

Status: Semiprivate course

Tees: Championship: 5,578 yards, par 70, USGA 68, slope 123.
Men's: 5,249 yards, par 70, USGA 66.5, slope 111.
Ladies': 4,202 yards, par 70, USGA 64.5, slope 111.

Fees: $119 for morning tee times in high season to $52 for same times in low season; includes cart rental.

Facilities: No lockers, large pro shop (lessons available).

Comments: Two minutes from the beach, the course is set on 140 acres in a wildlife area; alligators, bald eagles, and other local species are always evident. This is a popular course and features 70 acres of water.

Eastwood Golf Course

Established: 1977

Address: 4600 Bruce Herd Lane, Fort Myers 33905

Phone: (941) 275-4848

Status: Public course

Tees: Championship: 6,772 yards, par 72, USGA 72.3, slope 130.
Men's: 6,226 yards, par 72, USGA 70.7, slope 125.
Ladies': 5,116 yards, par 72, USGA 68.9, slope 120.

Fees: $55 for morning tee times in high season; includes cart rental.

Facilities: Snack bar, driving range.

Comments: Very popular course, where more than 75,000 rounds of golf are played annually. Designed by Devlin Von Haage.

El Rio Golf Club

Established: 1970s

Address: 1801 Skyline Drive, North Fort Myers 33903

Phone: (941) 995-2204

Status: Public course; six executive par-4 courses—three on the front, three on the back

Tees: Men's: 3,004 yards, par 60, USGA 57.1, slope 90.
Ladies': 2,401 yards, par 60, USGA 53.1, slope 81.

Fees: $20 for morning tee times in high season; $30 with cart

Facilities: Clubhouse, snack bar, rental clubs (men's and women's, left- and right-handed clubs).

Comments: This isn't one of the new courses that appear to pop up overnight, this is a tried and true executive course and one of the area's most popular.

Gateway Golf & Country Club

Established: 1989

Address: 11360 Championship Drive, Fort Myers 33913

Phone: (941) 561-1010

Status: Semiprivate course

Tees: Championship: 6,974 yards, par 72, USGA 74.1, slope 129.
Men's: 6,225 yards, par 72, USGA 70.1, slope 121.
Ladies': 5,847 yards, par 72, USGA 73.9, slope 133.

Fees: $90 morning tee times in high season, $30 low season; includes cart rental.

Facilities: Pro shop (lessons available), restaurant.

Comments: Located near Southwest Florida International Airport; off-season, more locals play the Tom Fazio–designed course.

Lochmoor Country Club

Established: 1973

Address: 3911 Orange Grove Boulevard, North Fort Myers 33903

Phone: (941) 995-0501

Status: Semiprivate course

Tees: Championship: 6,908 yards, par 72, USGA 73.6, slope 132.
Men's: 6,514 yards, par 72, USGA 71.9, slope 130.
Ladies': 5,152 yards, par 72, USGA 69.9, slope 117.

Fees: Winter rates are $50 before 1 p.m., $20 after 3 p.m.; includes cart rental.

Facilities: Full practice facilities, restaurant, halfway house, pool, tennis, club rentals.

Comments: Bill Mitchell designed this course, located about one-half block from the historic Caloosahatchee River.

Olde Hickory Golf & Country Club

Established: 1992

Address: 14670 Old Hickory Boulevard, Fort Myers 33912

Phone: (941) 768-2400

Status: Semiprivate course

Tees: Championship: 6,601 yards, par 72, USGA 72.5, slope 135.
Men's: 6,155 yards, par 72, USGA 70.1, slope 130.
Ladies': 5,738 yards, par 72, USGA 73.1, slope 131.

Fees: $125 rates during high season (January–March); includes cart rental.

Facilities: Restaurant, bar, clubhouse, fitness center, locker room, pool.

Comments: Located ten minutes from the airport at Exit 21, this course is state-of-the-art.

Sabal Springs Golf & Racquet Club Ltd.

Established: 1989

Address: 17540 North Tamiami Trail, North Fort Myers 33917

Phone: (941) 731-0101

Status: Semiprivate course; an executive course, with two nine-hole courses and limited par 4s

Tees: Men's: 3,279 yards, par 60, USGA 58.9, slope 95.

Ladies': 2,196 yards, par 60, USGA 53.0, slope 83.

Fees: $39 for morning tee times during high season; includes cart rental.

Facilities: Snack bar, club rental.

Comments: The course was designed by Gordon Lewis and is located five miles north of the Caloosahatchee Bridge.

Tiburon Golf Club

Established: 1998

Address: 2620 Tiburon Drive, Naples 34109

Phone: (941) 394-2040

Status: Semiprivate course

Tees: Championship: 7,179 yards, par 72, USGA 74.5, slope 137.

Men's: 6,525 yards, par 72, USGA 71.2, slope 121.

Ladies': 5,140 yards, par 72, USGA 70.6, slope 124.

Fees: $215 for morning tee times during high season, $80 during low season (May14–September)

Facilities: Putting green, chipping green, golf academy, restaurants, bar, locker rooms.

Comments: Designed by Greg "The Shark" Norman. Tiburon is Spanish for "shark."

Twin Eagles

Established: 1999

Address: 11725 Twin Eagles Drive, Naples 34120

Phone: (941) 352-0002

Status: Private course

Tees: Championship: 7,197 yards, par 72, USGA 75.5, slope 141.

Men's: 6,299 yards, par 72, USGA 71.5, slope 131.

Ladies': 5,455 yards, par 72, USGA 71.7, slope 126.

Fees: $125 in high season; includes cart rental.

Facilities: Clubhouse, restaurant, locker room.

Comments: Jack Nicklaus–designed course, part of the Bonita Bay group. Eighth hole has two different greens: one at 397 yards, another at 445 yards.

BICYCLING

Sanibel Island is peppered with bike routes, and several roads (Summerlin is one) in Fort Myers and others in Naples and Marco Island are designated bike paths. Before you rent a bike, request a map of the bike trails.

Watch the traffic and enjoy some of the outstanding bike trails in the region. Bike rental shops include **Bike Route** (locations at 2330 Palm Ridge Road, Sanibel, (941) 472-1955; and at 14530 South US 41, Fort Myers, (941) 481-3376), **Finnimore's Cycle Shop** (2353 Periwinkle Way, Sanibel; (941) 472-5577), and **Trikes, Bikes, and Mowers** (3451-53 Fowler Street, Fort Myers; (941) 936-1851). **Colliers Seminole State Park** (20200 E. Tamiami Trail, Naples; (941) 394-3397) offers more biking opportunities.

BIRD-WATCHING

Birders enjoy Marco Island's smaller, uninhabited sister islands that are home to a wide range of rare and endangered wading birds. **Everglades National Park,** one of the nation's largest wildlife sanctuaries, is home to more than 200 species of birds—egrets, herons, ibis, osprey, and the American Bald Eagle. **Cape Coral** has the state's largest number of burrowing owls— estimated at about 10,000 pairs. They grow to about nine inches and have a wingspan of over 20 inches. Some birders claim 300 species live on this coast. We think **J.N. "Ding" Darling National Wildlife Refuge** on Sanibel Island offers some of the best birding in the state (if not the country), but the Everglades and other nature parks all over the area are rife with birders.

CANOEING AND KAYAKING

Southwest Florida's Sanibel and Captiva Islands have found their way onto *Paddler* magazine's list of ten best kayaking destinations in the nation. *Paddler* publisher and editor Eugene Buchanan kayaked on the Lee Island Coast and says, "besides the islands having a strong community feel, the area's temperate climate is great for year-round kayaking, and its easy access and close proximity to other areas are ideal for paddlers." For more information, contact the following: **Captiva Kayak and Wildside Adventures** (11401 Andy Rosse Lane, Capitva Island; (941) 395-2925); **Estero River Outfitters** (20991 South Tamiami Trail, Estero; (941) 992-4050); **Gulf Coast Kayak** (The Olde Fish House Marina, 4530 Pine Island Road, Matlach; (941) 283-1125); **Tropic Star of Pine Island, Inc.** (16499 Porto Bello Street, Bokeelia; (941) 283-0015); **Canoe Adventures, Inc.** (716 Rabbit Road, Sanibel Island; (941) 472-5218); **Briggs Nature Center** (401 Shell Island Road, Naples; (941) 775-8569); and **Naples Nature Center** (1450 Merrihue Drive, Naples; (941) 262-0304).

SCUBA DIVING AND SNORKELING

The Gulf of Mexico along the Southwest Florida coast offers some dive sites with visibility approaching 50 feet. Artificial reefs are plentiful and made up of old culverts, the old Edison Reef, and a ship called the *Pegasus*. The Caloosa Dive Club has been exploring underwater sites for three decades. For more information, contact **Scuba Quest** (11705-3 Cleveland Avenue, Fort Myers; (941) 826-7566) or **Seahorse Scuba** (15600 No. 19 San Carlos Boulevard, Fort Myers; (941) 454-3115).

SAILBOATS AND SAILING SCHOOLS

Sailing on the Gulf of Mexico is an exhilarating experience, and thousands of sailors have learned their skills at the **Offshore Sailing School** (16731 McGregor Boulevard, Fort Myers; (941) 434-1700), founded 26 years ago by Olympic and America's Cup winner Steve Colgate. Offshore teaches at South Seas Resort on Captiva Island (call (941) 454-1700) and Hawk's Cay in the Florida Keys, as well as at other locations throughout the Caribbean and United States. Other sailboat rentals and schools include: **Captiva Kayak and Wildside Adventures** (11401 Andy Rosse Lane, Captiva Island; (941) 395-2925); **Florida Sailing and Cruising School** (3444 Marinatown Lane, NW #19, North Fort Myers; (941) 656-1339); and **Sanibel Island Adventures** (call (941) 826-7566).

FISHING

Fishing on the Gulf Coast can be fishing from almost anywhere. It can be by boat in the backcountry, inshore or offshore. Called a fisherman's paradise by those who know about such things, the opportunities are so varied that they appeal to anyone who loves the water and has ever picked up a fishing rod. Snook, redfish, spotted sea trout, sheepshead, jack, crevalle, mangrove snapper, and other varieties of fish can be caught in mangrove shorelines; over the open flats; around bridges, piers, and docks; and by wading. Shark, grouper, bonito, barracuda, permit, black fin tuna, cobia, and Spanish and king mackerel can be caught over natural or artificial reefs offshore.

During the months of April, May, and June, tarpon migrate by the thousands from Boca Grande pass to the reefs off Sanibel Island and Fort Myers Beach. They can be fished many ways. In Boca Grande Pass (known as the world capital of tarpon fishing), anglers in 20- or 30-foot boats employ a controlled drift-fishing technique with heavy tackle using live bait. Along the beaches of Boca Grande, Cayo Costa, North Captiva, and Captiva and Sanibel Islands, as well as the backcountry, anglers pursue tarpon in smaller boats and flat skiffs. Light tackle with live crabs or 11 to 15 weight fly rods with various flies are used. On the reefs in water 20 feet deep or more, anglers use live bait and heavy tackle.

Freshwater fishing targets bass, crappie, blue gill, shell crackers, catfish, and Oscars, using poles, plug casting outfits, spinning reels, or fly rods. Bait can be plastic worms, wild shiners, artificial lures, crickets in the spring, and fly-fishing flies.

Fishing Guide Referral Services	
Boca Grande Fishing Guides Association	(800) 667-1612
Fish Southwest Florida	(888) 347-4793
Pro Guides Co-op of Southwest Florida	(800) 945-9858

Party Boats

No fishing license is required on party boats, and fishers of any age can go out. Tackle is supplied, and boats are usually 60–100 feet with a rest room and a small galley. Average cost for a half day is $25 per person ($40 for a full day).

Charter Boats

No fishing license is required, and anglers can charter a captain and boat for a half-day or full day. Tackle is supplied; costs range from $150 for half-day to $400 for a full day.

Anyone can fish from beaches, piers, bridges, or docks. A saltwater license is required for nonresidents over the age of 16 and can be obtained from the Lee County Tax Collector (phone (941) 339-6000) or through Florida Marine Patrol (phone (941) 332-6966). The Marine Patrol also provides information on fishing regulations and closed seasons for specific types of fish.

More than 50 marinas are available on the Lee Island Coast alone. Here's a sampling, offering bait, charters, fishing equipment, and customized trips:

Southwest Florida Marinas		
Marina	**Location**	**Phone**
Sanibel and Captiva Islands		
Adventure Sailing Charters	Couth Seas Plantation	(941) 472-7532
Captain Jim's Charters	Tween Waters Marine	(941) 472-1779
Castaways Marina	6460 Sanibel-Captiva Road	(941) 472-1112
Sanibel Marina	634 North Yachtsman Drive	(941) 472-2723
South Seas Plantation	Yacht Harbor	(941) 472-5111
Tarpon Bay Recreation, Inc.	900 Tarpon Bay Road	(941) 472-8900
Fort Myers Beach (Estero Island)		
Calusa Coast Outfitters	2668 Shriver Drive	(941) 332-0709
Captain Dan's Fishing	416 Crescent Street	(941) 463-4166

Southwest Florida Marinas (continued)		
Marina	Location	Phone

Fort Myers Beach (Estero Island) (continued)
Fish Tale Marina	7225 Estero Boulevard	(941) 463-3600
Island Lady Deep Sea Fishing	702 Fisherman's Wharf	(941) 482-2005
Moss Marine	450 Harbor Court	(941) 463-6137

Fort Myers
| Adventures in Paradise | 14341 Port Comfort Road | (941) 472-8443 |
| Sanibel Harbour Marina | 15051 Punta Rassa Road | (941) 267-3717 |

Cape Coral
| Cape Coral Yacht Basin | 5819 Driftwood Parkway | (941) 454-0141 |
| Lazy Day Charters | 1428 SW 53rd Lane | (941) 549-9366 |

Bonita Springs and Beaches
Bonita Bay Marina	27598 Marina Point Drive SE	(941) 495-3222
Captain Ron LePree	9971 Puopolo Lane	(941) 498-9992
Estero Bay Boat Tours	5231 Mamie Street SW	(941) 992-2200

North Fort Myers
| Captain Jack Stanaland Fishing Charters | 11650 Deal Road | (941) 731-0812 |
| Captain Van Hubbard/ Let's Go Fishing, Inc. | P.O. Box 821 | (941) 697-6944 |

SPECTATOR SPORTS

Baseball

Southwest Florida has been a baseball town for more than 100 years, and "batter up" is a cry heard year-round. The area hosts two of the twenty major league teams in the Florida Grapefruit League, a Winter Baseball League team, and a Florida State League team.

The first baseball team in Lee County was organized in January 1896, playing its first game the following July 4. Baseball continued as a major player in the region, and in 1925, the Philadelphia Athletics became the first major league club to train in Fort Myers. Cornelius McGillicuddy, better known as Connie Mack, was the team manager. Mack's grandson and namesake was a U.S. senator from Lee County. From 1939 to 1940, the Cleveland Indians made Fort Myers their spring training headquarters. And in 1955 the Pittsburgh Pirates came to town.

Terry Park is not a "park" in the true meaning of the word—it's comprised of four baseball fields. Don't expect playground equipment or picnic facilities. This is the headquarters for Lee County Parks & Recreation

(3410 Palm Beach Boulevard, Fort Myers; (941)338-3300). Terry Park does have quite a history, including its role as the site of the annual Lee County fair for some 50 years. It was also home to Kansas City Royals spring training from 1968 to 1988.

The **Lee County Sports Complex** in south Fort Myers (which includes the William H. Hammond Stadium) is spring training headquarters for the **Minnesota Twins** and the summer home to the **Fort Myers Miracle.** The 7,500-seat stadium opened in 1994 and boasts 4 regulation major league practice fields, 2 half-fields, 4 softball practice fields, 10 indoor batting cages (4 in the main stadium), and 30 practice pitching areas with mounds. The handicapped-accessible stadium is located at 14100 Six Mile Cypress and Daniels Parkway, Fort Myers; phone (941) 768-4270 or (941) 768-4210.

The Minnesota Twins are the fifth team in more than 65 years to train in Lee County; call (941) 768-4270 for tickets. The Class-A Fort Myers Miracle became affiliated with the Twins. Actor Bill Murray and songwriter Jimmy Buffet are part-owners of the Miracle and have been known to attend games; call (941) 768-4210 for tickets.

The **City of Palms Park** (2201 Edison Avenue, Fort Myers; (941) 334-4700) in downtown Fort Myers is the spring training home of the **Boston Red Sox.** The ten-year-old, 6,800-seat stadium resembles Chicago's Wrigley Field or Boston's Fenway Park.

Hockey

In 1998, the East Coast Hockey League's **Florida Everblades** made their permanent home in the area at an ice and inline rink, **The Fort Myers Skatium,** a 71,000-square-foot facility featuring laser tag, indoor soccer and volleyball, a pro shop, and off-ice practice and warm-up areas. Individual and group lessons in figure skating and hockey are offered.

The Everblades belong to the East Coast Hockey League and compete with 26 other franchises in the eastern half of the country. The Skatium is located at 2250 Broadway, Fort Myers; (941) 461-3145.

Shopping

STROLLING AND WINDOW SHOPPING

Fifth Avenue South   Naples' Fifth Avenue South is a wonderful street for taking a delightful walk, window shopping, buying the perfect gift, or picking up something special for the new baby next door. Shoppers of the world love this avenue, with its wonderfully colorful array of shops, galleries, boutiques and restaurants. Most clothing stores feature a collection of pricey leisure and golf wear (and a lot in bright colors—strictly Florida-deco hues—are sure to catch your eye!).

Other popular stores throughout the region offer golf gear for men and women, fishing clothes and accoutrements, and galleries galore. Some of these are branches of stores from Martha's Vineyard, Nantucket, Palm Beach, and other resort centers. Stores generally close between 5 p.m. and 6 p.m., but some shops are open until 9 p.m. on Thursday, Friday, and Saturday. Some stores are open on Sundays during high season; others stay closed on Sundays year-round.

Fifth Avenue South is home to **Back of the Bay** (555 Fifth Avenue South; (941) 263-4233), offering one-of-a-kind women's sweaters and outerwear, plus hand-painted apparel, shoes, and jewelry. **GH Collections** (727 Fifth Avenue South; (941) 649-4356) features men's and women's clothing and original artwork by Guy Harvey, a famous marine wildlife artist. **Glad Rags Etc.** and **Glad Rags Too** (655 and 757 Fifth Avenue South; (941) 261-0675 and (941) 262-3222) are a pair of stores hawking bright colors and Lily Pulitzer and Fresh Produce resort wear for women; they also sell sportswear featuring wonderful floral and sea life prints in yet more bright and cheery colors. Like lime green and turquoise? Purple and pink? Blue and yellow? This one's for you.

Other Fifth Avenue South shops include **Giggle Moon** (720 Fifth Avenue South, Suite 105; (941) 643-3833), a children's boutique featuring local and European designs; **The Paddle** (300 Fifth Avenue South; (941) 262-4688), a men's store specializing in sportswear with a local flavor; and **The Wind in the Willows** (793 Fifth Avenue South; (941) 430-2100), a ladies' wear and gift shop with a literary theme. For shells and a coral gallery (this is high quality we're talking about), try **The Blue Mussel** (478 Fifth Avenue South; (941)262-4814).

Dennison-Moran Gallery at (696 Fifth Avenue South; (941) 263-0590) and **Gallery on Fifth** (680 Fifth Avenue, South, (941) 435-7377) are but two of the many fine galleries on the street. Both stock contemporary art.

Elsewhere in Naples   Don't miss a visit to the **Ted E Bear Shoppe** (2120 Tamiami Trail North; (941) 261-2225 or (800) 814-bear) for everything imaginable connected with teddy bears—cocktail napkins, Christmas decorations, pillows, keepsake bears, and collectibles of all kinds with prices tags from $5 to $2,000. This is but one of six bear-y nice stores where you can even have your old mink coat made into a teddy bear.

For an area with a large number of golf courses, what would you expect but a huge collection of women's golf wear? The best selection awaits the shopper at **For the Love of Golf** (976 South Tamiami Trail North; (941) 566-3395), where you can find all the newest and sharpest gear for the next 18 holes.

Tin City in Naples on US 41 (1200 Fifth Avenue South and East Goodlette Road; (941) 262-4200) is a collection of 40 waterfront restaurants and shops. Of course there are the ubiquitous T-shirt shops, souvenirs, jewelry, and tourist-tempting goodies, but the waterfront setting makes it a great place to pass the time.

Other shopping opportunities include: **Coastland Center** (1900 Tamiami Trail North, Naples; (941) 262-7100), built in a Key West style; **Third Street South,** a group of stores now on the National Register of Historic Places; and **Waterside Shops** (5415 Tamiami Trail North, Suite 320, Naples; (941) 261-0030), an upscale mall anchored by Saks Fifth Avenue and Jacobson's department stores. **Prime Outlets** (7222 Isle of Capri Road, Suite 121, Naples; (941) 775-8083) offer more than 40 stores, including Mikasa (#112 6060 Collier Boulevard, Naples; (941) 793-7171); Harry & David (#26 6060 Collier Boulevard, Naples; (941) 417-5530); Dansk (#4 6070 Collier Boulevard, Naples; (941) 793-5533); and Etienne Aigner (#65 6060 Collier Boulevard, Naples; (941) 793-0654).

Marco Island   Expect to find numerous resort boutiques and bathing suit shops, as well as stores for sandals, sunglasses, and sunscreen. They include **The Beach House** (1300 Third Street South; (941) 261-1366) and **The Cricket Shop** (326 13th Avenue South; (941) 262-6791).

Fort Myers   **Edison Mall** (4125 Cleveland Avenue; (941) 939-5465) is the largest mall in the region and includes Florida-based Burdines and Dillards plus the usual mall fare. **Tanger Sanibel Factory Outlet Stores** (20350 Summerlin Road, just before the Sanibel Causeway; (941) 454-1974 or (888) 471-3939) offers 55 shops. The upscale, Mediterranean-style **Bell Tower Shops** (corner of US 41 and Daniels Parkway; (941) 489-1221) just completed a multi-million-dollar renovation. Bell Tower Shops houses Saks Fifth Avenue, dozens of other name retailers, and a variety of restaurants.

Miromar Outlets (10801 Corkscrew Road, Estero; (941) 948-3766) hosts DKNY, Ellen Tracy, NIKE, FILA, and Bose outlets; and **Promenade Shops at Bonita Bay** (South Bay Drive off US 41, Fort Myers; (941) 334-7001) are also not to be missed on a rainy day.

SPECIALTY SHOPS

Antiques

World Antiques (1111 Fifth Avenue South, Naples; (941) 263-0609) features global antique furniture and decorative arts for serious collectors and gift-buyers alike. **Antique Mall at Treasure Island** (950 Central Avenue,

Naples; (941) 434-7684) and **Tenth Street Antiques** (183 10th Street South, Naples; (941) 649-0323) are other good options.

Books

Barnes & Noble (13751 S. Tamiami Trail, Fort Myers; (941) 437-0654) has more than 100,000 book titles and CDs. **The Book Store** (Coralwood Shopping Center, Cape Coral; (941) 574-2225); **MacIntosh Book Shop** (2365 Periwinkle Way, Sanibel Island; (941) 472-1447); **The Book Trader** (170 10th Street North, Naples; (941) 262-7562); **Dunn & Dunn Booksellers** (1300 Third Street South, Naples; (941) 435-1911); and **The Wise Old Owl** (826 Neapolitan Way, Naples; (941) 263-3249) are other good options.

Cigars

Timmy Tobacco (852 Fifth Avenue, South, Naples; (941) 403-3550) has the oldest walk-in cigar humidor in the area.

Fruit

Sun Harvest Market (Big Green Packinghouse, Metro Parkway and Six Mile Cypress Parkway; (941) 768-2686 or (800) 743-1480) sells gift packs and fresh Florida fruits and food for shipping to the folks back home.

Shells

In an area known for its shelling, what could be a better souvenir than a shell? **The Shell Factory** (2787 North Tamiami Trail, North Fort Myers; (941) 995-2141) has been one of the region's most famous shopping experiences for more than five decades. Last year the mega-store reopened and claims to have the world's largest collection of rare shells, sponges, and fossils from the seven seas. Sprawling across more than 65, 000 square feet, the Shell Factory has shell jewelry (ranging from costume to fine) and shell magnets, T-shirts, night lights, chimes, mobiles, key chains, towels, and candles, among many other options. There's also a video game area, a glass blower, a seafood restaurant, a live animal area called "Journey into Africa," the Railroad Museum, and bumper and paddle boats. Not as pretty as Sanibel Island, but the shells are easier to find.

Shoes

Visit **Ellie's Pricey Shoes** (10063 East Tamiami Trail, Naples, (941) 732-1322; and 16520 South Tamiami Trail, at Island Park Plaza, Fort Myers, (941) 432-2384) for discounted big name shoes. **Naples on the Run** (2128 9th Street North, Naples; (941) 434-9786) has a good selection of running shoes. And **Pratt's Shoe Salon of Naples** (1183 Third Street South, Naples; (941) 261-7127) has a wide assortment of dressy and casual shoes.

Swimwear

Swim World (13300-53 South Cleveland Avenue, Fort Myers; (941) 481-3350) offers a variety of swimwear in the latest styles, fabrics, and colors.

Winery

Eden Vineyards Winery (19850 State Road 80, 10 miles east of Fort Myers at I-75 and Exit 25, Alva; (941) 992-2411) is the southernmost winery in the country. Wine tastings are offered daily and include unique carambola wine.

FLEA MARKETS

Visit **Fleamasters Flea Market** (State Road 82, one-and-one-quarter mile west of I-75 at Exit 23, Fort Myers; (941) 334-7001) for kitschy Florida souvenirs, T-shirts (tacky and trendy alike), produce, and craft items.

Attractions

On Florida's Southwest Coast, a perfect day might include a variety of things. It could be golf on any one of more than 100 golf courses or a day sea-fishing for tarpon. The sport of tarpon fishing actually originated in Southwest Florida's Pine Island Sound in the late 1880s, and Boca Grade Pass, the opening between Cayo Costa and Gasparilla Islands, is considered the "tarpon fishing capital of the world."

Other ideal days could be spent luxuriating at a posh spa, shopping 'til you drop, or just enjoying the sun and sea with a cool drink at your elbow on any of the beautiful beaches along the Gulf of Mexico.

Unlike other parts of The Sunshine State, where "nature" is relegated to landscaping at high-end hotels or restaurants, nature lovers in the Fort Myers/Naples area get a big bonus with a number of outstanding facilities where wildlife and the environment take center stage. Local parks include more than one million acres of nature sanctuaries—most with paths or boardwalks—which permit visitors to see unspoiled wetlands where they can experience the beauty of the state in pristine condition.

These include **J. N. "Ding" Darling National Wildlife Refuge,** the **Sanibel-Captiva Nature Conservation Foundation,** the **Calusa Nature Center, Carl E. Johnson Park** at Lovers Key, **Matanzas Pass Wilderness Preserve, Babcock Wilderness Adventures, Gulf Coast Kayak, Ostego Bay Foundation, Corkscrew Swamp Sanctuary, Big Cypress Preserve,** and **Everglades National Park.** For most parks, a flat fee is charged for parking or entry for a car full of people. Some request donations from visitors.

Sure, there are malls, movie theaters, restaurants, and dozens of shopping centers (and we describe these in separate sections), but nature is big business in this part of Florida. You won't find world-class art exhibits on tour here, but you will find some of the most wonderful scenery in the world.

Other spots to visit include **Children's Science Center** (2915 NE Pine Island Road; (941) 997-0012); **Palm Tree Park** (corner of Edwards Drive and Lee Streets, Fort Myers; (941) 334-0839), sporting palm trees from all over the world; **Sun Harvest Citrus** (14810 Metro Parkway; (941) 768-2686), a huge fruit-packing house that allows a look at Florida's citrus industry; and **Mound Key** (just east of Lovers Key, Fort Myers Beach; (941) 418-5941), where people believe the Calusa Indians lived more than 1,000 years ago and built the island from shells. Amateur and professional archaeologists do research on the site.

Most of the attractions dotting the region are nature-oriented and many are outdoors, so heed our warnings about wearing sunscreen and hats, carrying plenty of water, and wearing comfortable shoes.

We've tried to prioritize your touring at a glance. You'll find all the information you'll need, plus the author's rating from one star (don't bother) to five stars (don't miss) and a brief look at the attraction. Art museums with changing exhibitions are not included. Most museum-type attractions offer group rates for ten or more people.

A Time-Saving Chart

Name	City	Author's Rating
Amusement park/petting zoo/shops		
The Shell Factory	Fort Myers	★★
Aquarium		
Imaginarium	Fort Myers	★★
Home and Garden Tour		
Edison/Ford Winter Estates	Fort Myers	★★★
Lighthouse		
Sanibel Lighthouse Boardwalk	Sanibel Island	★★
Museums		
Calusa Nature Center & Planetarium	Fort Myers	★★
Fort Myers Historical Museum	Fort Myers	★★★
Imaginarium	Fort Myers	★★
Useppa Museum	Useppa Island	★★
Parks and Nature Experiences		
Babcock Wilderness Adventures	Punta Gorda	★★★½
Cayo Costa State Park	Costa Island	★★

A Time-Saving Chart (continued)		
Name	City	Author's Rating
Parks and Nature Experiences (continued)		
Corkscrew Swamp Sanctuary	Naples	★★
J.N. "Ding" Darling National Wildlife Refuge	Sanibel Island	★★
Koreshan State Historic Site	Estero	★★
Lakes Park	Fort Myers	★★
Lovers Key	Fort Myers Beach	★★
Manatee Park	Fort Myers	★★
Six Mile Cypress Slough Preserve	Fort Myers	★
Planetarium		
Calusa Nature Center & Planetarium	Fort Myers	★★
Train Excursion		
Seminole Gulf Railway	Fort Myers	★
Vineyard and Winery		
Eden Vineyards	Alva	★
Water Park		
Sun Splash Family Waterpark	Cape Coral	★★

ATTRACTION PROFILES

Babcock Wilderness Adventures

Type of Attraction: Wildlife woods and waters of Telegraph Cypress Swamp

Location: 8000 State Road 31, Punta Gorda 33982

Admission: Adults, $19.21; seniors, $18.21; children ages 3–12, $10.65

Hours: November–April, daily, 9 a.m.–3 p.m.; May–October, mornings only—call for times

Phone: (800) 500-583 or (941) 489-3911

When to Go: Early morning or late afternoon

Special Comments: The Ranch has won an Environmental Stewardship Award due to its dedication to working in harmony with nature.

Overall Appeal by Age Group:

Pre-school	Grade School	Teens	Young Adults	Over 30	Seniors
★	★★★	★★★	★★★	★★★	★★★

Author's Rating: ★★★½

How Much Time to Allow: Minimum of three hours

Description and Comments   One of the best of the nature trips in the region, with a museum, snack bar, and 90-minute swamp buggy tour. The tour provides a glimpse of panthers, bison, alligators, exotic birds, and boar, and an amazing overview of the exciting wilderness that makes up the Babcock Ranch—which has been in the same family since 1914.

Touring Tips   Bring water and pick up snacks at the snack bar. Be sure to make reservations. *Note:* The swamp buggy tour may be rough on those with bad backs.

Other Things to Do Nearby   Head back west over the bridge and spend the rest of the day at The Shell Factory—a 20-minute ride from Babcock—or stop by Manatee Park.

Calusa Nature Center & Planetarium

Type of Attraction: Natural history concentrating on the background of the Calusa Indians and their place in the history of the Southwest Coast

Location: 3450 Ortiz Avenue, Fort Myers 33905

Admission: Museum: Adults, $4; children ages 3–12, $2.50. Planetarium: adults, $3; children, $2

Hours: Monday–Saturday, 9 a.m–5 p.m.; Sunday, 11 a.m.–5 p.m.

Phone: (941) 275-3435

When to Go: Any time

Special Comments: Handicapped access; laser show offered first Friday of the month. Call for times.

Overall Appeal by Age Group:

Pre-school	Grade School	Teens	Young Adults	Over 30	Seniors
★	★★	★★★	★★★	★★★	★★★

Author's Rating: ★★

How Much Time to Allow: Two hours

Description and Comments   A great display of Southwest Florida's history, including information on the Calusa Indians who ruled the area from 800 to 1700 A.D.

Touring Tips   If you have little ones, take the stroller onto the mile-long boardwalk.

Other Things to Do Nearby   Hit the Edison Mall for air-conditioned comfort and shopping.

Cayo Costa State Park

Type of Attraction: State park

Location: Cayo Costa Island between North Captiva and Boca Grande in the Gulf of Mexico; accessible only by boat.

Admission: Parking is 75 cents an hour, maximum of $3

Hours: Daily, 8 a.m.–sunset

Phone: (941) 964-0375

When to Go: Any time

Overall Appeal by Age Group:

Pre-school	Grade School	Teens	Young Adults	Over 30	Seniors
★★	★★	★★	★★★	★★★	★★★

Author's Rating: ★★

How Much Time to Allow: At least two–four hours

Description and Comments This is one of the largest uninhabited barrier islands in the state, and it sports some unique vegetation. Cayo Costa lies in a transition area between the temperate southeastern coastal plain and subtropical South Florida. If you love the outdoors, natural beauty, pine flatwoods, oak-palm hammocks, and grassy areas, and you enjoy swimming, fishing, hiking, and camping, this one's for you.

Touring Tips Take the ferry from Pine Island (phone (941) 283-0015). The island has rest rooms, cold showers, and drinking water. Bring everything else with you, including snacks, hats, and sunscreen.

Other Things to Do Nearby Nothing—this is a true tropical island. It's a great place to play Robinson Crusoe, but don't expect a Burger King around the corner or a supermarket on the next block. It makes a nice day's outing.

Corkscrew Swamp Sanctuary

Type of Attraction: Natural forest

Location: 375 Sanctuary Road (Exit 17 of I-75), Naples 34120

Admission: Adults, $6.50; college students and National Audubon Society members, $5; school children through 12th grade, $3; children under age 5 free

Hours: Daily, 7 a.m.–5 p.m.

Phone: (941) 348-9151

When to Go: Any time; early in the day or late in the afternoon will be cooler, as it gets pretty hot out on the boardwalk.

Special Comments: The watershed is owned and operated by the National Audubon Society; it features wading and migratory birds and other wildlife on a two-mile trail though the largest virgin bald cypress forest in the country.

Overall Appeal by Age Group:

Pre-school	Grade School	Teens	Young Adults	Over 30	Seniors
★	★★	★★	★★★	★★★	★★★

Author's Rating: ★★

How Much Time to Allow: Two–three hours

Description and Comments This is Florida at its finest, 180 degrees from the hectic sun and fun of Florida's beaches. Corkscrew offers exquisite natural beauty. The birds are magnificent, the quiet unbelievably serene, and the experience thoroughly enjoyable. Younger children will likely get bored, but birders will love it. And the boardwalk through the pinelands, hammock, and cypress ponds offer some spectacular natural sites.

Touring Tips Go early. It gets hot quickly, so don't forget to bring water and hats (and your camera).

Other Things to Do Nearby Head for anything in Bonita Springs or Naples after a tour of Corkscrew. It might be a good time to head to the beach and veg out. If the kids have been patient while you hung out with the herons, take them to Clam Pass Beach and enjoy the sun, sand, and shelling. Shells you might see include the Sunray Venus, Thorny Sea Star, Alphabet Cone, Horse Oncch, Lettered Olive, Florida Fighting Conch, Pear Whelk, Apple Murex, Sand Dollar, Atlantic Giant Cockle, Lightning Whelk, and more.

J.N. "Ding" Darling National Wildlife Refuge

Type of Attraction: Wildlife preserve

Location: One Wildlife Drive, Sanibel Island 33957

Admission: Cars, $5; walkers or bikers, $1; Visitors center is free

Hours: Saturday–Thursday, 7:30 a.m.–6 p.m.; closed Friday

Phone: (941) 472-1100

When to Go: Any time

Overall Appeal by Age Group:

Pre-school	Grade School	Teens	Young Adults	Over 30	Seniors
★★	★★	★★★	★★★	★★★★	★★★★

Author's Rating: ★★

How Much Time to Allow: Two hours

Description and Comments Named after an early conservationist, this 6,000-acre wildlife refuge is located on the northeast side of Sanibel Island. "Ding" Darling was Chief of the U.S. Biological Survey—the forerunner of the U.S. Fish and Wildlife Service—and saw the need to protect natural habitats. See alligators, roseate spoonbills, snow egrets, great blue herons, and more.

Touring Tips The five-mile drive is best done slowly to enjoy the surroundings and wildlife.

Other Things to Do Nearby Shelling. Again! This is Sanibel, you know. Pick and choose from some of the widest variety of shells in the country.

Eden Vineyards

Type of Attraction: Vineyard and winery
Location: 19709 Little Lane (Exit 25 off I-75), Alva 33920
Admission: Adults, $2.50
Hours: Daily, 11 a.m.–4 p.m.
Phone: (941) 728-9463
When to Go: Any time
Special Comments: Adults only, of course.
Overall Appeal by Age Group:

Pre-school	Grade School	Teens	Young Adults	Over 30	Seniors
—	—	—	★★	★★★	★★★

Author's Rating: ★
How Much Time to Allow: One hour

Description and Comments Set on 20 acres, this vineyard has been operated by the Kiser family for more than 20 years and is the country's southernmost winery. Take an informal tour and sample the six wines produced here. While Southwest Florida isn't about hardcore vineyards, the wine is pretty good. One wine is made from tropical star fruit and has been called Florida's alternative to California blush. If you've never been to a winery and want a change of activity, this is ideal.

Touring Tips Eden Vineyards wines make nice gifts. Groups of 12 or more must be arranged by prior appointment.

Other Things to Do Nearby Visit Manatee Park to watch the endangered West Indian Manatee in its natural environment.

Edison/Ford Winter Estates

Type of Attraction: Old home of multi-millionaire, plus lab and gardens

Location: 2350 McGregor Boulevard, Fort Myers 33901

Admission: Adults, $12; children ages 8–12, $5.50; children under age 6 free

Hours: Monday–Saturday, 9 a.m.–5:30 p.m.; Sunday, noon–5:30 p.m.

Phone: (941) 334-3614

When to Go: Any time

Special Comments: Don't miss the gigantic banyan tree out front near the entry. A gift from Harvey S. Firestone (the tire guy), the tree was planted in 1925 when it was only four feet tall. It's now over 400 feet in circumference.

Overall Appeal by Age Group:

Pre-school	Grade School	Teens	Young Adults	Over 30	Seniors
★	★★	★★★	★★★★	★★★★	★★★★

Author's Rating: ★★★

How Much Time to Allow: Two hours or more

Description and Comments In 1884, Thomas Alva Edison, whom we thank for inventing the light bulb, phonograph, and dozens of other things electrical, decided to make his winter home in Fort Myers. The home was built in 1886 and donated to the city of Fort Myers in 1947 by Edison's widow Mina Miller Edison. See not only his home, laboratory, experimental gardens, and museum but also rare antique cars and some 200 Edison phonographs among the memorabilia. Edison convinced his buddy Henry Ford to visit Fort Myers, and Ford also became a winter resident. A gate between the two properties is called the "Friendship Gate."

Touring Tips Take a guided tour so you don't miss anything.

Other Things to Do Nearby Fort Myers Historical Museum to put things in perspective—not all settlers lived so well.

Fort Myers Historical Museum

Type of Attraction: National history museum

Location: 2300 Peck Street, Fort Myers 33901

Admission: Adults, $6; seniors, $5.50; children, $3

Hours: Tuesday–Saturday, 9 a.m.–4 p.m.

Phone: (941) 332-5955

When to Go: Any time

Special Comments: Commemorates the region in the days during World War II, when there were more military in the area than civilians. Also explains the term "Florida crackers" (they were cowboys and cattle ranchers who cracked whips).

Overall Appeal by Age Group:

Pre-school	Grade School	Teens	Young Adults	Over 30	Seniors
★★	★★★	★★★	★★★	★★★	★★★★

Author's Rating: ★★★

How Much Time to Allow: Two–three hours

Description and Comments This wonderful museum of Floridiana is housed in an old Atlantic Coast Line railroad station built in 1923 (there's Esperanza, a private rail car on the siding next door). The museum offers a fairly comprehensive record of the region's history: Native Americans, military, agricultural beginnings, cowboys, more military during World War II, and a big-time boom in growth these last 40 years. There's a collection of carnival and Depression glass—one of the first gifts to the museum.

Touring Tips Take a guided tour and take your time. It's worth it.

Other Things to Do Nearby Spend the rest of the day touring the Edison/Ford Winter Estates and see how the millionaires lived. It's impressive.

Imaginarium

Type of Attraction: Hands-on museum and aquarium

Location: 2000 Cranford Avenue, Fort Myers (4 miles west of I-75, Exit 23 in downtown Fort Myers) 33916

Admission: Adults, $6; students and seniors, $5.50; children under age 13, $3; children under age 3 free

Hours: Tuesday–Saturday, 10 a.m–5 p.m.; Sunday, noon–5 p.m.; closed Monday

Phone: (941) 337-3332

When to Go: Any time

Special Comments: Kids will enjoy this interactive learning center geared to explore the principles of science.

Overall Appeal by Age Group:

Pre-school	Grade School	Teens	Young Adults	Over 30	Seniors
★★	★★★	★★	★★★	★★	★★★★

Author's Rating: ★★

How Much Time to Allow: Two hours

Description and Comments Good for all ages. See a giant Pipe-O-Saurus at the wetland area entry, stand in a Florida thunderstorm without getting wet, and surf the Internet or broadcast the weather from a TV center.

Touring Tips Take your time. This can be fun for the whole family.

Other Things to Do Nearby Visit Fort Myers Historical Museum.

Koreshan State Historic Site

Type of Attraction: State park
Location: South US 41, Estero 33928
Admission: $3.25 per vehicle
Hours: Daily, 8 a.m.–sunset
Phone: (941) 992-0311
When to Go: Any time
Overall Appeal by Age Group:

Pre-school	Grade School	Teens	Young Adults	Over 30	Seniors
★	★★	★★★	★★★	★★★	★★★

Author's Rating: ★★
How Much Time to Allow: Two hours minimum

Description and Comments A religious sect was created on these grounds. The sect was headed by Dr. Cyrus Teed, a Union Army Medical Corps veteran inspired by a vision or "divine illumination," which prompted him to change his name to Koresh (Hebrew for Cyrus) and move his followers to Southwest Florida. He thought he'd create a city of ten million people. Although it never materialized—the settlement had nearly 250 residents—13 of the original 60 buildings are left. Teed's home is one of the remaining buildings. Be sure to see the one-of-a-kind globe illustrating Koreshan belief that man resides on the inside surface of the earth, gazing at the solar system within. This is also a state park, with nature trails, boat ramp, canoeing, fresh- and saltwater fishing, and camping.

Touring Tips Wear comfortable shoes, a hat, and sunscreen.

Other Things to Do Nearby Anything in Bonita Springs or Naples; you are right on the Tamiami Trail, which offers a smorgasbord of restaurants, shops, movie theaters, and more, all within minutes of Koreshan.

Lakes Park

Type of Attraction: Park
Location: 7330 Gladiolus Drive, Fort Myers 33908
Admission: Parking is 75 cents an hour; admission is free
Hours: Daily, 8 a.m.–8 p.m.; closed Christmas Day
Phone: (941) 432-2000

When to Go: Any time

Overall Appeal by Age Group:

Pre-school	Grade School	Teens	Young Adults	Over 30	Seniors
★	★★	★★	★★★	★★★	★★★

Author's Rating: ★★

How Much Time to Allow: Three hours

Description and Comments   Diversions include swimming, nature trails, bike and boat rentals, and picnic areas with barbecue grills and showers. Check out the Fragrance Garden, created especially for persons with visual impairments. Names of herbs are printed in Braille and include chamomile, basil, sage, and rosemary.

Touring Tips   The park is a dream family destination. We recommend it as a multigenerational chance to enhance the senses and enjoy nature in a lovely setting. You'll find walking and hiking trails, a beach, bike and boat rentals, and picnic areas.

Other Things to Do Nearby   Anything on US 41; you're just a half-mile away. Wander through any of the dozen strip-mall shopping centers. Kids will love The Ted E. Bear Shoppe, and a variety of golf and tennis shops appeal to sports enthusiasts. Enjoy the air-conditioning in these shops.

Lovers Key

Type of Attraction: State park

Location: 8700 Estero Boulevard, Fort Myers Beach 33931

Admission: One person, $2; two–eight people in vehicle, $4; walk-ins and bicyclists, $1 per person

Hours: Daily, 8 a.m.–sunset

Phone: (941) 463-4588

When to Go: Any time

Special Comments: Canoe and kayak explorations are available.

Overall Appeal by Age Group:

Pre-school	Grade School	Teens	Young Adults	Over 30	Seniors
★★	★★	★★	★★★	★★★	★★★

Author's Rating: ★★

How Much Time to Allow: All day if possible

Description and Comments   This romantic park with 2.5 miles of white sand beaches is a new addition to the area's parks and offers excursions to view endangered West Indian manatees and bottlenose dolphins. It's ideal for those who merely love the beach or those who want to see more wildlife. Loggerhead sea turtles nest along the beach in season. From May to October, 300-pound big mama turtles come ashore nightly to dig their nests above high-tide line along the beach. Sixty days later, the babies break out of their Ping-Pong-sized eggs. A lights-out policy is in effect during nesting and hatching periods and year-round on Sanibel. Fishing, bird-watching, and various boat rides are also on tap on Lover's Key.

Touring Tips   Don't forget the sunscreen, hat, and comfortable shoes.

Other Things to Do Nearby   Visit another beach or stop off at one of the shopping centers dotting the Tamiami Trail.

Manatee Park

Type of Attraction: Marine park
Location: State Road 80, Fort Myers 33905
Admission: Parking is 75 cents per hour; $3 maximum per day
Hours: April–September, daily, 8 a.m.–8 p.m.; October–March, 8 a.m.–5 p.m.
Phone: (941) 694-3537
When to Go: Any time; climate and weather conditions determine whether the manatees will be resting or feeding on the river.

Overall Appeal by Age Group:

Pre-school	Grade School	Teens	Young Adults	Over 30	Seniors
★★	★★	★★★	★★★	★★★	★★★

Author's Rating: ★★
How Much Time to Allow: Two hours

Description and Comments   See the endangered West Indian Manatee in its natural habitat from three observation decks during the winter months. Year-round facilities include picnic areas, fishing, and canoeing. The park's restored native plant habitats and butterfly gardens are lovely.

Touring Tips   Bring a picnic basket and enjoy. Dress for the outdoors— comfy shoes are a must.

Other Things to Do Nearby   Eden Vineyard or Babcock Wilderness Park are two good possibilities.

Sanibel Lighthouse Boardwalk

Type of Attraction: Lighthouse
Location: East tip of Sanibel Island, 33957

Admission: Parking is 75 cents an hour

Hours: Daily, 8 a.m.–sunset

Phone: (941) 472-6477

When to Go: Any time

Special Comments: Great photo op; park in fishing pier lot.

Overall Appeal by Age Group:

Pre-school	Grade School	Teens	Young Adults	Over 30	Seniors
★	★★	★★	★★★	★★★	★★★

Author's Rating: ★★

How Much Time to Allow: One hour

Description and Comments   This is a beautiful open lighthouse, probably one of the most photographed spots on this scenic island. The lighthouse has been a landmark since 1834.

Touring Tips   The boardwalk is 400 feet long and wheelchair accessible. Bring your camera to take home your own version of the lighthouse.

Other Things to Do Nearby   Shell on any of the nearby beaches.

Seminole Gulf Railway

Type of Attraction: Train excursions

Location: Metro Mall Station, at Colonial Boulevard and Metro Parkway, Fort Myers 33919

Admission: Varies

Hours: In summer the train operates Wednesday–Sunday, but call for locations and exact departure times.

Phone: (941) 275-8487 or (800) 736-4853; www.semgulf.com

When to Go: Check schedules

Overall Appeal by Age Group:

Pre-school	Grade School	Teens	Young Adults	Over 30	Seniors
★	★	★★	★★★	★★★	★★★

Author's Rating: ★

How Much Time to Allow: Varies, whether you take the dinner tour, murder mystery tour, or train ride; evening tours are 3½ hours long.

Description and Comments   A unique take on the area's history while riding in a 1930s–1950s vintage railroad car. The dinner tour offers a five-course meal with wine and other beverages. The daytime tour provides narration and a snack bar.

Touring Tips   Take the evening trip.

Other Things to Do Nearby   Spend the day outdoors or at the beach before you take the dinner train. The train leaves around 6:30 p.m., so you can still see the passing scenery.

The Shell Factory

Type of Attraction: Amusement park/petting zoo/shops
Location: 2787 North Tamiami Trail, Fort Myers 33903
Admission: Free
Hours: Daily, 10 a.m.–9 p.m.
Phone: (941) 995-2141
When to Go: Any time
Special Comments: A little bit of this, a little bit of that, and hundreds of thousands of shells of every size, shape, and description.

Overall Appeal by Age Group:

Pre-school	Grade School	Teens	Young Adults	Over 30	Seniors
★★	★★	★★★	★★★	★★★	★★★

Author's Rating: ★★
How Much Time to Allow: One–two hours

Description and Comments   There's a railroad museum, video arcade, bumper and paddle boats, and a petting zoo. The Shell Factory is a little tacky, but it's worth wandering through the enormous building and out-buildings. Never before has such a big area been dedicated to seashells.

Touring Tips   Since Southwest Florida is best known for its shelling, this property pays homage to the shell—and shell novelties. Buy your souvenirs here—the choices are many. Skip the video games but enjoy the bumper boats and petting zoo.

Other Things to Do Nearby   This might be the day to head out to Babcock Wilderness Adventures and commune with nature (including a swamp buggy ride with a trained naturalist discussing the bison, deer, and alligators you'll see throughout Telegraph Cypress Swamp) before shell shopping.

Six Mile Cypress Slough Preserve

Type of Attraction: Nature park
Location: 7751 Penzance Crossing (off Six Mile Cypress Parkway), Fort Myers 33912
Admission: $2 parking fee

Hours: Times vary by season; call first; summer: 8 a.m.–8 p.m., with guided tours at 9:30 a.m. on Wednesday and Saturday

Phone: (941) 432-2004

When to Go: Any time

Overall Appeal by Age Group:

Pre-school	Grade School	Teens	Young Adults	Over 30	Seniors
★	★★	★	★★	★★	★★

Author's Rating: ★

How Much Time to Allow: One–two hours

Description and Comments   This wetland ecosystem with a 1.2-mile-long boardwalk offers self-guided and free guided walks year-round. Keep your eyes peeled for turtles, alligators, river otters, white-tailed deer, and blue herons, among other wildlife. In the flora department, you can see five distinct plant communities, including cypress swamp.

Touring Tips   Take a camera.

Other Things to Do Nearby   For even more nature action, check out Calusa Nature Center & Planetatirum (3450 Ortiz Avenue, Fort Myers; (941) 275-3435).

Sun Splash Family Waterpark

Type of Attraction: Water theme park

Location: 400 Santa Barbara Boulevard, Cape Coral

Admission: Adults and children 48 inches and taller, $9.95; smaller children, $7.95; children under age 2 free

Hours: Friday, 11 a.m.–5 p.m.; Saturday and Sunday, 10 a.m.–5 p.m.

Phone: (941) 574-0557

When to Go: Early in the day

Overall Appeal by Age Group:

Pre-school	Grade School	Teens	Young Adults	Over 30	Seniors
★	★★	★★★	★★★	★★	★★

Author's Rating: ★★

How Much Time to Allow: Two–three hours

Description and Comments   Zoom Flume, Cape Fear (a popular tube slide), and the new Electric Slide are the main attractions here but don't overlook the inner-tube river and children's play area. Outside food and beverages are not allowed in the water park proper; however, you can eat and drink all you want at the picnic area outside the gates. U.S. Coast Guard life jackets are the only ones approved for use in the park (a limited supply is available at the park).

Touring Tips   Pack a lunch, enjoy it at the outside picnic area, then attack the slides.

Other Things to Do Nearby   You won't need more, but if you do, consider the Children's Science Center also in Cape Coral on NE Pine Island Road.

Useppa Museum

Type of Attraction: Historical museum
Location: Useppa Island; mailing address: P.O. Box 640, Bokeelia 33922
Admission: $3
Hours: Tuesday–Friday, noon–2 p.m.; Saturday and Sunday, 1–2 p.m.;
   closed Monday and holidays
Phone: (941) 283-9600
When to Go: Any time
Special Comments: The island is accessible only by boat.
Overall Appeal by Age Group:

Pre-school	Grade School	Teens	Young Adults	Over 30	Seniors
★	★★	★★	★★	★★★	★★★

Author's Rating: ★★
How Much Time to Allow: One hour

Description and Comments   A 30-minute audio tour is available, and don't miss a forensic restoration of Useppa Man, taken from a skeleton found during an archeological dig in 1989.

Touring Tips   Tie it into a Captiva Island visit.

Other Things to Do Nearby   Head back to Captiva, which will seem overly civilized after visiting Useppa.

Dining and Restaurants

Known primarily as a laid-back sun-and-surf destination, Southwest Florida's burgeoning restaurant scene offers some of the usual suspects as well as many gastronomic surprises. With a year-round population of more than a half-million people as well as nearly four million visitors a year, the area attracts ever more of the major chains along with scores of smaller concerns. Visitors will find many of the old reliables—Perkins, Applebee's, Steak & Shake, TGI Friday's, Bennigan's, and Tony Roma's, among them.

The area's culinary stature rose several points in 1999, when Roy Yamaguchi, the celebrated West Coast chef, opened his first restaurant east of the Mississippi in Bonita Springs, a small city between Fort Myers and Naples. Known for innovative style that fuses Pacific Rim, Californian, and European ingredients, **Roy's** has become one of the region's most popular dinner destinations.

For those who love Italian food, there are dozens of restaurants from which to choose. Options range from the big boys, such as **Carrabba's, Olive Garden,** and **Buca di Beppo,** to mom-and-pop affairs that seem to have been lifted whole from New York or Chicago and set down in the subtropics. In virtually all of them, expect large portions and relatively modest prices. Almost as plentiful are steakhouses such as **Outback, Angus,** and **Lone Star,** along with several upscale versions, including **Don Shula's** and **Mike Ditka's** in Naples and accomplished local concerns with multiple locations, including **Sanibel Steakhouse** and **Bogert's Chop House.** Most ethnic cuisines are well represented, with Mexican, French, Chinese, and Japanese most prevalent.

EATING LIKE A NATIVE

Diners looking for local flavor should seek out a restaurant specializing in fresh seafood or Floribbean fare (a blend of Caribbean and Florida flavors). Florida seafood includes grouper, a lean, firm fish frequently served in a sandwich as well as grilled, fried, or blackened; Florida lobster tails, which are less rich than their New England counterparts and are actually large crawfish tails; and the much-heralded stone crab claws, taken from crabs without killing them, which allows them to regenerate their limbs. The claws, in season from mid-October through mid-May, can be eaten hot or cold and are served much the same way as lobster: partially cracked, with a shell cracker, cocktail fork, lemon, and drawn butter. Do not be alarmed at the sight of dolphin on the menu. It is not the mammal, but a fish species also known as mahi-mahi. Most good seafood houses also serve fresh shrimp, tuna, yellowfin, salmon, snapper, and swordfish. Depending on how busy they are, some restaurants will cook a customer's fresh catch. Call first to make sure.

It takes some searching, but there are a few restaurants that serve another local species, found in abundance both in the wild and at commercial farms: Florida gator. While it has a well-earned reputation for toughness, gator tail can be a tasty alternative protein when prepared by an expert. It's often served fried, although it appears in chowders as well.

Not surprisingly, many people want to dine where there's a water view. There are quite a few restaurants located on such high-rent real estate. Many, however, seem to believe that by offering a great view, customers will fail to notice that the food is below average while the prices are not.

For a glimpse of the inspiration behind Jimmy Buffett's hit, "Cheeseburger in Paradise," hop a water taxi for a trip to Cabbage Key, a small barrier island off the coast accessible only by boat. The walls are lined with thousands of signed dollar bills of past patrons and the somewhat pricey lunch menu features shrimp and cheeseburgers.

CHOOSING A TIME AND PLACE

As is the case at stores and on streets and beaches, the area's restaurants are more crowded from Christmas to Easter, when winter residents and sun-seeking vacationers flock to the area. During the winter tourist season, it's wise to make a reservation if the restaurant accepts them. Otherwise, expect to wait.

Given its reputation as a prime beach resort area, Southwest Florida embraces the casual lifestyle. As a result, even most of the nicest establishments have few regulations regarding dress beyond requiring shoes and shirts. Only a few even suggest that gentlemen wear jackets.

That doesn't mean there's no place to go for a special occasion. The Ritz-Carlton, Naples, has several restaurants, two of which have won international acclaim for food, service, and atmosphere. **The Dining Room,** where jackets are required, has been a repeat winner of both Mobil five-star and AAA five-diamond awards. **The Grill Room** next door has won widespread acclaim as well. Other special-event-worthy choices are **Peter's La Cuisine** in Fort Myers, **Chez Le Bear** at the Sanibel Harbour Resort & Spa in south Fort Myers, **Lafite** at The Registry Resort in Naples, and **Roy's** in Bonita Springs.

At the other end of the scale, there are lots of little eateries serving on-the-run food—such as pizza and hot dogs—for those who don't want to waste a second of precious beach time indoors.

EXPLAINING THE RATINGS

We have developed detailed profiles for the restaurants we think are the best in each county. Each profile features an easily scanned heading that allows you, in just a second, to check out the restaurant's name, cuisine, star rating, cost, quality rating, and value rating.

Star Rating   The star rating is an overall rating that evaluates the entire dining experience, including style, service, and ambience, in addition to the taste, presentation, and quality of the food. Five stars is the highest rating possible, meaning the place has the best of everything. Four-star restaurants are exceptional and three-star restaurants are well above average. Two-star restaurants are good. One star is given to average restaurants that demonstrate an unusual capability in some area of specialization, for example, an otherwise forgettable place that has great corned beef.

Cost . Below and to the left of the star rating is an expense category giving the general price range for a complete meal. A complete meal for our purposes consists of an entrée with vegetable or side dish, and choice of soup or salad. Appetizers, desserts, drinks, and tips are excluded. Categories and related prices are listed below.

Inexpensive	$14 or less per person
Moderate	$15 to $30 per person
Expensive	More than $30 per person

Quality Rating   On the far right of each heading appears a number and a letter. The number is a food quality rating based on a scale of 0 to 100, with 100 being the best rating attainable. The quality rating is based expressly on the taste, freshness of ingredients, preparation, presentation, and creativity of food served. There is no consideration of price. If you are a person who wants the best food available and cost is not an issue, you need look no further than the quality ratings.

Value Rating   If, on the other hand, you are looking for both quality and value, then you should check the value rating, expressed in letters. The value ratings are defined as follows:

A	Exception value, a real bargain
B	Good value
C	Fair value, you get exactly what you pay for
D	Somewhat overpriced
F	Significantly overpriced

Payment   We've listed the type of payment accepted at each restaurant using the following codes:

AMEX	American Express (Optima)
CB	Carte Blanche
D	Discover
DC	Diners Club
MC	MasterCard
VISA	Visa

About These Choices

We have chosen restaurants that, while we can't guarantee their staying power, have proven to operate successfully for some time. We've also selected restaurants with a following among local professionals, residents, and tourists. We have included a mix of restaurants that are well known and some that are low-profile, and in the process we have tried to provide something for everyone. Bon appetit!

The Best of Southwest Florida Restaurants

Restaurant/Type	Star Rating	Quality Rating	Value Rating	City
American				
Bistro 41	★★★★	94	C	Fort Myers
Mel's Diner	★★★½	90	A	Fort Myers, south Fort Myers, Bonita Springs, Naples
British-Style Pub				
The Mucky Duck	★★★½	87	B	Captiva Island
Caribbean				
Tommy Bahama Tropical Café & Emporium	★★★★	94	B	Naples
Continental				
Peter's La Cuisine	★★★★½	96	C	Fort Myers
Euro-Asian				
Roy's	★★★★½	96	C	Bonita Springs
European				
Varian's	★★★★	95	C	Fort Myers
French				
The Dining Room at The Ritz-Carlton	★★★★★	99	C	Naples
Le Bistro	★★★★½	97	B	Naples
Viva	★★★★½	96	C	Captiva Island

The Best of Southwest Florida Restaurants (cont.)

Restaurant/Type	Star Rating	Quality Rating	Value Rating	City
Indian				
India Palace	★★★★	93	B	Fort Myers
Italian				
Fernando's of Martha's Vineyard	★★★	84	B	Fort Myers, Fort Myers Beach
Kosher-Style Deli				
Miami Connection Bagel & Deli	★★★★½	96	B	Fort Myers
Middle Eastern				
Bha! Bha! A Persian Bistro	★★★★	93	C	Naples
New American				
Mad Hatter	★★★★½	95	C	Sanibel
Annabelle's	★★★★	93	D	Old Naples
Seafood				
Fernando's of Martha's Vineyard	★★★	84	B	Fort Myers, Fort Myers Beach
Southern				
Farmer's Market	★★★★	95	A	Fort Myers
Steakhouse				
Sanibel Steakhouse	★★★★	91	D	Sanibel Island, Fort Myers, Bonita Springs
Thai				
Siam Hut	★★★★	94	B	Cape Coral
Tropical				
Yabba Street Grill	★★★★	94	C	Naples

ANNABELLE'S ★★★★

New American	Expensive	QUALITY
		93

494 Fifth Avenue South, Old Naples
(941) 261-4275

	VALUE
	D

Reservations: Strongly recommended
When to go: Dinner
Entree range: $15.95–36.95
Payment: VISA, MC, AMEX, D
Parking: Street
Bar: Full service
Wine selection: Gargantuan and award-winning, with more than 500 selections; $26–2,100 by the bottle; 13 by the glass, $6–12
Dress: Stylishly casual downstairs; jackets preferred upstairs
Disabled access: Yes
Customers: The chic and chic wannabes

Dinner: Upstairs: Monday–Saturday, 6–10 p.m.; downstairs: Monday–Thursday, 5–10 p.m., Friday and Saturday, 5–11 p.m.

Menu recommendations: Heart of palm and Maytag blue cheese casserole appetizer; salmon cured with fine teas and spices; pan-roasted Chilean sea bass with crab and asparagus ragout; charbroiled dry-aged prime New York strip with tomato chips and demi glace; warm apple tart with butterscotch sauce a la mode.

Comments: Not all tables are created equal in this tony two-restaurants-in-one. Downstairs features small-plate Asian cuisine and a lively setting that includes a wall of water and a glass bar that glows. The more formal restaurant with French influences is upstairs with its own set of curiosities, including a few curtained booths and 26-foot ceilings. Request a window seat or, for true intimacy, one of the booths with curtains.

BHA! BHA! A PERSIAN BISTRO ★★★★

Middle Eastern	Moderate	QUALITY
		93

Pavilion Shopping Center, 847 Vanderbilt Beach Road,
Naples; (941) 594-5557

	VALUE
	C

Reservations: Recommended
When to go: Dinner
Entree range: $14.95–17.95
Payment: VISA, MC, AMEX
Parking: Free lot
Bar: Beer and wine
Wine selection: Not large but nicely varied; $20–80 by the bottle; $5–7.50 by the glass
Dress: Stylishly casual
Disabled access: Wheelchair accessible
Customers: The culinarily adventurous and gourmets in the know

Lunch: Monday–Thursday, 11:30 a.m.–3 p.m.; Saturday and Sunday, 11:30 a.m.–2:30 p.m.

Dinner: Monday–Saturday, 5–10 p.m.; Sunday, 5–9 p.m.

Menu recommendations: Roasted butternut squash soup; duck in pomegranate sauce; charbroiled lamb drizzled with homemade yogurt; Persian ice cream with saffron and rose water.

Comments: Except during the busiest winter months, expect entertainment by a belly dancer on Thursdays and a fortune teller on Fridays. The menu includes some Middle Eastern classics as well as innovations by chef/owner Michael Mir. The decor reflects that same diversity. Servers are usually well informed and helpful.

BISTRO 41		★★★★
		QUALITY
Eclectic American	Moderate	94
		VALUE
Bell Tower, 13499 South Cleveland Avenue, Fort Myers (941) 466-4141		C

Reservations: Recommended for dinner
When to go: Dinner
Entree range: $10.95–23.95
Payment: VISA, MC, AMEX
Parking: Free lot
Bar: Full service

Wine selection: Wide-ranging; $18–180 bottle; 12 by the glass, $5 - $7.50
Dress: Chic casual to moderately dressy
Disabled access: Wheelchair accessible
Customers: Professionals, vegetarians, families, friends

Lunch: Monday–Saturday, 11:30 a.m.–2:30 p.m.

Dinner: Sunday–Thursday, 4–10 p.m.; Friday and Saturday, 5–10:30 p.m.

Menu recommendations: Bistro 41 salad; roasted chicken; meatloaf with mashed potatoes; vegetables en papillote; chocolate bourbon bread pudding.

Comments: Located in the trendy Bell Tower shopping center, Bistro 41 offers both classic comfort food and cutting-edge cuisine. Many dishes are offered in half portions. It's directly across the parking lot from a 20-screen theater. Tables can feel somewhat close when the dining room is full. When the weather is good, the covered outdoor dining area affords great people-watching.

THE DINING ROOM AT THE RITZ-CARLTON ★★★★

		QUALITY
Eclectic American	Moderate	**99**
		VALUE
280 Vanderbilt Beach Road, Naples		**C**
(941) 598-3300		

Reservations: Required
When to go: Dinner or Sunday jazz
 brunch
Entree range: Three courses, $65; four
 courses, $70; five courses, $80; eight-
 course blind tasting menu, $85–130
Payment: VISA, MC, AMEX, D
Parking: Free lot; valet available
Bar: Full service

Wine selection: Encyclopedic—the list
 comes with a table of contents.
 $35–$18,000 bottle, $7.50–15 by the
 glass
Dress: Very dressy
Disabled access: Yes
Customers: Hotel guests, knowledgeable
 and well-heeled locals, celebrants

Brunch: Sunday, 10:30 a.m.–2:30 p.m.

Dinner: Tuesday–Saturday, 6–10 p.m.

Menu recommendations: Artichoke salad with goat cheese coulis, arugula, tomato and lemon confit; ginger-crusted foie gras with turnip tatin; pompano scented with nori and served with lobster jus; chocolate soufflé.

Comments: This is the ultimate in service and gracious ambience, both of which measure up to the inventive menu that relies heavily on local produce and seafood. For a special occasion, it's hard to top. The Sunday brunch is elegant, complete with a jazz trio. Expect expert pampering at this consistent Mobil five-star/AAA five-diamond restaurant. Jackets are required for men.

FARMER'S MARKET   ★★★★

		QUALITY
Southern	Inexpensive	**95**
		VALUE
2736 Edison Avenue, Fort Myers		**A**
(941) 334-1687		

Reservations: Not accepted
When to go: Any time
Entree range: $4.50–9.95
Payment: Cash only
Parking: Free parking lot
Bar: None

Wine selection: None
Dress: Casual to Sunday best
Disabled access: Yes
Customers: Florida natives, Sunday
 church crowd, professionals, construc-
 tion workers

Open: Monday–Saturday, 6 a.m.–8 p.m.; Sunday, 6 a.m.–7 p.m.

Menu recommendations: Southern fried chicken; meatloaf; barbecued ribs; chicken and dumplings; corn muffins; collard greens; black-eyed peas; mashed potatoes with gravy; coconut cream pie.

Comments: Southern hospitality reigns at this Fort Myers institution, where heaping helpings of classic down-home fare are complemented by a cheery, clean, and smoke-free dining room that's usually full. Don't be discouraged; turnover is fairly rapid. Arrive hungry. Large entrees come with three vegetables plus rolls.

FERNANDO'S OF MARTHA'S VINEYARD		★★★

Italian and seafood	Moderate	QUALITY 84
7381 College Parkway, Fort Myers (941) 939-5060		VALUE B

4675 Estero Boulevard, Fort Myers Beach
(941) 463-0026

Reservations: Recommended for weekends
When to go: Lunch or dinner
Entree range: $11.95–20.95
Payment: VISA, MC, AMEX, D
Parking: Free lot
Bar: Full service

Wine selection: Limited, mainly Italian with some California selections; $23–85 per bottle, $4–4.50 by the glass
Dress: Casual
Disabled access: Wheelchair accessible
Customers: Families, couples, tourists

Lunch: Daily, 11:30 a.m.–2:30 p.m.

Dinner: Daily, 4:30–10 p.m.

Menu recommendations: Stuffed eggplant appetizer; chicken Saporito (with olives, sun-dried tomatoes, garlic, and white wine); gamberi alla Toscana (grilled shrimp over Tuscan-style beans); tiramisu.

Comments: In a region rich in Italian restaurants, Fernando's sets itself apart with a menu that includes some of the classics and some lesser-known dishes. The Fort Myers location has a bar with live music, which can be heard in the adjoining dining room. The Fort Myers Beach location has a waterfront view.

INDIA PALACE ★★★★

		QUALITY
Indian	Moderate	**93**
Dragon Plaza, 11605 Cleveland Avenue, Fort Myers (941) 939-2323		VALUE **B**

Reservations: Yes
When to go: Any time
Entree range: $8.50–15.95
Payment: VISA, MC, AMEX, D
Parking: Free lot
Bar: Full service
Wine selection: Mostly Californian;

$14–50 bottle, $3.25–3.95 by the glass
Dress: Casual
Disabled access: Wheelchair accessible
Customers: Indian expatriates, professionals, young and old

Lunch: Monday–Saturday, 11:30 a.m.–2:30 p.m.

Dinner: Daily, 5–10 p.m.

Menu recommendations: Dal (lentil soup); chicken or vegetable curry; eggplant bartha; nan (buttery pita-like bread); tandoori dinner for one.

Comments: The restaurant sits back quite a way from the highway, so look for the Dragon Plaza sign. With numerous meatless dishes, it's a prime pick for vegetarians. Take care when ordering dishes hot; even the mild dishes have a distinct bite. Service can be a bit slow on busy weekends, but customers are never rushed out of their tables, either.

LE BISTRO ★★★★½

		QUALITY
Country French	Expensive	**97**
842 Neapolitan Way, Naples (941) 434-7061		VALUE **B**

Reservations: Strongly recommended
When to go: Dinner before curtain at the nearby Philharmonic Center for the Arts
Entree range: $20.50–34.50
Payment: VISA, MC, AMEX, D
Parking: Free lot
Bar: Beer and wine

Wine selection: Substantial list of primarily French and Californian labels; $24.50–175 bottle, $5.95–6.95 by the glass
Dress: Stylishly casual
Disabled access: Wheelchair accessible
Customers: Theater crowd, Francophiles

Dinner: Monday–Saturday, 5:30 p.m.–last seating 8:30 p.m.

Menu recommendations: Lobster bisque; mussels with cream sauce; bouillabaisse Marseillaise; roasted duck l'orange; grilled swordfish; crème caramel; poached pear with vanilla ice cream and cinnamon sauce.

Comments: Worth finding in a busy shopping center. Cool Mexican tile floors, crisp white linen tablecloths, and a bubbling fountain soothe the soul while classic French food nourishes it. Service is friendly and efficient without being chummy. Make reservations as the smoke-free dining room is small and the clientele large.

MAD HATTER ★★★★½

New American	Expensive	QUALITY
		95
6460 Sanibel-Captiva Road, Sanibel		VALUE
(941) 472-0033		C

Reservations: Strongly recommended
When to go: For sunset dinner
Entree range: $25.95–33.95
Payment: VISA, MC, AMEX
Parking: Free lot
Bar: Beer and wine

Wine selection: Five dozen choices, primarily Californian; $18–175 bottle; 15 by the glass, $5.50–8.50
Dress: Stylishly casual
Disabled access: Yes
Customers: Tourists and romantics

Lunch: Monday–Saturday, 11:30 a.m.–2 p.m.

Dinner: Daily, 5 p.m.–closing varies

Menu recommendations: Baked goat-cheese-and-green-onion-filled pillows; bibb salad with gorgonzola dressing; yellowfin tuna with orange chipotle peanut crust; beef tenderloin; anything on the dessert tray.

Comments: An *Alice in Wonderland* decor lends an air of whimsy and informality, while the food and service measure up to the prime beachfront real estate. The sunset's visible through large windows that run the length of the dining room. Smallish tables for two can feel cramped. The dining room is smoke-free.

MEL'S DINER ★★★½

American	Inexpensive	QUALITY
		90
4820 South Cleveland Avenue (US 41), Fort Myers		VALUE
(941) 472-0033 or (941) 275-7850		A

19050 Tamiami Trail (US 41), south Fort Myers
(941) 985-2220

28601 Trails Edge Boulevard, Bonita Springs
(941) 949-1590

3650 Tamiami Trail (US 41), Naples
(941) 643-9898

Reservations: Not accepted	Wine selection: Minimal; $1.99 per glass
When to go: Any time	Dress: Casual
Entree range: $3–9	Disabled access: Yes
Payment: VISA, MC	Customers: Retirees, families, diner
Parking: Free lot	devotees
Bar: Beer and wine	

Open: Daily, 6:30 a.m.–9 p.m.

Menu recommendations: Homemade chicken noodle soup; Greek salad; roasted chicken on open-face sandwich with mashed potatoes and gravy; burgers; fried onion rings; mile-high banana pie; chocolate bread pudding.

Comments: All but the Fort Myers branch are new, cheery Art Deco buildings, with the classic silver diner exterior. Inside, the 1950s, the height of diner-dom, reign with pictures of period celebrities everywhere. Service is folksy and efficient. Portions are generous.

MIAMI CONNECTION BAGEL & DELI ★★★★½

Kosher-style deli	Moderate	QUALITY
		96
11506 Cleveland Avenue, Fort Myers		VALUE
(941) 936-3811		**B**

Reservations: Not accepted	Wine selection: None
When to go: Breakfast or lunch	Dress: Casual
Entree range: $4.95–9.95	Disabled access: Wheelchair accessible
Payment: VISA, MC, AMEX, D	Customers: Transplanted Northeastern-
Parking: Free lot	ers, families, professionals, blue-collar
Bar: None	workers

Open: Daily, 7 a.m.–3 p.m.

Menu recommendations: Piled-high pastrami or corned beef on rye bread; onion bagel with kippered salmon, cream cheese, onion and tomato; potato knishes; rugelach (small pastries with cinnamon and nuts) or halvah (sesame-seed paste-based candy).

Comments: A long-time favorite with locals who crave a two-fisted sandwich, this deli is almost always busy. Find it along the highway by the mural of Israeli holy sites—Jewish, Christian, and Moslem—that spans the entire northernmost exterior wall.

THE MUCKY DUCK   ★★★½

British-style pub	Moderate	QUALITY
		87

11546 Andy Rosse Lane, Captiva Island
(941) 472-3434

	VALUE
	B

Reservations: Not accepted
When to go: For sunset dinner
Entree range: $12.97–18.54
Payment: VISA, MC, AMEX, D
Parking: Free lot
Bar: Beer and wine

Wine selection: Primarily domestic;
  $15–120 bottle; 13 by the glass, $3–8
Dress: Casual
Disabled access: Wheelchair accessible
Customers: Tourists, island residents

Lunch: Monday–Saturday, 11 a.m.–2:30 p.m.; May–November, lunch starts at 11:30 a.m.

Dinner: Monday–Saturday, 5–9:30 p.m.

Menu recommendations: Barbecued shrimp; charcoal-grilled lobster tail; roast duckling l'orange.

Comments: There's almost always a lively crowd—with charismatic owner Victor Mayeron often leading the pack—at this popular waterfront pub. Because of its prime sunset view, seats are hardest to get just before sunset. Within, it's filled with wood and British memorabilia. Outdoors, tables overlook the beach and the Gulf of Mexico. This is a good choice for families who don't want to worry about how much noise the kids will make. The volume's generally high enough that it won't matter.

PETER'S LA CUISINE   ★★★★½

Continental	Expensive	QUALITY
		96

2224 Bay Street, Fort Myers
(941) 332-2228

	VALUE
	C

Reservations: Recommended
When to go: Dinner
Entree range: $24.95–34.95
Payment: VISA, MC, AMEX
Parking: Metered street parking, free after
  6 p.m.
Bar: Full service
Wine selection: A broad range of French
  and American labels, including 22

champagnes and sparkling wines;
  $23–$225 bottle; 8–10 by the glass,
  $4–6
Dress: Moderately dressy
Disabled access: Yes (except to rooftop
  bar)
Customers: Well-heeled professionals and
  retirees, the arts and theater crowds,
  special-occasion celebrants

Lunch: Monday–Friday, 11:30 a.m.–2 p.m.

Dinner: Daily, 5:30–9:30 p.m.

Menu recommendations: Lobster bisque; oven-baked goat cheese tart; grouper stuffed with crab and lobster; grilled Peking duck a l'orange; mousse of white and dark chocolate; bananas Foster.

Comments: Small and elegant, this downtown establishment offers lots of special-occasion atmosphere, a knowledgeable and accommodating wait staff, and food that's artful and imaginative. Located in the downtown arts and entertainment district, it's convenient to the Arcade Theatre as well as numerous bars and clubs, including two on the floors above the dining room. Street parking can be hard to come by on weekend nights.

ROY'S		★★★★½
		QUALITY
Euro-Asian	Expensive	**96**
		VALUE
The Promenade at Bonita Bay		**C**

The Promenade at Bonita Bay
26831 South Bay Drive, Bonita Springs
(941) 498-7697

Reservations: Should be made well in advance

When to go: Dinner

Entree range: $14.95–27.95

Payment: VISA, MC, AMEX, D

Parking: Free lot

Bar: Full service

Wine selection: Extensive, including some specially bottled for Roy's; $23–250 bottle, $5.75–11.75 by the glass

Dress: Casual chic

Disabled access: Yes

Customers: Trendsetters, organized sorts who make reservations well in advance

Dinner: Sunday–Thursday, 5–10 p.m.; Friday and Saturday, 5–10:30 p.m.

Menu recommendations: Crispy coconut tiger shrimp sticks with spicy pineapple chili sauce; teriyaki short rib pizza; blackened rare ahi tuna; a chocolate soufflé for dessert.

Comments: The large dining room tends to be noisy when full, and it's full most of the time. The 160-seat restaurant is smoke-free with an artfully designed dining room with big, multilayer ceilings, recessed lighting, and a tantalizing view of the kitchen. A good-sized bar up front provides a strategic spot for people-watching. Expect plenty of attention from the well-trained waitstaff.

SANIBEL STEAKHOUSE ★★★★

		QUALITY
Steakhouse	Expensive	**91**

	VALUE
1473 Periwinkle Way, Sanibel Island (941) 472-5700	**D**

13401 Summerlin Road, Fort Myers
(941) 437-8325

24041 North Tamiami Trail, Bonita Springs
(941) 390-0400

Reservations: Recommended
When to go: Dinner
Entree range: $16.95–29.95
Payment: VISA, MC, AMEX, D, DC
Parking: Free lot
Bar: Full service
Wine selection: Wide range of wines, including champagne; $20–200 bottle, $5.95–9.95 by the glass
Dress: Stylishly casual to dressy
Disabled access: Yes
Customers: Theatergoers, tourists, beef devotees

Lunch: (Fort Myers location only) Monday–Friday, 11:30 a.m.–2:30 p.m.

Dinner: Monday–Friday, 5–10 p.m.

Menu recommendations: Shrimp cocktail appetizer; oysters Rockefeller; sautéed lump crab cakes; dry-aged prime rib-eye steak; Porterhouse steak for two; profiteroles.

Comments: All locations emphasize good service and aged beef. As is the case at many steakhouses, everything on the menu is a la carte. Raised panels, muted colors, and subtle lighting create a clubby feel. The Fort Myers branch is convenient to the Barbara. B. Mann Performing Arts Hall, while the Sanibel one is minutes from the island's two playhouses.

SIAM HUT ★★★★

		QUALITY
Thai	Moderate	**94**

	VALUE
4521 Del Prado Boulevard, Cape Coral (941) 945-4247	**B**

Reservations: Recommended on weekends
When to go: Dinner
Entree range: $6.95–10.95
Payment: VISA, MC
Parking: Free lot
Bar: Beer and wine
Wine selection: Limited to sake, house wine, and plum wine; $12.95–15.95 carafe, $2.50–3.95 by the glass
Dress: Casual
Disabled access: Wheelchair accessible
Customers: Multiethnic melting pot

Lunch: Monday–Friday, 11:30 a.m.–3 p.m.

Dinner: Monday–Saturday, 5–10 p.m.

Menu recommendations: Tom kha gai (a fragrant coconut-milk-based soup); Siam rolls (spring rolls); pad Thai (traditional rice noodles); panang curry or green beans in hot and spicy chili paste with chicken or tofu.

Comments: A nondescript storefront belies the well-appointed dining room within that includes two tables at which customers sit on the floor with their legs resting in a recessed space below the table. The management is careful to prepare dishes as mild or spicy as desired.

TOMMY BAHAMA TROPICAL CAFÉ & EMPORIUM ★★★★

Caribbean	Moderate	QUALITY 94
1220 Third Street South, Naples (941) 643-6889		VALUE B

Reservations: Limited, subject to weather conditions	**Bar:** Full service
When to go: On a sunny day or starry night	**Wine selection:** Concise, with low to moderately priced labels; $18–65 bottle; 14 by the glass, $4.25–6.75
Entree range: $17–27	**Dress:** Casual
Payment: VISA, MC, AMEX	**Disabled access:** Wheelchair accessible
Parking: Street	**Customers:** Everyone

Open: Daily, 11 a.m.–11 p.m.

Menu recommendations: Fandango mango chicken salad; St. Bart's BLT; Tommy's Tahitian tacos (wonton shells stuffed with grilled mahi-mahi, black rice, and mango salsa); pina colada cake; Tommy's original bread pudding.

Comments: With most of its seating along the broad expanse of sidewalk, this restaurant affords a great view as well as a chance to savor the great outdoors, provided the weather's good. When it isn't, tables can be hard to come by. Despite the island theme, the decor is understated and tasteful. Check out the adjoining his and her boutiques featuring the Tommy Bahama clothing line.

VARIAN'S   ★★★★

Seasonal European	Expensive	QUALITY
		95

33 Patio De Leon, Fort Myers
(941) 461-2727

VALUE
C

Reservations: Recommended
When to go: Any time
Entree range: $13.50–22.50
Payment: VISA, MC, AMEX
Parking: Metered street parking, free after
6 p.m.
Bar: Full service

Wine selection: Thirty selections, primarily Californian, French, and Italian; $29–159 bottle, $5–6 by the glass
Dress: Casual to dressy
Disabled access: Yes
Customers: Actors (real and imagined), downtown crowd, professionals

Lunch: Monday–Friday, 11 a.m.–2 p.m.

Dinner: Daily, 6–11 p.m.

Menu recommendations: The lunch menu changes weekly; the dinner menu changes with the seasons. Previous standouts include Salad of the Icy Season (greens with roasted apple and goat cheese in potato vinaigrette); lamb with potato crust; lobster and crab crepes; terrine of wild berries with marzipan ice cream.

Comments: Just slightly off the beaten path—on a pedestrian-only brick courtyard between two downtown streets—Varian's changes menus every three months. The dining room is a clever blend of industrial chic and tables dressed in crisp white linens. There's also dining upstairs at the bar as well as at tables on the sprawling balcony that overlooks Patio de Leon. Street parking can be difficult on weekend nights.

VIVA   ★★★★½

French	Expensive	QUALITY
		96

15050 Captiva Drive, Captiva Island
(941) 395-9494

VALUE
C

Reservations: Recommended
When to go: Dinner
Entree range: $22.95–28.95
Payment: VISA, MC, AMEX, D
Parking: Free lot
Bar: Beer and wine

Wine selection: Excellent, including port and dessert wines; $26–170 bottle; 12 by the glass, $5.95–12.50
Dress: Upscale casual to dressy
Disabled access: Wheelchair accessible
Customers: Tourists, islanders

Open: Monday–Saturday, 5:30–9:30 p.m.

Menu recommendations: Assorted homemade pâtés; New Zealand mussels stuffed with spinach and glazed with mousseline sauce; cold asparagus salad with white truffle oil and balsamic vinaigrette; coq au vin; grilled filet mignon; black cherry tart.

Comments: Lots of concrete, dramatic angles, and a front wall of glass give this French gem a futuristic look, a striking departure from most of the island's restaurants. Food is prepared in an efficient and quiet open kitchen, providing a show for those seated nearby. An eclectic art gallery fills a third of the building.

YABBA STREET GRILL		★★★★
Tropical	Moderate	QUALITY 94
711 Fifth Avenue, Naples (941) 262-5787		VALUE C

Reservations: Yes	Wine selection: Upwards of 120 choices;
When to go: Dinner	$22–215 bottle; 14 by the glass,
Entree range: $8.95–21.50	$4.75–12.95
Payment: VISA, MC, AMEX	Dress: Stylishly casual
Parking: Street	Disabled access: Yes
Bar: Full service, including 40 types of	Customers: Social butterflies, searching
rum	singles, people-watchers

Open: Daily, 11 a.m.–10 p.m.

Menu recommendations: Bahamian conch chowder; tuna Negril appetizer; jerk chicken Cubano; lobster island stir-fry; fudgy flourless chocolate cake with rum and raspberry sauce.

Comments: Eat indoors or out at this trendy, high-volume restaurant in Old Naples. Inside, the dining room sports a tin-ceiling and walls awash in vivid azure and lime. Service can suffer during peak times, such as weekend nights. This isn't the place for an intimate dinner for two, but it fills the bill for a lively night out and is next door to the Sugden Theatre.

Entertainment and Nightlife

The party-all-night scene may flourish on Miami Beach, but in Southwest Florida, after-dark activities are considerably more staid and limited. In most cases, the people you'll find out on the gulf beaches in the wee hours are likely to be volunteer members of the sea turtle patrol, keeping a protective eye out for egg-laying turtles that come ashore as well as their tiny hatchlings that must swim out to sea on summer nights.

On Sanibel and Captiva islands, in fact, where there aren't any traffic signals, streetlights, or neon signs, nightlife generally consists of going out for dinner after watching the sun set. But for those who simply must find a place to drink, dance, and/or carouse, the larger hotels have clubs that stay open later than most island establishments.

THE CLUB SCENE ... WHAT THERE IS OF IT

By law, bars must close by 2 a.m., and most shut down before then. While there are a great many scattered along US 41, clusters of clubs can be found in historic Old Naples; in downtown Fort Myers; and along Estero Boulevard, the main drag through Fort Myers Beach (which is at its wildest during March, when chilled Northern college students head south for spring break). In any of these places, it's possible to park and travel by foot from club to club. Beware of driving intoxicated, however: the police know where the clubs are, too, and are vigilant about enforcing the 0.08 blood-alcohol limit.

The Naples club scene tends toward a slightly older demographic: 30- and 40-something professionals, energetic retirees, and patrons of the arts. By night, inhabitants of downtown Fort Myers can range from preteens on inline skates to multiply pierced and tattooed young adults to tourists who took a wrong turn to the beach. On Fort Myers Beach, the heart of action is at Times Square, where singles in their late teens and early twenties mingle while looking for a match.

THEATER AND OTHER CULTURAL PURSUITS

Southwest Florida offers an increased awareness of the fine arts with new venues and opportunities. In February 1992, the Lee County Alliance of the Arts opened the 12,100-square-foot, $1 million **William R. Frizzell Cultural Center.** The Center consists of an exhibition gallery, the 200-seat Claiborne & Ned Foulds Theatre, an outdoor amphitheater, and art education classrooms. Many festivals are set at the Frizzell, in addition to a professional equity theater group, the Film Society of Southwest Florida, the Southwest Florida Historical Society, and the Lee County Art in Public Places program.

The **Philharmonic Center for the Arts** in Naples (5833 Pelican Bay Boulevard; (941) 597-1900 or (800) 597-1900) and the **Barbara B. Mann Performing Arts Hall** in Fort Myers (8099 College Park Way; (941) 481-4849) provide forums for national touring companies of big stage productions such as *Les Miserables, Phantom of the Opera,* and *Miss Saigon.* Well-known comedians, musicians, and dance troupes perform there, too.

There are more than a dozen theater companies between Naples and Fort Myers, including professional and amateur troupes. The primary theater season is November through April, and several of the groups produce summer shows, too. The **Broadway Palm Dinner Theatre** in Fort Myers (1380 Colonial Boulevard; (941) 278-4422) and the **Naples Dinner Theatre** (1075 Piper Boulevard; (941) 514-7827) operate year-round, serving up buffets and plays—most often musicals. Most first-run movies debut locally in a timely fashion, but foreign and art films are in short supply.

MONEY TO BURN?

Gamblers should hit the **Naples-Fort Myers Greyhound Track** in Bonita Springs (10601 Bonita Beach Road; (941) 992-2411); The Big "M" Casino (end of Third Street, Fort Myers Beach; (941) 765-7529), a boat that spends a few hours in international waters; and the **Seminole Indian Casino** (506 South First Street, Immokalee; (941) 658-1313 or (800) 218-0007), a barebones casino near Naples that's one of the few places open all night.

The Best of Southwest Florida Clubs			
Name	Cover	Cost	City
Bars			
Calvin's Crabtrap	$1	Inexp	Naples
Liquid Café	None	Mod	Fort Myers
Shooters	None	Mod	Fort Myers
Dance Club			
Atlantizz	$3–5; higher for touring bands	Mod	Fort Myers
Live Music			
Atlantizz	$3–5; higher for touring bands	Mod	Fort Myers
The Brick Bar at Peter's La Cuisine	$3 on weekends	Mod	Fort Myers
Calvin's Crabtrap	$1	Inexp	Naples
Shooters	None	Mod	Fort Myers
Lounge			
The Club at the Ritz-Carlton, Naples	None	Exp	Naples

CLUB PROFILES

ATLANTIZZ

Sunken city for singles
Who Goes There: The young and the restless

3057 Cleveland Avenue, Fort Myers; (941) 461-0550; www. atlantizz.com

Cover: $3–5; higher when touring bands perform	Beer: $2.75–$3.75
Minimum: None	Food available: None
Mixed drinks: $3–8	Hours: Open daily during the winter; closed Monday and Tuesday through summer
Wine: $2.75	

What goes on: It's a showcase for local rock bands as well as touring bands; singles mingle, with the 18- to 35-year-old set dancing to top 40 tunes or live bands, which take to the stage on Thursday nights.

Comments: The name, a variation on the mythical island of Atlantis, takes the sunken city theme to heart. Through the club's windows, deep sea coral, sunken buildings and mermaids glow in the black light. A dress code allows for casual attire but prohibits muscle shirts, baseball caps, windbreakers, trench coats, and shirts that are not tucked into pants. Anyone 18 and older can enter, but customers must be 21 and older to buy alcohol. Concerts of touring bands can be extremely crowded.

THE BRICK BAR AT PETER'S LA CUISINE

Live music in stylish setting for stylish patrons
Who Goes There: Young professionals, music-loving couples, clusters of downtown workers

2224 Bay Street, Fort Myers; (941) 332-2228

Cover: $3 on weekends	ster bisque, baked Brie with fruit and bread, pot stickers
Minimum: None	
Mixed drinks: $4–6	Hours: Monday–Friday, 4 p.m.–1:30 a.m.; Saturday and Sunday, 5:30 p.m.–1:30 p.m.; happy hour 4–7 p.m. weekdays with 2 for 1 drinks
Wine: $4–8	
Beer: $3–6	
Food available: Bistro menu includes lob-	

What goes on: Live R&B nightly draws everyone from 20-somethings to retirees. Happy hour is the domain of downtown workers winding down with the sunsets. On weekends, a younger crowd joins in, dividing time between the Brick Bar's soulful sound and the more raucous activities at the Sky Bar on the roof.

Comments: This third-story bar, with brick walls, plush banquettes, and live music, hearkens back to the classy bars of yesteryear. One story above that on the roof is the trendy Sky Bar, where customers flip coins during happy hour (if they win, they don't pay for that round) and singles connect under the stars.

CALVIN'S CRABTRAP

Raw bar with a family ambience
Who Goes There: Families, tourists, locals

11901 Tamiami Trail North, Naples; (941) 566-7011

Cover: $1	half shell, oysters or clams Rockefeller,
Minimum: None	clams casino, chicken wings
Mixed drinks: $4	Hours: Sunday–Thursday, 4 p.m.–
Wine: $3	midnight; Friday and Saturday,
Beer: $2.50–6	4 p.m.–1:30 a.m.
Food available: Full raw bar, oysters on the	

What goes on: Live music most nights means there's dancing most nights. Some customers are there for the music, while others pay more attention to the fresh raw bar, where 50 cents buys an oyster, clam, or chicken wing.

Comments: Expect a crowd through most of the winter season. Lots of families find it a good choice for dinner in the restaurant followed by music in the bar, so most of the action is G-rated.

THE CLUB AT THE RITZ-CARLTON, NAPLES

Sophisticates seeking same for dancing, romancing
Who Goes There: Well-heeled travelers, conventioneers, people-watchers

280 Vanderbilt Beach Road, Naples; (941) 598-3300

Cover: None	Beer: $5.50
Minimum: None	Food available: None
Mixed drinks: $6.75–8.25	Hours: Tuesday–Saturday, 9 p.m.–1 a.m.
Wine: $7–15	

What goes on: Older singles check one another out, business deals get sealed, locals work hard at seeing and being seen, and special occasions are celebrated

Comments: This is not the place to slouch into after a day on the beach. Business casual is the minimum and it goes up from there. The music appeals to a more mature patron who is also accustomed to fine service and subdued lighting. Tables are set far enough apart to allow easy access to the dance floor when the mood strikes. Given that it's located inside the marble-and chandelier-laden Ritz-Carlton resort, servers are well versed at making customers feel pampered.

LIQUID CAFE

Café by day, bar by night
Who Goes There: Downtown workers, musicians, music lovers, Goths, hippies, theater people

2236 First Street, Fort Myers; (941) 461-0444

Cover: None
Minimum: None
Mixed drinks: None
Wine: $5.50–9.50
Beer: $3–5
Food available: Baked Brie with strawber-ries, Caesar salad, smoked salmon and cream cheese sandwiches, assorted baked desserts
Hours: Monday–Saturday, 11 a.m.–2 a.m.

What goes on: Wine, beer, and song are dispensed in generous quantities (and usually at high volume) in this popular downtown hangout. For less smoke and lower volume, there is seating outside—prime people-watching right in the heart of the city's burgeoning arts and entertainment district.

Comments: If there's live music, as there is most evenings, the entertainers will set up wherever they can fit in the stage-less room. Seating is catch-as-catch can, with quieter options in an alcove beyond the bar and outside at the sidewalk tables. Tuesday is open-mic night, where all manner of aspiring musicians, singers, poets, and comedians may step up.

SHOOTERS

Tropical waterfront watering hole complete with tiki hut
Who Goes There: Downtown workers winding down at happy hour, singles gearing up for the weekend

2220 West First Street, Fort Myers; (941) 334-2727

Cover: None

Minimum: None

Mixed drinks: $3.50–6

Wine: $4–7

Beer: $3–4

Food available: Grouper sandwich, combo nachos, spinach dip, fried mozzarella sticks, chicken fingers

Hours: Inside bar: daily, 11 a.m.–midnight; tiki bar: Wednesday–Sunday, 11 a.m.–midnight (or until the crowd winds down); drinks and some appetizers are half-price during happy hour, Monday–Friday, 4–7 p.m.

What goes on: The crowd forms early, jockeying for the best sunset view. There's live music or a DJ Tuesday–Sunday, ranging from tropical pop to blues to reggae, jazz, oldies, and folk.

Comments: With one bar inside and one outside, there's almost always room for a few more people. The outdoor tiki bar sees the most action, with seating on all four sides, three of which are ideal for watching the sunset. Lots of tables, some covered, also allow for a seat with a view of the sun, the moon, and the boat traffic along the river.

Part Eight

The Everglades

Introduction

If a restless urge hits you to do more than just laze on the beach, traipse through resort towns, or vibrate in sync with Miami's caffeine-fueled rhythms, take a day trip to a place that feels like it's a million miles away—the Everglades.

While eyes adjusted to the gaudiness of Miami's beaches and urban landscapes need time to adapt, the Everglades is a unique destination that offers a satisfying contrast to the high-tempo city—and it's not much more than an hour away by car. But be warned: some folks fall in love with this subtly gorgeous, tranquil place and don't want to leave.

IT'S NOT A SWAMP

The Everglades ecosystem encompasses a major chunk of South Florida, including the 2,100-square-mile Everglades National Park, the second largest national park (after Yellowstone) in the lower 48 states. To many people who have never been here—or have only driven through—the Everglades may seem to be nothing to get excited about. It looks like just a broad expanse of grass, water, and trees. In other words, just another swamp.

They're wrong. The Everglades is, in fact, the last remaining subtropical wilderness in the continental United States. This huge expanse of water, sawgrass, clumps of trees called "hammocks," and pockets of tropical jungle is also an unparalleled wildlife sanctuary containing an astounding variety of mammals, reptiles, birds, and fish. Our advice: Folks who enjoy the outdoors and thrill to seeing wildlife in its natural environment should put the Everglades on their "A" list during a visit to South Florida.

A trip to the Everglades entirely removes visitors from the hubbub of daily life in the big city. It's all replaced by the cries of birds, the splash of

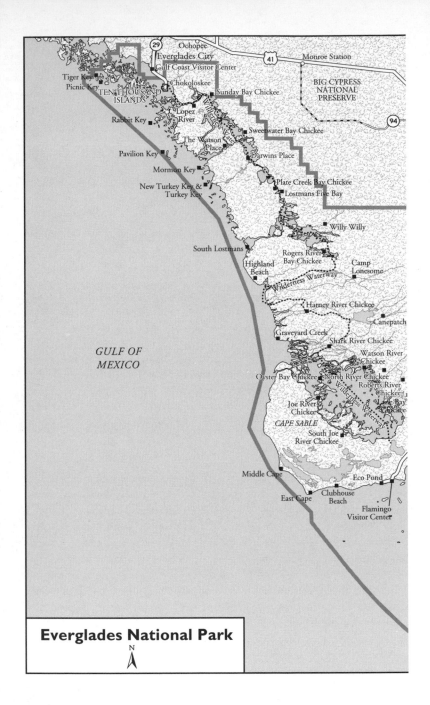

Everglades National Park

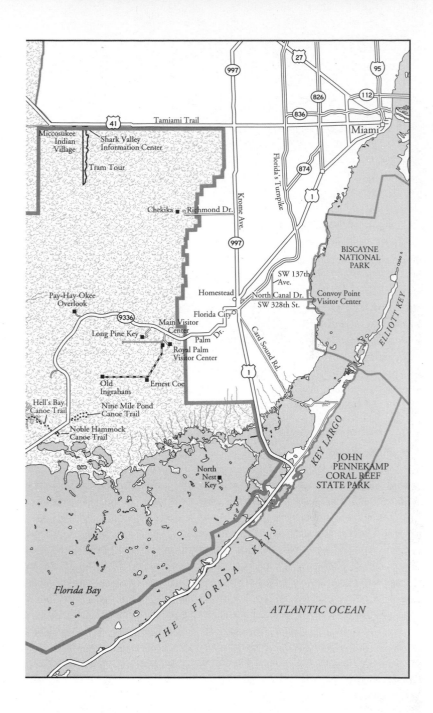

fish leaping from the water, and the sound of the wind rippling through the sawgrass. The almost limitless expanses of natural beauty remind us that humans are not really the center of the universe.

A VAST, SLOW-MOVING RIVER

Admittedly, the Everglades doesn't look like very much when viewed through a car window: seemingly endless expanses of grass and water fade into the distance, with only an occasional clump of trees to break the monotony. These apparently empty spaces, however, are deceiving: the landscape is teeming with life and activity. The Everglades is a complex, evolving ecosystem that is the result of a unique combination of climate, topography, and vegetation. To experience the Everglades—and to find out what's so special about it—you've got to get out of your car.

To appreciate the Everglades, it helps to understand what's going on here. This huge expanse of grass and water is a vast, slow-moving, shallow river that's flowing over land nearly as flat as a pool table. For eons, the overflow of Lake Okeechobee to the north has moved south slowly over this land into Florida Bay, nourishing millions of acres of sawgrass as the water ebbs and flows.

In her best-selling 1947 book, *The Everglades: River of Grass,* Florida environmentalist Marjory Stoneman Douglas popularized the notion of the Everglades as a river. Douglas, who died in 1998 at the age of 107, continued to write and speak out about preserving this unique ecosystem until the end of her life. She did so because the Everglades is in serious danger of being destroyed.

The Everglades used to encompass everything south of Lake Okeechobee, but encroaching civilization has pushed its perimeter back, until today the Everglades is only a fraction of its former size. Today's Everglades National Park makes up only about one-seventh of what's left of the Everglades, and it's the only portion of the ecosystem that's federally protected. New initiatives to save this unique ecosystem include $200 million in funds provided by Congress in 1996 and a $7.8 billion, 30-year restoration plan approved by Congress in November 2000. But true restoration, experts say, is a long-term goal and will be very expensive. Pick up almost any edition of the *Miami Herald* and you'll find news articles reporting the raging controversies surrounding efforts to protect the remaining—and seriously threatened—portions of this unique environment.

While the Everglades is subtle and doesn't easily give up its charms to short-term visitors, day-trippers can still gain an appreciation of the area and enjoy a rewarding visit—at least during the winter months, when the mosquito population is down. We don't recommend visiting the Everglades April through October, when mosquitoes and other biting insects make a visit unbearable. (But even in winter, apply insect repellent on an

Everglades visit.) Another reason to visit in the winter is that you'll see more wildlife. Winter is the dry season, and a vast array of animals and birds congregate near the remaining water.

Where to Go

SHARK VALLEY

From Florida's east coast, the closest entrance to Everglades National Park is **Shark Valley,** located on Route 41 (the Tamiami Trail) about 35 miles west of downtown Miami. Another entrance, the Western Water Gateway at Everglades City on the Gulf Coast, is more convenient for visitors traveling from Florida's west coast. To avoid a seemingly endless procession of traffic lights on SW 8th Street (Route 41 in the city), take Route 836 (the Dolphin Expressway) west to the Florida Turnpike, and go south one exit to Route 41 west. Admission to the park is $10 and is good for a week at this and other park entrances. For more information, call Everglades National Park at (305) 242-7700.

Take the Tram

If a day trip to Shark Valley is your only visit to the Everglades, our advice is to take the two-hour, motorized-tram tour that leaves from the Shark Valley parking lot on the hour from 9 a.m. to 4 p.m. daily in the winter and at 9:30 a.m., 11 a.m., 1 p.m., and 3 p.m. daily in the summer. The cost is $10.50 for adults, $9.50 for seniors, and $5 for children under age 12. Try to arrive early; the parking lot is small and this is a popular visitor destination. Reservations are recommended for tram tours; call (305) 221-8455.

Soon after the open-air tram leaves the visitor center, you'll discover what all the excitement is about as you view an incredible number of birds, alligators resting beside the narrow road, and a beautiful landscape. Well-informed and enthusiastic guides do a good job of explaining the unique topography and pointing out the unusual fauna. The tram stops often to let visitors view and photograph the wildlife and terrain.

The tram follows a 15-mile paved loop road. At the halfway point, visitors disembark at an observation tower for one of the best views in South Florida: a 360-degree, 18-mile panorama of the Everglades. Rest rooms, vending machines, and water fountains are available at the 20-minute stop.

Rental Bikes and Binoculars

Another option when visiting Shark Valley is to rent a bicycle at the visitor center. Single-speed bikes rent for $4 an hour between 8:30 a.m. and 3 p.m.; bikes must be returned by 4 p.m. And don't forget to bring binoculars when you visit; if you forget, rent a pair at the visitor center.

Airboats

Another highlight of a Shark Valley excursion: taking an **airboat ride.** While the motorized contraptions are illegal inside the national park, small airboat operations found all along Route 41 offer visitors 30-minute rides into the 'Glades. The excursions may not be "ecologically correct"—the boats are big, extremely noisy, and, some say, destructive to the environment—but a ride on one sure is fun.

Most drivers make a stop at a hammock (a small, wooded island) that features a re-creation of an Indian village. Your driver will often try to locate some alligators, usually small specimens two or three feet in length. "They look cute," my driver said as he tossed pieces of bread into the water to attract the critters, "but they've got as many teeth as an adult." We kept our hands inside the boat.

Note: Airboats are so incredibly loud that customers are given wads of cotton to stuff in their ears. You need them. Very small children may be frightened by the noise. The price for a half-hour ride ranges from $7 to $9 per person.

AN INDIAN VILLAGE

The Miccosukee Indians are descendants of Seminole Indians who retreated into the Everglades to escape forced resettlement during the 19th century. They lived on hammocks in open-sided "chickees"—thatched-roof huts built from cypress—and hunted and fished the Everglades by canoe. They also learned how to handle alligators.

At the **Miccosukee Indian Village,** on Route 41 a mile or so west of the Shark Valley entrance to Everglades National Park, alligators are the stars of the show—and if this your only opportunity to visit the Everglades, this is your chance to see an alligator do more than snooze in the sun. Alligator wrestling exhibitions are offered at 11 a.m., 12:30 p.m., 1:30 p.m., 3 p.m., and 4:40 p.m.; admission to the attraction is $5 for adults, $4 for seniors, and $3.50 for children ages 4–12. Airboat rides are $10 per person. The hours are 9 a.m.–5 p.m. daily. For more information, call (305) 223-8380.

In addition to seeing a Miccosukee Indian put a live gator through its paces, you'll get a peek at Miccosukee culture and life on a tour of the "village" (a small collection of open-air chickees and alligator pens) and a small museum. Lots of crafts and tacky souvenirs are also offered for sale.

THE ROYAL PALM VISITOR CENTER

Another option for both day-trippers to Everglades National Park and folks who want to spend a few days in the Everglades starts south of Miami near Florida City at the **Royal Palm Visitor Center,** located at the park's main entrance. To get there, take Route 9336 from US 1 at Homestead for ten miles to the gate; admission is $10 per car and is good for a week.

The new visitor center (it replaces the one destroyed by Hurricane Andrew) features interactive displays, a small theater, and an enclosed walkway to a "borrow"—a water-filled pit created when coral was excavated. Visitors can pick up free brochures, view educational displays, obtain information on boat tours and canoe rentals, and get a map to the many trails that intersect with the 38-mile main road that leads to Flamingo. While Flamingo is a stretch for day-trippers, the village there is the park's largest visitor complex, featuring a motel, a restaurant, a small grocery store, campgrounds, boat tours, a marina, and another visitor center.

Easy Walks

The two-lane road also serves as the jumping-off point for short walking explorations into the Everglades. This end of the park, by the way, is a better destination for folks who prefer walking and exploring on their own over the guided tram tour offered at Shark Valley.

A well-planned day here will quickly reveal much that's fascinating about the Everglades. The nearby **Anhinga Trail** is a half-mile boardwalk that takes visitors through areas teeming with wildlife and shows off the subtle beauty of the region at its best. The adjacent **Gumbo Limbo Trail,** on the other hand, is completely different: the one-third-mile-long asphalt-covered path takes visitors through a dense jungle unique to South Florida.

Other stops visitors should make along the road to Flamingo include the *Pa-hay-okee Overlook; Mahogany Hammock,* featuring the largest stand of mahogany trees in the United States; and a number of ponds that offer views of bird life that may be unequaled anywhere else in the world. All the trails are on boardwalks, so there's no need to worry about wet feet.

Flamingo

The end of the road is the village of **Flamingo,** which offers visitors boat rides on Florida Bay, canoe rentals, birding cruises, backcountry boat excursions, a restaurant, a marina, and the only overnight sleeping facilities in the park (outside of primitive camping). If you've got the time and interest, it's a great place for an extended visit. *Note:* Services are limited in Flamingo during the summer.

Overnight visitors should plan to take a sunset cruise on the *Bald Eagle,* a large pontoon boat that cruises Florida Bay for 90 minutes several times a day. The views of the bay, dense mangrove forests, and the shoreline are spectacular, and the guide narrating our tour offered first-time visitors a few words of wisdom: "A lot of people blast down here from Homestead at

65 miles per hour, get here and ask us, 'What is there to do?' Folks, that's not the way to do it."

His suggestion: "There's a lot of subtle beauty here and you've got to relax to see it. Get away from your car, walk one of the trails or rent a canoe." As the guide spoke, huge flocks of birds were leaving the mainland and flying across the bay through the light of the setting sun to roost on uninhabited keys. His point was made.

The sight-seeing tour of the bay is $10 for adults and $5 for children ages 6–12. Other services visitors can use to explore the Flamingo area include canoe rentals ($22 for a half-day and $32 for a full day) and bicycle rentals ($8 for a half-day and $14 all day).

Rates at the **Flamingo Lodge Marina & Outpost Resort's** comfortable (but not fancy) motel range from $95 to $115. Fully equipped cottages and houseboats are also available for rent. Call the lodge at (941) 695-3101 for more information and at (800) 600-3813 to make reservations.

AN ALLIGATOR FARM

Outside the park entrance near Florida City is another small, private attraction worth a look: the **Everglades Alligator Farm.** More than 3,000 alligators (most of them little guys in "grow out" pens), a collection of snakes and crocodiles (including an eight-and-a-half-foot-long speckled caiman), two mountain lions, two lynxes, and a black bear reside in this minizoo. The farm is located on SW 192nd Avenue; follow the signs out of Florida City.

The two main attractions are a 20-minute alligator show (a handler "wrestles" a gator and answers questions from visitors) and the only airboat rides on this end of the Everglades (no airboats are allowed in the national park). Alligator feedings, alligator shows, and snake shows alternate on the hour. Don't plan to stick around for all three shows, though. This attraction is too small to invest that much time.

The park is open 9 a.m.–6 p.m. daily; admission is $14.50 for adults, $8 for children ages 4–12, and free for children age 3 and under, which includes a 30-minute airboat ride. Skip the ride and admission is $9 for adults and $5 for kids. Our advice: Go for the ride. For more information, call the gator farm at (800) 644-9711 or (305) 247-2628.

Index

Unofficial Guide **Reader Survey**

If you would like to express your opinion about South Florida or this guidebook, complete the following survey and mail it to:

Unofficial Guide Reader Survey
P.O. Box 43673
Birmingham, AL 35243

Inclusive dates of your visit: _____

Members of your party:	Person 1	Person 2	Person 3	Person 4	Person 5
Gender:	M F	M F	M F	M F	M F
Age:					

How many times have you been to South Florida? _____
On your most recent trip, where did you stay? _____

Concerning your accommodations, on a scale of 100 as best and 0 as worst, how would you rate:

The quality of your room? _____ The value of your room? _____
The quietness of your room? _____ Check-in/check-out efficiency? _____
Swimming pool facilities? _____

Did you rent a car? _____ From whom? _____

Concerning your rental car, on a scale of 100 as best and 0 as worst, how would you rate:

Pick-up processing efficiency? _____ Return processing efficiency? _____
Condition of the car? _____ Cleanliness of the car? _____
Airport shuttle efficiency? _____

Concerning your dining experiences:

Including fast-food, estimate your meals in restaurants per day? _____
Approximately how much did your party spend on meals per day? _____
Favorite restaurants in South Florida: _____

_____

Did you buy this guide before leaving? ☐   while on your trip? ☐

How did you hear about this guide? (check all that apply)

Loaned or recommended by a friend ☐   Radio or TV ☐
Newspaper or magazine ☐   Bookstore salesperson ☐
Just picked it out on my own ☐   Library ☐
Internet ☐

What other guidebooks did you use on this trip? _____

_____

_____

_____

On a scale of 100 as best and 0 as worst, how would you rate them?

_____

_____

_____

Using the same scale, how would you rate *The Unofficial Guide(s)?*

_____

Are *Unofficial Guides* readily available at bookstores in your area? _____

Have you used other *Unofficial Guides?* _____

Which one(s)? _____

_____

_____

_____

_____

Comments about your South Florida trip or *The Unofficial Guide(s):*

_____

_____

_____

_____

_____

_____

_____

_____

_____

_____

_____

_____

_____